NEW CENTURY BIBLE COMMENTARY

General Editors

RONALD E. CLEMENTS	MATTHEW BLACK
(Old Testament)	(New Testament)

The Gospel of JOHN

THE NEW CENTURY BIBLE COMMENTARIES

Other titles in preparation

NEW CENTURY BIBLE COMMENTARY

Based on the Revised Standard Version

The Gospel of JOHN

BARNABAS LINDARS

WM. B. EERDMANS PUBL. CO., GRAND RAPIDS

MARSHALL, MORGAN & SCOTT PUBL. LTD., LONDON

Copyright © Marshall, Morgan & Scott 1972
First published 1972 by Marshall, Morgan & Scott, England
Softback edition published 1981

Reprinted 1995

All rights reserved
Printed in the United States of America
for
Wm. B. Eerdmans Publishing Company
255 Jefferson Ave. S.E., Grand Rapids, Mich. 49503
and
Marshall, Morgan & Scott
'A Pentos company
1 Bath Street, London EC1V 9LB
ISBN 0 551 00848 2

Library of Congress Cataloging in Publication Data
Lindars, Barnabas.
The Gospel of John.

(New century Bible commentaries)
Reprint of the ed. published by Oliphants, London,
which was issued in series: New century Bible.
Bibliography: p. 13
Includes index.
1.   Bible.   N.T.   John — Commentaries.   I.   Title.
II.   Series.   New century Bible commentary.
III.   Series: New century Bible.
[BS2615.3.L54   1980]   226'.507   80-18297
ISBN 0-8028-1864-1

CONTENTS

To the Memory of
Brother Peter, S.S.F.

PREFACE

The Fourth Gospel has attracted the interest of an overwhelming number of scholars, because of the range and intricacy of the problems which it presents. But for most people its attraction lies in what it is in itself—a strange but compelling picture of the irruption of Jesus Christ on to the stage of history to claim the allegiance of men. My own interest was aroused in the mid-1950s, when for several years I conducted a daily Bible study for the mission team of a Mission to hop-pickers in Kent, led by the late Brother Peter, S.S.F. (J. P. Searle). The subject was always St John. Sitting round trestle-tables in a disused oast-house, we sought to unlock the riches of the Fourth Gospel, and discovered that it is pre-eminently an evangelistic work. Subsequently I was asked at very short notice to deputize for one of the principal speakers at the Fourth Theology and Ministry Convention at Oxford in 1956. The lecture had to be produced in a single afternoon, without access to any reference books; it was published under the title of 'The Fourth Gospel an Act of Contemplation' in the conference volume, *Studies in the Fourth Gospel*, edited by F. L. Cross (1957).

Since then my work has taken me into other fields. But the request to contribute the commentary on St John for the present series was one which could not be refused. The work has had to be done more rapidly than I could have wished; but I hope that the result will commend itself to scholarly judgment, and will be found useful by students and the general reader alike.

It has been my primary aim to show the vital contact between John's presentation of the Gospel narrative and the living tradition of the words and deeds of Jesus. Discussion of the sources of the Fourth Gospel has been dominated by what I can only regard as false criteria: it is only in recent years that a proper employment of form-critical techniques has begun to appear in Johannine studies. I have tried to interpret the Gospel afresh from this point of view, so as to expose the underlying traditions which John had at his disposal, and to trace his creative use of them for his theological design.

The literature listed in the bibliography is confined to works which are actually mentioned in the course of the commentary, but I have added publications of my own in which some of my thinking on John has been worked out. It will be evident from the commentary which are the authors to whom I am most deeply indebted. At the time of writing only the first volumes of the commentaries of R. E. Brown (The Anchor Bible) and of R. Schnackenburg (Herders theologischer Kommentar) were available.

I would like to thank my colleagues in the Faculty of Divinity for kindly arranging to free me from teaching duties during the past academic year, and for their help and encouragement.

B. L.

28th October 1969

ABBREVIATIONS

9

AV	Authorized Version 1611
BDF	*A Greek Grammar of the New Testament and other Early Christian Literature,* trans. and rev. by F. Blass, and A. Debrunner's *Grammatik des neutestamentlichen Griechisch,* by R. W. Funk (Cambridge, 1961)
BJRL	*Bulletin of the John Rylands Library,* Manchester
BZ	*Biblischer Zeitschrift,* Paderborn
BZNW	*Beihefte zur Zeitschrift für die neutestamentliche Wissenschaft,* Berlin
CBQ	*Catholic Biblical Quarterly,* Washington (D.C.)
CQ EG	*De Congressu Quaerendae Eruditionis Gratia* (Philo)
ET	*Expository Times,* Edinburgh
EvTh	*Evangelische Theologie,* Munich
FRLANT	*Forschungen zur Religion und Literatur des Alten und Neuen Testaments,* Göttingen
HE	*Historia Ecclesiastica* (Eusebius)
HTR	*Harvard Theological Review,* Cambridge (Mass.)
IDB	*Interpreter's Dictionary of the Bible,* 4 vols (New York and Nashville, 1962)
JB	The Jerusalem Bible (London, 1966)
JBL	*Journal of Biblical Literature,* New York
JJS	*Journal of Jewish Studies,* London
JTS	*Journal of Theological Studies,* Oxford
LSJ	*A Greek–English Lexicon,* by H. G. Liddell and R. Scott, rev. H. S. Jones, 2 vols (Oxford, 1925–40)
LXX	Septuagint
MM	*The Vocabulary of the Greek New Testament, illustrated from the papyri and other non-literary sources,* by J. H. Moulton and G. Milligan (London, 1914–29)
MS(s)	Manuscript(s)
NEB(mg)	The New English Bible (London, 1970), (margin)
NT(Sup)	*Novum Testamentum,* Leiden, (Supplements)
NTS	*New Testament Studies,* Cambridge
para(s)	parallel(s)
RB	*Revue Biblique,* Paris
RGG	*Die Religion in Geschichte und Gegenwart.* 3rd edn, 6 vols (Tübingen, 1957–62)
RV(mg)	Revised Version (1884), (margin)
RSV(mg)	Revised Standard Version (1952), (margin)
SB	*Kommentar zum Neuen Testament aus Talmud und Midrasch,* by H. L. Strack and P. Billerbeck, 5 vols (1922–55)
SBT	*Studies in Biblical Theology,* London
TDNT	*Theological Dictionary of the New Testament,* translation of

	G. Kittel's *Theologisches Wörterbuch zum Neuen Testament*, by G. W. Bromiley, 1964–.
TLZ	*Theologische Literaturzeitung*, Leipzig/Berlin
TNT	*Twelve New Testament Studies*, by J. A. T. Robinson (London, 1962)
TU	*Texte und Untersuchungen zur Geschichte der altchristlichen Literatur* Leipzig/Berlin
TZ	*Theologische Zeitschrift*, Basel
ZNW	*Zeitschrift für die neutestamentliche Wissenschaft und die Kunde der älteren Kirche*, Berlin

BIBLIOGRAPHY

COMMENTARIES CITED BY AUTHOR

Barrett   Barrett, C. K. *The Gospel according to St John* (London, 1955, 1978²) (References are to the first edition.)

Bauer   Bauer, W. *Das Johannesevangelium* (Tübingen, 1933³)

Bernard   Bernard, J. H. *A Criticial and Exegetical Commentary on the Gospel according to St John* (Edinburgh, 1928) 2 vols

Brown   Brown, R. E. *The Gospel according to John*, 2 vols (New York/London, 1971)

Bultmann   Bultmann, R. *Das Evangelium des Johannes* (Göttingen, 1941); Eng. trans. as *The Gospel of John* (Oxford, 1971). (References are to the English edition.)

Holtzmann   Holtzmann, H. J. *Evangelium des Johannes* (Freiburg-i-Br., 1908³)

Hoskyns   Hoskyns, E. C. *The Fourth Gospel*, ed. F. N. Davey (London, 1947²)

Lagrange   Lagrange, M.-J. *L'Évangile selon Saint Jean* (Paris, 1936⁵)

Lightfoot   Lightfoot, R. H. *St John's Gospel*, ed. C. F. Evans (Oxford, 1956)

Loisy   Loisy, A. *Le Quatrième Évangile* (Paris, 1903 edn.)

Marsh   Marsh, J. *The Gospel of Saint John* (Harmondsworth, 1968)

Mastin   (*see:* Sanders)

Sanders   Sanders, J. N. *The Gospel according to Saint John*, ed. B. A. Mastin (London, 1968)

Schnackenburg   Schnackenburg, R. *The Gospel according to Saint John*. I *Introduction and commentary on chapters* 1–4 (London/New York, 1968), II and III (Herders Kommentar, Freiburg, 1971, 1976)

Strathmann   Strathmann, H. *Das Evangelium nach Johannes* (Göttingen, 1963¹⁰)

Wellhausen   Wellhausen, J. *Das Evangelium Johannis* (Berlin, 1908)

Westcott   Westcott, B. F. *The Gospel according to St John* (London, 1908)

Wikenhauser   Wikenhauser, A. *Das Evangelium nach Johannes* (Regensburg, 1958)

GENERAL

Aland, K. 'Neue neutestamentliche Papyri II', *NTS* IX (1962–3), pp. 303–13; X (1963–4), pp. 62–79; XI (1964–5), pp. 1–21; XII (1965–6), pp. 193–210.

Albright, W. F. 'Recent Discoveries in Palestine and the Gospel of St John', in *The Background of the New Testament and its Eschatology*, ed. W. D. Davies and D. Daube (Cambridge, 1956, pp. 153–71).
— *The Archaeology of Palestine* (Harmondsworth, 1960[2]).
Bacon, B. W. *The Fourth Gospel in Research and Debate* (New Haven, 1918[2]).
Bailey, J. A. *The Traditions Common to the Gospels of Luke and John*, *NT Sup* VII (1963).
Bammel, E. 'Philos tou Kaisaros', *TLZ* LXXVII (1952), cols 205–10.
— 'John did no Miracle: John 10.41', in *Miracles*, edited by C. F. D. Moule (London, 1965), pp. 179–202.
Barrett, C. K. 'The Old Testament in the Fourth Gospel', *JTS* XLVIII (1947), pp. 155–69.
— 'The Holy Spirit in the Fourth Gospel', *JTS*, n.s., 1 (1950), pp. 1–15.
— 'The Lamb of God', *NTS* 1 (1954–5), pp. 210–18.
Beasley-Murray, G. R. *Baptism in the New Testament* (London, 1962).
Becker, J. 'Wunder und Christologie: zum literarkritische und christologischen Problem der Wunder in Johannesevangelium', *NTS* XVI (1969–70), pp. 130–48.
Behm, J. 'Paraklētos', *TDNT* v, pp. 800–14.
Benoit, P. *L'Évangile selon saint Matthieu* (Paris, 1950).
— 'Prétoire, Lithostroton et Gabbatha', *RB* LIX (1952), pp. 531–50.
Berger, K., 'Die Amen-Worter Jesu', *BZNW* XXXIX (1970).
Birdsall, J. N. 'John 10.29', *JTS*, n.s., XI (1960), pp. 342–4.
Black, M. 'Does an Aramaic Tradition underlie John 1.16?', *JTS* XLII (1941), pp. 69–70.
— *The Scrolls and Christian Origins* (London, 1961).
— *An Aramaic Approach to the Gospels and Acts*, (Oxford, 1967[3]).
Blank, J. *Krisis: Untersuchungen zur johanneischen Christologie und Eschatologie* (Freiburg-i.-Br., 1964).
Blenkinsopp, J. 'John 7.37–39: another Note on a Notorious Crux', *NTS* VI (1959–60), pp. 95–8.
Blinzler, J. *The Trial of Jesus* (Westminster (Maryland), 1959).
Boismard, M.-É. 'Problèmes de critique textuelle concernant le Quatrième Évangile', *RB* LX (1953), pp. 347–71.
— 'Importance de critique textuelle pour établir l'origine araméenne du quatrième évangile'; in *L'Évangile de Jean*, Recherches Bibliques III (Bruges, 1958), pp. 41–57.
— 'De son ventre couleront des fleuves d'eau (Jn. 7.38)', *RB* LXV (1958), pp. 523–46; LXVI (1959), pp. 369–86.
— 'Saint Luc et la rédaction du quatrième évangile', *RB* LXIX (1962), pp. 185–211.
— 'Les traditions johanniques concernant le Baptiste', *RB* LXX (1963), pp. 5–42.

Bonner, C. 'Traces of Thaumaturgic Technique in the Miracles', *HTR* xx (1927), pp. 171–81.
Bonsirven, J. 'Les araméïsmes de S. Jean l'Évangéliste', *Biblica* xxx (1949), pp. 405–31.
Borgen, P. *Bread From Heaven*, *NT Sup* x (Leiden, 1965).
Bornkamm, G. 'Die eucharistische Rede im Johannes-Evangelium?', *ZNW* xlvii (1956), pp. 161–9.
Bowker, J. W. 'The Origin and Purpose of St John's Gospel', *NTS* xi (1964–5), pp. 398–408.
— 'Speeches in Acts: A Study in Proem and Yelammedenu Form', *NTS* xiv (1967–8), pp. 96–110.
Bowman, J. 'Samaritan Studies', *BJRL* xl (1958), pp. 298–327.
Braun, F.-M. *Jean le Théologien*, Études Bibliques, 3 vols (Paris, 1959–68).
Brown, R. E. 'The Paraclete in the Fourth Gospel', *NTS* xiii (1966–7), pp. 113–32.
Brown, S. 'From Burney to Black: the Fourth Gospel and the Aramaic Question', *CBQ* xxvi (1964), pp. 323–39.
Buchanan, G. W. 'The Samaritan Origin of the Gospel of John', in *Religions in Antiquity: Essays in Memory of E. R. Goodenough*, edited by J. Neusner, *Numen Sup* xiv (Leiden, 1968), pp. 149–75.
Büchsel, F. '*Elenchō*', *TDNT* ii, pp. 473–5.
Burkitt, F. C. *The Gospel History and its Transmission* (Edinburgh, 1906).
Burney, C. F. *The Aramaic Origin of the Fourth Gospel* (Oxford, 1922).
Caird, G. B. 'The Glory of God in the Fourth Gospel: an Exercise in Biblical Semantics', *NTS* xv (1968–9), pp. 265–77.
Colpe, C. 'Mandäer', *RGG* iv (1960), cols 709–12.
Colwell, E. C. *The Greek of the Fourth Gospel* (Chicago, 1931).
Colwell, E. C., and Riddle, D. W. *Prolegomena to the Study of the Lectionary Text of the Gospels* (Chicago, 1933).
Connolly, R. H., ed., *Didascalia Apostolorum; The Syriac Version* (Oxford, 1929).
Cranfield, C. E. B. *The Gospel according to Saint Mark* (Cambridge, 1959).
Cullmann, O. *Early Christian Worship*, *SBT* x (1953).
— 'Samaria and the Origins of the Christian Mission'; in *The Early Church* (London, 1956), pp. 183–92.
— 'L'Opposition contre le Temple de Jérusalem, Motif Commun de la Théologie Johannique et du Monde Ambiant', *NTS* v (1958–9), pp. 157–73.
— *Peter: Disciple, Apostle, Martyr* (London, 1962²).
Dalman, G. H. *Grammatik des jüdisch-palestinischen Aramäisch* (1905²).
— *Jesus-Jeshua* (Leipzig, 1929)
Daube, D. *The New Testament and Rabbinic Judaism* (London, 1956).
Deissmann, A. *Light from the Ancient East* (London, 1911).

Dekker, C. 'Grundschrift und Redaktion im Johannesevangelium', *NTS* XIII (1966–7), pp. 66–80.

Derrett, J. D. M. 'Water into Wine', *BZ* VII (1963), pp. 80–97.

— 'Law in the New Testament: the Story of the Woman Taken in Adultery', *NTS* X (1963–4), pp. 1–26.

Diaz, J. R. 'Palestinian Targum and New Testament', *NT* VI (1963), pp. 75–84.

Dibelius, M. *From Tradition to Gospel* (London, 1934).

Dodd, C. H. *The Apostolic Preaching and its Developments* (London, 1937).

— *The Interpretation of the Fourth Gospel* (Cambridge, 1953).

— 'A New Gospel'; in *New Testament Studies* (Manchester, 1953), pp. 12–52.

— 'Note on John 21.24', *JTS*, n.s., IV (1953), pp. 212–13.

— *Historical Tradition in the Fourth Gospel* (Cambridge, 1963).

— 'A Hidden Parable in the Fourth Gospel'; in *More New Testament Studies* (Manchester, 1968), pp. 30–40.

— 'Behind a Johannine Dialogue'; *ibid.*, pp. 41–57.

Dunn, J. D. G. 'John vi—a Eucharistic Discourse', *NTS* XVII (1970–1), pp. 328–38.

Eckhardt, K. A. *Der Tod des Johannes als Schlüssel zum Verständnis der johanneischen Schriften* (Berlin, 1961).

Edwards, R. A. *The Gospel according to St John: its Criticism and Interpretation* (London, 1954).

Ellis, E. E. *The Gospel of Luke* (London, 1966).

Emerton, J. A. 'The Hundred and Fifty-three Fishes in John 21.11', *JTS*, n.s., IX (1958), pp. 86–9.

— 'Some New Testament Notes', *JTS*, n.s., XI (1960), pp. 329–36.

— 'Binding and Loosing—Forgiving and Retaining', *JTS*, n.s., XIII (1962), pp. 325–31.

Eppstein, V. 'The Historicity of the Gospel Account of the Cleansing of the Temple', *ZNW* LV (1964), pp. 42–58.

Evans, E. 'The Verb *agapān* in the Fourth Gospel'; in *Studies in the Fourth Gospel*, ed. F. L. Cross (London, 1957), pp. 64–71.

Field, F. *Notes on the Translation of the New Testament* (Cambridge, 1899).

Filson, F. V. 'Who was the Beloved Disciple?', *JBL* LXVIII (1949), pp. 83–8.

Fleming, W. K. 'The Authorship of the Fourth Gospel', *The Guardian*, 19th Dec. 1906, p. 2118.

Fortna, R. T. *The Gospel of Signs*, Society for New Testament Studies Monograph Series XI (Cambridge, 1970).

Freed, E. D. *Old Testament Quotations in the Gospel of John*, *NT* Sup XI (Leiden, 1965).

— 'Did John write his Gospel partly to win Samaritan converts?', *NT* xii (1970), pp. 241–56.

Gächter, P. 'Zur Form von Joh. 5.19–30'; in *Neutestamentliche Aufsätze*, ed. J. Blinzler, O. Kuss and F. Mussner (Regensburg, 1963), pp. 65–8.

Gardner-Smith, P. *Saint John and the Synoptic Gospels* (Cambridge, 1938).

Gärtner, B. *John 6 and the Jewish Passover*, Coniectanea Neotestamentica xvii (Lund, 1959).

Goguel, M. *Le Quatrième Évangile*, Introduction au Nouveau Testament ii (Paris, 1924).

Goodspeed, E. J. *Problems of New Testament Translation* (Chicago, 1945).

Grant, R. M. 'One Hundred Fifty-Three Large Fish (John 21.11)', *HTR* xlii (1949), pp. 273–5.

Guilding, A. *The Fourth Gospel and Jewish Worship* (Oxford, 1960).

Hart, H. St J. 'The Crown of Thorns in John 19.2–5', *JTS*, n.s., iii, (1952), pp. 66–75.

Hatch, W. H. P. 'The Meaning of John 16.8–11', *HTR* xiv (1921), pp. 103–5.

Hooker, M. D. *The Son of Man in Mark* (London, 1967).

Horvath, T. 'Why was Jesus brought to Pilate?', *NT* xi (1969), pp. 174–84.

Howard, W. F. *The Fourth Gospel in Recent Criticism and Interpretation*, rev. C. K. Barrett (London, 1955).

Hügel, F. von. 'Gospel of St John', *Encyclopaedia Britannica* (London, 1911[11]) xv, pp. 452–8.

Hunger, H. 'Zur Datierung des Papyrus Bodmer II (P[66])', quoted in B. M. Metzger, *The Text of the New Testament* (Oxford, 1968[2]), p. 40, n. 1.

Hunter, A. M. *According to John* (London, 1968).

Jaubert, A. *La Date de la Cène* (Paris, 1957).

Jeremias, J. *Golgotha*, Angelos i (Leipzig, 1926).

— '*Amnos tou Theou—pais Theou*', *ZNW* xxxiv (1935), pp. 115–23.

— *The Rediscovery of Bethesda, John* 5.2, New Testament Archaeology Monographs i (Louisville, 1966).

— *The Eucharistic Words of Jesus* (London, 1966[2]).

— *Jerusalem in the Time of Jesus* (London, 1969).

— *New Testament Theology*, i (London, 1970).

Johnston, G. *The Spirit-Paraclete in the Gospel of John*, Society for New Testament Studies Monograph Series xii (Cambridge, 1970).

Jonge, M. de, and Woude, A. S. van der. '11Q Melchizedek and the New Testament', *NTS* xii (1965–6), pp. 301–26.

Juster, J. *Les Juifs en l'Empire Romain* (Paris, 1914), ii.

Käsemann, E. *The Testament of Jesus: a Study of the Gospel of John in the Light of Chapter 17* (London, 1968).

Kragerud, A. *Der Lieblingsjünger im Johannesevangelium* (Oslo, 1959).
Kümmel, W. G. *Introduction to the New Testament* (London, 1966).
Laurentin, A. '*We-attah—kai nun*, formule charactéristique des textes juridiques et liturgiques, à propos de Jean 17.5', *Biblica* xlv (1964), pp. 168–97, 413–32.
Leaney, A. R. C. 'Jesus and Peter: The Call and Post-Resurrection Appearances', *ET* lxv (1953–4), pp. 381–2.
— 'The Resurrection Narratives in Luke (24.12–53)', *NTS* ii (1954–5), pp. 110–14.
— *A Commentary on the Gospel according to St Luke* (London, 1958).
— *The Rule of Qumran and its Meaning* (London, 1966).
Lietzmann, H. *The Beginnings of the Christian Church* (London, 1937).
— 'Der Prozess Jesu', in *Kleine Schriften* ii (*TU* lxviii (1958), pp. 251–76).
Lightfoot, R. H. *History and Interpretation in the Gospels* (London, 1935).
Lindars, B. 'The Fourth Gospel: an Act of Contemplation'; in *Studies in the Fourth Gospel*, ed. F. L. Cross (London, 1957), pp. 23–35.
— 'The Composition of John 20', *NTS* vii (1960–1), pp. 142–7.
— *New Testament Apologetic: The Doctrinal Significance of the Old Testament Quotations* (London, 1961).
— '*Dikaiosunē* in John 16.8 and 10', in *Hommage à Béda Rigaux* (Gembloux, 1970).
— 'Two Parables in John', *NTS* xvi (1969–70), pp. 318–29.
— *Behind the Fourth Gospel* (London, 1971).
Lindblom, J. *Gesichte und Offenbarungen: Vorstellungen von göttlichen Weisungen und übernatürlichen Erscheinungen im ältesten Christentum*, Acta Reg. Societatis Humaniorum Litterarum Lundensis lxv (Lund, 1968).
Lohse, E. 'Wort und Sakrament im Johannesevangelium', *NTS* vii (1960–1), pp. 110–25.
Lossky, V. *The Mystical Theology of the Eastern Church* (London, 1957).
Macdonald, J. *The Theology of the Samaritans* (London, 1964).
MacGregor, G. H. C., and Morton, A. Q. *The Structure of the Fourth Gospel* (Edinburgh, 1961).
Martyn, J. L. *History and Theology in the Fourth Gospel* (New York, 1968).
Meeks, W. A. *The Prophet-King: Moses Traditions and Johannine Christology*, *NT Sup* xiv (Leiden, 1967).
Metzger, B. M. *The Text of the New Testament* (Oxford, 1968²).
— trans. [Coptic] *Gospel of Thomas;* in Aland, K., *Synopsis Quattuor Evangeliorum* (Stuttgart, 1964), pp. 517–30.
Milik, J. T. *Les 'petites grottes' de Qumran* (Discoveries in the Judaean Desert iii, by M. Baillet, J. T. Milik and R. de Vaux) (Oxford, 1962).

Moffatt, J. *An Introduction to the Literature of the New Testament* (Edinburgh, 1918³).

Moule, C. F. D. *An Idiom Book of New Testament Greek* (Cambridge, 1959²).

— 'The Influence of Circumstances on the Use of Christological Terms', *JTS*, n.s., x (1959), pp. 247–63.

— 'The Individualism of the Fourth Gospel', *NT* v (1962), pp. 171–90.

— *The Birth of the New Testament* (London, 1966²).

— *The Phenomenon of the New Testament*, *SBT*, 2nd ser. 1(1967).

—, ed. *The Significance of the Message of the Resurrection for Faith in Jesus Christ*, *SBT*, 2nd ser. VIII (1968).

Moulton, J. H., and Howard, W. F. *A Grammar of New Testament Greek* II (Edinburgh, 1929).

Neirynck, F. 'Les Femmes au Tombeau: Étude de la rédaction Matthéenne', *NTS* xv (1968–9), pp. 168–90.

Niewalda, P. *Sakramentensymbolik im Johannesevangelium?* (Limbourg, 1958).

Nineham, D. E. *The Gospel of Saint Mark* (Harmondsworth, 1963).

Noack, B. *Zur johanneischen Tradition* (Copenhagen, 1954).

Odeberg, H. *The Fourth Gospel interpreted in its relation to Contemporaneous Religious Currents in Palestine and the Hellenistic-Oriental World* (Uppsala, 1929).

O'Neill, J. C. 'The Silence of Jesus', *NTS* xv (1968–9), pp. 153–67.

— 'The Prologue to St John's Gospel', *JTS*, n.s., xx (1969), pp. 41–52.

Parker, P. 'John and John Mark', *JBL* LXXIX (1960), pp. 97–110.

— 'John the Son of Zebedee and the Fourth Gospel', *JBL* LXXXI, (1962), pp. 35–43.

Perry, M. C. 'The Other of the Two: A Fresh Look at John 1.35ff', *Theology* LXIV (1961), pp. 153–4.

Pollard, T. E. *Johannine Christology and the Early Church*, Society for New Testament Studies Monograph Series XIII (Cambridge, 1970).

Porter, C. L. 'John 9.38, 39a: A Liturgical Addition to the Text', *NTS* XIII (1966–7), pp. 387–94.

Rawlinson, A. E. J. *St Mark* (London, 1925).

Reitzenstein, R. *Poimandres: Studien zur griechisch-ägyptischen und frühchristlichen Literatur* (Leipzig, 1904).

— *Das Mandäische Buch des Herrn der Grösse und die Evangelienüberlieferung*, Sitzungsberichte der Österreichischen Akademie der Wissenschaften (Vienna, 1919).

Rengstorf, K. H. '*Apostolos*', *TDNT* I, pp. 413–20.

Richter, G. 'Zur Formgeschichte und literarischen Einheit von Joh. 6.31–58', *ZNW* LX (1969), pp. 21–55.

Robinson, J. A. T. 'Elijah, John and Jesus', in *Twelve New Testament Studies*, *SBT* XXXIV (1962), pp. 28–52.

— 'The Parable of the Shepherd (John 10.1–5)', *ibid.*, pp. 67–75.
— 'The Destination and Purpose of St John's Gospel', *ibid.*, pp. 107–25.
— 'The Relation of the Prologue to the Gospel of St John, *NTS* IX (1962–3), pp. 120–9.
Roloff, J. 'Der johanneische "Lieblingsjünger" und der Lehrer der Gerechtigkeit', *NTS* XV (1968–9), pp. 129–51.
Ruckstuhl, E. *Die literarische Einheit des Johannesevangeliums* (Freiburg-i.-Br. 1951).
Schniewind, J. *Die Parallelperikopen bei Lukas und Johannes* (Darmstadt, 1914).
Schweizer, E. *Ego eimi: Die religionsgeschichtliche Herkunft und theologische Bedeutung der johanneischen Bildreden, zugleich ein Beitrag zur Quellenfrage des vierten Evangeliums, FRLANT* LVI (1939).
— 'Das johanneische Zeugnis vom Herrenmahl', *EvTh.* XII (1952–3), pp. 341–62.
Sherwin-White, A. N. 'The Trial of Christ in the Synoptic Gospels'; in *Roman Society and Roman Law in the New Testament* (Oxford, 1963), pp. 24–47.
Singer, S. *The Authorised Daily Prayer Book of the United Hebrew Congregations of the British Empire* (London, 1956).
Smalley, S. S. 'The Johannine Son of Man Sayings', *NTS* XV (1968–9). pp. 278–301.
Smith, D. M. 'The Sources of the Gospel of John: an Assessment of the Present State of the Problem', *NTS* X (1963–4), pp. 336–51.
Smith, G. A. *The Historical Geography of the Holy Land* (London, 1931[25]; republ. 1966).
Spitta, F. *Das Johannes-Evangelium als Quelle der Geschichte Jesu* (Göttingen, 1910).
Stather Hunt, B. P. W. *Some Johannine Problems* (London, 1958).
Stauffer, E. 'Agnostos Christos: Joh. 2.24 und die Eschatologie des vierten Evangeliums'; in *The Background of the New Testament and its Eschatology*, ed. W. D. Davies and D. Daube (Cambridge, 1956), pp. 281–99.
Stemberger, G. *La Symbolique du Bien et du Mal selon Saint Jean* (Paris, 1970).
Taylor, V. *The Gospel according to St Mark* (London, 1955).
Titus, E. L. 'The Identity of the Beloved Disciple', *JBL* LXIX (1950), pp. 323–8.
Torrey, C. C. 'The Aramaic Origin of the Fourth Gospel', *HTR* XVI (1923), pp. 305–44.
Vermes, G. *The Dead Sea Scrolls in English* (Harmondsworth, 1962).
Vincent, L.-H. 'Le Lithostrotos évangélique', *RB* LIX (1952), pp. 513–30.

Wead, D. W. 'We have a Law', *NT* xi (1969), pp. 185–9.
Wiles, M. F. *The Spiritual Gospel: the Interpretation of the Fourth Gospel in the Early Church* (Cambridge, 1960).
Wilkens, W. *Die Entstehungsgeschichte des vierten Evangeliums* (Zollikon, 1958).
— 'Die Erweckung des Lazarus', *TZ* xv (1959), pp. 22–39.
Windisch, H. *Johannes und die Synoptiker* (Leipzig, 1926).
— *The Spirit-Paraclete in the Fourth Gospel* (Philadelphia, 1968).
Winter, P. *On the Trial of Jesus* (Berlin, 1961).
Zimmermann, H. 'Das absolute *ego eimi* als die neutestamentliche Offenbarungsformel', *BZ* iv (1960), pp. 54–69, 266–76.

INTRODUCTION

1. THE CENTRAL MESSAGE OF THE FOURTH GOSPEL

The Gospel according to John is a book with a message. The author wants to bring the reader to the point of decision. As he says in 20.30f. (the original conclusion of the book), he has done his work 'that you may believe that Jesus is the Son of God, and that believing you may have life in his name'. His purpose is expressed with equal clarity in the 'miniature gospel' of 3.16: 'For God so loved the world that he gave his only Son, that whoever believes in him should not perish but have eternal life.' This is no vague statement. It presents two possibilities: 'to perish', or 'to have eternal life'. John knows no middle course. He sees mankind as inexorably faced with these solemn alternatives. Man is involved in a power struggle between cosmic forces. On one side is the darkness (more often put in other terms: 'blindness', 'evil', 'this world', 'the prince of this world'); this leads to destruction and death. On the other side is the light (associated with sight, the Spirit, 'the water of life', 'the bread of life', 'the light of the world', fellowship with God); this leads to salvation and life in the New Age. Consequently the decision between the light and the darkness affects a man's whole existence.†

John believes passionately that the crucial factor in this decision is one's attitude to Jesus Christ. This is because the appearance of Jesus on the plane of history is the irruption of the light from the divine realm into the created order, where evil is rampant. Thus the power struggle is fought out, not only at a cosmic level, but also in the historic events of the life of Jesus. In this strife the Cross is central. It is 'the hour' (12.23; 13.31) when the powers of darkness appear to have brought their enemy down. But with magnificent irony John shows that it is the darkness which is vanquished, and that in the Cross the victory is won (3.14; 8.28; 12.34). By faith in Jesus men may share his victory; to John this means entrusting oneself to Jesus with full personal commitment; man does not thereby escape his share in the strife (15.20), but his victory is assured (16.33).

The modern reader may find difficulty with the world-view

---

† These all-pervading Johannine themes are the subject of an attractive study by G. Stemberger, *La symbolique du bien et du mal selon saint Jean* (1970).

which is here presupposed. But in reading the Gospel he will find again and again that it touches the depths of human existence. The urgency of the message remains undiminished.

2. JOHN AND THE SYNOPTIC GOSPELS

If John's purpose is primarily practical in this way, the question arises why he has chosen the Gospel form. We tend to think of the Gospels as biographies of Jesus. But none of them is rightly regarded as such.[1]

(a) The Greek *evangelion* refers to the proclamation (*kērygma*) of the good news (Mk 1.15). It is derived from *evangelizō*, used in the Septuagint of Isa. 52.7 to translate the Hebrew *biśśēr* (= bring good tidings). It thus refers to the activity of preaching (cf. 1 C. 1.21). The most primitive preaching asserted that the prophecies are fulfilled and the New Age is inaugurated by the coming of Christ: he was born of the seed of David; he died according to the Scriptures, to deliver us from the present evil age; he was buried; he rose on the third day according to the Scriptures; he was exalted to the right hand of God; and he will come again as Judge and Saviour of men.[2] Here already can be seen the framework of the Gospels, which thus may be called kerygmatic statements filled out with biographical material.

(b) The biographical material was ready to hand, for the primitive instruction (*catechēsis*) made use of memories of the life of Jesus as illustrative material (healing miracles, parables, etc.). Similarly, small collections of the moral teaching of Jesus came into existence to meet the need for simple rules for the guidance of Christians. These could be learnt by heart.

The Gospel form arises from the convergence of these two forms of the traditions about Jesus as a further development of the accepted ways of teaching and preaching. It is highly probable that Mark was the originator of this form. It corresponds with changing needs, as the Church moved further from its origins and developed a more complex internal life. It was necessary to provide a definitive account of the distinctive Christian beliefs in the face of distortion of the original tradition (cf. Lk. 1.1–4). This

---

[1] Numbered footnotes are to be found at the end of the Introduction (pp. 68f.).

coincides with John's motive in adopting the Gospel form, and suggests that he writes primarily for those who are within the Church rather than for outsiders.

John's use of this form at once puts his Gospel in the same category as the Synoptics.[3] But this only raises more acutely the problem of his relation to them. He uses only a small number of biographical incidents (the Signs), and he makes them the basis of extended discourses, which have no counterpart in the Synoptics; in matters of detail his account is frequently irreconcilable with them. This raises the crucial problem of historicity, for both cannot be right. The dilemma was felt as soon as the Fourth Gospel came into general use in the second century. The Muratorian Canon (A.D. 170) says that John wrote on behalf of Andrew and the other Apostles—evidently to reassure those who doubt the Gospel's authenticity. The Alexandrians got round the difficulty by putting John on a different level: 'Last of all John, perceiving that the external facts (ta sōmatika) had been made plain in the Gospels, being urged by his friends and inspired by the Spirit, composed a spiritual gospel (pneumatikon . . . evangelion).'[4] Origen even suggests that the discrepancies cannot and must not be harmonized, because the needs of spiritual truth demand the abandonment of strict historical accuracy (Comm. in Joh. x.4–6). This position has a modern counterpart in the argument of Hoskyns (p. 82) that John knew, and expected his readers to know, the Synoptic material (not necessarily the Synoptics as we have them), but presented it differently to bring out its true meaning. Hence John is the key to the others.

The problem remained acute as long as it was held that John actually knew the Synoptic Gospels. Burkitt was frankly sceptical of the historical worth of John. But direct dependence was challenged by Schniewind (1914), Windisch (1926), Gardner-Smith (1938) and Wilkens (1958). Though it is retained in some degree by Howard, Barrett and Bailey, most scholars today favour the view that John made use of independent parallel traditions. Three factors have to be taken into account.

(a) *Order of material.* John allows room for a Judean ministry of Jesus unknown to the Synoptics (2.22). He also brings Jesus up to Jerusalem for the festivals (2.13; 5.1; 7.2; 10.22). He places the Cleansing of the Temple at the beginning of the ministry (2.13–21) instead of at the end (Mk 11.15–19). On the other hand, a series of events in chapters 5, 6 and 9 roughly corresponds with the Marcan sequence. But as the most telling features are to be found in chapter 6, which is probably an addition to the original form of the Gospel (see below, p. 50), not much can be made of this. The Cleansing of the Temple also probably originally occupied the Synoptic position. But really neither John nor the Synoptists are much interested in historical sequence, so that the argument from the order of events gives little support either way.

(b) *Common material.* John shares many incidents with the Synoptics (the Baptism of Jesus, the Call of the Disciples, the Cleansing of the Temple, the Healing of an Official's Son, etc.). But in every case the time or location is changed and the whole scene is differently imagined. Moreover there is much Synoptic-type material which is peculiar to John (the Marriage at Cana, the Shepherd parable, the Raising of Lazarus). Sayings of Jesus which have Synoptic parallels rarely show verbal agreement. The differences between John and the Synoptics cannot all be due to his theological purpose. It is more likely that they are due to the non-Synoptic sources, from which his additional material is derived. It is not necessary to hold with Noack that these sources were entirely oral.

(c) *Exact verbal links.* These are few, but are too striking to be brushed aside. Thus Jn 5.8 = Mk 2.9, including the colloquial *krabbaton*, avoided by Matthew and Luke; Jn 6.7 has 'two-hundred denarii', exactly as in Mk 6.37; Jn 12.1–8, the Anointing at Bethany, has even more impressive links with the Marcan and Lucan versions of the story. Brown is compelled to suppose that these are due to a final redactor (who also added chapter 21), who was familiar with Mark. Boismard even supposes that Luke himself was the final editor. A source theory such as Bultmann's has to allow contact either in the prior stage—i.e. in the Signs source—or in the final work of the ecclesiastical redactor. But the difficulty is overcome if we assume that John's sources were at some points either identical with, or closely similar to, the sources used by Mark and Luke. There is no reason why some at least of these sources should not have been in written form.

If John did not use the Synoptic Gospels, the way is opened for an independent assessment of the historical value of his material. It cannot be taken for granted that he is more reliable than the Synoptists, or less so. Each item has to be taken on its own merits.

The crucial question is the authority of John himself as a transmitter of the traditions. And this depends on who he was. Hence the question of authorship is inextricably bound up with the central problem of the Fourth Gospel.

3. AUTHORSHIP

I. JOHN THE APOSTLE

The traditional view is that the evangelist was John son of Zebedee, and that he is the person referred to in the Gospel itself as 'the disciple whom Jesus loved'. This view still has its supporters.[5] Even such critical commentators as Brown and Schnackenburg retain it up to a point. But the objections to it are formidable.[6]

To begin with, it must be observed that this attribution of the Gospel to the Apostle John cannot be traced back to the earliest days. Justin Martyr, writing in the middle of the second century, seems to include slight reminiscences of the Fourth Gospel (1 *Ap.* lxi; *Dial.* lxii; lxxxviii; xci). But when he speaks of John (*Dial.* cvi.3) he makes no mention of the Gospel, even though he ascribes the Apocalypse to him (*Dial.* lxxxi.4). Hence John the Apostle was already identified with the John of Rev. 1.4, 9, but not with the evangelist. By the time of the *Homily on the Pasch* of Melito of Sardis (*c.* A.D. 165), the use of the Fourth Gospel is certain, but there is still no mention of John by name. For the evidence of Papias, see below.

However, the Gospel was already known and valued by the Valentinian Gnostics, who found in it much to support their heretical views. Irenaeus (*Adv. Haer.* I.viii.5) quotes Ptolemaeus' exposition of the Prologue, which he ascribes to 'John, the disciple of the Lord'. This is clearly an allusion to the Beloved Disciple, and suggests that the identification of the author was derived from the internal evidence of the Gospel itself. It has been plausibly suggested that the Valentinians were the first to make the identification of him with John the Apostle, as the authority of the Apostle's name would naturally strengthen their case. They were so successful that some Christians rejected the Fourth Gospel as a heretical work. Thus Hippolytus speaks of the 'Alogi', who ascribed both the Gospel and the Apocalypse to the Gnostic Cerinthus.[7] The *Acts of John* (a heretical popular work of the mid-second century), however, appears not to know that John was the author of the Gospel, though apparently making some use of it. It is the earliest work to link John with Ephesus.

By this time those Church Fathers who accepted the Fourth Gospel were beginning also to accept the claim of apostolic authorship, though the Muratorian Canon and Clement of Alexandria both attest a certain element of doubt (cf. above, p. 26). The first indisputable statement is that of Irenaeus (*Adv. Haer.* iii.i.1f.): 'Then John, the disciple of the Lord, who also lay on his breast, himself published the gospel, while he was staying at Ephesus in Asia.' Thereafter the attribution to John the Apostle is generally accepted. Lagrange was disposed to give weight to the unanimity of the Fathers, but it looks as if the tradition really goes back to the Valentinians, who themselves derived it from the internal evidence of the Gospel itself. But, before we look at this, it is necessary to review the evidence of Papias, which has been used to support another theory of authorship— i.e., not John the Apostle, but an Elder of the same name.

2. JOHN THE ELDER

The five books of Papias' *Exposition of the Sayings of the Lord* are lost; but a fragment preserved by Eusebius (*HE* iii.xxxix.1–7) tells how Papias gathered his information at the end of the first century: 'If anyone who had been a follower of the Elders came, I enquired about the words of the Elders—what Andrew or Peter said, or what Philip, or what Thomas or James, or what John or Matthew or any other of the disciples of the Lord (said), and the things which Aristion and the elder John, disciples of the Lord, were saying. For I thought that the things which come from books would not be so useful to me as the things which come from a voice that is still alive (lit. "a living and abiding voice").' Eusebius points out that Papias here mentions two Johns, the first now dead (whom Eusebius assumes to be the evangelist), and the second still alive (to whom he ascribes the Apocalypse). Jerome (*de viris inl.* xviii) gives the same quotation from Papias, but suggests more plausibly that John the Elder was the writer of 2 and 3 John, in which the writer actually styles himself 'the Elder' (*presbyteros*). The title does not necessarily refer to an official position, but can be applied to any revered teacher, as in Jewish usage (cf. Mk 7.5).

Nevertheless, whatever Eusebius and Jerome thought, it is clear that Papias himself has no knowledge of the Gospel, and ascribes it to neither of these two Johns. It has been left to modern scholarship to propose John the Elder as the evangelist. Harnack, followed by Bernard, assumed that the Elder wrote the Gospel on the basis of the Apostle's teaching, and subsequent tradition confused the two Johns. But there is no solid evidence for this theory in Papias. It is a deduction, supported by the opening words of 2 and 3 John, assumed to be by the same hand as the Gospel and 1 John. We are not hereby exempted from the need to give primary attention to the internal evidence.

3. JOHN AT EPHESUS

Before leaving the patristic evidence, there is a further point about the connection between John the Apostle and Ephesus, already mentioned. Polycrates, bishop of Ephesus (c. A.D. 190), proudly tells of the Christian heroes buried there, and continues: 'And, moreover, John, who lay on the breast of the Lord, who had been a priest wearing the plate (*hiereus to petalon pephorekōs*, cf. Exod. 28.36), and was a witness and a disciple—he also sleeps at Ephesus' (Eusebius, *HE* iii.xxxi.4). Actually there were two tombs there, which Eusebius (iii.xxxix.6) connects with the two Johns mentioned by Papias.

But any connection of the Apostle with Ephesus, and indeed any possibility of his authorship of the Gospel, have been challenged by the theory that he had been martyred along with James (Ac. 12.2). Though accepted by several modern scholars (Wellhausen, Moffatt, Bacon, Burkitt), this view must really be regarded as a red herring; in fact, it seems to be a deduction from Mk 10.39 on the fate of the sons of Zebedee. Philip of Side (c. A.D. 430) gives another quotation of Papias to the effect that 'John the Theologian and James his brother were killed by Jews'. But, although the brothers are bracketed in this way, Papias may mean that John's martyrdom was much later than that of James, and this certainly must be how Philip took it, seeing that he attributes the Gospel, 1 John and the Apocalypse to him.

The Chronicle of George the Monk (IX cent.) also quotes this passage of Papias, directly connecting it with Mk 10.38f. He quotes Origen (*Comm. in Mt.* xvi.6) to the effect that John was martyred, but points out that Eusebius (*HE* iii.i.1) speaks of his

death at Ephesus. So again it seems that John's martyrdom is long
after that of James. In fact, there is probably behind these
references a confusion in the Greek *martys*, which can mean both a
witness in the legal sense and a martyr in our modern sense; this
confusion would be encouraged by Mk 10.39.
    Barrett gives further evidence from two martyrologies. A
Syriac martyrology of A.D. 411 gives for 27th December: 'John
and James the Apostles in Jerusalem'; and the Calendar of
Carthage (A.D. 505) has for the same day: 'Commemoration of St
John the Baptist and of James the Apostle whom (singular,
referring to James only) Herod slew'. Even if, as is probable, 'the
Baptist' is an error for 'the Apostle', this does not prove martyrdom
on the same day. Nothing can be built on this fragile testimony.

4. THE BELOVED DISCIPLE

Turning to internal evidence, obviously the first thing we must do
is to consider the claim that the Beloved Disciple was the author,
for this is actually made in the Appendix (21.24). It is also
necessary to decide if the traditional identification of him with
John the Apostle is correct.

    (a) The 'disciple whom Jesus loved' is so named only at the
Last Supper (13.23), the Crucifixion (19.26), the Empty Tomb
(20.2), and in the Appendix (21.7, 20). But he might be the unnamed disciple in 1.35 (the other of the two being Andrew, 1.40).
He could also be the 'other disciple' who gained entry into the
High Priest's house (18. 15f.), and he might be the witness of the
Piercing of Jesus' side (19.35). When all these references are put
together in the light of 21.24, a consistent and attractive picture
emerges. He is one of the first disciples, and gains a special place
in the affection of Jesus. This appears in the Last Supper, and also
in Jesus' consignment of his mother to his care. We have to
assume that he returned after taking her home (19.27), if he is the
witness of 19.35. But the most important thing is that he is the
first to believe the Resurrection. Later his long life is covertly
foretold (21.22). Finally, his writing of the Gospel, as an eye-
witness long after the events, is attested by an editor.
    But appealing as it is, this picture is open to serious objections.
    (i) There is no warrant to see a reference to the Beloved Disciple
in 1.35, and no hint is given there that the unnamed one will

spring to importance at the end of the story. Similarly the 'other disciple' of 18.15f. must be left out of consideration, as the designation of him as the one 'whom Jesus loved' is lacking (contrast 20.2). The witness of the Piercing (19.35) also lacks the proper description; in fact, this verse may well be a gloss (see the notes *ad loc.*). Obviously if this verse could with confidence be taken as a reference to the Beloved Disciple, it would strengthen the claim that he was the author. But it must be excluded; the only authentic references to him are 13.23; 19.26; 20.2; and the Appendix.

(ii) The story in the Appendix (21.1–23) may be accepted as authentic work of the evangelist, even though it was not part of the Gospel. Here, and here only, the personality of the Beloved Disciple is evidently the subject of speculation. But the whole point is that the question about his future (verse 21) should never have been asked. Jesus makes an existential demand ('Follow me!', verse 22), and refuses to give a straight answer. The story was, then, intended to *stop* speculation about the Beloved Disciple, which had arisen from the Gospel already completed. But the evangelist's method left an air of mystery which only aroused further speculation! A promoter of the Gospel concluded that the reason for the concealment of the Disciple's identity is that he is in fact the author himself. So verse 24 was added, and perhaps also 19.35.

(iii) But the idea that the title is a self-designation of the author is far from convincing.[8] It is bound to lead to the conclusion that the three passages in chapters 13, 19 and 20 where he appears are eye-witness accounts. But all three incidents have parallels in the Synoptic Gospels in which the Beloved Disciple plays no part. It will be shown in the commentary that John's sources at these three points stood close to the Synoptic accounts. It is precisely the presence and function of the Disciple in John's presentation of them which it is so hard to explain on historical grounds. This takes us to our second question, who really *was* the Beloved Disciple?

(b) It has always been recognized that John the Apostle is the most likely candidate. In favour of this identification it is urged that, according to the Synoptics, he was one of the inner group of three who were present at the raising of Jairus' daughter, the Transfiguration, and Gethsemane. But this is no argument, for the Fourth Gospel does not include any of these three occasions when the group is singled out for special mention. It is true that Luke mentions John along with Peter (Lk. 22.8; Ac. 3.1, 11; 4.13; 8.14), but this proves nothing either way. Finally, the Appendix lists seven disciples, including 'the sons of Zebedee, and two others of his disciples' (21.2). Obviously 'that disciple whom Jesus loved' in verse 7 must be one of these four; but the fact that the author is so careful to hide his identity makes it more likely that he is intended to be one of the two unnamed, rather than one of the sons of Zebedee. Thus the identification with John the Apostle is not only unproven, but also distinctly doubtful. Other suggestions are:

(i) *Lazarus* (Fleming, Filson, Sanders, Eckhardt), because his return to life (11.44) and further association with Jesus (12.9–11) would account for the fact that the Disciple is first mentioned at the Last Supper (13.23). The cardinal factor is that 'Jesus *loved* . . . Lazarus' (11.5, cf. verses 3, 11, 36). But the theory is scarcely tenable: if the Disciple is named in these passages, it is hard to see why he is not named in chapters 13, 19 and 20. But, as 11.1–44 and 12.9–11 probably were added by the evangelist into the second edition of his work (see below, p. 50), it could be argued that he decided to abandon the anonymity of the Disciple at this stage. However, this still does not account for the elaborate concealment of his identity in the Appendix.

(ii) *John Mark* (Wellhausen, Parker), because of the attribution of the Gospel to 'John', and because his house seems to have been the headquarters of the early church in Jerusalem (Ac. 12.12). Some think that he was not the Beloved Disciple, but the evangelist who used the Disciple's reminiscences (Sanders: Mark used Lazarus' notes, which were in Aramaic; Marsh: Mark used traditions stemming from John the Apostle). If so, the second Gospel could not be attributed to Mark. But there is no evidence for his connection with the Fourth Gospel. It only adds to the confusion to bring in yet another John on such slender grounds.

(iii) *Paul* (B. W. Bacon), on the basis of Gal. 2.20 ('who loved me'), as the retrojection of a later figure into the past. The suggestion is grotesque. *Matthias* (E. L. Titus) is equally improbable.

The anonymity of the Beloved Disciple must be taken seriously: John did not wish his identity to be known. This leads to the question whether he can rightly be regarded as an historically identifiable character at all. He may then be an ideal figure (Loisy, Bultmann). Here we must be careful to keep the issues distinct. The Disciple certainly has a *symbolic* function as the ideal disciple, who remains true where Peter fails (he is not necessarily the type of the Gentile church, as Bultmann supposes). But this does not mean that he is not intended to be an actual historical person: he is definitely one of the Twelve. But John has felt the need of representing one of them as the perfect disciple. He has taken advantage of the facelessness of most of them in the tradition to impose on one of them the features which are needed for his purpose. John knows that Peter was the leader of the Twelve (cf. 6.68); but Peter's failure at the time of Jesus' trial disqualified him for the function which John needed to represent at this point, i.e. someone who does not deny the Passion, but pierces beyond it to the Resurrection. This role demands an Apostle more discerning and more loyal than Peter, and closer to the mind of Jesus. The tradition contained no clear candidate for this position among the Twelve, and John wisely decided not to commit himself to any particular one of them.

5. THE EVANGELIST

Our search for the author of the Fourth Gospel has produced only negative results. The attribution of it to John the Apostle is not well founded. The Beloved Disciple is not the author, nor even a person who could have supplied eye-witness information, in spite of 21.24. We simply do not know who the author was; in this commentary he will be called 'John' for the sake of custom and convenience.

It follows that the Fourth Gospel can lay no claim to special historical reliability. In fact, the fictional approach to descriptions of character, exemplified in the figure of the Beloved Disciple, warns us against giving too ready credence to the numerous circumstantial details of the narrative. On the other hand, we may still hold that John has excellent sources. Moreover we can find out a good deal more about him by studying the background of his thought.

4. BACKGROUND OF THOUGHT

The Fourth Gospel was valued by the Gnostics because it was congenial to their Greek ways of thought. It has been similarly valued in modern times for its mystical kind of spirituality, notably by von Hügel,[9] and scholars have frequently sought for the origins of its ideas in Hellenistic speculative thought. More recently attention has been turned to the Jewish background, especially in the work of Hoskyns and of Barrett. This has received striking confirmation from the discovery of the Dead Sea Scrolls.

In fact, we must distinguish carefully between the background of the author's thought and that of his readers. Obviously he writes against his own background, but he will have to adapt himself to that of his readers to some extent, if theirs differs greatly from his own. In the case of the Fourth Gospel, it is clear that the author derives his thought from the Jewish and Christian tradition; but it is altogether probable that he writes for Greeks, and duly takes their way of thinking into account.

I. THE CHRISTIAN BACKGROUND

It has already been shown that John's choice of the Gospel form puts him in line with the primitive *kērygma*. John accepts the Fatherhood of God, the idea of God as sole Creator (in spite of a measure of dualism), and the messiahship of Jesus. He is quite definite about the real humanity of Jesus, emphasizing the flesh (1.14), probably in reaction to Docetism (cf. below, pp. 61ff.). He presupposes the institutions of baptism (4.1) and the Eucharist (6.52–8). His emphasis on the role of faith in adherence to Jesus and on the idea of love as the expression of moral obedience have their counterparts both in the Synoptic tradition and in the epistles of Paul.

But John's Christianity, like Paul's, is a developed Christianity. Both think of Jesus as pre-existent, using Jewish Wisdom categories (Jn 1.1–18; Col. 1.15–17), and call him 'Son of God', not simply as a messianic designation (cf. Ps. 2.7), but as a metaphysical reality. To both the Crucifixion and the Resurrection constitute the central act of redemption, though Paul thinks in terms of justification (Rom. 5), whereas John thinks in terms of victory over the forces of evil (12.31f.; 14.30; 16.33). Both retain the consistent eschatology which gave such urgency to the message of

Jesus, but for both of them the centre of gravity has shifted from preparation for the coming Kingdom to the concept of being 'in Christ' (Rom. 8; Jn 15), which makes an equally stern ethical demand.

But John's thought is not derived from Paul. In some ways it is more primitive, as in his use of the Son of Man figure. This stems from the Synoptic tradition, but is still recognizably related to the basic picture in Dan. 7.13; but he does not have Paul's Adam typology, which is based on it. Again, John's idea of the glory revealed in the Passion is not found in Paul, and conversely Paul's doctrine of the 'body' has no place in John. But it seems that John is later in time than Paul: the Judaizing controversy, so important for Paul, is a thing of the past; and in John the break with the synagogue is almost, if not quite, complete, whereas Paul still has hopes of winning the Jews for Christ. So, too, John presupposes that the Church has a normal, established life; whereas Paul is taken up with the problems of newly planted Christianity.

2. THE JEWISH BACKGROUND

If John is so firmly based on the Christian *kērygma*, it follows that he is affiliated to its Jewish matrix; there is no Marcionite attempt to cut the Church from its Jewish moorings. So John includes many quotations from the Old Testament, which not only reproduce passages common to the Christian tradition (e.g. Isa. 6.10, quoted in 12.40; cf. Mk 4.12), but also show knowledge of the wider context (cf. 6.31; 12.41). John also makes a broad use of Old Testament themes—e.g., the creation and Sinai theophany (1.1–18), patriarchal narratives (4.12), the Son of Man and resurrection ideas of Dan. 7 and 12 (5.19–29), the manna and the Law (6.25–51), messianic texts (7.41f.), the story of Abraham (8.56), etc.[10]

But John's Jewish lore is not only book-learning. He gives numerous topographical details of Jerusalem and its environs, which suggest either personal acquaintance with the sites, or at least very detailed information. He is also familiar with Jewish customs: he is familiar with the feasts (Passover, 'the feast' = Tabernacles, Dedication) and ceremonies connected with them (7.37), and knows about ritual purification (2.6); and he knows about the Samaritans, and understands their relation to official

Judaism (4.20–25).† He can also translate technical terms (e.g. Messiah, *rabboni*).

Moreover John is familiar with contemporary rabbinic disputes. The argument on the Sabbath in 5.17 involves a point of controversy which is not found in the primitive Gospel strands. The discourse of chapter 6 turns on a rabbinic equation of the manna with the Law given at Sinai, and also includes a specific rabbinic argument (6.45). The idea of the hidden Messiah (7.27) is known from rabbinic sources, but is not found in the Old Testament. The discourse of chapter 8 is also thoroughly rabbinic in style. We are here dealing with a facet of the Gospel which cannot be attributed to good sources, but is an essential part of its content and style. It is most natural to conclude with Bowker that John has had personal contact with Jewish and Christian discussions.[11] This suggests that the work was begun before the exclusion of the Christians from the synagogue (*c.* A.D. 85), and finished somewhat later.

This conclusion is reinforced by the Gospel's attitude to the Jews. We hear no word of the Sadducees, the leading party in the time of Jesus, or of the Zealots, to whom one of the Twelve probably belonged (Simon the Cananean, Mk 3.18). Only the Pharisees are named, and they are the undisputed leaders. This reflects the situation after the Jewish War of A.D. 68–73, when the Sadducees and Zealots were virtually liquidated and the Pharisees were left in sole possession of Jewish loyalty.

John also has very special links with the thought of the Dead Sea Scrolls. In spite of far-reaching differences between the Qumran sect (identified by many scholars with the Essenes) and the primitive Church, in some ways it provides the closest parallel of thought in Judaism at the time of Jesus. Like the Christians, these sectaries thought of their own history as the fulfilment of

† Recent studies have laid much stress on John's knowledge of the Samaritans, suggesting a closer community of ideas than has been formerly recognized. J. Bowman ('Samaritan Studies', *BJRL* XL (1958), pp. 298–327) and E. D. Freed ('Did John write his Gospel partly to win Samaritan converts?', *NT* XII (1970), pp. 241–56) have pointed to a number of possible influences on John. W. A. Meeks (*The Prophet King* (1967)) claims that he is writing for the benefit of converts from Samaritanism. G. W. Buchanan has taken these possibilities even further ('The Samaritan Origin of the fourth Gospel', in *Religions in Antiquity*, ed. J. Neusner (1968), pp. 149–75). It must be stressed, however, that all these studies are highly speculative.

prophecy; they had a similar eschatological orientation, and they handled Scripture in much the same way. Moreover, they showed a system of thought in which some of the Hellenistic, or at least Iranian, elements were already present, so that we do not have to look outside Judaism to account for their presence in early Christianity; in particular, we find in the Scrolls the clearest expression of the contrast between the light and the darkness, which is a central theme in John. The *Manual of Discipline* begins with an exposition of the basic spirituality of the sect, in which it is asserted that there are two spirits contending for the domination of men, variously described as 'the Spirit of Truth' and 'the Spirit of Error', or 'the Angel of Light' and 'the Angel of Darkness'. So John speaks of the devil as 'the father of lies' (8.44), and of the Holy Spirit as 'the Spirit of truth' (14.17; 15.26; 16.13).

Some kind of influence of the sect on John seems inescapable. But this need not have been more than his contacts with Judaism in general; for at this time, even though the sect probably came to an end with the Jewish War, its ideas were probably widespread and influential. The work of the triumphant Pharisaic party was not achieved all at once, and ideas which were later rejected or simply superseded and forgotten could survive for some time. Moreover, the rabbis largely assimilated them by adaptation rather than rejected them outright, as witness the rabbinic doctrine of the two inclinations in man (the *yēṣer haṭ-ṭōb* and the *yēṣer hā-raʿ*, the good and the bad inclinations), which is a sophisticated form of the Two Spirits doctrine, shorn of its dualistic basis.

It is evident that the Jewish element in John is far too important to be merely derived from the continuation of Jewish ideas in the Church, and demands actual contact with Judaism. But the same is not true of his readers, for whom he often provides an explanation of Jewish items (1.41; 4.9; etc.). It is highly probable that he had to reckon with Hellenistic elements in their outlook, and to these we now turn.

3. THE HELLENISTIC BACKGROUND

In the three centuries following the death of Alexander the Great (323 B.C.), the three centres of ancient civilization—Egypt, Mesopotamia and Greece—became largely fused into a single cultural unit. The aesthetic achievements of classical Greece provided the superficial style, but the nature religions of the ancient Orient lived on, though they became more sophisticated, and to some extent adapted to Greek philosophy. This Hellenistic culture penetrated Judaism to a great extent, but encountered the fierce opposition of the Maccabees when Antiochus Epiphanes attempted to impose oriental religious forms on the Jews early in the second century B.C. But the Jewish community at Alexandria came under the influence of Greek thought. So we begin with the Hellenistic Jewish thought of Alexandria, of which the great representative is Philo.

(a) *Philo*

Philo's active period of writing was in the first half of the first century A.D. He endeavoured to understand his own Jewish faith in the light of the synthesis of Platonic and Stoic thought made by Posidonius (*c.* 100 B.C.). The aim of the religious man is to bring his life into relation with reality, so as to attain his true end— immortality. But there is an impassable gulf between the real world of the divine ideas and the existing world, which is subject to change and decay. However, on this Platonic basis is superimposed the Stoic notion of the Logos (Word). By this 'Philo means the Platonic world of ideas, conceived not as self-existent, but as expressing the mind of the One God.'[12] Hence the Logos is the image of God, impressed on the multitudinous forms of the created order. It is also found within Man, supremely in his intelligence, enabling him to perceive ultimate truth and so to rise to communion with God. The Law, as the perfect expression of the Logos, is thus concerned with the activity of the soul. So Philo indulges in wholesale allegorizing of the Scriptures, in which persons and events are identified with the virtues and vices and the activity of the soul.

We are at once reminded of two features of the Fourth Gospel: (i) John speaks of the Logos in the Prologue in rather a similar way. But this is derived from certain key passages, notably Prov. 8.22–31 and Sir. 24, to which Philo also is indebted. The crucial difference is that, in John, the Logos 'became flesh' (1.14). Philo has nothing of this, which indeed runs counter to his system. In fact, John shows no acquaintance with Philo's works, so that this similarity is likely to be a parallel development rather than direct borrowing (see further the notes on 1.1). (ii) John occasionally uses *alēthinos* ('real, true') in a way which could be compared with Philo (1.9; 6.32; 15.1); but in these passages we have metaphor, but not the characteristic Philonic allegory. There is really no connection with Philo's thought, which must be counted out of the influences on the Fourth Gospel.

(b) *The Hermetic Literature*

What Dodd has called 'the higher religion of Hellenism' is well represented in the *corpus Hermeticum*. It is a sophisticated form of Egyptian religion, influenced by the Platonic and Stoic traditions. The tractate *Poimandres* has many words and phrases which are reminiscent of John. According to this work, there is an archetypal Man in the world of eternal forms, and men only reach their true end of the vision of God when they become fully identified with the archetype. But the creation myth (probably under Jewish influence) recognizes that, when the archetypal Man came into the sensible world to become the race of men, corruption took place, and men lusted after other creatures and lost the capacity for the vision of God. So some form of redemption is needed, and another tractate, *peri Palingenesias*, shows how man may be purified by a rebirth through the agency of Hermes Trismegistus, who has himself been through the process. We are reminded of Jn 3.3–12, where Jesus is the agent of rebirth, being the one who comes from above. But, as will be shown in the commentary, it is not necessary to go outside Christian sources to account for John's ideas. But it may well be that John echoes this kind of language at this point for the benefit of readers to whom it is meaningful to speak in this way about the religious quest.

c) *The Saviour Myth*

The mystery religions of the ancient world seem like Christianity, because they offer salvation to men from the wheel of Fate by a sacramental initiation into the myth of a dying and rising god, derived from the old vegetation cults of Syria and Asia Minor. Whereas these think of salvation in terms of an *ex opere operato* sacramentalism, the Gnosticism which invaded Christianity early in the second century used a comparable mythology to express salvation in terms of a secret knowledge by which men pass to the divine realm. In some forms of Gnosticism this is imparted by a saviour sent from the divine realm (as in the *Hermetica*), so that one may speak of a 'Saviour Myth'. The saving knowledge is mediated in some systems through a prophet, and in others (especially in the Docetic form of Christian Gnosticism) by the heavenly Jesus, who appears to be (but is not really) in human form. John's language is capable of being understood along these lines (cf. 3.13, 31; 6.62; 16.28; 17.3).

The question thus arises whether there was a pre-Christian Gnosticism from which John derived his ideas. Bultmann argues that this was so, and that it flourished on the Syrian fringe of Judaism. His contention is based on the Syriac *Odes of Solomon*, which are certainly Gnostic and contain many Johannine expressions (but this is probably due to Johannine influence);† and also on the Mandean literature of a sect which survives in Iraq to this day. The saviour-hero in this religion is a divine being called Manda d'Ḥayyē ('knowledge of life'), who is sent from heaven to fight the powers of darkness, and rises victoriously 'to the realm of light and reunion with the Great Life and all the celestial society.'[13] Initiation is by baptism, and John the Baptist has an honoured place in the system of thought.

Hence it is argued (i) that the Johannine interpretation of the death and resurrection of Jesus is derived from a Baptist group (such as we find at Ephesus in Ac. 19.1–7); and (ii) that this is the origin of the language of descent and ascent, which is foreign to Jewish thought. Kümmel asserts that this compels us to look for the origins of John's ideas to some such sources as Mandean Gnosticism. With regard to the first point, though there is some evidence for Baptist groups in Syria at this time, from which Mandaism is derived, it is virtually certain that the Gnostic elements are due to later syncretism.[14] With regard to the second, it is of course recognized that ascent is normal in apocalyptic, so that the exaltation of Jesus is pictured in terms of the ascent of the Son of Man (Dan. 7.13). On the other hand a Jewish origin

† There is really no consensus among scholars about the provenance of this work. Recently J. H. Charlesworth ('The Odes of Solomon—not Gnostic', *CBQ* xxxi (1969), pp. 357–69) has called for a fresh assessment of the problem. He places the *Odes* in the class of Jewish apocalyptic mystical literature of the first century A.D., along with Ethiopic Enoch, the *Thanksgiving Hymns* of Qumran (1QH), the fragment of a *Book of Mysteries* (1Q27), and 2 Esdras, which forms one of the tributaries to the Gnosticism of the second century. If this is right, the relationship of the *Odes* to John would be not a matter of dependence on either side but of sharing a common background of speculative Jewish thought. The Saviour-myth plays no part in the *Odes of Solomon*.

for the notion of descent is ready to hand in the Wisdom tradition already referred to in connection with the Logos (p. 39 above). The correlation of descent and ascent is an inner-Christian development, resulting from the application to Christ of two highly significant ideas of Judaism which had not previously come together. It can be documented in strands of the New Testament which precede John's use of these ideas: it is found in the pre-Pauline hymn of Phil. 2.5–11 and in the deutero-Pauline Eph. 4.1–16, especially verse 9 (cf. also Col. 1.15–20). Paul himself shows the development by using the idea of the *sending* of the Son of God (Rom. 8.3; Gal. 4.4). This is not the Gnostic idea of a descent through the cosmic powers, but the thoroughly biblical idea of the predetermined plan and purpose of God coming to fruition in the person of Jesus. John frequently uses the idea of sending (3.17, 34; 5.24, 36f., etc.).[15]

Seeing that John undeniably uses the key Old Testament passages both for the Wisdom idea of descent and for the apocalyptic idea of the ascent of the Son of Man, it is altogether probable that he builds on current Christian ideas rather than on an alien system of thought. Here again it seems that John writes out of a Christian and Jewish background, but uses expressions which can appeal to the wider world of Hellenistic seekers after truth within the Christian community.

5. DATE AND PLACE

It has already been shown in dealing with the Christian and Jewish background that the most probable date of composition is about A.D. 85–95; in fact, the process, involving at least two editions, could have spanned the whole of this time. On the other hand, the lack of any references to the Gospel in the letters of Ignatius and Polycarp (c. A.D. 115) might suggest that it was not written until much later. Polyc. vii.1 seems to be derived from 1 Jn 4.2f., but not as if it is a conscious quotation. Yet Irenaeus (*Letter to Florinus*) claims to have had personal knowledge of Polycarp, who 'would speak of his familiar intercourse with John, and with the rest of those who had seen the Lord'. But this is only relevant if the attribution of the Gospel to John had been made before Polycarp wrote his letter, at least thirty years before

Irenaeus knew him. All we can say is that before A.D. 115 the Gospel was not yet widely diffused or widely accepted as an apostolic writing. But its diffusion was already beginning, for we soon find that it was being copied in Egypt. The John Rylands papyrus (P52), comprising Jn 18.31–4, 37–8, is the oldest manuscript of the New Testament known; Aland considers that it was written by A.D. 130 at the latest. Also the Bodmer papyrus (P66), generally dated about A.D. 200, is put as much as fifty years earlier by Hunger. Again, the fragment of a non-canonical gospel (Papyrus Egerton 2) is certainly based on Jn 5;[16] as this seems to have been written before A.D. 150, it is clear that the Fourth Gospel had been long enough in circulation for other works to be based on it.

The traditional place of composition is Ephesus. This has several points in its favour: (i) Some kind of connection between the Apocalypse and the rest of the Johannine literature seems certain, though they cannot have been by the same authors; and Rev. 1.9, 11; 2.1 points to Ephesus as the home of the Apocalypse. (ii) Although they do not know the Fourth Gospel, Ignatius and Polycarp both echo its style of language, which points to Asia Minor, where their letters were written. (iii) Hellenistic sects flourished in Asia, and there was a Baptist group at Ephesus (Ac. 19.1–7). (iv) Ephesus had a large and important Jewish community (Ac. 18.19, 24–8; 19.8–20).

The case is hardly a strong one, and so other places have been proposed: (i) Alexandria, because of the finds of papyrus in Egypt, and because of Philo's Logos doctrine. But *all* the most ancient manuscripts of the New Testament come from Egypt, thanks to its preservative climate, and John's lack of knowledge of Philo actually precludes Alexandria from consideration. (ii) Antioch, or elsewhere in Syria, because (a) it is close to Palestine, whose language and customs John knows well; (b) Ignatius was bishop of Antioch; (c) the pre-Christian Gnosticism which lies behind Mandaism flourished in Syria; (d) the first non-heretical commentary was by Theophilus of Antioch. But the Valentinians were using John in Egypt before Theophilus wrote his commentary; the pre-Christian Gnosticism is probably irrelevant; and the other two points are not decisive. But Syria is by no means impossible as the place of origin. (iii) Palestine itself, however, though attractive in view of the strong Jewish aspects of John, is scarcely possible, because after the Jewish War the Christian community there became more and more isolated, estranged from the Jews, and cut off from the main development of the Church of the Gentiles. That John, with his advanced Christology and broad understanding of Hellenistic religious aims, belonged to this group is hardly thinkable. Hence the choice lies between Ephesus and Syria, but no certainty on this issue is possible.

6. THE LANGUAGE OF JOHN

The connection of John with Palestine, which seems to be demanded by the importance of the Jewish background, could be explained if John is dependent on much earlier work, perhaps an Aramaic original. Jesus spoke Aramaic, and Papias tells us that Matthew 'arranged the sayings in the Hebrew [i.e. Aramaic] dialect',[17] which may be a reference to the Aramaic original of the postulated sayings-source Q.

There has been a lively debate concerning the language of the Fourth Gospel.[18] Burney[19] argued from the syntax of the Gospel that the whole work is a translation from an Aramaic original. His conclusions were challenged by Colwell[20] and Bonsirven[21], who showed that the *koinē* Greek of New Testament times has all the main points of syntax which Burney took to be Aramaisms. The most recent study of M. Black[22] takes the view that, as most of the Aramaisms are found in sayings of Jesus, John was using Aramaic sources, although he wrote in Greek. Nevertheless the Aramaic is so near to the surface, that some of the MS. variations in the transmission of the Greek text are to be traced to alternative translations of the same Aramaic original. But such cases are few, even including further examples found by Boismard, and none is conclusive. The most important cases are discussed in the commentary.

In fact, John wrote good, if not very stylish, Greek. Some of his sources undoubtedly go back to Aramaic originals, but it is by no means certain that any were still in Aramaic. Where they agree verbally with the Synoptics (cf. p. 27 above) they must have been in Greek. But it is possible that Greek was not John's mother-tongue, so that his use of it is rather circumscribed. The following points may be noted:

(a) John's vocabulary is exceptionally limited, though adequate to his purpose. He uses synonyms for the sake of variation, but tends to do so without discrimination between them (the classic example is *agapān* and *philein* = love; see the commentary on 21.15–17).

(b) Unlike classical Greek, John uses parataxis (sentences strung together with 'and'), which is normal in Hebrew and Aramaic, and also asyndeton (no connecting particle), which is a special feature of Aramaic. When he does use a particle, it is often *oun* (= therefore), but deprived of its inferential meaning, so that it only means 'next', 'then', or even (at 9.18) 'but' (see also the Greek at 12.1–3).

(c) John often uses the demonstrative adjective *ekeinos* as a pronoun ('he'), whereas *houtos* is far more commonly used in this way in normal Greek. But resumption of the pronoun after a relative with which it agrees (e.g. 1.27, 33) seems always to be derived from sources which have a Semitic base.

(d) Epexegetical clauses with *hina* and *hoti* ('that') are very common, and the two particles are almost interchangeable. *Hina* properly introduces a final clause, but the sense of purpose is often lacking in John. This has been explained as mistranslation of the Aramaic *dᵉ*, which has a wide range of meaning. But it is unlikely that a translator would *choose* the wrong rendering, when the particle allows such latitude. These conjunctions are used, not so much incorrectly, as loosely, and with weakened meaning.

(e) The tenses of verbs (historic present; periphrastic ways of expressing present and imperfect) look like the Aramaic participial construction, but are common enough in the *koinē*. Occasionally a cognate noun in the dative represents the Hebrew (not Aramaic) infinitive absolute construction (see 3.29), but this is due to underlying Semitic tradition.[23]

It certainly seems probable that Greek was not John's first language, and that he acquired it too late to allow him to gain full mastery of the language. This restores confidence in his contact with old and authentic traditions, even though he writes late in the first century, with contemporary developments in view. Moreover the distribution of linguistic traits covers the whole Gospel. This weakens the theory of multiple written sources, some of which might have been in Aramaic, and rather suggests that the writing, editing and reshaping are all the work of one man.

Differences noted (e.g. by Schweizer) between the Greek of the narratives and the discourses are probably no more than is inevitable in the handling of different kinds of subject matter.

7. THE MAKING OF THE FOURTH GOSPEL

Though the language and style of John are remarkably consistent, suggesting that it is one man's work, there are abrupt transitions and apparent dislocations, which make it impossible to regard it as written all in one piece. It has either been subjected to much alteration in the process of composition, or it suffered disturbance at an early stage. Various theories, not necessarily mutually exclusive, have been put forward to account for this: that John was redacting (not quite successfully) written sources; that accidental displacements occurred; or that the addition of supplementary material in successive editions disturbed the original plan. It will be argued below that the third is the most satisfactory solution, and that the Gospel had its genesis in homilies preached by John, which he used as the basis for his work.

1. THE QUESTION OF SOURCES

It has long been observed that the enumeration of Signs in 2.11 and 4.54 points to a collection of such stories, from which John has taken his narrative material. This Signs Source would have been a collection rather like the Synoptic Gospels. If it was a written source, it can only be reconstructed by assuming that John has transcribed excerpts from it almost verbatim (so Bultmann).† In any case it seems as if John took over the feature of enumeration from it to begin with, but soon abandoned this.

The Gospel is not arranged by signs, but by the Jewish feasts, whereby Jesus is repeatedly brought to Jerusalem. This arrangement suggests editorial work to impose a pattern on rather shapeless material. In this case it is possible to think of a Discourse

---

† The Signs Source as an entity has been studied by J. Becker ('Wunder und Christologie', *NTS* xvi (1969–70), pp. 130–48), and a complete reconstruction of the text has been attempted by R. T. Fortna (*The Gospel of Signs* (1970)). I have presented a detailed criticism of the theory in my *Behind the Fourth Gospel*, chapter 2.

Source, which has been correlated with the signs selected from the other source, and arranged under the heading of the feasts.

The chief exponent of this theory is Bultmann. His work stems from the success of the source-criticism of the Synoptics, but also constitutes a brilliant application of the ideas of the History of Religions school, which was influential in the 1920s. He takes the Discourse Source to be Aramaic poems (like the Prologue), comprising the revelations of the Heavenly Man, the Revealer of the Gnostic Saviour-myth (cf. above, p. 40). A Greek translator christianized them by identifying the Revealer with the historical Jesus. They contain the real Johannine doctrine, which is not truly represented in either the Signs Source or the Passion narrative.

But source analysis of this kind is open to objections. (i) Schweizer, Ruckstuhl and others have shown that John's style and diction run through the whole work. The scissors-and-paste method of source-criticism cannot be used for John. (ii) The tradition of Synoptic type is not confined to the Signs, but occurs in sayings of Jesus in the Discourses, which are too important to be relegated to a secondary position. (iii) Some Signs and Discourses are so closely bound together that the Signs must be taken as the source for the Discourses, which have been built up from themes discovered in them by the evangelist (e.g. chapters 9 and 11).[24]

A proper approach to the question of sources must proceed along the lines of Synoptic criticism. This does not mean that John is a redactor of written sources; but he certainly made use of some written work and of oral tradition in a fairly fixed form. The right lines have been laid down by C. H. Dodd in his *Historical Tradition in the Fourth Gospel*. Here numerous sayings and narrative details are shown to be parallel to, but independent of, items in the Synoptic Gospels. By these comparisons, further non-Synoptic items of traditional material can be detected. It is one of the aims of this commentary to draw attention to such early material in John. Here just two points may be mentioned.

(i) John had short written collections closely parallel to the *sources* of the Synoptic Gospels. Thus details in chapters 2, 3 and 5 show knowledge of the sequence in Mk 2.1–3.6, well known to be a self-contained pre-Marcan collection.[25] Jn 6.1–21 (the Feeding of the Multitude) has affinities with both Mk 6 and 8, but is not dependent on either. In chapters 11 and 12 (Mary and Martha),

20 and 21 (the Resurrection) John uses sources used also by Luke, who indeed perhaps wrote later than John.[26] It is also likely that John's Passion narrative is from a written source.

(ii) Synoptic-type sayings of Jesus have a far more important place in the structure of the Gospel than has been previously recognized.[27] So far from being incidental to the Discourses, they are often the starting-point of the whole argument. Very often John draws attention to this with the formula 'Truly, truly, I say to you', which is not merely a stylistic device;† in nearly every case it points to the use of a traditional saying (see 1.51; 3.3, 5, 11; 5.19, 24f.; 6.26, 32, 47, 53; 8.34, 51, 58; 10.1, 7; 12.24; 13.16, 20f., 38; 14.12; 16.20, 23; 21.18).

2. DISPLACEMENTS

Whatever we think about John's sources, we still have to account for the signs of dislocation in the Gospel as it has come down to us. Bernard marshalled evidence to show that accidental displacements of whole blocks of material could be due to the disarrangement of some of the leaves of a codex, assuming that each block would exactly fill one or more leaves. This theory has not won wide acceptance, and is disregarded in the computer analysis of MacGregor and Morton.[28] To some extent the effects of displacement have been smoothed out, so that something other than accident is required. Hence the 'secretary' hypothesis, which assumes that a final editor has tried unsuccessfully to put together the material which was in the form of completely disarranged notes. A theory of this kind is essential to Bultmann, as he holds that the original christianized Gnostic poems, which are the nucleus of the discourses, can only be recovered by dissecting and reassembling the existing material, so as to bring

† Scholars so diverse as J. Jeremias (*New Testament Theology* I (1971), p. 35f.) and E. Käsemann (see the quotations in C. F. D. Moule, *The Phenomenon of the New Testament*, SBT, 2nd ser., I (1967), p. 67f.) maintain that this formula, involving a unique use of 'amen', certainly goes back to Jesus himself. But this assumption has been challenged by V. Hasler (*Amen: Redaktionsgeschichtliche Untersuchung zur Einführungsformel der Herrenworte 'Wahrlich, ich sage euch'* (1969)) and K. Berger (*Die Amen-Worter Jesu, BZNW* xxxix (1970)), who have argued independently that the formula can only have arisen in a Hellenistic–Jewish milieu. This does not alter the fact that the sayings introduced by the formula preserve very primitive, and for the most part certainly authentic, tradition of the words of Jesus.

together the *disjecta membra* of thematic compositions. Thus the typical Johannine feature of cross-references and repetitions is regarded as no true part of the original design. The principle suggestions are as follows:

(a) 3.22–30 is transposed to follow 3.36 (Bernard), or to follow 2.12 (Moffatt). This brings together 3.13–21 and 3.31–6, which are obviously closely related. Schnackenburg, followed by Blank, takes these in the order 3.31–6, 13–21, regarding them as late insertions of authentic material.

(b) Chapter 6 is transposed to precede chapter 5, because 7.23 refers back to 5.1–18. Alternatively 7.15–24 is removed from its context and placed after 5.47.

(c) Chapter 10 is rearranged, because the allegory of the Shepherd is taken up again on a much later occasion, and the earlier part of it spoils a cross-reference to chapter 9. So the proposed order is 10.19–21, 22–9, 1–18, 30–9. But this is really impossible, because it leaves no explanation of the 'division among the Jews' (verse 19) if the allegory has not yet been given; verses 26–9 can hardly precede the allegory, for they presuppose the results of what is only slowly and methodically built up in the course of it; and the allegory forms the transition from the theme of sight and blindness in chapter 9 (now applied to true and false shepherds) to the theology of the Passion which begins with the note of a new occasion in verse 22.

(d) 12.44–50 is placed (with partial support from Tatian's *Diatessaron*) after 12.36a, thus bringing the sayings of Jesus together before the evangelist's comments.

(e) Bernard rearranges the Supper Discourses thus: 13.1–30; 15.1–16.33; 13.31–8; 14; 17. Bultmann has a similar but more complex sequence. The object is to bring 'Rise, let us go hence' of 14.31 to the conclusion, and to ease an apparent contradiction between 13.36 and 16.5. This arrangement spoils the teaching on the Paraclete, which must begin with 14.16. But again Schnackenburg regards the Paraclete passages as subsequent insertions of authentic material.

(f) Spitta rearranges 18.13–28 in order to cope with the mention of *two* high priests, Annas and Caiaphas. His proposed sequence (18.13, 19–24, 14–18, 25b–28—25a being editorial repetition of 18) has some support from the Sinaitic Syriac, though that is probably governed by the desire to approximate to the Synoptic order.

These rearrangements will be considered in the course of the commentary. All are open to objections; in fact, some of them would never have been suggested if John's methods of composition had been properly understood. It is part of his technique to hold over part of the material from one section to form the nucleus of the next section. This applies to 7.15–24 and 10.26–9 (cf. (b) and (c) above), and the position given to 3.31–6 in (a) can be given a rather similar explanation. Others are better explained as due to the introduction of supplementary material by John himself, whereby he very considerably enlarged his original work.

3. SUPPLEMENTARY MATERIAL

It is convenient to regard the following blocks as additions for the second edition of the Gospel, though they were not necessarily all added at the same time. Detailed arguments for taking them to be additional will be given in the commentary.

(i) *The Prologue* (1.1–18) replaces the original opening, which began with John the Baptist, as in Mark. Verses 6–8 and 15 belong to this original opening.

(ii) *Chapter* 6 is obviously a self-contained unit.[29] Although the discourse is ostensibly an exposition of the Feeding miracle, it is really a sustained piece of biblical exegesis. John has inserted it after 5.47 as an example of Jesus' claim that Moses 'wrote of me' (5.46). This fact has not been generally noticed by commentators.

(iii) *The Lazarus material* (11.1–46; 12.9–11) has been added to prepare for the Passion of Jesus. This not only breaks the connection between chapters 10 and 12, but also has led John to make further rearrangements for the second edition. It will be argued in the commentary that in his original edition he had an order of events closer to that of the Synoptics, comprising the Triumphal Entry (12.12–19), the Cleansing of the Temple (2.13–22), the Priests' plot (11.47–53), and the Anointing at Bethany (12.1–8). John has removed the Cleansing to chapter 2 in order to make the raising of Lazarus the prime motive for the Priests' plot, and brought the Anointing into closer relation with the Lazarus material. Originally it had a more obvious connection with the Last Supper (chapter 13).

(d) The best explanation of 'Rise, let us go hence' in 14.31 is that only chapter 14 belongs to the first edition. Chapters 15 and 16 are a supplementary discourse added in the second edition (the

Paraclete passages were inserted into chapter 14 at the same time). It is probable that the Prayer of chapter 17 also belongs to the second edition, so that originally there was no break between 14.31 and 18.1.

To recover the original plan of the Gospel, we must not only remove these additions and make the necessary adjustments to chapters 2 and 12, but also remove the post-Johannine additions. These are the *pericope de adultera* (7.53–8.11), which only found its way into the manuscript tradition long after the Gospel was written; the appendix (chapter 21), which probably embodies the evangelist's own work in verses 1–23, but was added by an editor perhaps after his death; and all or part of 19.35. The main Christological argument of the book, beginning (1.19–34) and ending (10.40–2) with the witness of John the Baptist, then stands out very clearly, before the introduction of the Passion narrative with its traditional events in chapter 12.

4. THE HOMILIES OF JOHN

John's technique of holding over material from one section to the next (above, p. 50) indicates that he has used large, self-contained pieces as the basis of his work, splitting them up to some extent in the process of making a connected narrative. It is very likely that most of these underlying pieces were homilies which he gave to the Christian assembly, possibly at the eucharist. Chapter 6 obviously suits this setting. Some pieces are more likely to have been composed specially for the Gospel, which does not consist *only* of homilies strung together. These often incorporate fragments of homilies not used *in extenso* (e.g. the Paraclete passages in the Supper discourses, and cf. the analysis of chapter 7 in the commentary).

There are two main objections to this theory: (i) Much of John's writing, even in the discourses, is in dialogue form, so that it would appear to be the record of disputations rather than of homilies. (ii) The content is largely concerned with issues of the Jewish and Christian debate, whereas homilies are more likely to be directed to the edification of the faithful. With regard to the first point, it can hardly be supposed that John has given verbatim reports of actual disputations (though J. Louis Martyn holds that such disputations are reflected in his *History and Theology in the Gospel of John* (1968), p. 69f.). There is no reason why John should not have adopted the style of 'telling a story' about Jesus in making his homilies. The disputations are simply part of the story. The second point presupposes too rigid a distinction between the liturgical assembly and the debating chamber. No better form of edification could have been devised than these inspiring compositions, which embody the points of crucial concern to a group of Christians in vital contact with Judaism. In any case, as just pointed out, John had to adapt his homilies and to compose a certain amount of fresh material for the making of the Gospel.

This homiletic view of the making of the Fourth Gospel has been gaining ground in recent criticism (cf. Barrett, Braun, Brown, Schnackenburg, Sanders), but it must be proved from examination of John's technique.† A single example will suffice to show his literary method and its homiletic basis: chapter 5, with which, of course, must be included 7.15–24.

5.1 is an editorial note to maintain the narrative sequence, and the homily begins at verse 2. It consists of an opening Sign (2–9a), a transitional dialogue (9b–18), the discourse (19–47), and a closing dialogue (7.15–24).

(a) The Sign is the healing of a paralysed man, drawn from John's stock of traditions about Jesus. It will be shown in the commentary that it is a fusion of a non-Synoptic Jerusalem tradition and the well-known Galilean story in Mk 2.1–12. Thus, as an experienced preacher, John begins with a story to arouse the interest of his hearers; and like many a Christian teacher who has retold stories of Jesus in giving instruction, he has unconsciously fused two different versions.

(b) Next he has to work round the theme to lead into the serious matters which he really wishes to teach. This is done by means of the dialogue of 9b–18, which has a close parallel in the dialogue of 9.13–41. In both cases the issue of the Sabbath is arbitrarily attached to a tradition in which originally it played no part; moreover, in both cases the absence of Jesus when the dialogue begins allows the terms of the argument to be set out before the fundamental statement is reached (5.17 thus prepares for verse 19). The characterization is limited and stilted, the paragraph being really devoted to the process of thought; it is probably entirely

† See, further, my *Behind the Fourth Gospel*, chapter 3.

artificial. Many a preacher will remember the contortions needed to proceed from a given text to the real point at issue.

(c) The discourse is not really based on the Sign, but has its own text in the form of a parable stemming from non-Synoptic traditions of the words of Jesus (see the commentary on verses 19–20a). Though other traditional material can be discerned in verses 24, 30, 32–6, the whole is really a Johannine composition in the form of a speech by Jesus himself. Some may feel that John is morally wrong to do this, but it is to be explained simply as his homiletic method. He is using the device of the dramatic monologue; all preachers know how gripping this can be—it is a method which can be illustrated from Christian homiletic works down the ages, e.g. Thomas à Kempis in the fourteenth century and R. M. Benson in the nineteenth. The preacher feels that he has the mind of Christ (cf. 1 C. 2.1–16), and that what he says is a legitimate extension of his teaching. It is likely that John was held by his fellow Churchmen to be a prophet (cf. 1 C. 14.1–5).

(d) The closing dialogue in 7.16–24 (verse 15 is an editorial link) is not so much the end of the homily as further material from it. It shows another characteristic device of John—return to the *beginning* of the argument at each new section (thus 5.30 and 7.16 both go back to 5.19).

In general, it may be said that John shows a strong feeling for drama, but this shows itself more in the discourses than in the narrative. He knows how to order his material to lead to a most impressive climax. He is an acknowledged master of the art of dramatic irony, but this is found as much in paradoxical statements as in situations. The most famous example is the theme of kingship in the trial before Pilate (18.33–8; 19.1–16). For other examples, see 1.9–13; 2.19; 3.10; 4.11, 19, 33; 5.18, 46; 7.24, 34–6, 41f., 52; 8.22, 33, 41, 56f.; 10.33; 11.12, 16, 48; 12.27; 13.2, 21–30, 36; 15.25; 16.3, 30; 18.5, 14, 28; 19.9f., 14f., 21, 28; 20.27, 29. John also has a favourite trick of making Jesus' hearers misunderstand his meaning, so that a finer distinction may be drawn and the subject taken deeper (cf. 3.3–5; 4.10–15, 32–4, etc.). This is good theatre, but improbable in real life.

John's sense of drama, however, does not extend to the exploration of character. There is a lack of human warmth in the portrait of Jesus that requires the complement of the Synoptic picture to convey the truth. Other characters are mostly foils to Jesus; as soon as they have made their point, they are dismissed from the stage (e.g. Nicodemus in 3.1–15). Attempts at differentiation are clumsy. Peter, Andrew and Thomas are stock figures representing different functions, and the same is true of the Beloved Disciple.

One reason why this picture of Jesus (which Strathmann calls 'kerygmatic stylization') is so unsatisfactory arises directly from John's theology. Jesus, being admitted to the divine counsels, knows all that must befall him and is in complete control of his destiny. He has insight into character (2.25), knows Judas will betray him (6.71), delays to respond to an urgent message for higher reasons (11.11), seeks divine assurance only for the sake of others (11.42; 12.30), and, above all, knows when his 'hour' is to come (2.4; 7.6, 30; 8.20; 12.27; 17.1; cf. 18.4). In this way John superimposes upon Jesus the apologetic interests of the early Church, for which the Passion, and particularly the failure of Judas, demanded explanation. It was held that these embarrassing facts were part of the plan of God, foretold in Scripture. In fact, John reproduces some of the stock passages used in this connection (e.g. 19.24, 28).[30] The result is that his portrait of Jesus tends to make him a superhuman figure. This has the unfortunate effect that the Christ of the Fourth Gospel, so far from being anti-Docetic, flings the door wide open to a Docetic Christology, which John himself would no doubt have repudiated with horror (cf. pp. 61ff. below).

8. THE HISTORICAL VALUE OF THE FOURTH GOSPEL

The last remarks are bound to lead to a degree of scepticism concerning the value of the Fourth Gospel as an historical document. We have seen in earlier sections that John cannot be regarded as an eye-witness of the events which he records, and that he writes at a time long after they occurred. In any case, his presentation of them is dominated by his theological purpose; he may have access to excellent traditions, but he recasts them radically to suit his interpretation of the meaning of Christ. The historical value of his work cannot be confined to matters of historical facts, persons and places which can be recovered by stripping off his interpretation to expose the underlying traditions;

nor is it enough to point further to the information which the
Gospel implies about the state of the Church in his own day. The
question of crucial importance for the modern reader is whether
John's interpretation of Jesus is true. Making due allowances
for an inevitable degree of distortion, can we accept John's
interpretation as a true account of what was *really* going on when
Jesus lived and worked among men?

As far as the facts go, it is doubtful if the Gospel adds much to
the knowledge which we have from the Synoptic Gospels. The
order of events has to be corrected to some extent to accord closer
with them, and in any case John's habit of bringing Jesus to
Jerusalem for the feasts is a literary device rather than historical
reminiscence. It is, however, probable that Jesus visited Jerusalem
more frequently than the Synoptists suggest. On the other hand,
many scholars are disposed to take the brief notes of an early
Judean ministry of Jesus (3.22; 4.1) as an authentic item which
they have omitted. In matters of detail, John's underlying non-
Synoptic traditions have much to give, both of sayings and incidents, to fill out the Synoptic picture; but these can only be
recovered by careful analysis of the material as it stands.

Information about the Church in John's day has already been
indicated in the section on his background of thought, especially
with regard to the Jewish background. Here we may note that a
further Jewish feature—the exclusion of Christians from the
synagogue—is alluded to in chapter 9. See further the next
section.

With regard to John's interpretation of the events, there can be
no doubt that John himself was absolutely convinced that his
presentation of Jesus—his Christology—is true. Whether we can
agree with him depends largely on our own religious presuppositions. There is a magisterial quality about John's writing
which appears to admit of no contradiction; but we should not be
tricked by this into supposing that his thought is completely
homogeneous and systematized. To some extent he is still groping.
His Christology of the Logos is confined to the Prologue, which
belongs to the second edition of his work; elsewhere we see a
fusion of the title Son of Man, used by Jesus as a self-designation
in the Synoptic tradition, and of the Father and Son relationship
attested in Jesus' specially intimate address to God as 'Father'
(cf. Lk. 11.2; 22.42). Very often the statements are so ambivalent

that it is not clear whether John means by the Father–Son relationship the spiritual relation of any devout person with his God, or the metaphysical relation which applies solely to Christ as the Man from Heaven. Consequently, there are some statements which can only seem outrageous to the Jewish mind (cf. 8.48–59; 10.30–9). There are moments when he appears to contradict himself flatly—e.g. 10.30: 'I and the Father are one' and 14.28: 'the Father is greater than I'. Questions about the meaning of Christ were being asked from the earliest days, and the contradictory texts of John were the subject of controversy for several centuries. It was not until the Council of Chalcedon in A.D. 451 that a formula for the two natures in Christ, divine and human, was devised. Those whose faith is built on this dogmatic foundation will inevitably tend to understand the Johannine Christ in Chalcedonian terms, forgetting that the Definition was not forged until 350 years later. The fact that John's not always self-consistent expressions paved the way for this Definition shows the cardinal importance of the Fourth Gospel in the history of the Church.

The historical value of John's presentation of Christ is that it is a most telling witness to the long-term effects of the astounding impact of Christ himself. The inconsistencies suggest that his idea of the meaning of Jesus stands midway between the original experience of the disciples and the beginnings of a formal system of thought, containing both a measure of truth and a measure of distortion. The fact remains that it is still possible to claim, as has been done many times through the centuries, that no one has grasped the meaning of Jesus better than John. The importance of his work depends not so much on accurate reporting as on his intellectual capacity to pierce through the tradition and bring to expression its inner meaning. If it is a prerequisite for understanding the saving activity of God that the divine meaning of an event depends upon fact *and* interpretation, then it is the special achievement of John that he has given the clues for the interpretation of the facts.

9. SPECIAL ISSUES

To some extent the Fourth Gospel stands apart from the rest of the New Testament. Hence it is possible to argue, not only that

John reflects new issues that were arising in the Church of his day, but also that he stands outside the mainstream of Christianity and is actively opposed to it.

1. THE DELAY OF THE PAROUSIA

Jesus preached the imminent expectation of the Kingdom of God. His death and resurrection were interpreted as the decisive act in the transition from the age that was passing away to the new age that was to come. But, according to apocalyptic expectation, this should be marked by the general resurrection of the dead and the judgment (Dan. 12.1f.). The first preaching of the Apostles asserted that Jesus would shortly appear in glory to claim his own. But time went on, and Jesus did not appear. Some of those who had embraced Christianity died. We can see the problem this posed in 1 Th. and 1 C. 15. Without exactly denying the problem, Paul concentrates on response to God in Christ: if a man is in Christ, the point of decision, the actual judgment, is in a sense already past; the delay of the Parousia no longer matters. The idea of the Kingdom is replaced by the concept of being in Christ.

The same applies in John. He never refers to the Kingdom of God, except at 3.3, 5. On the other hand, he frequently asserts that faith in Jesus opens the way to present enjoyment of the blessings of the coming age. He may use the language of consistent eschatology ('the hour is coming' (5.25)), but he qualifies it in the same breath ('and now is'). The believer will not only be raised up 'at the last day' (6.39, 40, 44), but even now 'has eternal life' (6.47). He can even say that the believer 'shall never die' (11.26). The fate of the Beloved Disciple (21.20–3) is probably related to this problem: would he survive until the Parousia? The answer is unsatisfactory; Jesus seems to hedge round the question. The idea of the Parousia, one may conclude, is not to be considered seriously.

Modern criticism more and more denies the possibility of a thoroughgoing realized eschatology. The language of consistent eschatology in John is to be taken seriously; Bultmann's decision to excise such passages (e.g. 5.26–9) as the work of the ecclesiastical redactor is purely arbitrary, dependent on his identification of the Johannine doctrine with Gnosticism. But, really, the whole point is that the historic event of Christ anticipates the End, and also reveals him as the designated judge. So adherence to Christ means that the judgment is anticipated in the case of the believer, and he already knows something of the final bliss. For such a person the future is not only anticipated in the present, but also guaranteed ultimately (cf. 10.27f.). But there is no suggestion that salvation consists in a kind of timeless mysticism.

Nor is there any sign that John is consciously opposing a different view. He uses apocalyptic expressions ambivalently, so that they apply both to the present by anticipation and to the future. But he does not overtly set a timeless present over against a futuristic eschatology; he is not telling his readers to cease to concern themselves with 'the times and the seasons' (1 Th. 5.1), as if he had to correct mistaken ideas. We can say that the delay of the Parousia is an underlying influence, which accounts for the emphasis on present anticipation of the End through faith in Christ, so that John gives, not an 'interim ethic', but an interpretation of the Gospel that is true for all time. But there is no sign that this is an issue which divides John from the main body of Christians of his day.

2. POLEMIC AGAINST SACRAMENTALISM

The next issue arises from the first. If John's spirituality places all the emphasis on the interior response of the believer, it can be argued that he is opposed, not only to the crude apocalypticism of the Church of his day, but also to the whole paraphernalia of the externals of Church order and worship. John unaccountably omits the institution of the Eucharist from his account of the Last Supper (chapter 13). He uses eucharistic themes (the Bread of Life (6.26–58); the Vine (15.1–17), but these are not directly related to liturgical acts, and are not distinguished from other themes which have no liturgical significance (the Water (4.7–15); the Light (8.12); the Life (11.25f.)). Modern scholars are divided on this issue. Bultmann was by no means the first to see an anti-sacramental strain in John, but his theory of the Gnostic origins of the discourses positively requires it. The themes just mentioned are various aspects of the truth brought by the Revealer, which is concerned not with cultic practices but with the inner orientation of the mind. Bultmann does not deny that there is direct allusion to the eucharist in 6.51b–8, but he ascribes these verses to the ecclesiastical redactor, who had a definite interest in bringing the Gospel into line with conventional ideas and practice. Similarly, he regards the commissioning of the Apostles to forgive sins (20.23) as an old tradition reworked by the Evangelist (not the same as the ecclesiastical redactor), so as to apply it to the Christian community as a whole (pp. 690, 693).

The theory is based on a general impression of the Gospel reinforced by the dangerous argument from silence. It entails excisions from the received text on doctrinaire grounds without a secure basis of literary criticism. The themes of Water, Light and Life, which are certainly metaphorical in the higher religion of Hellenism, are not necessarily without liturgical significance in John's hands, for they may well include a reference to baptism. There is room for disagreement how far John intends to make such allusions. Cullmann and Niewalda undoubtedly go too far in seeing liturgical allusions everywhere. But whereas the sacraments and Church order have in the past been considered to be extraneous additions to the original message of Jesus, modern research tends to confirm that they belong to the most primitive strands of the tradition. The Qumran sect has given us an idea how a Jewish sect would embody such institutions, even without the superstructure of Christian theology. If the homiletic view of the composition of John is correct, the silence is due, not to disapproval, but to the fact that sacraments and Church order are presupposed. For the homilies were actually given in the course of the Eucharist. For John the Christian institutions are not only the form of Church life which is received from the past, but they bear an integral relation to the essential meaning of the life and work of Jesus himself. This connection is expressed in the allegory of the Vine, and in the teaching on persecution which follows from it (chapter 15). As this chapter is set in the Last Supper, it is most natural to see allusion to the wine of the Eucharist in this allegory. As in the first issue, it is unsound to suspect a polemic which is not brought to the surface.

3. POLEMIC AGAINST THE BAPTIST SECT

The Fourth Gospel attaches special importance to John the Baptist as the primary witness to Christ (1.6–8, 15, 19–36; 3.22–30; 5.30–6; 10.40f.). Although these passages have a positive function—to enhance the unique position of Jesus—they can be interpreted as hostile, because they proceed by way of contrast. Jesus is in every way *better* than the Baptist. When we find that the Baptist's disciples continue to work in a way parallel to the disciples of Jesus (3.22f.; 4.1), the question arises whether the position reflects rivalry between Christian and Baptist groups in John's own time.

Undoubtedly the relation between the Baptist and Jesus needed explanation in the early days of the Church; cf. Mt. 11.2–19. The position finally adopted was that the Baptist was the last of the line of the prophets, fulfilling the function of Elijah, who was expected to return to prepare people for the Day of the Lord (Mal. 4.5f.; cf. Lk. 1.13–17). It is probable that behind this explanation there lies the embarrassing fact that Jesus had broken away from the Baptist, whom many regarded as the Messiah. This embarrassment shows through in Matthew's version of the baptism of Jesus (Mt. 3.14f.).

Evidence for the continuation of the Baptist's following in later times may be seen in Acts. There was a small group of his disciples at Ephesus (Ac. 19.1–7), and Apollos of Alexandria was also a disciple (Ac. 18.25). Outside the New Testament, the *Clementine Recognitions* (third century, but based on older writings) assert that various sects grew up to thwart the infant Church. These included the Baptist's disciples, who claimed, on the authority of Mt. 11.11, that he was the Messiah. This is often taken to mean that there was a Baptist sect which made this claim in the second century; but this is not exactly what is said, and the assumption may be quite erroneous. But the possibility of the continuation of Baptist groups in Syria is supported by the Mandean traditions, though the system does not identify him with the Man from Heaven, so that he still has a subordinate role.[31] There is also patristic evidence that certain Gnostics traced their origins to Simon Magus and Dositheus, who had been followers of the Baptist in Samaria (the Mandean texts know nothing of this). Out of these scraps of evidence the theory has been built up by Reitzenstein and others that there was a large and important Baptist movement, which could have been a serious threat to Christianity in Syria. The theory is adopted for obvious reasons by Bultmann, but it is far too insecure to be taken as a guide to understanding John's references to the Baptist.[32]

It is far more likely that John contrasts him with Jesus for the same reason as the Synoptists—that it was known that Jesus was in some way affiliated to him, and that this was cause of embarrassment in Christian apologetic to the *Jews*, who held it against Christian claims. From this point of view the Fourth Gospel affords evidence only of the Jewish and Christian encounter. The need to postulate opposition to active Baptist groups becomes redundant.

4. POLEMIC AGAINST DOCETISM

The case for a polemic against Docetism is much stronger, and has been persuasively presented by Hoskyns (pp. 48–57). Docetism, often called the first Christian heresy, is a tendency rather than a formulated dogmatic position. The description of certain Christians as Docetists (*dokētai*) first appears in a letter of Serapion.[33] He gives a warning against a certain book which asserts that the Saviour only *appeared* (*dokein*) to have a created human body and only *appeared* to die on the Cross. This links up with the use of *dokein* in Ignatius (*Trall.* x), who was much concerned with this issue. The heresy arises from the dualism of Hellenistic thought, which sees the created order as belonging to the side of evil and mortality, over against the divine realm of good and immortality. If Jesus is the Saviour of men (so the argument runs), he must belong to the divine realm, and so cannot really have had a human existence. This doctrine is the presupposition of most of the Gnostic systems, but would be equally liable to arise wherever Hellenistic ideas prevailed.

The expansion of the Church among the Gentiles was bound to lead to difficulties at this point. 'Flesh' (*sarx*) was a bad word among people with these ideas. They could agree with Paul that 'God has done what the law, weakened by the flesh, could not do . . .' (Rom. 8.3a). It was harder to accept *how* he had done it. 'Sending his own Son in the likeness of sinful flesh and for sin, he condemned sin in the flesh' (Rom. 8.3b). But 'likeness' is ambiguous; Paul is more definite in Col. 1.22: 'He has now reconciled (you) in his body of flesh by his death.' The troubles are more apparent when we reach the Pastorals. The author not only asserts that 'he was manifested in the flesh' (1 Tim. 3.16), but also refers to the practical consequences of the heresy: 'Everything created by God is good, and nothing is to be rejected if it is received with thanksgiving' (4.4). When we reach the Johannine epistles, the issue is a burning one: 'Every spirit which confesses that Jesus Christ is come in the flesh is of God, and every spirit

which does not confess Jesus is not of God. This is the spirit of
antichrist' (1 Jn 4.2f.; cf. 1.1–3; 2.22; 2 Jn 7). Imagine then the
effectiveness of the climax of the Prologue to the Gospel: 'And the
Word became flesh' (1.14).

The point is that salvation conceived in dualistic terms makes
the present world order of no account. First, it leads to asceticism,
as the spiritual person will have no interest in the motions of the
flesh (cf. 1 Tim. 4.4, quoted above). Then, under pressure of the
flesh itself, it leads to sheer antinomian immorality, as the person
who is enlightened feels himself free from the trammels of the
flesh, which can then do what it likes without being able to touch
his real self, secure in the higher life. The monotheistic and strongly
ethical basis of Christianity, derived from Judaism, could not
allow such perverted notions. Salvation is the transition from one
age to the next, already reached with the exaltation of Christ. It
is essentially a linear view, requiring the language of eschatology,
and only approaches the timelessness of Greek metaphysics in so
far as stress is laid on the present anticipation of the coming age
(cf. pp. 57f. above). The indispensable requirements for participation in the new age are repentance and faith (cf. Mk 1.15).
Thus moral categories are all-important. The idea of 'the flesh' in
Jewish and Christian thought sometimes seems ambiguous. It is
properly morally neutral, but, when it stands for the created
order in contrast with God, it tends to emphasize the weakness of
mere createdness (cf. Isa. 31.3; Mt. 16.17; Rom. 8.3a, quoted
above). It is this contrast which is intended in Jn 3.6, where the
flesh is set against the Spirit (see the notes *ad loc.*, and cf. 1 C.
15.50). But the transition from one age to the next has been
accomplished in Christ's person. It has been done on the level of
this world. It is essentially a *moral* achievement. Hence it is vital
to hold that it was done in the flesh, on the level of humanity
where man belongs.

1 John is so definite on this subject that it is at once to be
expected that the Gospel should be specially concerned with it.
Käsemann denies this, on the grounds that John's Christology
actually exhibits the tendency to Docetism (cf. p. 54 above). It
is true that the key passages do not belong to the first edition of
the Gospel (1.14; 6.51b–8—but cp. 6.63, which *perhaps* points in
the opposite direction; 19.35). But Käsemann's view only becomes
plausible when attention is confined to distinctive ideas, and what

John has in common with the rest of the New Testament is
ignored; and it has been argued above that the overall unity of the
Gospel is too great to allow any theory which requires carving
up the book into different strands embodying irreconcilable views.
John not only refers to Jesus as the Messiah and the apocalyptic
Son of Man, but also retains the central Christian tenet that,
contrary to expectation, he died a criminal's death. There is no
hint that Jesus only seemed to die; the fact that Gnostics, holding
Docetic views, were the first to value the Fourth Gospel only shows
that it is possible to interpret it in this way, given their presuppositions, and it does not prove that John would have agreed with
them. If, as seems probable, 1 John is by the same author, and
written later than the Gospel, then we can conclude that the anti-
Docetism, which begins to be apparent in the second edition of
the Gospel, eventually became a more serious preoccupation of
the author. Possibly this was because of misinterpretation and
misunderstanding of the Gospel itself.

10. THE PERMANENT VALUE OF THE FOURTH GOSPEL

The Fourth Gospel is such a masterly work and so deeply moving
as an interpretation of Christ that it is hard to believe that its
origins are so obscure and that it made its way into the life of the
Church so slowly. But this happened at a critical stage. The control
exercised by living memory of Jesus was passing away, and expansion in the Gentile world brought Christianity to the notice of
men of powerful intellect, whose minds were conditioned by
Hellenistic culture; the rise of Gnosticism attests the problems
which exercised the minds of these men. Above all, it was the
problem of reconciling Christian faith with their cosmological
presuppositions which most urgently demanded solution and
presented the gravest dangers. For the tendency was, as it has
always continued to be, that the solution should be a reflection of
the *Zeitgeist*, the outlook of the time. It was only too easy to lose
the essence of the Gospel in the process; Docetism is a case in
point. The intellectual struggle of the first five centuries is the
record of the clash of irreconcilable views, and of the hammering
out of an agreed and acceptable solution.

The Fourth Gospel was written just when these issues were

beginning to be felt. It was seized by the Gnostics because it appeared to offer support for their views. Then it began to make its way in orthodox circles. It is not too much to say that its 'discovery' had a profound influence on the survival of orthodox Christianity. For it had the unique advantage of taking some account of the questions which were crying out for solution, at the same time as being securely anchored in the historic facts of the primitive tradition.[34] Origen makes this point when he complains that too many give 'their whole attention to Christ as the Logos, to the virtual exclusion of the many other titles ascribed to him' (*Comm. in Joh.* i.21). It was, of course, this element above all which provided a way of reconciling Christian faith with the cosmology of the time.

The point which chiefly concerns the patristic period, and which explains the concentration on the Prologue, was the explanation of Christ in terms of the doctrine of the Incarnation. This is indeed a matter of lasting value, but modern readers may well be equally impressed by another unique Johannine feature— the concept of the glory of God displayed in the Passion of Christ. This appears in the double meaning of the phrase 'lifting up the Son of Man' (3.14; 8.28; 12.34), which refers both to the Cross and to the exaltation of Jesus. Then there is the dramatic declaration that 'now' is the time when 'the Son of Man is glorified' when the moment of the Passion is reached (12.23; 13.31). This emphasis, coupled with the Incarnation, gives two poles which are both essential to Johannine Christology. The resulting portrait, for all its deficiencies, gives a most compelling idea of the ethical relationship between Jesus and the Father. 'The Father loves the Son, and shows him all that he himself is doing . . . I can do nothing on my own authority . . . I seek not my own will but the will of him who sent me' (5.20, 30). The Incarnation is the act of 'sending'. The Passion is the ultimate test of filial obedience (12.27f.). Hints of the relationship between the Father and the Son reverberate all through the Gospel, and come to a climax in 10.30: 'I and the Father are one'. Without considering the possible metaphysical implications of this verse, we can certainly see a unity of will here, a perfect communion between the Father in heaven and the Son on earth.†

John's conception of the relation between the Father and the

† See further T. E. Pollard, *Johannine Christology and the Early Church* (1970).

Son is rooted in the earlier tradition, but obviously it owes something to his own experience. He had the capacity to enter imaginatively into the meaning of the tradition; his own spiritual-ity was such that he could conceive of Jesus' relation to the Father in this way. Moreover, he is at pains to show that the same experience is open to the disciples—i.e., to the reader—as well. Unlike the Gnostics, John gives no suggestion that it applies only to a privileged élite. All men are invited to share through Christ in his communion with the Father (14.20; 17.20f.). They will have to bear their part in the Cross (15.18–27), but in him they will find peace (14.27). To communicate this experience is one of John's central aims.

Today, when the advance of science renders the world-view of New Testament times untenable without radical reinterpretation, the experience enshrined in the Fourth Gospel is likely to have special importance. Bultmann has led the way here, for he has translated the Gospel from its mythical cosmology to the modern concern with the meaningfulness of existence. We may not agree with his source analysis of the Gospel, but no one can quarrel with the seriousness of his aim. The Fourth Gospel does indeed enable us to see in Jesus the affirmation of the meaningfulness of existence in terms of human personality; the theology of the Incarnate Word gives status to the centrality of morals in a mechanistic universe; and the life, death and Resurrection of Jesus affirm the meaningfulness of existence in the face of the harsh realities of living and dying in the universe as we know it. This affirmation takes the form of personal, ethical response to the Word, which is the utterance of created existence. The Word which is heard through meditation on Jesus is the Word that is to be obeyed by a loving motion of the will and of the mind and of the heart. It is no accident that 'to hear' and 'to obey' are one word in Hebrew (šāmaʿ; cf. 5.25). True hearing is inseparable from obedient response; the filial attitude of Jesus, as the Son to the Father, is the proper mode of response to the meaningfulness of existence.

If the Fourth Gospel lends itself to reinterpretation in existential terms, it means that the experience which it contains is not necessarily tied to a rigid doctrinal frame, but can be the common property of all who are seekers after truth. But it is essential that it should first be understood within its own terms of reference. It would be fatally easy to repeat the mistake of the early Gnostics, and to press it into the service of a system of thought which is alien to its spirit. Only when its essential message has been mastered can it make its contribution to solving the problems of the future. In the Prologue John says: 'No one has ever seen God.' To us today this represents more than a rabbinic dogmatic position. It represents the uncertainty of life and of the future, which hangs over men and can lead them to despair. But John has an affirmation to make in the same breath: 'The only Son, who is in the bosom of the Father, he has made him known.' And in the chapters which follow he draws out of the reader the response of faith, which leads to a new dimension of hope as he discovers the meaning of life in Christ.

THE TEXT

The Greek text used in preparing this commentary is that of the Württembergische Bibelanstalt, Stuttgart, in the *Synopsis Quattuor Evangeliorum*, edited by Kurt Aland (1965²). Textual notes are based on the *apparatus criticus* of this edition, and on the fuller information in *The Greek New Testament* of the United Bible Societies, edited by K. Aland, M. Black, B. M. Metzger and A. Wikgren (1966).

Textual authorities are mentioned in the notes only to draw attention to notable variants or to present disputed readings. In the latter case, the evidence is not given in full, but only sufficient for a fair picture of the problem, so as to show how a decision may be reached. The following list gives the authorities mentioned in the notes. Though it contains all the most important witnesses, it is by no means complete; but it may be found useful by readers who use this commentary with a critical Greek text

PAPYRI

Symbol	Century	Name	Location	Contents
P5	III	—	Philadelphia	fragments of Jn 1, 16 and 20
P45	III	Chester Beatty	Dublin	fragments of Jn 10 and 11
P52	II	John Rylands	Manchester	Jn 18.31–4, 37f.

| P66 | II–III | Bodmer | Geneva | complete; some lacunae |
| P75 | II–III | Bodmer | Geneva | Jn 1.1–15.8; some lacunae |

UNCIALS

Symbol	Century	Name	Location	Contents
ℵ	IV	Sinaiticus	London	complete
A	V	Alexandrinus	London	*omits* Jn 6.50–8.52
B	IV	Vaticanus	Rome	complete
C	V	Ephraemi rescriptus	Paris	many gaps
D	VI	Bezae	Cambridge	*omits* Jn 1.16–3.26
E	VIII	—	Basle	complete
F	IX	Boreelianus	Utrecht	many lacunae
G	IX	Seidelianus I	London	some lacunae
H	IX	Seidelianus II	Cambridge	some lacunae
K	IX	Cyprius	Paris	complete
L	VIII	—	Paris	Jn 1.1–21.14
N	XI	purpureus	Leningrad	fragmentary
S	X	—	Rome	complete
T	V–VI	Borgianus	Paris and Rome	fragmentary
W	IV–V	Freer	Washington	complete
X	X	—	Munich	some lacunae
Z	VI	—	Dublin	[Matthew only]
Γ	IX–X	—	Oxford and Leningrad	complete
Δ	IX–X	—	St Gall	*omits* Jn 19.17–35
Θ	IX	Koridethi	Tiflis	complete
Λ	IX	—	Oxford	complete
Ψ	VIII–IX	—	Athos	complete
070 070 } 0124	VI	—	Oxford Paris	fragmentary

Additional symbols: * = first hand
                     1, 2, 3 or a, b = first, second, third corrector
                     corr = various correctors

MINUSCULES

Symbol	Century	Location	Symbol	Century	Location
1	XII	Basle	69	XV	Leicester
13	XIII	Paris	225	XII	Naples
33	IX	Paris	565	IX	Leningrad

'Lake group' = *family* 1, a group of MSS. of same text-type as 1.
'Ferrar group' = *family* 13, a group of same text-type as 13.

VERSIONS

Latin

(a) Old Latin

Symbol	Century	Location	Symbol	Century	Location
a	IV	Vercelli	ff²	V	Paris
b	V	Verona	l	VII–VIII	(lost)
e	V	Trent	q	VII	Munich
f	VI	Brescia	r¹	VII	Dublin

m = patristic quotations in the early medieval *Speculum*.

(b) Vulgate: the Latin translation of St Jerome.

Syriac

(a) Old Syriac

This very ancient version only survives in two MSS., the Curetonian
(V, London, Jn 1.1–42; 3.5–8.19; fragments of 14) and the Sinaiticus
(IV, Mt Sinai, some lacunae).

(b) Peshitta

The later common translation.

Coptic

(a) Sahidic

Translation in the dialect of upper Egypt, undertaken in the third
century.

(b) Bohairic

Translation in the dialect of lower Egypt, about a century later.

FOOTNOTES TO INTRODUCTION

[1] Cf. Moule, *Birth of the New Testament*, chapter 5.

[2] Condensed from Dodd, *Apostolic Preaching*, p. 28.

[3] Contrast the Synoptic source Q and the Gnostic *Gospel of Thomas*, which are
amorphous collections without narrative framework.

[4] Clement of Alexandria, quoted by Eusebius, *HE* VI.xiv.7.

[5] For a fresh and attractive presentation of the traditional view, see Edwards,
The Gospel according to St John.

[6] See the list of objections assembled by Parker in *JBL* LXXXI.

[7] Quoted by Epiphanius, *Pan. Haer.* li. 3.

[8] Schnackenburg has suggested that the first person 'I' originally stood in the tradition, which was changed to third person ('the disciple whom Jesus loved') by the Johannine School responsible for compiling the Gospel.

[9] See his article in the 11th edition of the *Encyclopaedia Britannica*.

[10] The OT themes in John are treated at length by Braun, *Jean le Théologien* II (1964).

[11] Bowker, 'The Origin and Purpose of St John's Gospel'.

[12] Dodd, *Interpretation*, p. 68. Philo can even refer to the Logos metaphorically as the offspring or son of God (p. 71).

[13] Dodd, *Interpretation*, p. 117.

[14] Cf. Colpe, 'Mandäer'.

[15] See further Excursus VI. 'The Gnostic Myth of the Redeemer and the Johannine Christology', in Schnackenburg, pp. 543–57.

[16] See Dodd's essay, 'A New Gospel', in his collection of *New Testament Studies*, pp. 12–52.

[17] Quoted by Eusebius, *HE* III.xxxix.16.

[18] Cf. S. Brown, *CBQ* XXVI.

[19] Burney, *Aramaic Origin*.

[20] Colwell, *Greek of the Fourth Gospel*.

[21] Bonsirven, in *HTR* xx.

[22] Black, *Aramaic Approach*.

[23] For other linguistic features, see Barrett, pp. 7–11, and Schweizer, *Ego Eimi*, pp. 87–99.

[24] For a sympathetic critique of Bultmann's theory see D. Moody Smith, 'The Sources of the Gospel of John: An Assessment of the Present State of the Problem', *NTS* x (1963–4), pp. 336–51.

[25] Cf. Lightfoot, *History and Interpretation*, p. 110.

[26] See Ellis, *Gospel of Luke*, pp. 55–8, for the current debate on this question.

[27] Conveniently collected in the popular work of Hunter, *According to John*, chapters 8 and 9.

[28] MacGregor and Morton, *Structure of the Fourth Gospel*.

[29] Within this chapter, 6.51b–8 are held to be a later insertion by many scholars. Brown has suggested that some of the material in the discourses existed in duplicate forms, both of which were used by the final editor. Thus he takes 6.35–50 and 51–8 to be doublets, in spite of the great differences between them.

[30] Cf. my *New Testament Apologetic*, chapter 3.

[31] Cf. Colpe, art. cit.

[32] Cf. Robinson, *TNT*, p. 49, n. 49.

[33] Bishop of Antioch, A.D. 199–211. The letter is preserved in Eusebius, *HE* VI.xii.

[34] The issues are dealt with in Braun, III (1968).

SYNOPSIS OF THE FOURTH GOSPEL

1.1–2.12 THE MANIFESTATION OF THE DIVINE GLORY IN JESUS

   1.1–18 Prologue: Jesus in his Cosmic Setting
   Cosmology, 1–5—Witness, 6–8—History, 9–13—Salvation, 14–18
   1.19–51 The Baptist and the First Disciples: Jesus in his Historical Setting
   Questioning of the Baptist, 19–28—The Baptism of Jesus, 29–34—The First Disciples, 35–42—The Testimony of Nathanael, 43–51
   2.1–12 The Marriage at Cana: Jesus in the History of Salvation

2.13–3.36 THE NEW ORDER INAUGURATED BY THE COMING OF JESUS

   2.13–22 The Cleansing of the Temple: The New Place of Worship
   Jesus in Jerusalem, 23–5
   3.1–21 Discourse with Nicodemus on the New Life of the Spirit
   The Discourse, 1–15—The Challenge, 16–21
   3.22–36 Testimony of the Baptist: The New Order
   Baptizing by Jesus and by John, 22–4—The Baptist's Testimony, 25–30—Jesus the Heavenly Revealer, 31–6

4.1–54 NEW LIFE MADE AVAILABLE BY THE COMING OF JESUS

   4.1–26 Discourse with a Samaritan Woman on the Water of Life
   Jesus Leaves Judea, 1–3—The Water of Life, 4–15—The True Teacher, 16–26
   4.27–42 Testimony of the Samaritans and Reflections on the Missionary Task
   4.43–54 Healing of an Official's Son: New Life Displayed
   Jesus Comes to Galilee, 43–5—The Healing of the Official's Son, 46–54

5.1–47 THE LIFE-GIVING WORD OF JESUS AND THE QUESTION OF HIS AUTHORITY

   5.1–18 A Paralyzed Man Healed on the Sabbath
   5.19–47 Discourse on the Authority of Jesus
   The Son Performs the Father's Work, 19–24—The Coming Judgment, 25–9—The Testimony to Jesus' Equality with God, 30–47

6.1–71 JESUS IS THE BREAD OF LIFE

   6.1–25 Jesus Feeds the Multitude and Walks on the Water
   The Feeding of the Multitude, 1–15—Jesus Walks on the Sea, 16–21—The People Follow Jesus to Capernaum, 22–5
   6.26–59 Discourse on the Bread of Life: Maintenance of Life in Christ

THE GOSPEL ACCORDING TO
JOHN

THE MANIFESTATION OF THE DIVINE GLORY IN JESUS 1.1–2.12

The Gospel opens with an episodic narrative, woven together by the mention of successive days (1.29, 35, 39, 43; 2.1). It builds up to a climax, expressed in the statement that Jesus 'manifested his glory' (2.11). As it now stands, the narrative is introduced by the Prologue (1.1–18), which does not fit into this close time-scheme, but leads up to it by a rapid transition from the Creation 'in the beginning' to the appearance of the Word upon the stage of history (1.14). Notice here the mention of 'his glory', which will be picked up again at the end of the section in 2.11. This is an example of the homiletic device of '*inclusio*', rounding off the thought by bringing it back to the beginning, which is frequent in John. This points to the over-arching plan of the section. It 'places' Jesus, first in his cosmic setting (1.1–18), then in his historical setting (1.19–51), and finally in the history of salvation (2.1–11). Thenceforward the reader is familiar with the central character of the story. He knows who Jesus was in relation to God; he knows the group of people to which he belonged; and he has been given a vivid and evocative story, which, by its symbolism, provides a clue to the meaning of the coming of Jesus into these historical circumstances.

This overall unity is important, because it shows the care with which John has composed the opening sequence as a whole. Nevertheless it is probable that the Gospel did not originally include the Prologue. It probably began with a briefer way of introducing Jesus in connection with the witness of the Baptist, like the beginning of Mark; traces of this original opening survive in 1.6–8, 15. Even so, it is likely that there was mention of 'his glory' (hence the intrusion of 15 immediately after 14), so that the *inclusio* was a feature of the primary plan. Thus, when John first wrote his Gospel, the setting of Jesus was confined to historical considerations and to the history of salvation. Subsequently, and partly, perhaps, as a result of reflection on his own completed work, John has felt it desirable to place Jesus in the cosmic setting of his relationship to the Father, which is everywhere presupposed in the Gospel, but not treated systematically. So the Prologue was added for the second edition of his work (on the stages of composition, see the Introduction, pp. 46–54).

PROLOGUE: JESUS IN HIS COSMIC SETTING 1.1–18

The Prologue is a work of immense assurance and literary power. It moves with measured steps from the Creation to the climactic moment of the Incarnation (verse 14), and then indicates the fulness of revelation which results from it—like the dawn gradually illuminating the sky until the sun suddenly bursts above the skyline and sends its rays horizontally across the earth.

Cosmology 1.1–5

The eternal being of God includes the Word (Gr. *logos*), which is his thought, or self-expression. Though inseparable from him in essence, it can be distinguished from him conceptually; it thus partakes of the nature of God, preserving Jewish monotheism. But it can also be thought of separately from him, and even personified, so that it is spoken of as a Person in the closest possible relation to him. The Word in the Prologue thus corresponds with the position of Wisdom in Prov. 8.22–36; Sir. 24.1–22; Wis. 7.22–8.1, and these passages have undoubtedly influenced the Prologue. Following the same tradition the Word, like Wisdom, is regarded as the sole agent or assistant of God in creation. This is very apt, as the work of God in creation is effected by his utterance (cf. Gen. 1.3, etc.). So also the characteristics of man as the apex of Creation are ascribed to the Word: life, which man shares with the animal kingdom, but which in its fullest sense is shared only with God himself; and light, which refers to the illumination of man's mind and conscience through his special capacity to receive divine revelation. This means that the activity of the Word does not stop at the initial act of Creation, but continues through time. So, finally, the shining of the light in the darkness, which is one way of describing the creation itself (cf. Gen. 1.2, 3), is a continuous factor. John does not describe the origin of evil, any more than the Genesis account of Creation, but he presupposes that it exists as a perpetual threat to the fulfilment of God's purpose in creation. So also the revelation of God in Man through the Word is threatened with extinction, but has always been stronger and survived.

Witness 1.6–8

These verses form a parenthetical comment on verse 5. The fact that the light has never been quenched is proved by the witness of the prophets, above all by the witness of John the Baptist, the last of the prophets and the herald of Christ. But his function as witness has to be clearly distinguished from that to which witness is given—the light, which became flesh in Jesus Christ. Although these verses are probably additional to the Prologue as originally composed, they thus fit well into their present position.

History **1.9–13**

In the paragraph leading up to the Incarnation (verse 14) there are two levels of meaning running along parallel lines. From one point of view the theme of the light of revelation in men (verses 4 and 5) is traced through history. First it (or, rather, he, for the light is the Word conceived personally) came to the world in general, but went unrecognized. Then he made entry into 'his own people', i.e. the chosen people of Israel (again following a Wisdom model; cf. Sir. 24.7f.), but was largely rejected. But, as the light was never quenched, so some of the people did receive him. The principle on which they were able to receive him is carefully explained. It was not through human generation, as the selection of a special people might imply, but through the divine initiative meeting with the response of faith. So the ground was prepared for the Incarnation. But from another point of view all these facts can be applied to the reception accorded to Jesus in his incarnate life. His Incarnation has already been hinted at in the witness of the Baptist in verses 6–8. His coming to his people followed the same pattern. They rejected him, and put him to death on the Cross. But where the response of faith was found the purpose of God was accomplished, and those who believe in him have become the children of God (cf. 11.51f.). Many scholars hold that this latter interpretation is the primary meaning of this paragraph; but this ruins the climax of verse 14, where the Incarnation is definitely expressed for the first time. In fact the second meaning only becomes possible when this verse is reached. It is an example of John's most effective device, his capacity for irony (cf. Introduction, p. 53). Bultmann (p. 46) stresses the continuity of creation and redemption which this implies.

Salvation **1.14–18**

With the birth of Christ the Word of God was wholly identified with human life, revealing the full purpose of God; in him, therefore, men may see the glory of God, and experience his covenanted mercy. This is the fact to which the Baptist's witness points: those who have seen him, and by response of faith have accepted him as the Word made flesh, are thus able to receive all that God intended to offer out of his divine mercy, or grace. This was prepared for by the revelation of God in the old dispensation, when the Law was given to Moses. But only in the flesh-taking of the Word of God is the full revelation given and the full purpose of grace achieved. One aspect of this revelation appears in the fact that it took the form of a human birth. It is the essentially personal character of the relation of the Word to God, which in human terms can only be expressed as the relation of a Son to a Father (verses 14 and 18). It will appear later in the Gospel, as it has already been intimated in verse 12, that the salvation of men also involves a personal relationship which is best expressed in terms of sonship.

The crucial point in the whole composition is the Incarnation in verse 14. A reader with the dualistic world-view of Hellenistic thought might accept the argument up to that point (not, however, understanding verses 9–13 in terms of the history of salvation, but rather of timeless inward apprehension), but he would be horrified by the thought of the Word becoming flesh. For the flesh, in dualistic thought, is fundamentally incompatible with the divine; and the object of salvation is precisely to release man, as an intelligent being, from the prison of the body, so that he may join the realm of pure spirit, which is divine. Conversely a Jewish reader would object to the anthropomorphism implicit in the claim that a man known to history was himself the revelation of the invisible God, rather than an inspired messenger like the prophets (the objection is explicitly raised in chapter 10). God always remains above man, and the Jewish concept of salvation did not take kindly to the idea of the deification of man. Rather it was concerned with successive ages under the rule of God. Salvation is a coming era of blessedness (*hā-ʿōlām hab-bāʾ*), in which the troubles of this present age (*ha-ʿōlām haz-zeh*) are done away, but human life goes on much as before, though in idyllic conditions. Thus Jewish thought is primarily eschatological, whereas Hellenistic thought is metaphysical.

It is thus a distinctively Christian idea which John propounds. It implies a notion of salvation in terms of relationship (sonship) which is consistent with the peculiar ambiguity of the Christian time-scheme—that the end-time is still future, and yet has been reached in Christ. By the entry of the Word into human flesh, the way has been opened for men to be brought into the relation of sonship to the Father even now, although the final consummation still lies in the future (cf. Introduction, pp. 57f.). Moreover, the emphasis on the Incarnation helps to counteract the tendency to Docetism, which was already becoming current within the Church when John was writing his Gospel, and is more noticeably attacked in parts of it which (like the Prologue itself) belong to the second edition (Introduction, pp. 61–3). Jesus is not a divine person who only seemed to be a man, and who did not really suffer death on the cross; he actually entered the darkness, but was not overcome by it. The divine glory was seen in him (some editors think that verse 14 alludes to the Transfiguration, but there is no sure indication that John actually knew the episode). This glory kept breaking through in his human life, in the words and deeds which will form the substance of the narrative of the Gospel. In Christ, God was present in the midst of human life.

The Prologue is a triumph of Christian exposition, written with complete mastery of the delicate issues handled. It is not surprising that it has been the foundation of the classic Christian formulations of the doctrine of Christ, and no future attempts at restatement can afford to neglect it.

THE ORIGINAL FORM OF THE PROLOGUE

The above analysis has drawn attention to certain passages in the Wisdom Literature which are concerned with the Creation, Prov. 8.22–36; Sir. 24.1–22; Wis. 7.22–8.1. These are poems, written in the regular form of Hebrew poetic parallelism. Much of the Prologue has a comparable poetic character, and this has led scholars to postulate a similar Semitic original, which John either has composed himself, or has taken over and adapted to serve as the opening statement of his work. In the OT passages, the subject is Wisdom (Heb. *ḥokmāh*, Gr. *sophia*), often personified as a woman. She was beside God in all his acts of creation (Prov. 8.30), and those who find her find life (8.35). Thus the concept of Wisdom enabled the Jewish thinkers to explain the diversity of creation as an expression of the one God, and to relate man's apprehension of the divine plan in creation to the moral sense. The *Odes of Solomon* (Syriac poems of the second century A.D.) continue this tradition, but use Word instead of Wisdom, and so afford a parallel to John's Prologue. But in fact it is most probable that these Christian Gnostic poems have been influenced by John (cf. Introduction, p. 41).

Numerous attempts have been made to reconstruct the original of the Prologue along these lines, both by selection of verse-lines in the Greek, and by retranslation into the presumed underlying Aramaic. Although the results vary, all necessitate the exclusion of certain phrases and whole verses. Bernard (p. cxlv) gives the following criteria, which are applicable to all these reconstructions: (a) In accordance with the character of Semitic poetry, the verse-lines must be short, roughly the same in length, and fall into parallel clauses. (b) As it is a hymn, it must consist of statements, so that argumentative verses (13, 17, and perhaps 18) must be excluded. (c) As it is an abstract statement, proper names (John, Moses, Jesus Christ) are to be excluded (i.e. verses 6–8, 15, 17). (See further on these points Brown, p. 22.) A rough idea of a possible version of the original poem may be obtained by reading through verses 1–5, 9–12, 14, 16.

The proposal is attractive, but may well be misconceived. If John has composed it himself, we should expect to find him using poetic form elsewhere, but attempts to isolate poetic passages in the discourses are equally problematical. It would be more likely that he took over an existing hymn and adapted it. This supposition is in fact essential to Bultmann's theory of an early Gnostic Aramaic source, similar to the *Odes of Solomon*. But, as Barrett (p. 126) has pointed out, the distinction between prose and verse cannot be drawn sharply, and the vocabulary is Johannine throughout, with the exception of the key word *Logos* and of 'grace' (*charis*) in verses 14 and 16. The general poetic character of the Prologue is just as easily accounted for by the theory that John was consciously modelling his opening statement on Prov. 8.22–36 and similar passages; he had a precedent for this in the Pauline hymns (Phil. 2.5–11; Col. 1.15–20) and in Heb. 1.1–4, which is based on these passages. There was no need for him to keep tightly within the limits of the poetic models, because his own composition was not a poem, and was serving a different purpose. He wishes it not only to provide the theological basis for his Gospel, but also to lead up to the historical situation with which it begins. For this purpose, the use of proper names is appropriate and necessary, and some measure of argumentation is not out of place. In fact, he subtly alludes to many of the themes which will be taken up in the rest of the Gospel—or, rather, have already been developed in it, if we think of the Prologue as belonging to the second stage of the composition. 'Life' and 'light' are central to the Gospel; verse 5 (the darkness) alludes to 12.35f.; the rejection motif of 10f. reappears in 5.43f.; the spiritual birth of verse 13 in the discourse with Nicodemus (3.5f.); the witness of Moses (17) in 5.45f.; 6.32; 9.29f.; and the invisibility of God (18) in 5.37; 6.46. It is not difficult to imagine John writing the Prologue as a curtain-raiser for the Gospel, like the overture of an opera, using a Wisdom poem as his model, and bringing in various themes which he has explored in the course of his work.

In fact the form and structure of the Prologue are in conformity with John's discourse style, as analysed above (Introduction, pp. 52f.). Each fresh phase of the argument takes up what immediately precedes it, but also recaptures the opening statement of verse 1 (verses 9 and 14). The central section (9–13) has the characteristic Johannine pathos and irony. The whole builds up to an impressive climax. John's technique here has been compared by P. Borgen (*NTS* xvi (1969–70), pp. 288–95) to that of the Jerusalem Targum, which is, of course, primarily a homiletic work. If John first composed it as a homily, albeit with the first edition of his Gospel in mind, it becomes easier to understand why it has been fitted to the Gospel rather artificially.

Seen in this light, the Prologue can have been composed as a whole, exactly as we have it. But the arguments for the exclusion of the references to the Baptist remain strong. Verses 6–8 interrupt the sequence of thought, and anticipate the historical fact of the Incarnation, which is not reached until verse 14; and verse 15 again breaks the sense, and anticipates the narrative of 1.26–34. These insertions have been made to tie up the Prologue with the existing opening of the Gospel. It is very likely that verse 6 was the original opening sentence. The Prologue, leading up to the Incarnation of Jesus, lacked close connection with the opening sequence on the Baptist (1.19ff.). This was made good by transferring the opening words to their present position in verse 6, for the reason suggested in the analysis above. It was then necessary to explain the function of the Baptist as witness by adding verse 7, and to guard against misinterpretation by adding verse 8. Verse 15 then shows the Baptist performing his function of witness, in words drawn from verse 30. In this way, the transition from the Prologue to the narrative is easy and almost inevitable, and completely avoids the abruptness that would otherwise have happened.

Cosmology 1.1–5

1.1. In the beginning: a deliberate allusion to Gen. 1.1, cf. Prov. 8.22.

was (*ēn*) is past continuous, and so virtually timeless, different from the historic 'was' (*egeneto*) of verses 3 and 6.

Word: *Logos* replaces *sophia* (wisdom), used in all the OT passages.

Hence Bultmann contends (p. 21) that its origin here must be sought elsewhere. There are three non-biblical possibilities. (a) Greek speculative thought. The Greek *logos* refers primarily to the expression of thought, and in the hands of the Stoics it was used to denote the rational principle of the universe. This principle alone was regarded as divine. Consequently there is no place for God alongside the Logos, and therefore no precedent here for John's Prologue. (b) In the work of Philo this difficulty is overcome. Here the Logos of the Stoics is identified with the Wisdom of the OT passages, with results strikingly similar to John's. But Philo uses the concept far more widely. In particular, his application of it to man's cognitive faculty blurs a distinction which John is most careful to observe, between the Creator and the creature, which he expresses by distinguishing between the Logos and the light. John's thought is thus in some degree parallel to Philo's, but not derived from it. There is, in fact, no evidence that John knew the works of Philo (cf. Introduction, pp. 39f.). (c) The Aramaic *mē'mrā'* of the Targums is not really comparable, as it is there a stylistic device to soften the anthropomorphisms of the OT, so that 'the word of the Lord' is simply a synonym for 'the Lord'. We are thus driven back to the OT for the origins of John's Logos, though not to the Wisdom passages as such. Even Bultmann admits that Logos in the *Odes of Solomon* goes back to the wider OT usage.

Two points may be noted. (a) The Genesis creation account mentions God's speaking (Gen. 1.3, etc.), and this is echoed in such passages as Isa. 40.8; 55.11 (Heb. *dābār*, LXX *rhēma*) and Ps. 33.6 (Heb. *dābār*, LXX *logos*). (b) 'The word of the Lord' is a phrase often used to denote prophetic speech (e.g. Ezek. 1.3), and the idea of revelation is as important for the Prologue as that of creation. In rabbinic thought it was the Law which filled the place of revelation, and that also could be called God's word, being his wisdom in the form of speech.

We conclude that the origins of John's use of 'the Word' are not to be sought outside the biblical tradition. This, however, does not yet explain his choice of the term. Other words might have been equally suitable. Two reasons may be suggested. (a) John uses 'Word' rather than 'Wisdom' because he needs a masculine noun (*sophia* is feminine) to express the Incarnation. (b) The Incarnate Son is not only the revealer of divine truth, but he is himself the content of the apostolic preaching (cf. 1 C. 1.18).

There is continuity between the Word who **was in the beginning
with God** and the Word of life (1 Jn 1.1) which is the message
of the Gospel.

with God: Gr. *pros* ('in company with'; hence *NEB:* 'dwelt
with'). The usage is not classical, but is found elsewhere in the
NT, e.g. Mk 6.3. There may be allusion here to Prov. 8.30
('beside him').

was God: i.e. not separable from God himself. There must be
no suggestion of ditheism. It is unlikely that the phrase means
'was divine', though a Greek might so understand it.

2. He was in the beginning: Verse 1a, b is resumed to rein-
force its timeless character. Otherwise the three clauses of verse 1
could be taken as successive steps. It also prepares for the act of
creation in the next verse. As the act of creation is performed by
the utterance of God (Gen. 1.3: 'And God said'), the Word is
not only essentially inseparable from God, but also proceeds from
him in the creative act. John probably alludes to Prov. 8.22:
'The Lord created me at the beginning of his work', perhaps
understanding 'created' as 'possessed' (against the LXX, but
according to the usual meaning of the Hebrew; cf. *AV, RV*).

3. were made: The verbs in this sentence are the historic past
'was', or 'came into being' (Gr. *egeneto*; contrast verse 1).

through him: Cf. Prov. 3.19; 8.30. The negative **without him**
excludes other intermediaries, and so upholds the essential Jewish
and Christian monotheism.

that was made: The punctuation is a notorious crux. The margin
**was not anything made. That which has been made was
life in him** is the reading of the oldest mss. (P75 C* (D) G I W Θ),
versions (Lat. Syr^Cur Sah) and patristic citations of verse 3, which
usually stop short at **was not anything made.** The external
support for it is thus overwhelming, though many modern editors
reject it on internal grounds (cf. B. F. Westcott and F. J. A. Hort,
Notes on Select Readings, p. 74), for it is difficult to see what the
margin means. Sanders (p. 71) construes 'in him' as 'in it', which
involves no change in the Greek, and translates: 'As for that
which is in being, in it he was the life' (cf. *NEB*: 'All that came to
be was alive with his life', a paraphrase which conceals the obscurity of the Greek; the usual punctuation is given in *NEB mg*).
The use of appositional clauses is a feature of John's style; cf.
1.12; 6.39; 18.9. But against this it must be said that here the

use of an appositional clause serves no purpose, and the subject
'he' has to be supplied, although it is too important to be omitted.
The ancient reading may be a false inference on stylistic grounds,
whereby each verse can consist of two balanced clauses:

> All things were made through him,
>   and without him was not anything made.
> That which has been made was life in him,
>   and the life was the light of men.

But although this was how the ancients read it, they soon discovered that it was open to heretical interpretation. If *all* things
came through him, what about the Holy Spirit? Is he one of the
creatures? To exclude this interpretation it was necessary to show
that verse 3 applied only to that which has been made, as opposed
to what is uncreated. Hence the punctuation in the text ultimately
prevailed. For the point at issue, see Wiles, *Spiritual Gospel*, p. 103.

   4. In him was life: If we accept the punctuation given in the
text, the verse makes a new beginning, similar to the first words
of verse 1, and describes the state of affairs which has obtained
(**was** = *ēn*, past continuous again) since the Creation.
life: The Word, like Wisdom, performs the function of the Spirit
of the Lord (Gen. 1.2; cf. Wis. 1.6f.), and there is probably a
reference here to the second account of the creation of man,
Gen. 2.7: 'God . . . breathed into his nostrils the breath of life;
and man became a living being.' The life is thus primarily the
physical breath, without which creatures die and return to dust
(Ps. 104.29). But in the OT it already has a much richer meaning:
just as death denotes a weakened existence, stripped of all good
things and cut off from God, so life includes all the positive aspects
of social well-being and fellowship with God (cf. Isa. 38.10–20;
Ezek. 37.1–14). Life and salvation are associated with light in
Ps. 27.1; life and light occur together in Ps. 36.9; according to
Prov. 8.35, those who find Wisdom find life. It is with this large
range of meaning that life constitutes one of the great themes of
the Fourth Gospel (the word occurs thirty-seven times), frequently
defined as 'eternal life' (seventeen times).
light: Again the primary reference is to the creative work of the
Spirit and the first act of creation (Gen. 1.2, 3), but again there
are rich religious overtones (cf. Psalms mentioned above). It
denotes both that which gives light and the light which is received;

thus Wisdom herself is 'a reflection of eternal light' and also the illumination of men, as 'in every generation she passes into holy souls' (Wis. 7.26f.). This Wisdom passage is applied to Christ in Heb. 1.3. Light is another of the key words of the Fourth Gospel (twenty-two times).

the light of men is not restricted to the idea of conscience, but includes the widest range of man's intellectual apprehension of God and his purposes, and so carries with it the idea of revelation. As the light in the creation preceded the creation of the heavenly bodies (Gen. 1.3, 14; Wis. 7.29), so man's spiritual illumination by the Word is more far-reaching than his physical sight, which is illuminated only by the created lights. Light in this sense of saving revelation has a special application in the idea of God's self-revelation in the giving of the Law (cf. Exod. 34.29–35, referred to by Paul in 2 C. 3.7–4.6). This theme recurs in rabbinic texts (see the examples in Barrett, p. 131). But to John the Law is only a witness to the true light (verses 9 and 17).

John's use of the themes of light and life depends not only on the creation passages on which he models the Prologue, but also on the universal employment of them in the religious language of his times. We do not have to think of a debt to any particular range of literature. They figure in Philo (Dodd, *Interpretation*, pp. 55f.) and in the Hermetic writings (*ibid.*, pp. 30–6) on the Hellenistic side, and in the Dead Sea Scrolls on the Jewish ('light' (= revelation) is frequent in the *Thanksgiving Hymns*; life is usually indicated by other expressions).

5. darkness: According to Gen. 1.2 there was a primeval darkness before God's first act—the creation of light—and in Hebrew thought darkness retained its mythological character as a symbol of danger and death (Ps. 23.4). As it precedes the Creation, it could be taken as an ultimate principle, opposed to God, in a dualistic world-view. Under Persian influence late Jewish apocalyptic thought took on a strongly dualistic colouring, seeing the historical process as the battle-ground of a supramundane conflict (cf. Rev. 12.7–12). But Jewish monotheism was strong enough to resist the idea of an ultimate dualism, just as the Jewish linear view of history resisted the associated notion of an endless cycle of conflicts. So the apocalyptic works all agree that God is in ultimate control and will triumph in the end. Nevertheless there is in them a cosmic dualism, and it is untrue to say that Judaism knows only a moral dualism. There is also a moral dualism, for the cosmic struggle is reflected in the inner life of individuals, who are torn between the competing claims of light and darkness, good and evil. These ideas are vividly expressed in the Dead Sea Scrolls: moral dualism is related to demonology, so that each man is the battlefield of two opposed spirits, *both* of which have been created by God (1QS iii.20–5); and the final struggle of these forces in the near future is forecast with elaborate military details in the War Scroll (1QM i.1). John accepts this modified dualism of the Jewish background, and points of contact with the thought of the scrolls will be noted in this connection in later chapters. But the word darkness is rare in John (only nine times), and its relevance to the conflict of good and evil has to be inferred from the context—a fact which differentiates his thought from the presumed pre-Christian Gnosticism preserved in the Mandaean texts, in which the opposition of light and darkness is an important issue (cf. Introduction, p. 41). Some scholars therefore refuse to see here the notion of conflict, regarding darkness negatively as the absence of light. But see the next note.

overcome: The verb means 'to grasp', and so yields two possible translations. (a) To 'understand' (cf. *AV* 'comprehended it not') is adopted by those who do not recognize the element of conflict in this verse. Schnackenburg (p. 246) argues that the connection with verse 4 means that it is the darkness *of the world of men*, who fail to understand the light, as will be said explicitly in verse 10. (b) But to 'overcome' is certainly the meaning of the very same phrase in 12.35, where the primary thought is that of the darkness overtaking the light at nightfall (see the notes on 6.17). This suggests a background in Wis. 7.29f.: 'Compared with light she [wisdom] is found to be superior, for it is succeeded by the night, but against wisdom evil does not prevail.' This supports the second meaning, as adopted in the text. Whereas the light, having once shone in the beginning, shines continuously (hence the present tense), there has never been an occasion when it was completely extinguished. This interpretation is that of Origen and most of the Fathers. Some editors see both meanings here, but this is scarcely possible. To the Christian reader the verse already contains a hint of the Passion and Resurrection of Jesus (cf. 12.23–36).

Witness **6–8**

For the reasons for regarding these verses as insertions into the formal composition of the Prologue see above, p. 82.

6. There was a man: This is typical Hebrew narrative style for the opening of a prose story, cf. 1 Sam. 1.1; Job 1.1. The verse, which is perhaps consciously in OT style, may have· been the original opening of the Gospel, before the Prologue was added, cf. J. A. T. Robinson, *NTS* IX (1962–3), pp. 120–9.

sent: regularly used of the prophets—e.g. at Jer. 7.25. It is the word from which 'apostle' is derived.

7. testimony, to bear witness: The words are from the same root in the Greek (*marturia, marturein*), and our word 'martyr' is derived from it. It is an important root in the Johannine literature (forty-six times in the Gospel, eighteen times in the Epistles). In John's handling of the Gospel traditions, it is the chief function of the characters who figure in the story to give witness to the truth revealed in Jesus. Even Jesus' own words and deeds serve this purpose (5.36–47). The problem of the relation of the Baptist to Jesus was solved in the primitive Christian tradition by making him the forerunner of the Messiah, so that he is cast in the role of Elijah *redivivus* (cf. Introduction, p. 60). John takes this up by making him the special witness to Christ.

believe: The verb expresses the essential relation to Jesus whereby men may have the life which he brings (cf. 20.31). It occurs ninety-eight times in the Gospel and nine times in 1 John, as against 136 times in the rest of the NT. It is an active concept, denoting the orientation of the mind and heart towards Jesus (hence the frequent construction with *eis*, as in verse 12), and not merely assent to propositions about him. Significantly, the corresponding noun *pistis* (faith), which is very common in Paul, never occurs in John (but once in 1 John). The testimony of the Baptist, as also of others who bear witness, is given to promote this active believing in Jesus.

through him: through the Baptist's witness.

8. He was not the light: Contrast 5.35: 'He was a burning and a shining lamp, and you were willing to rejoice for a while in his light.' There is no real contradiction here, for John has made it plain that the light which shines through the prophets is a light which is only received and passed on by them. It is in

fact the Word of God. The repetition of 7b implies that John
feels the need to guard against misinterpretation, possibly because
of the apparent contradiction of 5.35, which already existed in the
first edition of his Gospel. There is thus no necessary implication
here that followers of the Baptist were claiming him as the
Messiah, though the possibility is not excluded.

History **9–13**

   9. true: or 'real' (*alēthinos*); cf. Introduction, p. 39.
enlightens: The phrase picks up 4b and anticipates the next
verse. The verb (*phōtizein*) is a technical term of the mystery
religions for the imparting of saving knowledge, and occurs in
baptismal contexts in Christian thought; cf. Heb. 6.4. But it is
unlikely that there is a baptismal overtone here, as the reference
is universal. Barrett, arguing that light in John is concerned with
judgment (cf. chapter 9), translates 'casts light upon [with a view
to judgment]'. But the thought is surely closer to Wis. 9.9–18,
where Wisdom, identified with the Holy Spirit, is the source of
revelation, which men may only too easily fail to perceive.
was: this verb is emphatic in the Greek (*ēn*), and recalls the use
of the same verb in the opening statement of verse 1.
coming: grammatically, this verb could be taken with **every
man,** which would mean that the light enlightens each man as he
comes into existence (cf. *AV*). This is supported by the fact that
'everyone coming into the world' is a rabbinic phrase for 'all
men' (*SB* II. 358). If this is adopted, **man** must be bracketed as a
gloss on the phrase (so Bultmann). But the analogy of 12.46
suggests that the *RSV* is right. It refers to the continuous coming
of the light as the source of revelation to mankind (not, then, to
the specific coming of the Word in the Incarnation; cf. the analysis
of the Prologue above). It is probable that this verse has been
adapted to some extent on account of the insertion of 6–8; hence
the addition of **true**, and perhaps **that enlightens every man**
is additional.
world: the created order, but, as the next verse shows, here
meaning the world of men. John's use of the term oscillates between a neutral sense, as here, and a hostile sense, i.e. the world
of men apart from God and under the control of the devil (cf.
12.31). In the neutral sense it denotes the area in which there is
the possibility of response to God.

10. He was in the world repeats verse 9. It is a mark of John's style to repeat the preceding thought, with a slight modification to open up the next thought. As *phōs* (light) is neuter, the pronoun could be translated 'it', but in the final phrase (**knew him not**) it is definitely masculine, and so the whole verse must be taken personally of the divine Word, who is the light. This is made clear by the next phrase **and the world was made through him,** which points up the contrast between the world as the area of human response to the light and the fact that that response has been withheld.

knew him not: Personal recognition, implying not only the intellectual apprehension of the revelation but personal response to its source. 'To know' in Greek is connected with verbs of seeing, and so denotes intellectual awareness. In Hebrew thought it is much more a word of relationship; cf. Hos. 4.1. John's usage combines both emphases.

11. his own home: Gr. *ta idia* ('his own things'). The phrase can be used of one's belongings, one's affairs, or one's home. It should not be taken as a vivid metaphor here (contrast 19.27, where it literally means 'home'). It virtually repeats 10b, and means 'he came to the world which he had himself created' (*NEB:* 'his own realm'). But the variation of phrase forms a subtle transition to the next phrase **his own people,** which is the same word in the masculine instead of the neuter (Gr. *hoi idioi*). The word **came** refers to a definite act in time. But it still does not mean the Incarnation primarily, but the choice of Israel as God's special people. There is allusion here to Wisdom's search 'in whose territory I might lodge' and God's reply 'Make your dwelling in Jacob, and in Israel receive your inheritance' (Sir. 24.7f.). The history of the chosen people shows many occasions when they refused to receive the light, thus anticipating the rejection of Jesus.

12. all who received him: The aorist tense implies 'all who actually did receive him', for indeed the light has never been extinguished (verse 5), and some have made response. The next words **who believed in his name** (which are omitted in some patristic citations, and may be a gloss; they come at the end of the verse in the Greek) explain the nature of this response. For **believed,** cf. the notes on verse 7. To **believe in his name** means to 'accept what his name proclaims him to be' (*AG,*

p. 667a). In OT usage the name is the revealed character of the
person who bears it; cf. Am. 5.8, 27; etc. So Yahweh acts 'for his
name's sake' (Isa. 48.9), i.e. according to his character. To 'praise
the name of the Lord' (Ps. 113.1) is to praise him for what he is in
himself. So in later usage it easily passes into a periphrasis for
God, in order to avoid pronouncing the ineffable name of Yahweh.
In speaking of Jesus, John usually says simply 'believe in him'.
'In his name' occurs only here and 2.23; 3.18.

power: Greek *exousia* has a wide range of meanings. It indicates
that one is in the position to do something: it is a practical possibility. So it can mean 'right' or 'authority' in the sense of a legal
capacity, 'power' in the sense of personal capability, or even
supernatural power conferred on someone. John does not mean
that those who respond have a mysterious power within themselves, nor does he mean that they have personal rights against
God. He means that the way is opened for God's purpose to be
fulfilled in them. But it must be admitted that his expression is
open to misunderstanding, as the next verse shows.

children of God: according to Wis. 7.27, Wisdom 'passes into
holy souls, and makes them friends of God and prophets'. But
the idea of the people of God as his sons is also found in the OT—
e.g. Exod. 4.22; cf. Hos. 11.1; Wis. 16.21. Metaphorically the
father–son relationship is used of teachers and scholars (frequent
in Proverbs), of the inhabitants of a city, and so of those who
belong to a particular group (cf. 'children of Abraham', 8.39).
The phrase **children of God** is specially used of Christians to
express their relation to God through incorporation into Christ
(Rom. 8.16, 21; 9.8). John uses the idea again at 11.52. The
closest parallel to the present passage is Lk. 7.35: 'Yet wisdom
is justified by all her children'. This denotes those who are under
the guidance of Wisdom, those in whom she is operative. So here
it means those in whom the Word can achieve fellowship with
God, which is his purpose for them. The OT would use 'sons'
(Gr. *huioi*). But John and Paul both prefer **children** (*tekna*), 'son'
being reserved for the unique relation of Jesus to the Father. See
further the notes on 10.34ff.; 12.36.

13. born (lit. 'begotten'), continuing the metaphor of 'children
of God', and specifying with greater precision 'all who received
him'. The whole verse is aimed at eliminating the misunderstanding latent in the ambiguous word 'power' and in the use of

the birth metaphor. These might well suggest that the saved are
a race of supermen, who have been injected with some divine
substance not available to the rest of men; and thereby the ethical
basis of response and relationship, which is absolutely essential
to John's thought, would be lost. John has to explain that this
'birth' has nothing whatever to do with physical generation
through the sexual act. The three phrases that express this are
virtually synonymous: **blood** is plural (*haimatōn*, bloods), and
perhaps refers to the theory of conception, found in rabbinic
sources, that the seed of man is derived from his blood and mixes
with the blood of the woman. Hoskyns points out that in Christian
usage the singular 'of blood' would have been understood as a
reference to the sacrifice of Christ; **the will of the flesh** means
the impulse of man's natural endowment, and so refers to sexual
desire. There is no suggestion, however, that flesh is inherently
evil; in biblical usage it is applied to the createdness, and therefore weakness, of human or animal nature in contrast with God
(cf. Isa. 31.3). But for this reason it is sometimes thought of as
allied to sin against God (frequent in Paul; cf. 1 Jn 2.16). The
point, then, is that human nature and sexual power are not *capable*
of effecting God's purpose; **the will of man** (Gr. *anēr*) certainly
means the husband (cf. 4.16); otherwise John would use *anthrōpos*,
and so brings in the idea of paternity, in contrast with the following **of God**. The three almost synonymous phrases cover the
stages of reproduction in reverse order, in an attempt to trace it to
its source: the forming of the child in the womb through the
mixing of blood is preceded by the sexual union, and this (in
the masculine outlook on family life of NT times) goes back to
the will of the man to beget children.

The verse raises a number of problems. Surely not even a pagan
would confuse the spiritual birth with normal physical birth? John
tends to write with almost painful literalness in order to point a fundamental contrast, and we shall see the same point in 3.3–6. What he
means is that only God can do God's work, and man has no power of
his own to achieve it. Then why does he make the point so elaborately?
Why pile up the phrases? The reason is certainly connected with the
fact that he is just about to mention the birth of Christ, which is the
climax of the Prologue. In the incarnate Word there is the full glory
of the light that was constantly shining, and it is manifested in the relation of sonship which he bears to the Father. There is thus continuity

with the revelation of the Word in history. But there is also dis-
continuity, for the Incarnation is a unique event, and Jesus is the Son
of God in a different sense from men in general, who are his children.
Thus, just as the spiritual birth cannot be effected by human art, so
the flesh-taking of the divine Word involves more than physical
generation in the process of human history. It is an act of God, not of
men, unique in kind and unique in time. Thus verse 13 both prepares
the reader for the climax of the birth of Christ, and warns him against
misunderstanding of it.

Does the verse, then, imply knowledge of and belief in the virgin-
birth of Jesus? This was certainly the opinion of Irenaeus and Tertullian
and many of the Fathers, and of many modern editors. One Old Latin
MS. (b) reads 'who *was* born' (*qui . . . natus est*), supported by some of
the patristic quotations (though these may be accommodated). But
even without this reading, the Johannine irony would suggest that
he has this at the back of his mind. If Boismard (*RB* LVII (1950),
p. 403f.; cf. J. C. O'Neill, *JTS*, n.s., xx (1969), p. 43) is right in
thinking that the three synonymous phrases are the result of a con-
fluence of variants in the early stages of transmission, and that originally
the text was shorter, then the expansion at this point would suggest a
growing desire to make the allusion to the virgin-birth more explicit.
But this would reduce the likelihood that John himself intended it.
In fact, although such an allusion is certainly possible, it is difficult to
prove. There are other passages which seem to imply knowledge of the
virgin-birth (1.45; 6.42; 7.42; 8.41), but none is decisive. If we did
not know of the virgin-birth from other sources, i.e. the birth narratives
of Matthew and Luke, we would not detect an allusion to it here, for
it is not self-explanatory. It is not as if John were ironically alluding to
a theme which he actually handles in the Gospel (like the theme of
the Kingdom in 18.33ff.). John's point is, not that a miracle attended
the birth of Jesus, but that the Incarnation is essentially an act of the
divine initiative, and this holds good, even though it took the form of
human birth. Thus the possibility of allusion to the virgin-birth remains open, but the balance of probability is against it.

Salvation 14–18

14. **Word:** Mentioned for the first time since verse 1. Characteristically John reverts to his opening statement at the beginning
of a fresh paragraph; cf. p. 53 above.
became flesh: not just 'a man'. The Word is allied to that which
is earthly (see on 'flesh' in last note) in contrast with that which is
divine. The weakness of flesh apart from God is movingly expressed in 1QH iv.29: 'But what is flesh (to be worthy) of this?

What is a creature of clay for such great marvels to be done, whereas he is in iniquity from the womb and in guilty unfaithfulness until his old age?' (Vermes' translation). It is precisely at this point of weakness that the full revelation of the Word has been given. **Word** and **flesh** are juxtaposed in the Greek, to make the fullest impact. There is probably a polemic against Docetism here (cf. Introduction, p. 61).

dwelt among us: The verb *skēnoun* (in the NT only here and four times in Rev.) is connected with *skēnē* ('tent'), and implies temporary residence. The Word was known in human flesh at a particular time and place in history. The generalities of verses 1–13 have been left behind. The pronoun **us** is equally surprising by its particularity. It refers to the people who knew Jesus in the flesh, and associates the evangelist and his readers with them. The unusual verb for **dwelt** has rich overtones. (a) It probably alludes to Sir. 24.8, where Wisdom says, 'The one who created me assigned a place for my tent (*skēnēn*). And he said, "Make your dwelling (*kataskēnōson*) in Jacob." ' Thus Wisdom finds a home with the chosen people, making God known through the worship of the Temple and the Jewish scriptures. There is probably an ancient mythology behind the idea of Wisdom's tent (cf. Ps. 19.4c; 1 Enoch 42.2). (b) The Temple at Jerusalem is referred to as the *skēnē*, especially when the tent-church of the wilderness wanderings is in mind; cf. Sir. 24.10: 'In the holy tabernacle (*skēnē*) I ministered before him.' This carries with it the idea of a localized presence of God. (c) The word may also have been chosen because of its similarity in sound to the Hebrew *šᵉkīnāh* of Mishnaic times. It is a circumlocution for God, which can perhaps best be translated 'presence', derived from the common Deuteronomic phrase 'to make his name dwell there (viz., in the Temple)', Dt. 12.11, etc. (cf. also the Hebrew *miškēn* from the same root, regularly used of the Tabernacle in the wilderness). In Num. 9.18 the cloud, which in the Priestly strand of the Pentateuch was the sign of the presence of God, remained (lit. dwelt, *yiškōn*) above the Tabernacle. This cloud both concealed and indicated the glory of God. Although it is difficult to be sure whether all these ideas were present to John's mind, there is undoubtedly a reference to OT ideas. The Word made flesh is the revelation of the Father (cf. verse 18), to be compared and contrasted with the OT theophanies.

full of grace and truth: These words are appended at the end
of the verse (cf. *AV*), but grammatically agree with **the Word**
(or, more probably, *plērēs* **full** is to be regarded as genitive,
agreeing with **his** in the phrase **his glory**, cf. *BDF* § 137.1; one
MS. (D) makes it agree with **glory**, but this is certainly wrong).
The whole phrase recalls the theophany to Moses at Mt Sinai,
Exod. 33.12–34.8: 'Moses said: "I pray thee, show me thy
glory" (33.18) ... The Lord passed before him, and proclaimed:
"The Lord, the Lord, a God merciful and gracious, slow to anger,
and abounding in steadfast love and faithfulness" ' (34.6). The
last words 'abounding, etc.' (*raḇ ḥeseḏ weʾemeṯ*) can be correctly
translated 'full of grace and truth'. In fact John has given a more
literal translation than the Greek of the LXX, which shows that
he is working from the Hebrew scriptures. **grace and truth** describe the character of God as one who is loyal to the covenant
which he has made with his people. This OT background excludes
any interpretation in abstract terms of truth and beauty, and
stresses the element of relationship. The incarnate Word reveals
the God who is loyal to his covenant of mercy, and the Incarnation
is itself the supreme demonstration of this mercy. **grace** (*charis*,
here better translated 'mercy') is common in Paul, but in John
only occurs here and in verses 16–17; **truth**, on the other hand,
is a favourite word (twenty-five times in Jn; twenty in 1–3 Jn).
Its meaning oscillates between the more Greek idea of absolute
truth and the more Hebraic idea of steadfastness to one's character (cf. Barrett, *JTS*, n.s., 1 (1950), p. 8).
beheld his glory: As Moses did (see last note), or Isaiah (cf.
12.41). The word translated **glory** (*doxa*) properly means 'good
opinion', but was adopted by the LXX translators as the regular
rendering of the Hebrew *kāḇôḏ* (root-meaning 'weight', but always
applied to '(regal) splendour', and so associated with ideas of
brightness). It is not as common in John as might be expected,
though he frequently uses the related verb *doxazō*; and more often
it means 'good opinion' or 'praise'. Here the OT allusion fixes
the meaning **glory**, as in 12.41. But it is a hidden glory, perceived
only by those who know who Jesus is, and who recognize that his
Incarnation is the revelation of the divine mercy. So **beheld**
(*etheasametha*), though it should refer to outward gaze, is really the
perception of faith (Bultmann).
as of the only Son from the Father: the nature of his glory is

now specified, and it is (as the last note indicated) not an outward glory but a unique filial relationship. **the only Son** is a rather free translation of *monogenēs*, which means either 'one only-begotten' or 'one unique in kind'. The former meaning is suggested by the context (cf. verse 13), and by the OT background, as the corresponding Hebrew word often means 'a beloved son', and there may even be a hint here of the tradition of the baptism of Jesus (cf. Mk 1.11). But the latter meaning is supported by Wis. 7.22, where Wisdom is said to be 'unique' (*monogenēs*), and perhaps by verse 18, though there are difficulties about this verse (see the notes below). **Son** is not in the Greek here, but it is added in 3.16, 18; 1 Jn 4.9, where *monogenēs* occurs again. But the phrase **of the Father** (not 'of *a* Father', in spite of the omission of the article in the Greek, cf. *BDF* § 257.3) is decisive for 'only-begotten'.

From this point onwards Jesus is never again referred to as the Word, but always as the Son (cf. 5.19–23).

15. John bore witness to him, and cried: the verbs are in the present tense (the perfect *kekragen* has present meaning; see *AG*, p. 448b), applying to the reader and for all time. For the insertion of this verse, see the analysis above, p. 82. It forms almost a liturgical response, a sort of 'Amen', and gives a moment to take a breath, after the intense concentration of meaning in verse 14. The words of the Baptist, based on verse 30, express the paradox that, just as Jesus came late in time, and yet 'was in the beginning with God', so his ministry comes **after** that of the Baptist, but he **ranks before** him. The past tenses in the words **This was he of whom I said** put the comment from the point of view of the Baptist's eventual recognition of Jesus: 'the one who was born then is the one of whom I said later . . .' It is thus unnecessary to follow Torrey in supposing confusion arising from a postulated Aramaic original, in which the pronoun *hū'*, used for the copula 'is', has been misread as the perfect *hᵃwā' =* 'was'. An attempt to ease the sense by reading 'This (i.e. the Baptist) was the man who said' is found in some early mss. א^a B* Origen), but is clearly wrong.

16. And: The major uncials read 'For', and this is probably correct. This follows naturally from verse 14, but the intrusion of verse 15 has led to **And** in the *textus receptus* (omitted by *NEB*).

fulness: The abundance of grace and truth of verse 14. It is unnecessary to see here a hint of the use of the word (*plērōma*) to express the sum of the divine attributes, which is found in the Valentinian and other Gnostic systems (against Sanders). **we all received** it as a result of 'believing in his name' (verse 12). One ms. (W), apparently misunderstanding the partitive, has 'we all received life from his fulness', which is a fair interpretation of what is meant.

grace upon grace: lit. '*and* grace *instead of* (i.e. in addition to) grace'. The 'and' is explicative in OT style, and can be dispensed with in English. The phrase refers to progressive mercies in the Christian life out of the abundance. For the phrase, cf. Sir. 26.15 'adds charm to charm' (lit. 'grace on grace', *charis epi chariti*). It is unlikely that John intends a contrast between the old covenant of mercy and the new, as John thinks of the era of Grace as following on the era of Law, which bears witness to it (see the notes on the next verse). Black's suggestion that there is an Aramaic word-play on two different words *ḥisdā* (i.e. 'grace instead of shame') is ingenious, but is foreign to John's estimate of the OT elsewhere.

17. The verse appears to contrast the old and the new dispensations (antithetic parallelism). It has thus been taken to be an erroneous explanatory addition to verse 16; and this impression is reinforced by the unexpected full designation **Jesus Christ** (cf. above, p. 81). There is, of course, a very important contrast between the Law and Jesus in John's thought, expressed explicitly in 5.39, and underlying the great themes of the Water of Life and the Bread of Life (chapters 4 and 6), etc. But the difference between them is, as Dodd (*Interpretation*, p. 84) points out, that of shadow and substance, rather than direct opposition. We must see this verse in its context, effecting the transition to the conclusion in verse 18 by way of a chiastic structure. Thus 17 answers to 16, just as 18 answers to 14. In verse 14, as we have seen, the Incarnation is described in terms which unmistakably echo the theophany to Moses, but in verse 18 it is asserted that there has been no real theophany apart from the Incarnation. The giving of grace in verse 16 also recalls Moses at Mt Sinai, for there he received the Law. According to Sir. 24.23–9 the Law was the highest manifestation of Wisdom; and the grace and truth of God are revealed in the Law according to rabbinic exegesis (*Midrash Ps.* on Ps. 25.10, where the phrase *ḥeseḏ we'ᵉmeṯ* occurs). But now it is asserted that there has been no real gift of grace and truth except in Christ. It is really a case of synthetic parallelism (so J. Jeremias): *just as* the law was given through Moses, *so* grace and truth (which the law prefigures) came into being (*egeneto*) through Jesus Christ.

Christ: Already in the Pauline epistles **Christ** is used almost as a surname, to distinguish Jesus from others of the same name (cf. Col. 4.11), without regard to its technical meaning as a rendering of the Jewish Messiah. But John always has its proper meaning in mind, except here and 17.3, and this throws some doubt on the authenticity of the verse. But in favour of it, it may be urged that (a) there may be a contrast intended here between Moses as lawgiver and Jesus as Messiah, cf. 5.46; (b) the mention of Jesus by name in verse 29 implies that he has been already introduced, and the full title is appropriate for the first occasion when the Son of God is named.

18. No one has ever seen God: Direct sight of God was in early times regarded as extremely dangerous (Jg. 13.22), and in the theophany to Moses only a partial manifestation is given (Exod. 33.20). The view of later Jewish piety, however, was that it is beyond man's capacity to see God, or at any rate to know him as he is (Sir. 43.27–33). At quite an early stage, texts which mentioned seeing God were altered to 'appear before God', e.g. Exod. 23.15, though not quite consistently (cf. Isa. 6.5). In this case, however, the Targum softens it by expanding 'My eyes have seen the King' to 'My eyes have seen the glory of the presence (*s^{e}kīnā'*) of the King of the ages'; and there are other examples. This is a fact which John takes for granted, but he makes the point that the personal relationship with God established through the Incarnation of the Word completely fulfils the purpose of seeing God. It is a manifestation by means of relationship (cf. 1 Jn 4.12, where the precise phrase is used in this connection). It is straining the sense of the Greek to take it to mean 'No man has *ever yet* seen God', as if the door was being left open for full sight in the future.

the only Son: this is the standard text, and is supported by John's usage in 3.16, 18; 1 Jn 4.9. But the more difficult reading of the margin, 'the only-begotten one, God, who is in the bosom of the Father' has much too strong MS. attestation to be set aside. (*monogenēs theos*: P^{66} B א* C* L Syriac Peshitta; *ho monogenēs theos*: P^{75} א^3 A C^3 Γ Δ). It can be accepted if 'God' is taken to be in

apposition to 'only-begotten one', meaning 'who is divine in
origin' (so Bernard, Schnackenburg). Sanders has revived the
suggestion of Blass and Resch that the original text had only
'the only-begotten one' (so two Vulgate MSS. and quotations in
Ephrem, Aphraates, Cyril of Jerusalem and Nestorius). In this
case it is postulated that the relative *hos* was inserted, and that
this was misread as *theos* in abbreviated form (there is actual MS.
evidence for just this confusion at 1 Tim. 3.16). But it is difficult
to see how *hos* (which has no MS. support) can have got into the
text in the first place. The change from *theos* to *huios* (**Son**) is so
natural that it needs no explanation. The harder reading has the
merit of bringing the thought back to verse 1, and so constitutes
another case of the Johannine *inclusio*. 'God' here has the same
meaning as 'and the Word was God' (1c). The point is that only
God can reveal God. This is fundamental to the thought of the
Prologue. For the importance of this disputed reading in the
Arian controversy, cf. Wiles, *op. cit.* p. 121.

who is in the bosom of the Father: These words, like 'God'
in the preceding phrase, recall verse 1, though they do so by means
of a bold anthropomorphic metaphor. The idea of the bosom
companion, which occurs in both Jewish and classical sources,
comes from the nursing of a child (Ruth, 4.16; 2 Sam. 12.3),
from the embrace of husband and wife (Dt. 13.6), and from the
rather similar position of the most privileged guest when reclining
at dinner (cf. the Beloved Disciple, 13.23). Rabbinic sources
speak of the bosom of the righteous as the place of honour in the
heavenly banquet of the blessed (SB II.226; cf. Mt. 8.11), and
Lk. 16.22f. speaks of Abraham's bosom in this way. Here the
preposition *eis* (properly 'into' rather than 'in') implies that Jesus
has access to the innermost being of God (cf. 1b). At the same
time the metaphor combines with the verbal allusions to verse 14
to emphasize the filial relationship, so that the idea is personal and
ethical.

he: Emphatic, picking up the whole of the preceding ideas.
made him known: John uses a word (*exēgēsato*, only here) which
is almost a technical term in Greek literature for the declaration
of divine secrets by an oracle or priest, and so he may have a
Hellenistic audience in mind. But it is also used by Josephus
(*BJ.* i.649; ii.162; *Ant.* xviii.81) of the exposition of the Law, and,
in view of verse 17, it is at least as probable that he is thinking in

Jewish thought-forms. In either case the verb implies the revelation of God by means of human speech, which fittingly represents
the activity of him who is the Word of God. The suggestion of
something visible is avoided. The revelation is meaning conveyed
by the Word, to be apprehended by faith.

THE BAPTIST AND THE FIRST DISCIPLES: JESUS IN HIS HISTORICAL SETTING 1.19-51

A series of short episodes introduces Jesus to the plane of history.
John follows roughly the order of Mark: first John the Baptist
appears on the scene; then his baptism of Jesus is recorded; and
after that the first few disciples are called. The only thing that is
missing is Jesus' forty days' fast in the wilderness immediately
after his baptism. Either John did not know of it, or else he chose
not to include it because he wished to put the call of the disciples
in direct relation with the witness of the Baptist.

The narrative can be viewed quite simply in historical terms,
as a record of what happened when Jesus began his public
ministry. But John is never content with simple historical reporting. He is much more concerned with the fact that the appearance
of Jesus constitutes the manifestation of the divine glory. Hence
his material is carefully organized to lead up to a succession of
confessions of faith and Christological statements. The Baptist
and the first disciples give their testimony to the meaning of
Jesus, using titles commonly ascribed to him (Christ, Son of God,
etc.). The following chapters will take these titles for granted, but
will greatly enrich the reader's understanding of them.

The section is notable for its use of Synoptic material and for its
familiarity with OT themes. It is not likely that it is based
directly on Mark; in fact, the verbal parallels are distributed
almost equally between the three Synoptic Gospels. But there is
certainly traditional material of a very similar character underlying it. John makes use of this material allusively, without
reproducing it in detail. The most remarkable feature of his work
is that the baptism of Jesus is not narrated, but referred to in a
flash-back (verses 29-34). This gives the impression that he can
take a certain amount of knowledge on the part of his readers for
granted (cf. Schnackenburg, p. 285). This leaves him free to
concentrate on the Christological titles, which are his real concern.
These do not follow any special sequence, but the effect of climax

is produced by reserving the most impressive narrative-item until the end of the section (the testimony of Nathaniel, verses 43–50), and by adding the vivid picture of the future glory of the Son of Man as a closing comment (verse 51).

The historical value of the section is difficult to estimate. The questioning of the Baptist by Jewish officials (verses 19–28) is possible, but is not attested elsewhere. In any case John's theological motives completely dominate his account of it. But many scholars think that John is right in representing Jesus' first contact with some of his disciples as a direct result of meeting them in the circle of the Baptist's followers. This could have happened before Jesus withdrew to the wilderness. Then the actual call of them to form the apostolic band could have taken place later in Galilee, when they had returned to their fishing. If so, John preserves authentic independent tradition, which does not conflict with the Synoptic evidence. But again we have to recognize that John's narrative is artificially constructed to lead up to the successive confessions of faith, so that the only aspect of the tradition that really carries conviction is the bare fact that some of the disciples had first been among the Baptist's followers, which may well have been the case. Although John locates the narrative in Judea, there is some evidence to suggest that his sources for the call of the disciples had a Galilean setting (see the notes on verse 43). If so, it is more likely that we have an alternative to the Synoptic call stories, rather than the record of a separate historical occasion.

This last observation leads us to suspect some reworking of older material on the part of John. Out of scraps of tradition he has worked up a series of scenes (identified as a Johannine style-characteristic by J. Louis Martyn), in order to make a profound emotional impact. It is noteworthy that the contact with underlying tradition becomes progressively weaker, so that in the final scene of the conversation with Nathanael it is reduced virtually to vanishing point. Although John is writing narrative, his literary style here has much in common with the discourses (cf. *Behind the Fourth Gospel*, chapter 3). But the repetitious character of the narrative, and the fact that verses 19–28 and 29–34 are virtually doublets, have led many scholars to postulate a more complicated literary evolution. Bultmann (p. 85) isolates a single narrative, which has been worked over to bring it into line with the Synoptic accounts of the baptism. Boismard thinks of two parallel

narratives which have been composed at different times for the
opening of the Gospel, replacing yet another which is now found
in 3.22–30. The final editor decided to retain all three. But this
makes a far too complex prehistory to be convincing.

Questioning of the Baptist 19–28

The questioning falls into two parts, and it is even possible that
John means two successive deputations (see the notes on verse 24).
The first leads up to the Baptist's quotation of Isa. 40.3, which
defines his own position in relation to Christ. The second relates
his baptismal activity to the messianic expectations which are
fulfilled in Jesus. These are both classic Christian explanations of
the person and work of the Baptist, and as such seem improbable
on his lips before Jesus has become known. It is thus possible that
the questioning reflects an anti-Baptist polemic at a later time (cf.
Introduction, pp. 59ff.). But it is equally possible that it is a
literary device to expose the Baptist's function as witness in the
Gospel; cf. verse 7. In either case John may have modelled it on
traditions of questioning about Jesus himself, such as are preserved
in Mt. 11.2 para.; Mk 6.14–16 paras.; Mk 8.27–29 paras. The
Synoptic tradition does also contain some questioning about the
Baptist, cf. Mt. 11.7–15 para.; Mk 11.29–32 paras; Lk. 3.15.

19. And: This links the narrative to the Prologue, softening the
change of literary genre; but it also suggests the loss of the original
opening (cf. 6–8).

this is the testimony of John is the heading of the paragraph,
but the **when** clause should not be separated from it. For **testimony,** cf. verse 7.

the Jews: John's usage often means the people of the province of
Judea; cf. 11.45. Here he is referring more specifically to the
ruling authorities, cf. 3.1.

priests and Levites are the two grades of the temple staff of
post-Exilic Judaism. The distinction between them is carefully
preserved in the Jewish ecclesiastical polity, even in sectarian
circles (e.g. the Qumran sect), where there is no connection with
the existing Temple. They are mentioned by John only here, and
the combined designation does not occur elsewhere in the NT.
There is nothing improbable in such a deputation seeking to find
out what the Baptist's activity is about; his whereabouts are not
explained until verse 28, although it is already implied in verse 23

that it is somewhere in the desert region. Some knowledge of the Baptist on the part of the readers is thus presupposed.

20. confessed: The emphatic repetition, with the synonymous phrase **he did not deny,** places the Baptist alongside the Christian martyrs. The language seems to be derived from a tradition similar to Mt. 10.32f. (= Lk. 12.8f.). The confession of faith is of vital importance to John, cf. 1 Jn 2.22f.; 4.1–3; 5.1–12.

not the Christ: The answer is not to the actual question of verse 19, but to the question implied by it; cf. verse 8 and Lk. 3.15. Since the Prologue has already named the Word become flesh 'Jesus Christ' (see the notes on verse 17), the claim to messiahship is the immediate question at issue, and it dominates the rest of the chapter.

21. Are you Elijah? The dialogue occurs in very similar form in Mk 6.14–16 paras.; Mk 8.27–9 paras., but is there concerned with the identity of Jesus after the Baptist's death. Even if John is modelling the present passage on such traditions as these, it is certainly probable that the questions asked about Jesus had first been asked about the Baptist, and were asked afresh when Jesus became prominent after the Baptist's death. Elijah is named because there was a popular expectation that this great prophet would return to prepare men for the messianic age; cf. Mal. 4.5f.; Sir. 48.9f.; Justin, *Dial.* viii.4; xlix. This idea developed wide ramifications in later rabbinic thought.

I am not: It is obvious that the Baptist should deny being the Messiah, but less easy to see why he equally definitely denies being Elijah, thus contradicting Mt. 17.10–13 (= Mk 9.11–13), where the identification is explicit. This need not be taken as direct repudiation of the view expressed in the Synoptic Gospels, especially when we assume that John was working on parallel independent traditions. It is better to regard it as a different estimate of the Baptist, in which identification with Elijah *redivivus* has not yet been made. It is scarcely probable that, as a matter of history, the Baptist saw himself in this role (cf. J. A. T. Robinson, 'Elijah, John and Jesus', *TNT*, pp. 28–52). Luke represents a mediating view, in which the Baptist comes 'in the spirit and power of Elijah' (1.17), but also Jesus' own activity is seen to be the antitype of Elijah's work of old (7.11–17). If we go back to the fundamental passages (Mal. 3.1; 4.5f.), it is clear that Elijah's function can be understood in two ways: he is the herald

of the coming of the Lord, and he has a social task in preparation
for it. As far as we can gather, the Baptist's actual work was more
like the latter, but the Church resolved the problem of his relation
to Jesus by concentrating on the former. John is so anxious to
present the Baptist solely as herald, that he refuses to allow the
identification with Elijah, which would give him the status of a
social reformer in his own right.

the prophet: The use of the article implies that a particular
prophet is intended, and it has long been held that this must be
the prophet of Dt. 18.15–18, whom Moses promises will mediate
the word of God after his death. This figure was given messianic
significance by NT times. The Samaritans, whose scriptures were
confined to the Pentateuch, used this text as the foundation of
their messianic ideas (see the notes on 4.25). It is probable that
Jesus, who was widely held to be a prophet in his lifetime (cf.
Mt. 21.11), was identified with this figure by some elements in
early Christianity (cf. Ac. 7.37). If any doubts remained, they
have been dispelled by the Dead Sea Scrolls, which prove beyond
question that the Prophet was a figure of messianic expectation
in the time of Christ. The Qumran sect expected his arrival,
along with the two Messiahs of Aaron and Israel (1QS ix.11; cf.
4Q *Testimonia*), presumably performing much the same kind of
preparatory role as Elijah *redivivus*. So, as before, we have a
quasi-messianic figure, who in some circles seems to have been
identified with Jesus himself, and John cannot allow the Baptist
to be equated with him.

22. John prepares for the climax by a much fuller form of
question, repeating the first of the preceding terse questions
(verse 19).

23. the voice: The Baptist is thus simply and solely a herald,
and this accords with his proper Johannine function of giving
witness. All the words from **the voice** onwards are from Isa.
40.3, not merely the words indicated as a quotation. This verse
is quoted with reference to the Baptist in the Synoptic Gospels
(Mk 1.3 paras.). The form of the quotation closely follows the
LXX, except that John characteristically abbreviates the text by
telescoping two parallel lines into one: 'Prepare *the way of the
Lord, make straight* . . . a highway' (John's *euthunate* corresponds
with LXX *eutheias poieite*). The LXX differs from the Hebrew in
making the wilderness the place where the voice cries; in the

Hebrew the wilderness is the place where the way of the Lord is to be prepared. Christian interpretation of the prophecy was developed with the aid of the LXX version, so that the fact that the Baptist was active in the desert is felt to be an exact fulfilment of it. The Hebrew text would only be relevant if the Baptist had actually called men to go out to the desert in preparation for the Lord. This may have been the case, but not in the Christian understanding of it. For Jesus, whom he heralded, performed his ministry, not in the desert, but in the cities and homes of the people. On the other hand, the men of Qumran applied this text to their own company as a whole, and made it the warrant for their withdrawal to the wilderness (1QS viii.14; ix.19). It is possible, then, that the text was first applied to (or by) the Baptist in a similar sense, and later adapted in Christian usage. John is not ignorant of Jewish language and customs, and his use of the LXX version in this instance shows his dependence on the developed Christian interpretation.

24. the Pharisees: the verse appears to conflict with verse 19 and seems redundant, and so is bracketed by Schmiedel, though it is found in all our MSS. The matter is complicated by a textual variation. The received text, supported by AWΘ, has 'those who had been sent', i.e. the priests and Levites. But the evidence for **they had been sent** is strong, and includes both P⁶⁶ and P⁷⁵. This *could* mean a fresh deputation of priests and Levites (so Dodd), or part of the original deputation (so *NEB*, though it is unlikely that John would omit *tines* in this case, in spite of 16.17), but it is just as likely that it means the whole of the original deputation, so that **from the Pharisees** refers back to those who had sent the priests and Levites—i.e., 'the Jews'. In either case the identification of them with the Pharisees looks strange, seeing that the Sadducees were the dominant party in the Temple. But in fact many priests and Levites belonged to the Pharisaic party, because of their concern for strict observance of the Jewish Law. Moreover John, writing from the standpoint of Judaism after the fall of Jerusalem, simply identifies the Jewish rulers with the Pharisees (cf. Introduction, p. 37). Hence **the Pharisees** here is best taken as a further description of 'the Jews' of verse 19. So, in characteristic style, John introduces a new element in his account, in order to open up a further issue (cf. 5.19, and the remarks on it in the Introduction, p. 53). For the dialogue now turns to the purpose of John's baptism, and it is natural to ask whether it was done in order to promote strict observance of the Law or not. The answer is that it prepares men for the Coming One, Christ, and so the witness given in verse 23 in terms of Isa. 40.3 is taken a stage further towards its full import.

25. if you are neither . . .: it is not that to be the Messiah or Elijah or the Prophet necessarily involves the activity of baptizing, but that, if John had been one of these three his work would have been explicable as a ceremony of initiation into the coming Kingdom. This, at any rate, is what baptism became in Christian usage. The Jewish purification rites involved elaborate regulations for the removal of ritual taboos. Total immersion was required for a person in a state of ritual uncleanness in theory, but in practice this was only insisted on in the case of menstruous women and of proselytes before being received into Judaism, at any rate after the destruction of the Temple. The Qumran Covenanters laid stress on the need for interior repentance at the same time (1QS iii.4–9; cf. A. R. C. Leaney, *The Rule of Qumran and its Meaning*, pp. 139–42). The connection between the external act and the inner intention already appears in Sir. 34.25f., where the Greek has *baptizein* in the technical sense of ceremonial immersion. All such acts fitted into the scheme of Jewish life under the Law, and were thus of great importance to the Pharisees. But John the Baptist has only claimed to be 'the voice', so that his credentials are in doubt.

26f. The Baptist's answer in these two verses is extremely close to the tradition preserved in the Synoptic Gospels (Mt. 3.11f. = Mk 1.7f. = Lk. 3.16), the closest parallel being with Luke. If John is not dependent on them, his source at this point must have been almost identical with theirs, for his adaptation is not comprehensible without the Synoptic version. For there the baptism with water is contrasted with the Coming One's baptism 'with the Holy Spirit and with fire'. This presumably means the eschatological judgment, and the preceding water-baptism is to cleanse men, so that they may be free from condemnation at this greater ordeal. But John has omitted this element of the contrast, so that his description of the Coming One seems quite illogical. But, in fact, he is familiar with it, but he is saving it up for the next paragraph (verse 33). It is not difficult to see why John has done this. Christian thought had already explained the Baptist's activity as preparation for the work of Jesus, rather than for the final ordeal, and Jesus' work can be loosely described as 'baptism with the Holy Spirit' (note that in verse 33 John omits 'with fire', and cf. 7.37–9). So John sees the Baptist's work as preparation for the coming of Jesus, and therefore as a pointer towards him. It thus serves the same purpose as the description of the Baptist as 'the voice', or herald of Jesus.

whom you do not know: according to some Jewish teachers, the Messiah would be kept hidden until the moment of his appearance to begin his appointed task; cf. Justin, *Dial.* viii.4; xlix.1; cx.1. But Schnackenburg (p. 295) denies that there is a reference to this belief here.

27. **who comes after me:** cf. verse 15. **he who comes** is not a standard messianic title, but there is evidence that it had some currency as such in early Christianity; cf. Mt. 11.3 (= Lk. 7.19). It probably alludes to an OT passage, e.g. Ps. 118.26; cf. Lk. 13.35. **whose sandal:** The construction in the Greek involves a Semitism (cf. Introduction, p. 44; Black, p. 101); it is also found in Mk 1.7 (= Lk. 3.16). This implies that John's source was already in Greek, but taken from an Aramaic original. To untie the sandal was the work of a slave, preparatory to washing the feet of his master or of a guest on arrival from a journey. The point is that there is the greatest possible distance between the Baptist and the one whom he announced. This is an allusive way of saying that he is the Messiah. But John himself probably means to imply more than he takes over from the tradition. It is the distance between a man and the pre-existent Son of God (cf. 30, 34, 49). Hence the same baptismal tradition has been used by John as the basis of a comment in the Prologue (verse 15).

28. **Bethany:** This is the reading of the best MSS. and the principal versions. Bethabara (sometimes corrupted to Betharaba) is found in the Old Syriac and Sahidic versions, and in some Greek MSS. It was preferred by Origen (*Comm. in Joh.* vi.40), because he could not find a Bethany by the Jordan. The exact location remains unidentified. The -*abara* component in the alternative name means both 'ford' and 'beyond', which suggests that the corruption is due to speculation about the locality. It is called **Bethany beyond the Jordan** to distinguish it from the village near Jerusalem (11.1). It is possible that this topographical detail is derived from trustworthy independent tradition about

the Baptist's activity. John introduces this information here, instead of at the beginning, because he is now going to give the Baptist's witness in the course of his work.

The Baptism of Jesus 29–34

After the two testimonies of verses 23 and 26f., it is only to be expected that the Messiah should 'come', instead of being hidden in the crowd, and that 'the voice' should proclaim him. The proclamation itself (verse 29) is quite unexpected, and has given rise to endless discussion. John writes as if someone has objected that the Baptist himself was not in a position to recognize him (verse 31). It is then revealed that the work of baptizing actually provided the opportunity whereby the Messiah could be made known; this has already been implied by John's handling of the dialogue in verse 26. From John's point of view, then, the Baptist's work has no value in itself, but only as the setting for the divine revelation. This is stated finally in terms which probably allude to the divine words as given in the Synoptists (verse 34). The reason why John has given the traditional material in this topsy-turvy fashion is that he wants to take the Baptist's testimony through to a climax.

29. The next day: for possible symbolic significance, see on 2.1. Jesus is introduced with astonishing abruptness. As the underlying tradition states that he was one of the crowd (verse 26), John assumes that he is present.

coming may be an intentional allusion to verse 27. No description of him is given, because his identity will be indicated by the testimony which follows.

the Lamb of God: this is the opening testimony of the Baptist, and it must be seen in relation to what follows. Jesus is the one who takes away the sin of the world, who takes precedence over the Baptist (verse 30), who baptizes with the Spirit (33), and who is the Son (or Elect) of God (34). This testimony arises directly out of the work of baptizing (33). The first impression, then, that he is **the Lamb of God, who takes away the sin of the world**, may be connected with the initial act which starts the series of testimonies—i.e., Jesus' submission to baptism. That this is in John's mind is implied by the next two verses, which reflect the Church's embarrassment that Jesus was just one of the crowd and was not at first recognized as the Messiah by the Baptist (this embarrassment lies behind Mt. 3.14f.). It is thus unlikely that this is an item of historical fact, and we need not try to discover how the Baptist could possibly have used this description, which seems so improbable on his lips. But what does it actually mean? Dodd argues on the basis of I Enoch 90 and *Test. Joseph* xix.8 that **Lamb of God** was a messianic title in some Jewish circles. But as both contexts are full of animal imagery, this is not really convincing; nor does it explain the motif of removing sin.

If, as we have suggested, John is dependent on Christian thinking, it is most natural to suppose that the whole title is based on the Christian application of the poem of the Suffering Servant in Isa. 53 to Jesus, especially verse 7, 'like a lamb (LXX *amnos*, as in John) that is led to the slaughter', and verse 11, 'he shall bear their iniquities', cf. verses 4 and 12. John's **takes away** (*airōn*; lit. 'lifts up') corresponds with the meaning of the Hebrew. By the time that John was writing, this poem had already established itself as a classic expression of the atoning efficacy of the death of Jesus. Burney favoured the suggestion that the title was a mistranslation of an Aramaic phrase using *talyā'*, which can mean both 'lamb' and 'servant'; but it is unlikely that an Aramaic rendering of Isa. 53 would use this word rather than the more usual *'abdā'*. But this does draw attention to the difficulty of the use of Lamb rather than Servant, if this poem alone lies behind the title.

Another symbol was already current for the death of Christ, the Passover lamb. Although the Passover was not technically an atonement sacrifice, the Exodus which it celebrated was interpreted in terms of deliverance from the power of sin in Christian thought; cf. 1 C. 5.7; 1 Pet. 1.19. Moreover, Christian baptism was a sacramental sharing in Christ's death with its atoning effects (Rom. 6.3f.). As John uses the symbolism of the Passover elsewhere in the Gospel, it is altogether probable that it is included in the range of ideas here; hence 'Lamb' rather than 'Servant'. There may, too, be some connection with the picture of the 'Lamb . . . as though it had been slain' of Rev. 5.6.

We conclude that the title is based on Isa. 53, interpreted in the light of the Passover sacrifice. The title is chosen because it expresses Jesus' submission to baptism, which he received not for his own sins, for he was sinless, but in token of his vocation to an atoning death. It is the first element in the baptismal mystery which is now to be recounted: each stage unlocks further items of revelation. His willingness to be baptized comes first, and this evokes the opening testimony; but the Baptist can only give this testimony subsequently, because, from the narrative point of view, he did not recognize Jesus as the Messiah until the next stage (verse 32).

30. who ranks before me: referring back to verse 27, where these words are actually added by many MSS. The Greek means literally 'who came into being in front of me', and can refer either to rank or to temporal sequence. The idea of rank was implied by the comparison of the Baptist to the slave in verse 27, which was taken over from the source. The idea of temporal precedence is now introduced by the addition of **for he was before me.** This implies pre-existence, which is an essential element in the build-up towards the full testimony of verse 34. It is possible that this verse again corresponds with the progress of the baptism of Jesus, for it represents the Baptist's deference as in Mt. 3.13; but this can be no more than surmise. This verse is the basis of the parenthesis in the Prologue (verse 15).

31. This verse, recalling verse 26, forms the transition to the account of the baptism, which it is assumed has already taken place. **revealed to Israel** is reminiscent of Lk. 1.80, but there is no literary connection. It defines the purpose of the Baptist's ministry as John understands it.

with water prepares the reader for the other element of the contrast which was omitted in verses 26f.

32. bore witness: cf. verse 15. The words are inserted to prepare for the climax.

I saw: according to Matthew and Mark Jesus saw the Spirit's descent (though Matthew makes the divine words audible generally). Luke leaves open the possibility that others may have seen it. Only John says that the Baptist saw it. But the words **the Spirit descend as a dove from heaven** are closer to Mark than to the others. John adds **and it remained on him,** indicating the permanent effect of the messianic anointing. There may be an allusion to the Hebrew text of Isa. 11.2. It is probable that the event was an inner experience of Jesus, which later elaboration has made out to be perceived more generally. John takes over the symbolism of the Dove from the earlier tradition (see Barrett, *The Holy Spirit and the Gospel Tradition*, pp. 35–9; Bernard, 1.49f.).

33. did not know him: Repeating the beginning of 31. The point is that the Baptist's testimony is not an inference from the vision of the Spirit, which might suggest to him that Jesus was the Messiah, but is his response to the fulfilment of a prearranged signal that this is how the Messiah would be indicated. For the Messiah is the one **who baptizes with the Holy Spirit.** When the Spirit comes down upon Jesus, he is at one and the same time singled out as the Messiah and empowered to perform his special task. This is the moment to which the Baptist's ministry of water-baptism has been solely directed (see the note on 31).

who baptizes with the Holy Spirit: Here at last is the contrast omitted in verses 26f. It amounts virtually to a messianic title. Matthew and Luke add: 'and with fire', and this has been interpolated into one MS. (C*) and the Sahidic version. But John is not interested in the horrific aspects of apocalyptic expectation. Baptism here does not have its literal meaning of immersion, but means purification from defilement. This spiritual purification is an aspect of Jewish thought about the End Time, but not usually attributed to the Messiah; cf. 1QS iv.20f.: 'Then God in his truth will make manifest all the deeds of man, and will purify for himself some from mankind, destroying all spirit of perversity . . ., and purifying him with a spirit of holiness (cf. Rom. 1.4) from all deeds of evil. He will sprinkle upon him a spirit of truth like waters for purification . . .' (Leaney, p. 154). To John this eschatological cleansing is already effected by the word of Jesus (15.3), who also gives the Spirit for future guidance (7.38f.; 14.16f.) and for the proclamation of forgiveness to the world (20.22f.).

on whom . . . remain: Black (p. 101) claims that this is a Semitism, as in verse 27; but it is more likely that it is simply due to the repetition of the phrases in verse 32.

34. borne witness: the words take the reader back, through verse 32, to the opening in verse 19, thus rounding off the paragraph with typical *inclusio.*

the Son of God: the Baptist's testimony finally states the truth to which the whole paragraph has been leading, that Jesus is the Messiah. Unfortunately there is uncertainty about the original reading at this point. The 'Western' text (P⁵ ℵ* e ff² Old Syriac and Sahidic) reads 'the chosen of God' (*eklektos*). Most modern editors, following Harnack, maintain that this must be the original, as the change to 'Son' is far more likely than the other way round. In either case it is virtually certain that the title is an allusion to the divine words at the baptism, which are not included in John's account. He has transferred the divine witness to the Baptist (cf. the notes on 3.29; 7.4). Mk 1.11 reads: 'Thou art my beloved Son; with thee I am well pleased.' This appears to refer to Ps. 2.7, in which 'Son' is a messianic title of the king as the adopted son of God. But it also refers to Isa. 42.1; 'my chosen, in whom my soul delights' (cf. Mt. 12.18). 'The Chosen One' occurs as a messianic title in Lk. 23.35 and 1 Enoch 39.6, cf. also Lk. 9.35. In the latter passage the Greek word is adjectival (*eklelegmenos* instead of *eklektos*), corresponding with 'beloved' (*agapētos*) in Matthew and Mark, but closer to the literal meaning of Isa. 42.1. This suggests a tradition nearer to the original Semitic form of the divine words, but not different in meaning. The 'choice' of Jesus by the Father means in John's thought the Incarnation (cf. 10.36); it does not mean that a new status is conferred on him at the moment of baptism. Thus the climax of the Baptist's witness, whether we read here **Son** or 'chosen', is that the baptism reveals the truth of the Incarnation, though it is expressed in words which primarily simply state messiahship; cf. below on verse 49.

The First Disciples **35–42**

According to John, the first disciples follow Jesus, not in response to a call *in vacuo*, as it were, but as a direct result of the Baptist's witness. This agrees with his idea, which is consistent throughout the Gospel, that witness evokes faith, and faith leads to adherence to Jesus; cf. 12.37; 20.31. It is probable that he was familiar with traditions similar to the call stories of the Synoptic Gospels; cf. 21.3–6, 19, 22. On the other hand, the material in the present paragraph seems to be based on an independent tradition of these call stories, as it shows no close links with the Synoptic accounts. But, like them, it was a Galilean tradition (see the notes on verse 43), transferred to a Judean setting to bring it into close relation with the Baptist.

35. two of his disciples: only John tells us that these two (one of whom was Andrew, verse 40) had been followers of the Baptist, but it is quite possible historically. That he had a group of disciples similar to Jesus' group is confirmed by Mk 2.18. Apparently John also imagines that Jesus was included in the group, as he still seems to be in the Baptist's company some days after his baptism, whereas according to the Synoptists he went off immediately after his baptism for his retreat in the wilderness.

36. a repetition of verse 29, with slight verbal variations. Just enough is given to imply that the whole of the Baptist's witness, given in 29–34, is passed on to the disciples.

the Lamb of God is merely an *incipit*, so that it is not necessary to suppose that the disciples were expected to understand this title without the rest. The Baptist is really pointing Jesus out as the Messiah (cf. verse 41). His function is now completed, and he drops abruptly out of the story.

37. heard: the word includes the notion of obedient response as in the OT (e.g. Ps. 81.11).

followed: This word (*akolouthein*) is used in all the Synoptic call stories and frequently in contexts of discipleship; cf. Mk 10.21 paras. Here, however, it really has a double meaning: (a) literally, to walk behind, as the narrative requires; (b) metaphorically, to be a follower of, as in the underlying traditions.

38. Jesus turned: cf. 21.20, which seems to be modelled on this verse. The scene is quite vividly imagined, with Jesus walking on ahead and the two disciples trying to catch him up.

what do you seek?: i.e. 'what do you want?', as in 4.27, where the same word is used. The fact that the disciples are trying to catch up is enough to suggest that they have a request to make.

Rabbi: the usual way of addressing a religious teacher after A.D. 70, and perhaps as early as the lifetime of Jesus. The disciples use it, because they are not yet ready to commit themselves to the implications of the title used by the Baptist. John is usually careful to translate his Jewish terms for the benefit of his Greek readers.

where are you staying: this request shows psychological insight, for it is the sort of exploratory question likely to be asked by those who are uncertain what to make of Jesus, but wish to find out more about him. The word for **staying** is *menein*, translated 'abide' in the allegory of the Vine. Hence some commentators find here a symbolical overtone: it is the quest for the Saviour, who will be found in the place where he abides—i.e. in the life of the Church (cf. 15.4ff.). But this reads too much into the text.

39. Come and see: the invitation moves at two levels, and so explains the plot at this point, without resorting to the symbolical interpretation just mentioned. (a) Jesus entertains the two disciples. John is not interested where it was. (b) Jesus promises them

spiritual illumination (cf. verse 51) which will confirm the beginnings of faith that are stirring within them. As a result, Andrew is
able to make his testimony in verse 41.

the tenth hour: i.e. 4 p.m., according to the usual Jewish
reckoning of twelve hours from dawn to dusk. Westcott favoured
the reckoning from midnight, which would give the whole day for
the disciples' stay, and allow time for Andrew to find Peter. It is
the kind of circumstantial detail which raises the whole question
of the historical accuracy of John's writing. From one point of
view, it appears so artless that it must be taken at its face value;
from another, it is a typical vivid touch of the story-teller's art
(cf. Introduction, p. 34). From the latter point of view, it is
simply a narrative device to get the disciples into Jesus' entourage,
so that they are with him when he goes to Galilee (verse 43; 2.2);
this makes 4 p.m. the more likely time.

40. Andrew: in the Synoptic tradition Andrew and Peter
together were the first two to be called. **Simon Peter's brother**
anticipates the next verse (cf. 11.2), and (if it is not a marginal
note brought into the text) it presupposes knowledge of the facts
on the part of the reader. But here Andrew is one of the first two,
but the other is not named. Chrysostom (*Catena Aurea*) records the
suggestion that this is intentional, for he is John the Apostle, the
presumed author himself, and this view is still held by conservative
scholars. The 'Alogi' (Epiphanius, *Pan. Haer.* 51; cf. Introduction,
p. 28), who regarded the Gospel as heretical, denied the genuine-
ness of verses 40–2, presumably because of this issue. The unnamed
disciple could quite well be John, without raising the question of
authorship, seeing that James and John are the next two to be
named in the Synoptic tradition. But Schnackenburg brackets
verse 43, and takes him to be Philip (so Perry, Boismard). But it is
equally possible that he is left unnamed, because John's narrative
did not require further mention of him.

41. first: this presumably means 'first of all' (Gr. *prōton*), but
nothing is said about what he did next. It can be taken to mean
before going to see where Jesus was staying, so that Peter in effect
joins the party in verse 39. But this is certainly awkward, and the
difficulty was felt from the beginning. The Curetonian Syriac,
Tatian, Chrysostom and Augustine simply omit the word. The
received text, supported by ℵ*, reads *prōtos* = 'he as the first',
i.e. being the first person to act in a missionary capacity. But this

scarcely carries conviction. A third alternative is to accept *māne* ('in the morning'), the reading of a few Old Latin texts, which suggests an original reading in the Greek *prōï*, perhaps supported by the Sinaitic Syriac's 'on that day'. *Prōton* would then have arisen from dittography, the whole phrase being *prōï ton adelphon*. Although this is attractive at first sight, it is equally arguable that this has arisen by haplography from *prōton ton adelphon*; if John really meant to say 'the next day', he would surely have written *tē epaurion*, as in verses 29, 35 and 43. Bernard, Sanders and Marsh accept *prōï*, but Schnackenburg argues that *prōton* is more likely, because it is both strongly attested, and also constitutes a *lectio difficilior*. The sense is eased if Philip is identified with the unnamed disciple, who subsequently (i.e. in the second place) acted like Andrew (verse 45).

Messiah: having 'seen' Jesus (verse 39), Andrew is able to give his testimony. The title is used, as in 4.25, because John does not wish to include Christian overtones at this stage. It corresponds with the final statement of the Baptist's testimony (verse 34).

42. looked at him: cf. verses 47–9. John makes much of Jesus' penetrating insight, perhaps deriving it from genuine impressions of his personality. But to John it has dogmatic implications, cf. Introduction, p. 54.

So you are: it is not certain that this should be taken as a question.

son of John: this is the best attested reading, but 'Jonah' is a variant, both here and in 21.15–17. It seems probable that the latter was the real name of Peter's father, in view of the transliteration of the Aramaic in Mt. 16.17 (Bar-Jona). As Jonah is rare, but John very common, the change is more readily explained if Jonah is original. Barrett argues that *Iōna* is a variant spelling of *Iōanēs*, rather than a different name, but if so this can only have been in the Greek tradition, as the names could hardly be confused in Aramaic.

Cephas: Better 'Kephas', transliterating the Aramaic *Kēphā'* = a rock. *Petros* (= a stone) is used as the Greek equivalent for the sake of the masculine ending, instead of the feminine form *petra* ('a rock'). The Aramaic form is sometimes used by Paul, e.g. 1 C. 1.12. Mk 3.16 reports the nickname in the list of the Apostles, but without explanation. Mt. 16.17f. connects it with Peter's confession of faith at Caesarea Philippi, though the name has already occurred previously. John here makes it the result of Jesus' estimate of Simon's character, and there is no hint of the Matthean symbolism of the foundation of the Church. Origen suggests that Jesus subsequently said: 'You are Peter . . .' (Mt. 16.18), because he had already formed this estimate of Simon. The nickname was presumably given to distinguish him from other Simons, and John may well be right in connecting it with the impression of his personality.

The Testimony of Nathanael **43–51**

The narrative continues without a break. But in verses 44f. we suddenly discover that the setting is in or near Beth-saida, a fishing village at the northern end of the Sea of Galilee, about seventy miles from the scene of the Baptist's ministry. It is, of course, possible that Nathanael is called before the intention of going to Galilee (verse 43) is actually carried out. But then we get into fresh difficulties, as the wedding at Cana, in the Galilean hills, takes place only two days later. The difficulties are not resolved by the omission of verse 43, though it may well be that they are the reason for its insertion. It must be confessed that John's topographical care deserts him at this point. The simplest solution is that he is working on Galilean traditions, which he has only partially transferred to the Judean setting.

The story itself has no counterpart in the Synoptics, and is presumably derived from independent tradition. Nathanael does not occur in the Synoptic lists of the Twelve, but as there are variations in them, it is quite possible that his name was found in a non-Synoptic list. John's reworking of his source is too heavily dominated by his theological motives to enable us to recover the original. It has been prepared for by two motifs in the preceding paragraph, Jesus' insight (verse 42) and Andrew's testimony (41), which are now considerably developed to compose an effective climax.

43. The *RSV* translation hides the fact that the subject of **decided** and **found** is not expressed, and that **Jesus** goes closely with **said to him.** If we bracket **decided to go to Galilee** as in any case an addition to the underlying source, the subject of **found** could then be Andrew, doing his second missionary activity (cf. verse 41), or the unnamed disciple (Bultmann), or Peter taking his turn (Bernard). If we follow Schnackenburg and bracket the whole verse, Philip can then be regarded as the unnamed disciple of verse 40, whose fortunes are now followed up after Andrew has been dealt with. But, awkward as it is, the text can stand, and the *RSV* can be taken as a right interpretation, though not a literal translation (so *NEB*). Whichever view is adopted the verse is primarily aimed at bringing Philip on to the stage, because of his part in what follows.

Philip is only mentioned in the Synoptic Gospels in the lists of the Apostles. As he is placed next after Peter, James, John and Andrew, he may have been more important than the rest, and this may account for his prominence in the Fourth Gospel; cf. 6.5; 12.21; 14.8.

44. Beth-saida: Bethsaida-Julias is at the point where the upper waters of the Jordan empty into the northern tip of the Sea of Galilee. As this was just over the border of Galilee in the tetrarchy of Philip (cf. Lk. 3.1), another Beth-saida has been postulated further west. But this is very doubtful. It may well have been the home of Philip, but, according to Mk 1.29, Peter and Andrew came from Capernaum, only a few miles to the west. This area has the richest associations with the ministry of Jesus.

45. Nathanael: only mentioned in this story, and at 21.2, where he is said to be from Cana in Galilee (cf. 2.1). He has been traditionally identified with Bartholomew, or with other lesser apostles, to bring him into the number of the Twelve. In Mk 3.18 Bartholomew is paired with Philip, and as this is a patronymic ('son of Ptolemy', or 'Talmai') it is not impossible that his personal name was Nathanael, but there can be no certainty about this.

we have found: The plural subject associates Philip with Andrew and Peter, and may be intended to include the reader; cf. verse 14.

Moses ... wrote: The messianic testimony is enlarged by allusion to the OT scriptures, cf. Lk. 24.27. This reference was noted by the Fathers, who then identified the unnamed disciple of Lk. 24.13, 18 with Nathanael (Epiphanius, *Pan.* XXIII.vi.5).

of Nazareth, the son of Joseph: At the same time Jesus' human identity is given in fuller detail. So far he has appeared without historical background, but these details are necessary for the following dialogue. **son of Joseph** does not exclude the virgin-birth (see the notes on verse 13 above), but it may imply that Jesus' family was held to be insignificant, cf. 6.42.

46: There is no external evidence to explain Nathanael's low estimate of Nazareth, though the fact that it is never mentioned in the OT or early rabbinic literature indicates that it was a place of little importance. But it is very probable that Jesus' Galilean origins were held against Christian claims by the unbelieving Jews; cf. 6.42; 7.41, 52. The tradition of his birth at Bethlehem may have arisen in response to this criticism. The Galileans were of mixed stock, and had been forcibly Judaized by John Hyrcanus (135–105 B.C.). They were despised by Jews of pure descent, of whom Nathanael is here evidently to be regarded as a representative. Nazareth means a look-out place (Heb. *nāṣar* to watch), and stands on a promontory of the hills overlooking the Plain of Esdraelon. Another Hebrew root yields the noun *nēṣer* = a branch, used of the 'shoot of Jesse' in the messianic passage, Isa. 11.1, and this could be taken to indicate a closer relation between Jesus' messianic status and his place of origin than appears on the surface. But there is no hint of this in the present passage, which is concerned with the contrast between his origins and his true identity.

47. Jesus saw: cf. verse 42.
an Israelite indeed: it is essential to the story that Nathanael is a man of pure Jewish stock, in spite of the fact that he is apparently resident in Galilee, and this is emphasized by the use of **Israelite** (used only here in the Four Gospels; for its nationalistic significance, cf. 2 Co. 11.22). The addition of **in whom is no guile** indicates his religious and moral integrity; cf. Ps. 32.2. Nathanael is the devout Jew whom the Christian may hope to convert by a reasonable exposition of the messianic claims of Jesus, but there is an initial prejudice to be overcome.

48. know: the verb (*ginōskein*) is not the same as in verses 31 and 33 (*eidenai*), and is capable of a deeper meaning, though John tends to use the two verbs almost interchangeably. Jesus' insight is enhanced by the fact that he had formed a correct opinion of Nathanael even before Philip approached him.
under the fig tree: Another subtle reference to the pious Jew whom Nathanael represents; cf. Mic. 4.4; Zech. 3.10. According to the Midrash Rabba on Eccles. 5.11, some rabbis taught the Law under a fig tree (cf. *SB* 1.858; 11.371). This apparently gratuitous detail of the story thus has symbolical significance, which must clearly affect our estimate of the historical value of it.

49: Nathanael's confession of faith is so daring, and such a complete reversal of his contemptuous question in verse 46, that it seems to the modern reader an impossible conclusion to draw from Jesus' display of insight, and even strikes him as ludicrous. It is to avoid this impression that some commentators turn it into a question: 'Rabbi, are you . . .?' But the next verse forbids this expedient. In fact Nathanael's confession says no more than had been implied in Philip's words in verse 45. His *belief* has been evoked by Jesus' insight, but the *content* of it is not derived from it, but from Philip's announcement. From the outset only two alternatives have been open to him—either to believe that Jesus is the Messiah, or to deny it. There is no mediating position, as that Jesus might be a holy man or a prophet. John's writing can be blamed for compressing the thought too much, but his logic is sound.

Son of God . . . King of Israel: the phrases are virtually synonymous, cf. the note on the reading 'Son of God' in verse 34. Though John certainly holds the metaphysical implications of **Son of God,** as outlined in the Prologue, he correctly understands it as, from a scriptural point of view, a messianic title derived from Ps. 2.7, cf. 2 Sam. 7.14; Ps. 89.26f.; 2 Esd. 7.28f.; 13.52; 14.9; I Enoch 105.2. This is how it might be understood by the pious Jew represented by Nathanael, though not without some demur, for it was not a normally current messianic title. It would have been easier if **King of Israel** had come first; as it stands, the latter appears to be an explanation of the other, so as to avoid misunderstanding from a Jewish point of view (so Lagrange). **Son of God** is thus the climax of the whole series of confessions of faith, the most far-reaching of the messianic titles, unique in the series, if we read 'chosen' in verse 34. Much of the rest of the Gospel will be concerned with its implications, whereas the explanatory equivalent, **King of Israel,** will be handled in the trial before Pilate.

50. This verse provides the link between the climax of Nathanael's confession of faith in the last verse and the fresh climax of the prophecy of Jesus in verse 51. As the latter is not to be regarded as part of the original homily on the call of the disciples, but belongs to the larger structure of the Gospel as a whole, it follows that this verse has only been composed in the process of making the Gospel (cf. Bultmann, p. 98). The link is effected by a comment on Nathanael's confession suggesting three

stages in the revelation of Jesus' glory. First there is Jesus' penetrating insight, which has evoked his belief. It is a witness, or sign,
of the truth of the claims made about him.

you shall see: the verb is singular (contrast the next verse),
addressed to Nathanael alone. He will see **greater things**, i.e.
further, more compelling signs. This is the second stage in the
revelation of Jesus' glory. For the special use of **greater,** cf. 5.20;
14.12. Some editors take this verse closely with 2.1–11, which is
a specimen Sign, and so regard verse 51 as intrusive. But it is
better to take it more generally, applying to the unfolding of
Jesus' glory throughout the Gospel.

51. The prophecy of Jesus, addressed to the whole company,
gives a preview of the future glory of the Son of Man when his
mission is accomplished. This is the third stage of revelation,
which goes beyond the previous two stages. It is a vision of
fulfilment. As such, it forms a comment on the whole section,
which began with vision (verse 32) to some extent corresponding
with what is now foretold: both tell of a rift in the heavens and
spiritual traffic between God and Jesus.

Truly: the Greek transliterates the Hebrew *'āmēn. RSV* leaves it
in the form 'Amen' only in liturgical contexts (e.g. Rom. 1.25).
It is used with **I say** as an asseverative particle only in the sayings
of Jesus (e.g. Mt. 5.18). John always repeats it, as here, thus
giving it more solemn effect. It is sometimes doubled in liturgical
use (e.g. Ps. 72.19; 1QS i.20; ii.10, 18; 4Q *Words of the Heavenly
Lights*). But the asseverative use has no real parallel (Jer. 28.6 is the
nearest to it in the OT), and seems to have been a special feature
of Jesus' authoritative style of speaking, which may be used more
frequently by the evangelists than they found in their sources. For
the special use of it in John, cf. Introduction, p. 48.

you will see: the verb is plural. For the change from address to
an individual to a general statement implying a wider audience;
cf. 3.11. The saying which follows is based on traditional words of
Jesus, being reminiscent of a number of other sayings about the
future glory of the Son of Man (cf. S. S. Smalley, *NTS* xv (1969),
pp. 287ff.). The foundation-text is the vision of Dan. 7.13f., applied
there to the vindication and glory of the Jewish people in the life-
and-death struggle of the Maccabean revolt (168 B.C.). The figure
of the Son of Man can be thought of either as a collective, a
symbol of the people as a whole, or as an individual whose destiny

in some way represents that of the whole nation. From the latter point of view it was an easy transition to identify him with the Messiah, and this is done in I Enoch (cf. M. D. Hooker, *The Son of Man in Mark*, pp. 33–48). The Gospel sayings certainly imply this identification in a number of instances.

The question whether Jesus saw himself in the role of the Son of Man is extremely complex, and has given rise to a vast amount of literature in modern study. But there can be no doubt that the primitive church came to the conclusion that Jesus was the Son of Man, and John stands in the same tradition. The key passage for our present purpose is the answer of Jesus at his trial before the high priest: 'The high priest asked him, "Are you the Christ, the Son of the Blessed?" And Jesus said, "I am; and you will see the Son of man sitting at the right hand of Power, and coming with the clouds of heaven" ' (Mk 14.61f. paras.). Though this saying raises numerous problems, it is clear that the heavenly session of the Son of Man is held to be the vindication of Jesus' claim to be the Messiah. The Matthean form of the saying has actually influenced the text of our verse, in that some MSS. have inserted 'hereafter' (*ap' arti*) before **you will see** (cf. Mt. 26.64). Other passages which should be compared with this are Mt. 16.28 (just before the Transfiguration, which is an anticipatory vision of the glory of the Son of Man); Mk 13.26 paras.; Ac. 7.55f. Thus the point of departure for the present saying is the promise that the disciples will see Jesus risen and glorified as the messianic King, fulfilling the Jewish expectations which surround the claim to messiahship.

heaven opened: the idea is of a rift in the blue dome of the sky (the 'firmament'), allowing sight into the abode of God above it, according to the ancient cosmology of the three-storey universe; cf. Ezek. 1.1. It is a feature of the baptismal vision of Jesus (Mt. 3.16 paras.), from which John has presumably derived it.

angels: the ministers of God in the heavenly court, cf. Dan. 7.10; I Enoch 1.9; Jude 14. Here John has introduced an entirely original feature by linking the conventional picture to Jacob's dream (Gen. 28.12), where 'the angels of God were ascending and descending on' the ladder, joining the place where Jacob lay to heaven. Strangely enough, this allusion was not perceived by any ancient commentators before Augustine (*Contra Faustum* xii.26; cf. Bernard, 1.71).

upon the Son of man: it seems that John substitutes **the Son of Man** for the ladder of Jacob's dream. It is possible that he is making use of rabbinic exegesis at this point, which is first attested in Targum Neofiti at Gen. 28.12. Thus *Gen. Rabba* lxviii.18; lxix.3 take 'on it' and 'above it' of Gen. 28.12 and 13 respectively to be 'on him'—i.e. on Jacob. One of the explanations given for this obviously erroneous interpretation is that the 'image' of Jacob is in heaven while his body sleeps on earth, and the angels maintain contact between them. John does not have this explanation, but the interpretation 'on him' may have been current in rabbinic circles in his time. It depends on the Hebrew text, as the Greek for 'ladder' is feminine, so that the LXX's 'on it' (*ep' autēs*) is unambiguous. But, in adopting this exegesis, John is certainly using the motif of the angels to suggest the inauguration of vital contact between heaven and earth. The point is that Jesus is *on earth*, and the revelation of his glory as the Son of Man does not have to wait for his exaltation to heaven.

At this stage in the argument we have to observe a further element of the Son of Man imagery, which has not so far been mentioned. This is the fact that suffering precedes glory: in Daniel, the suffering of the Jewish people before their vindication; in the Synoptic Gospels, the Passion of Jesus before his resurrection; cf. Mk 8.31; 9.31; 10.33. One of John's most original and daring ideas is that the glory of God is already revealed in the Passion of Jesus, cf. 12.23–32, where 'Son of man' is used. Hence, while Jesus is still on earth, the vision of his heavenly glory is given to those who have eyes to see it, and earth and heaven are joined.

The verse is comprehensible without elaborate exegesis (which could hardly be expected of the reader) if it is realized that (a) the symbolism of the angels represents contact between heaven and earth, and (b) the use of the title Son of man in John's thought is a technical messianic designation for Jesus as the one who fulfils the role of the suffering Son of Man, who is vindicated and receives power and authority to execute judgment, as implied in Dan. 7.13f. and the literature related to it. For the judgment theme in John, cf. 5.27.

THE MARRIAGE AT CANA: JESUS IN THE HISTORY OF SALVATION
2.1–12

The opening sequence of the Gospel is rounded off with the
miracle at Cana, symbolizing the new element which has entered
the history of salvation with the arrival of Jesus, the Word made
flesh. His 'glory' was seen in his incarnate life (1.14). Up to this
point it has remained concealed, though witness has been given
to it. Now it is 'manifested' for the first time (2.11). This confirms
the faith of the disciples, which has been expressed in their
confessions of Jesus' messiahship, and so the story goes closely
with the preceding chapter. At the same time it is the first act of
what is to follow. It is the first of a series of signs which constitute
John's account of the ministry of Jesus. These signs are from one
point of view Jesus' credentials, the proofs that he *is* the Messiah.
But to John they have greater importance in that they unfold
what it means to have faith in him. As we might expect, the first
of these signs is concerned with the new dimension of the coming
of Christ, rather than with a particular aspect of its meaning. God
has been active in history since the beginning of time. But now
something new has occurred which completely overshadows all
the past: **you have kept the good wine until now.**

It is at once clear that the story which we are now to study
differs from the preceding series in that its meaning is to be found
in its symbolism. The account of the first disciples was told as
narrative, even if we have to regard it as to some extent artificially
constructed by John, and the meaning was found in the confessions of faith. There was no sign of allegorizing of details. Now,
however, we have a miracle-story in which the miracle itself is
unimportant and all the interest lies in the symbolical possibilities
of the event. Inevitably there is some degree of allegorizing. In
fact, once the search for allegorical detail is begun, the possibilities
seem to be endless. Then the problem is to decide how much
John really intended to imply. Schnackenburg utters a warning
against the tendency of some exegetes to read into it far too much.

All critics recognize that some degree of symbolism is to be
found in this story. This naturally raises questions about its
historical accuracy, which is liable to be distorted when symbolical
motifs are the dominant factor. Consequently commentators for
the most part seem either to be preoccupied with the problem of

accounting for all the details on strictly historical grounds, in spite of the symbolical overtones, or else to be dazzled by the immense range of symbolism to such a degree that all other considerations fall into the background. In either case, there has been a curious failure to tackle the story along form-critical lines, such as it would have received if it **had** been found in the Synoptic Gospels. Each of these three aspects **must** now be briefly examined in turn.

(a) Although John has evidently written up the story in his own way for his purposes, it can hardly be supposed that he has spun it out of his head. Many scholars think that John derived it from a Signs-source (cf. Introduction, pp. 46–8). It is not necessary to accept Bultmann's elaborate version of the theory in order to agree that the two numbered Signs (the present story and 4.46–54) came to John from some short collection, perhaps including some other items which he has used elsewhere. The underlying story need not have had the symbolical overtones. It could have been an example of Jesus' kindly concern at a wedding, to which his family was invited. Afterwards it was seen to be almost prophetic, a hint of the mighty works of his public ministry. From this point of view the historicity of the story is accepted, and the symbolism is regarded as subsequent elaboration, probably already operative to some extent in the form in which it came to John.

We may at once agree that John himself accepted it as historical, and that he wrote it up in good faith, even though adapting it to some degree in the process. There are, however, two considerations which reduce the likelihood of an authentic historical episode at the back of it, and may drive us reluctantly to the conclusion that in this case there is no firm foundation of fact. The first is the fact that the symbolism cannot be successfully strained out of the story, as will appear from the form-critical analysis below. The second is that the motif of changing water into wine is well known from pagan sources. But the final result will not be wholly negative; for though the narrative as history disappears, an authentic tradition of Jesus comes to light.

(b) As already indicated, the symbolical possibilities present an *embarras de richesses*, and the critic must tread warily. The following points should be observed. (i) The timing on the third day suggests that the whole story points forward to the blessings of the Resurrection, when the glory of Jesus is complete. This is not

quite certainly John's intention, though it is by no means impossible. More importantly, this detail does not belong to the
underlying story. (ii) The setting of a wedding is a standard
symbol of the eschatological banquet, the coming time of blessing
when all the enemies of God's people have been destroyed. For the
idea of the banquet, cf. Isa. 25.6–8; for the marriage-feast, there
are the parables of Jesus in Mt. 22.1–14; 25.1–13; cf. also Rev.
19.7–9. Wedding imagery also appears in the saying of Jesus in
Mk 2.18–20 paras.; cf. Jn 3.29f. Jesus' reply in Mk 2.19: 'Can
the wedding guests fast while the bridegroom is with them?' is
tantamount to a claim that the time of the wedding-feast has
arrived in the new order which he himself has inaugurated. This
saying is thus extremely close to the interpretation of the present
passage. (iii) The motif of the wine is central to the story. The
Marcan saying just quoted is followed by another very similar
one, or rather pair of sayings, about the new patch on an old
garment and the new wine which bursts the old wineskins (Mk
2.21f.). Here there is more emphasis on the inadequacy of the old.
The regulations of the old dispensation under the Jewish Law cannot contain the new wine of the era that Jesus announces. This
motif can be seen in the Cana story in several details: the failure
of the old wine, the vast supply of the new wine produced by
Jesus, the fact that it is superior to the old. As this is the point of
the story as John presents it, the question arises why Jesus' part in
producing the good wine is kept secret, being only known to Mary
and the servants, and presumably the disciples (but see the notes
on verse 12). It is evidently a hidden sign. This makes it impossible to assert that Jesus used a domestic occasion to bring out his
first public expression of the coming of the messianic kingdom.
The apparent reason for this feature is that the steward's com-
mendation of the wine is an unsolicited testimony to the excellence
of the new order. But see further under (c) below.

So far we have been within the bounds of the necessary symbolism of the story. Dodd and others are impressed by the connection
of wine and marriage symbolism with the Eucharist, and so see a
reference here to the liturgical life of the Church. This is possible,
but there is no warrant for interpreting the story as a symbol of the
refreshing of men's souls with the sacramental wine of the
Eucharist. It has also been suggested that the wine is a reference to
the blood of Christ shed in his Passion (cf. 19.34). The story could

then be symbolical of the inexhaustible grace that flows from his saving death. This is supported by the allusion to the Resurrection in the timing on the third day, and more particularly by Jesus' reply to his mother: 'My hour has not yet come'; for the hour of Jesus is the manifestation of his glory in the Passion, cf. 12.23. But John does not use the theme of the blood of Christ in this way; the reference to the Passion is too muted to be taken as the controlling factor in the interpretation of the whole piece. Finally, Catholic theology has laid much stress on the function of Mary, whose intercession with her Son is so fruitful. Again, this can hardly be the central motif of the story, and in fact her function in it is to be explained on other lines, as will be shown below.

(c) Form-critical analysis can begin with the observation of Bernard (1.80): 'the story does not lead up to any great saying of Jesus, or to any discourse like that which John appends to the Feeding of the Five Thousand'. Schnackenburg points out that the essence of the story is contained in verse 10; 'You have kept the good wine until now.' This verse is, then, to be taken as the nucleus of the whole story.

Let us imagine that we are in the same position as the steward, knowing nothing of the miracle, and let us treat his words in isolation from the setting of the story: 'Every man serves the good wine first; and when men have drunk freely, then the poor wine; but you have kept the good wine until now.' Now compare this with Mk 2.22: 'No one puts new wine into old wineskins; if he does, the wine will burst the skins, and the wine is lost, and so are the skins; but new wine is for fresh skins.' The latter saying is a short parable, almost a proverb—what the Hebrews would call a māšāl—extremely characteristic of the teaching of Jesus. The same applies to Lk. 5.39: 'And no one after drinking old wine desires new; for he says, "The old is good." ' But, surely, exactly the same could be said of the steward's words in verse 10.

I suggest therefore that we have here an authentic saying of Jesus, one of the 'submerged parables' to be found in various places in John (see the notes on 5.19). But the saying cannot have stood alone just as we have it now. It has got to have some kind of a setting. It could have been something like this: 'the kingdom of God is like a wedding-feast; and the steward of the feast called the bridegroom and said to him . . .' (cf. verse 9).

The next stage in the formation of the tradition is the provision of a narrative setting for the saying. It is at this stage that we may suspect influence from pagan sources. For the motif of changing water into wine is found in the cult of the Greek wine-god Dionysus, which has left widespread traces in the Greco-Roman world. It is referred to in Euripides, *Bacchae*, 704ff. Miraculous springs of wine are attested by Diodorus Siculus at Teos, and by Pausanias at Elis. Pliny tells us of a similar spring which produced wine on the nones of January—i.e. the time of the Christian feast of Epiphany. The temple of Dionysus at Corinth provides archaeological evidence for cultic 'miracles' of this kind; this is probably also the case with the church at Jerash (Gerasa), where a basin can be seen which was used precisely in this way in an Epiphany ceremony, for it very likely is the Christianizing of the pagan cult. The cult was known to Philo, who applies it allegorically to the Logos under the guise of Melchizedek, who 'brought wine instead of water' (*Leg. All.* iii.82). It would be a mistake to suppose that this was applied directly to Jesus, as one who is better than the Greek god, for (as Dodd remarks) the age of this kind of apologetic had not yet been reached. But it is not difficult to see how a folk-legend of this type could be applied to Jesus in connection with this very memorable little parable.

Finally, we must note that the resulting pre-Johannine story belongs to a special class of folk-legend. It is a story of the early life of Jesus, when he is still with his mother and his brothers (cf. verse 12), and it probably did not include mention of the disciples. Stories of this kind abound in the apocryphal infancy gospels, and we have one very beautiful example in Lk. 2.41–52. The point is always the same. A domestic incident, usually involving a miracle, is prophetic of what Jesus will accomplish when he is grown up and begins his ministry. Just as in the Lucan story, there is a pathetic touch, in that the action serves to put Jesus at a distance from the control of his mother. John has worked over it lightly to make it a Sign to the disciples at the outset of the ministry. The remarkable thing is that the original point of the parable, contained in verse 10, has been preserved intact in the transformation from saying to legend and in John's adaptation of the legend for his Gospel.

The above analysis cannot claim to be a final solution of the problem of the story, and many readers may prefer to take it historically, in spite of all difficulties. But it should be noted that

Dodd has tentatively put forward a similar solution in his *Historical Tradition*, p. 227, although his work generally tends towards more conservative conclusions. But he has missed the point, which to me is fundamental, that verse 10 not only preserves the conclusion of a genuine parable of Jesus, but also comprises it almost in its entirety.

1. the third day: the phrase immediately suggests the day of Resurrection, though John does not actually use it in his Resurrection narratives. If we count the days since the questioning of the Baptist in 1.19ff., allowing an extra day at 1.39f. and a day for travelling to Galilee after 1.43, this makes it the eighth day of the first week of Jesus' ministry; or, omitting one of the extra days, it is an exact week of seven days. This suggests a sort of 'creation week', or perhaps an artistic balance with Holy Week at the end of the ministry. From either point of view it may be concluded that the Sign at Cana is symbolic of the beginning of a new era. The suggestion is attractive, but John has not said enough for us to be sure that he actually intended to mean this.

Cana: mentioned only by John in the NT. In 21.2 it is said to be the home of Nathanael. Jerome thought that Simon the Cananaean (Mt. 10.4) means Simon of Cana, but this is rarely accepted today. There are two possible sites in Galilee, the more probable being Khirbet Qana, 9 miles north of Nazareth. It is designated **of Galilee** to distinguish it from the Cana (Kanah) near Tyre, mentioned in Jos. 19.28.

mother: John does not use the name Mary, perhaps to distinguish her from Mary of Bethany (Mary Magdalene). She only appears in this story and in 19.25–7, though she is mentioned in 6.42.

2. with his disciples: it is probable that John has added this, or even altered an original 'with his brothers'; see the above analysis and the notes on verse 12. It is natural to think of the Twelve, though John has in fact told us of only five.

3. the wine failed: only the barest detail of the setting is given, so as to go straight to the point of the story. If we are right in seeing allegorical meaning in some of the details, this presumably represents the failure of the Jewish Law, which in its turn stands for the inadequacy of all religion before the coming of Christ (Bultmann). The Synoptic Gospels have a similar allegorical reference in the parable of the fig-tree (Lk. 13.6–9, cf. Mk 11.12–14

= Mt. 21.18f.). The text is ambiguous by the standards of
classical Greek, and ℵ* is an early example of the tendency to
'improve' style, reading 'they had no wine, because the wine of
the marriage was used up'. There is no suggestion, then, that the
wine was not considered good enough. Mary's concern about it
has been explained by the custom of guests to give provisions for
the occasion; cf. J. D. M. Derrett, 'Water into Wine', *BZ*, N.F.
VII (1963), pp. 80–97.

4. O woman: the address, like Peter's 'Man, I am not' in Lk.
22.58, sounds unnatural to English ears, but is normal usage.
Modern English would say 'mother' (so *NEB*).

what have you to do with me: a Semitic idiom, though found
also in colloquial Greek. It is used to indicate that the speaker
feels that a suggestion is an intrusion into his private judgment;
cf. 2 Sam. 16.10; 19.22, but more commonly to complain of
active hostility; cf. 1 Kg. 17.18 ('What have you against me?').
The latter meaning occurs in the Synoptic Gospels, when the
demons use this phrase; cf. Mk 1.24; 5.7. The former is the
meaning here, and like the address is not to be taken as disrespectful. Most editors, however, remark that it implies a certain
dissociation on the part of Jesus. According to our analysis this is an
essential motif of the genre of this story; cf. Lk. 2.48.

my hour: this is John's special word for the moment of the
manifestation of the glory of Jesus in the darkness of the Cross;
cf. 12.23. It is derived from Jesus' sayings on watchfulness, in
which he impresses on his hearers the urgency of the situation in
terms of apocalyptic expectation; cf. Mt. 24.42, 44; 25.13; Mk
13.35; Lk. 12.39f. Commentators are divided whether the word
in the present context refers to the moment of the first public
display of Jesus' power or to the moment of his Passion. I would
suggest that the source meant the former (if the word in fact was
used in the source), but that John, having further ranges of
symbolism in mind, thinks also of the latter. Jesus is not yet ready
to display the Sign of what is to be the climax of his whole work.
However, in spite of his demur, he accedes to his mother's request.
Some critics find this awkward, and avoid it by treating **My
hour, etc.,** as a question (Gregory of Nyssa, Theodore of Mop-
suestia, as well as many moderns). This makes it virtually
equivalent to assent. But, in the context of the pre-Johannine
story, it makes better sense as a statement, as Jesus knows that he

has powers that are not yet ready to be used, and his mother's request, made quite innocently, poses to him the problem of whether to hold back or not. For John similarly it is not so much a refusal as a comment which opens up some of the deeper implications of the event.

5. servants: Gr. *diakonois.* The word quickly gained the technical sense of 'deacon' in Church usage, and some think that its use here is prompted by the eucharistic symbolism of the feast. But it is quite common in the Synoptic sayings in the general sense of servant.

6. six stone jars: water was required for cleansing vessels and pouring over the hands (elaborate rules are given in the Mishnah tractate *Yadaim*); cf. Mk 7.3f., and so had to be stored within easy reach in a Jewish household. The number **six** is taken by some to be symbolical (the inadequacy of the Law, as six is one less than the perfect number seven), but it is doubtful if any special significance attaches to it. The pots were made of **stone**, because it does not contract uncleanness, whereas pottery has to be smashed if that happens (*SB* II.406). John explains the purpose of them for the sake of Gentile readers.

twenty or thirty gallons: Gr. 'two or three *metrētai*', roughly corresponding to the Hebrew *baṭ* (Ezr. 7.22, where one Greek version uses this word), and generally estimated to be nine gallons. The enormous quantity of water, and so ultimately of wine, may represent the inexhaustible supply of grace which Jesus brings; cf. 7.37f.

7. fill: the artificial, and to some extent allegorical, nature of the story forbids us to ask such awkward questions as: Were the jars empty? Would it be necessary to drain them off first? How long would it take to fill them from the well when such a large quantity was required? But we may again see a symbol in the fact that they are now filled **up to the brim.**

8. draw: as the verb (*antlein*) is the usual one for drawing water from a well, Westcott sought to reduce the exaggeration of the miracle by supposing that it is further water, drawn after the jars had been filled, which became wine, and this would only be enough to satisfy actual requirements. But the verb properly means to bale out (of a ship), and so it probably means here dipping a basin into the water. Moreover '*the* water' in the next verse grammatically refers back to verse 7.

steward: Gr. *architriklinos*, the head waiter, or butler. But in the next verse he is distinguished from the servants, and so his position seems rather to be that of toastmaster, for which another Greek word (*sumposiarchos*) should be used. But Jewish customs differed from Greek, and John, or his source, may not have known which word to use.

9. now become wine: the miracle is described only allusively. The point of the story does not lie in the transformation of water into wine as such, but in the comment of the steward, who does not even know that it has happened. If the form-critical analysis given above is accepted, the transformation is regarded as unhistorical, so that the miracle requires no explanation. But if the narrative is accepted as substantially historical, it is essential to accept the miraculous element along with it, and to assume that Jesus could and did perform the miracle as it is described. Naturalistic explanations—that Jesus set an example of enjoying water *as if* it were wine and the steward played up to it splendidly, for instance—are desperate expedients to save the historicity without the dogma.

and did not know: Bultmann points out that the parenthesis really begins here. The steward neither knew that the wine had come from the water-jars nor understood that it was really supplied by Jesus the Messiah; cf. 4.11, 14 (Schnackenburg, p. 333). John retains the theme of the underlying story that the episode precedes the public ministry, so that the miracle is known only to Jesus' family circle and the servants involved.

bridegroom: the marriage ceremony took place at the bridegroom's house, and he was responsible for the banquet.

10. good wine: the new wine is superior to the old, contrast Lk. 5.39, which may be related to the original saying here. From a symbolical point of view this indicates the superiority of Jesus over the old Law. Bultmann (p. 118, n. 4, quoting Windisch) asserts that the opposite custom, of saving the better wine till later in the meal, was the usual practice. Sanders (p. 113) denies that there is reference here to a fixed custom, and calls it 'a bit of peasant humour' on the part of the steward. In fact, if we adopt the form-critical analysis given above, and take it as a detached saying of Jesus, it is a shrewd observation of life in general rather than a reference to specific wedding customs.

11. Once the point of the story has been reached, nothing further needs to be said. This verse is a comment, presumably adapted from the source, which also contained 4.46–54.

first: The Greek word (*archē*) may perhaps replace *prōton* (the usual word for first, cf. 4.54) in the source. It means 'beginning', and so recalls the opening words of the Prologue, 1.1.

signs: (**his** has been supplied by the *RSV* translator.) The word (*sēmeion*) denotes a significant act, which is not necessarily miraculous. Following the Synoptic tradition, John generally refers to miracles in speaking of Jesus' works, but his use of this term indicates that it is the *meaning* of them that is really important to him. In this case the sign is not so much Jesus' power to change water into wine, but the fact that this act reveals the unique position of Jesus in the history of salvation.

manifested his glory: John further defines the meaning of the act by adding this phrase, which again brings the reader back to the Prologue; cf. 1.14. Jesus' **glory** consists both in his power to do mighty works and in the revelation of God which they disclose. The purpose of this display is thus to illuminate the minds of men, and so to produce faith. John is thus careful to note that **his disciples believed in him**, here and at each stage in the ensuing story, again picking up a point in the Prologue. cf. 1.12.

12. It is assumed in this commentary that the Prologue was added when John revised his first edition, and if so, he must have adapted the wording of verse 11 at the same time. This verse, which now appears to be a pointless addition, may have stood in much closer relation to the story before the changes were made. The move to **Capernaum** is relevant to the second Sign, which may have taken place there rather than at Cana (see the notes on 4.46). It is generally identified with Tell Ḥûm on the north-west shore of the Sea of Galilee, and Jesus is said to have taught in the synagogue there (Mk 1.21; Jn 6.59).

went down is a correct topographical use, as there is a considerable descent from the Galilean hills to the lake in the Rift Valley (700 feet below sea level). But this may be from John's source, rather than his personal knowledge.

brothers: obviously they would have been included in the family party at the wedding. It was suggested above that John has replaced them by the disciples in verse 2. Here apparently he did not feel it necessary to make the same alteration, for **and his disciples** is missing from ℵ and the Old Latin version, and misplaced in W, and may well be an interpolation. According to Christian tradition as early as the second century, the brothers of Jesus were sons of Joseph by a former marriage (Origen, *Com. in Matt.* x.17, quoting 'the gospel of Peter or the book of James'), but there is no evidence for this in the NT. In the Synoptic Gospels they are occasionally mentioned in a way which implies a neutral attitude to Jesus. In Jn 7.3–10 they appear to be positively hostile, but in the Resurrection narratives they are regarded as part of the nucleus of the Church (Mt. 28.10; Jn 2c.17; Ac. 1.14). This is supported by 1 C. 9.5 and the tradition that the James of Ac. 12.17; 15.13; 21.18; Gal. 2.9, 12 was a brother of Jesus (cf. Jas. 1.1). Their attitude, cautious at first, may well have changed.

THE NEW ORDER INAUGURATED BY THE COMING OF JESUS 2.13–3.36

Having described the coming of Jesus, John now begins to unfold the meaning of his coming. The Baptist and the first disciples have given their testimony that he is the Messiah. The marriage at Cana has shown that he brings a new and better way of access to God, and this theme is repeated in the cleansing of the Temple (2.13–22). This symbolic act of Jesus indicates a radical break with the existing religion of Judaism. After this there is a conversation with Nicodemus, which leads into the first example of John's most characteristic literary device, the discourse (3.1–36), which is interrupted by a further testimony of the Baptist (3.22–30). Nicodemus is a representative of official Judaism, who, we discover later (7.50f.; 19.39), becomes a follower of Christ. In the next section we shall see how the gospel spreads to a Samaritan (4.1–42) and to a Gentile (4.46–54), reflecting the spread of the Church as it is described in Ac. 1–11. The discourse with Nicodemus expresses even more strongly than the marriage at Cana and the cleansing of the Temple the radical break with the past, involving nothing less than a new birth from above. It concludes by posing the alternatives in sharpest contrast in terms that are permanently relevant to man's condition before God and challenge the reader to a decision.

Although the main thrust of the section can be thus simply

summarized, even a cursory reading of it reveals that it is far from uniform. In fact, this section presents the critic with all the major problems of the Fourth Gospel in an acute form. There is first the question of historicity. Did the cleansing of the Temple take place at the very outset of Jesus' ministry, before he began his work in Galilee? Or are the Synoptic Gospels right in placing it at the very end, only five days before the Crucifixion? Did Jesus really have what seems an improbable conversation with Nicodemus, apparently an important person, though unknown from other sources? Did Jesus and his disciples practise baptism (3.22) in rivalry with the Baptist, or was the latter already imprisoned by the time Jesus began his mission, as Mark asserts? Even if these questions can be answered satisfactorily, there is next the problem of literary composition. There are three distinct types of material, which appear to correspond with different sources. Two of these, the narrative of the Cleansing and the diatribe of the discourse, are easily distinguished, and are clearly derived from very different strata of tradition. The third, including the testimony of the Baptist, appears to have some relation with the traditions used in chapter 1 and perhaps with the marriage at Cana. But we also have to take into account the short editorial links (2.23–5; 3.22–4), which many recent writers say preserve reliable independent tradition.

But the literary problem is not merely that of sources, but of the disposition of the material in the section as we have it. It has been argued in the Introduction (p. 50) that the Cleansing has been moved from chapter 12 to its present position by John himself for the second edition of his work, but there is no general agreement among scholars about this. In chapter 3 the disruption caused by 3.22–30, and the difficulty of tracing the connections of thought in the rest of the material, have led critics to propose a variety of theories of alteration after the completion of the Gospel, either due to interpolation of additional authentic matter or resulting from accidental displacements (cf. Introduction, pp. 48–50). It will be argued below that in spite of the manifest difficulties, it is best to take the order of the text as it stands as preserving John's intentions.

The most serious problem of all, however, is that of interpreta- tion. The discourse with Nicodemus uses categories of thought which unmistakably recall ideas of Gnosticism—the dualism of flesh and spirit and of earthly things and heavenly things, the need for a rebirth from heaven, the descent of the revealer of the divine secrets. Moreover the language might easily be applied to Christian baptism, but there is no reference to the sacrament as such. This raises the question of the relation of John to sacramentalism. Finally the testimony of the Baptist suggests once more the question of an anti-Baptist polemic in the Fourth Gospel. These issues have been discussed in the Introduction (pp. 58–61).

It is obvious that these various problems are interdependent, though different facets are presented by the different types of material. Discussion of them is thus best left to the closer analysis of each subsection.

The Cleansing of the Temple: The New Place of Worship 2.13–22

The paragraph opens with a note that Jesus travelled to Jerusalem at the time of a pilgrimage feast, expressed in language absolutely typical of John (cf. 5.1; 7.2, 10; 11.55). This point is taken up in verse 23 for a short general statement of Jesus' activity, described as 'signs'—we naturally think of healing and other miracles. It would be very awkward to try to refer this plural word to the cleansing of the Temple, in which, indeed, the word 'sign' occurs (verse 18), but with a rather different sense. When we go on to chapter 3, we discover that this short summary has been given mainly to provide the introduction for the discourse with Nicodemus (cf. 3.2). It thus seems probable that 2.13, 23–5 is the transition from the marriage at Cana to the discourse with Nicodemus, which has to take place at Jerusalem because it is appropriate for disputes with the Jewish authorities to take place there. When we note further that chapter 3 has clear links with chapter 1, and continues thematically from 2.1–11, but has no obvious connection with the cleansing of the Temple—however suitable it may seem to be—it begins to be probable that 2.14–22 did not originally stand in its present position.

If the Cleansing did not originally belong here, it is obvious that its proper position is the same as in the Synoptic Gospels, closely connected with the triumphal entry into Jerusalem and the events leading up to the Arrest a few days later (cf. Mk 11.15–18 paras.). This is probable on internal grounds. Brown notes that John's version of the Cleansing has features which correspond with three separate items of tradition in the Synoptics: the action itself (verses 14–16) (cf. Mk 11.15–18); the question of Jesus' authority (18) (cf. Mk 11.28); and the saying about the destruction of the Temple (19) (cf. Mk 14.58; 15.29). These three all belong to the Passion narrative and associated material. Two further details point in the same direction: the quotation in verse 17 is from Ps. 69, which is frequently quarried for texts to account for Jesus' passion in the NT (see the notes *ad loc.*); and the repeated intimation of the disciples' subsequent exegetical work in verses 17 and 22 has a close parallel in 12.16, John's account of the triumphal entry itself. It is quite likely, as Brown himself believes, that the three Synoptic items had already been fused in the tradition of the Cleansing which John was using, and it is at least possible that it already contained the note about the scriptural exegesis of the disciples. But it certainly looks as if it came to John in company with the triumphal entry (12.12–19), and that he used it in that chapter in the first instance.

The reason why he has transferred it to chapter 2 is that he introduced the raising of Lazarus (11.1–44) in the second edition, giving it a pivotal position as the climax of the Signs and the curtain-raiser for the Passion and Resurrection of Jesus, and so made it the reason for the plot to arrest him. There is a possible hint of an original connection with Jesus' activity in the Temple in the allusion to 'our place' (11.48 margin) in the complaint of the chief priests. Chapter 2 was the natural alternative, because it already had Jesus in Jerusalem at Passover time; moreover, the theme of the destruction of the old order was ready to hand. Many commentators have observed that John's placing of the event is (in Barrett's words) 'theological rather than chronological'. Naturally this raises the whole question of the integrity of John's handling of historical tradition. In the case of the marriage at Cana, this was not in doubt, because the tradition had already been historicized before it came to him. To do John justice, he does preserve the main outline of the gospel history as we know it from the Synoptics, though it is equally clear that his work is highly creative and controlled mainly by theological considerations. But it may well be that, to his mind, there was a certain identity between one Passover and another, so that the transference in the present instance was less difficult to him than it would be to us. Certainly the timing of the Bread of Life discourse is guided by his interpretation of the Feeding miracle (6.4). We must grant that he had a different conception of the scope of an author's licence than we do today (on the whole question see Introduction, pp. 54–6).

Finally we want to know what really happened on this dramatic occasion. There need be no hesitation that the tradition is based on fact. Jesus came boldly into the Temple, and made an open protest. But what was the point at issue? We do not know enough about the business side of the Temple in the first century to be sure whether the conduct of the money-changers really warranted the description 'a den of robbers' (Mk 11.17; cf. Jer. 7.11), but it is generally supposed that control was good and that Jesus is unlikely to have been concerned about specific abuses of the system. Nor is it probable that he aimed at opening the Temple to the Gentiles, for they already had the right to worship in the Court of the Gentiles. The only other alternative is that he was attacking the whole idea of the Temple and its sacrificial system (as the Johannine account suggests) in the manner of Jeremiah of old (cf. Jer. 7.1–14, from which 'a den of robbers' is quoted). This does not necessarily entail a rejection of Temple and cultus as such, but it does mean a radical criticism of the presuppositions on which they are maintained. This is consistent with Jesus' known attitude to the laws of purification; cf. Mk 7.1–23. Moreover it would seem altogether probable that it was this event which precipitated the plot to arrest him. The Johannine dating—or apparent dating—at the beginning of the ministry has its advocates among modern scholars (e.g. Vincent Taylor, J. A. T. Robinson, V. Eppstein), partly because the Synoptic time-scheme puts far too much into one short week in Jerusalem, and partly because the Question on Authority (Mk 11.27–33 paras.) unexpectedly refers to the work of the Baptist. But John does not really support this view, for, as we have seen, both the literary and the internal evidence favour the Synoptic position.

13. Passover: according to the analysis above, this verse is to be taken with 23–5. John frequently uses a pilgrimage feast to bring Jesus to Jerusalem; cf. 5.1, etc. For the sake of his Gentile readers, he explains that it was a feast **of the Jews.** Many commentators suppose that John also wishes to distinguish the feast from the *Christian* Passover, but 7.2 has the same phrase with the feast of Tabernacles, which has no Christian counterpart.

went up: geographically correct, as Jerusalem is on high ground. But the verb is almost a technical term for pilgrimage. It implies that John does not imagine that Jesus was normally resident in Jerusalem.

14f. The scene is described in much the same terms as the parallels in Matthew and Mark (Luke abbreviates drastically). The **temple** (*hieron*) means the whole area including the outer courts. Mark mentions 'those who sold (*pōlountes*, as in John) and those who bought' in a general way, before specifying 'those who sold pigeons' (*peristerai*, as in John). He may thus intend to imply the **oxen and sheep,** which in fact only John actually mentions. There is some uncertainty whether these animals for sacrifice were actually sold within the Temple area, but Eppstein (*ZNW* 55 (1964), pp. 42-58) gives reason to believe that this practice was introduced by Caiaphas. John's omission of the purchasers is not significant. For **money-changers** he has a word (*kermatistai*) not found elsewhere in Greek (it is a derivative of *kerma* = a small coin), but in verse 15 he uses the Synoptic word (*kollubistai*, derived from *kollubos* = exchange rate). Money for offerings had to be paid in Temple coinage because the Roman imperial currency, stamped with the head of Caesar (Mk 12.16) and sometimes with the image of pagan deities, was felt to be a defilement of the holy place. It is often supposed that Jesus was protesting against exorbitant exactions, but it seems that under Caiaphas the business of exchange was carefully controlled. It is more likely that Jesus objected to the outward show of piety which insisted on a 'pure' coinage without corresponding purity of heart. That he was concerned for the sacredness of the place is suggested by the further detail, found only in Mark, that he tried to stop people from using the Temple precincts as a right of way (Mk 11.16).

15. whip: only John has this detail, which may well be authentic, especially if his source is, as seems probable, not Mark but a parallel tradition. No weapons were allowed in the Temple, so Jesus seized some rope or string which would obviously be available for handling the animals (though the word for **cords** originally meant string made of rushes, it is hardly likely that Jesus used rushes strewn about for the purpose).

with the sheep and oxen: as these words are in poor apposition to **all,** which definitely refers to the persons, and as they employ a usage not normal in John (. . . *te* . . . *kai* . . .), they are probably an editorial addition, though found in all MSS.

16. At this point John and the Synoptists go their separate ways. But the agreement between them is more important than the differences; for the meaning of the act is defined by the words that are spoken, and these in both John and the Synoptics are based on a considered scriptural exegesis. If we may give John equal value with the Synoptic account for the preservation of primitive tradition, we have no warrant to prefer the Synoptic words rather than his. Both alike record the act, and so we may assume that this was a fixed item of the traditions about Jesus. But the spoken words that follow it are the fruit of subsequent reflection on the event, seeking to estimate its significance in the light of scriptural prophecy, and we have independent developments of this in the two different accounts. The keyword is **house,** used in the sense of 'temple'. The Synoptic account quotes Isa. 56.7: 'My house shall be called a house of prayer for all the nations.' Although Matthew and Luke (independently of each other) drop the final phrase, and so concentrate on the theme of sanctity, which is indeed close to Jesus' intentions, it is probable that the full text given in Mark is the reason for the choice of this passage, and that it represents an interpretation in favour of the Church's mission to the Gentiles. The Synoptists also have a phrase from Jer. 7.11, as we have seen, describing the 'house' as 'a den of robbers', which appears to reflect the opinion that Jesus was concerned to expose abuses. This represents the primary desire to find a scriptural warrant for Jesus' action, rather than an interpretation of it. When we turn to John, we find that the exegesis starts from the same point. The saying in verse 16: **You shall not make my Father's house a house of trade,** is also directed simply to explaining the action taken against the traders, without going more deeply into the matter. It is not a quotation from the OT, but it alludes to the prophecy of Zech. 14.20f., which describes the holiness which will attend the whole city when the new age dawns. According to this rather naïve prophecy, the universal holiness will make it unnecessary to have special arrangements for the sanctification of sacrifices in the Temple, and therefore 'there shall no longer be a trader in the house of the Lord of hosts on that day'. It should be noted that the correlation of this text with the Johannine saying is only possible from the Hebrew, as the LXX differs at the significant point. It is probable that the saying has been formed in the pre-Johannine stage, using **Father** as

frequently in the tradition of the words of Jesus. We shall continue to
see this exegetical work on the key word **house** in verses 17 and
19, but first one more comment needs to be made on the scriptural
interpretation in general. Many commentators think that Jesus
was staging a fulfilment of Mal. 3.1–4. Brown, commenting on the
position of the *pericope* at the beginning of the ministry, says that,
whereas Mal. 3.1: 'Behold, I send my messenger to prepare the
way before me' is applied to the Baptist (cf. Mt. 11.10; Mk 1.2),
the parallel clause: 'and the Lord whom you seek will suddenly
come to his temple' could be applied to Jesus, and so bring about
correlation of the activities of both. There may be something in
this speculation, but the notable thing is that so much Scripture
surrounds the Cleansing story, but there is no verbal allusion to
this obvious passage. It is hazardous to build any theory on this basis
(*contra* J. A. T. Robinson, 'Elijah, John and Jesus', *TNT*, p. 40).

17. The verse is a parenthesis, interrupting the narrative. Roloff
(*NTS* xv (1968–9), pp. 129–51) notes that it is the first of a series
of comments in which John points to the Church's understanding
of an event afterwards, cf. verse 22 and, among other examples,
7.39; 20.9. The proof text has the usual words of introduction (**it
was written**) which John employs when citing Scripture from
the exegetical tradition (6.31, 45; 10.34; 12.14). The quotation is
from Ps. 69.9, following the LXX. The future verb is found in
some LXX texts, but may be an accommodation to the context.
Ps. 69 has been quarried for quotations by NT writers more than
any other OT passage, and the second half of the very same verse
is cited by Paul in Rom. 15.3. John quotes from it again in the
Passion narrative (19.28, alluding to Ps. 69.21), following a tradition already found in the Synoptic parallels (cf. Mt. 27.34, 48);
and probably also 15.25 ('they hated me without a cause') refers
to Ps. 69.4. Moreover Paul quotes from it in Rom. 11.9f. (= Ps.
69.22f.), and Ps. 69.25 is used in connection with Judas Iscariot
in Ac. 1.20. Study of these passages shows conclusively that the
original use of this psalm was to account for Jesus' sufferings. It
was not generally expected that the Messiah should die (cf. Lk.
24.26), and the Christian claims about Jesus had to meet this
objection. The use of this passage, made possible by the key word
house, thus connects the Cleansing with the Passion, and so
accounts for the arrest of Jesus as a result of his open protest. His
zeal for the house of God precipitated the plot against him. John

includes this important quotation at precisely this point in the story, instead of leaving it until the end, because it indicates the proper interpretation of the dialogue which now follows.

18. sign: the request of the **Jews** (i.e. the Temple authorities; cf. 1.19) has several Synoptic parallels (Mt. 12.38f.; 16.1–4; Mk 8.11–13; Lk. 11.16, 29). Jesus acts like the Messiah, and they want convincing proof that he *is* the Messiah. Of course Jesus did numerous signs (cf. verse 23), but these could be taken to be the acts of a wonder-worker, and so the significance of them was equivocal. In fact, the discourses of chapters 5–10 are largely concerned with this issue, and show that it was possible to dispute the claim to messiahship. The real point at issue is Jesus' *authority* for his action. Just as Jesus refused to give a sign when challenged in this way (Mt. 12.38f.), so he refused to specify his authority according to the Synoptic tradition (Mk 11.27–33 paras.). John confirms this tradition, arguing in the discourses that the Jews must *look* at what Jesus is doing, and then they will find the answer. Here, however, he gives an answer, but it is suitably cryptic.

19. The saying comes twice in Matthew and Mark (it is not found in Luke), first as the charge of the false witnesses at the trial before the High Priest (Mt. 26.61 = Mk 14.58), and secondly as a taunt of the crowds at the Crucifixion (Mt. 27.40 = Mk 15.29). As neither evangelist asserts that Jesus had actually said it, only that it was attributed to him by his enemies, it comes as a surprise to find it here as a genuine saying of Jesus. But it is probably basically authentic, and the witnesses may well have heard him say it on this actual occasion. On the other hand, it is possible that it has come into John's source from another context, because of the key word **temple** (variant of **house** of the other texts). This time the word is *naos* (= the Temple proper, not the whole precincts; cp. verse 14). The vocabulary of the saying is virtually identical with Mk 15.29, except that John has the simple verb (*lusai*) for the compound (*katalusai*) for **destroy,** which is not significant, and *egeirein* for *oikodomein* for **raise,** which is (see below). But there is an important grammatical difference: in Mark Jesus is the subject of both verbs ('I will destroy . . . I will build', Mk 14.58), but in John the first clause is imperative plural, implying that the subject is the Jews. Before trying to decide what to make of this, we must first attempt to establish what is likely to be the original text.

It will be noticed that the form of the saying in Mark shows that it has already been subjected to interpretative adaptation:

(a) In Mk 14.58 Jesus is reported to have said, 'I will destroy this temple *that is made with hands,* and in three days I will build *another, not made with hands.*' The italicized words are clearly additional. They make the saying a prophecy of a *new* Temple, of a different kind from the old. Presumably this means the abrogation of the old worship; cf. Heb. 10.1–10. Mt. 26.61 omits the additional phrases, not necessarily on the authority of an independent tradition, but more likely for closer agreement with the form in the crucifixion scene, where he follows Mark.

(b) Mk 15.29, 'Aha! You who would destroy the temple and build it in three days, save yourself . . .', naturally uses participles, but keeps Jesus as subject of both verbs. Otherwise the text is not altered from what may be regarded as the original form. It could imply that Jesus was going to restore the *same* Temple by a miracle. But the point here is that, though he had made such an extravagant claim, on the Cross he was powerless to save himself! There is an almost Johannine irony here. But what is really important for our purpose is the fact that the irony goes deeper, for the reader will discover that the true Temple *was* raised in three days. Hence the use of this saying as a taunt implies that it is already being interpreted as a prophecy of the Resurrection as we have it in John.

It follows from this that it is at least possible that 'I will destroy' in Mark is due to the application of the saying to Jesus' death and Resurrection. Obviously Jesus does not destroy or raise himself, but it is put in this form to show that he is master of his destiny. When applied to the Temple, it is even more inappropriate. We know that Jesus forecast its destruction (cf. Lk. 19.44), but it is most improbable that he said he would destroy it himself. It is much more likely that he said: '*If* it be destroyed . . .' Dodd (*Interpretation*, p. 302, n. 1) has pointed out that the imperative in the Johannine form of the text can be taken as an idiom for exactly these words (for the construction, cf. Isa. 8.10: 'Speak a word, but it will not stand', i.e. 'Though you speak . . .').

Returning to John, we can feel some confidence that he has preserved the original form of the saying. Many commentators refuse to accept Dodd's point about the first clause, as they take it to be a threat or an ironical challenge: 'Pull it down yourselves!' i.e. 'Do your worst!' (Bultmann compares Am. 4.4). But everything turns on the originality of the second clause. John's **raise** is per-

fectly good Greek for erecting a building, but, as a word frequently
used of the Resurrection, does seem to be an accommodation to
the Christological interpretation. But **in three days,** both in
Mark and John, is not quite the same as the Resurrection phrase
'on the third day'. Accordingly Bultmann says it is an allusion to
Hos. 6.2, where the idea of the third day is idiomatic for a short
space of time (though the text here is 'on the third day'!). This
seems to me reasonable; so that the saying need not be taken to
be a Resurrection prediction in its original form, and there is no
need to take the second clause as an addition after the event.
The whole saying then means 'Even if this temple be destroyed,
I will build it in a trice'—an extravagant claim rather than a
challenge to the hearers, no doubt intended to shake them into
thinking again what the Temple really is (cf. the interpretation of
Mk 14.58). John, of course, sees it as a prediction of the Passion
and Resurrection. The quotation in verse 17 has prepared the
way for this interpretation, and verses 20 and 21 make it explicit.

20. forty-six years: in typical Johannine style, the Jews understand Jesus quite literally, and therefore miss the point. Their
answer already begins the true interpretation, because they have
nothing whatever to say about the destruction of the Temple, only
its resurrection. The contrast between the long time of **years** and
the brief **three days** fixes attention on this mysterious phrase.
Herod the Great had begun rebuilding the Temple on a grand
scale in 20 B.C., and the work was still unfinished. The characteristic huge stone blocks of the walls can still be seen by travellers,
especially at the Wailing Wall. In fact, the Temple was not
finished until A.D. 63, and so it is difficult to see what the number
forty-six refers to. It might refer to a restricted part of the
structure which was finished by this time; alternatively, it might
mean 'building has been going for forty-six years' without implying
completion. Most commentators say the latter is impossible, in
view of the aorist *oikodomēthē* (for omission of augment, cf. *BDF*
§ 67.1), but Bernard cites Ezr. 5.16, where the LXX has the
same word for the unfinished building of the second Temple. The
number in this case is then a reference to the presumed date, i.e.
A.D. 26. If Jesus was born in 4 B.C., this would make him thirty
years old (cf. Lk. 3.23, and the notes on Jn 8.57).

21. Jesus gives no answer. In fact, the narrative is at an end.
Looking back, we see now that the continuity from verse 16

onwards has been in the progress of exegesis, punctuated with the
questions of the Jews in verses 18 and 20. The present verse gives
the key to interpretation of the climactic verse 19. To use the idea
of a temple as a metaphor for the body is a commonplace of
religious writing (Philo, *de Op. Mundi*, 136f.; cf. 1 C. 3.16; 6.19.
Here, however, there is no generalized sense. The application is
restricted to **his body,** a word which John only uses elsewhere in
connection with the burial of Jesus. It is meant, then, quite
literally. The Jews want a Sign (verse 18), and the only Sign
which will really meet their need is the death and Resurrection.
The destruction of the Temple is not the Sign, even if Jesus
prophesied it, for John has provided the key to interpret the saying
—viz., for **temple** read **body;** there is no hint of further related
ideas. We might suppose that, because the cleansing of the Temple
is concerned with the holiness of the place, John is thinking of the
consecration of Jesus' body (cf. 17.19), and so of his death as the
new and sufficient sacrifice. Or we might suppose that, as the
Temple is a place where men gather for worship, his body is to
be taken in the larger metaphorical sense of the church, which it
has in Paul (e.g. 1 C. 12.12–27). If he had based a discourse on this
pericope, he might well have developed such ideas as these. But he
has not done so, and it is a false exegesis which would read into
the verse anything more than the sole idea that the sign which
Jesus gives is the *fact* of the Resurrection.

22. was raised: Gr. *ēgerthē*, the same verb as in 19. This
comment removes all doubt about the preceding verse. For the
significance of **remembered,** cf. verse 17. The fact that the life
and death of Jesus followed the course which he had himself foretold is an important facet of John's teaching. The precise agreement between (i) **the scripture,** i.e. Ps. 69.9 cited in 17, (ii)
the word of Jesus himself, i.e. his prophecy in 19, and (iii) the
actual event of the Resurrection, clinches the argument and compels belief. Many commentators think that **the scripture** means
prophecies of the Resurrection in general, though all recognize
that it properly refers to a specific passage. Barrett complains that
the quotation in verse 17 does not mean the death and Resurrection, but the point is that it is a fragment of a whole psalm which
is known to be a Passion proof text in the thought of the primitive
Church.

Jesus in Jerusalem **23-5**

These verses, which, as we have seen, should follow on verse 13, are a link between the Sign at Cana and the discourse with Nicodemus, and may be compared to the Synoptic summaries (e.g. Mt. 4.23-5).

23. at the Passover feast: (lit. 'at the Passover at the feast'.) The expression is stilted, and probably **at the Passover** has been inserted when verses 14-22 were introduced. *NEB* omits 'at the feast'.

signs: we have to assume that John means some healing miracles, which he does not trouble to describe. It certainly does not refer to verse 18.

24. trust himself: the same word as 'believed' in the preceding verse. This usage has no exact parallel in the NT, though it is found in other Greek works. Jesus' reserve, which on any showing is a wise discretion, prepares the reader for the inconclusive character of the conversation with Nicodemus.

25. bear witness of man: his capacity to size up a man (cf. 1.42, 47) was so infallible that he needed no confirmation of it from any other source. In this respect Jesus is like God himself, who 'knows the thoughts of men, that they are vain' (Ps. 94.11; the idea is frequently expressed in the Qumran literature, e.g. 1QH i.7, 23f.; vii.13; etc.). This is another facet of John's insistence that Jesus foreknew all things and was in complete command of the situation (cf. verse 22). No doubt this is an apologetic motif rather than a direct personal reminiscence, though not without some basis in fact (see the notes on 1.42). The divine knowledge becomes an attribute of Jesus by way of the Wisdom Christology based on Prov. 8.22ff. (for a parallel development in the case of the spirit Metatron, cf. 3 Enoch 11 (cited by Odeberg, p. 45)). It is unlikely that there is here, as Stauffer has suggested, an allusion to the Marcan 'messianic secret'.

DISCOURSE WITH NICODEMUS ON THE NEW LIFE OF THE SPIRIT **3.1-21**

The abrupt narrative opening (cf. 1.6) might lead us to suppose that another self-contained incident is to be described, but we very soon discover that we have moved into a quite different literary genre. Nicodemus provides the opening gambit (verse 2), and remains a while as a foil to the words of Jesus (verses 4 and 9). Then he quietly disappears, and the rest is monologue. This is the style of the Johannine discourse, in which the evangelist gives us the fruit of his own deep thinking on the meaning of Christ. It requires of the reader 'an energy of understanding' (to use Hoskyns' phrase), which will be rewarded by a grasp of the essential message of the Fourth Gospel.

The basic text is the statement that salvation is only possible for those who are born from above (verse 3; see the notes below). This is a birth 'of water and the Spirit', which makes God the controlling influence of a man's life (verses 5–8). It is implied that the desired salvation is wholly God's gift, because of the fundamental distinction between 'flesh' and 'Spirit' (verse 6). In the same way only God can reveal 'heavenly things'; and Jesus has the unique position of being one who has come from heaven, and so of being the revealer of them (verses 9–13). He does this not so much by teaching as by action, for the Cross is the supreme act of revelation which leads to belief and so secures salvation (14f.).

Such, in brief paraphrase, is the thread of the argument. It is followed by two supplementary paragraphs: '(a) Verses 16–21 take up the last point about the purpose of the revealing act of God in Christ. It is the act of salvation for those who believe, but those who refuse to believe are self-condemned. This takes the thought back to the distinction between the 'once-born' and the 'twice-born' with which the discourse started. (b) Verses 31–6, which now depend on the testimony of the Baptist in the intervening paragraph, obviously belong to the same range of material. This piece reverts to the theme of the unique function of Jesus as the revealer from heaven, explaining it in greater detail, and finishes with a solemn warning of the peril of disbelief.

The question obviously arises why verses 31–6 have been separated from the rest and attached to a paragraph set in a completely different time and place (cf. verse 22). This is so awkward that many commentators assume accidental transposition. The simplest and most natural solution is to place verses 22–30 after verse 36, bringing them into close relation with 4.1–3 (so Bernard). Other proposals have been mentioned in the Introduction (p. 40). But we must distinguish between John's sources and the use he makes of them. In this case his material on the testimony of the

Baptist has a clear connection with the theme of the unique function of Jesus. So he has held over this paragraph for use in conjunction with it. There is a similar procedure in chapter 10,
where some of the Shepherd material is held over for an entirely
separate occasion (10.22–30). We may also note in passing that
the two paragraphs, 16–21 and 30–6, are distinct and by no
means doublets, as Brown supposes. They are self-contained pieces,
developing two different points of the discourse. This, again, is
characteristic of John's way of composition.

Now another question arises. We have used the word 'source'
to explain the distinct character of the discourse. Was there, then,
a Discourse Source available to John? It has been argued in the
Introduction (pp. 46–54) that it is unlikely that there was a
Gnostic source, which the evangelist has adapted, such as Bultmann proposes. Rather John is himself the author of his source,
for he bases his writing on homilies which he has himself delivered.
His method is to take a narrative for the setting, so as to engage
his hearers' attention, then to pass by means of dialogue to the
point which he really wants to press home. In this case the narrative setting is minimal, merely someone coming to ask a question.
In view of the answer which he receives in verse 3, we may conjecture that the underlying tradition was something like the Rich
Young Ruler (Mk 10.17 paras.; only Luke tells us that he was a
ruler), though there is some affinity with the Question about the
Tribute Money (Mt. 22.16 paras.). The dialogue which follows is
then concerned with entry into the Kingdom of God. The two
supplementary paragraphs are addressed to the hearers for a
decision, though expressed in the third person.

Unfortunately the dialogue raises two further problems: (a) As
the subject is entry into the Kingdom, it is natural to look for
hints of the Christian sacrament of baptism. Much depends on
the interpretation of verse 5. The view taken here is that John is
writing with the sacrament in mind, not, however, to argue for
its efficacy as a divine act, but to pose the radical decision to the
conscience of men which it involves. This is supported by his
placing of this homily in close connection with the Baptist's testimony and with an unexpected reference to Jesus' own work of
baptizing (verse 22). (b) John expresses his teaching in terms
which have a decidedly Gnostic ring (cf. pp. 134f. above). It is this
passage more than any other which supports Bultmann's theory of

adaptation from a pre-Christian Gnostic source. It is, then, necessary to observe carefully what John is doing. We may assume that Gnostic language is likely to appeal to a Gentile audience rather than to Jews. But the piece, as it stands, is a dialogue with a Jew. Most of the words (water, Spirit, flesh, ascended, descended) are common to both Judaism and Gnosticism. The ideas of the Kingdom of God and of the Son of Man are already deeply embedded in the Synoptic tradition. Even rebirth has its Synoptic counterpart. The one point which appears to demand a Gnostic original is the assertion that Jesus comes from the heavenly realm, so that he does not truly belong to the world of men (verses 13 and 31). But John has provided his own explanation of this in the Prologue, where, as we have seen, he shows that he is thinking in terms of the Jewish Wisdom tradition. Although it has been argued above that the Prologue was composed subsequently for the second edition of the Gospel, it must none the less be accepted as the definitive exposition of John's intentions. But the most telling point is the climax, that the Revealer must die, and that his death is the high point of revelation. This fact is adduced with a striking OT allusion (verse 14). It seems, then, that Jewish categories are fundamental to the discourse. They can hardly be stripped off, leaving a Gnostic original. It is more reasonable to suppose that John presents what is basically Jewish and Christian teaching in words that may be expected to be meaningful to a Gentile audience, familiar with the ideas of Hellenistic religious aspirations.

One more point remains to be considered. The language of the discourse frequently shows points of contact with the Prologue, so that it could even be said that it is an explication of the Prologue's themes. But according to our analysis the Prologue was composed for the second edition of the work. It is in fact such a highly concentrated composition that it is at least as likely that it is dependent on chapter 3, rather than the other way round. John here adumbrates ideas which remained fundamental to his Christological thinking, and which he brought to the greatest refinement of expression in that masterly work.

The Discourse **3.1–15**

   1. a man: Gr. *anthrōpos*, instead of the indefinite *tis*, as in 1.6; but there may be an intentional allusion to the same word at the end of 2.25. He is **a ruler of the Jews,** like the rich young man in Lk. 18.18. At the time when John was writing, all the rulers were Pharisees. Like all John's characters, he has a symbolical function, whether he is an historical person or not. He represents official Judaism in a situation of openness before the claims of Christ. Although he seems not to accept them (verse 11), he appears in a good light in 7.50f., and in the end is counted among the disciples, 19.39. He thus may stand for the sort of response which was still possible in some Jewish circles when John wrote the first edition of his work.

Nicodemus: though it is a Greek name, it is known in the form Naqdimon as the name of Jews in this period. A wealthy man of this name is known to have been in Jerusalem at the time of the Jewish War (*B. Taanith*, 20a), whom some have identified with Nicodemus. But this is unlikely, if he was already a ruler forty years earlier. *B. Sanhedrin*, 43a, mentions five disciples of Jesus, one of whom is called Naqai, a name which Dalman (*Grammatik*, p. 179) asserts is an abbreviated form of Naqdimon. But we have no facts to go on, as we do not know whether John has chosen the name as a typical one for a Jewish ruler, or derives it from some reliable tradition otherwise unknown. In any case his identity is of no consequence for the story.

2. by night: presumably to avoid notice, but the detail seems unnecessary. But the darkness is often symbolical in John; cf. 9.4; 11.10; 13.30. In the Prologue it is the area in which the light shines, 1.5. The present discourse leads to the idea of coming to the light to be exposed, verse 21. Thus Nicodemus' nocturnal visit is a search for truth in which he himself will be exposed. It is a detail which only becomes meaningful when the whole piece has been read.

Rabbi, we know: Nicodemus begins politely by acknowledging Jesus' position as **a teacher come from God,** even though he does not hold an officially authorized position. It is a deduction from the evidence of the **signs** (cf. 2.23). This formal opening is very similar to that of the Pharisees before they ask the question about the tribute-money (Mt. 22.16 paras.), a version of which has actually been influenced by our present text in the fragments of an unknown gospel preserved in B.M. Pap. Egerton 2 ('Teacher Jesus, we know that you have come from God, for what you do bears witness more than all the prophets . . .'). It there prepares the way for a very awkward question, in which prejudices might be

deeply involved. Here it represents open-mindedness on the part
of an authority, who might be expected to resent the position
which Jesus is gaining for himself among the people. It also has
a deeper relation to the following dialogue, in that the argument
will turn on Jesus' unique function as the bringer of revelation
from God (11–13). Black (p. 160) claims that the form of the
sentence, consisting of two balanced clauses, is an example of
Semitic poetic parallelism, but this is hardly convincing.
God is with him: cf. Ac. 10.38.

3. After the introduction, we expect Nicodemus to ask a question, but it is anticipated by Jesus' reply. We can deduce that it
was something like that of the Rich Young Ruler, 'What must I
do to inherit eternal life?' (Mk 10.17). John perhaps intends us
to understand that Jesus knows the question before it is asked,
because of his special insight (cf. 2.25). The answer is a solemn
statement (for **Truly, truly,** cf. 1.51), and as such requires no
preliminaries. It is, then, the text on which the homily will be
preached, for which verses 1 and 2 have merely provided a suitable lead-in. The statement asserts the essential condition for
participation (for this sense of **see,** cf. 1 Pet. 3.10) in **the kingdom
of God.** The latter phrase is not characteristic of John, and indicates that he has taken this text for his sermon from the tradition
of words of Jesus. In fact an extremely close parallel is preserved in
Mt. 18.3: 'Truly, I say to you, unless you turn and become like
children, you will never enter the kingdom of heaven.' It is a
demand for a radical reorientation.

born anew: These words replace Matthew's 'turn and become
like children'. The word *anōthen* means (i) from above, of place;
(ii) from the beginning, of time. The latter meaning can be
weakened to anew, afresh, as here (cf. Gal. 4.9). As the Matthean
parallel shows, the underlying tradition probably meant anew,
so that the translation is formally correct. But, in view of the
following argument, it is virtually certain that John meant it
spatially, i.e. from above (cf. *RSV mg*). It is, then, equivalent to
'from heaven', which is certainly the meaning in verse 31 and also
in 19.11. (In 19.23, the only other place where John uses it, it
means 'from the top'.) It is customary to see here a play on two
meanings. In the present verse it is regarded as ambiguous. Then
Nicodemus, assuming the ideas of rebirth, misses the point of
Jesus' statement (verse 4). In the next verse Jesus corrects it,

showing that he really meant birth from heaven. Bultmann, however, (p. 135, n. 1) points out that John's device of a misunderstanding, which we have already encountered in 2.20, never
depends on a verbal ambiguity. He insists that the word must be
translated 'anew'. The misunderstanding is that Nicodemus supposes that this fresh birth is the same as physical birth. But
Schnackenburg points out that, as this is a matter of the *kind* of
birth, it does not depend on the meaning of *anōthen*; and as he is
impressed by the unquestionable usage in verse 31, he insists on
the translation 'from above'. The idea of a *fresh* birth is not
expressed until verse 4, where *deuteron* ('a second time') is used.
Of course the idea of rebirth is certainly present whichever way
we translate *anōthen*, because it is implied by the whole context.
It is not, then, surprising that it was translated **anew** by the Old
Syriac version and understood in this sense by Justin Martyr
(*I Ap.* lxi). But a closer look at the context clinches the argument
that John in fact intended 'from above'. In verse 2 Nicodemus has
referred to Jesus' credentials as a teacher by suggesting his origin—
i.e. 'from God'. Now, in reply to his unspoken question, Jesus
states that the kingdom of God is open only to those who have
the same origin. For to be born from heaven is equivalent to
being born from God (cf. 1.13; 1 Jn 2.29; 3.9; 4.7; 5.1, 4, 18).

4. Nicodemus' question is entirely taken up with the idea of
birth. Obviously Jesus' statement requires some form of rebirth,
for it is addressed to persons who are already in existence. In a
crudely literal way Nicodemus points out that to repeat the physical process is impossible. We notice that he says: **'How can a
man be born . . .?',** leaving out the crucial phrase 'from above'
(which is, however, supplied by some inferior MSS. and versions).
He presses home the point by suggesting that it would involve
the whole process **a second time** (*deuteron*). This word is not a
substitute for *anōthen*, as it qualifies **enter,** and has been omitted
from the first clause. Nicodemus concentrates on the idea of
birth to the exclusion of the question of origin. In fact his words
do contain a kind of substitute for *anōthen*, and that is **his
mother's womb;** the contrast is between physical and spiritual
birth. This is another verse in which Black sees poetic parallelism;
but the two clauses are not equivalent, for the second is explicative
of the first.

5. of water and the Spirit: Jesus repeats verse 3 with this explanation of the key word 'from above' (the other variation, **enter** for 'see', is merely stylistic). It must be remembered that this is an answer to the question: 'How?' It is not disputed that the birth is to be 'from above', though by pressing the metaphor to the limit Nicodemus has virtually denied it. To be **born of** (lit. from) **water and the Spirit** can only mean 'as a result of', as in 1.13. The spatial idea has fallen into the background. It refers to an act, and that act can only be water-baptism and the giving of the Spirit which that conveys. It is not absolutely necessary to assume that John is referring to the Christian sacrament of baptism when he uses this phrase. The symbolism of water in connection with the Spirit is frequent in the OT (e.g. Ezek. 36.25f.) and in the Qumran texts (e.g. 1QS iv.19–21) where the context requires spiritual cleansing and renewal, cf. also 7.37–9. But the impression that Christian baptism is meant is hard to resist. John is not concerned with the outward aspect of it, and so **water** plays no further part in the argument. It is only mentioned as an act which entails a radical break with the past and opens a new chapter of life under the control of **the Spirit** (for the *act* of baptism as a break so fundamental that it represents a new beginning *as if* one were to be born afresh from the womb, cf. Justin Martyr, *I Ap.* lxi, which includes quotation of verse 3). Modern commentators have attempted to evade the reference to the sacrament in two ways: (a) Wellhausen, followed by Bultmann, takes **water and** to be an ecclesiastical insertion. This has no MS. support, and is a purely arbitrary decision. (b) Odeberg adduces rabbinic evidence for water = semen, and so takes it to mean 'of both physical and spiritual generation'. But if John had meant this he would have said 'of blood' (*ex haimaton*), as in 1.13.

   6. flesh . . . spirit: the meaning of the spiritual birth is now explained by contrasting it with the physical. At first sight it seems so obvious that it is scarcely worth saying. But it is a necessary step in the argument. In verses 3 and 5 John has used the Greek 'from' both spatially ('from above') and causally ('as a result of water and the Spirit'); this must now be taken through to the end-product. The result of physical generation is **flesh,** i.e. something that belongs to the created order and has all the weakness which that implies (see the notes on 1.13). The result of spiritual generation, which, it must be remembered, is overlaid on the physical existence of man 'when he is old', is to transfer

him to the spiritual order with all the freedom and power which
that implies (cf. 1.33). It is tempting to see a radical dualism
here, as if man consists of two parts, flesh and spirit, and only his
spiritual part is of any true value. But the argument speaks of a
second *birth*, and the whole man is in mind both before and after
it. The **Spirit** is not a component part of man, but the influence
which directs the *whole* man once he has been reborn. This influence is analogous to the wind (verse 8). The man born from the
flesh is man as he is by nature, impelled by the forces of his own
natural endowment. The man born from the Spirit is man as he
is when open to the influence of God, with all his natural forces
brought under the control of the Spirit. This modified dualism is
closely parallel to (but not identical with) the doctrine of the
Two Spirits in the Dead Sea Scrolls (cf. Introduction, p. 38). In
these texts the contrast is not between flesh and spirit, but between
flesh under the control of the Spirit of Error and flesh under the
control of the Spirit of Truth. But it is still a matter of influence
over the whole man. So there is a striking parallel to the present
verse in 1QS iii.19: 'Those born of truth spring from a fountain of
light, but those born of falsehood spring from a source of darkness'
(Vermes' translation). The fundamental difference between the
Scrolls and the NT is that in the NT the Spirit of truth (light) is
always identified with the Holy Spirit, or Spirit of God, whereas
in the Scrolls it is equivalent to an angel, and sometimes referred to
as such. The teaching of Paul in Rom. 8.1–17 should be compared with John's exposition, with which it is in essential agreement.

7. you must: the pronoun is plural, and the change to second
person (instead of the impersonal 'one' of 3 and 5) conveys a
hint of personal challenge to the reader. In this verse **anew** must
certainly be corrected to 'from above', as in the margin.

8. At this point in the argument we expect Jesus to establish
his opening assertion that entry into the kingdom is impossible
unless one is born of the Spirit. So far we have only been told
what that form of birth is. Unfortunately this next step of the
exposition is obscure.

The point of the verse is that entry into the Kingdom requires
the spiritual birth on the principle that like answers to like. As
Paul says, 'flesh and blood cannot inherit the kingdom of God'
(1 C. 15.50). The spiritual man, however, is like the source of

spirit—i.e. God. So the verse draws a comparison between the Spirit and the spiritual man, and it does so by means of a parable. Spirit and **wind** are the same word in both Greek (*pneuma*) and Hebrew (*rûaḥ*), and we can only deduce that this is a parable from the fact that it **blows** and its **sound** can be heard. Bernard denies the translation **wind,** as he considers it to be an impossibly harsh change of nuance, and he points out that it was not recognized by the early Fathers in commenting on this verse; also the NT always uses a different word for wind elsewhere (e.g. *pnoē*, Ac. 2.2); but the verse was taken to be a parable by John Chrysostom. Modern scholars take it to be an authentic parable of Jesus, which John has incorporated (Hunter, p. 79). The point is that the origin and final direction of the wind cannot be observed, and this makes it analogous to God himself, who exists before the creation and on into eternity. The same is true of the man **who is born of the Spirit,** not because he belongs to a different order of being from other men, but because he is controlled by the Spirit, the effluence of the eternal God, without beginning or end (cf. Heb. 7.3). There is a rather similar idea in Ec. 11.5 referring to the unknowable source of the breath of life in the newborn child born from the flesh of his mother. Ignatius, *Philad.* vii.1, describes the activity of the Spirit in strikingly similar terms, perhaps alluding to the underlying parable, if not actually dependent on John.

9. This time Nicodemus' question is really an expression of incredulity, cf. verse 11. Though it obviously seems to mean: **How can this** [lit. these things] happen?', which is virtually the same as verse 4, it can be taken to mean: 'How can these things exist?'—i.e. how can they be accepted as true? This is required by the course of the argument, for the discourse now turns to the question of the source of Jesus' teaching, taking up the motif of his authority as a teacher from verse 2. It will be shown that the teaching has to be 'from above', just as much as the spiritual birth which has been the content of the teaching.

10. a teacher: lit. '*the* teacher', one who represents the official Jewish teaching authority. Jesus' question is ironical; as a well-instructed rabbi, Nicodemus should have been in possession of the facts to enable him to **understand** Jesus' teaching and to acknowledge its authenticity. The fact that he does not, or perhaps rather will not, believe illustrates the failure of the old Law.

11. Truly: the solemn formula marks a formal break, though the thought runs on. The verse puts in general terms the complaint that Jesus' teaching was not accepted, and this is specially applicable to official Judaism (cf. 1.11). But the sudden change to plural pronouns (**we . . . you**) indicates the transition from a private conversation to general teaching addressed to the readers. But after this verse the **we** is not maintained, though the **you** remains plural. Brown suggests that it is merely stylistic, a sort of parody of Nicodemus' own use of it in verse 2. But this does not explain why it is abandoned in verse 12. Schnackenburg is nearer the mark when he compares 9.4, which is the proverbial 'we'. By using the plural Jesus associates himself with all others who are similarly frustrated, cf. the proverb in Mt. 11.17. In fact the use of the **truly** formula is a sign that this is a verse which John has taken over almost verbatim from the tradition of words of Jesus, as in verse 3. It is the appeal to a special revelation, characteristic of prophets and religious pioneers, which always meets with some opposition; cf. Jer. 15.15–21. The vocabulary of the saying is Johannine, but the synonymous parallelism of the first two clauses suggests a Semitic original.

12. earthly things: this is always a puzzle to expositors. The verse is an *a fortiori* argument (a frequent rabbinic device), the question in the apodosis being equivalent to a second negative statement. It is implied that Jesus has so far taught only **earthly things,** and has not yet reached **heavenly things.** But how can the substance of verses 5–8 be regarded as anything less than **heavenly things**? There is, however, a sense in which it can be regarded as earthly wisdom, for it ought to be possible to understand the point at issue, that only one born of the Spirit may inherit the Kingdom, even by the exercise of human intelligence without the aid of a special revelation from above, difficult though this may be (cf. Wis. 9.16f.). This interpretation suits the rebuke implicit in verse 10, and has the same ironical effect. At the same time it prepares the reader for the statement in verse 13. Even before the incarnation it was possible for men to gain the wisdom that is from above, if only they would believe, cf. 1.12. But now, with the coming of Christ, a greater apprehension of the divine glory has become possible (1.14).

13. No one has ascended: the heavenly wisdom cannot be attained by Man himself, straining to reach heaven for it, but is

JOHN 3.14 156

the gift of God himself; and this gift has taken the form of the incarnation of the Word of God, so that what is hidden in heaven is accessible in human form on earth. The idea of the inscrutability of heaven is a commonplace of Jewish thought; cf. for example Prov. 30.4 and the elaborate use of the theme in 2 Esd. 4. The idea of straining to heaven for the divine knowledge appears in Dt. 30.12, only to be rejected because God has made himself known in the Law (Paul adapts this text to a Christian interpretation in Rom. 10.6–9). It is not a question of bringing knowledge *from* the heavenly world, but of gaining access *to* it, in order to discover the divine secrets. Odeberg suggests that there may be a polemic here against Jewish *merkaḅah* mysticism, the tradition of heavenly ascent based on the chariot-vision of the ascension of Elijah (2 Kg. 2.11f.). But John's intention is probably more inclusive than this, taking in all claims to access to heavenly knowledge. On the other hand his use of the word **ascended** must be taken seriously. Most readers, and many commentators, suppose that he must be referring by contrast to the ascension of Jesus, although this is an awkward anticipation of events from the point of view of the timing of the discourse, and puts the cart before the horse by making the ascent appear to precede the descent, which certainly means the Incarnation. But the combination of ascending and descending has been used already in a Son of Man saying in 1.51 to express the link between heaven and earth: Jesus' *future* glory is already made visible to the eye of faith in his Incarnation and Passion (see the notes *ad loc.*). It is not intended to imply that he ascended first before he descended, but that, whereas no one has ascended, *he* has come down bringing the knowledge of heavenly things. The addition of 'who is in heaven' in many MSS. (some have 'who is from heaven') is aimed at making this clear, and could be original, as Barrett thinks (though it is not in P[66] and P[75]). The *content* of the heavenly knowledge is only fully represented in the future glory of Jesus (this is the point of using the title **Son of man** here), but even this is accessible now to those who recognize in the incarnate Jesus the Son of man who is to be glorified.

14. As . . . so . . .: typical of John's style in the discourses, cf. 5.21. **Lifted up** is not a word-link with 'ascended' in the preceding verse. The relation of thought (broken by Schnackenburg's insertion of 31–6 at this point) is contained in the idea of **the Son**

of man. The essential point to remember in John's use of this title is that it refers to Jesus in his future glory, and that this is only visible in his incarnate life to the eye of faith. By a supreme paradox, faith sees his glory most fully in the darkness and humiliation of the Cross. So the title frequently takes the thought to the Passion, and this is what happens here. The paradox is expressed in the actual choice of verb, **lifted up,** which expresses both the exaltation of the Son of Man and the act of Crucifixion. John seems dazzled with this evocative phrase, and uses it several times; cf. 8.28; 12.32, 34. The Greek verb (*hupsōthēnai*) is appropriate to the exaltation, and occurs twice in this sense in Ac. 2.33; 5.31. It is far from being appropriate to the Crucifixion, and we only know that this sense is also in mind because of the comparison of **the serpent in the wilderness,** an allusion to Num. 21.9. To 'lift up' is not the same as to 'set on a pole' (Num. 21.9) or 'fix to a cross' (*stauroun*, usually translated 'crucify'). It simply means elevation upwards, whether literal or metaphorical. But here it becomes almost a technical term for crucifixion, while retaining the notion of exaltation.

How has this come about? There are two possible answers. (a) The great Passion prophecy of Isa. 53 begins with the announcement that 'my servant' shall be 'lifted up and glorified' (Isa. 52.13 (LXX); *RSV* has 'lifted up, and shall be very high'). This refers to the final estimate of the Servant after his death. But the juxtaposition of death and exaltation is ready made, and could have suggested the idea of taking **lifted up** in two ways i.e. both metaphorically of exaltation and literally of the rearing up of Jesus on the cross. (b) The Aramaic verb *zᵉqap* does have both meanings. It occurs within the Aramaic portions of the OT itself in Ezr. 6.11, where it is translated 'impaled', and in Syriac it is regularly used for 'crucify' in the NT. But it also can mean to be exalted, and occurs in this sense in the Targum to Job 13.11 found in Qumran Cave 11. If this is the right answer (though both may be right, for the idea may have been reached as a result of more than one factor), we shall have to assume that John is here dependent on previous work in Aramaic (as argued by Black in *ZNW* LX (1969), pp. 1–8). This is quite possible, because our present text is clearly the result of scholarly activity. It includes the interpretation of the Cross as having saving efficacy by adducing 'the serpent in the wilderness'. This is a legend in which Moses is directed to make a serpent of brass and set it on a pole when a plague of serpents is inflicting deadly wounds on the people: 'If a serpent bit any man, he would look at the bronze serpent and live.' The legend had already been treated symbolically in Jewish thought. In Wis. 16.6 any superstitious idea of magical effect is rejected by calling it 'a token of deliverance to remind them of thy law's command'. Such reinterpretations appear in various rabbinic texts. The application of the legend to the Crucifixion (which to John is the clue to the double meaning of **lifted up**) is taken up by many of the Church Fathers, e.g. Barnabas, xii.5–7.

15. At last we reach a statement of the *purpose* for which the heavenly knowledge has been made accessible to men through the incarnate and crucified Son of man. It is, of course, as was said in verse 3, that men may see the Kingdom of God. But a new set of terms is used to express this.

believes in him: this is the reading of ℵ and the great majority of mss, but, instead of the usual *eis auton*, A has *ep' auton*, P66 and L have *ep' autō*, and P75 B W and others have *en autō*. The last of these is so unusual in combination with **believes** that the other readings are best taken as attempts to improve it. But for the same reason it is probably the correct reading, and the difficulty is overcome if we take it, not with **believes,** but with **may have eternal life** (so *NEB* and most recent commentators). It is **life in him** that the believer receives, i.e. a share in his glory when he is exalted (the other sense of 'lifted up') as the Son of man.

eternal life: see the notes on 1.4. Here the fuller phrase is used for the first time (John has it 17 times). It is quite common in the NT, and in fact occurs in the question of the Rich Young Ruler (Mk 10.17). As the Kingdom (or reign) of God in Jewish thought belongs to the Coming Age, so eternal life, i.e. the Life of the Age, is another way of describing the same thing. On a strictly linear view it means the Coming Age *on earth*, which follows the end of the present world order. But it carries with it a sense of the timelessness of an abiding fellowship with God, and this is uppermost in John's thought. Hence his use of the phrase here is an interpretation of the words in verse 3.

The Challenge 16–21

16. We now come to the first of the two supplementary paragraphs. This one arises immediately from the last two verses,

and restates that great affirmation in terms which put the fundamental alternatives before the reader. John does this in a sentence
which is the most celebrated expression of the Gospel to run from
his pen. Here for the first time (if we may for the moment discount
the Prologue) he mentions God's personal initiative. Here for the
first time he uses the word **love** (*agapān*), which will recur frequently in the Supper discourses. This word had been chosen by
the LXX translators to represent the Hebrew *'āheḇ*, partly perhaps
for its similarity of sound. It is used of God's love for his people in
Dt. 7.8 and many similar passages. But here it has universal
application, and is not confined to the Chosen People (**world** is
morally neutral, as in 1.9f.).

gave his only Son: these words replace the descent of the Son
of man of verse 13, and convey the idea of both Incarnation and
Passion. Both **gave** and **only** contribute to the emotional force of
the statement, which has already been begun by the emotive
loved. It is possible that there is allusion here to the great OT
type of such a sacrifice in the story of Abraham and Isaac (Gen.
22.12). Paul has a very similar statement, expressed in equally
emotive words, in Rom. 8.32. This is the only time that **gave** is
used in such a context in John. Elsewhere he uses 'sent', as in the
next verse. This whole phrase is the basis of the use of 'only'
(*monogenēs*, as here) in 1.14, 18.

should not perish: The negative possibility is put first, thus
heightening the positive statement of salvation, which is repeated
from the preceding verse. Thus the two alternatives are set, and
consideration of them will occupy the rest of the paragraph. John
thinks in terms of absolute opposites (cf. Dt. 30.15–20), and admits
no middle position between them. But, as the next verse shows, he
holds that God's purpose is the salvation of all men.

17. sent: John's usual word, instead of 'gave'. It could suggest
the sending of the Revealer in the Gnostic redeemer-myths, but
it is used by Jesus of his mission in several Synoptic sayings, e.g.
Mt. 15.24; Mk 9.37; Lk. 4.43. Cf. the notes on 1.6.

the Son: The absolute use of **the Son** also occurs in Synoptic
sayings (Mk 13.32; Mt. 11.27 = Lk. 10.22). Schnackenburg
(p. 400) points out that it is always used with God or 'the Father'
used absolutely, and denotes their complete community of
thought and action.

condemn: properly 'judge' (so *NEB*), but often meaning con-

demnation or punishment. 'Condemn', with its correlative **saved,**
repeat the alternatives of the preceding verse, but with a new
slant. They turn attention to the criterion for deciding whether a
man is to perish or to have eternal life. The theme of judgment is
frequent in the apocalyptic literature of NT times, and many of
the parables introduce it (e.g. the Great Assize (Mt. 25.31–46)).
Much of the teaching of Jesus is concerned with the present judgment of the individual confronted by the arrival of God's Kingdom, whose status before God is determined by the moral decisions
of daily life.

saved: *sōzein* and its cognates are rare in John, perhaps out of a
conscious desire to avoid a word common in Hellenistic religion.
He generally prefers 'live', which is more biblical. In contexts
where personal salvation is virtually equivalent to having eternal
life, Hebrew would naturally use *ḥāyāh* = 'live'. The word
hōšīaʿ = 'save' generally refers to deliverance from some specific
trouble.

18. The criterion for John is belief in, i.e. response to, Jesus.
As this is an attitude of mind which is either adopted or refused
when a man is confronted by Jesus, the judgment does not have to
wait for a final day of reckoning (cf. Dodd, *Historical Tradition*,
pp. 357f., who compares Mk 16.16). This does not mean a universal process in the souls of men, but the transposition of eschatology into 'a radical understanding of the appearance of Jesus as
the eschatological event' (Bultmann, p. 155).

the name of the only Son of God: cf. 16, and (for **name**) 1.12.
What John says here about confrontation with Jesus is set in a
wider context in the Prologue. There it is response to the light
that was in man before the Incarnation; here it is response to the
light made manifest.

19. judgment: the cognate noun to 'condemn' in verses 17f.
Here too 'condemnation' would be a better rendering, but it carries with it also the idea of 'the decisive thing' (Bultmann, Blank).
the light has come: yet another expression for the Incarnation,
this time identifying Jesus with the principle of moral goodness
which is implicit in the Creation from the beginning, and is represented by light as opposed to darkness. Before the Incarnation,
this was an internal light from the strictly moral point of view.
To use Qumran terminology, men of moral goodness are under
the sway of the Angel of Light, whereas evil men are under the

Angel of Darkness. The Incarnation can be thought of as a sudden flood of light, in which the hidden, inner, realities of man's moral state are exposed. The thought and vocabulary are closely related to 1.5–9.

loved . . . rather than: the verb does not have the emotional content which it had in verse 16, but has a weakened sense, so that the whole phrase simply means 'preferred . . . to' (as *NEB*); cf. 12.43.

deeds were evil: being under the domination of darkness, they followed an evil course of action, which made them incapable of the desired response to Jesus when he confronted them. John appears not to leave open the possibility of a change of heart. But of course no man is wholly under the sway of darkness; the two principles of light and darkness struggle for mastery over him. It is always possible that a man may eventually respond to the light. Although John sets the contrast with the utmost rigour, there would be no point in writing at all if he did not believe in the more generous statement of verse 17. In fact the whole Gospel is directed to evoking the response of faith.

20. exposed: the Greek word (*elenchein*) can have a neutral sense, but frequently passes over into ideas of convicting, reproving or punishing. Here it is strictly parallel to 'be clearly seen' (*phanerousthai*) = 'be brought to light' in the next verse (against Büchsel (*TDNT* II, pp. 473–5); cf. Schnackenburg, p. 406, n. 160). John is referring to a familiar fact of psychology, which accounts for the difficulty of bringing one who is under the sway of darkness to the point of accepting the truth.

21. does what is true: the correlative to 'does evil' in the series of antitheses. The choice of phrase (instead of the more obvious 'does good') is again reminiscent of the Dead Sea Scrolls. The actual phrase 'to do truth' (*ʿāsāh ʾemet*) occurs in 1QS i.5; v.3; viii.2. The decision of faith when a man is confronted by Jesus 'brings to light' (cf. the last note) what a man really is, and so fulfils the potentialities of his nature.

wrought in God: i.e. done in fellowship with God; cf. the force of 'in him' in verse 15. Belief in Jesus, and all that that entails for eternal life, is the natural outcome of the relationship with God which such men have always had. The Incarnation of Jesus, with the response to him of belief or unbelief, is thus the focal point of the cosmic struggle between light and darkness, truth and evil. Such are the wider implications of the decisive act of Christian baptism, for which the confession of faith is in John's eyes the central issue.

TESTIMONY OF THE BAPTIST: THE NEW ORDER 3.22–36

Before going on to the second of the supplementary paragraphs to the discourse with Nicodemus, John inserts a quite different range of material about the Baptist. The insertion is appropriate, because the preceding discourse has been based on a baptismal theme. It has followed the beginning of the Gospel, which was concerned with the baptism of John, and it has presupposed the subsequent practice of baptism in the Church. The Church's activity is rooted in the teaching of Jesus, though it is also a continuation of the practice of the Baptist. If Jesus posed his challenge to faith in terms which reflect the practice of both the Baptist and the Church, it is only reasonable to suppose that he himself also administered baptism, either personally or through his disciples. In fact one would imagine that John's baptism would be at an end, having attained its object (cf. 1.31), and that Jesus would have taken it over completely, adding in the new element of the gift of the Spirit (1.33). There must have been some kind of continuity between John's baptism and the Church's. But the extraordinary thing is that the Synoptic record gives no hint of any baptizing either by Jesus or his disciples. On the other hand, it complicates the whole issue by implying that the Baptist's disciples continued to be active at the same time as Jesus (Mk 2.18; Mt. 11.2f.).

It is, then, at least clear enough that some kind of clarification is needed, both of the relation of John's baptism to the Christian sacrament of baptism and of the relation of the Baptist himself to Jesus. John tackles this problem by using some traditional material left over from the sources of 1.19–2.12. He says that Jesus practised baptism in much the same way as John did, so that the two movements were parallel for a time; but the Baptist soon began to lose ground, and acknowledged that this should be regarded as cause for joy rather than for envy. Thus, as John sees it, the Baptist's ministry is still a work of preparation for Jesus, making men ready to receive him, even though it continues after his arrival. The final verses from the discourse (31–6) suitably follow on from this, as they are concerned with acceptance of the one 'who comes from above'.

How far is all this historically true? Many scholars today hold that the information in verses 22–4 is derived from authentic tradition. After his own baptism, Jesus may well have spent some time in the area of the Jordan baptizing, before he began his preaching ministry in Galilee. We know so little about the *real* relation between him and the Baptist that we can only guess whether they began in co-operation and gradually drifted apart, possibly because of a deep disagreement on the content of the eschatological message. Jesus preaches that the Kingdom is already present, whereas John the Baptist is warning men of a coming cataclysm for which they must ensure their safety by declaring themselves to be on the right side (rather like the men of Qumran). At any rate, quite early on the imprisonment of the Baptist (verse 24) radically altered the situation: from then onwards Jesus had the advantage of being in a position of active leadership, while the other's hands were tied.

One of the ways in which the difference between them came to the surface was the attitude to the ever-increasing strictness of some religious teachers (i.e. the Pharisees) on fasting (Mk 2.18) and ritual purification (verse 25). Jesus takes what appears to be a lenient view, but he bases it on theological considerations (Mk 2.19–22). We have already seen that John is dependent on tradition closely parallel to this little Marcan paragraph in the story of the marriage at Cana. Now he uses further material from it for his version of the relation between the Baptist and Jesus (verses 29f.). If so, we must take the Baptist's words, not as actually spoken by him, but as a variant of genuine teaching of Jesus which has been adapted to fit him as the speaker.

Consequently, the view taken here is that verses 22–30 are based on two items of tradition, the first being a note on Jesus' baptizing ministry, the second being teaching of Jesus justifying his lack of strictness with regard to fasting and purification. But it is not necessary to suppose that John wrote them up originally for a different place in the Gospel (e.g. to follow after 2.12), which solves some problems only to create new ones. Nor is it likely that Boismard is justified in seeing here an *alternative* to 1.19–28 or 29–34.

It must finally be asked whether this material reflects rivalry between Christian and Baptist groups in the post-Resurrection period. The discourse with Nicodemus certainly shows signs of theological discussion between Christian and Jew at a later time. But it is not at all the same with the present short section. It is true that it reflects the Church's embarrassment about the relation between Jesus and the Baptist; but, as has been pointed out in the Introduction (pp. 59ff.), this issue is more likely to have been yet another subject of discussion between Christian and Jew than a reflection of existing rival groups.

Baptizing by Jesus and by John **22–4**

These verses, very likely embodying reliable tradition, are put in simply to prepare for verses 25–30. It is necessary to change the scene from private discussion in Jerusalem, and to show Jesus actively engaged in the baptismal activity which has been its theme.

22. into the land of Judea: as it stands, this presumably means a move from the city to the Jordan valley. But if it is taken with the source material of chapter 1, in which the call of the disciples originally had a Galilean setting, it could have meant a journey from Galilee in the first place. It appears that it was quite a long stay. This is the implication of **remained** (*dietriben*), a word which occurs only here and as a variant at 11.54 in John, though it is fairly common in Acts. We have no information at all about this period of Jesus' life, which is completely unknown to the Synoptic writers.

23. Aenon near Salim: if Jesus is active in the Baptist's old haunts, the latter has apparently moved to a fresh field. This indicates the break between them; but not too much should be made of this, as the idea of separate, but parallel, activity is necessary background for the following verses. Neither place has been identified with certainty. The sixth-century Madeba map marks two different places as Aenon, presumably because both claimed to be the site and were attracting pilgrims. One is very close to Bethabara (cf. 1.28 notes), which is hardly likely; the other is much further north near Beth-shan (Scythopolis), on the basis of identification of Salim with a village there called Salumias; but neither proposal is convincing. Aenon is obviously connected with the Hebrew ʿ*ain*, which occurs in numerous place names to denote a spring or well. But both the above identifications are much too near the Jordan for the Baptist to choose either of them on the grounds that **there was much water there.** A third possibility has been put forward by Albright. He has pointed out that there is a Salim only a few miles from Shechem and a village, now called Ainun, close by. There are many springs in this area, for it is the point where the Wadi Farah rises. The only difficulty about this proposal, which from all other points of view is absolutely convincing, is that it is in the heart of the Samaritan territory. But as there is some evidence for the Baptist's influence in Samaria (cf. Introduction, p. 60), this is not insuperable. It is possible, of course, that the place was really associated with the activity of *later* Baptist groups, and has been retrojected to the life of John himself.

24. A parenthetical explanation, perhaps an editorial note, to account for the discrepancy with the Synoptic record. The Baptist's imprisonment is not referred to elsewhere by John. Besides the well-known story in Mk 6.17–29 para., there is a different version of the legend in Josephus, *Ant.* xviii.116f.

The Baptist's Testimony 25–30

That the piece is composite is suggested by the discrepancy between the question on purification (verse 25) and the complaint of Jesus' success (26). It consists of traditional material, which has left traces only in 25 and 29 (not even 27, *pace* Bultmann). The rest is John's free composition, largely based on what he has himself already written in chapter 1.

25. At first sight it seems that the situation has nothing whatever to do with Jesus. It is simply a matter of a discussion **between John's disciples and a Jew** (perhaps a Temple authority, cf. 1.19). **purifying** is the same word as was used in 2.6; some editors think it is an exceptional variation for 'baptism'. It could, indeed, *include* baptism, and was presumably intended by John to do so. But this does not solve the real difficulty, that verse 26 is concerned with Jesus' success, not with the meaning of baptism. We can gain a slight improvement of connection if we accept the conjecture that **with a Jew** (*meta Ioudaiou*, which is impossible Greek) is a corruption of 'with Jesus' or better 'with the [disciples] of Jesus'. Though this has no ms. support, something like it must be right. The mistake may be due to early influence from 2.6. But even this conjecture still fails to produce a satisfactory connection with verse 26.

There is, however, quite good MS. support (P⁶⁶ ℵ* G Θ, the Lake and Ferrar groups, Curetonian Syriac and some Old Latin texts) for the reading 'Jews' (so *NEB*), but this does not help the difficulty. The solution is not to be sought only by textual emendation, but lies in the pre-history of the tradition. We may assume that this was comparable to Mk 2.18. Here the Baptist's disciples are mentioned along with the Pharisees in connection with fasting, and the question is put to Jesus why he does not follow the same practice (his answer includes bridal imagery, as in verse 29). If we turn to the parallel in Mt. 9.14, we find that Matthew has simplified the text, so that the disciples of the Baptist themselves come to Jesus and ask the question. Our verse here looks very like the situation in Mark, in that the disciples of the Baptist and the Jew (or the disciples of Jesus) are bracketed together in order to introduce the subject (purification); but like Matthew, in that the disciples of the Baptist then come and ask the question (hence verse 26 replaces a continuation such as 'and they came to *Jesus* and said . . .').

The point at issue is that the Baptist sides with other Jews (the Pharisees?) in requiring strict adherence to the purificatory laws, whereas Jesus is notoriously lax (cf. Mk 7.1–23; Jesus' *reason* is given in Mk 2.15–17). We have other evidence of a deep disagreement between the Baptist and Jesus on this kind of issue in the attractive parable of the Children in the Market Place (Mt. 11.16–19 = Lk. 7.31–5).

26. Rabbi: the title is 'not very appropriate' (Barrett) in an address to the Baptist. It is possible that it is a relic of the address to Jesus which originally followed verse 25 (cf. the last note).
who was with you . . . bore witness: the whole description is derived from 1.28, 34. It is quite clear from these words that John does not think of the Baptist as being in Transjordan, and this supports Albright's identification of Aenon in verse 23.
baptizing: derived from verse 22.
going to him: the same words as 'coming toward him' in 1.29.
27. John answered: but no question has been asked, merely a statement which implies a question. This feature of Johannine style occurred in 3.2f. and the answer itself reflects the discourse with Nicodemus; it might almost be a fragment from it. It is a universal statement (**one** = *anthrōpos* for *tis*), not really answering a question, but providing the basis for the particular application which is to follow. If we follow the *RSV* translation it seems to mean that one has to be content with what God gives, and the application

to the Baptist himself is clear enough. But this is not what the Greek means: we must at least translate it **No one can receive anything** *unless it be* **given him from heaven** (we note in passing that **from heaven** is simply a variation of 'from above'; cf. verse 31). But even this leaves the reference of *it* undecided. Does it mean **anything,** or does it mean the *capacity* to **receive anything**? The present text is ambiguous, but there is a remarkable parallel to this sentence in 19.11: 'You would have no power over me unless it had been given you from above.' Here the disagreement between 'power' (*exousia*, fem.) and 'it be given' (*dedomenon*, neut.) shows that 'it' means the whole verbal idea, to have power. So here it is the capacity to receive which is God-given. The sentence summarizes one aspect of verses 11–13, that of the capacity to receive Jesus' testimony; applied to the situation of the Baptist, this means that not only the degree of success in his work, but the whole meaning of his baptizing ministry, is limited by the fact that he is not the Christ, not the heavenly Revealer, not one who has ascended to the place of heavenly things, not the one to whom response of faith gains entry to eternal life.

28. The application to the Baptist can, then, be briefly stated in the words **I am not the Christ,** quoting 1.20. His own position is that of the forerunner, one **sent before him,** an allusion to 1.30, but this time unmistakably recalling the classic proof text for the Baptist, Mal. 3.1 (cf. Mt. 11.10 = Lk. 7.27; also Mk 1.2): 'Behold, I *send* my messenger before thy face, who shall prepare the way *before thee*.' It should be noted that the text (quoted here from Matthew) has been correlated with Ex. 23.20, an indication of exegetical work in the Church.

29. The same point is now put in the form of a parable, extending as far as **voice.** As it stands it is an allegory, in which Jesus is the bridegroom and the Baptist is the best man (it would be a mistake to go further and identify the bride with the Church, as happens for instance in Eph. 5.25). Unlike the Galilean customs presupposed in the Cana story, a Judean wedding was arranged and presided over by the *Shōshbīn*, roughly corresponding with our best man.

But what would it mean if it were originally not, as it is presented here, the testimony of the Baptist to a relationship with Jesus which history does not justify in view of the disagreement between them, but the answer of *Jesus himself* to the question about

purification in verse 25? When the Baptist's disciples asked him
about his lax practice, what did he say? In Mk 2.19 Jesus used
the imagery of a wedding to represent the new conditions of the
kingdom of God, and this justified his practice of refusing to fast,
because it is obviously a time of feasting. Here the application is
not quite so simple. First we must take seriously the fact, which is
of no consequence in its present application, that **he who has
the bride is the bridegroom.** Jesus' lack of strictness over purification was part of his set policy to make himself accessible to
'tax-collectors and sinners' (Mk 2.16). If he has gained them for
the joy of the kingdom, from which they are usually held to be
excluded, it is as if God has gained his bride. It then ill becomes
the best man to raise objections. Rather he should have the
generosity to join in the gaiety. Who then is the best man? Surely
precisely those whose strict application of the Law is aimed at
fulfilling God's purpose, but in fact fails to do so because of
its exclusiveness. The parable is, then, an appeal to those who
insist on strict laws of purification to abandon their exclusiveness
and rejoice in what Jesus is doing, instead of being critical of it.
If it is right to see here a parable of *Jesus*, in spite of the fact that
we have to postulate the phenomenon of the transference of a
dominical saying to a different speaker (cf. the notes on 1.34; 7.4),
a further interesting point emerges. Jesus uses the parable, not only
to explain his own actual contact with the outcasts, but also to
suggest the theological basis of his behaviour. Very delicately he
implies that there is a direct relation between his own activity
and the care of God himself for the outcast. On this point see
further the notes on 11.9f.

The final words, **therefore this joy of mine is now full,**
employ typical Johannine vocabulary (cf. 15.11; 16.24), and
represent John's application of the parable to the situation of the
Baptist. Finally, in verse 30, the point is repeated with epigrammatic conciseness.

It should be mentioned that Black (pp. 147, 173) found Semitic
parallelism in this parable, and by taking it through to verse 30
proposed an intriguing paronomasia (bride, *kall⁽ᵉ⁾ta*' voice, *qālā*';
fullfilled *k⁽ᵉ⁾lal;* decrease, *q⁽ᵉ⁾lal*). He also transposed the final words of
verse 29 to follow 30, to get a better strophic arrangement.
Obviously the parable has a Semitic basis, but I feel that the language of 29b, 30 is too dissimilar from it and too close to John's

own diction to be regarded as an original part of it. The fact that retranslation into Aramaic can produce puns is no proof that an Aramaic original actually existed.

Jesus the Heavenly Revealer 31–6

We now return to the theme of the discourse with Nicodemus for the second supplementary paragraph. Verses 27 and 28 have confirmed the point that no one, not even the Baptist, can lay claim to the unique position of Jesus described in verse 13. The consequences of this are now worked out in more detail.

31. He who comes: for this quasi-messianic title, cf. 1.27.
from above takes us back to verses 3 and 7 (cf. *RSV mg*), and is synonymous with **from heaven** at the end of the verse (cf. verse 27). Both really mean 'from God'.
above all: properly spatial, but here perhaps there is a double meaning, as the phrase can be used of authority over people, cf. Lk. 19.17. Because Jesus is in a class by himself, he is superior to all others from the point of view of conveying God's gift of eternal life.
of the earth: all others, then, are inferior, and can convey only such truth as belongs to 'earthly things' (verse 12). For the deliberate tautology of this sentence, cf. verse 6. Black (p. 148) suggests that the tautology is due to mistranslation of an Aramaic original, which meant 'he who is of the earth is inferior to him', but in order to obtain this it is necessary to suppose confusion of the Aramaic consonants rather than straight mistranslation, and so it fails to convince. Although the words are meant in a most general sense, it is obvious, in view of the insertion of the Baptist's testimony, that they apply particularly to him too. For the 'earthiness' of humanity, cf. Gen. 2.7; 1 C. 15.47.
is above all: this phrase at the end of the verse (omitted by *NEB*) is missing from P75 ℵ* D, the Lake group, Old Latin and Curetonian Syriac. But this may be accidental, for John has a liking for repetition. If, however, the omission is correct, it means that **he who comes from heaven** is the subject of the next verse, and this certainly improves the flow of the argument. But accidental omission is more likely than needless insertion (so Barrett, Schnackenburg).
32. seen and heard: it does not seem possible to distinguish between the tenses in these words (perfect and aorist respectively),

though attempts have been made to do so (cf. *BDF* § 342.2). The
verse repeats the teaching of verse 11.

no one is really too strong, but is modified by the next verse, in
exactly the same way as in the Prologue (cf. 1.11f.).

33. sets his seal: like certifying a document; cf. Est. 8.8. The
word is used metaphorically for 'confirm' or 'guarantee'; in 6.27
Jesus gives *God's* bread as God's accredited agent ('for on him has
God the Father set his seal'); in Rom. 15.28 Paul looks forward
to completing the collection from the Gentile Churches for the
Church in Jerusalem, for by means of it he will have 'sealed to
them (the Christians of Jerusalem) this fruit', i.e. the spiritual
fecundity of the Gentile churches, which the collection of money
for material needs attests (Rom. 15.28, *RSV mg*; the text gives a
false interpretation). So here, **he who receives his testimony,**
i.e. believes that the teaching of *Jesus* is true, certifies not only
that Jesus is true, but that **God** himself **is true.** This is because
Jesus is not only the unique Revealer of God, but what he reveals
is the *whole* truth of God. There can be no fear that further aspects
of divine truth are kept hidden, which might jeopardize the
promise of eternal life. This is explained in the next verse.

34. sent: cf. verse 17. Here it has the full value, which belongs
properly to the cognate 'apostle', of denoting an accredited agent.
In this capacity Jesus reveals the heavenly things of verse 12, for
he **utters the words of God.**

he gives the Spirit: Who is **he**? The progress of the argument
suggests that Jesus' capacity to speak divine truth is derived from
the unstinting (**not by measure**) endowment of God, and this
suggests that God is the subject of the verb. But it is also true to
say that, having this endowment, Jesus himself gives unstintingly
in passing it on to those who will receive his message; this makes
Jesus the subject. If the object (**the Spirit**) were not expressed,
we should naturally suppose that God was the subject, and the
sentence would mean 'for God gives [his words] to him unstintingly'. This may well be the true text, as Sanders holds. Many of
the later MSS. actually insert 'God' in order to make this clear.
There is also slight MS. warrant for the omission of **Spirit** (it is not
in B* or the Sinaitic Syriac). In fact the Old Syriac illustrates the
difficulty which was felt about this verse from early times. The
Curetonian, much damaged at this point, reads 'not by measure
the Father [gives] to the Son [the Spirit]'. The Sinaitic, also very

difficult to decipher, has apparently 'not by measure gives God
the Father to the Son'; but 'God' may in fact be a misreading for
'Spirit', which is attested in the quotation of Aphraates (details in
F. C. Burkitt, *Euangelion da-Mepharreshê* (1904) I, *ad loc.* and
Appendix I). On balance, the evidence for the omission of **Spirit**
is too slight, and it is better to accept it as an allusion to verses
6–8. Hoskyns and Schnackenburg are prepared to see a double
meaning in the sentence: Jesus receives and passes on the Spirit
unstintingly (cf. 7.38f.). But the argument really requires God as
subject: he gives his **words,** and in so doing gives **the Spirit** (a
more comprehensive notion), and so Jesus has 'all things' (the
most complete endowment) as his own to give, as the next verse
states.

35. loves the Son: John repeats the point just made (the full
measure of the divine gift) by expressing the relationship which
this implies with the aid of the emotive word **loves,** which he has
already used so effectively in verse 16.

all things: the limitless endowment, not to be taken as omni-
science and omnipotence in a speculative sense. It refers to the
capacity to give eternal life, as the next verse shows.

into his hands: The preposition is exceptional (*en* for *eis*), and
Sanders translates the phrase, on the basis of Gal. 3.19: 'by his
means'. If this is right, it means that the Father gives **all things**
(eternal life) *to men* through his Son.

36. The discourse ends with an epigram, which condenses the
contrast set out in verses 17–21 into a single sentence.

does not obey: The Greek verb *apeithein* (only here in John)
properly means 'disobey', but occasionally is used for 'disbelieve'
(e.g. Ac. 14.2; Rom. 15.31). But it retains its moral emphasis,
and so denotes a wilful refusal to believe. So here it combines the
implications of 'he who does not believe' (verse 18) and 'every
one who does evil' (20), whose condition blinds him to the truth
of the Gospel. Hence he **shall not see life,** i.e. participate in
God's kingdom; cf. verse 3.

the wrath of God rests upon him: The exact opposite of what
the Baptist saw in the case of Jesus himself (1.32f.). The words are
similar, and indeed typical of John's diction, but there is not
necessarily an intentional allusion. The one exception is **wrath**
(*orgē*), which occurs only here in John. This is a concept much
used in eschatological, especially apocalyptic, contexts, in which

great natural disasters are attributed to the effect on God of men's resistance to his will (cf. Rom. 1.18–32). His power is bound to take a destructive form. But the remarkable thing about the NT is that the idea of God's wrath is never conceived in a highly emotional or vindictive or capricious way, but much more in terms of cause and effect. Here the idea is so stereotyped that it means little more than saying that wilful unbelief reaps its own inevitable unpleasant reward. Even the idea of permanence implied in **rests** (or remains, Gr. *menei*) is only valid in so far as the refusal of belief is maintained. It would be a gross distortion of John's meaning to suggest that a person who is an 'honest disbeliever' on the grounds of intellectual difficulties is in this position. But the threat is put here at the end of the discourse to induce the reader to take the whole argument with the utmost seriousness. (On the wrath of God in the NT, cf. *TDNT* v, pp. 422–47.)

NEW LIFE MADE AVAILABLE BY THE COMING OF JESUS 4.1–54

In the last chapter John showed how membership in God's Kingdom, both here and hereafter, requires two things: first rebirth from above, giving control to the Spirit of God; and secondly acknowledgment that Jesus is the Revealer from above, so that response of faith to him is the means by which the new birth is effected. Having made these two points, John proceeded to underline the crucial importance of the decision of faith.

It is now necessary to give a fuller idea of the content of what is gained by this new birth, of what is meant when the expressions 'Kingdom of God' or, more usually, 'life' or 'eternal life' are used. This is the subject of chapter 4. The discourse with a Samaritan Woman (verses 1–26) uses the symbolism of a gushing spring of water to express the richness of this new life. The metaphor is apt in itself, and there are parallels to it in numerous religious writings, both in the Bible and in other works. There is probably, too, an intentional link with the baptismal theme of chapter 3, where water has been barely mentioned (3.5, 23) but the idea has been present. The cleansing aspect of baptismal water was indicated in 1.25–33. The link with the Spirit in 3.5 has now prepared the way for consideration of its life-giving property.

One of the biblical parallels to John's use of the water-symbolism makes it a metaphor for the Jewish Law as the fountain of wisdom. Chapter 4 has a background of Jewish religious issues, and so this parallel is likely to be near the surface. It helps us to understand the transition in the middle of the discourse to a different theme, the identity of Jesus himself. It transpires that he replaces the Law, because, as messiah conceived in Samaritan terms, he is the true teacher, himself a fountain of knowledge (verse 25). Thus the discourse really follows the same pattern as 3.1–15.

The discourse is set in the framework of a narrative about a Samaritan woman, who meets Jesus at a well. This narrative continues in verses 27–42, which describe the effect of their conversation on the villagers. It is a little model of the future missionary work of the Church, and so some reflections on this work, put in the form of the imagery of sowing and reaping, are inserted into the narrative. If Nicodemus was a typical Jew, and so represented the mission to the Jewish people, that was only a very muted theme in chapter 3. But in this chapter the idea of mission is brought to the surface. It is part of the fecundity of the new life that springs from Jesus.

The section ends with the brief narrative of Jesus' second Sign, the healing of an official's son (verses 43–54). If the official was a Gentile, as is possible, it might carry the missionary theme further. But we cannot be sure about this, because John does not say that he was a Gentile, although the language of Christian mission is not altogether absent (cf. verse 53). But the main purpose of recording the Sign at this point is that it very suitably rounds off the teaching of chapters 3 and 4. For it hinges on two principal ideas, the response of faith and the new life demonstrated in the healing. Thus the teaching of the two discourses is put into action. So, just like the wedding at Cana, with which it has a certain literary connection, it points backwards rather than forwards, and there is no fresh discourse built on the foundation of it; on the other hand, it has enough links with chapter 5 to act as a bridge to the next section, and some commentators prefer to take it closely with that chapter. (On this view the discourse of chapter 5 is based on *two* miracles. Chapter 6 is adduced as another case where John does this. But that is not at all the same, because the two miracles of 6.1–21 belong together in the underlying tradition, and the discourse is exclusively based on the *first* of them.)

In this section we are free from the acute problems which we had to face in the last one. Verses 1–42 have evidently been composed as a whole. In so far as it is based on a source, the composition has only one item of tradition behind it, apart from verses 31–8, which John has taken from his stock of sayings of Jesus, and adapted for his purpose. The Sign of verses 43–54 also comes from a stock of tradition parallel to, but independent of, the Synoptic Gospels, and probably belongs to the same source as the wedding at Cana.

DISCOURSE WITH A SAMARITAN WOMAN ON THE WATER OF LIFE 4.1–26

A simple reading of these verses at once shows a considerable difference from chapter 3, the only other specimen of the Johannine discourse which we have so far encountered. Unlike Nicodemus, the woman is well characterized, more background information is given, and the dialogue is kept up to the end. There is no drifting away into a monologue, as in chapter 3 and as we shall find again in chapter 5; it is far more like chapter 11, where discourse and action are completely welded together. On the other hand, all John's favourite literary devices come into play. The argument moves by means of misunderstandings. These often bring in a subtle irony, as the woman speaks more truly than she realizes. Some of the circumstantial detail seems exaggerated (verse 8: *all* the disciples go for food, leaving Jesus alone; verse 18: it appears that the woman has been married six times). Characteristic Johannine language is used at the points of climax (10, 14, 23f., 26). The whole is contrived to lead up to a self-revelation of Jesus. It seems, then, that story and discourse are interwoven.

Moreover, the discourse is not simply developed out of a story, which merely provided the basic motif for the argument. In this case the background to the story, the setting in the province of Samaria, is closely related to the background to the thought of the discourse, which is fully aware of the issues dividing the Samaritans from the Jews. The story necessitates mention of the Jewish refusal to use a vessel handled by a Samaritan woman, which Jesus seems ready to waive (verse 9). It is less likely that the exact topographical knowledge (5), including the history of the well (12), derives merely from story details. Nor can they account for knowledge of the rivalry between the Jews and the Samaritans

concerning the site of the Temple (20) and the true source of
salvation (22), or of the specifically Samaritan form of messianic
expectation (25).

What then of the original story? We cannot say that the whole
piece is almost a verbatim report (told either by Jesus or by the
woman, as there were no witnesses), for it is patently a Johannine
construction, and this time we have no Synoptic parallels to help
us. Bultmann suggests that the story might have begun with
verses 7–9; at verse 10 John takes over and begins his discourse
material, so that the original reply of Jesus is lost. However, a
remarkable Indian (Buddhist) parallel suggests what it might have
been. Ananda, a disciple of Buddha, asks a low-caste maiden for
water. When she explains her position, he replies: 'My sister, I do
not ask about your caste or your family; I only ask for water, if
you can give it me' (refs. in Bultmann, p. 179). If Jesus said something like this, it ought to be the end of the story. But Bultmann
thinks verses 16–19 are also part of it, leading into a statement
similar to 25, and then concluding with 28–30, 40. But this will
hardly do, for these verses have the very Johannine theme of the
special insight of Jesus; cf. 1.47. The most that can be said is that
the Indian parallel provides a clue about the kind of incident
that the story seems to presuppose, and accounts for the setting
as far as verse 9. All the rest of the story grows out of the argument
of the discourse. The factor which binds together both story and
discourse is the detailed knowledge of the Samaritan position.
John's sustained imaginative power to keep up the narrative interest to the end is to be traced to this factor.

This means that the key to the whole piece is the evangelist's
unexpected familiarity with the Samaritans. Either by personal
experience from his travels or by having access to excellent sources
of information, he knows both topography and customs and beliefs.
The one thing which strains credulity is the suggestion of a mission
to the Samaritans, or at least the conversion of a whole village, in
the course of the public ministry of Jesus. The Samaritans are
expressly excluded from his mission charge (Mt. 10.5f., reinforced
by Mt. 15.24). Luke records a rather hostile encounter on the
journey to Jerusalem (Lk. 9.51–6). It is true that Luke shows
Samaritans in a favourable light (Lk. 10. 33; 17.16), but it must
be remembered that Luke is the latest of the Synoptic Gospels.
Much more to the point is the fact that he records a very successful

mission to the Samaritans in the early days of the Church (Ac. 8.4–25). Cullmann ('Samaria and the Origins of the Christian Mission', in *The Early Church*, edited by A. J. B. Higgins (1956), pp. 185–92) has suggested that there is a close link between this and our present chapter. Without accepting all his arguments, we can at least agree that successful work among the Samaritans gives a good basis for some Christians to be well informed about them. This is sufficient to account for John's knowledge, without entailing a full-scale tradition stemming from the ministry of Jesus himself. We should not forget that much of John's thought shows an awareness of Christian discussion with the synagogue. So here it is noteworthy that Jesus is represented as maintaining the Jewish case against the Samaritans, at the same time as asserting that both Jewish and Samaritan aspirations are alike fulfilled in his person (verses 20–3). (For recent work on John and the Samaritans, see Introduction, p. 37.)

Jesus leaves Judea 4.1–3

These verses are merely a stage direction, to bring Jesus back to Galilee, where he will perform the Second Sign (verses 43–54). That will conclude the present sequence of teaching, and John will bring Jesus back to Jerusalem for another feast for the start of the next sequence (5.1). The reason for his departure from Judea must be explained, especially as we have been given the impression that his preaching is proving very successful (3.22, 26). It is implied that, for this very reason, the Pharisees (whom John takes to be the ruling authority) are showing hostility. It must be assumed that Jesus withdraws, not from fear, but 'because his hour had not yet come' (7.30); unfortunately, the verses show some signs of confusion as a result of later editorial 'improvements'.

1. The beginning of the sentence is extraordinarily clumsy. To say that **the Lord knew that . . . Jesus** is as awkward in Greek as it is in English. **The Lord** can be simply a title of respect, but it is complicated for NT usage in reference to Jesus, because it was the normal Jewish way of referring to God, so as to avoid uttering the divine name. In the Synoptic Gospels it usually means God, and only rather rarely Jesus (chiefly in Luke). On the other hand it is commonly applied to Jesus in the Epistles, usually with definite religious implications. It is probably to be connected with the Christian use of Ps. 110.1 (cf. Ac. 2.34–6) and the bap-

tismal confession of faith (1 C. 12.3), in which the lordship of
Christ is acknowledged, rather like acknowledging a king or
ruler; cf. Thomas's confession in 20.28.

On this basis it is capable of two developments: (a) making
Jesus virtually equivalent to the God of the OT, e.g. Rom.
10.9–13; (b) weakening the sense, so that it becomes merely a
convenient designation for Jesus, as here. It is only natural that
the latter usage should become more common as time goes on.
Consequently there is every likelihood that its occurrence in this
verse is due to a glossator. Several important MSS (א D Θ, Old
Latin, Curetonian and Peshitta Syriac, and some Bohairic) have
'Jesus' instead, but this can hardly be original, as the alteration
then becomes inexplicable. Barrett suggests that originally no
subject was expressed, and it has been supplied variously. All are
agreed that it was put in to remove the ambiguity of the opening
words. But it seems to me best to assume that the text originally
began: 'Now the Pharisees heard' (cf. 9.40). This would give
quite a good sense, but leave open a slight awkwardness at the
change of subject at verse 3, which would account for the addition
of the whole of the first clause (**when the Lord knew that** (in
order to make the sense less awkward, *NEB* transfers the clause to
the beginning of verse 3). The Johannine **Now** (*oun*), belongs to
the original text). This explanation is very similar to Bultmann's.

2. Grammatically the verse is a parenthesis, and, like 3.24, may
well be an editorial addition, to bring John into line with the
Synoptic tradition, though it is found in all MSS. Sanders objects
that a glossator would have inserted it at 3.22, but the habits of
glossators are not always logical. Bernard and Schnackenburg
remark that **although** (*kaitoige*) is contrary to John's style.

The Water of Life 4–15

4. through Samaria: i.e. the province, not the city (called
Sebaste in NT times). It was part of the territory of Pontius
Pilate, and so, like Judea, under direct control of the Romans.
When the old northern kingdom of Israel fell in 722 B.C., the
Assyrian conquerors carried out mass deportations, so that the land
was repopulated with people of five different races (2 Kg. 17,
corroborated by Assyrian records). Two centuries later, when the
Persians came to power, there was a province of Samaria, and
this included Judea, the southern kingdom, now also fallen. When

the Jews returned from the Exile, they were thus part of the Persian province of Samaria. During the fifth century B.C. there was a gradual separation of the two communities, resulting in deep and lasting bitterness. The Jews gained their independence, and Judea became a separate province. Eventually the Samaritans set up their own centre of worship on Mount Gerizim as a rival to Jerusalem, though their form of religion was in all essentials identical. So bitter was the feeling that Jews plying between Judea and Galilee would very often prefer to avoid Samaria by crossing over to Perea (Transjordan), as Jesus did according to Mk 10.1. But necessity (so here Jesus **had to pass**), as for instance the need to get to Jerusalem quickly for a feast, frequently caused Jews to take the shorter route through Samaria (Jos. *Vita*, 269; *Ant.* xx.118). Presumably the opposition of the Pharisees is intended to be the reason for Jesus' haste.

5. Sychar: the identification of this place is a tantalizing problem; we have plenty of facts and John's information is clearly accurate. The question is whether this means ancient Shechem or the site of the modern village of ʿAskar. The latter seemed obvious, because of the similarity of the name, when the site of Shechem was thought to be identical with Nablus (Neapolis) west of the gap between the heights of Gerizim and Ebal. For Jacob's well (verse 6) is east of the gap, much nearer to ʿAskar, and within a stone's throw of another village called Balāṭah. But modern archaeology has proved beyond question that ancient Shechem was actually at Balāṭah. The excavations are some of the most impressive of the Holy Land, and illuminate numerous OT references. Shechem was an important city, and the real centre of the Samaritans as a religious group at the time of the split with the Jews. It was frequently devastated, and seems to have been finally destroyed by John Hyrcanus about 107 B.C. In NT times it was merely a village, and the description **city** does not seem very appropriate, though perhaps the designation survived as a relic of its past. If **Sychar** means ʿAskar, we want to know why the woman came all the way to Jacob's well for water, when there was an adequate water-supply at the village itself. If, however, it means Shechem (Gr. *Sychem*), it would be more natural for her to use it. Only the Old Syriac version actually reads Shechem, but Jerome argued that this is what was meant. Albright suggests Sychem had been accidentally written Sychar because of the preceding

Samaria, but this is hardly likely. G. A. Smith (*Historical Geography*, 1966 reissue, pp. 240–6) suggests what may be the true solution, provided that ʿAskar preserves a genuinely ancient name, which Albright denies (it simply means 'camp'). Though there is plenty of water both at ʿAskar and at Balāṭah, Jacob's well is unnecessarily deep (about 100 feet), going far below the water-table. The water is clear and good, and may well have been preferred for drinking purposes to that of the local streams. If this is so, the woman might just as well have come from ʿAskar as from Balāṭah, disregarding the other sources of supply. As the textual evidence overwhelmingly supports Sychar against Shechem, it seems that the identification with ʿAskar is to be retained (so Schnackenburg). **field:** the reference is to Gen. 33.19, which tells how Jacob bought the land from the Shechemites; to Gen. 48.22, where he bequeathes it to Joseph (this depends on a pun on Heb. *šᵉkem* = shoulder); and to Jos. 24.32, which describes how Joseph's bones were eventually buried there after the Exodus and conquest of Canaan. It is thus the oldest part of the Holy Land to belong to the Israelites by right of purchase. The Samaritans laid great store by their connections with the scene of the patriarch's transaction. Evidently John knows the correct site, i.e. the mound at Balāṭah, which is quite close to the well and much nearer to ʿAskar than is Nablus.

6. Jacob's well: though the patriarchal narratives of Genesis tell of the digging of many wells, this one is not mentioned. But it is certainly very ancient, and being in Jacob's land would obviously have a traditional connection with him.
wearied: John feels no difficulty about ascribing normal human emotions and physical needs to Jesus. It is mid-day (**the sixth hour**), time for rest and refreshment on the journey. These facts are not mentioned for realistic effect, but because they are necessary for the story.
beside the well: perhaps on the parapet surrounding it. This would not be possible if the well were as it is today, for the square stone parapet is rather narrow. But at Dothan there is a typical well, with a wide circular parapet. Unlike Jacob's well, which is enclosed in a Christian shrine, this one stands in the open outside the village, and the women still come to draw water from it. Jacob's well may have been like this in NT times.

7. to draw water: the situation is reminiscent of the meeting of Abraham's servant with Rebekah (Gen. 24.10–27) and of Jacob

with Rachel (Gen. 29.1–12), but there is no hint of literary allusion. It is true that the whole passage is so full of patriarchal
allusions that it would be quite possible to imagine John composing
the whole story from his imagination as an allegory (cf. the notes
on verse 18). But this is not John's way. All the indications of the
literary technique of the Gospel suggest that he limits the scope
of his creative imagination to developing the theological meaning
which he sees in actual historical traditions at his disposal. Whether
the present incident actually took place or not we cannot tell, for
we have no other evidence to corroborate it. But, when all allow-
ance is made for John's free exercise of his imagination in reproducing traditional material, we must still recognize that he himself
thought that he was describing something that actually happened
and meant the story to be taken at its face value. Note that *NEB*
reverses the order of verses 7 and 8.

8. to buy food: the original detached tradition may have had
no mention of the disciples; but John's interpolation of the incident into the journey to Galilee implies that they are accompany-
ing Jesus, and so it is necessary to remove them from the stage.
The device is not altogether convincing, because it is not really
likely that all should go, leaving Jesus alone, unless he specially
wished to be left undisturbed. The idea of obtaining food also
introduces a secondary motif similar to the primary motif of the
living water, which will be taken up by John in verses 31–8. We
can conjecture that when John first gave this discourse as a
homily it did not contain verses 8 and 27, 31–8, which he has
only introduced in the process of dovetailing the homily into the
book.

9. a Jew: no hint is given how the woman knew that Jesus
was not a Samaritan. We might rather expect her to recognize
him as a Galilean. But as the Galileans sided with the Jews against
the Samaritans, this would amount to the same thing. Out of
courtesy she gives him the opportunity to weigh up whether to
insist on his request or to avoid possible subsequent embarrassment
on account of ceremonial defilement. From a strict Jewish point
of view a Samaritan woman was to be avoided, because the
Samaritans were careless about ceremonial purification, so that
'the daughters of the Samaritans are deemed unclean as menstru-
ants from their cradle' (*Niddah*, iv.1). Consequently Jesus could
not even touch her water-pot without risk of contracting unclean-

ness and being liable to the consequent disabilities. But, as we have seen in seeking to uncover the underlying tradition of 3.25, 29, Jesus in fact refused to allow such considerations to place a barrier between himself and the outcasts of society. Later on we shall find that the disciples wonder that he has been talking to a *woman*, but show no sign of objection on the score that she is a Samaritan (verse 27). This is perfectly consistent, for there could be no question of incurring uncleanness merely by having a conversation with her.

no dealings: this explanatory note is missing from ℵ* D a b e, but it accords with John's habit of elucidating points unfamiliar to Gentile readers. It could, in fact, be taken to be part of the woman's speech (so, apparently, *AV*). Controversy surrounds the precise meaning of **have no dealings.** D. Daube (*The New Testament and Rabbinic Judaism*, 1956, pp. 373–82) has argued that the verb (*sunchrōntai*) means the 'co-use' of vessels, as implied in the last note. It is a technical term, stemming from a decree- of the Sanhedrin of A.D. 65/6, from which the harsh quotation about Samaritan women above is derived. It cannot, then, have been operative in the time of Jesus, though it could well have been known to John. The difficulty of this view is that it fails as an explanation for Gentiles, being a case of expounding *ignotum per ignotius*; also the verb has no object, so that 'vessels' has to be understood. On the other hand the meaning 'to have commercial dealings with' is attested for the early second century. This supports the more general idea here, especially if the sentence be regarded as a second-century gloss. The point of the explanation is then likely to be that the Jews do not eat and drink with Samaritans, treating them exactly as if they were Gentiles. This suits the actual relations between them over a long period (cf. Sir. 50.25f.). In the course of the second century relations between them improved.

   10. the gift of God, and who it is: whatever may have been the answer of Jesus in the underlying tradition, it is clear that in this verse we have the enunciation of the theme of the ensuing discourse. Both aspects of it are included in these few words. The **gift of God** is the living water, which is the subject of 11–15; **who it is** is the 'true teacher', which is the subject of 16–26. The word used for gift (*dōrea*) is a special one reserved for expressing divine bounty, and not used of the presents given by men, both in

classical and biblical Greek. It is to be noticed that the verse is not
a proper answer to the question, but arises from it by taking its
implications to extremes. Not only is there reason why Jesus
should not have asked the woman for water, but, if the situation
were rightly understood, she should **have asked him.**

living water: i.e. running water, especially water bubbling up
from a spring, as in verse 14. The phrase occurs in Zech. 14.8.
This tells of the eschatological fountain, following the same tradition of the renewal of the paradisal streams as Ezek. 47.1–12,
where fresh water that supports life is distinguished from the salt
waters of the Dead Sea. The phrase thus has symbolical overtones;
cf. also Jer. 2.13: 'They have forsaken me, the fountain of living
waters.' But it can be taken simply as a way of distinguishing
spring water from well water.

11. the well is deep: following his customary style, John
represents the woman as only understanding the practical sense
of Jesus' reply. Here she uses a different word for well (*phrear*)
from the word used in verse 6 (*pēgē*, properly source or spring).
It means a cistern or artificial shaft. She does not admit that the
water might not be 'living' at the bottom of it, merely that without
a rope and a bucket it cannot be obtained. Jacob's well is in fact
very deep. It is not quite clear whether there is a spring at the
bottom of it, or whether the water collects there by infiltration.
We must assume that John imagines that the woman has brought
her own rope, though one might have expected that a rope and
bucket for filling jars were always handy.

12. The thought that Jesus might know of a superior source of
fresh water has occurred to the woman, but it is an affront to
her Samaritan pride in possession of the patriarch's well. If G. A.
Smith is correct in saying that she used it because of the superiority
of its water, no difficulty is caused by the fact that many other
sources of supply are available in the vicinity, for she knows that
none is better. So, for Jesus to claim that he has a better source,
is to claim that he is a **greater** man than **Jacob** himself. The
question is sarcastic, but ironically it is perfectly true. Moreover,
by mentioning the **cattle** (and Jacob had vast flocks and herds
(Gen. 31–3)), the woman hints that it must be a very copious
supply of water. This makes Jesus' claim seem even more impossible, but takes the irony further, for in fact his waters are inexhaustible. Thus what appears to be an artless allusion to the

history of the site turns out to be a subtle step in the progress of
the discourse. Cf. also 8.53.

13. thirst again: the difference between the two kinds of water
is first indicated by the effects. Natural water quenches thirst only
for a short time; Jesus' water has lasting effect. Even when it is
realized that he is speaking metaphorically, it may seem surprising
that he should say this. In Sir. 24.21 Wisdom, claiming to be
much better than earthly delights, says: 'Those who drink me will
thirst for more.' However, this is explained in the next verse.

14. whoever drinks: the Greek phrase (*hos d'an piē*—aorist
subjunctive) makes it perfectly plain that a single draught is
meant, as opposed to the frequentative participial construction
of the last verse. It is only necessary to drink once. This means a
decisive act, which reminds us of the baptismal setting of chapter 3.
never: very emphatic, lit. 'not for unlimited duration'.
a spring of water welling up to eternal life: it is a special
mark of John's teaching style that he frequently moves the argument forward by a repetition of what he has just said, which
nevertheless incorporates a new and more far-reaching definition
of it. So here he repeats **the water that I shall give him** from
the first half of the verse, but the rest of the sentence is a fuller
and more explanatory equivalent of 'living water' in verse 10. It
now becomes clear why a single draught of it has such lasting
effect. It is an inner principle of spiritual life which is not bound
by the limits of earthly existence. It is what results from the new
birth from above (3.3–8). To describe it with the metaphor of an
internal fountain, gushing up inexhaustibly, is to suggest something of the richness of the new life that is made available through
faith in Christ; the idea is immensely comprehensive. We can see
something of what is involved from the obvious OT references: 'the
fountain of life' of Ps. 36.9: 'the wells of salvation' of Isa. 12.3;
the offer of 'waters' in Isa. 55.1; the waters that flow from the
Temple in the idealized picture of Ezek. 47.1, and the use of
'living waters' to describe them in Zech. 14.8. Besides these general
ideas, we should not forget the connection of water and the Spirit
(see above on 3.5) and the application of both ideas to Wisdom
(especially in 1 Enoch and Mandaean texts—refs. in Odeberg,
p. 168). The application to Wisdom comes, as we have seen, in
Sir. 24.21–31, but here there is a further equation which became
very important for later Jewish and rabbinic thought, that the

flowing stream of Wisdom is canalized in the Law of Moses. In the Damascus Document the patriarchal wells are actually interpreted to mean the Law (CD iii.16; vi.3–9; xix.34: 'the well of living waters'). For NT references, cf. 1 C. 10.4; Rev. 22.17, and, of course, Jn 7.37–9. It would be a mistake to try to tie John down to one particular interpretation. The metaphor is intended to be very inclusive. In 3.5–8 we learnt that the Spirit is the controlling influence over the whole life of those who participate in eternal life through incorporation into Christ. The metaphor of water suggests what this influence produces: a flow of thoughts and words and actions which accord with God's will and inspiration and continue into eternal life. It is not easy to think of the metaphor purely in terms of relationship, so that it is not surprising that it has often been expounded as if it meant a quasi-physical substance in man, derived from God, or the possession of an esoteric doctrine. The Gnostic *Gospel of Thomas* includes a passage, clearly referring to this verse, in which Jesus asks what the disciples think he is like. Thomas refuses to attempt a comparison, but addresses him 'Master' in the usual way. Then 'Jesus said: I am not your master, because you drank (and) became drunken from the bubbling spring (*pēgē*) which I have measured out' (*logion* 13 (Metzger's translation)). The sequel (and also *logion* 108) shows that this means that Jesus is not his master, because, as the possessor of the secret doctrine, Thomas has become one with him. Such a mystical merging of identities is quite foreign to John's thought. His constant reiteration of the necessity of believing in Jesus ensures that response and relationship are the proper categories of thought. But the Jewish idea of the Law as the water of life is probably below the surface, so that the aspect of true teaching certainly belongs to the range of thought. For it must not be forgotten that the magnificent assertion of this verse is not set in a vacuum, but against the backcloth of the historic division between the Jews and the Samaritans.

15. give me this water: almost identical with 6.34 (where 'Lord' should be rendered 'Sir' as here, cf. verse 1). The woman has only half understood what Jesus has said, i.e. 13–14a, but not 14b. So she thinks of his gift only as a labour-saving device. In order to expose the meaning of 14b it is necessary to abandon the metaphor of water and to turn attention to the giver of the water, for who he is reveals the nature of what he gives. Conse-

quently there is a sudden break in the flow of the argument, just
as there was at 3.9.

The True Teacher 16–26

16. here: Marsh notices that the repetition of this word (Gr.
enthade) from verse 15 helps to maintain the continuity (which is
obscured by the free translation of *NEB*). In every other way the
verse seems strangely inconsequent. However, a plausible sense can
be made from it in line with the preceding conversation: the
woman has asked for Jesus' special water, without realizing what
it really is; Jesus can begin to open her understanding by telling
her that it applies just as much to her husband as it does to her,
which would hardly be the case if he were talking about physical
water, which it was her domestic duty to fetch. This may be what
John intends to imply, though of course his real purpose is to
introduce his other topic, and to achieve it he will resort to his
favourite theme of Jesus' exceptional insight. Some scholars
think that the sudden mention of the husband is a call-up sign
to warn the reader that the underlying allegory is coming to the
surface. Her husband is her Samaritan religion, sorely in need of
spiritual enlightenment, as the sequel shows. But we have already
seen reason to doubt a full-scale allegorical interpretation in considering verse 7, and the objection still holds good. The woman is,
of course, a representative of the Samaritans, just as Nicodemus
was a representative of a certain type of Jew. But the story details
are meant to be quite factual, and the force of the argument gains
nothing from the attempt to turn some of them into allegorical,
and therefore non-narrative, factors.

17. no husband: the woman simply tells a white lie; there is
no suggestion that she is hiding the truth out of shame. The
reason could be that she wants to get the water without going all
the way back to Sychar first, which would certainly be a natural
reaction. But we do not have to seek the motive, for it is really
part of John's manœuvre to bring the argument to the important
theme of verse 19. It may be observed that the allegorical interpretation breaks down at this point, as the Samaritans certainly
had a form of the Jewish religion, and were proud of it.

18. five husbands: Jesus suddenly displays his special insight
by confronting her with her life-story (cf. 1.47). As this is a recurring feature of John's portrait of Jesus, this need occasion no

surprise to the reader, even if it is felt on other grounds to be improbable. It is not quite clear whether the present husband is meant to be the last of the five or a sixth; the point, however, is that in Jesus' eyes her present union does not constitute a true marriage, so that her white lie is ironically correct. Can these details be accepted as plausible items of the story? The number five certainly seems unnecessarily exaggerated, if John is inventing this part of the story and nothing was contained in the underlying tradition (as in fact is probable). The best solution is that it suggests a scandalous way of life which bears out the Jews' low opinion of the Samaritans. Jewish law permitted remarriage after divorce, but a person who was married more than three times was considered reprehensible (*SB* 11.437). According to the Synoptic tradition, Jesus disapproved of divorce altogether (Mk 10.2–9 paras.).

But there is no stress laid on the morals of the situation here. The revelation of the woman's past actually serves two positive functions in the subsequent development of the argument: (a) Jesus' insight attests the truth that he is the Christ (verses 19 and 29); (b) Jesus affirms the Jewish attitude to the Samaritans at the same time as claiming to supersede both (verses 21–3). If John has Jewish readers in mind, it would never do to give the impression that Jesus sided with the Samaritans (cf. 8.48); nor do the Synoptic Gospels suggest that he did so. So the woman has to be shown as morally inferior to the Jews, and to this extent she is representative of how they felt about all Samaritans. This really is sufficient to account for the number five; but it looks odd, and so invites speculation. In fact it is the trump card of the allegorical interpretation. For in 2 Kg. 17.24 we are told that the Assyrians repopulated the cities of Samaria with people of five different nations, who naturally brought their own forms of worship. The same account (verses 30f.) gives the names of seven gods, but Josephus (*Ant.* ix.287) manages to reduce them to five. The result was a religious syncretism abhorrent to the Jews still holding out against the Assyrians in the southern kingdom. On the allegorical view, the woman with five husbands is the Samaritan religion contaminated with five forms of idolatry; but the details must not be pressed, for she did not have her husbands concurrently, as the suggestion of syncretism naturally implies. It can then be argued that the next step of the argument follows naturally on this indication of impurity of religion. For first Jesus is described

as a prophet, and the OT prophets specialized in denouncing
religious syncretism. Then he goes on to talk about the true worship in spirit and truth, by contrast with the Samaritan religion.
But this will not really hold, for in NT times Samaritan religion
was not seriously syncretistic, and was firmly based on the Law of
Moses (the Samaritan Pentateuch has only minor differences from
the Hebrew); and the most remarkable fact of the whole discourse
is its awareness of *current* issues. To drag up a piece of ancient
history by means of a doubtful allusion is simply not relevant. The
allegorical view is rejected by Bernard, Bultmann, Brown, Sanders
and Schnackenburg, among recent commentators.

19. a prophet: simply because of his power of perception.
Jesus has denounced neither the woman's character nor the
Samaritan religion, although he has indicated disapproval with
a touch of Johannine irony. It is not for this reason that she thinks
he is a prophet. This is an important step in the argument, because
it shows that she has begun to realize that religious issues are at
stake, in spite of her failure to understand verse 14b. And if Jesus
is *a* prophet, it opens the possibility that he is *the* prophet (cf. 1.21).
As the Samaritans only recognized the Pentateuch as canonical,
they based their messianic expectations not on OT prophecy but
on the promise of a Prophet like Moses in Dt. 18.15–18, whom they
called the *Taheb* (= the restorer, or the one who returns). He was
thought of as a true teacher, rather than as an anointed king (cf.
J. Macdonald, *The Theology of the Samaritans* (1964), pp. 362ff.).
Jesus' revelation that he is the fulfiller of this role will be the
climax of the discourse (verse 26).

20. For the moment she thinks of Jesus as a Jewish prophet,
and so, mindful of her local pride (cf. verse 12), raises the central
religious issue of the Samaritan position. When the Samaritans
were forbidden (or self-excluded) from worship at the Temple at
Jerusalem, they set up their own temple on Mount Gerizim (**this
mountain**). The law of Deuteronomy requires that sacrifice
should be offered in one place only (Dt. 12.1–14). As the place
is not named, it could be argued that Jerusalem was not what
was intended. In fact the immediately preceding paragraph (Dt.
11.26–32) mentions a ceremony of blessing and cursing, those who
utter blessings being on Mount Gerizim, and those who utter
curses on Mount Ebal. These two heights, divided by the gap
through which the road passes to Nablus and Samaria (Sebaste),

have a commanding position, from which on a clear day one can
see the Mediterranean in the west and the winding stream of the
Jordan in the rift valley to the east. Immediately below on the east
side is the site of Shechem, the ancient rallying point of the
tribes of Israel. Thus it was not without reason that the Samaritans
argued that Mount Gerizim was the one proper place of worship;
their descendants still go up to the top to celebrate the Passover
each year. But the Samaritan temple was probably rather lower
down towards the gap, where there are now the ruins of a Hellenistic temple. For **place** = temple, cf. 11.48 and Dt. 12.5.

21. Woman: not disrespectful; cf. 2.4.
believe me: the Greek phrase (*pisteue moi*) is unique in the NT.
Bernard suggests that it serves the same purpose as John's usual
'truly, truly'.
the hour is coming: a technical expression in John for the eschatological event, which he sees as bound up with the destiny of
Jesus, especially with the paradox of his glory revealed in the
Passion; cf. 2.4. Here only the future idea of the eschatological
event is meant; the reference to Jesus himself will only be introduced in verse 23. The Samaritan temple had already been destroyed, and Jesus forecasts the destruction of the Jerusalem temple
also.
you will worship: the subject of the verb is plural—i.e. the
Samaritan people.
the Father: for the absolute use of 'the Father', see on 3.17. It
should not be taken to mean worship of the universal Father in a
non-sectarian (Jewish, Samaritan, or even Christian) way, which
would be quite foreign to John's theology, but worship in and
through the Father–Son relationship which is made possible by
incorporation into the Son. This will be clarified in verses 23f.

22. what you do not know: not a contemptuous assertion of
Jewish superiority, but a reflection of the actual position of Christianity, that the Incarnation took place in a Jewish setting and
Christ is heir to the promises made to the Jews. Before Jesus can
expound the new worship which will replace that of Jerusalem
and of Mount Gerizim, he must make this fundamental point
plain: **salvation**—i.e. deliverance in its richest sense—**is from
the Jews**—i.e. arises from God's promises to the Jews. We think
at once of the great prophecies of Isaiah: the messianic prophecies
of the early chapters (Isa. 9 and 11), and the salvation prophecies

of the chapters that belong to the exilic age (e.g. 45.8, 17; etc.); none of these were accepted by the Samaritans, but to Christianity they are essential. Hence, as Hoskyns points out, this is not as if Jesus were simply taking the Jewish part in the controversy, but it is a veiled messianic claim, even though by saying **we** Jesus speaks as one of the Jews. Odeberg, followed by Bultmann, thinks this is impossible, and says the **we** must mean the Christians, as in 3.11; accordingly, he has to bracket the last clause as a gloss. Schnackenburg says that 'but' at the beginning of the next verse proves that it is part of the text, for it means that even the Jewish claim is superseded.

23. and now is: by the addition of these words, Jesus brings eschatological prophecy into the present. Though the destruction of the Temple lies in the future, the coming event of the establishment of true worship is present in principle in the person of Jesus; cf. 5.25.

in spirit and truth: the contrast is not between the forms and ceremonies of the Temple and the spiritual worship of the Church, but between worship apart from Jesus and worship within his filial response to the Father, soon to be revealed in his Passion. This is worship **in spirit,** for it is the response of the man who, by belief in Jesus, is open to the influence of the Spirit (3.6), and it arises from the inner spring of the water of life (verse 14). It is also **in truth,** for it accords with the truth revealed in Jesus (1.14, 17), which is another aspect of the water of life.

for such the Father seeks to worship him: the verb must be translated 'demands' or 'requires', cf. next verse (so *AG*, p. 339). Though this last clause is missing from a few MSS. (chiefly the Lake group), it must certainly be retained, as it leads into the explanation of the new worship which is the purpose of the next verse.

24. God is spirit: the point is that like requires like: the Father demands such worshippers because he is himself spirit. The argument is exactly the same as 3.8: the God-like person (in 3.8 compared to the wind) alone can have fellowship with God (3.3, 5), and the God-like person alone can offer true worship to God. Through their birth from above (3.3, 5), or, in other words, through their draught of the water of life (verse 14), men have the Spirit, and worship in spirit and truth is the natural outcome. What was promised in the last verse as an eschatological event

coming true in the present is here restated as a generally necessary
(**must**) truth. This is because it alone accords with God's nature.
God is spirit is not a metaphysical statement but much more a
character-description, like 'God is light' and 'God is love' (1 Jn
1.5; 4.8). Although it is true that the Church abandoned the
Jewish ceremonies and, in common with many thoughtful people,
placed the emphasis on the heart and the mind (cf. Heb. 13.15),
there is here no polemic against forms and ceremonies as such.
'That true worship is set over against idolatry, and over against a
cult restricted to one sanctuary, is not more than incidental'
(Barrett, p. 200). The fundamental thing is that worship expresses
a relationship between God and men. This has to be a spiritual
relationship, because God is spirit, and therefore men too must
have the Spirit. This, according to John's theology, is precisely
what has been established in Jesus. Consequently, when Jesus says
that the new worship is coming *now*, and that men of the Spirit
are *required*, it is tantamount to a messianic claim and a demand
for personal allegiance to himself. If we think of the setting of this
discourse within an act of worship, as a homily or devotional
address, it is not difficult to see how the Christians would see the
now as applying to their own situation, and the demand for worship in spirit and truth as the very essence of their awareness of
their membership in the living Christ.

25. The woman can hardly be imagined as being in a position
to understand the full import of Jesus' words; nor is it necessary
to the argument that she should do so, for the purpose of the discourse has not yet been reached. This is to draw the listeners to
fix their gaze on Jesus, who is the giver of the water of life and the
agent of the true worship in the Spirit. It is sufficient, therefore,
that the woman should only be aware that Jesus is speaking of an
eschatological event, and it is important for John's purpose that
she should speak of it in terms of the Samaritan beliefs; for Jesus
is to be shown as the fulfilment of the Samaritans' hopes at the
same time as confirming the Jewish expectations. By this means,
the universal scope of the Christian mission can be suggested.

I know: some MSS. have 'we know', but this is probably a correction to agree with **us** at the end of the verse. It is a personal statement of conventional teaching, which she here reproduces, in
exactly the same way as Martha in 11.24 reproduces standard
Jewish teaching. Her words are not quite accurate, because the

Samaritans did not use the title **Messiah.** She should have said
'I know that the *Taheb* comes, whom you call the Messiah.'
Odeberg, noting that the explanation is quite unnecessary, as it
has already been given in 1.41, even suggests that *Taheb* originally
stood in the text. But, as a piece complete in itself, the discourse
would need the explanation, and it is probable that John intentionally used the Jewish equivalent rather than the Samaritan
title, because of the next verse.

show us all things: performing his teaching function, like the
prophet of Dt. 18.18; cf. 1QS ix.11. The words are reminiscent
of the description of the Paraclete, or Counsellor (14.25; 16.13–15).
As this is one aspect of the inner spring of living water offered in
verse 14, it only remains for Jesus to show that he fulfils this
Samaritan expectation, and then the woman's understanding may
be regarded as complete.

26. Jesus' words are, literally: 'I am, who speak to you.' It is
the first occasion when Jesus uses the 'I am' revelation-formula,
a special feature of the Fourth Gospel; cf. 6.35; 8.12, 58; 11.25.
The formula is normal in a theophany, when God introduces
himself, both in the OT (e.g. Gen. 17.1) and in pagan literature.
Here it has the same very solemn ring about it, but comes as the
climax at the end of the conversation. It is not clear how far we
should see here an allusion to the name of God in Exod. 3.14:
'I AM WHO I AM', or to 'I am he' in Isa. 41.4; 43.10. These
will certainly have to be considered in connection with 8.58 and
some of the other passages where the Greek *egō eimi* (I am) occurs.
In these passages Jesus, as it were, takes to himself the name of
God because he is the revealer of God's character, God's self-
expression made flesh. The revelation-formula is thus an invitation to the reader to pass beyond the flesh of Jesus to his origin in
God, and to understand his work and person in the light of it.
But it is not necessary to suppose that these implications are
present in this verse. Jesus' reply to the woman simply affirms
that he *is* the Messiah, the *Taheb*, the true teacher. That is in
itself revelation enough for the time being. On the whole subject
see Bultmann, p. 225, n. 3; Brown, pp. 533–8; E. Schweizer,
pp. 4–45; H. Zimmermann, in *BZ* IV (1960), pp. 54–69, 266–76.

TESTIMONY OF THE SAMARITANS AND REFLECTIONS ON THE MIS-
SIONARY TASK   4.27–42

Although the discourse is finished, the story continues without a
break. The Samaritan woman goes to her people—for now at last
she is ready to share Jesus' offer and to obey his instruction in
verse 16—and spreads the exciting news (verses 28–30). First many
of them accept her word, then they have personal experience of
Jesus' ministry, and finally they are able to give their own testimony in terms that go beyond the revelation that he is the
Messiah, asserting that he is 'the Saviour of the world' (39–42).
The story is, then, more than a revelation-discourse. It is a model
of the mission of the church. It has been suggested above (p. 176)
that John composed it on the basis of the mission that was actually
undertaken there in the years following Pentecost. New life in the
Spirit leads to spiritual fecundity (verse 14) and to mission. It is
very unlikely that the underlying story of the woman coming to
the well contained more than the slightest hint of these themes. It is
probable that it was little more than a peg on which to hang
them. But the Gospel tradition contained just enough indication
that Jesus did have some contact with Samaritans to make this a
plausible expansion of the story for John's purpose. He is anxious
to show that the new life in Christ inevitably breaks out of its
Jewish setting and is as universal as the light that enlightens
every man (1.9). In chapter 12 he will introduce some Greeks
so as to keep the theme of universal mission in view; here he can
use a detailed knowledge of the Samaritan religion and the fact
that Christian missions had been successful among them to make
the point very effectively within the context of the life of Jesus.

For the purpose of dovetailing the story-discourse into the
larger composition of the Gospel, John has represented Jesus as
being accompanied by the disciples (how many he does not say;
presumably more than the original five) on his journey to Galilee.
So their return from shopping is mentioned in verse 27 (a verse
which spoils the connection between verses 26 and 28). Whereas
the woman's function is to provide water, the disciples' is to provide food. Jesus refuses it, and so a little parallel to the main discourse on the water is begun. It is not, however, developed in discourse style, but seems rather to be a collection of sayings on the
theme of sowing and reaping, very similar to the parables of

growth in the Synoptic Gospels. The purpose of this interpolation (verses 31–8) is to relate the story to the Church's missionary work, which is a continuation of Jesus' public ministry. This point will be dealt with at length in the Supper discourses. John has inserted these verses into the story in such a way as to fill in the time while the woman is going home and her friends are coming out to Jesus. This device is a well-known characteristic of Mark (his 'sandwich' construction; cf. Mk 5.21–43; 11.12–21).

27. marvelled: Proverbs contains many warnings of the dangers of talking with a strange woman, a tradition continued by the rabbis (*Pirqe Aboth* i.5). Jesus, as a rabbi with disciples under his care, might be expected to be specially cautious in this respect. The fact that the woman is a Samaritan appears not to be relevant (cf. above on verse 9).

none said: the disciples' reticence reflects the sense of awe aroused by verse 26, and helps to prepare for Jesus' refusal of food in verse 32. Their unspoken questions should perhaps be translated: 'What are you asking? or what are you talking with her about?' **Talking** (*laleis*) is the same word as 'speak' in verse 26. For a similar reticence, cf. 21.12.

28. went away: one MS. (Θ) adds 'running', and most commentators suppose that the woman left her water-jar because she was in haste to spread the news. Chrysostom (*Hom.* xxxiv.1) suggests that she forgot it in her excitement. Less likely is Barrett's idea that she left it so that Jesus could drink. If the detail is more than a human touch, it may be intended to indicate that the woman is going to *return*. By leaving her property she shows that she is not going away altogether, and the story is not yet finished.

29. The Samaritan woman's testimony corresponds with the two stages of argument in the preceding discourse. First she adduces the evidence of Jesus' insight, which had led her to believe that he was a prophet (verses 16–19); then she makes the further suggestion, which really goes beyond this evidence, that he might be the Christ (25–6).

Can this be the Christ: the Greek particle *mēti* implies the answer 'no' (*BDF* § 427.2). But the implications of verse 42 hardly allow this. John *means* it to be an expression of cautious faith (cf. 7.26, where *mēpote* is used).

30. This verse belongs closely with verses 39f. Presumably the woman herself goes with the people. On the way (verse 39, which has been expanded on account of the addition of 31–8) it is noted that many of them are persuaded by her testimony; and at verse 40 they arrive at the well.

31. Meanwhile: Gr. *en tō metaxu*, only here in the NT.

32. food: Gr. *brōsis* (properly 'eating') for the more correct *brōma*, which is used in verse 34. Jesus' refusal of what the disciples have brought is not given an explanation at the purely narrative level. The disciples think of a possible explanation, but it is wrong. It is John's teaching method, in order to work in the teaching of the following verses.

33. In the best Johannine manner, we have here the usual misunderstanding, which, at another level, is ironically near the truth. For, though no one has brought any food, Jesus has had the deeper satisfaction of seeing his word bear fruit in the beginnings of a successful mission. For the irony, cf. verses 11f.

34. the will of him who sent me: the whole phrase occurs again at 5.30 and 6.38f., but there are many equivalent expressions. For this is one of the most important ideas of John's Christology. His concept of the unity of the Father and the Son is first and foremost in terms of a moral unity. It is this complete identity of will, or in other words the complete obedience of Jesus to his Father, which justifies Jesus' unique and exclusive claim on men's allegiance (cf. 3.16–21, 31–6). The idea is found in the Synoptic tradition (cf. Mt. 11.27). But when this obedience is described as **food,** we are naturally reminded of Dt. 8.3, cited in the story of the Temptations (Mt. 4.4): 'Man shall not live by bread alone, but by every word that proceeds from the mouth of God.' Though there may not be an allusion here to this precise verse, the theme of the bread in the wilderness as a type of the teaching from heaven was certainly well known to John, and is treated at length in chapter 6.

to accomplish his work: Not 'works' (plural; cf. 5.36), which are only Signs, but the whole purpose for which he has been sent, his mission. His personal task will be completed in his Passion (17.4; 19.30); but, from the point of view of mission in the broad sense, that will only be the beginning.

35. At this point, John's discourse-style, which has begun so characteristically in verses 32–4, is abandoned, and the rest consists of traditional material, which gives us a glimpse of what John's material looked like before he worked it up into the full-

scale discourses. Here there are two proverbial sayings (35 and
37), each followed by a comment which, though distinctly Johannine in its present form, has links with the Synoptic tradition.
Verses 35–7 describe the 'work' of verse 34 in terms of the harvest,
suggested by the idea of food, in an entirely general way. It is
only at verse 38 that it is applied to the disciples, so that they are
associated with Jesus' vocation.

do you not say: you is emphatic, referring to people in general
(not just the disciples), and dissociating Jesus himself from them.
The saying is a proverb, though not known from other sources,
based on a Semitic original (the **yet . . . then** [lit. 'and] construction, as in Jon. 3.4). It conforms roughly with the pattern of
agriculture in the Holy Land. Sowing took place after the autumn
rains, i.e. in Nov.–Dec. As it was done by scattering on the soil,
and the seed was not covered (cf. the Parable of the Sower), it
could not be done while the heavy rains lasted, for fear that it
would be washed away. The barley harvest began at Passover
time, i.e. early April, and the wheat in May. This agrees with the
Gezer Calendar (? ninth cent. B.C.), which lists the work appropriate to each month. There is no necessary implication that the
time when Jesus is speaking is actually the time of sowing, though
some commentators have attempted to date the whole episode
by this verse. But, if this is an item of genuine tradition taken over
by John from his sources, it may well be that Jesus originally gave
the teaching of this and the next verse at the time of sowing in some
circumstances which made it specially appropriate.

I tell you, lift up your eyes: RSV has suppressed 'Behold'
(NEB 'look') at the beginning of this clause, which serves to give an
adversative sense (cf. Isa. 40.15). For **lift up your eyes** (obscured
by the paraphrase in NEB), cf. Mt. 17.8; Lk. 6.20; etc.; these are
Semitic features. The observation that the harvest is ready even
now contradicts the experience of the proverb, which implies four
months of inactivity while the seed is growing (cf. Mk 4.26–9). This
can be taken as a parable of the Kingdom of God, like the seed
parables in Mk 4. The point is that, unlike the normal conditions
of agriculture, the grain is already ripening, even though it is the
time of sowing. With the continuation in the next verse, it is comparable to the mission charge of Mt. 9.37f. (cf. Lk. 10.2): 'The
harvest is plentiful, but the labourers are few; pray therefore the
Lord of the harvest to send out labourers into the harvest.' It is

the same idea of the eschatological event being realized in the
present as we found in John's 'the hour is coming, and now is' in
verse 23.

already: this word stands last in the sentence in the Greek, which
is an unusual position for this particular expression. C* D and
other MSS. and versions (Old Syriac and some Old Latin and
Bohairic) take it with the next verse, which is more in accordance
with John's style (cf. 7.14; 9.22; 15.3), and may well be right (so
RV, mg). It greatly improves the sense of the next verse.

36. rejoice together: i.e. at the same time, for the four
months' gap between the two activities is done away, and they are
virtually simultaneous. With such miraculous productivity, no
wonder there is cause for rejoicing! At this stage there is no point
in trying to decide who is the sower and who is the reaper. We are
still talking about agriculture, with the one unusual factor of the
miraculous time-scale to make its point as a parable of the Kingdom. For **receives wages** there is a further parallel in the mission
charge (Lk. 10.7; cf. Mt. 10.10): 'The labourer deserves his wages'
(quoted also, as if from Scripture, in 1 Tim. 5.18; *Didache* xiii.1f.).
gathers fruit for eternal life refers to the next task—storing up
the grain in the barns—which all adds to the rejoicing. It occurs
in an eschatological context in Mt. 3.12 (= Lk. 3.17); cf. Mt.
13.30. But by specifying **eternal life,** John has dropped the
metaphor and provided the application. For the theme of the
whole parable, Bernard compares Am. 9.13: 'The ploughman
shall overtake the reaper.'

37. the saying: another proverb, not ascribed to Jesus in the
Synoptic tradition, though Sanders points to a reference to it in
the Parable of the Talents (Mt. 25.24, cf. Lk. 19.21). It was
widely current in ancient times. Barrett mentions Greek parallels
and quotes one from Aristophanes. In the OT (Dt. 20.6; 28.30;
Mic. 6.15; Job 31.8) the idea is brought up as a form of punishment, so contradicting the norm that each man gains what he has
himself sown; hence in the OT it is not a proverb about the wry
injustices of fate, as it is here; but it may well have been current
in this sense in the Holy Land in NT times. At first sight, it
appears to contradict verse 36, in which the distinction between
sower and reaper has been virtually eliminated. In fact, however,
it is introducing a modification necessary for the application in
the next verse. **Here** (lit. 'in this'; *NEB* 'that is how') refers

forward, as in 9.30 and 13.35 (Greek text). Thus it is in the one factor that is just going to be mentioned that the proverb holds good and the distinction between sower and reaper still applies.

38. sent: implying that Jesus has already given his mission charge, though John actually reserves this until 20.21; but cf. 17.18. However, the charge has really been implicit in the apostolic call from the beginning.

others have laboured: great controversy surrounds this verse. How we interpret it depends on the perspective from which it is seen:

(a) In the context of the original mission charge, the work of reaping takes the form of proclaiming that the promises of God made through the prophets have now been fulfilled and the Kingdom has arrived. In this case the prophets are the **others.** (b) If the saying is taken strictly in relation to the conversion of the Samaritans, it is possible that the ground had been prepared by the Baptist and his disciples, cf. 3.23 (J. A. T. Robinson). (c) Schnackenburg asserts that **sent** here and in 17.18 means Jesus' decision to send the disciples in the future (20.21), and then they will work in the soil he has himself prepared. The **others** then refer to Jesus himself alone. (d) If a post-Resurrection perspective is taken, the verse could refer to the contemporary church, and the **others** are either Jesus and the Apostles in general (Loisy, Hoskyns), or the Hellenists of Ac. 8 who converted Samaria (Cullmann).

(a) is the traditional interpretation, and seems right. The verse follows naturally on what has just been said, and needs to be interpreted in the same way—i.e., not as a comment of the evangelist, but as an item of traditional material closely related to the mission charge. In the Lucan context of the mission of the Seventy we read (Lk. 10.23f.): 'Blessed are the eyes which see what you see! For I tell you that many prophets and kings desired to see what you see, and did not see it, and to hear what you hear, and did not hear it.' This is not dissimilar to the theme of the present verse. The point surely is that, whereas in the exciting eschatological perspective of Jesus' preaching sowing and reaping coincide, nevertheless the *former* labourers (i.e., the prophets), have died before seeing the harvest. There may perhaps be a verbal allusion to Jos. 24.13, where the same word for labour (*kopiān*) is used in the LXX.

39. see above on verse 30.

many . . . believe: cf. 2.23.

40. two days: cf. 11.6. It seems to be a way of expressing a short period of time, and is unlikely to include symbolical significance.

42. The story ends with the testimony of the Samaritans to their belief in Jesus himself. In the Church's missionary work the missionaries give witness to Christ, but their task is not achieved until the people reach personal faith in him.

the Saviour of the world: this phrase occurs only here in the Gospel, but it is found in 1 Jn 4.14. A D Θ and many later MSS. add 'the Christ' to bring it into line with verse 29, but it is characteristic of John to substitute a title which goes beyond what has been said before. Jesus is not only the Messiah of Jewish expectation, but the universal Saviour. This word is applied to God in Deutero-Isaiah, e.g. Isa. 43.3, referring to the divine activity in the Exodus and the coming return from exile, which is a repetition of it. It is as the agent of a new Exodus that it might be applied to Jesus, but in NT times the word was widely used as a title of pagan deities, and so there was probably reluctance to use it in the early days. It is regularly applied to Jesus only in the Pastoral Epistles. Thus it follows much the same pattern as the corresponding verb: 'to save' (cf. 3.17). As a title which came into use in the Gentile mission of the Church, it makes a fitting climax to the section.

HEALING OF AN OFFICIAL'S SON: NEW LIFE DISPLAYED   **4.43–54**

The offer of living water has been extended in the discourse just ended, and now John records a miracle from his stock of tradition to show it in action. First there is an editorial paragraph, resuming the larger narrative framework, in which Jesus arrives in Galilee and receives an enthusiastic welcome. Short as it is, it is not without some perplexing problems.

The healing miracle illustrates the teaching on saving belief given in chapter 3, and on the gift of life, the theme of chapter 4. The story has such an obvious similarity to the healing of the centurion's servant in Mt. 8.5–13 (= Lk. 7.1–10), that it is very probable that both go back ultimately to the same event in the life of Jesus. But although there are some close similarities of phrase, the differences are too great to suggest that John is dependent on the Synoptic accounts. It is better to suppose that

it comes from a parallel development of the same original tradition. In view of the cross-references to the marriage at Cana, and
some slight affinities with the way John handled that tradition, it
seems likely that it has been taken by him from the same source.

The story has been remembered as a striking example of the
value of faith in the life-giving word of Jesus. Most of the miracle-
stories show Jesus in personal contact with the sick person. In this
case there was no contact at all. The Synoptic account makes this
point most effectively, because the centurion draws an analogy
between his own position, in which he expects his word of
command to be obeyed, and that of Jesus, who need 'only say
the word, and my servant shall be healed'. It is possible that there
was a comparable motif in John's source; but it would hardly suit
his picture of Jesus to suggest that the man himself should tell him
how to do his job, and so there is a typical Johannine variation
at this point. On the other hand he increases the distance between
Jesus and the sick person, and lays considerable stress on the fact
that, in spite of it, there was a direct relationship between the
word of Jesus and the boy's recovery. Just as in the case of the
Samaritans (verses 39 and 42), there is an initial act of faith which
is subsequently confirmed (verses 50 and 53).

It is not possible to reconstruct exactly what happened. It might
be suggested that it was all a happy coincidence: the boy took a
turn for the better at the same time as Jesus happened to counsel
faith, but there was no real relation between these. Or it may be
a matter of attributing to Jesus a theme beloved of folk-lore.
There is another example of a healing at a distance in the story of
the Syrophoenician woman in Mk 7.24–30 (= Mt. 15.21–8),
which has some points of contact with our present passage; but
there is also an even closer parallel in a rab'.nic story of Rabban
Gamaliel II (early second century A.D.) recorded in *B. Berakoth*
34b (see the notes on verses 50 and 52). But to John himself the
story is based on a tradition which he does not question. To him
it is important as a Sign of something of much greater value, which
he has indicated in the far more inclusive and far-reaching
promise of verse 14.

Jesus comes to Galilee **43–5**

43, 45. In this transitional note, John works back through his
chronological references: **two days** refers to verse 40; **departed**

for Galilee resumes verse 3, where the reason for Jesus' departure was given as Pharisaic opposition aroused by his successful baptismal activity (3.22); **all that he had done in Jerusalem at the feast** refers to 2.23–5. Two points need to be observed. (a) The miracle at Cana is disregarded, though it is just about to be mentioned in verse 46, perhaps because it was done in private. The grounds for belief are then exactly the same as for the people of Jerusalem; but, whereas the latter's response was equivocal (2.25), **the Galileans welcomed him.** (b) The journey in between can be seen as a sort of triumphal progress, once Jesus has left Jerusalem. First there is the baptizing mission in Judea, then the success among the Samaritans, and finally the enthusiasm of the Galileans.

44. Into the midst of this quite intelligible picture, John has inserted a proverbial saying of Jesus which does not seem to fit. It is found in all three Synoptic Gospels (Mt. 13.57; Mk 6.4; Lk. 4.24) and also in the *Gospel of Thomas*, 31. The vocabulary is close to that of Matthew and Mark, but the form is nearer to Luke; there may also be an allusion to the Lucan version in 'welcomed' (*edexanto*) in the next verse, from the same verb as Luke's 'acceptable' (*dektos*). In all three Synoptics the point is the same: whereas Jesus had met with considerable success in Galilee as a whole, in Nazareth he was too well known, and the people were sceptical. It is important to realize that, though the proverb says **in his own country** (*patris* = fatherland), the application is not to the whole of Galilee, but is restricted to the city of Nazareth. This is clearer still in the *Thomas* version, though it has no context to define its meaning: 'Jesus said: No prophet is acceptable in his village; no physician works cures on those who know him' (Metzger's translation). This seems to be based on the Lucan version. John also knows that Jesus' work was successful in Galilee in general, but that he had some opposition at home; cf. 7.1–9. But the difficulty here is that the proverb has the wrong application. It can only be intended to explain Jesus' move to Galilee, and so must apply to the first hints of opposition in Jerusalem. Attempts to get round this—arguing for instance that he has heard of trouble in Galilee and comes to put it right, apparently very successfully—fail to convince, because they require too much complicated amplification of the text. Bernard and Brown feel the difficulties are insuperable, and suggest that the verse is a misplaced gloss. R. H. Lightfoot takes it to apply to *all* the places where Jesus worked, none of which gave him the true honour which belongs to him in his real *patris*, i.e. the bosom of the Father. But there is no hint of such a spiritualizing reinterpretation in the context, which remains quite factual. The solution surely lies in the fact that John is not making direct use of the Synoptic Gospels, and that the proverb came to him without a specific context, as in the *Thomas* version. Thus the *patris* is only identifiable by the fact that it is the place of opposition, and this to John is, not Galilee nor Samaria, nor even Judea, but only the city of Jerusalem. It is possible that he knew of a tradition comparable to Lk. 13.33, which also sounds proverbial: 'It cannot be that a prophet should perish away from Jerusalem.' Thus the insertion of the proverb at this point maintains the recurring theme that Jerusalem, the religious centre of Judaism, was 'his own home' from the point of view of the history of salvation (cf. Sir. 24.8–12), but 'his own people received him not' (1.11).

The Healing of the Official's Son 46–54

46. he came again: a further editorial sentence, linking the story following with the first Sign, and providing a suitable setting for it. There is no reason to suppose that the miracle actually took place at Cana, but it makes a suitable place in the light of the need to suggest some distance from Capernaum (see on verse 52). Brown argues that it must have been in the source, because of the correct use of 'come down' in 47, 49 and 51. But the decision to represent a considerable distance is alone sufficient to suggest a setting somewhere in the uplands, so that this feature necessarily belongs to the Johannine version, even without specification of Cana.

And at Capernaum: the story begins at this point (*NEB*: 'An officer . . .'). In the Synoptic accounts Jesus is himself at Capernaum, and there is no suggestion that the centurion comes from another town. The healing has to be done without contact with the sufferer, not because he is far away, but because the centurion, as a devout Gentile deeply respectful of Jewish customs, feels unworthy to entertain Jesus in his house. It was remarked in the notes on 2.12 that it is probable that the same was true of John's source at this point. If so, we must assume that the use of 'come down' is due to his editing, and also the whole of verses 52f., in which the motif of the large distance appears. This is not impossible, for the story really finishes with verse 51 (or even 50). In favour of this opinion is the very clear sign of John's editing in the phrase: 'Jesus had come from Judea to Galilee' in verse 47. Thus John also adds further verses, because he likes to press home the evidence which clinches the point. We shall see this feature again in his treatment of the feeding miracle in chapter 6.

an official: the word (*basilikos*) means a royal person, and probably refers to an official in the service of King Herod rather than a member of the royal family. Similarly the centurion of the Synoptic account is to be regarded as an officer of Herod's army, which was modelled on the Roman pattern. In both cases he could be a Jew (Galilean), or just as likely a Gentile, as mercenaries were much used; but the Synoptists definitely regard him as a Gentile.

son: Gr. *huios*. Matthew has 'boy' (*pais*), distinguished from 'servant' (Mt. 8.9) in the same context, but probably meaning a personal servant or batman. Luke uses 'servant' (*doulos*) in Lk. 7.2, 10, but 'boy' in verse 7. 'Son' may be an alternative rendering of the ambiguous 'boy' of the original tradition, which is probably the correct text in verse 51.

ill: the original probably did not say what the illness was, and no indication is given in Luke. Mt. 8.5 says the boy was paralysed, but this is probably due to the influence of Mk 2.3, also set in Capernaum. Eventually (verse 52) we discover that John thought it was a fever.

47. he went: this agrees with Matthew, but Luke makes the centurion act through a deputation of Jewish elders, followed by a group of friends. In John there is a hint of a deputation in verse 51, but this is only after the miracle has been done. It is likely that Matthew is nearest to the original tradition. We note that the deputations in Luke and John serve to emphasize precisely the point which interests each evangelist. Luke is interested in the distance of social status that has to be covered, the honorific approach to Jesus and the extreme self-abasement of the highly respectable Gentile. John, as we have seen, is interested in the geographical distance. Whereas the Synoptic version, and especially Luke's expansions to the source, contain the suggestion that Jesus might not be willing to go to a Gentile's house, and have to counterbalance this by turning the whole story into a charter for

the Gentiles, John avoids the suggestion by making it *impossible*
for Jesus to come straight to the patient.

at the point of death: Cf. Lk. 7.2.

48. Here John introduces his first major change to the story.
In Matthew and Luke Jesus agrees to come, and then the centurion answers: 'Lord, I am not worthy to have you come under
my roof; but only say the word, and my servant will be healed.'
This is the central feature of the original story, carefully preserved by Matthew, somewhat expanded by Luke. It is difficult to
believe that it was not in John's source too, and his version of it
is the poorer for omitting it. Like the original, he keeps to an
act in two stages: (a) the approach to Jesus and his response;
(b) the renewed approach and the healing by word of command.
But he substitutes a slight rebuff for the willing response of Jesus,
and so the second approach has to be a repetition of the first,
losing all the interest in the centurion's answer in the Synoptic account. Technically it serves the same purpose, which is to lead on
to a finer quality of faith. But in the Synoptic story this quality
of faith is produced voluntarily by the centurion himself, whereas
in John it has to be evoked by Jesus putting the man to the test.
The slight rebuff employed is similar to the marriage at Cana
(2.4) and to the Syrophoenician woman (Mk 7.27). It really
amounts to a refusal to do anything; the man must believe without seeing any action taken.

signs and wonders: a conventional expression (only here in
John) for the great acts of God in redemption (e.g. Dt. 4.34) and
in apocalyptic contexts (e.g. Mt. 24.24). It is applied to the works
of Jesus (Ac. 2.22) and to comparable acts of the Apostles (Ac.
2.43; 5.12; etc.; 2 C. 12.12), as signs of the new age; so they are
guarantees of the messianic claims about Jesus, and grounds for
belief in him. John does not deny this, but it is his thesis that the
Signs belong to the incarnate life, and thereafter they will not be
required for faith (but cf. 14.12). At the close of the book he
commends faith without sight (20.29, 31). So here Jesus demands
of the official the kind of faith which John hopes that his readers
will attain. Bultmann even suggests that John is deliberately correcting the more naïve view of the earlier tradition.

49. As we should expect, John does not show the official rising
immediately to the faith which Jesus requires. But he heightens
the narrative by stressing the urgency. With such a long distance

to traverse, speed is essential, and Jesus seems bent on delay. The word **child** (*paidion*) is a diminutive form of 'boy' (*pais*), used either for variation or for emotive effect.

50. Jesus acts more quickly than the official could have thought possible. It is enough, as the original story maintained, that Jesus 'only say the word'. The word **Go** (*NEB*: 'return home') probably comes from the source; cf. Mt. 8.13. But whereas there it is the word which confirms the centurion's faith already expressed, here it creates the demand for faith, and the officer at last rises to the occasion, achieving faith without sight, and so goes as he has been bidden. The situation is comparable to the story in *B. Berakoth*, 34b. This tells how Rabban Gamaliel sent two disciples to Rabbi Hanina b. Dosa, to ask him to pray for his son who was ill. After praying awhile upstairs, Hanina came down and said to them, 'Go, for the fever has left him' (cf. verse 52). After he had explained to them how he could achieve such certainty in his prayers, they noted down the time and returned to Gamaliel, and found that the boy had recovered at that precise moment (full text in Barrett, p. 208).

your son will live: lit. 'lives'. It is a declaration, rather than a promise, and is repeated in verses 51 and 53, thus giving it great emphasis. For this word as an expression for recovery from sickness, cf. 1 Kg. 17.23; Num. 21.8 (referred to in 3.14f.); Mk 5.23; in an ethical sense Lk. 10.28. It has been deliberately chosen to point to the fulfilment of the promise of life already given in the discourse with the Samaritan woman. It thus carries with it the larger sense of salvation, or eternal life, which is the point of John's insertion of this story here.

believed the word: the conversation ends with the official's acceptance of Jesus' **word,** which has had a healing and creative effect. This is the true kind of belief, by contrast with verse 48.

The story is really at an end. What follows is only to give confirmation of his belief, for the benefit of the reader.

51. his servants met him: 'The reason why the father does not simply confirm the healing on his return home, but has to be told the news of the cure on the way by his servants, is that they cannot know the reason for the cure and are thus beyond suspicion as witnesses' (Bultmann, p. 208).

son: This is the reading of P[66c] D and some other MSS. and versions, but probably 'boy' (*pais*) should be read here (so *NEB*).

52. If, as has been suggested above, we are now dealing with a Johannine elaboration of the original story, it may well be that he has incorporated a feature drawn from some other source, not necessarily a tradition about Jesus at all. At this point the similarity to the rabbinic story is very impressive, not only the precision concerning the hour, but also the unexpected words: 'the fever left him', which introduce a specification of the illness omitted before. Both stories may ultimately go back to the same original, which was probably not identical with the tradition about Jesus which lies behind verses 46–50 and the Synoptic story. But see the note on **the fever** below.

began to mend: Hoskyns remarks that the colloquial English 'got better' would be a more accurate rendering, because the Greek aorist tense implies complete recovery all at once. The *RSV* and *NEB* translations are a mistaken attempt to reproduce the comparative in the Greek *kompsoteron*.

yesterday at the seventh hour: i.e. about 1 p.m. on the previous day. Cana is about 17 miles from Capernaum, so it is not impossible that the two parties should not meet until after sundown, especially if they waited until the heat of the day was past before setting out; alternatively both could have delayed until the next morning. But we cannot be sure that John knew the distance between the two places, and this is the kind of detail which is invented for verisimilitude rather than preserved in the various stages of transmission unchanged.

the fever: besides the rabbinic parallel, there is an exact parallel to the Greek text in the story of the healing of Peter's mother-in-law, which comes immediately after the story of the centurion in Matthew (Mt. 8.15). This suggests yet another possibility of the filling out of one story with details from another. Such permutations are frequent in the oral transmission of folk-lore. The fusion of two similar stories will be postulated again when we deal with the next chapter.

53. household: a word from the vocabulary of Christian mission; cf. Ac. 10.2; 11.14; 16.15, 31–4; 18.8; Rom. 16.5; 1 C. 1.16; Phm. 2. The servants have confirmed the official's faith, but in so doing have themselves discovered faith. So the missionary motive of verse 42 is recalled.

54. the second sign: this must belong to the source, as it does not take cognizance of the signs in Jerusalem (verse 45), or even

suggest that he has visited the city since the marriage at Cana.
The new life which Jesus came to bring has been impressively displayed, and the first act of the drama of the ministry of Jesus is
ended.

THE LIFE-GIVING WORD OF JESUS AND THE
QUESTION OF HIS AUTHORITY 5.1–47

An analysis of this chapter has been given in the Introduction
(pp 53f.), as an example of John's literary technique. It is the
clearest specimen of his characteristic style. A healing miracle,
drawn from traditional sources (verses 1–9a), serves as the basis
of a brief dialogue, which introduces the real point to be considered (9b–18). In this case Jesus' action has involved a breach
of the divine ordinance of the Sabbath, and this raises the whole
question of the relation of his work to the will of God. The Jewish
authorities naturally feel that he cannot be a true servant or
agent of God if he breaks God's law. Jesus defends himself by
asserting that God himself is above the Law, and that what he
has done is God's work, and is therefore above reproach, in spite
of being a formal breach of the Law. This puts Jesus on the side of
God over against men. Such a provocative claim is bound to
arouse hostility (verse 18). The discourse which follows works out
the implications of Jesus' position.

Various issues are treated successively, and it looks as if the
opening miracle, the Sign, has been lost sight of, though in fact
it is in the background all the time. First of all Jesus shows that his
participation in God's work means that he has the divine prerogatives of giving life and acting as judge (verses 19–24). It is easy
to see how the act of healing (especially when we remember the
prominence given to the gift of life in 4.46–54) is a hint of the
first of these prerogatives, although the connection is not explicitly
stated. Next Jesus shows how his present work already anticipates
the future exercise of these prerogatives, especially that of judgment (25–9). Here again the connection with the Sign does not
come to the surface, but the act has necessitated a decision to
override the Sabbath of God, which means that Jesus has already
anticipated this prerogative in one sense. After this Jesus leaves
the subject of his part in God's work, and turns to the evidence

for it (30–47). Again the Sign is not mentioned as such, but the drift of the argument shows that, as a divine act, it is part of God's own testimony that what Jesus claims is true. Finally, in a kind of appendix to the discourse which is held over for a future occasion, Jesus returns to the basic point that the work of God fulfils the true purpose of the Sabbath, even when it necessitates a formal breach of it (7.15–24). But even this does not quite exhaust the discussion. The question whether Jesus' claims really are substantiated by God himself, treated in verses 30–47, turns on men's capacity to recognize that God is his Father in a unique sense. So this part of the discourse is recalled in 8.13–20, which leads into a fresh discourse occupying the rest of that chapter.

It is evident from the above brief précis that chapter 5 is only the beginning of a much larger and more sustained, and far more complex, argument than we have met with so far. It takes us into the great central section of the book, which is generally found to be the most difficult part to understand. It is the section in which John is working out his understanding of the relation of the historical Jesus to the one true God. His work is perhaps tentative and fumbling, gyrating around its themes rather than presenting them logically; but it is also creative and inspiring, paving the way for the more polished and assured pieces of the second edition of his book—the Prologue and chapters 6 and 11.

It has been mentioned that 7.15–24 belongs to the same range of material, and this raises the question whether the book is in its proper order as we now have it. Various suggested rearrangements have been considered in the Introduction (pp. 48–50). Bernard's may be taken as typical, being followed by a number of modern commentators: he places chapter 6 before chapter 5; 7.15–24 immediately follows 5.47, and 7.1–14, 25–end comes after that. This neatly solves a number of problems. As the material stands, nothing is said of Jesus' return to Galilee before 6.1; the transposition of the chapter avoids this difficulty, because Jesus is already in Galilee (4.54). The rearrangement of chapter 7 then brings together the material which obviously belongs to chapter 5 before Jesus returns to Galilee (7.1), and also produces a very attractive connection between 7.14 and 7.25f. on Jesus' public teaching. It may be useful to set beside this Bultmann's rearrangement. He also places chapter 6 before chapter 5; then the order of verses is: 5.1–18; original form of 7.19–24; 5.19–47; 7.15–18; later form of 7.19–24; 8.13–20. He is thus less interested in sorting out the present confusion than in recovering the original discourse.

These proposals are open to two objections: (a) In detail, though it must be confessed that 6.1 is awkward, it can mean a move from Jerusalem just as well as a move from Cana (probably it originally meant a move from Capernaum, however); 7.15 follows badly on 5.47, because of the harsh change of nuance of the Greek *grammata* in both verses; on the other hand, it fits in admirably after 7.14, so that 15–24 becomes a sample of the teaching which arouses the ensuing discussion. (b) In general, transpositions may not be impossible, and indeed it has already been argued that 2.13–22 has been transferred by John from chapter 12. But they are either purposeful or accidental; if the latter, they should surely give a more obviously confused impression than is the case here; but if they are purposeful, they belong to one or other of the stages of composition, and must be treated with due seriousness.

According to the two-stage theory of composition adopted in this commentary, the facts can be explained as follows: The original edition did not include chapter 6, but chapters 5, 7 and 8 were virtually in their present form. 7.15–24 is not the continuation from 5.47, but supplementary material, rather like 3.16–21, 31–6, going back to the start of the discourse rather than following from the end of it (7.15 is a link verse for its *present* context). John has used it to open up the Christological theme of chapter 7, for which he has no appropriate Sign in his stock of traditions. Similarly 8.13–20 resumes another issue of chapter 5—the witness of the Father (5.37)—as the basis of a further discourse, which continues from chapter 7 without a break. But this time the connection is not so close as to suggest that this is another piece of the discourse of chapter 5. It seems rather to have been composed for its present position, but with the deliberate intention of expounding a theme of chapter 5 at greater length. Finally, the independent homily of chapter 6 was inserted into its present position for the second edition. John's decision to do this, in spite of the fact that it damages the connection between chapters 5 and 7, was certainly no accident. Chapters 2–4 took place at Passover time, and in 6.4 the next Passover is 'at hand'. It was thus desirable to have at any rate one feast (chapter 5) in between. But a later position, e.g. after chapter 8, would have brought it too close to the *final* Passover. Furthermore, the narrative material of chapter 6 in its present position roughly corresponds with the sequence in Mark, a sequence which may have been beginning to take shape independently of Mark's written gospel.

Much the most important consideration, however, and one which makes the present position of chapter 6 the only right one, is the thematic connection with chapter 5. It is a full-scale example, and the only one which John has given us, of the important assertion that Moses 'wrote of' Jesus (5.46). It is a chapter which is concerned with the witness of scripture to Christ to a degree far greater than is generally recognized.

A PARALYSED MAN HEALED ON THE SABBATH   5.1–18

The discourse is introduced by a healing miracle from John's stock of tradition. It was argued in the Introduction (p. 53) that this is a fusion of two distinct stories. Whether the amalgamation is due to John himself, it is difficult to say. But if so, his motive is not far to seek. He needs for his purpose a miracle set in Jerusalem, and it has got to raise the issue of Sabbath observance. He has at his disposal a suitable tradition connected with a well-known pool in Jerusalem. Although the details will present us with perplexing problems, this is in fact another case of excellent topographical knowledge. But, in order to bring in the Sabbath motif, he has resorted to a range of Galilean material which has been preserved for us in Mk 2. The verbal similarity between 5.8–9a and Mk 2.9, 11–12a is so close that it can scarcely be doubted that an almost identical source lies behind them both. Now the whole sequence of Mk 2.1–3.6 seems to be based on a collection of traditions about Jesus all on the theme of his controversy with the Pharisees. This makes it possible that, instead of having in his stock only isolated sayings and stories which have Synoptic counterparts, John had in this case some little collection almost identical with the source of Mark at this point. A further glance at this section of Mark shows that we have already encountered several of its contents. On purification in 3.25, 29, we found the justification for Jesus' attitude in Mk 2.15–17, and comparable imagery in Mk 2.18–19. On the symbolism of the marriage at Cana, we found a link with the same paragraph, Mk 2.19 and 22. Now we look to the next two paragraphs, Mk 2.23–8 and 3.1–6, and we discover the final link in the chain. For neither the Jerusalem story nor the story of Mk 2.1–12 have included mention of the Sabbath, which John suddenly produces at verse 9b, and makes the basis of the discourse. It is very likely that he has taken it over from this other material in the collection.

The transition from story to discourse is effected by means of a dialogue, which appears to owe nothing to the source. In fact it is so strongly reminiscent, both in tone and in content, of the much longer cross-examination of the man born blind in chapter 9, that it can hardly be doubted that it is John's own free composition.

It thus seems that the story is made out of several different ingredients, and it may be objected that it is too homogeneous to have such a fragmentary origin. Brown in particular is impressed by the realism of the character of the man who is healed, and argues that he is no mere representative figure, like Nicodemus in chapter 3. But it is difficult to avoid subjective impressions in this kind of matter. Neither verse 7 nor 11—the only verses where the man himself speaks—have any necessary emotional colouring; they are simply statements of fact. The only thing that makes an inevitable impression—and that an unpleasant one—is the information about his apparent ingratitude in telling the Jews about Jesus. But this can be interpreted differently, and in any case is an absolutely necessary manœuvre to prepare for verses 16f. The characterization, such as it is, belongs to John's handling of the dialogue, and does not come from the sources. Lying behind these traditions there are several healing miracles—the Jerusalem healing of John's special material, the paralytic and the Sabbath healing of the material also preserved in Mark. John's amalgam is historical in the sense that it is typical of the kind of thing that Jesus was doing according to these traditions. But that it is an amalgam shows through in the poor workmanship of fitting them together. The Jerusalem-setting is entirely unnecessary to the actual healing in verse 8, which, to make sense of it, ought to have been an instruction to enter the pool at the right time unaided. On the other hand there has been no preparation for the central feature, that he carried his own pallet. It has to be assumed that he had one, which he either kept permanently by the pool, or else found someone to carry for him, in spite of the fact that he had no friend to take him to the pool. Contrast the Marcan story, where it is an essential feature from the beginning. So also the Sabbath is added in as an afterthought: contrast Mk 2.23; 3.2. Such clumsiness is not characteristic of John; in the last chapter we noticed how every detail of the introductory setting was necessary to the following narrative (4.5–7). The conclusion can only be that in 5.2–9 John is redacting his sources with the minimum of rewriting, contrary to his general practice.

1. a feast: the verse is editorial; cf. 2.13. The omission of the article before **feast** is unexpected, but is definitely the right read-

ing (P⁶⁶ P⁷⁵ B A D G W Θ and Ferrar group). Barrett says it
is intentionally vague. Those who transpose chapter 6 to precede
this chapter naturally take it to mean the Passover (Bernard,
Bultmann, Sanders), but this would require the article (א C
Lake group and most later mss.). One ms. actually adds 'of the
Passover', another adds 'Tabernacles'. If chapter 6 is not transposed, *the* feast would certainly mean Tabernacles, as the principal
festival of the year, in Jewish usage; or perhaps the *Rōsh ha-
Shānāh* (New Year), which shortly preceded it (so Westcott,
Guilding, Marsh). This coincides with the beginning of the
autumn rains (cf. p. 213 below). But, accepting the text as it
stands, we have really no right to specify the feast; one can only
guess that, as the next feast after the Passover of 2.13, it *might* be
Pentecost (Chrysostom, Epiphanius among the Fathers; see the
discussion in Brown (p. 206) and the remarks in the Introduction,
p. 46).

2. Now there is: anecdotal opening, cf. 1.6.

the Sheep Gate: this is where the difficulties begin. The word
Gate is not in the text, and has been supplied by the translator
from Neh. 3.1, 32; 12.39, where the whole phrase occurs. This gate
was at the NE. corner of the Temple area, somewhere near the
site of the present St Stephen's Gate, and got its name from the
fact that sacrificial animals were brought in this way. The trouble
is that the word for **Sheep** (*probatikē*) is adjectival, and the same
gender as **pool** (*kolumbēthra*), and many mss. make them agree as
adjective and substantive (both, then, having *iota*-subscript of the
dative case). Thus, whereas the *RSV* assumes the text to be 'there
is . . . by the Sheep—a pool called . . .', the other reading would
be 'there is . . . by the Sheep Pool what is called . . .', the phrase
'what is called' no longer having a noun with which to agree.
Obviously we have to supply 'pool', and so we have the rather
strange designation 'by the Sheep Pool a pool called . . .', as if the
latter could only be identified by the better-known Sheep Pool
nearby. Jeremias (*The Rediscovery of Bethesda. John* 5.2 (1966), p. 10)
has shown that all interpreters took it this way, and no one
thought of supplying 'gate' to ease the sense, until well into the
Middle Ages. This seems decisive support for the more difficult
rendering, which then has to be taken to mean 'by the Sheep Pool
a *place* called . . .' (so Barrett, Brown, Jeremias, *NEB*). But we
must take into account the fact that no one *thought* of supplying

'gate', as this is not a word like 'month' or 'day' which one would naturally omit by universal convention. Without it there is bound to be a tendency to take 'Pool' as the noun which goes with **sheep** for anyone who has a feel for Greek, in spite of the fact that the following phrase then becomes almost barbarous (cf. *BDF* § 412.2). **Gate** is therefore to be accepted as the correct *interpretation*, and its omission is to be attributed to the colloquial usage which goes with personal familiarity with the site. The reading of ℵ* ('there is a sheep pool, what is called Beth-zatha'), though favoured by Holtzmann, is an attempt to cope with the difficulty of the text. **Beth-zatha:** this comes as a surprise to readers familiar with the Bethesda of the *AV* (so *NEB*). The question of the true name of the pool is even more complex and difficult to decide than the last one. Transliterated names always give rise to endless variations in the mss., and frequently cannot be turned back into the underlying Aramaic with any certainty.

We can group all the variants under the two forms just given. (a) **Beth-zatha** ℵ 33 e l; *Belzetha* D a r[1]. This must be the same as *Bezetha* of Josephus *BJ* II. 328, 530; v.151, 246, and as *Beth-zaith* (or *Bezeth* or *Baithzeth*) of 1 Mac. 7.19. This certainly denotes the suburb N. of the Temple area, but it could either have given its name to the pool or taken it from it. Turning it back into Hebrew, it would seem most natural to take it as 'house of olives' (*Bēt-zait*), but Hoskyns and Sanders argue for an Aramaic *Bēt-sētā'* ('house of sheep') but not very convincingly, and Barrett suggested 'new house' (Heb. *Bait ḥādāš*) after Josephus' designation of it in Greek as 'the new city' in *BJ* II.530; v.151. Lagrange prefers the form *Bezetha*, which might represent an Aramaic word for 'ditch'. (b) **Bethesda** C A Θ Lake and Ferrar, later Greek mss., Syriac and some Old Latin; *Bethsaida* P[75] B W Vulgate, Coptic; *Bedsaida* P[66]. *Bethsaida* is clearly assimilation to the better-known name, but probably supports *Bethesda*. This is generally taken to be an equivalent of 'house of mercy' (this is explicit in the Syriac), but *could* be Barrett's 'new house' by metathesis of two letters (*Bethedsa* for *Bethesda*). However *Bethesda* has received dramatic, if doubtful, support from the Copper Scroll from Qumran, where Milik reads the name of a pool as *Bēt 'Ešdātayin* (3Q15 xi.12). The *-tayin* ending is the dual form, which suggests a double pool (see next note). Milik connects the *'Ešdā-* component with a Semitic root *'šd* = 'to flow'. Hence the whole name means 'house of the two springs'. It should be noted that, though this root is common in Syriac, the Syriac translators appear not to have thought that the Greek was a transliteration of it (taking it as *Bēṯ-ḥesḏā'* instead of *Bēṯ-'esḏā'*), though their own version may have been guided entirely by symbolical considerations ('house of mercy' fits the place as one where men are healed). But, impressive as it is, the evidence of the Copper Scroll can only be accepted cautiously, because the transcription is not absolutely certain and the identification with the pool of which John is speaking here lacks confirmation.

What is the solution of the problem? There can be no doubt that the pool was situated in the district known as **Beth-zatha** or *Bezetha*, and that, although it was *also* referred to as 'the new town' (so Jos. *BJ* II.530; v.151 is misleading), the meaning was 'house of olives', probably because there had formerly been orchards there. *If* the Copper Scroll evidence is valid, the name of the pool within this area was *Bethesda*, perhaps meaning 'house of two springs', but not 'house of mercy'. If it is *not* valid, *Bethesda* lacks external evidence as the name of the pool, which may be intended to be the same as that of the district. The question cannot be decided simply by text-criticism. Originally only one name stood in the text, either Beth-zatha or Bethesda. The bifurcation came about because *z*, *ds* and *sd* tend to interchange in transliterations. It would seem likely that *Bethesda* (whatever it means) is original, but the name of the pool was corrupted by this means at a very early stage into the better-known name of the district in which it was situated.

five porticoes: the site is in the grounds of the church of St Anne in the Bezetha district, though recent excavations show that the pool was actually no longer in use in the time of Jesus. The double pool was man-made as a kind of reservoir, 315 feet long, and 220 feet wide at one end, tapering to 165 at the other, divided into two by a partition. There were colonnades on the four sides and along the central divide, thus exactly corresponding with John's brief description. As it is on high ground, it is improbable that it was fed by perpetual springs, but it could have been fed by temporary springs in the rainy seasons. This would explain the phenomenon mentioned in verse 7 (but it cannot decide the feast of verse 1, as that is editorial). The five porticoes are thus a prominent identifying feature of the pool, and there is no need to indulge in the fanciful and irrelevant patristic exegesis, which saw in them the five books of the Law.

3. paralysed: lit. 'dried up' (*xēros*), not quite the same as *paralutikos*, which is actually added here by D, presumably to bring it into line with the Synoptic story where this word is used. There may be no difference of meaning between them, though one might expect *paralutikos* to refer to muscular weakness and *xēros* to visible disablement. In fact John does not tell us what the man's illness was (verse 5), and it is only the similarity to the Synoptic story which makes us assume paralysis.

3b, 4. These verses are relegated to the margin because they have insufficient textual support: they are missing from the Egyptian group, which includes some of the most important of our witnesses (notably ℵ and B), and also from P⁶⁶ and P⁷⁵; but D and W have 3b without 4. Brown thinks that 3b, *waiting for the moving of the water,* is original, and has been accidentally lost from the Egyptian texts. Others take this to be the first stage in elaborating the text by an allusion to verse 7 (though the vocabulary is different), in order to explain the presence of the sick folk. Then verse 4 is, on any showing, an explanation of the explanation, again dependent on verse 7, but this time in all probability misunderstanding it: *the moving of the water* is likely to be the bubbling up of intermittent springs below the water level; this is explained in verse 4 in terms of popular demonology, the *angel of the Lord* being the supposed unseen agent of the phenomenon. But the idea that its curative property is limited to the *first* to reach the disturbed water may be a false deduction: verse 7 may only mean that the man is crowded out, so that he cannot reach it before it has subsided, and so (according to the belief) lost its potency for healing. On this interpretation the presence of a multitude of invalids is an essential detail for the story.

5. thirty-eight years: the circumstantial detail, which John may have found in his source, makes the subsequent healing seem more remarkable (and to modern minds less credible); cf. Mk 5. 25 (twelve years). As it is not the conventional forty, it has naturally attracted speculation, as numbers always do. Apart from 1 Kg. 16.29 and 2 Kg. 15.8 (merely comparative dates), thirty-eight years only occurs in the OT at Dt. 2.14 as an item in the chronology of the wanderings of the Children of Israel, and so another flight of fancy presents itself to those who think that numbers must always have meanings.

6. knew: it is not clear whether Jesus is supposed to have made enquiries, or to have known the truth from his supernatural insight (cf. 1.48; etc.)—probably the former, as John is here sticking close to his source.

7. It is possible to imagine that Jesus' question has been prompted by the fact that this man has made no attempt to reach the water when it last bubbled up. His reply will then appear to be quite dignified and free from bitterness. The answer is: 'Yes, but experience has taught that it is hopeless to try.' **Sir:** cf. 4.11.

put: the verb (*ballein*) properly means 'to throw', but is here used in the weakened sense common in colloquial and later Greek.

8–9a. It has been argued above that these verses are taken from another source, which included much the same material as is found in Mk 2.

Rise, take up your pallet, and walk: word for word the same as Mk 2.9 (a very few MSS. have 'go home' for **walk,** as in Mk 2.11, probably by assimilation to it). The next words are almost identical with Mk 2.12, except that **the man was healed** replaces Mark's 'he rose', probably in order to recall the question of Jesus in verse 6. As will be seen in verse 10, the whole point of using this other material is so as to represent the man as carrying his pallet, i.e. doing something that is forbidden on the Sabbath day. We can only guess how the Jerusalem story finished. No doubt it would be quite similar, at least including an instruction to get up and walk. It is only the feature of picking up the pallet which seems unnecessary for it, though it is vital for John's purpose. But of course it is scarcely likely that it would have been expressed in words which so extremely closely follow the Marcan story. We can get an idea of how it might have continued from the very similar story, also set in Jerusalem, in Ac. 3.1–10, especially verses 6f. Contrast Ac. 9.33f., where the bed is the main motif.

pallet: Gr. *krabatos*, the poor man's bed, another colloquial expression. In the NT it is used only in Mk 6.55; Ac. 5.15; 9.33, apart from the several occurrences in Mk 2.1–12 and in the present passage (Matthew and Luke both take pains to avoid the word in their versions of the Marcan story).

9b. the sabbath: this essential piece of information is brought in by John only at the end of the tale in exactly the same way in 9.14. In neither case can it be regarded as a true part of the story itself. Of course the issue which is raised is one of the best attested in the Gospel traditions; cf. (besides Mk 2.23–3.6) Lk. 13.10–17; 14.1–6.

10. the Jews: as usual in these dialogues, this means the Temple authorities.

carry: the whole phrase comes directly from the source material in 8–9a. Bultmann says that the original motive for this feature in the healing story was to give proof of the miracle, but he does not allow for its true function in the Marcan story (in the crowded room it would have to be moved aside at the very least). But this is quite irrelevant here. John has taken over this feature with no other purpose than to provide the occasion for the objection in this verse. The actual law of the Sabbath (Ex. 20.8–11 (= Dt. 5.12–15)) does not specify the carrying of burdens, but it is already a definite rule in Jer. 17.21 and Neh. 13.19. Naturally the Mishnah tractate *Shabbath* gives elaborate rules (the *halākhōth*, or rabbinic decisions on the subject); in vii.2 the carrying of a burden is given as the last of a series of thirty-nine classes of work; in x.5 a couch may be carried if it is to transport an invalid on an errand which could in any case be performed on the Sabbath, but not otherwise—not even to carry out a dead man.

11. The man . . . said to me: cf. 9.11. Rather in the style of a rabbinic disputation, the healed man sets against the halakhic ruling of verse 10 the ruling of another authority—Jesus himself.

12. Who is the man: the Greek *anthrōpos* here might be contemptuous (so Bernard), but this is improbable. It is a serious request for information, because it appears that Jesus claims authority to dispense people from the accepted rulings. There is no hint as yet that Jesus' *act of healing* involves a breach of the Sabbath, as happens in the Synoptic stories, though this will be raised in verse 16 and 7.21–4.

13. As in chapter 9, the healed man is cross-questioned in the absence of Jesus. It seems to be a device of John's, whereby the deeper issue arising from the healing is brought into the centre of interest first, and then Jesus comes back into the picture to make a theological pronouncement about it.

14. you are well: the same word as 'healed' (*hygiēs*) in verses 6, 9 and 11. The whole composition keeps closely to the vocabulary-range of the preceding story in typical Johannine style.

sin no more: it was widely held in ancient times that illness and misfortune were divine punishment for sin. The issue is raised in 9.2, and Jesus there opposes the usual view. The words here may reflect the Synoptic story (cf. Mk 2.5 'your sins are forgiven'), where the healing is the proof of the divine forgiveness. But this is by no means certain, especially as we do not know whether the version of the Marcan story which John had in his source contained this feature or not (it is widely held that Mk 2.1–12 itself is a fusion of two stories). It is better to take it that John makes Jesus bring up the subject because of the conventional connection between sin and sickness; but he does so in a way that is not untrue to what we know of Jesus' attitudes. There is no word of blame for the past, but only a concern for the future: the man must take his newly gained health as a spur to strive to live well. What, then, is the **worse** thing he might suffer? It can be taken in a purely individual way, referring to the consequences of sin in a general sense, which (when rightly understood) are more damaging than physical disability; or it can be taken specifically of the eschatological judgment (Barrett compares Lk. 13.1–5). It is probably a mistake to choose between these, for the destiny of the individual and the cosmic eschatological perspective are inextricably united in John's theology. In this verse we have a faint premonition of the two functions of Jesus as Son of Man, which will be considered in the discourse—giving life and executing judgment.

15. told the Jews: this always seems ungrateful to modern readers, especially after the admonition in the last verse. But it is by no means clear that John imagined that the man was deliberately betraying Jesus to his enemies. He had cited Jesus as his authority for his breach of the Sabbath (verse 11), and the dispute could only be settled by a discussion between Jesus and the Jews; and until that had been done his own position would be ambiguous. Quite apart from the probabilities, however, it is a convenient way for John to bring the composition quickly to the point where the discourse can begin.

16. persecuted: the imperfect verb (*diōkein*, only here and 15.20) may be translated 'began to persecute' (Bernard; cf. *NEB*) or even 'tried to persecute' (Sanders). Whatever the healed man may have thought, the authorities took a very serious view of Jesus' refusal to observe the strict rules of the Sabbath, cf. Mk 3.6. Some MSS. add: 'and sought to kill him', anticipating verse 18.

he did this: the vagueness of the expression leaves it doubtful whether Jesus is to blame for causing someone else to break the Sabbath, or whether his own act of healing contravened it. The story so far would suggest the former, but Jesus' reply in the next

verse implies the latter; cf. 7.23. Possibly John now has the story
which underlies Mk 3.1–6 in mind, for it has supplied him with the
Sabbath motif.

17. It must be assumed that the Jews' 'persecution' of Jesus
meant that they searched for him at once, and having found him
(still in the Temple, perhaps; cf. verse 14) challenged him with
the point at issue. Jesus defends himself by relating his own activity
to the unceasing activity of God himself. It was of course recognized
that, in spite of the Sabbath rest of God in the creation story, his
activity in maintaining the universe continues without intermission;
cf. Ps. 121.4. The distinction is made explicit in *Genesis Rabba*, xi.10,
where R. Phinehas (*c.* A.D. 360) quotes R. Hoshaiah (*c.* 225) as
saying: 'When thou sayest that God rested on this day from all his
works, it means that he rested from work on his world; but he did
not rest from work on the unrighteous and on the righteous.' But the
issue was being discussed much earlier than this, as it is referred to in
a passage of *Exodus Rabba*, xxx.6, which can be dated to *c.* A.D. 95.
Philo has the same point (*Leg. All.* i.5f.; *de Cherub.* 87), under the
influence of Greek philosophy. But the point here is that Jesus
deduces from this fact, which everyone is likely to accept, that he
has himself a right to override the Sabbath. Although the saying
in this verse has no direct parallel in the Synoptic tradition, it
certainly conforms to what we know of Jesus' attitude to the
Pharisaic rules. He goes behind the *halākhāh* to the original divine
command (cf. Mk 10.2–9). The argument here is that the Sabbath
does not stop God's work, and therefore the obligation may be set
aside that God's work may be done. This seems to be the point
of the non-canonical saying preserved in the Greek text of Codex
Bezae (D) at Lk. 6.5: 'On the same day he saw someone working
on the Sabbath, and said to him: "Man, if you know what you
are doing, you are blessed; but if you do not know, you are
accursed and a transgressor of the law." ' But, as so often, what
appears to be a general statement in Jesus' teaching, in John's
handling of it becomes a Christological affirmation. It is not just
that 'the sabbath was made for man, not man for the sabbath',
but that 'the Son of man is lord even of the sabbath' (Mk. 2.27f.).
Whether these two sayings belonged together in the underlying
tradition, and how we should interpret 'the Son of man' in the
second one, are both disputed questions among scholars. But it
may well be that the second one was known to John, as he goes on

to speak of the functions of the Son of Man in the ensuing discourse. Thus, while John confirms the principle that God's work
may override the Sabbath, he puts it in the form of a personal
claim on the part of Jesus: *'My* **Father . . . and** *I* **am working.'**
His authority (cf. verse 12) derives from his special relation to the
Father, and the fact that health has resulted from the exercise of
it is proof that this is no empty boast.

18. his Father: Gr. *idion*—i.e. *his own* Father, in contrast with
the sense in which God is the Father of all men.

equal: this is the implication of what Jesus has said, for the expressions 'My Father is working still' and 'I am working' are
completely parallel. Nothing could be more provocative to Jews
who did not accept his claim. It was not only the ultimate folly
to put oneself on a level with God, but absolute blasphemy, and
it is understandable that **the Jews sought all the more to kill
him** (cf. Mk 14.64). It is unlikely that the policy of Jesus really
involved this claim in quite such a simple way. But that it was
possible for people to assume that his exercise of religious authority
implied such a claim is already implicit in the Marcan account of
the healing; cf. Mk 2.7–10. This again suggests a connection
between John's source and Mark (but note the caution expressed
in the note on verse 14). The situation is certainly parallel. Jesus
takes an initiative which belongs to God. It is assumed that this
implies a divine claim, and so is regarded as blasphemy. The
evangelist (both Mark and John) is aware of the irony of the situation, for he knows that the claim is true, and that therefore no
blasphemy is involved. It is probable that this kind of argument
reflects the dispute between Church and synagogue *arising from*
Jesus' attitudes to the Jewish Law.

DISCOURSE ON THE AUTHORITY OF JESUS **5.19–47**

The rest of the chapter is a monologue, expounding the saying in
verse 17. The issue of the Sabbath is left on one side. Jesus is
concerned only with defending his saying as it has been interpreted
in the light of verse 18. His work is equivalent to the Father's,
because the Father has delegated to him his own prerogatives of
giving life and of judging the dead at the end of the age. The
healing of the paralysed man is a token of this function, doing
for one man now what is applicable to all men at all times and to
the end of the world. If there is a hint of the Marcan element of

the divine forgiveness of sins in verses 14 and 18, this may be taken similarly as a token of the function of judgment; alternatively the function of judgment may be considered to have been implicit in Jesus' decision to override the Sabbath.

These two functions belong to the figure of the Son of Man (cf. the notes on 3.14). Thus what Jesus is here describing is his position when he reaches his future glory after the Passion. Thus he speaks for the most part in the third person, in a quite theoretical way, about the work of the Son of Man in the coming crisis. This suggests that he is referring to current speculations about the Son of Man, such as are found in Enoch. However, in two crucial verses (24 and 25), both starting 'Truly, truly', these theoretical reflections are related directly to Jesus himself, and it is precisely in these verses that we are presented with an alteration of the temporal perspective. The discourse changes from consistent futuristic eschatology to present fulfilment in relation to the response to Jesus. As far as the individual is concerned, the final events are anticipated in his response to Jesus. John does not deny the language of futuristic eschatology; but his concern is that it should be intensely real to the reader as a matter of immediate decision. See further, Introduction, pp. 57f.

At verse 30 the first person form is resumed. Here Jesus is not speaking theoretically, but dealing with the proofs that he is the Son of Man who exercises these functions. He begins by recalling verse 19, which is the basic comment on verse 17. If Jesus' work is his Father's work, it must have his authority. From this point of view no human witness is sufficient, not even that of John the Baptist. But the works, such as the healing of the paralysed man, may be adduced as evidence, for they are God's own saving activity. Finally Jesus turns the argument back on the Jews themselves, for they profess to be true to the Scriptures, and yet fail to see that Jesus' works are actual fulfilments of Scripture. If they saw that, they would realize that God had already provided the key to interpreting Jesus through the inspired word of Scripture. Thus the accusation of the Jews is refuted on their own ground. Everything depends on the interpretation of Scripture (again a subject of debate between Church and synagogue). It is not that they have not the proofs before them, but that they have not the will to believe.

The fact that the discourse reflects disputes between Christians and Jews hardly needs demonstration. The theoretical character of much of verses 19–29, and the argument on the interpretation of Scripture in 39–47, strongly suggest such debates. Odeberg has shown that it is permeated with rabbinic diction (see his table of phrases (pp. 232–4)). Barrett draws attention to the reminiscence of passages in Paul which deal with the relation of Christianity to Judaism, notably Rom. 9–11 and Gal. 4, without any suggestion that John may be dependent on Paul. Gächter has attempted to analyse the discourse by separating the first person verses from the third person passages, but this is a mistake, for it is the first person verses which are the key to the argument of the whole. Nor is Brown likely to be right in taking verses 19–25 and 26–30 as doublets—the second being an earlier form presupposing a consistent eschatology, the first revising it in the interests of a realized eschatology—for that is to misunderstand the double polarity of John's eschatology, which is at once future and realized in the person of Christ (cf. J. Blank, *Krisis*, pp. 172–82). It is more fruitful to look for signs of dependence on primitive Gospel sayings of Jesus, which have been worked into a typical Johannine discourse. We shall see some signs of these in the 'Truly, Truly' verses.

The Son performs the Father's work **19–24**

19–20a. In verse 17 Jesus has hinted at a direct relationship between his own work and that of God. The discourse begins by putting this in the form of a general rule. *All* his activity is copied from the Father. Both Dodd and Gächter have independently observed that this general rule may well be an authentic parable of Jesus. If we read **Son** and **Father** without the capital letters, and take the article to be the generic use common in Semitic speech (i.e. 'a son can do nothing . . .'), we have a little picture of an apprenticed son learning his trade in his father's shop, as Jesus himself did at Nazareth; Dodd cites Egyptian papyri which lay down the rule of exact imitation which such apprentices must follow. So Jesus teaches that all his acts are done in obedience to God. This makes an excellent starting-point for the discourse, in which John is going to show that Jesus' imitation of his Father is not confined to the visible acts, such as the healing of the paralytic, but extend to the ultimate acts of redemption. (Perhaps the *same* parable of Jesus lies at the basis of Mt. 11.27 = Lk. 10.22 (cf. J. Jeremias, *New Testament Theology* I, pp. 56–61)).

20b. greater works: this is where John's application of the parable begins. These **greater works** will be described in the next two verses. They will cause men to **marvel,** because what they have so far seen is only a faint shadow of the full scale of the eschatological task which Jesus will perform when he is glorified; cf. verse 28.

21. raises the dead: only God can raise the dead; cf. 2 Kg. 5.7, where death and sickness, life and health, are related in typical Hebrew fashion. Although the stories of Elijah and Elisha contain miracles of raising the dead, Hebrew thought in general did not allow any return from the grave. But in the time of the Maccabean revolt the idea that the martyrs would not lose their reward was beginning to be established; cf. 2 Mac. 12.44. Dan. 12.2 speaks of a general resurrection at the end of the age, with final judgment. By NT times the popular belief in personal resurrection was strongly upheld by the Pharisees (cf. Ac. 23.6–9), for which there is abundant rabbinic evidence. So the second of the Eighteen Benedictions reads: 'Thou, O Lord, art mighty for ever, thou quickenest the dead, thou art mighty to save' (Singer, *Authorised Daily Prayer Book*, p. 44).

gives life to whom he will: this divine prerogative is to be delegated to the Son of Man. **whom he will** sounds arbitrary (for this reason the Old Syriac version has substituted 'those who believe on him' from 3.16), but Jesus is still speaking of the present anticipation of the end: it means that those who are healed, or raised to life, by Jesus are selected examples of what is to be universal at the end of the age. This final perspective will become explicit in verses 25–9. There may be a hint here of the raising of Lazarus (so Sanders), but as on other grounds it is likely that chapter 11 belongs to the second edition of the Gospel, it is probably better to leave the reference vague. We should not forget the thrice repeated 'your son will live' in 4.46–54.

22. judges no one: God is 'the Judge of all the earth' (Gen. 18.25). The idea is frequent in contexts which speak of his universal dominion, e.g. Ps. 82.8, and therefore in eschatological passages, e.g. Jl 3.1–3. The heavenly court is thought of as a great assize in apocalyptic visions, often very vividly imagined. Such is the setting of the vision of the Son of Man in Dan.7. It is much elaborated in the Similitudes of Enoch (1 Enoch 37–71), introducing a feature which is important for our present passage, that the function of judging is delegated to the Son of Man. So here, when it is said that God **judges no one,** it must be taken to mean that, though this function properly belongs to him alone, he delegates it to the Son in the final act of history. According to the usual ideas of the apocalyptic programme, the resurrection of the dead precedes the judgment (cf. Rev. 20). Thus, just as in the last verse Jesus' acts of healing were regarded as anticipations of his function of raising the dead at the end of the age, so he will perform the task of judgment which follows it, and this too has anticipations in his present activity. In fact Jesus does not exercise this prerogative now (cf. 8.15; 12.47), any more than he raises the dead (for the miracles are selected Signs only, as we have seen). The way in which he does both functions in the present will be explained in verse 24.

23. honour the Son: this is the whole point of the paragraph. Jesus has shown that all his activity is done in direct obedience to the Father. He has also asserted that the Father has delegated to him the divine functions of raising the dead and giving judgment at the last day. It follows that he has the right to the same respect as is due to God himself, and to refuse him this respect is equivalent to refusing respect to God. This is the direct answer to the objection raised by the Jews in verse 18. The idea has frequent parallels in John (cf. 12.44f.; 13.20). But what is more interesting is that it also has Synoptic parallels, which indicates that John is here building his Christology on a deposit of traditional sayings; cf. Mt. 10.40; 18.5; Lk. 10.16. John is thus developing the implications of a striking element in the teaching of Jesus, his consciousness of being the focal point of men's allegiance to God.

24. The two 'truly, truly' sayings in this and the next verse look like doublets, and it is not easy to decide the right point for the division of paragraphs. The first theme of the discourse, that Jesus can rightly 'make himself equal with God', has reached its logical conclusion in the last verse (notice how the Father and Son language of verse 23 picks up the parable of verse 19). The *RSV* paragraphing then takes verse 24 to be a kind of afterthought, rather than the beginning of a new theme. This seems to be right, because it is John's practice to use these sayings either at the beginning or at the end of a paragraph, but he does not string them together. This is very clear at 13.20f., the only other place where they come in two adjacent verses. This means that, if the present verse is an appendix to verses 19–23, we must see the connection chiefly in the words **he who hears my word and believes him who sent me.** This is evidently yet another variant of the traditional saying underlying verse 23, this time showing most affinity with Mk 9.37. As 'truly, truly' sayings generally preserve traditional material, this verse, along with the parable of 19–20a, must be regarded as the scaffolding of the rest of the paragraph. True to the underlying teaching, it is an assertion that the final decision does not have to wait until the last day. A man's fate can be decided in advance by his response to Jesus now. There can be enjoyment of **eternal life** already, as if the general resurrection had already taken place, and the future **judgment** can be regarded as already past. This is not a thoroughgoing realized eschatology, as the next verses will show. It is an anticipated eschatology, corresponding with the fact that the future judge is already present in the person of Jesus. Thus the theoretical, third person, statements of verses 21f., become present and immediate in the actual life of Jesus. It is an obvious corollary of this that response to him even after his withdrawal from earthly life continues to have the same meaning for people at all times and places. It is almost the Pauline doctrine of justification by faith, cf. Rom. 8.1.

The coming Judgment 25–9

25. and now is: these words are missing from ℵ* a b, but there can be no doubt that they are a true part of the text. We are at once reminded of 4.23. It may not be possible to identify a traditional saying this time, but these words strike the authentic note of crisis in the present, which is a theme repeated in Jesus' teaching. Thus we have here (a) the **Truly, truly** which opens up the new paragraph, (b) the traditional theme of the crisis in the present, and then (c) the announcement of the theme of the paragraph, which is the general resurrection at the last day.

The whole of this paragraph is concerned with the future in terms of consistent eschatology. Verses 26f. are almost a direct repetition of 21f.; the difference between them is that the last paragraph was dealing with the eschatological functions from the point of view of Jesus' *present* work and the honour which is due to him *now*, whereas this paragraph is concerned with the *future* which Jesus' present work both anticipates and guarantees. Thus the paragraph serves a different purpose from the last one, and they can hardly be regarded as doublets. It reaches its climax in the solemn alternatives of verse 29, and thus is to be taken as a serious warning, similar to 3.18–21.

the Son of God: we should expect 'the Son of man', as in 27. K S and a few other MSS. accordingly make the correction. But John's Christology tends to blur the distinction between the titles. Here the relation of Jesus to the Father is in mind; so that **Son of God** is appropriate—though **of God** is perhaps a very early gloss.

those who hear: Brown observes that the word is used in two senses in this verse. Here it means to obey.

26. life in himself: not quite the same as 1.4, because here it refers in the first place to the self-subsistent being of God, which makes him the author of all life (cf. Gen. 2.7), and in the second place to the Son's derivative capacity to renew the act of creation in the final resurrection. The special idea of the Prologue, that the Word is the agent of God in the creation at the beginning, is omitted, though not contradicted. It should be noted that this is a slightly different formulation of the resurrection from verse 21, to which it is so similar. For there the point of comparison was God's prerogative of raising the dead, whereas here it is the creation. Inasmuch as Jesus' acts are creative now, they anticipate his final function of being the agent of a new act of creation. This verse is, then, timeless, but gives the grounds for the future statements of 28f.

27. judgment: similarly the second function belongs to Jesus, and, as we have seen in 3.17–21, the **judgment** is already taking place. But, exactly the same as with the function of giving life, this present possession of authority is an earnest of the future, and this is the point which John now wishes to stress. So at the end of the verse he opens up the apocalyptic picture of **the Son of man,** here mentioned in the text for the first time in the discourse. This seems to us perfectly natural, as it acts as a kind of code-sign that what is to follow will be a matter of consistent eschatology.

But there are two difficulties. (a) The phrase is unique in John because the article is omitted with both words (*huios anthrōpou* instead of *ho hu. tou an.*), so that it might be taken to mean 'a son of man', i.e. a human being. In this case it would mean that the Father has delegated judgment to the Son because he has experienced the Incarnation, and thus knows the human side as well as the divine side, which could make him strictly impartial. But such considerations never come to the surface in this discourse. Much the more likely explanation is that the verse is a direct allusion to Dan. 7.13f., from which the imagery is derived. For there both LXX and Theodotion have 'son of man' without the article, exactly as here, and LXX has precisely the same words for **has given him authority** (Theodotion has a different word for 'authority'). (b) It seems then that we should not press the notion of humanity in this context, but there is a natural tendency to do so. To the later Greek fathers 'Son of Man' was a phrase to express the humanity of Jesus over against his divinity, as much as it is with many people today. Hence this verse was a crux of interpretation; for the function of final judgment can hardly be regarded as conferred on Jesus by virtue of his humanity, but rather belongs to his divine glory. Accordingly some tried to take these words, very awkwardly, with the next verse (cf. Wiles, pp. 114f.).

28. Do not marvel: cf. verse 20b. Here the progression of thought is reversed. That Jesus should hold such exalted positions *now* is not so surprising when it is understood that he will exercise the full corresponding functions at the last day. So the text goes straight into a completely conventional apocalyptic picture of the resurrection of the dead and the judgment, naïve in its literalism and devoid of John's subtle reinterpretations. It is not surprising that some critics have found it difficult to believe that John himself wrote it; but there is no need to question it. It is not John's purpose to rewrite the conventional doctrines, only to make them absolutely real to the present situation of his readers. When he is speaking simply of the future, he has no need to abandon the usual language, which in any case refers to the future; what he is saying is that those who believe the standard eschatology should not be surprised to find the eschatological functions already in operation (cf. Hoskyns, p. 271). It is no accident that the phrase **the hour is coming** is not followed by 'and now is'; for if he wished to put it in the form which applies to the present, John would have to rephrase it in the terms of verse 24.

29. The ideas are very close to Dan. 12.2; cf. Mt. 27.52f.; Rev. 20.11f. The crude simplicity and literalism of the picture is thoroughly Jewish and owes nothing whatever to Greek thought.

But it is not for this reason impossible that John should have written it. The fact that the present world order is to come to an end, and that Jesus will have the key part to play at that moment, is something he takes for granted. As the present discourse has shown, it is in fact a fundamental presupposition of his Christology.

The Testimony to Jesus' Equality with God 30–47

30. I can do nothing: again this is a verse which hovers between two paragraphs uncertainly. But as it refers back to verse 19 it is better to take it as the opening of a new theme in the discourse, which takes up a different aspect of the original point at issue. The allusion to verse 19 goes back to the beginning by way of the whole argument of the verses in between. Jesus' function of judging (just mentioned at the end of the last verse) does duty also for his function of raising the dead. Both are done in obedience to the Father. The judgment is completely impartial, for it is done without a trace of self-seeking. Jesus is the obedient apprentice of the parable of verse 19, and this justifies the identity between his work and the Father's in the original provocative statement of verse 17. For **the will of him who sent me,** cf. 4.34. The longer phrase here recalls the prayer of Jesus at Gethsemane, especially Lk. 22.42.

31. bear witness: the last verse has brought the thought away from Jesus' functions and back to the Father, but it has not given any indication of the new theme that is now to be tackled. But it is one thing to make the magnificent assertions of verses 19–29, which certainly justify the implied claim of verse 17 if they are true, but quite another to prove them. As they refer to the future in order to justify the present, they cannot provide the proof without further evidence. Jesus begins this vital aspect of the issue by excluding certain possible kinds of evidence as inadmissible. The first is his own testimony. In a passage of the Mishnah dealing with marriage cases, it is stated: 'None may be believed when he testifies of himself', not even when he speaks on oath (*Ketuboth* 2.9). That John is familiar with Jewish legal practice is clear from 8.17. Jesus is speaking *ad hominem*, for of course the word of Jesus is the embodiment of *the* truth, and as such does not rely on any human witness (verse 34); so there is the precise opposite of this verse in 8.13f. But for the moment he is speaking of such witness as the Jews may be expected to accept on their own legal principles.

32. another: intentionally vague, so as to make the hearers curious to know the answer. So far he merely says that he has witness outside himself, such as the Jews would themselves regard as admissible. It is natural to suppose that he means the Baptist (so Chrysostom and some moderns), but it turns out that Jesus has reason to exclude his witness also. Hence it can only be the Father (verse 37), and this explains Jesus' complete confidence in his testimony (so Cyprian and most moderns).

I know: the variant 'you know' (ℵ* D Old Syriac) is probably due to taking **another** to be the Baptist.

33. You sent: referring to the deputation of 1.19. The Baptist's testimony was both negative (refusing the messianic title for himself) and positive (claiming divine inspiration, 1.32f.).

34. Even if the Jews had accepted the Baptist's witness, it would not have been adequate from Jesus' point of view. For the matter requiring proof is the relation of Jesus to the Father, and this cannot rest on the Baptist's surmise (1.34), which goes beyond the inspiration mentioned in 1.33. In the last analysis only God can testify to divine relations, just as only those begotten afresh from God can come to God (3.5f.), and only those who are like God can worship God truly (4.23f.). Jesus cannot accept the witness of men, as that would mean 'that there is a commensurable relationship between human and divine standards' (Bultmann, p. 264). The Baptist's witness served a different purpose. It was a pointer to Jesus as the agent of salvation, so that men might turn to him and be saved. But it was not a proof in the legal sense which is here required.

35. lamp: Gr. *luchnos*. The metaphor is carefully chosen to drive home the point just made. It is not a self-subsistent light (*phōs*), but it is **burning and shining**—i.e. it shines when it is kindled and kept supplied with oil. The small clay lamps of Palestine are well known—like a tiny teapot without a handle; the wick is placed in the spout, and the top open for refilling with oil. The Jews had been attracted (**you** perhaps means Jews in general) when the Baptist first preached, but they were not willing to accept the real consequences of his message. It is probable that the application of this metaphor to the Baptist is derived from the Christian comparison of him to Elijah; cf. Sir. 48.1: 'His word burned like a torch.'

36. greater than that of John: the adjective is predicative

with suppressed comparative (lit. 'greater than John'), which
RSV interprets correctly. According to Moulton, the reading
meizōn in some MSS. is not the nominative, but the accusative
meizō with added *n*, and therefore does not require an alternative
rendering.

the works: obviously one thinks first of the Signs, such as the
healing of the paralytic. They prove Jesus' special relation to the
Father, because they are done with his power and authority and
fulfil his redemptive purpose. Bultmann thinks that the *whole* of
Jesus' activity is meant, not only the Signs, but this seems to me
doubtful. The point is made with considerable emphasis, because
these acts can be cited as evidence quite apart from anything
Jesus may say about himself (cf. verse 31).

37. the Father . . . has himself borne witness: at last we
reach the most convincing evidence of all (cf. verse 32). The rest
of the chapter is concerned with this form of witness. It is not at
first explained in what way the Father has given witness, but it
becomes clear that it is through the Scriptures. Here there should
be common ground with the Jews, for they acknowledge the
Scriptures as the one source of revealed truth.

His voice . . . his form: before coming to this point, Jesus
suggests ways in which God might have been expected to give
witness, only to rule them out. The Jewish rabbis would certainly
agree with Jesus about this—which goes to show once more that
John is familiar with rabbinic reasonings. For in NT times the
theophanies of the OT, e.g. on Mount Sinai, were generally
ascribed to angelic agency (cf. Ac. 7.35), and divine words were
regarded as a *baṭ qōl* (= echo), in order to preserve the divine
transcendence; cf. 1.18. Odeberg makes a great point that Jesus
does not here deny the *baṭ qōl*, and this is surely right; what he
does deny, and what the rabbis would undoubtedly deny too, is
that there could be *direct* sight or hearing of God. It is unlikely
that this verse contains any reference to the experience of Jesus at
his baptism.

38. his word: another possibility for the Father's witness is
that it might be direct inspiration, like the prophets of old, like the
endowment promised for the age to come (Jl 2.28-32, quoted in
Ac. 2.17-21), and like the Christian experience of the Holy Spirit
(16.12-15; 1 Jn 5.10). This is not ruled out *a priori*, but fails in the
present instance because of the Jews' lack of belief.

39. You search the scriptures: this leaves only **the scriptures,** and this should be sufficient, for it is the chief object of rabbinic endeavour. **Search** (Hebrew *dāraš*) is a technical term for rabbinic study (cf. *SB* II.467). The *AV* imperative: 'Search the scriptures!' follows a venerable tradition, going back to Origen and Tertullian, and is perhaps motivated by the desire to avoid the implication that it might be a fruitless search. But it breaks the careful build-up of the argument, and is rejected by all modern commentators (it involves no change in the Greek). Here there is real hope that the Jews might be able to perceive the Father's witness, for they approach the Scriptures in the hope that in them they may **have eternal life,** and the Scriptures are the divinely given **witness to** Jesus. It is thus all the more tragic that even this form of witness fails (verse 47).

in them: the construction in Greek (*hoti . . . en autais*) is quite acceptable, but there is a variant in the quotation of this verse and verse 45 in Fragment 1 verso of B.M. Pap. Egerton 2, which reads *en hais*. Black (p. 73) claims that both these readings go back to an Aramaic original, differently translated in the two versions (the Aramaic particle *d*ᵉ). Barrett denies this, claiming that John is more forceful, and that the papyrus is smoothing out the Greek. We have already come across another fragment of this papyrus, which seems to be part of an unknown Gospel (see p. 149 above). The fragment reads:

> Jesus said to the lawyers: 'Punish every transgressor and lawless man and not me; for if . . . does the law, why does he do it?' Then, turning to the rulers of the people, he said this word: 'Search' (or 'You search') 'the scriptures, in which you think you have life; it is they that bear witness to me. Do not think that I came to accuse you to my Father; it is Moses who accuses you, on whom you set your hope.' When they said: 'We know well that God spoke to Moses, but as for you, we do not know where you come from', Jesus replied: 'Now your unbelief accuses you . . .'

The fragment thus contains verses 39 and 45, and (for the people's saying) an adaptation of 9.29, but appears to be quite alien to John in the opening words. The theory that it is based on John as we know it, rather than on John's source, is that which is most widely held today.

40. The Jews' hope of gaining eternal life from the study of Scripture is bound to fail for the same reason that they do not perceive how it is the divine witness to Jesus himself. This starts a little digression (omitted by the fragment) on the inadequacy of their approach to scriptural exegesis, and this no doubt reflects something of the bitterness about this thorny subject in Jewish and Christian debate. Jesus does not wish for the praise of men, but of God, and if the Jews truly loved God, they would give him due recognition. As it is, they are easily swayed by those who make claims for themselves, and are so concerned to gain a good opinion of themselves from their own colleagues that they neglect to seek for the approval of God. It is implied that, if they were less concerned for their own reputation, they would not make mistakes in their estimate of others, and so would be able to recognize Jesus as God's Son, which is what would really win them approval in God's sight. The argument thus puts the Jews in the wrong on their own terms, and so prepares for the final indictment of verses 45–7. There is ample evidence elsewhere in the NT that the early Christians held that the unbelieving Jews were guilty of culpable blindness in their refusal to accept the christological interpretation of Scripture; cf. Rom. 9–11. Perhaps today we should be less bitter about this issue.

41. glory means in this context praise or good opinion. Jesus is not in the least concerned to win the approval of men, for the witness of Scripture (which is the witness of God) is far better. The words are almost identical with verse 34a.

42. the love of God: does this mean being open to the love which God has for men, so that it may take root in them and give them the capacity to understand the Scriptures rightly (Bernard, Wikenhauser)? Or does it mean having love for God, which is the only right disposition for studying Scripture (Lightfoot, Barrett, Bultmann, *NEB*)? The latter seems to be favoured by the use of this phrase in 1 Jn 2.5, 15; 3.17; 4.12; 5.3, and also suits the context best; cf. verse 44.

43. in my Father's name: Jesus is a teacher come from God. His coming was foretold in Scripture, and now he is in the midst of the rabbis, laden with the vast responsibilities of the Father's delegated power (Barrett sees a reference here to the whole argument from verse 19). If the rabbis approached the Scriptures with the right disposition, they would receive Jesus into their own fraternity as one of themselves, and give him due honour as the supreme teacher and revealer of God.

another: there has been much speculation who this might be. As
it is an alternative to Jesus, most commentators suppose that it
is a reference to false messianic claimants; cf. Mk 13.6, 21f. It
has even been suggested that it might be a specific reference to
Bar Cochba, who led the revolt of A.D. 132–5, and was hailed as
the Messiah; but this would give an impossibly late date for the
composition of the Gospel. Odeberg compares 8.44, and says that
it is a sarcastic allusion to the Devil. But surely these suggestions
take the issue outside its terms of reference. Jesus is speaking of
receiving the praise of men (verse 41). The Jews refuse him,
because of their lack of the right disposition, i.e. love for God.
But **another**—i.e. any other man who makes claims for himself
as a rabbi—they will be prepared to admire and to accept as one
of themselves.

44. glory from one another: this is precisely the point. The
opposition to Jesus comes from a group of teachers who are a sort
of 'mutual admiration society', and have a vested interest in maintaining their own traditions. This sounds harsh, and may be
exaggerated, though it is probable that there is some actual
experience behind John's attack, which may be compared with
Jesus' indictment of the Pharisees in Mt. 23.1–36. The desire to be
admired is the besetting sin of petty officialdom everywhere. It is
much more tragic when it occurs among religious teachers, for it
blinds them to the truth of their appointed task.
the only God: God is missing from P66 P75 B W a b Curetonian
Syriac, Sahidic, some Bohairic texts and some quotations in Origen
and Cyril. This is surprising, as the word is, as Bultmann says,
really indispensable; cf. 17.3. Most commentators assume that it
has been lost by haplography before **not,** which follows in the
Greek (*ou*, with which the abbreviated form of *theou* would be
almost identical). For an opposite view, cf. Sanders, p. 172, n. 4.

45. Having exposed the hypocrisy of the rabbis, which prevents
them from interpreting the Scripture correctly, Jesus now returns
to the main argument, and incidentally the papyrus fragment
continues at this point (see above on verse 39). As Jesus has come
from the Father and the rabbis have refused to accept him (verse
43), he might well be expected to **accuse** them **to the Father.**
It is the metaphor of the law court, but it does not resume the
theme of Jesus' own function as judge of verse 22. This little inconsistency may be allowed, for the idea of Jesus as prosecuting wit-

ness is only brought in as a foil to the real point that the Scriptures themselves contain the indictment.

Moses: as the presumed author of the Pentateuch, the only part of the OT universally accorded canonical status, **Moses** can stand for the Scriptures. But by mentioning the person rather than the book, Jesus can represent the Scriptures as the counsel for the prosecution in the forensic metaphor. The figure of Moses was immensely important to the rabbis, who regarded him as the mediator between God and Israel. They have **set** their **hope on** him in as much as they expend their energy on keeping the Law of Moses, which they regard as the complete revelation of God's will for mankind.

46. The irony of their position is that they do not realize that the Law of Moses is itself the Father's witness to Jesus. It is not easy for us today to see how this is so. John does not mean specific proof texts which may be applied to Jesus; he means something much more fundamental and pervasive. The whole of the Scriptures reveal God and his redemptive purpose for mankind, and this is what is fulfilled in Jesus. In the discourse of chapter 7 John will take up the question of certain proof texts. But that is only one aspect of what is meant here. We should dearly love to have a specimen of the way in which John understood the OT witness to Christ; fortunately, for the second edition of his work, he has provided precisely such an example in his great interpolation of chapter 6, in which the whole issue is treated at length. We generally think of chapter 6 as the discourse on the Bread of Life, but it is much more a discourse on the interpretation of Scripture, as we shall see.

47. The discourse ends with an unanswerable question, and we may assume that the Jews are left speechless. But so many issues have been raised that John continues the disputations in chapters 7 and 8, using some material left over from this discourse. For the purposes of this continuation, it is necessary to make a break, and to bring Jesus back to Jerusalem for another feast (7.1–14). But first chapter 6 must claim our attention.

JESUS IS THE BREAD OF LIFE 6.1–71

After the obscurities of the progression of thought in chapter 5, it is a relief to come to a chapter in which a single theme can clearly be discerned even on a superficial reading of it. Jesus is the Bread of Life: he feeds the hungry multitude; he patiently unfolds in the course of a carefully constructed sermon how he is himself the spiritual food of mankind; and though many of his disciples are offended and forsake him, he wins the enthusiastic allegiance of those who are most close to him. The whole chapter has such a clear internal unity and self-consistency, it is so well balanced and articulated, that it ranks as one of the finest products of John's pen. But at the same time it bears so little relation to the progress of the Gospel as a whole that it seems best to take it as an independent composition, inserted by John into the second edition of his work.

It is not necessary to repeat here the arguments for retaining the chapter in its present position presented in the Introduction and in the introductory remarks to chapter 5. In spite of the fact that very many modern commentators, including even so cautious a scholar as Schnackenburg, place it before chapter 5, the present position of it is peculiarly suitable because of the way in which it serves as an illustration of Jesus' claim in 5.39, 46f. For this is the most biblical section of the whole Gospel. The discourse is not merely a development of the implications of the miracle of feeding with which the chapter opens; on the contrary, that is really a brilliant use of traditional material as an opening gambit for a discourse which is fundamentally an exposition of an OT text— the story of the manna in the Wilderness in Exod. 16. The meaning of that chapter, universally regarded in ancient times as the writing of Moses himself, can be summed up in the words 'He gave them bread from heaven to eat' (verse 31), even though they are more likely to be a quotation of Ps. 78.24 than of a particular verse of Exod. 16 (see below, p. 275). The whole discourse is built on these words, repeating them again and again with subtle variations, until the final verse (58). And the point of the whole argument is that they have a deeper meaning than the historic event of the giving of the manna. They properly refer to the one who has been sent from heaven, and this is none other than Jesus himself. And, whereas the manna was merely for physical sustenance during the desert wanderings, Jesus supplies the means of eternal life. This is the Christian interpretation of Scripture, which the Jews of chapter 5 reject. But, as we shall see when we come to study the discourse in detail, the Christian interpretation does not come like a bolt from the blue, but has been prepared for by the Jewish tradition of exegesis of the manna miracle, which had already been interpreted in terms of the Wisdom of God and his gift of the Law. This tradition is essential to understanding the argument of the discourse, and provides the strongest proof that John was well acquainted with rabbinic teaching.

Lest it be objected that the above is all too simple, it may be well to draw attention now to some of the perplexing problems which we shall have to face in considering the discourse. The relation of the teaching of the discourse to the Christian institution of the Eucharist is much disputed. Closely bound up with this issue there arises the question of the provenance of verses 51–8: Do they really belong to the rest, or have they been added by a later hand? If so, are they part of the missing eucharistic narrative in John's narrative of the Last Supper (chapter 13)? This leads to the further problem of the disciples who withdraw in verse 60. John elsewhere always shows the Jews as the opposition to Jesus; here, and here only, is it his own disciples. What is the reason for their taking offence? How does it relate to the life of the Church? Is 'flesh' in verse 63 to be taken to refer to 51–8 or is it to be interpreted strictly without reference to these verses?

Then there are questions which concern the background of thought of the whole discourse. How does it relate to rabbinic and other Jewish literature? Is it possible to detect a model for the structure of the discourse in Jewish homiletic, or does the influence extend only to the ideas? If the form and structure can be traced to Jewish influence, can the scriptural content be traced to the synagogue lectionary? Is there, perhaps, a danger of over-stressing the Jewish background, and ought we to take into account pagan parallels? Finally, there is the relation of the whole chapter to the Synoptic tradition to be considered. This is clearly going to be an important issue for the two miracles of the Feeding of the Multitude and Walking on the Sea with which the chapter begins. But it also concerns the final part after the conclusion of the discourse, and (to a very slight extent) the discourse itself.

These points will be weighed up as we go along, but it will perhaps be helpful if the views adopted in the commentary are briefly summarized here. John is aware all the way through that the divine gift of the Bread of Life in the person of Jesus has its ceremonial enactment in the Eucharist. Accordingly, verses 51–8 only make explicit an aspect of the subject which has been implicit from the beginning, and may be retained as an integral part of the discourse. They are dependent on the traditions of the Last Supper, but were never part of John's plan of chapter 13. The disciples in verse 60 stand for Christians who have lapsed into heresy in John's own day, just as 'the Jews' represent the contemporary synagogue. The issue is Docetism, but the offence is *not* the provocative 'carnal' language of 51–8, but a more fundamental objection.

The Jewish background is decisive, and pagan parallels have only marginal interest. The discourse has been modelled to some extent on a synagogue homily, following the characteristic form, and the underlying lections can be determined with some confidence (one of them, Exod. 16, for certain). The narrative framework of the whole chapter is dependent on a sequence of Gospel traditions which correspond fairly closely with Mark, but are more likely to be an independent collection which Mark has used as a source. The situation is, then, exactly the same as we found in the case of chapters 2–5, where John evidently had a sequence corresponding with Mk 2.1–3.6, but not identical with it. So here we have further evidence for the existence of short collections of Gospel traditions, some of which were incorporated by Mark in his longer work.

JESUS FEEDS THE MULTITUDE AND WALKS ON THE SEA **6.1–25**

The most surprising thing about this chapter is the fact that John felt it necessary to record not only the feeding, but also the walking on the sea. If he were simply selecting a sign as the basis for a discourse, he could surely have been content with just the feeding. As it is, he has used the second miracle quite effectively: it adds a great deal of mystery to the personality of Jesus (notice especially verse 20), which prepares for the revelation concerning himself made in the discourse (cf. verse 35); and it creates the situation out of which the dialogue springs, so as to lead in to the discourse without a break. But it is most improbable that John would ever have thought of this, had it not been for the fact that the walk on the sea was already connected with the feeding miracle in his source, exactly as it is in Mt. 14.13–36 (= Mk 6.32–52). In these two parallels we have therefore important comparative material for the whole section. But the Synoptic Gospels have more than this to offer. For there is a strikingly similar sequence, consisting of a second feeding miracle, return by boat, the Pharisees' request for a sign, and then a strange conversation in the boat which refers to *both* feedings (Mt. 15.32–16.12 = Mk 8.1–21). Luke, however, is surprisingly deficient. He records only the first feeding, and that without the walking on the sea (Lk. 9.10–17).

When these various accounts are compared in detail some interesting facts emerge. John's description of the setting in verse 2f. shows a relation to Mt. 15.30, immediately preceding Matthew's version of the second feeding. The question of Jesus in verse 5 is similar to Mk 8.4, again the second feeding, though the vocabulary reflects Mk 6.36. Philip's answer (verse 7) corresponds closely with Mk 6.37, the five loaves and two fish (verse 9) with Mk 6.38. The command to sit down and the mention of grass (verse 10) reflect Mk 6.39f. The specification of the number, 5,000 persons, at this point corresponds roughly with the Lucan position (Lk. 9.14), whereas in both the Marcan and the Matthean accounts it is left until the end, but this may be only coincidental agreement with Luke. John's word for 'given thanks' is used in the second feeding in Matthew and Mark, but both have a different word in the first (this again may be due to other reasons). 'Left over' in verse 12 is found in Mt. 14.20, but is missing from Mk 6.43; on the other hand it occurs in both Mt. 15.37 and Mk 8.8. The twelve baskets of fragments closely correspond with Mk 6.43. It is not to be supposed that John was borrowing a word from here and a word from there, with all these versions in front of him. The only probable explanation is that his source was a variant of Mk 6.32–44, exhibiting some features which are reflected in Mk 8.1–10. If the two feedings in Mark, and indeed the larger contexts in which they are found, are ultimately variants of the same sequence of events, it is safe to conclude that John's source represents an earlier stage in the history of the transmission of the sequence than Mark. It is held (for instance, by Vincent Taylor) that the second Marcan sequence is more primitive than the first, though it also shows signs of far greater disruption by Mark's own interpretative interests. John's source appears to hold a middle position between them.

John has not simply copied out his source without alteration; he has introduced some characteristic features of his own. Verse 4 (the Passover) not only gives the date, but suggests an important factor for the interpretation of the following discourse. The personal details—Philip, Andrew and the lad—are generally traced to John's liking for vivid circumstantial details, though Brown thinks they might have been found in the source, which is certainly not impossible, once it is recognized that this was in any case not identical with the Synoptic versions. Jesus' own inner assurance (verse 6) is an obviously Johannine feature. The command to gather up the fragments in verse 12 introduces a change of emphasis to the original account which is best explained in terms of the manna story to be treated in the discourse. It is thus a rare occasion when it may be allowed that John has been guided by symbolical considerations in narrative composition. The reactions of the people (verses 14f.) are also recorded only by John, though not entirely without support in the Synoptic material.

The relation of the Johannine account of the walking on the sea to the Synoptists will be dealt with when we reach verse 16. Here it may be said that his version strongly suggests that his source had it in a more primitive form than either Matthew or Mark.

Concerning the historicity of the feeding miracle, the account is so well attested that there is no need to doubt that a real incident lies behind it. The figure (5,000, or even 4,000) seems improbably high, but we can allow for some exaggeration. But what actually happened? It may be taken as a miracle in the strict sense. Jesus used his supernatural powers to create the bread as he broke it in his hands. The theme of the twelve baskets of fragments is precisely to attest this miraculous aspect. Whether the reader is willing to accept this must depend upon his presuppositions concerning the divine-human personality of Christ. Or the story may be regarded as a miracle in this way, but its historicity may be doubted on the grounds that it conforms to folk-lore tradition— cf. the stories of Elijah and Elisha in 1 Kg. 17.8–16; 2 Kk. 4.1–7. Or the story may be accepted in its main outlines, but given a naturalistic explanation. John's account has been used to explain it on behalf of all four Gospels. It is suggested that the lad, whom he alone mentions, set an example of sharing such food as he had,

and others then followed suit, and so everyone was satisfied. This
is the 'lunch basket' theory; it can scarcely be regarded as a
serious possibility.—Whether there was a miraculous element about
it or not, the story has been *remembered* for its symbolical importance. The wording of the blessing and distribution of the bread
in all four Gospels shows a close relation to the Last Supper
accounts. It is thus probable that the story has been remembered
and valued as a type of the Christian Eucharist. This suggests
that the actual event had a quasi-sacramental character: the meal
was important for its meaning, rather than for the physical
nourishment of the people. From this point of view a very little
piece of bread for each person would suffice, and the miraculous
aspect can be dispensed with; on the other hand, if it was miraculous, attention to the meaning explains why Jesus should use his
powers in this way. For a very similar miracle, but on a much less
exaggerated scale, probably having a sacramental intention, cf.
2 Kg. 4.42–4. If the feeding was sacramental, it must have been
related to the teaching of Jesus on the coming Kingdom, and so is
to be regarded as an anticipation of the eschatological banquet,
which is one aspect of the Last Supper itself (cf. Mk 14.25).
John's discourse on the Bread of Life contains eschatological
themes which he handles in characteristic style, and it is probable
that he regarded both the feeding miracle and the Eucharist in this
light. We have seen the theme of the eschatological banquet in
connection with the marriage at Cana (2.1–11).

The Feeding of the Multitude 6.1–15

1. the other side: it is implied that Jesus is already in Galilee,
anticipating 7.1. But even there John says nothing about the
journey from Jerusalem. If 4.46–54 was located in Capernaum in
the source (though we cannot be sure that this comes from the
same source), it may well be that Capernaum was the starting-
point for the crossing, especially as Jesus later returns there (verse
17). The sea trip is a feature of the Synoptic accounts. The destination was presumably some point on the NE. coast of the Sea of
Galilee, not too far for the crowd to come on foot (Mk 6.33).
Luke says it was Bethsaida. In any case it can hardly have been
Tabgha, the traditional site of the miracle: this is W. of Capernaum, and not sufficiently remote.
Tiberias: the name of the city built by Herod Antipas on the

SW. side of the lake, which he made the capital of his tetrarchy. Hence it gave its name to the lake, and John mentions it as likely to be better known to his Gentile readers. But the Greek is a little awkward (lit. 'of the Sea of Galilee of Tiberias'),) and Brown accepts the addition: 'to the district of Tiberias' found in D Θ b e r[1]. This would make the event on the SW. shore. But the additional phrase is likely to be due to reminiscence of Mk 8.10.

2, 3. The vocabulary of these two verses is slightly closer to Matthew than to Mark; for **a multitude followed,** cf. Mt. 14.13, but also Mk 6.34. For the healing miracles the most obvious parallel is Mt. 15.30, which also supplies the words **into the hills, and there sat down.** This is part of the context of the second feeding. But before we jump to the conclusion that Matthew is the original here, against Mark, on account of the agreement with John, it must be observed that the same vocabulary range occurs in Mark itself in the paragraph which immediately follows the Sabbath sequence (Mk 3.7-13a). Thus the comparison with Matthew only serves to draw attention to the fact that the source had a summary of healings and an ascent of the hills which are conventional items of the Galilean ministry, and the phrases recur in both Matthew and Mark. In fact **into the hills** (*eis to oros*; collective) is exactly the same phrase as 'on the mountain' at the beginning of the Sermon on the Mount (Mt. 5.1).

4. the Passover: cf. 2.13. The phrase is typical of John. It has been suggested that the name of the feast should be omitted, on account of the silence of some patristic quotations, but it is found in all MSS. The Passover coincided with the Feast of Unleavened Bread, which, according to Jos. 5.10-12, commemorated not only the flight from Egypt, but also the first food from grain when the Israelites reached the promised land, signifying the moment when the manna ceased. But John's reference to the feast here is probably more general: the Last Supper was the Passover meal (or preparation), commemorated in the Eucharist (1 C. 11.26). The feeding miracle is then to be interpreted in the light of it, with all its eschatological associations.

5. Lifting up his eyes: the same phrase, and following word for to **see** (*theasthai*), as in 4.35. It may well have stood in John's source.
Jesus said to Philip: In the Synoptic accounts of the first feeding, *the disciples* draw attention to the people's need, and

Jesus tells them to make provision. This evokes their question how they are to do it (Mk 6.37; Mt. 15.33 = Mk 8.4). Both versions in both Matthew and Mark have given adequate explanation of the people's need. John, however, brings up the subject while the people are still arriving, instead of at the end of a long day, and places the question on Jesus' lips. John's omission of the obvious reason for providing food not only indicates that he is not interested in this matter, but also that here he has tampered with his source; this makes it improbable that Philip and Andrew were named in the source; they are mentioned because John has already characterized them as individuals (cf. 1.40–4). It is, in fact, always in dialogue that John tends to be most arbitrary in his use of sources, and the dialogue here has been adapted in typical style. Jesus' question, **'How are we to buy bread . . .?'**, is reminiscent of Mk 8.4, but the wording is nearer to Mk 6.36f. Philip's reply in verse 7 is clearly related to Mk 6.37. Andrew's information in verse 9 takes its operative phrase ('has five . . . loaves and two fish') from Mk 6.38, but the Greek is almost identical (apart from the number) in Mk 8.5. It would seem, then, that the source included the question of the disciples, as in Mk 8; the suggestion of buying two hundred *denarii*-worth of bread, as in Mk 6.37; and the information about the available supply, as in Mk 6 and 8. John has taken all three items, and has redistributed them between three speakers, Jesus, Philip and Andrew. But in so doing he has introduced his favourite device of misunderstanding. Jesus asked the question, but—verse 6—**he himself knew what he would do.** As always in John, Jesus is in complete command of the situation; it is a **test** question. The remote position makes the question unanswerable in terms of the usual practical solution of darting into the shop round the corner. It is therefore intended to teach that the food of Jesus belongs to another level of reality (cf. 4.32).

7. Philip fails miserably. The positive suggestion of the source —that they should actually go off to buy food—is reduced to a lament that it would still be inadequate even if that were possible; and thereby John heightens the effect of the miracle.

two hundred denarii: of all the parallel accounts, this phrase is only found in Mk 6.37. Though worth about 17d (*RSV*, *mg*) (= 7p), a *denarius* was a day's wage for a labourer (cf. Mt. 20.2). *NEB*'s 'twenty pounds' takes it to be equivalent to 10p.

9. a lad: mentioned only by John; we can only speculate whether he found this vivid and attractive detail in his source, or introduced it himself. In all the Synoptic accounts the disciples have themselves brought the food. The word for **lad** (*paidarion*) can be used of either sex, and is often applied to a young slave boy or girl.

five barley loaves and two fish: as in Mk 6.38 paras. Only John specifies **barley,** which was generally used by the poorer people. Possibly it is an allusion to the date, as the Passover was the time of barley-harvest. John's word for **fish** (*opsarion*) is not used in the NT except in this *pericope* and 21.9f., 13. It can mean dried or pickled fish, used as a relish with bread.

among so many: Mark makes no comment on the absurdity of the small amount, but both Mt. 14.17 and Lk. 9.13 vary the text to bring this out a little. John makes Andrew echo Philip's lament, so as to heighten further the wonder of the miracle.

10. sit down: as in the Synoptic accounts. It seems that the people have been standing while Jesus has been teaching (Mk 6.34), as for the reading of the Law (cf. Neh. 8.5); but this does not apply in John, as the people have only just arrived. To **sit down** (properly 'recline') for the fellowship meal also accords with liturgical practice. The **grass** is a feature of Mk 6.39.

five thousand: again the number comes from the first feeding. Luke is the only one of the Synoptic accounts to give the figure at roughly the same point in the narrative. The rest save it until the end in both feedings. No doubt it was at the end in the source, and John has brought it forward in order to change the climax from the sheer size of the miracle to the reactions which it prompted (verses 14f.).

11. took . . . given thanks . . . distributed: as at the Eucharist, which has probably influenced all the accounts at this point. Mk 6.41 has 'taking . . . looked up to heaven . . . blessed . . . broke . . . gave'. Mark's account of the Last Supper (Mk 14.22) is the same, except for the omission of 'looked up to heaven', which nevertheless is probably taken for granted. John's **given thanks** (*eucharistēsas*) differs from the Synoptic 'blessed' (*eulogēsen*), but is used in the second feeding (Mt. 15.36 (= Mk 8.6)) and in the Last Supper narratives (Lk. 22.19; 1 C. 11.24). The two words are alternative translations of the Hebrew *bērēk*, used in grace before meals and in the blessing of the bread and the cup etc. in the

Passover. The variations may reflect differences in the eucharistic
formula. **Distributed** (*diedōken*) combines the ideas of 'broke'
and 'gave'. After this word D Θ and later MSS. insert 'to the disciples, and the disciples' before **to those who were seated,** by
influence of all the Synoptic accounts. It would seem likely that
this feature (which is reminiscent of the deacons in the Eucharist)
was included in the source. If so, John has omitted it to make
Jesus himself the giver of food to all.

12. fragments left over: the words come from both Mk 6.43
and 8.8. In the Elisha story (2 Kg. 4.43f.) the leavings are a sign
of the abundance of food, and this is no doubt the motive in the
underlying tradition (Bultmann). The command: **'Gather up ...
that nothing may be lost'** seems strange. Bernard tries to make
it plausible by making it the morsel saved for the servitors at a
meal, but it is difficult to avoid seeing a symbolical feature here;
verse 39; 11.52; 17.12; 18.9 show that we have here an important
idea in John's theology; cf. 3.17. He has taken this item of the
tradition and applied it to the Christian mission. The word
gather (*sunagein*) is typical of John's vocabulary, but it is not used
in the Synoptic accounts. There may be an allusion to Exod.
16.16, where it is used by the LXX in describing the arrangements
for collecting the manna. If so, we have here a feature of the
narrative which has been affected by the biblical background to
the discourse. The eucharistic prayer of the *Didache* (ix.4) has been
influenced by John: 'As this broken bread was scattered on the
hills and was gathered up and so became one, so may thy Church
be gathered up from the ends of the earth into thy Kingdom.' In
fact, as Moule has shown (*JTS*, n.s., VI (1955), pp. 240–3), Jn 6
provides the only satisfactory explanation of this text.

13. twelve baskets with fragments: The same words in
Mk 6.43. The second feeding has a different word for 'baskets',
but neither word gives any indication of size. We may well ask
how, if there were only five little round loaves and two dried fish
available, there could be twelve baskets handy. Possibly the
original tradition mentioned the baskets merely as a way of esti-
mating the leavings, i.e. as much as would fill twelve baskets; but
all the evangelists take it quite literally (cf. Mk 8.19f.). The
obvious possible symbolism of the number twelve plays no part in
any of the four accounts.

14f. These two verses should be taken more closely together than the paragraphing in *RSV* suggests. There is nothing corresponding with them in the Synoptic accounts; but John has probably interpreted the situation correctly to this extent, that he recognizes that the feeding is essentially more than a miracle—it is also a sign of the imminent approach of the coming age. This fact inevitably provokes speculation whether Jesus is himself the Messiah or not. Indeed, from John's point of view the feeding is a divine act, and therefore is a definite sign of his messiahship. The connection between the feeding miracles and growing speculation about Jesus can be detected in both the Marcan sequences: in Mk 6 Herod begins to be anxious at the increasing influence of Jesus (Mk 6.14–16). In Mk 8 the feeding is followed by a curious conversation in the boat, in which the 'leaven of Herod' is mentioned; then, after the healing of a blind man, which certainly is put into the context to suggest the enlightening of the minds of the disciples, there is the confession of Peter (Mk 8.14–30). But John is not dependent here on either of these.

sign: P75 B a read plural 'signs'. Brown is disposed to accept this, but it is probably due to the influence of verse 2.

This is indeed: the people's confession of faith is in Johannine form; cf. 4.42.

the prophet again means the Prophet like Moses of Dt. 18.15, as in 4.19, cf. 1.21, and is definitely messianic, as in 4.25. This is proved by the words **who is to come;** cf. the notes on 1.27 (Barrett). Consequently (verse 15) the people regard Jesus as **king;** cf. 1.49. Thus these two verses bring together the various messianic titles which John uses in Jewish contexts.

15. Perceiving: this again implies Jesus' supernatural knowledge (Barrett). The Synoptic tradition contains no hint of such a popular move, but in view of the anxieties of Herod just mentioned, it is certainly a possibility, and John may have good information at the back of his statement. Josephus tells of a number of such movements in Galilee, in which a popular leader is hailed as a 'prophet' or as a 'deliverer' (*Ant.* xvii.271f.; xx.97f., 169; *BJ* ii.261). For an interesting explanation of Jesus' reticence concerning such messianic claims, see J. C. O'Neill, 'The Silence of Jesus', *NTS* xv (1969), pp. 153–67. As a matter of history, Jesus would not accept popular acclaim, but awaited a sign from God himself. This is a fact which John has correctly understood; cf. 5.30–47.

withdrew again to the hills: here John links up once more with
the source; cf. Mk 6.46. According to Mark, Jesus sent the disciples
on ahead, while he dismissed the crowd. This seems an odd procedure. By making Jesus escape—from the disciples as much as
from the crowd—John has found a plausible way of producing
the required situation for the following *pericope* of the walking on
the sea. For **withdrew** Sanders and Brown prefer the more vivid
'fled' (*pheugei*) of א* Old Latin and Curetonian Syriac. Many
commentators feel that there is a parallel here to the third temptation (Mt. 4.8–10), but there is no hint of this in the text. No
temptation is involved; Jesus does not want a public acclamation
at this stage in his ministry.

Jesus walks on the Sea 16–21

The comparative material for this *pericope* includes not only the
parallel in Mt. 14.22–33 (= Mk 6.45–52), but also the stilling of
the storm (Mt. 8.23–7 = Mk 4.35–41 = Lk. 8.22–5). There are
considerable similarities between these two stories, and they may
well be ultimately variant traditions of the same event. The point
in both is that the presence of Jesus brings calm and safety to the
disciples (compare Mk 4.39 with Mk 6.51); but the miraculous
element has been developed differently in the two versions. The
abiding presence of Jesus is a feature of the Church's eucharistic
teaching (cf. Lk. 24.13–35); this may explain why the walking on
the sea was attached to the feeding at an early stage of transmission. John's version mostly follows Mk 6.45–52, though it is much
briefer. But the 'strong' (lit. 'great') wind of verse 18 may come
from Mk 4.37; 'frightened' in verse 19 from Mk 4.41 ('filled with
awe' is the same Greek word); and 'other boats' in Mk 4.36 may
have suggested the '[other] boats' in verse 23. If these are features
of John's source, it may be surmised that the source was not so
fully developed as Mk 6.45–52, and retained some phrases which
have found their way into the variant story of Mk 4.35–41. In
that case it is possible that Mark has heightened the effect by the
suggestion that 'they thought it was a ghost' (Mk 6.49). Matthew
goes further in the direction of the miraculous by adding the legend
of Peter (Mt. 14.28–31).

If this is a true account of the development of the tradition,
the question arises whether a miracle was really involved at all.
Walking on the sea (verse 19) could be translated walking *by* the

sea, especially in Aramaic, in which the preposition ʿal (ʿon')
regularly means 'beside' in such contexts. In this case the boat
could have been close to the shore, but unable to pull in because
of the strong wind. John's version may preserve a hint of this,
seeing that the boat was immediately able to come in to land
when the wind dropped (verse 21). Thus the underlying story of
both the Marcan accounts would have been the miraculous stilling of the gale. Bernard, followed by Sanders, has argued that this
is not only what actually happened, but also all that John himself
intends his readers to understand; John never thought of it as a
miracle of walking on the surface of the water. But it requires a
very strained exegesis of verse 21a to maintain this, not to mention
the implications of a miraculous crossing contained in verses 22–5.

It has already been pointed out that John uses this story, which
he had ready to hand in his source, to create the situation required
for the discourse in verse 26, and that he valued it for the saying
in verse 20: 'It is I' ('I am'; Gr. *egō eimi*). It may also be asked
whether the dating of the whole sequence at Passover is a factor,
giving it a symbolical connection with the crossing of the Red
Sea during the Exodus. It goes without saying that this was one
of the most important of all the Passover themes. But it must be
admitted that John takes no pains to bring this to the surface, so
that the possibility of such an allusion must be considered
improbable.

16. When evening came: cf. Mk 6.47.
His disciples: cf. Mk 6.45. John imagines that they were left
with the crowd when Jesus fled.

17. got into a boat . . . across: for these words, cf. Mk 6.45.
to Capernaum: Mark says Bethsaida, but apparently they landed
at Gennesaret (Mk 6.53), which is much nearer to Capernaum,
but a little further west. Hence Capernaum may perhaps have
stood in the source.
It was now dark: this is in the position of 'when evening came'
in the Marcan account, and so we must assume that John has
here used a different phrase for stylistic variation. The word for
dark (lit. 'darkness', *skotia*) is the same as he uses in 1.5 and 12.35;
hence the reading 'darkness overtook them' in ℵ and D, bringing
the expression into line with these two verses. But the deeper
theme of light and darkness is hardly present here.
not yet come: it is strange to mention this *after* the disciples have

set out. Mk 6.47 is much more natural: 'The boat was out on the sea, and he was alone on the land.' The Greek for 'he alone' (*autos monos*) has been used by John in verse 15 ('by himself'). John's version suggests that the miracle of walking on the sea is bound to happen.

18. a strong wind: cf. the 'great storm of wind' in Mk 4.37. It is toned down to a headwind in Mk 6.48. Sudden storms are a feature of the Sea of Galilee.

19. three or four miles: lit. 'twenty-five or thirty stadia'. The Greek *stadion* is a little more than 600 feet. The Sea of Galilee is a little less than seven miles at its widest part, but obviously the disciples would be going northwards rather than out into the middle. **walking on the sea:** the identical phrase of Mk 6.49. John's addition of **drawing near to the boat** certainly gives the impression that he means *on* rather than *by* the sea. There is no suggestion that he was wading out towards the boat from the shore. **frightened:** this could be deduced from Jesus' words in the next verse, but the exact word occurs in Mk 4.41. But John may have the true reading of the source at this point, changed by Mark into the much longer sentence of Mk 6.49b, 50a. Sanders argues that they were afraid of the severe conditions of the sea, but John has hardly made this plain. In fact his word **saw** (*theōrein*) tends to be used of something spectacular; cf. verse 62.

20. The verse is almost identical with Mk 6.50c. Consequently the *egō eimi* ('I am' = **it is I**) cannot be taken as the divine name of Exod. 3.14; it is simply self-identification. But, as the climax of the story, it brings Jesus to the centre of thought as the Saviour, and so we cannot exclude the possibility that John regarded it as an anticipation of the 'I am' saying of the discourse (verse 35).

21. they were glad: the plain sense of the Greek is that their fears were allayed when Jesus spoke to them, and so *they were willing* (cp. *NEB*) to take him on board. The verb is used in its normal volitional sense, as in 1.43; 5.35. According to the non-miraculous interpretation of Bernard, they were so near the shore that, though they *wanted* to take him in, it proved unnecessary, as the wind dropped and the difficulties were over. For the same verb with an unfulfilled intention, he compares 7.44; 16.19. This interpretation evades the impression that the disciples were overawed by Jesus. John's wording, though not quite the same as Mk 6.51a, may be that of his source, and does not really support this interpretation. On any showing, John ought now to explain that the wind dropped, as in Mk 6.51b; cf. Mk 4.39; but, instead, he goes straight on to record that **immediately the boat was at the land to which they were going.** It is quite likely that these words also stood in the source, as elsewhere John only has the form *eutheōs* (**immediately**) where he is using source material (5.9; 18.27). Mark at this point obscures the source by the explanatory addition of Mk 6.52. The word-picture is reminiscent of Ps. 107.30 (in fact, the whole story reminds one of verses 23–30), but there are no actual verbal links. Once more we cannot exclude the possibility that John had an eye to the symbolism of arrival at the haven and the attainment of eternal life through faith in Jesus (verses 35–40).

The People follow Jesus to Capernaum 22–5

The object of these verses is to provide the setting for the discourse. John has to explain not only how all the relevant people met up once more at Capernaum, but also how, as far as the crowd could understand it, Jesus himself could not possibly have arrived except by some miraculous means. But in order to put it briefly John has written in a rather confused way, just as in 4.1f., and here (as there) it has given rise to some textual uncertainty.

22. On the next day: John's favourite expression. But the action it refers to is the people's decision to sail over to Capernaum, verse 24b. Everything that comes in between is a long parenthesis, to explain why they took this decision. But grammatically it can only mean that **on the next day they saw that,** etc., which is picked up by 'saw' in verse 24. But the rest of verse 22 is not the same as 'they saw that Jesus was not there', though it gives the reason for it. Hence most commentators translate the verb for **saw** as if it had been pluperfect, 'had seen' (so *NEB*), though this still fails to make the sentence read naturally, even when verse 23 is treated as a parenthesis. It is thus not surprising that attempts to improve the grammar appear at an early stage in the MS. tradition, notably the first hand of א, which by means of rather drastic changes has produced tolerably good Greek.

on the other side: i.e. to the east, where the feeding miracle took place.

remained: lit. 'stood', perhaps meaning 'who had been standing and listening to Jesus on the day before'; cf. verse 10 and 12.29.

23. However, boats: Gr. *alla . . . ploiaria.* The word *alla* is ambiguous, as it can be either the adverb **however** or the adjective 'other'. The difference would appear in an accented text, but accents are not used in the early MSS. But the many variant readings at this point mostly suggest that it was understood as 'other', though then the lack of a connecting particle makes it rather harsh. It is less so, if the verse is not treated as a parenthesis, for then we have narrative sequence with characteristic asyndeton: 'On the next day the people saw . . .; other boats arrived . . .; so . . . they got into the boats.' If this is right, then we may hazard the guess that 'other boats' were mentioned in John's source for the miracle just described, as in Mk 4.36, and that he has held over this feature for the present paragraph.

from Tiberias: cf. verse 1. Again the confusion is such that Tiberias could be taken to be the locality of the feeding, although it is on the W. side, and this is how it is understood by ℵ*. We have to assume that these boats were out fishing. It is a happy coincidence, which John does not try to explain. Bernard, who brackets the whole verse as a gloss, nevertheless has to admit that it is necessary to the narrative.

after the Lord had given thanks: this final phrase, however, must certainly be bracketed as a gloss. It not only contains the later usage of **the Lord** (cf. the notes on 4.1), but also is missing from D 69 Old Syriac. Interpolations are frequent in D so that its omissions are 'always noteworthy' (Barrett). Both Bultmann and Brown reject this phrase.

25. when did you come here: Bultmann points out that the people's innocent question is an unconscious attestation of the miracle, like the steward in 2.9f. The straight answer to it would be to tell them of the miracle of verses 16–21. But Jesus does not answer it directly. The question expresses the fact that they have been 'seeking' him (verse 24) and in verse 26 he turns the attention to the motive of doing so. Thus very deftly John starts a dialogue which goes straight into the discourse, which is the real object of the chapter.

DISCOURSE ON THE BREAD OF LIFE: MAINTENANCE OF LIFE IN CHRIST **6.26–59**

The theme of the discourse is the bread that comes from heaven. The feeding miracle is not mentioned after verse 26. Instead, the teaching of Jesus is based upon an exposition of the miracle of the manna in the Wilderness, the OT type of a celestial food. Although numerous pagan parallels to the idea of the celestial food can be given (cf. Bultmann, pp. 223f.), it is totally unnecessary to bring them into consideration, not only because the OT basis of the discourse is so clear, but also because the development of the thought can be traced to Jewish traditions of exegesis. Within the OT itself we can see the beginnings of this homiletic tradition. According to Dt. 8.3, the manna was given as an object-lesson, so that the people should know 'that man does not live by bread alone, but that man lives by everything that proceeds out of the mouth of the Lord'. This thought is echoed by Philo (*Decal.* 15–17), but he also speaks of the manna itself as a type of the Wisdom that comes from God (*Mut.* 260; *CQEG* 173–4), or with the Word of God (*Leg. All.* 162). Borgen (*Bread from Heaven, NT Sup* x (1965)), has shown that Philo's language often shows a similarity to that of the later rabbinic exegesis, and argues that behind the latter there is a very long-standing tradition of the homiletic usage of Scripture, to which Philo was indebted in the first century. But he also shows that the same can be said of Jn 6, which is also comparable to the rabbinic homilies in a strikingly similar way.

Before following up this last point further, let us consider the consequences of the Jewish tradition for the interpretation of the discourse. It means that when Jesus says: 'I am the bread of life', he is designating himself as the Wisdom of God and as the Word of God coming to mankind; as such, he is the fulfilment of the Law which was given on Mount Sinai. These ideas are expressed in the discourse in verses 35 and 45. He is also the giver of the life of the age to come (verses 37–40, 49f., 58). This fits exactly with the meaning of Jesus which has appeared in previous discourses, notably chapters 3 and 5. This must be regarded as the primary purpose of the discourse. We have already seen enough of John's teaching to know that such ideas are not bound to exclude a consistent futuristic eschatology, cf. 5.25–9. Bultmann, of course, does not accept this point, and so here, as there, he wishes to bracket all eschatological references, especially verses 37–40. The issue need not be argued afresh here.

But is this interpretation—which may be called briefly 'the sapiential interpretation'—compatible with a reference to the Eucharist? It is only in verses 51–8 that such a reference becomes inescapable, and then it seems to predominate to the exclusion of the sapiential ideas. Many scholars feel that these verses cannot be regarded as part of the original discourse, not only Bultmann and his school, but cautious Roman Catholic scholars like Brown and Schnackenburg. Brown thinks that verses 51–8 are a doublet of 35–50, a reworking of its basic ideas using material from John's account of the Last Supper, which he did not include in chapter 13. Odeberg tries to escape from the problem by interpreting even 51–8 strictly in line with the sapiential exegesis, referring these verses to the spiritual meaning of the Incarnation, but excluding the Eucharist as such. Hoskyns, however, maintained that it is false reasoning to regard the sapiential and eucharistic interpretations as mutually exclusive. The issue would never have arisen if it had not been for the effect of the Reformation on Western theology. If the discourse has been composed by John on the basis of one of his own homilies at the Christian eucharistic assembly, it is only to be expected that the two levels of interpretation should co-exist, and interpenetrate one another. The discourse is not a handbook of eucharistic doctrine, and the sapiential interpretation is its real meaning and purpose. But the Eucharist is a meal of fellowship with the risen and exalted Lord, and when the Christians receive the sacramental elements they realize their fellowship with him, who is the Bread of Life who came down from heaven. Thus the eucharistic interpretation is latent beneath the sapiential section (35–50), and the sapiential continues without any diminution in the eucharistic section (51–8).

To return to the rabbinic homilies, we must now note that the form of the discourse follows rabbinic methods. Borgen has shown how the biblical quotation in verse 31 is expounded by means of word-by-word analysis, extending right through the discourse to verse 58, in much the same way as the rabbinic exegesis of a particular text. But does the *structure* follow rabbinic models as well? Various attempts have been made to trace in the discourse the pattern of the Jewish Passover Haggadah (i.e. the Passover liturgy), notably by Daube and Gärtner. But these have not produced very convincing results. Aileen Guilding sought to explain the whole Gospel as a presentation of the tradition of Jesus in the light of the OT scriptures read in the Jewish synagogue in the seasons of the various feasts which John mentions. Her theory has not won wide acceptance, but our present discourse is one point where her observations have proved valuable; for the unexpected quotation of Isa. 54.13 in verse 45 comes from a passage read during the season following the Passover. The synagogue lections consisted of the *sēder*, taken from the Pentateuch, and the *haphtarah*, from the Prophets and Writings. The *sēder* which lies behind the discourse is obviously Exod. 16, the story of the manna. Unfortunately, the passage Isa. 54.9–55.5 from which the quotation comes is not the *haphtarah* to this *sēder*. According to Guilding's reconstruction of the old synagogue lectionary on a triennial basis, it belongs to a different year and a different Sabbath. But her reconstruction has been heavily criticized, so that it cannot be taken as certain that these two passages did not belong together at some stage and in some places in the more fluid stage of the lectionary system.

The value of Guilding's work rests in the fact that it suggests another explanation for the structure of the discourse, and that is that it follows the pattern of an actual synagogue homily. This is the theory of Borgen himself. The structure consists of an opening text from the lection, in this case Exod. 16, which can be detected in verse 31; exposition of it, ending with a definite allusion to the same text; a subordinate quotation, here to be found in verse 45; further exposition, finishing with an allusion to the original text (verse 58). It cannot be claimed that this exactly corresponds with the structure of the rabbinic homilies that have come down to us, but it shows a recognizable family likeness.

Another study of such homilies has been made by J. W. Bowker in an article on the speeches in Acts (*NTS* xiv (1967), pp. 96–111). The homily is in answer to a question of the people. The preacher begins with a quotation from neither the *sēder* nor the *haphtarah*, but a text which can act as a bridge between them. Later on he may introduce a quotation from the *haphtarah*, and he may conclude with one from the *sēder*. If we may assume that the lections underlying Jn 6 were Exod. 16 and Isa. 54.9–55.5, we can see that it fits this scheme pretty well. There is a suitable question at the beginning of the discourse (verse 28). The first quotation is not directly taken from Exod. 16, but is more likely to be from Ps. 78.24, which can certainly act as a bridge between the two lections. The quotation in verse 45 is then from the *haphtarah*. Bowker himself does not consider the possibility that Jn 6 might be an example of this kind of homily, but the similarity of struc-

ture is certainly impressive. In any case we have to remember that,
if it were a Christian homily composed on Jewish models, it is
now adapted to its present position as a typical Johannine discourse. He has punctuated it with dialogue. Even the proemial
(introductory) text in verse 31 is placed on the lips of the Jews.
It is not, then, the homily as John preached it in the eucharistic
assembly, but as he has adapted it for his book. (This is important,
because there is a tendency to expect John to be too closely bound
by the rules of Jewish homiletic.) Thus G. Richter (*ZNW* LX
(1969), pp. 21–55) denies that verses 51–8 belong to the original
homily, because the form found by Borgen is complete without
these verses; he also complains that they contain ideas and phrases
which are very different from the preceding verses (but against
this, see J. D. G. Dunn, *NTS* XVII (1970–1), pp. 328–38). J. Heine-
mann (*JJS* XIX (1968), pp. 41–8) denies that fixed forms for
Jewish homilies can be traced back to NT times.

The argument of the discourse may be summarized as follows:

26–31. The feeding miracle is to be understood as a pointer to the
true food, which is gained by acceptance of Jesus as the one sent from
God. The Jews object that they cannot accept him unless he gives a
sign comparable to the manna miracle. They quote the proemial text:
'He gave them bread from heaven to eat.'

32–40. Exposition of 'he gave them bread from heaven'. The manna
was only a type of the truth. Jesus is himself the true bread, and offers
eternal life to all men.

41–51. Exposition of 'bread from heaven to eat'. Jesus is the truth
from heaven, to be received and taken into oneself as food is eaten
and digested. The sapiential idea is uppermost, and is expressed by
means of the *haphtarah* quotation: 'And they shall all be taught by
God.'

52–8. Exposition of 'to eat'. What is required is not merely an assimilation of ideas, but of the real Jesus, who was made man and died.
This is expressed in eucharistic language.

John has appropriately located this discourse in the synagogue
(verse 59). The whole piece is an exposition of a basic OT text,
split up into parts and expounded in order, until a complete
definition has been reached. It thus splendidly proves the point
that was made in 5.30–47, that the Scriptures, when rightly
understood, prepare for the revelation of God in Christ.

Introductory Dialogue **26–31**

26. The discourse begins with a **'Truly truly'**, saying, which we have learnt from past experience to treat as a possible indication of the use of source material. In verses 30f. we shall find that the people ask for a sign, and the present verse, so far from answering the question in verse 25, is a response to just such a request. Looking back at the Marcan sequences, we discover that the second feeding is immediately followed by a request for a sign, which shows linguistic affinity with these verses: 'The Pharisees came ... *seeking from him a sign from heaven*. And he ... said, "Why does this generation *seek a sign*? *Truly, I say to you*, no sign *shall be given* to this generation." ' (Mk 8.11f.). It has already been mentioned that the word **seek** is the link between the previous narrative and the discourse (verse 24). John has radically reconstructed the saying for its present context, but again we can be fairly confident that he found it in a form comparable to Mark's in his source. He has not altered the essential meaning of it, which is fundamental to what he is going to say. For the motive of the people's search does not arise from their perception that Jesus is attested by God himself as the Messiah. They may have understood the feeding miracle as a sign of imminent deliverance in the coming age, and even have hailed Jesus as the Messiah who was to perform the deliverance (cf. verses 14f.). But they have not understood it as a revelatory act. Thus, although they saw signs in one sense, they failed to do so in the sense of understanding.

ate your fill: Gr. *ephagete ... kai echortasthēte*. John used a different expression in verse 12, but here we have the precise words used at the corresponding point in the Synoptic accounts (Mk 6.42 paras.), which therefore also stood in John's source.

27. food which perishes ... endures: the contrast is not between perishable and imperishable foodstuffs, but between the effects of these foods in the recipient. The idea anticipates the contrast with the manna in verses 48–50. Here the word 'bread' is carefully avoided, and the emphasis goes on feeding in general. There is a precise parallel with the two kinds of water in 4.14. It is the eschatological **food** for which they should **labour**. Bernard and others have discerned here an echo of the invitation of Wisdom in Isa. 55.2a: 'Why do you spend your money for that which is not bread, and your labour for that which does not satisfy?' This allusion (which depends on the Hebrew text, and not the LXX) gains importance because it is included within the *haphtarah*, Isa. 54.9–55.5. Thus, although the proper exposition has not yet been reached, the verse anticipates the use of both *sēder* and *haphtarah*, already suggesting the sapiential interpretation.

the Son of man: he will perform the eschatological function of feeding, just like his other functions (cf. 5.19–23). There was a current belief among Jews that the miracle of the manna would be repeated in the coming age; cf. 2 Baruch 29.8; *Mekilta* to Exod. 16.25; *Eccles. Rabba*, i.9, 28. The last-mentioned reference may be quoted as an example: 'As the First Saviour [i.e. Moses] caused the manna to descend, as it is written "Behold, I will rain bread from heaven for you" (Exod. 16.4), so also the Last Saviour will cause the manna to descend, as it is written "There shall be bread of wheat upon the earth" (Ps. 72.16).'

set his seal: cf. 3.33. It means that he has already been marked out for this purpose, and so is a hint that he is none other than Jesus himself, though this is not yet stated. There is no need to see here a reference to the baptism of Jesus, on the grounds that the notion of sealing is applied to baptism in early Christianity (cf. 2 C. 1.22; Eph. 1.13).

28. to be doing the works of God: the verb is the same as 'labour' in the last verse. **The works of God** can only mean the spiritual labour which makes it possible to earn the enduring food, as opposed to labour for physical sustenance. The suggestion, recorded by Barrett, that **the works of God** are the *object* of the people's labour, something they do instead of working for the food which the Son of Man gives, is most improbable. Contrary to usual practice, John does not here employ his device of misunderstanding, but makes the people ask the right question, so as to bring the dialogue quickly to the desired point for the discourse. This question could perhaps correspond with the people's request for teaching in the homiletic form analysed by Bowker—a question on a point of *halakhah* with the demand *yᵉlammᵉdēnū rabbān* ('let our master teach us!'). The homily springs from this point.

29. The fact that **the work of God** (i.e. the spiritual labour) is to **believe in him whom he has sent** is exactly what we should expect from the teaching already given in 3.16–21. We may note how closely this approximates to the Pauline idea of justification by faith. The work is not a matter of doing certain

acts or observing a set of rules (e.g. the Law), but of accepting
and entrusting oneself to Jesus.

30. what work do you perform: it would be better to say
'what do you labour?', for this is the same verb as in the last two
verses. The dialogue is still playing upon the *haphtarah* allusion,
Isa. 55.2. The people are saying that, if they are to labour for the
spiritual food, Jesus must labour to show that he is the giver of it.
They want an action which will ummistakably express his function in the plan of God. We know already that, if they would
only realize it, the feeding miracle was precisely such a revelatory
act (cf. on verse 26). But, now that we have embarked on the
homily, we shall be well advised not to seek too close a relationship with the feeding miracle, which has been used to introduce it,
in spite of the fact that the two are woven together by the request
for a Sign. If we start at verse 27, where there is the first allusion
to the *haphtarah*, we can see that the people have been given something to do, and their question of *halakah* was the problem of how
to do it; the reply has taken the unexpected form of demanding
faith in Jesus. From this point it is only natural that they should
ask him to give a sign. For of course when John originally gave
the homily it was just based on the lections, and did not have the
feeding miracle to introduce it, though no doubt it was given in
the setting of the Eucharist.

that we may see and believe you: there is a parallel to these
words in *Gospel of Thomas*, 91: 'Tell us who you are, so that we
may believe in you.' The continuation of the *logion* is reminiscent
of Mt. 16.2–4, and dependence on John seems unlikely.

31. The people adduce the manna miracle as an example of the
sort of sign which they would find convincing. In view of the
expectations about the renewal of this miracle in the coming age
(see above on verse 27) it is a legitimate standard of comparison
to propose. But, seeing that they support their statement with a
quotation which is the proemial text of the discourse, we may
conjecture that in the original form of the homily the whole verse
was placed on the lips of Jesus: 'Your fathers . . .'

He gave them bread from heaven to eat: as so often in John,
the exact source of this quotation is very hard to determine. There
are three possibilities. (a) A conflation of Exod. 16.4 ('bread from
heaven') and 15 ('the bread which the Lord has given you to eat').
(b) Neh. 9.15: 'Thou didst give them bread from heaven for their

hunger.' (c) An abbreviated form of Ps. 78.24: 'And he rained
down upon them manna to eat, and gave them the grain' (LXX
'bread') 'from heaven.' 'Bread' occurs at the beginning of the
very next verse in the Hebrew. (b) can be ruled out, as it contains
nothing that is not in (a). (c) is preferable to (a), because it is in
the third person throughout, whereas (a) and (b) both employ
the second person. But it must be influenced by (a) to account for
the vocabulary. It is quite possible that John was familiar with
both the Hebrew and the LXX. It may then be tentatively assumed that John has taken his proemial text from Ps. 78.24, but
has abbreviated it with a conscious reminiscence of the *sēder* text,
Exod. 16. If this is so, does it make a suitable bridge to the
haphtarah text from Isaiah? A glance at the opening verses of Ps. 78
will show that it does so admirably, for the first eight verses are
concerned with the teaching of the Law, and the whole psalm is
aimed at showing the dreadful consequences of disobedience. Thus
the proemial text at once establishes the sapiential interpretation
which is going to dominate the discourse. For discussion of the
text of the quotation see E. D. Freed, *Old Testament Quotations in
the Gospel of John*, *NT Sup* XI (1965), pp. 11–16.

Jesus is the Bread from Heaven 32–40

32. Truly: as in the discourse of 5.19–47, this formal way of
speaking is usual for the opening of a fresh theme, and (less
commonly) for a summarizing statement. But we have also found
that it is often a sign that the saying includes traditional words of
Jesus. We shall see that this is the case here.

not Moses: the homily begins with the exposition of 'he gave
them bread from heaven'. First of all, the giver (God himself) is
indicated by the well-known debating technique, frequent in rabbinic debates, of dismissing an alternative possibility. Hence the
emphatic **not.** Obviously the Jews had not suggested that the
giver was Moses, but it is important to make the point clear,
because the common factor between the manna and the true
bread (i.e. Jesus himself) is the fact that both are the gift of God.
And of course Moses had a great deal of reflected glory in Jewish
estimation as God's agent; cf. the quotation from *Eccles. Rabba*,
i.28 given in the notes to verse 27.

my Father: the positive side of this first point takes the form of a
restatement of the proemial text, incorporating interpretative cor-

rections. 'He' becomes **my Father;** 'gave them' becomes **gives you;** 'bread' is qualified by the adjective **true,** i.e. real (*alēthinon*, cf. 1.9). Thus Jesus not only clarifies a point with regard to the manna miracle, but at once applies it to the feeding of his actual audience, and indeed (by implication) of all men at all times. But in correcting the proemial text in this way, John has produced a remarkable echo of a petition of the Lord's Prayer, which explains the sudden, and not strictly necessary, use of **Father** for God; cf. Mt. 6.9a, 11 (*RSV, mg*): 'Our Father who art in heaven . . . Give us this day our bread for the morrow.' The meaning of the last phrase is highly problematical, but one interpretation of it at least is that it refers to the food of the coming age, which is already available to those who belong to Christ. This exactly corresponds with the Johannine eschatology, in which the future events are anticipated by faith-relationship with Jesus. Although John does not reproduce the Lord's Prayer as such, there can be no doubt that he was familiar with it, as we shall come across further allusions to it in chapter 17. This, then, is the traditional material which lies behind this 'truly, truly' saying (cf. verse 34).

33. that which comes down: as the Greek word for **bread** is masculine, this could be translated 'he who comes down' (so *AV*). This is clearly wrong, for it anticipates verse 35, but the ambiguity is probably intentional. At this stage in the argument the aim is to expound 'the true bread from heaven' of the last verse in terms which will later be applicable to Jesus himself. For Jesus as the one who **comes down,** cf. 3.13.
life to the world: this expresses the qualitative difference of the true bread from the physical bread of the manna miracle, in much the same way as the living water in 4.14. It is a principle of spiritual life which leads into the eternal life of the coming age.

34. The people's request is similar to the response of the Samaritan woman in 4.15, and in the same way it implies only partial understanding of what Jesus is saying. Once more it constitutes an echo of the petition in the Lord's Prayer, even more compelling than the last, for **give us** is identical in the Greek. Moreover the rare word *epiousion* ('daily' in the familiar version, 'for the morrow' in *RSV, mg* quoted above) may perhaps mean 'continual' (it is so understood in the Old Syriac version), and would then be roughly equivalent to **always** in the present verse. John sees it as a petition to receive *now* the bread of the future age. It is thus possible that one of his aims is to correct inadequate interpretations of this petition of the Lord's Prayer.

35. I am the bread of life: Jesus has hinted that he is to be the giver of the bread of eternal life (verse 27); now he actually identifies himself with it. The **I am . . .** is simply explanatory, like Moses' explanation of the manna in the *sēder* text, Exod. 16.15: '*It is* the bread which the Lord has given you to eat.' But at the same time it constitutes a self-revelation, like 'I am the light of the world' in 8.12, and as such has been compared with the self-revelation of Isis in Egyptian Hellenistic religion (see the examples in Barrett, p. 242). To put it in Bultmann's terms (see his valuable note on *egō eimi*, p. 225, n. 3), the saying in its context is a 'recognition-formula', explaining how or what the bread is ('I am the bread which is under discussion'); but, taken by itself, it is a 'qualification-formula', declaring a particular quality of the speaker, that he is the means of eschatological nourishment ('I am bread for the hungry, water for the thirsty, . . .'). From this point of view, it is only natural to see it in Wisdom terms: just as in Sir. 24 Wisdom introduces herself, explains all her qualities, and finally issues an invitation to men to 'eat your fill of my produce' (Sir. 24.19), so Jesus not only identifies himself with the Bread of Life, but claims that this is a quality which makes him desirable to men for their salvation.

It is, then, not surprising that, in the beautifully balanced clauses of the remainder of the verse, he claims to satisfy not only hunger but also thirst. This is a reversal of Sir. 24.21, 'Those who eat me will hunger for more, and those who drink me will thirst for more', which we have already noticed in connection with 4.14. The satisfaction of thirst is a little unexpected in the present context, but at once seems perfectly natural when this Wisdom background is taken into consideration. The analogy with 4.14 would suggest that we are to think of water as the satisfaction of thirst (Sanders insists on this), but it could be a veiled allusion to the wine of the Eucharist (so Hoskyns). In fact the Wisdom background definitely tips the scales in favour of the latter, because the passage just quoted from Sirach is itself an allusion to Prov. 9.5, where Wisdom says: 'Come, eat of my bread and drink of the wine I have mixed.' Thus, quite regardless of whether verses 51–8 belong to the original form of the discourse, it is legitimate to see in *this* verse a hint of the Eucharist at the very point where the sapiential interpretation is absolutely inescapable. Finally, it should be noted that **comes to me** is strictly parallel to the more common **believes in me,** and may be a further hint of the Wisdom background (Prov. 9.5; Sir. 24.19). Compare also the *haphtarah* text, Isa. 55.1, where water is most prominent, but wine and milk are also mentioned.

36. This verse breaks the flow of thought, and substitutes personal address for the third person style of the exposition. In verses 37–40 Jesus is going to expound the Wisdom-invitation of verse 35 in terms of consistent eschatology, in a manner very similar to 5.25–9. As an exposition of the proemial text, this paragraph is concerned with the phrase 'from heaven', but it is much more dependent on the expanded form in verse 33, in which the emphasis falls on 'gives life to the world'. The present verse is a parenthesis, in which Jesus acknowledges that the hearers are not in a position to respond to the invitation of verse 35, and so to receive life. But it is not without a positive function at this point. For the exposition of this invitation in the following verses is made necessary by the people's lack of understanding, and forms a slight digression from the main line of the argument. The procedure is very like chapter 5, where a similar complaint (5.40) starts a short digression. The people's inadequacy is not a gratuitous assumption on Jesus' part, but is prompted by their lack of proper understanding in verse 34.

seen me: me is not in א A a b q Old Syriac, and is rejected by Bernard, Barrett and Sanders (cp. *NEB*). It is an obvious word to interpolate, especially in view of verse 40. Without it the object of **seen** would be 'the signs', and the verse is an allusion to verse 26. Verse 34 showed that the people still thought in terms of *physical* bread; consequently, in verses 35–40 the feeding metaphor is dropped. For the whole verse, cf. 15.24; 20.29.

37. All that the Father gives me: the neuter **all that,** instead of masculine 'everyone who', has been explained as due to thinking in Aramaic (Odeberg, p. 262), but Bernard (1.199) says that the collective use of the neuter singular 'is not unknown in classical Greek'. It occurs again in verse 39 and 17.2, 24. It is natural that here, as also in 17.2, we should assume from these words that some are predestined by God to salvation, and others not; but it should be observed that only the positive side is mentioned. We should, then, be on our guard against reading a rigid doctrine of predestination into this verse. We know from 3.17 that it is the desire of God that all men should be saved; but John is aware of the possibility of ultimate refusal. The point is that all those who *do* respond to the Father (or are 'drawn' by him (verse 44)) come to *Jesus*, because of the unique prerogatives which he has from the Father (cf. 5.20–3).

come to me is an allusion to verse 35, and so is exactly equivalent to 'believe in me', which will be taken up in verse 40.

not cast out: i.e. welcome heartily (an example of litotes, in which the negative is a way of strongly affirming the opposite). The metaphor of the banquet, implicit in the Wisdom allusions of verse 35, is the best explanation of this vivid phrase. In this part of the verse the idea is fully personal (**him who comes,** i.e. each individual).

38. come down from heaven: Jesus is still speaking of himself in terms of the proemial text, and this phrase is taken directly from the version of it in verse 33. But we can also hear in it an echo of 3.13. Jesus is explaining the reason for the magnanimity of the invitation. It is because it accords precisely with the purpose of his Incarnation, which is none other than the salvation of all men. First this is stated generally: the purpose is to carry out the Father's **will.** The words used are exactly the same as in 5.30. The argument of 5.19–30, on the complete accord between Jesus and the Father, is taken for granted.

39. this is the will: the repetition of phrases in this and the next verse succeeds admirably in drawing out the meaning of verse 35 with the utmost solemnity. The two verses take up the two halves of verse 37 successively. So here, as in 37a, the collective neuter singular is used throughout; but 'will come to me' is expanded in two ways, first by the negative formulation (**lose nothing**), which puts the point much more emphatically, and secondly by addition of **raise it up at the last day.** This gives eschatological significance to the invitation. The life that is promised is the life of the coming age, following the general resurrection (cf. 5.25–9).

lose nothing unmistakably recalls verse 12, and suggests the universality of God's plan of salvation.

40. The same ideas, but expressed in the fully personal manner of 37b. So 'him who comes to me' of that verse is specified in terms of a personal relationship with Jesus, i.e. **every one who**

sees the Son and believes in him. The word for **sees** (*theōron*—not the same as in verse 36) is unusual in this kind of context, and must have the idea of special perception or recognition (so Barrett, Brown). In view of the eschatological function involved, **the Son** presumably means the Son of Man. We can paraphrase the verse thus: 'Each individual who recognizes Jesus to be the Son of Man who will give life at the end of the age, and who puts faith in him even now, may have that life already, and also his part in the resurrection in the coming age.' Thus, whereas the last verse, with its neuter formulation, has been a general statement of consistent eschatology, the plan of God for the future, this verse brings the future into the present, anticipating the future at the level of individual response. All this is involved in the Wisdom invitation of verse 35.

Jesus is the Truth from above **41–51**

41. In the preceding section it has been asserted that it is *the Father* who gives the true bread, that this bread is *Jesus himself*, and the effect of it is a nourishment which continues into *eternal life*. What has not been made clear is how bread can be a suitable symbol to express this function of Jesus, although it is implicit in the sapiential background to verse 35. Thus it is necessary to go back to that point in the exposition, in order to give an idea of what it means to eat this bread. John does this by recalling verses 33 and 35, which are conflated to produce **'I am the bread which came down from heaven'**; and he makes it the substance of an objection by the audience, so as to give a fresh point of departure. **The Jews:** this comes as a surprise: we thought the audience was the nucleus of the Galileans who had been fed on the other side of the lake. It has been suggested that it means Judeans who have come to investigate Jesus' doings, but Bernard points out that it must mean Galileans, as they know Jesus' family. It is better to suppose that John has slipped into his usual way of designating Jesus' opponents in the discourses, which would be all the more likely when the discourse was an independent piece, before it was joined to the feeding miracle for the sake of the narrative. **murmured:** The word is rare in the NT, and it is very probable that it is used here in conscious allusion to the *sēder* text, for it occurs in Exod. 16.2, 7ff.

42. Is not this Jesus: the people's complaint is clearly depend-

ent on the tradition which is also preserved in Mk 6.2–4 paras.
This is pejorative, as in Mk 6.2. **The son of Joseph** replaces
Mark's 'the son of Mary' (cf. Lk. 4.22), but conforms to John's
style; cf. 1.45. The setting in Mark is Jesus' preaching in the
synagogue in Nazareth, but here it is the synagogue at Capernaum
(verse 59). The same context includes the proverb which John has
already used in 4.44. It was argued in the notes on that verse that
John's source did not specify any particular place, so that it was
possible for him to speak as if Jesus' *patris* was Jerusalem. But it
was therefore equally open to him to use the material in connection with the preaching at Capernaum. He knew in any case that
Jesus came from Nazareth (1.45). The objection in Mk 6.2f. is
that Jesus has assumed an authority which hardly suits his well-
known origin from a Nazarene family, an objection echoed by
Nathanael in 1.46. Here it is applied to the Christological claims
of the discourse.

I have come down: cf. verse 38. The objection, as so often, misunderstands Jesus' meaning. To be the son of Joseph and to be
the one sent from heaven are not mutually exclusive, as the Prologue makes clear. The word 'bread' is omitted, because the objection is concerned with the human personality of Jesus.

44. The Jews' objection was really a matter of 'the scandal of
the Incarnation'. As usual, Jesus does not make a direct reply,
but in fact he is concerned precisely with this issue. The Father's
purpose is that men should **come to** Jesus (verse 37), so that he
may give them a share in the resurrection to eternal life (verses
39f.).

This purpose cannot be achieved **unless the Father who sent
me draws him.** This is the key phrase, and it explains the necessity of the Incarnation; The Father **draws** men by inner attraction. There are several classic passages in the OT which express
the attractive power of the love of God, notably Jer. 31.3 (where
the LXX uses John's word) and Hos. 11.4. It will appear later
that John sees this attractive power in the sacrifice of Jesus; cf.
12.32, where he uses the same word. Jesus is the one who came
from heaven and gives his life for the world (verse 51). This verse
shows incontestably that John thinks of men's response to God in
fundamentally ethical and personal terms. This excludes any possibility of an interpretation of verse 37 in terms of predestination.

45. We seem to have moved away from the idea of the bread, but it is not far below the surface. John is now thinking of the manna miracle as a type of God's gift of the Law to the people in order to gain their obedience. So, instead of referring to the bread as such, he now introduces the quotation from the *haphtarah*. The whole discourse began with an allusion to Isa. 55.2 (verse 27). This is an invitation of Wisdom, and the very next words go on to express the sapiential meaning of the passage: 'Hearken diligently to me, and eat what is good . . . Incline your ear, and come to me; hear, that your soul may live' (Isa. 55.2b, 3a). It is thus perfectly natural to correlate with this the saying earlier in the same *haphtarah* passage: 'All your sons shall be taught by the Lord' (Isa. 54.13). Again John's text differs slightly from the original, but there can be no doubt about this allusion. The fact that he says vaguely **in the prophets** should not be taken to suggest that he is unaware of the source of the quotation; it is common usage, as in Ac. 7.42. It is unlikely that the text is influenced by Jer. 31.34, though the thought is similar. The effect of using this quotation at this point is that it makes the crucial connection between the future promise and the present offer of life in terms of the Incarnation. It is an offer to all, and no doubt John deliberately omits 'your sons', i.e. only the people of Israel, from the quotation. It is through the Incarnation that everyone may hear and learn from the Father. This will be explained in the next verse.

46. Not that any one has seen: the point is the same as was made in 5.37. But whereas that negative statement was made to show that the Father's *witness* could be found nowhere else than in the Scriptures, here it is to assert that only in the Incarnation of Jesus is God made known in visible form (cf. 1.18). The thought is thus closely parallel to the argument in 3.13, where the language of descent is used. It is unnecessary to bring into the discussion the possibility of a reference to Jewish mysticism, though this cannot be ruled out altogether. The point is that the true teaching of God, which the Jews held was given in the theophany on Sinai and the Book of the Law, and which was typified in the miracle of the manna, is actually given in the Incarnation of the Word of God in Jesus.

47. he who believes: this is the reading of the Egyptian group of MSS., and P[66] P[75] W Θ. The Old Syriac adds 'in God', which scarcely accords with Johannine diction; the *textus receptus* and

many MSS. have the obvious 'in me'. There can be no doubt that
the latter is the correct interpretation, even if it is not the original
text. The **truly** opening indicates that this brief verse is a concise
summary of what has just been said (in this case it does not seem
possible to detect a traditional saying of Jesus as the basis of it).
Those who receive Jesus, who is the bread from heaven, as the
revelation of the Father, already have the life that endures (cf.
verses 40 and 44).

48. Jesus repeats the self-revelation of verse 35, and so introduces a further phase of the argument. Having established the
sapiential interpretation of the bread with the aid of the *haphtarah*
text, he can now return to the *sēder*, the story of the manna, confident that it will no longer be misunderstood. So the next three
verses are concerned with the quality of this spiritual bread as food.
Verses 49 and 50 distinguish the two kinds of bread; then in
verse 51 Jesus identifies himself with the second kind of bread
once more and relates it to the Incarnation and the Passion.

49. and they died: the argument is the same as in 4.13f.
Although the manna was a heavenly gift, it was only intended to
support the Israelites on their way through the Wilderness, and
could never have the same effect as the true bread. But we can
read more into this verse in the light of the enlarged interpretation
opened up by the *haphtarah* text. The manna stands for the Law
of the Sinai covenant, which is equally without true life-giving
properties, and so is superseded (cf. Gal. 3.21).

50. This is the bread: This (Gr. *houtos*), referring to Jesus
himself, recalls the text of the *sēder*, Exod. 16.15: '*It* (*houtos*) *is the
bread* which the Lord has given you *to eat.*' Thereby it also recalls
the proemial text (verse 31), with the modification of verse 33.
This means 'the bread we are talking about now', which by contrast has lasting effects; but the verse does not quite conclude the
argument. Those scholars who regard the final eucharistic section
of the discourse as an addition feel that the exposition has come
to an end with this verse (Bultmann thinks it ends at 'for ever' in
verse 51). But John has suddenly introduced the word **eat,** which
has not been mentioned since the proemial text. There is, then,
further exposition to be done. The sapiential interpretation can
happily use a variety of symbols, such as water and light, and the
fact that it is bread which is under discussion has been rather lost
sight of. But John is going to insist that it has a meaning of its

own, denied to the other symbols. **eat** in this verse thus anticipates the subject which still remains to be treated.

51. Once more we have the self-revelation formula, identifying Jesus with the second kind of bread. It is yet another version of verse 33, this time giving special emphasis to the life-giving effects. **living bread** recalls the 'living water' of 4.10. There it could be taken quite simply as running water, but later (in 4.14) it transpired that it really meant the water of life. So here the phrase, which obviously can have no comparable literal meaning, is equivalent to 'bread of life' in verse 35.

will live for ever replaces 'and not die' of the preceding verse. It is not a doctrine of immortality, cutting out death, but a quality of life which survives death, continuing beyond the Resurrection.

and the bread which I shall give for the life of the world is my flesh: this final part of the verse not only comes rather oddly as an afterthought, but also suffers from textual uncertainty.

The latter point requires attention first. The *RSV* has adopted the order of words as it is found in ℵ m and Tertullian, whereby **for the life of the world** is brought into the relative clause, where it properly belongs. But this is surely an attempt at improvement. The best authorities (P⁶⁶ P⁷⁵ B D W Old Syriac, Old Latin and Vulgate, Sahidic) put this phrase at the end, so that the whole clause reads: 'and the bread which I shall give is my flesh for the life of the world'. Another attempt at improvement, found in the *textus receptus* and other MSS. and versions, is to repeat the relative clause: 'and the bread which I shall give is my flesh, which I shall give for the life of the world'. Bultmann treats **for the life of the world** as a gloss, but this is quite arbitrary. The unusual word-order of the best MSS. is to be accepted; we shall find on examination that it contains the answer to the question why John has appended this clause to the verse.

For the new factor of this section of the discourse, the word **eats,** opens up a fresh allusion, this time not to an OT text but to the eucharistic words of Jesus: 'Take, *eat*; this *is my body*' (Mt. 26.26); 'This *is my body which is given for* (*huper*) you' (Lk. 22.19, long text); 'This *is my body which is* [broken] *for* (*huper*) you' (1 C. 11.24). The point then is that bread must be *eaten,* and we now know enough about the bread to understand that it is the Word and Wisdom of God made *flesh* in the incarnation of Jesus. That is the essential fact which has to be swallowed, digested and assimilated by those who respond to Wisdom's invitation; and, moreover, this Bread from Heaven, this Word made flesh, reveals the Father supremely by giving himself in a sacrificial death **for** (*huper*) **the life of the world.**

As in 3.13–15, John will not speak of the Incarnation without the Passion. To him the Incarnation is primarily revelatory (cf. 1.18), and the Passion is the most revealing act of the incarnate Word. The idea does not come into the discourse at this late stage entirely unheralded. There has already been a hint of it in verse 44 (see the note on 'draws'). The unusual word-order—**'my flesh for the life of the world'**—is thus due to the eucharistic allusion, and the whole phrase is a definition of the bread in terms of both the Incarnation and the Passion. It should be noted that **flesh** (*sarx*) is a legitimate alternative to the 'body' (*sōma*) of the eucharistic texts. It is in fact a more literal rendering of the Hebrew *bāśār* ('flesh') which underlies both. The word also occurs in the *sēder* passage with reference to the quails given along with the manna. Exod. 16.8, 12 has *bāśār* in the Hebrew, though the LXX translates it *kreas* ('meat'). But according to Epiphanius, *Pan. Haer.* xxx.xxii.4f., this word was used in connection with the Passover lamb in the version of Lk. 22.15 given in the *Gospel of the Ebionites*. Ignatius uses *sarx* of the Eucharist in Rom. vii.3; Philad. iv.1; Smyr. vi.2.

The Flesh and Blood of the Son of Man 52–59

52. disputed: a stronger expression than was used in 41 (lit. 'battled'). The objection serves the same function, to make the transition to a new stage of the argument. For **the Jews,** cf. 41. **his flesh to eat:** most MSS. omit **his,** though it is supported by P66 B Old Latin, Syriac and Coptic versions. If the omission is original, there may well be an allusion to the 'murmuring' of the Israelites in Exod. 16.8, where Moses replies: 'When the Lord *gives* you in the evening *flesh to eat* and in the morning bread to the full . . .' If this is correct, the problem is not the scandal of a carnal view of feeding on Jesus, but another example of literal misunderstanding. The people cannot understand how Jesus is going to provide yet another foodstuff.

53. unless: cf. 3.3, 5, and note the **'Truly'** opening. This saying seems to be a variant of 3.3, just as that was recognizably a variant of Mt. 18.3. All these 'unless' sayings deal with the conditions of entry into the Kingdom of God. Here the eucharistic eating and drinking have been substituted for the idea of rebirth, and to **have life** for to enter the Kingdom. It is not necessary to suppose that John has invented the saying on the basis of 3.3, for it was probably current in a number of forms, but no doubt he has adapted it for its present context. The saying should not be taken in an exclusive sense, for the invitation is open to all (verse 39; cf. 44).

the Son of man: not only the giver of manna in the coming age, but also the one whose exaltation is by way of the Cross (3.14). The title thus again points to the Passion.

drink his blood: Wisdom's invitation is for drink as well as food (cf. verse 35 and Isa. 55.1; Prov. 9.5). The use of eucharistic language makes the introduction of this correlative to eating inevitable. It should be realized that there is no suggestion intended of the horrifying idea involved in a literal interpretation. The choice of phrase is again entirely controlled by the tradition of Jesus' words at the Last Supper (cf. Mk 14.23f.), and is again intended to draw attention to the Incarnation and the Passion. The metaphors of eating and drinking are not to be reduced to the vague notion of spiritual acceptance. Flesh and blood denote the real humanity of Jesus (cf. Mt. 16.17). It is the actual, historical Jesus who is to be taken and assimilated by the believer. According to 1 C. 11.26, in the Eucharist the Christians 'proclaim the Lord's death until he comes'. It is Christ, who lived and died and rose again, who is to be received as the revelation of the Father.

54. eats: here, and in 56–8, John uses a different word. So far he has used the aorist *phagein* throughout; now he uses the present tense, and, instead of the usual root employed for this tense (*esthiein*), he chooses *trōgein*, which properly means 'to munch, or nibble'. There are two reasons why he may have done this. *Trōgein* could be chosen to press the point home by its greater realism in the most uncompromising way, even at the risk of suggesting a 'carnal' view of the eucharistic meal. It would then very likely have a polemical motive, against the Docetists. Hoskyns and Brown take this view. Or it may be simply due to the limitations of John's Greek vocabulary. He must have known *esthiein*, for it is frequent both in the LXX and in the traditional Gospel material he has at his disposal, but *trōgein* is the word he finds most natural to use. He never uses *esthiein*, but he has *trōgein* again in a quotation in 13.18 (where LXX has *esthiein*). Elsewhere in the NT *trōgein* only occurs in Mt. 24.38, where it has no special meaning (Lk. 17.27 has *esthiein* in the parallel passage). This view, which is strongly argued by Sanders, seems to me to be more likely. As the next words show, the whole point of the verse is to correlate the eucharistic feeding with both present possession of eternal life, and participation in it after the general resurrection, exactly as in verse 40. The thought is moving away from the *nature* of the food (i.e. the incarnate and crucified Lord) to the *effect* of it, which is first put in the already familiar words of verse 40, and then has a new formulation in verse 56.

55. indeed: the Egyptian group of MSS., and with them P[66] and P[75], have the adjective 'true' (*alēthēs*), which differs from the adverb **indeed** by only one letter. In spite of this strong support, Barrett argues that for the sense 'real' John would have used the other adjectival form *alēthinos*, as in verse 32. It hardly affects the meaning of the verse, which is aimed at suggesting the comprehensive nourishment provided by Jesus.

56. abides in me: this is the climax of the discourse. All the metaphors are dropped, and the whole thing is put into terms of personal relationship. The mutual indwelling of Jesus and the disciples will be elaborated in the allegory of the Vine—again a eucharistic theme—in chapter 15. John's thought never moves in ontological or quasi-magical categories. As the mode of receiving Jesus is to 'come to' him and to 'believe in' him, so the effect must be put into terms of personal, ethical, relationship. It is this relationship which persists beyond the present age to the time of the general resurrection.

At the end of this verse D and some Old Latin MSS. add: '. . . as the Father is in me and I am in the Father. Truly, truly, I say to you, unless you receive the body of the Son of Man as the Bread of Life, you have no life in you.' That this is a homiletic addition, but not an original part of the text, is evident from the non-Johannine 'receive the body' (instead of 'eat the flesh'). Apart from this the interpolator has kept up the style well, taking verse 53 as his model. It is presumably aimed at making the eucharistic interpretation more explicit.

57. the living Father: the Father is self-subsistent and the source of all life. In 5.26f. Jesus traced his *authority* to his filial relationship to the Father. Here he traces his *capacity* to give life. The filial relationship is intimately personal, and the same applies to the relationship between Jesus and those to whom he gives life. Hence there can be no misunderstanding of the meaning of the otherwise shocking **eats me** (D changes this to 'receives me', in line with the interpolation).

58. The final verse recapitulates the whole discourse in words which recall the text of verse 31 from which it started. **This is the bread** is to be understood from the definition in verses 32–40; **which came down from heaven,** from verses 43–7; **not such as the fathers ate and died,** from verses 48–51; **he who eats** (cf. verse 54) **this bread will live for ever,** from verses 52–7. By itself, the verse would be open to misunderstanding; as a summary of the whole it brilliantly condenses the Christological exposition of the manna pericope into memorable form.

59. in the synagogue: D and the Old Latin MSS. which had the interpolation in verse 56 here add: 'on the Sabbath', probably as a result of the influence of Lk. 4.16. That Jesus should deliver a biblical exposition in the synagogue on the Sabbath is entirely credible; but the Christology of it suggests that in fact we have here an example of Christian preaching before the final split with the Jews. Visitors to the extensive remains at Capernaum can see a fine synagogue in classical style; it was not standing in the time of Jesus, but was perhaps built in John's day, though this is disputed. If so, it may well incorporate stones from the much smaller synagogue which stood on the same site in Jesus' day.

REACTIONS OF DISCIPLES AND CONFESSION OF PETER 6.60–71

Following his usual practice, John concludes the section with an indication of the response evoked by Jesus' teaching. We expect him to say 'many believed' (cf. 2.11, 23; 4.39–42). But here we have unbelief, and that not of the Jews who are opposed to Jesus, but of his own disciples, many of whom 'drew back' (verse 66). There is nothing like this in the Synoptic Gospels, but this does not exclude the possibility that it rests on authentic tradition. On the other hand the rapid growth of the Church after Pentecost hardly suggests that there had been a considerable defection only a year or so beforehand. When we come to the Supper discourses, and particularly to the Prayer of chapter 17, we shall see that John is much concerned about the problem of divisions within the Church. It is notable that all the references to division are in the parts of the Gospel which belong to the second edition. If we may also take 1 John as evidence, we can be certain that this was a live issue for John.

What was the issue which caused 'offence' (verse 61) to the disciples? It is generally held that they represent Christians who were lapsing into Docetism (see Introduction, pp. 61ff.). They object to the emphasis on the 'flesh' in verses 51–6; but in verse 63 Jesus appears to agree with them! This is generally explained in this way. The Docetists *assume* that Jesus' words imply the 'carnal' interpretation, taking it in a very crude and literal way. Verse 63 shows that this is the wrong level of interpretation. 'Flesh' here means the carnal interpretation, which 'is of no avail'; only a spiritual interpretation will do. But this line of explanation has recently been under attack. Brown objects that 'flesh' in verse 63 cannot have such a completely different meaning from 51–8, that it must mean (as it stands) the flesh of Jesus, and Jesus could not possibly say that his own flesh is of no avail. This is one reason why, in common with other scholars, he holds that 51–8 is a later insertion of parallel material. Bornkamm has pointed out that the thought-background of the verse is to be found in 3.6, where flesh and spirit are distinguished. E. Schweizer (*EvTh* XII (1952/3), pp. 361f.) had already shown that the polemic against Docetism is already implicit in verses 41f., for the real heresy of the Docetists is the denial of the Incarnation of Jesus, and so also of the reality of his death, and thus cuts at the heart of the entire discourse.

This is surely right, and in the above exposition of 51–8 care has been taken to show that the carnal interpretation is not even considered by John. His thought runs wholly along the lines of the Incarnation and the Passion, and the sacrament of the Eucharist is the means whereby men may have faith in union with him who came down from heaven and died on the Cross. From this point of view Bornkamm's observation may be accepted, without entailing the omission of 51–8; but this still does not meet the objection of Brown. How can John use 'flesh' in two such different ways? The difficulty is not insuperable. First we should remember that the discourse is a homily complete in itself, and that verses 60–71, like 1–25, are the narrative framework which John has used in order to bring it into the plan of the whole Gospel. Secondly, the

context of verse 63 shows further contact with the discourse with
Nicodemus, for the ascent motif in verse 62 comes from 3.13,
and this motif has been entirely omitted from the Bread of Life
homily, in spite of the fact that descent is one of its leading ideas.
Thus the meaning of verse 63 depends on the interpretation of
62, which has already taken the thought some distance away from
the particular issue of 51–8. Bultmann avoids the difficulty by
transferring this section to follow 12.33, first inserting 8.30–40.
But this depends on an unacceptable theory of the composition
of the Gospel; cf. Introduction, p. 48.

The narrative material of this section draws on traditional sayings on discipleship. This brings us once more to the Marcan
sequence following the second feeding miracle, which includes the
confession of Peter (Mk 8.27–9.1). Here again we must assume that
John's source is not Mark as such, but a tradition parallel to
Mark's source at this point.

The Offence of the Gospel 60–5

60. hard: not **hard** in the sense of 'harsh', but more like the
modern English usage of 'incredible', cf. Dt. 17.8 (a 'difficult'
case); 30.11 (a 'hard' commandment); Jer. 32.17 ('nothing is too
hard for thee'), where in each case the Hebrew word properly
means 'wonderful, extraordinary'.

61. knowing in himself: cf. 2.25.
murmured: cf. verse 41.
take offence: the verb *skandalizein* is derived from *skandalon*,
translated 'stumbling-block' in 1 C. 1.23 ('We preach Christ crucified, a stumbling-block to the Jews, and folly to the Gentiles').
It means properly to snare, and so to entice into sin, but in the
NT it has a special nuance, to cause hindrance to belief; cf.
Mt. 11.6. This seems to be derived from the use of Isa. 8.14 ('a
stone of offence, and a rock of stumbling') as a proof text, alluded
to in Rom. 9.32f.; 1 Pet. 2.8. As noted above, the teaching which
gives offence to these disciples is the necessity of the Incarnation
and the Cross in order that God may give life to the world. This
agrees with the quotation from 1 C. 1.23.

62. Then what if: the *RSV* attempts to cope with what is in
fact an incomplete sentence: 'Then if you were to see . . .?' This
needs to be completed with some such words as 'What would
happen?' The answer to this could be either 'the offence would be

all the greater!' (Bultmann), or 'you would see the truth which resolves the difficulty' (Bauer, Odeberg). Barrett, following Westcott, thinks both are possible, and suggests that the apodosis is omitted in order to leave both possibilities open. We have to bear in mind that the offence is caused by the great emphasis on Jesus' *descent* in the discourse. This means that John holds that the Incarnation is necessary for the real revelation of God (cf. 43–6). But he carries the thought through to the Passion, which is the climax of the Incarnation from the point of view of revelation (verse 44, and 51–8). The idea of the ascent of the Son of Man, which he now brings into the discussion, is derived from 3.13. It means the glorification of Jesus as the Son of Man figure, when his work on earth is done. But John sees this glory anticipated in the Passion. It is the point where revelation and glorification meet, and the descent and the ascent overlap. Thus, in so far as the ascent refers to the Passion, it makes the offence of the Incarnation even greater; but, as a hint of future glory, it must surely remove the offence. The future glory is the predominant notion, implied by **where he was before.** It may be right, with Barrett, to leave the interpretation open, but if a decision between the possibilities must be made the balance is in favour of the second. The disciples must have patience, and wait until the full story has been unfolded before they decide against it.

63. the spirit that gives life: it is only when this phrase is properly understood that the reference to **the flesh** can be interpreted correctly. John is speaking of the disciples' capacity to perceive the truth. It is one of his principles that only the spiritual man can perceive spiritual things. This was the point of the flesh/spirit contrast in 3.6, and it depends on the anthropology which he has received from Judaism. His words here are identical with Paul's in 2 C. 3.6 ('for the written code kills, but the Spirit gives life'), cf. 1 C. 15.45. This is derived from Gen. 2.7: 'God formed man of dust from the ground, and breathed into his nostrils the breath of life; and man became a living being'. Thus, by contrast, flesh here is the earthy part of man, man as he is by nature, his intellect remaining unilluminated by the revelation of God. It is only if he is open to the influence of God, that he can perceive divine things. Thus *in the composition of man* it is the Spirit that gives life, and the flesh is of no avail.

the words . . . are spirit and life: the reference may be simply to the preceding discourse or (as Barrett suggests) to the teaching of Jesus as a whole. This seems preferable, for this is a further general statement on the disciples' capacity to perceive the truth. Just as man can only receive spiritual things when illuminated by the Spirit, so it must be clearly understood that all Jesus' teaching belongs to the category of spiritual things. Here the phrase 'life-giving Spirit' is split up even to the extent of repeating the verb (lit. 'they are spirit and are life'). This distinction suggests that two aspects of the one idea are in mind: the source and the purpose. Jesus' teaching has its origin in the spiritual realm, and its aim and effect is to bring men into this realm, which is the gift of eternal life.

64. some . . . do not believe: in the light of the preceding verses this can only mean that John has in mind Christians whom he regards as not under the Spirit, but under the flesh, so that their minds are blind to the truth. (It is assumed that he actually means the Docetists.) John traces these back to false disciples even in the time of Jesus, Judas Iscariot being the most obvious example. The apologetic motive is here particularly strong; the issue can be traced elsewhere in the NT. For the problem of blindness to the truth, cf. the use of Isa. 6.9f. in Mk 4.12; Ac. 28.25–7; Jn 12.40; and the use of related texts in Rom. 11.7–10. For the special problem of Judas, cf. Mt. 27.3–10; Ac. 1.16–20; Jn 17.12.
knew from the first: cf. verse 61. **From the first** (*ex archēs*) could be an allusion to 1.1, where the word is used, but it is more likely to mean from the beginning of the ministry, cf. 2.11. The emphasis is on Jesus' complete foreknowledge of events.

65. To clinch the matter, Jesus refers back to verse 44, which was the reply to what was fundamentally the same objection. There can be no technique which by-passes the action of God in order to secure salvation. The point implicit in verse 63, that one must be open to the Spirit of God, and ready to receive from him, was in fact a major aspect of the teaching of the discourse itself (verses 44–7).

The Confession of Peter **66–71**

66. After this: the phrase (*ek toutou*) could equally well mean 'because of this'.
drew back: the phrase is unusual, and may be derived from a traditional saying such as Lk. 9.62, which is concerned with dis-

cipleship. The little anecdotes about men who refused the call
of Jesus in Mk 10.22 and Lk. 9.57–62 were remembered precisely
because of the Christians who fell away at a later stage.

67. the twelve: only mentioned in this paragraph and in
20.24. John takes it for granted that his readers know about them
as a special group among the disciples, though he has not mentioned the call of more than five men. The Synoptic Gospels
describe the choice of the Twelve, and Lk. 22.30 gives evidence
that the number was related to the tribes of Israel.

go away: Gr. *hupagein*. In view of 'back' (*opisō*) in the last verse,
it is just possible that there is an allusion to the strong words of
Jesus to Peter, when he questions the necessity of the Cross: 'Get
behind (*hupage opisō*) me, Satan!' (Mk 8.33), to which Matthew
adds: 'Your are a hindrance (*skandalon*) to me' (Mt. 16.23). For it
is the scandal of the Cross which has caused the others to draw
back.

68. Peter answered: even if the above allusion be considered
very doubtful, here John is certainly making use of material from
the same context in his source; cf. Mt. 16.16 paras. But before
the actual words of the confession (69b), Peter's speech prepares
for it by (a) an answer to verse 67 in the form of a rhetorical
question; (b) an assertion that Jesus has **the words of eternal
life** (a direct allusion to verse 63); (c) a solemn declaration of
belief (69a). He thus demonstrates what Jesus has just said about
the capacity to perceive the truth. He comes as one drawn by the
Father, he recognizes that the teaching of Jesus is 'spirit and life',
and accordingly he entrusts himself to him in faith and can make
acknowledgement of Jesus from personal experience. Thus at this
point Peter typifies the kind of response which John hopes his
readers will be led to make; cf. Mt. 16.17.

69. the Holy One of God: the Synoptic parallels all show variations. Mt. 16.16 has: 'You are the Christ, the Son of the living
God'; Mk 8.29: 'You are the Christ'; Lk. 9.20: 'The Christ of
God'. There are several different readings in the present case, as
the words have either been conformed to one or other of these
Synoptic parallels, or been influenced by the confession of
Nathanael in 1.49, cf. 20.31. The *RSV* (and *NEB*) **the Holy One
of God** follows the textual tradition which is least likely to have
come under these influences (P75 ℵ B D W Sahidic). It is reminiscent of the confession of the unclean spirit in Mk 1.24 (= Lk.

4.34) (cf. 'the Holy and Righteous One', Ac. 3.14). These references suggest that we have here a Semitism, in which a word for a consecrated person is used as a messianic title. John presumably found this form in his source, whereas the transition to more conventional titles has begun in Mark.

70. choose: the word is used in Luke's account of the choice of the Apostles (Lk. 6.13). John develops this point in 15.16.

a devil: the Greek *diabolos* properly means 'a slanderer', and was adopted by the LXX translators to render 'the Satan' (e.g. Job 2.1), which means 'adversary, or accuser' (cf. Rev. 12.10). According to 13.2, 27, Judas was under the influence of Satan (cf. Lk. 22.3). The underlying thought is that of the two spirits in Man (see the notes on 3.6). The reference to Judas at this point, immediately following Peter's confession, emphasizes the tragic element of false discipleship, which has already been brought to the fore in verses 60–5, and will be a special theme in the account of the Last Supper. It is tempting to find here, too, a reminiscence of the rebuke of Peter (Mk 8.33; see above on verse 67). John has transferred this element from Peter to Judas, because he likes to use characters symbolically, and Judas represents the Satanic influence in the Gospel story.

71. Judas the son of Simon Iscariot: only John tells us his father's name. The surname **Iscariot** is taken by most scholars to be a Hebrew phrase, 'man of Kerioth' (a place in southern Judea, about 15 miles W. of Masada; cf. Jer. 48.24; Am. 2.2). This is supported by the reading 'from Kerioth' in ℵ* Θ and the Ferrar group. The later MSS. take **Iscariot** with **Judas** (reading accusative instead of genitive). If this were right, the name could be descriptive, equivalent to *sicarius* ('assassin'), the most fanatical sect of Jewish nationalists at this time (cf. Ac. 21.38); but this view has been largely abandoned among scholars today. It is normal style to designate a man by either his father's name or his home town, or both.

betray him: cf. verse 64. The word is constantly used as a description of Judas; cf. Mt. 10.4; 26.25; 27.3; etc.

JESUS SUPERSEDES THE LAW BECAUSE HE IS THE SON OF GOD 7.1–8.59

Returning to the main narrative of the Gospel, we immediately plunge into the most difficult chapters in the book. There is no introductory episode from the tradition to provide a peg on which to hang a discourse. Dialogue there is in plenty, but it is confused for lack of a single theme. But not only does the subject-matter jump from topic to topic, but also the setting is constantly shifting. John seems to be uninterested in the unities of time and place and action. The most obvious case of this indifference is the mission of the Temple officers. Reference to 7.14, 32, 37 and 45 will show that it is two or three days before they report back to the Temple authorities, although the whole action takes place within the precincts. It is thus not surprising that numerous suggestions have been made to improve matters by carving these two chapters into pieces and reassembling them in a more logical order, even to the extent of transferring some groups of verses to quite remote parts of the Gospel (e.g. Bultmann places parts of chapter 8 in chapters 10 and 12).

One problem, however, is already solved for us. The episode of the woman caught in adultery (7.53–8.11) is not a true part of the text at all, being absent from the majority of the best MSS., and accordingly has been placed in a footnote in the *RSV* translation, and at the end of the Gospel in *NEB*. It is nevertheless a valuable item of tradition, and will be given due consideration in the commentary. But it cannot be taken into account in studying the structure and contents of these two chapters.

In chapter 7 we have to reckon with four distinct types of material: (a) verses 1–14 describe Jesus' private decision to go to Jerusalem for the feast of Tabernacles. The significant feature of this paragraph is the speculation among the people about Jesus (verse 12). This is continued in two other paragraphs, verses 25–31 and 40–4. It is clear that these belong together as far as their style and content are concerned. But it is equally clear that they require the background of Jesus' teaching activity provided in the verses that separate them. We cannot, then, simply detach these three blocks and treat them apart from the rest. (b) the discussion in verses 15–24. This section so obviously belongs with the discourse of chapter 5 that it seems best to regard it as supplementary material, which John has held over for this chapter. If this is so, and if it is not a case of accidental displacement, we may hope to find the clue to the composition of this chapter from John's decision to use it here. (c) the mission of the Temple officers and its results (verses 32–6 and 45–52). These paragraphs are also concerned with Jesus' identity. In fact, verses 33–6, in which the officers are not mentioned, could easily be taken with the material in (a); and verse 49 also alludes to that material. (d) the short paragraph in which Jesus offers the Water of Life (verses 37–9). This is specifically bound into the setting of the feast of Tabernacles, and many commentators hold that it is a deliberate allusion to the water-pouring ceremony at the feast (see further on this below). Our study of chapter 6, especially 6.35, suggests that this is to be taken as a Wisdom invitation, and will require the same kind of sapiential interpretation as the Bread of Life. The surprising thing is that it receives no comparable development into a discourse. This may be due to the fact that John has already given his teaching on this theme in the discourse with the Samaritan woman in chapter 4. We shall find that exactly the same is the case with the other Wisdom invitation in this section, 8.12 (the Light of the World).

If we reject transposition theories for this chapter, we are bound to make an effort to explain why John has produced such a patchwork of material at this point. It is evident, from the variety of its component parts, that he is working together bits and pieces, even if they are entirely his own work. He has certainly not penned this chapter in a single sitting. According to the homiletic view of composition of the book advanced in the Introduction, John based his work very largely on his own homilies in the Christian assembly. We should probably add to that other less formal teaching work. This would mean that he has far more material of his own than he needs to include in his book, and that there is very considerable overlapping of similar material used on different occasions and in connection with different traditional anecdotes. We may conjecture that one of his homilies for the feast of Tabernacles was on the Water of Life. But when he came to his account of the feast for the purposes of his narrative, at this particular point in his book, other considerations came to the fore. In chapter 5 he had already embarked on the major issue of the struggle between Jesus and official Judaism, leading eventually to the Passion. The Water of Life theme, which is a matter of the *effects* of belief in Jesus, had already been dealt with in chapter 4. What was needed was teaching which would take further the issues raised in chapter 5 and also build up the sense of mounting climax. As already indicated, he saved up part of the discourse of that chapter precisely for this reason (verses 15–24). It takes up the question of Jesus' breach of the Sabbath and

applies it to his authority as a teacher over against the authority of
the rabbis. Jesus neatly turns the argument into an accusation against
the rabbis themselves, whose determination to be rid of him is itself a
breach of the Law (verse 19). This gives the two motifs, of the question
of Jesus' identity and of the growing opposition to him, which are
found in the types of material under (a) and (c) above.

The (a) material (verses 1–14, 25–31, 40–4) is concerned with
questions of messianic expectation, and could quite easily have been
part of a longer and more consistent block of teaching, which John
has not wished to use as a whole in his book. He has edited it to fit
into the scene of Jesus' visit to the feast of Tabernacles, interspersing it
with the discourse material held over from chapter 5 and the opening
words of the Water of Life discourse which otherwise he has decided
to abandon. The (c) material (verses 32–6, 45–52) would then be
the concluding note about popular reactions, which John regularly
uses to round off his discourses, and (in view of verse 49) would seem
to be the conclusion of the (a) material. It will be noticed that the
latter presupposes discussion in the absence of Jesus for the most part,
but verses 32 and 45, belonging to (c), show that the same material
includes some teaching of Jesus. It is thus reasonable to suppose that
verses 33–6, which are the first intimation of the Passion in public
teaching, and also 8.21–30, which obviously belong to the same
stratum, give the teaching concerned.

The net result of this reasoning is that we may suppose that
chapter 7 is made up of a triple strand: (i) The setting at the feast
of Tabernacles, with fragment of the Water of Life discourse. (ii) A
series of excerpts from a discourse which included messianic
speculations (11–13, 25–31, 40–4), teaching on Jesus' departure
(33–6 and 8.21–30) and the mission of the officers (7.32, 45–52),
all of which has been adapted for its present arrangement. (iii)
The piece of the discourse of chapter 5, specially held over to be
the controlling factor of the resulting composition.

Chapter 8 can now be analysed along similar lines more briefly.
It is in fact a direct continuation from chapter 7, and implies the
same setting. Verse 12, with which it begins, is a short saying on
the Light of the World, comparable to 7.37. Like it, there is a
possible background in the ceremonies of the feast of Tabernacles,
the illumination of the Court of the Women; and in exactly the
same way it looks like the beginning of a discourse but remains
undeveloped. In this case also John has other material which over-
laps, the Man born Blind in chapter 9. Thus 8.12 merely announces

the theme, which is then held over for treatment later. Here it is simply used to lead in to the theme of the witness to Jesus, which is a further development of the discourse of chapter 5 (verses 13–20). The point of this section is the special relation between Jesus and the Father, which distinguishes him from the rabbis. The indictment against them (cf. 7.19) is presupposed, and John now inserts a piece more of the Passion teaching (verses 21–30). The rest of the chapter (31–59) is a continuous discourse, arising out of verses 13–20, in which the implications of the distinction between the rabbis and Jesus are taken to the limit. They are morally sons of the devil, but he is the eternal Son of God. The argument is worked out in terms of the meaning of descent from Abraham, along lines which recall Paul's arguments in Romans and Galatians, and no doubt owes much to disputes between church and synagogue.

Analysis of the chapters is not enough. Assuming that John has put together the material in its present order himself, we must ask how far the result is successful. He has certainly left some roughness, which has compelled us to assume that he is reworking existing material rather than composing afresh; but the total effect is impressive. We gain a picture of increasing interest in the identity of Jesus, popular speculations and official opposition, people taking sides, and Jesus exposing the deep ethical basis of the division, until finally the climax is reached: Jesus is essentially on the side of God, and the Jews, self-condemned, attempt to lynch him.

The overall purpose of the Gospel is well served. The orientation of the narrative has taken a definite turn towards the Passion, which will be maintained in chapters 9–12; and the exposition of the meaning of Jesus as the Christ, the Son of God (20.31), has gained the perspective of radical moral decision.

Jesus Goes up to the Feast: Rising Opposition 7.1–14

The chapter begins with a cross-reference to 5.18. If chapter 6 is taken as an addition at the second stage of composition, there is no difficulty in taking verse 1 as the original continuation from 5.47 (see below on verse 15 for other views). Nothing is recorded of the time spent in Galilee. If the feast of 5.1 was Tabernacles, it would be a whole year, which is hardly plausible; if it was Pentecost, it would give a suitable interval, and the question of Jesus' next visit to the capital would come up at the time of the next pilgrimage feast. Instead, then, of giving information about the time in Galilee, John provides a slight interlude by means of the discussion between Jesus and his brothers in verses 3–10. These verses have some basis in the tradition known from the Synoptic Gospels, but there is no parallel to the situation as a whole. Barrett thinks that it corresponds with Mk 9.30, where Jesus passed through Galilee secretly; but the verbal links are not close enough to suggest a common source, and in fact Mark (9.33) brings Jesus and the disciples to Capernaum. As it stands, the dialogue contains hints of the following discourse. The challenge of the brothers (verses 3f.) anticipates the Light of the World saying (8.12). Jesus' reply, explaining that the time is not ripe, is taken up in 7.30 and 8.20, and is linked with the teaching on his departure in 7.33f.; 8.21. The speculation of the people at Jerusalem prepares the way, not only for verses 25–31, 40–4, but also for some expressions in 47–9.

The historical basis for the section may well be the version in John's source of the rejection of Jesus at Nazareth (Mk 6.1–6 paras.), which he has already used in 4.44 and will use again in his second edition at 6.42. But if so, the strange behaviour of Jesus, whereby he appears to go back on his word, was no part of the source. The analogy of 11.6, where Jesus deliberately delays on receiving an urgent message from Mary and Martha, suggests that this is a Johannine motif. Jesus will not do what his brothers ask, because he is not ready yet to make a public display; nevertheless, he does it in his own way, in obedience to his calling from God. The antithesis of 'in secret' and 'openly' in verse 4 is reflected in verses 10 and 26. Barrett sees here a parallel to the Marcan 'messianic secret': whereas in Mark Jesus maintains a studied reserve about his messiahship until the Passion and Resurrection, in John the truth is always available to those who will believe, but hidden from those who do not.

1. would not go about (*NEB*: 'wished to avoid'): the Sinaitic Syriac adds 'openly', but the Curetonian and Old Latin, W and a few other Greek mss., Chrysostom and Augustine read 'did not have the ability to go about'. This seems right (so Barrett and Sanders). The well-attested **would not** is an early improvement to correct the impression that Jesus was not in control of events. But we already know that the Jews sought to kill him (cf. 5.18), and this is an ever-present danger throughout chapters 7 and 8. **Jews:** the footnote 'Judeans' does not depend on a difference of text, but indicates doubt about the meaning of *Ioudaioi*. Dekker (*NTS* xiii (1966), pp. 66–80) has argued that the usage in John varies, and even takes this as a criterion for different editors. In Palestine people used *Ioudaioi* for Judeans, i.e. those actually resident in the province of Judea. In the Diaspora it was used for Jews in general. Here, then, it is supposed that Jesus keeps out of Judea because the Judeans are after him. But, as we have often noticed, John generally uses *Ioudaioi* in an even more restricted sense still, to denote the Jewish authorities in Jerusalem. There is no reason why this should not be the case here. Jesus has gone to Galilee (the tetrarchy of Herod) to be out of reach of them.

2. feast of Tabernacles: this was the autumn feast (15–21 Tishri), and the most popular of the pilgrimage feasts while the Temple was still standing. The main feature was the custom of bivouacking in huts of wood and greenery, derived from the old vintage customs, but interpreted as a recapturing of the days of dwelling in tents in the Wilderness period. The feast lasted a week, plus an octave day in post-Exilic times. So much may be gathered from the OT (Lev. 23.39–43). But the Mishnah (*Sukkah*) tells us of two other practices which had evidently established themselves by NT times: the water-pouring with procession of the *lūlāb*, and the illumination of the Court of the Women. More will be said about these in the notes on verse 37 and 8.12. For the wording of this verse, cf. 6.4.

3. brothers: cf. 2.12. Their hostility is not mentioned elsewhere, but is not impossible historically. John may have deduced the fact from the version of Mk 6.4 in his source. We have seen a short form of this saying in 4.44, and an allusion to its context in 6.42. The full form of the proverb in Mk 6.4 is: 'A prophet is not without honour, except in his own country, *and among his own kin*, and in his own house' (the italicized words are found only in Mark). **your disciples may see:** it can hardly be supposed that they have been left behind in Jerusalem. The emphasis, then, falls on **the works.** Even those done in Galilee only become meaningful when related to messianic activity in Jerusalem, the centre of Jewish faith; only here can Jesus show himself to the world (verse 4). Barrett links the taunt with 6.66, suggesting a new display of power to recover the lost ground; but if chapter 6 is held to be a later strand of the book, the taunt can only mean that Galilee is too obscure. This is, in fact, the implication of the next verse.

4. in secret . . . openly: this is the essence of the brothers' taunt, and it is based on words of Jesus himself which occur in more than one form in the Synoptic tradition. (For other examples of words of Jesus applied to other speakers, cf. 2.10; 3.29.) The Synoptic parallels occur in two quite different contexts. (a) Mk 4.22 (= Lk. 8.17) has the following comment on the parable of the lamp under a bushel: 'For there is nothing hid, except to be made manifest; nor is anything secret, except to come to light' (Mk 4.22). John's **secret** and Mark's 'hid' are the same word (*kruptos*). John's **openly** (*parrēsia*) is not used, but Mark's 'manifest' is the same verb as **show yourself** in the next clause (*phaneroun*). The saying in this context is thus interpreted to mean the revealing of secret teaching, and it probably has the same idea in the *Gospel of Thomas*, 5: 'Jesus said: "Know what is before your face, and what is hidden from you will be revealed to you; for there is nothing hidden which will not be manifest."' (Pap. Oxyrhynchus 654.4, a fragment of the original Greek, has *krupton* and *phaneron* in the final clause, and adds: 'and buried which will not be raised'.) (b) Mt. 10.26 (= Lk. 12.2) reads: 'For nothing is covered that will not be revealed, or hidden (*krupton*) that will not be known.' Here the context is encouragement to the disciples not to be afraid to proclaim the Gospel in spite of persecution. The continuation is worth noting for its vocabulary-link with 8.12b: 'What I tell you in the dark (*skotia*), utter in the light (*phōs*); and what you hear whispered, proclaim upon the housetops' (Mt. 10.27). John's text is a little nearer to (a), but the contextual meaning is that of (b). As **openly** (*parrēsia*) is a Johannine word (7.13, 26; 10.24; 11.14, 54; 16.25, 29; 18.20), and is not found in the parallels, we may conjecture that the whole verse is expanded from an original shorter form 'no man works in secret, except to be made manifest'.

5. D Old Latin and Old Syriac add 'then' at the end of the verse, to harmonize with the post-resurrection evidence.

6. time: the word used here and in verse 8 (*kairos*) replaces the usual 'hour' (cf. 2.4, note). It never occurs elsewhere in John (except the spurious 5.4). On the other hand it is frequent in the Synoptic Gospels, especially in apocalyptic contexts, where it means the time of the manifestation of the Son of Man (Mk 13.33) or other aspects of the coming crisis. It is thus probable once more that John is adapting a traditional saying. He varies the verbs of which **time** is subject, but they are really synonymous (in this verse: *parestin* = is present, i.e. **has . . . come;** *estin hetoimos* = is ready, i.e. **is . . . here;** in verse 8 *peplērōtai* = is fulfilled, i.e. **has . . . fully come**). The last of the three is identical with Mk 1.15, but that cannot be the basis of the present context, as it is not concerned with Jesus' personal position. But there is some evidence for a floating saying: 'The (my) time is at hand!', which has found its way independently into Mt. 26.18 and Lk. 21.8. The latter passage is part of the triple tradition of the Synoptic apocalypse, in which the disciples are warned against false messiahs who may lead the people astray (*planān*), a word which occurs in verses 12 and 47 below. John may thus have taken his phrase from a similar apocalyptic context. The time to which Jesus refers can only be the time of manifestation of the Son of Man, in view of verse 4. Naturally John takes this, paradoxically, to be the moment of the Passion, which awaits the time appointed by the Father; so Jesus must not force the issue too soon. On the other hand the brothers have no such time, requiring careful calculation, and so are free to attend the feast if they wish.

7. **hate:** John has used this word in 3.20, in which he showed how the refusal of belief in Jesus is equivalent to being under the sway of evil, and therefore leads inevitably to condemnation. The verbal similarity between this verse and 3.20 is greater than the English suggests. This is the rationale of the opposition to Jesus, which will become a major theme in chapter 8. The word **hate** is used of persecution in 15.18, 19, 23, 24, 25; 17.14; and elsewhere only at 12.25.

8. **not going up:** this is the text of א D K Old Syriac, Vulgate and some Old Latin MSS. 'Yet' has been added in the majority of MSS. from the latter part of the verse, so as to remove the contradiction with verse 10. Commentators both ancient and modern have noticed a double meaning in **going up.** It is the usual word for a journey to Jerusalem for a feast; but it is also John's expression for the return of Jesus to the Father by way of the Cross; cf. 6.62. But it must also be pointed out that it is very infrequent in this sense; 1.51 and 3.13 are not strictly applicable to the Passion and exaltation (see the notes on these verses). This leaves only 20.17 where the word occurs (twice) in the sense of exaltation. All the other contexts where it is used require only the literal meaning, as in verse 10. If chapter 6 is a secondary stratum, 6.62 cannot

fix the meaning of the usage here. Caution forbids seeing more than the literal meaning in this verse. We cannot explain the contradiction between verses 8 and 10 by saying that Jesus does *not* go up in the sense of the final act of redemption, though he *does* go up in the literal sense. All we can say is that he does not go up *publicly*, because the time for public display has not arrived. While we are on this point, it should be observed that John's usual language for the Passion is that of 'going' (an entirely different word in Greek from 'going up'), and that this is used precisely in this sense in 7.33ff.; 8.21f.

fully come: see above on verse 6. In spite of the close similarity with Mk 1.15, it is doubtful if there is any real connection. The Greek word (*peplērōtai*) is a favourite of John's, and, as has been shown, is only one out of three virtual synonyms.

10. not publicly but in private: for the words (*ou phanerōs . . . en kruptō*), cf. verse 4. It is necessary that Jesus should continue to 'work in secret'—i.e. without making an open claim to be the Messiah, but allowing the conclusion to arise from the implications of his ministry. He thus appears in the Temple out of the blue, as it were, and this fact in itself points to one of the factors in messiahship (verse 27). But this means that he has moved out into the open (verse 26), so that there is implied a progression from obscurity to clarity, from darkness to light (cf. 8.12). It is no accident that it is precisely in the course of this movement into the light that Jesus gives his first public teaching on the Passion.

11. The Jews: although John's usage is not absolutely consistent, it is probably right to take this to mean the authorities, who are actively trying to arrest Jesus (cf. verse 1). They are not, then, to be identified with 'the people' of the next verse, who are the residents in Jerusalem (see below on verse 25) and those who have come on pilgrimage. They are not looking for him out of interest or curiosity (contrast 11.56), but with menacing seriousness.

12. muttering: this is the same word as 'murmured' in 6.41, 61, but used with a different nuance. There it was applied to the people's *complaints against* Jesus, and was probably derived from the text of Exod. 16. Here it refers to the people's discussion among themselves (Barrett calls it 'subdued debate') *about* Jesus, as also in verse 32. The word refers primarily to the low sound which is made on such occasions, and can even be applied to the cooing of doves (Pollux, *c.* A.D. 180).

leading the people astray: cf. verse 47, and the note on verse 6
above. The discussion is not about Jesus' identity, but about his
personal integrity. It presupposes, however, that the people are
aware that he may be the Messiah, and are concerned to distinguish between true and false claimants; cf. Lk. 21.8 paras.,
referred to under verse 6. The idea that Jesus led people astray
was a common Jewish opinion; cf. Mt. 27.63; Justin, *Dial.* lxix;
cviii; *B. Sanhedrin* 43a (quoted by Barrett, p. 259).

13. for fear of the Jews: cf. 9.22; 19.38; 20.19. This is the
first time that John mentions opposition, not only to Jesus, but
also to those who would take his part.

openly: the same word as in verses 4 and 26. So the people also
have to keep their opinions secret, though for less worthy motives
than Jesus.

14. the middle of the feast: this might be intended to be the
Sabbath that fell in the week of the feast, a suitable day for teaching. But more likely it is necessary stagecraft, to allow for Jesus'
late arrival and the Jews' search for him.

JESUS AND THE LAW OF MOSES: WHO THEN IS JESUS?   **7.15–36**

In spite of the complicated, scissors-and-paste method which John
has used in putting together his material for chapters 7 and 8,
it is nevertheless a well-balanced composition. Verses 15–36 and
37–52 have the same structure. First there is a specimen of Jesus'
teaching (15–24 and 37–9), then speculation among the people
(25–31 and 40–4), and finally the mission of the officers and its
consequences (32–6 and 45–52). The section 8.12–30 also divides
most naturally into three sections, though it is more drawn out
and the components do not tally in the same way. We have seen
already that the three parts of 7.15–36 were not originally composed for their present arrangement; but John has done a certain
amount of adaptation. Thus the first piece, 15–24, is carefully
fitted to verse 14. The words 'taught' (*edidasken*, verse 14) and
'teaching' (*didachē*, verses 16f.) are rare in John: the verb occurs in
6.59; 7.14, 28, 35; 8.20, 28; 9.34; 14.26; 18.20; the noun in
7.16, 17; 18.19; it is the fact of teaching which binds the two
pieces together. In the introductory setting (verse 14) Jesus is said
to teach in the Temple, for the first time in the Gospel; in the
following verses his credentials as a teacher are subjected to
scrutiny. In dealing with this issue, John uses some of the material

held over from chapter 5, which is obviously very suitable. For Jesus' act in breaking the Sabbath raises the question of his authority as a teacher over against Moses. The next paragraph (25–31) follows appropriately, because the people's questioning is about Jesus' origin. The immediate question is his authorization by contrast with Moses; but the discussion is in terms of the setting in the feast of Tabernacles, i.e. the Messiah's appearance out of obscurity (cf. verse 4). The word 'taught' reappears at the vital point in this discussion, where Jesus makes a solemn declaration about his origin from the Father (verses 28f.). In the third paragraph (32–6) Jesus gives a warning that his presence will soon be withdrawn. His words are misunderstood in such a way as to provide an unconscious forecast of the Gentile mission of the Church; and again the word 'teach' comes at the crucial point (verse 35). The Tabernacles setting has provided the theme of appearance and withdrawal, which is really an application of the more fundamental theme of light and darkness (8.12). The theme of teaching has been superimposed on this with the aid of the discourse material left over from chapter 5. The effect of this is to bring the whole issue of the origin of Jesus into relation with the Law. He supersedes the Law because he has come from God as the teacher whom God has sent. Odeberg maintains that it is this theme of teaching which is the real clue to the whole chapter.

Jesus supersedes the Law 15–24

15. marvelled: the imperfect implies that the Jews 'began to marvel' as they listened to Jesus; we are not told what he has been saying. Those who transfer this paragraph to follow 5.47 naturally apply it to the discourse of that chapter, but they still have to cope with a similar reaction in verses 25f., which then has no point of reference other than verse 14.

this man: pejorative, as in 6.41.

has learning: lit. 'knows letters' (*grammata*), cf. mg. It cannot mean 'literate', as mg. suggests, because most Jewish boys were taught in the synagogue to read the scrolls of the Law. But Jesus had not passed through the training in rabbinic disputation which Paul had (cf. Ac. 22.3). The Jews' astonishment is not at his capacity to read, but at his skill as a teacher (cf. Mk 1.22; 6.2; Lk. 2.47), and betrays professional jealousy. The word *grammata* occurs in John only here and in 5.47; to Bernard, Bultmann,

Sanders and many others who wish to transpose 7.15–24 to follow
5.47 this is the decisive link. Barrett, however, points out that it
makes the juxtaposition impossible. For *grammata* in these two
verses is used in entirely different ways. Here it refers to intellectual training, there to specific writings. We cannot even take
'knows letters' to mean 'is familiar with the writings of Moses',
because for one thing he would be bound to know them if he was
literate at all, and for another Jesus does not claim that his teaching is derived from Moses, either here or in chapter 5. It seems
more probable that this verse has been composed without any
direct reference to 5.47. The occurrence of *grammata* in both is
simply coincidence. Here it is a natural word to use, because the
passage is concerned with teaching. The verse is, then, a link between the setting of 1–14 and the discourse material of 16–24, providing the occasion for the statement of Jesus which now follows.

16. teaching: Gr. *didachē* (only in this context and 18.19) was
to become the regular word for the church's catechetical instruction, but it is used of Jesus' teaching in the synagogue in Mk 1.22.
The point is that the preaching of Jesus is directly derived from the
Father, and not from the precedents laid down by the succession
of duly ordained rabbis.

who sent me: the discourse begins by going back to a fundamental affirmation of the discourse of chapter 5—i.e. the
summarizing statement of 5.30. The rest of 5.30–47 was a
development of this point, applying it to the theme of the witness
to Jesus. Here Jesus goes back to the beginning again, to apply
it to the *source* of his teaching.

17. if any man's will is to do his will: the repetition of
will (verb and noun in the Greek) is reminiscent of the repetition of the noun in 5.30, and the sentence is to be understood in
the light of that verse. It means, then, anyone whose intentions
are the same as Jesus' own intentions, in which there is no element
of self-seeking, but entire submission to God. The allusion to 5.30
precludes Bultmann's suggestion that this verse is a relic of
another Wisdom invitation, in spite of the 'if any one' opening.
It is rather an essential step in the argument, as the Jews' questioning of Jesus' authority reflects back on themselves, and it is
their own integrity which will be called in question.

18. seeks his own glory: praise or good opinion, as in 5.41.
The two possibilities of verse 17 are tested by the motive of the

teacher. By abandoning the first person, and putting his remark into general terms, Jesus makes an attack on the blinding ambition of the rabbis, which evoked his complaint in 5.44. At the same time he shows that the unselfishness of his own motive is the proof of his integrity as a teacher; **true** here means honest in character (hence *NEB*: 'sincere'), and does not refer to the propositional truth of his teaching. Hence it is rightly explained by the synonymous phrase **in him there is no falsehood** (*adikia*, only here, but cf. 1 Jn 1.9; 5.17). This is forensic language, attributed by Bultmann to the ecclesiastical redactor, but without compelling reason.

19. Having established two interrelated facts: his own integrity and the derivation of his teaching from God, Jesus turns the tables on the rabbis and accuses them of just the opposite. The falsehood of their motive has already been exposed. Now Jesus shows up the true derivation of their teaching. We know that this is what Jesus has called speaking on one's own authority, as no other alternative has been admitted. But of course the rabbis claim that their teaching is derived from Moses, interpreted by the succession of teachers. So Jesus acknowledges that they take the Law of Moses as the foundation of their work, but accuses them of setting it aside in practice. They have, then, really set up their own authority. The situation is similar to the argument on the tradition of the elders in Mk 7.1–13, and to that extent strikes the authentic note of the teaching of Jesus. But he has still to bring an actual accusation against them. This comes very abruptly in the next words, **Why do you seek to kill me?** This takes us right back to 5.18, where the intention was related, at least partially, to Jesus' own breach of the Law in setting aside the strict observance of the Sabbath, the fourth commandment. Now, as a counter-charge—which admittedly is only implied and not stated—Jesus accuses the rabbis of breach of another commandment: 'You shall not kill'(Exod. 20.12); but, seeing that it is only at the stage of intention, and has not yet been put into effect, it is not strictly comparable. We should probably take it in the light of the teaching of Jesus in the Sermon on the Mount, where even the desire to kill is regarded as breach of this commandment (Mt. 5.21f.). We thus reach the equation, which will be important later on, that to refuse to accept Jesus is to seek to kill him.

20. The people: not, apparently, the rabbis themselves (whom John would have called the Jews). The distinction may be intentional, as in verse 26 we find that the rabbis have been silent. But, if 8.48 refers back to this verse, the distinction cannot be maintained. **you have a demon:** i.e. 'you are mad'; cf. 8.48; 10.20. In NT times insanity was popularly ascribed to demon-possession; cf. Mk 5.1–20. The accusation in the Synoptic tradition, in which Jesus is said to be in league with Beelzebul (Mk 3.21–7 paras.) is not a true parallel, because it is occasioned by Jesus' power over the demons, and there is no implication that he is himself possessed. **who is seeking to kill you:** the question is another example of taking Jesus too literally. The people have not understood that the real charge is that of spiritual murder incurred by the rejection of divine truth embodied in Jesus; cf. 8.40.

21. one deed: it seems most natural to take this to be the cure of 5.2–9, which caused general amazement because of its miraculous character. Bernard, however, takes it to mean 'one breach of the Sabbath', and everyone was amazed that Jesus should do such a thing (of course this still refers to the same act of healing on the Sabbath). In the ensuing verses it becomes clear that, whatever was intended by the vague charge of breaking the Sabbath in 5.16, here it is the act of healing which is meant. **at it:** the Greek (*dia touto*) means 'because of this', and there is uncertainty whether the phrase comes at the end of this verse or the beginning of the next. As the *RSV* take it, 'this' refers back to 'one deed'. Aland can only cite two MSS., X and q, in support of this, because of course early MSS. do not include punctuation marks; but Johannine usage certainly favours the position at the beginning of the next verse (5.18 is a case in point), and the translation of the Old Syriac implies it. The difficulty of taking it there is that it scarcely gives a satisfactory meaning (hence Bernard, Brown and Sanders side with *RSV*). John's characteristic usage is to have 'for this reason' at the beginning of a sentence, followed by 'because' (*hoti*), i.e. 'the reason why . . . is that . . .' (exactly as in 8.47). But here the reason is not given (hence *NEB* renders it as an interjection: 'But consider'). A parenthesis breaks the flow of the sentence, and thereafter the construction is changed. We should perhaps fill it out in this way: 'The reason why Moses gave you circumcision is precisely that such a work of healing should be done.' On this basis the argument proceeds with flawless logic, provided that an analogy between circumcision and healing is recognized. We have to assume that circumcision is not only an example of a law of sufficient importance to override the Sabbath (as is expressly stated in *Nedarim* 3.11), but that to make a man's whole body well (verse 23) is an extension of the principle of circumcision, and therefore, *a fortiori*, also overrides the Sabbath. In fact, we find this conclusion actually being drawn in the Talmud: Barrett (p. 264) quotes a saying of R. Eliezer (*c.* A.D. 100) from *B. Yoma* 85b: 'If circumcision, which concerns one of a man's 248 members, overrides the Sabbath, how much more must his whole body override the Sabbath?' The case in question is danger of death, which hardly applies to the man of 5.2–9. But again we find that in the Synoptic tradition Jesus defended acts of healing on the Sabbath, though without adducing the law of circumcision (Mk 3.1–6 paras.; Lk. 13.10–17). It can thus be argued that John is aware of Jesus' practice, and interprets it in the light of rabbinic discussion.

22. circumcision was to be performed on the eighth day after birth (Lev. 12.3), and in normal circumstances was done on that day, even if it was a Sabbath. Bultmann points out that the note in brackets (which he ascribes to the evangelist, as distinct from the presumed author of the source) is of purely academic interest, and does not affect the argument. He also lays stress on the insecurity of a law which can be broken, by contrast with the affirmation of God in Christ. The parenthetical note, which refers to the circumcision of Abraham (Gen. 17.10; 21.4), may however be an implied criticism of the Jews' reliance on Moses, and so may be a hint of the argument of Paul in Rom. 4 and Gal. 3. The introduction of the issue of circumcision into the discussion, which is concerned in the first place with Jesus' authority as a teacher, and in the second place with his setting aside of the Sabbath, may well be due to its prominence in Jewish and Christian debate. But it is a skilful device, for it provides a double-edged argument: on the one hand, it gives a precedent for Jesus' action, which justifies him on the Jews' own ground; on the other, it adduces an example of the way in which the Jews themselves break the Law, which is Jesus' accusation in verse 19. Thus the fact that the rabbis refuse to allow to Jesus the exercise of a principle which they themselves assert in the case of circumcision indisputably shows up their insidious intentions towards him.

23. The *a fortiori* argument ('from light to heavy') is well known in rabbinic debate. The rules for circumcision on the Sabbath are given in *Shabbath* xix.2–6. The argument requires that circumcision be regarded as indispensable, and thereby implies that Jesus' act of healing is so too. It is not then a case of taking advantage of a loop-hole in the rules to secure permission for something which falls outside them; it is a work which proceeds from God, typifying his will for the salvation of all men (3.16), and he who performs it on God's behalf has the divine prerogative to make his own halakhic decision when it conflicts with the rules. Thus the work of salvation surpasses the laws which prepare the way for salvation. **angry:** Gr. *cholāte*, only here in the NT. It is tempting to take this in conjunction with verse 19, and so to conclude that the rabbis' anger is breach of the command not to kill (Mt. 5.22). If so, all the points under discussion are brought into focus: the teaching and healing work of Jesus (making a man's whole body well) is vindicated as the will of the Father (verse 16); his apparent laxity with regard to the Law is justified on rabbinic principles; and the murderous intentions of the rabbis are exposed.

24. The Law contains several warnings on the necessity of integrity in making judgments; e.g. Lev. 19.15; Dt. 16.18f. In Isa. 11.3f. the promised messianic ruler 'shall not judge by what his eyes see . . . but with righteousness he shall judge . . .' It is possible that there is an actual allusion to this passage (Hebrew text), especially as the question of messiahship is central in this chapter. For the fact that Jesus has established his claim to judge rightly, by contrast with the rabbis, may well indicate that he is himself the Christ.

Messianic Origins (i) **25–31**

25. the people of Jerusalem: Gr. *Hierosolumitōn*, only here and Mk 1.5 in the NT. It does not seem possible to distinguish them from the people mentioned in verse 12, though they are obviously not to be confused with the Jews, i.e. the authorities. There is no indication that pilgrims are excluded, as if the word applied to residents only. What they say in this and the next two verses is not a set speech, but the summary of general discussion, couched in typically Johannine language.

26. openly: cf. verses 4 and 13, and the note on verse 10. The appearance of Jesus in the Temple during the feast suits the people's messianic expectations, but in fact his origins are known. On the other hand the fact that no action is taken against Jesus, although he has come out into the open, suggests that **the authorities** (*archontes*, the same word as 'ruler' in 3.1) have revised their opinion and believe that he is the Messiah. For **can it be that** (*mēpote*), cf. 4.29 (*mēti*).

27. where he comes from: the question at issue is whether Jesus, who is known to be from Galilee (verse 41), can qualify to be a messianic claimant. One qualification is descent from David, which will be discussed in verses 41f. Another, which appears to conflict with this, is that his origins will be unknown. That this was one strand in the manifold messianic expectations of the Jews is well known. There are, admittedly rather late, references to it in rabbinic literature (*SB* ii.489). It is mentioned by Trypho the Jew in Justin, *Dial.* viii. Earlier references suggest that the idea is taken from the figure of the Son of Man, fused with the Messiah in late Judaism. 1 Enoch 48.6 describes the pre-mundane designation of the Son of Man, who is kept hidden until the appointed time; 2 Esd. 13.52, at the end of a vision which is clearly derived from the Son of Man vision in Dan. 7, explains: 'Just as no one can explore or know what is in the depths of the sea, so no one on earth can see my Son or those who are with him, except in the time of his day.' From this point of view, the true Messiah will not be known until the moment when he is revealed by God. Although Jesus' baptism could be taken as such a moment (1.31–3), his work as a teacher in the Temple was aimed at producing a gradual conviction of his messiahship, and did not include a decisive display of divine power. It is precisely this issue which aroused the derision of his brothers (verses 3–8). As usual, there is an irony here: the people know where he comes from in the literal sense, but his real origin goes unrecognized; hence Jesus *does* pass this test. There may well be here a further allusion to the tradition of scorn of Jesus' origins in Mk 6.2f. (cf. the notes on verse 3).

28. proclaimed: the verb (*krazein*) was used of John the Baptist in 1.15; otherwise it occurs only here, verse 37 and 12.44. It implies inspired speech (Bultmann), and denotes, both here and in 37, a self-revelation of central importance. This is related to the theme of Jesus' emergence into the light by **as he taught in the temple;** cf. verses 14–16.

You know me: there is no indication in the Greek text that this

is to be taken as a question, challenging the supposition too readily
expressed by the people. It is more in accordance with John's
style to take it as superficial agreement ('Yes, indeed you know
me . . .'), only to be modified by what follows (so *AV, RV, JB,
NEB*). To know Jesus' place of origin is irrelevant when his divine
origin is not recognized.

of my own accord: lit. 'from myself', the same Greek as 'on my
own authority' in verse 17. Jesus' teaching is from God precisely
because he himself has been sent by God. Thus his teaching has
better authorization than that of the rabbis, and his claim to messiahship holds good.

true: Gr. *alēthinos* ('real'); cf. 1.9. It is applied to God again in
17.3. Generally it means in such contexts real as opposed to false
gods, but here it means true to himself, however erroneous the
people's ideas may be, and so is not significantly distinguished
from *alēthēs*. For the Jews' ignorance, cf. 5.37f. Failure to recognize Jesus as the Messiah is due to culpable refusal to respond to
God in faith (cf. verse 17), which is the only way to know God
(Hos. 4.1).

29. I come from him: lit. 'I am from his side', a phrase used
in 6.46. The preposition (*para*) denotes belonging to, or origina-
tion from, a person, and so expresses the close relationship between Jesus and the Father.

30. they sought to arrest him: in this and the next verse we
see the uncommitted people of Jerusalem dividing into opposed
groups. Some have been angered by the implicit messianic claim
in verses 28f.; but, as Jesus' proclamation has been too obscure to
constitute an actual offence, they cannot take positive action. This
accords with the Synoptic tradition, in which Jesus' opponents
have to resort to trying to trap him into an illegal statement to
gain grounds for arresting him (cf. Mk 12.13). From John's point
of view no action can be taken before the appointed hour; cf.
verses 6–8. The verse has a striking parallel in Lk. 22.53, which
suggests that John's thought may have been developed from the
Passion narrative.

31. many of the people believed: cf. 8.30. Again, it is the
common people, not the rabbis. For the plural **signs,** cf. 2.23.
According to verse 21, Jesus has done only 'one deed' in Jerusalem,
but it is characteristic of John's summaries to speak in this more
general way; cf. 12.37.

Jesus' Work will soon be Accomplished **32–6**

32. muttering: The low sound of discussion, as in verse 12.
The Pharisees are the rabbis, but not necessarily those who have
been concerned in the dialogue of 15–24 (which ultimately belongs
to a different stratum of John's material). They are the rulers
(authorities, verse 26), and so they **sent officers to arrest him,**
taking official action to contain the situation. When the temple
was standing the Sanhedrin was dominated by the Sadducees,
though there were Pharisees among them, whereas the Pharisees
became the acknowledged leaders after the catastrophe of A.D. 70.
The **officers** are the Temple guard (cf. 18.3), under the control
of the chief priests. John is always on the verge of anachronism
when he speaks of the Temple authorities, but saves himself by
saying **the chief priests and the Pharisees**; cf. verse 45. But
in *this* verse the phrase comes in awkwardly (we should expect
simply 'they'), and there are MS. variations in the order of words;
Brown therefore excises it as a corrector's gloss. This verse
clearly belongs with 45–52. As a serious attempt to silence Jesus,
the Pharisees' action makes a suitable point of departure for the
first public teaching on the Passion.

33. a little longer, and then I go: these words, with slight
variations of the Greek phrases, recur from now on to indicate
Jesus' expectation of the Passion; cf. 8.21; 12.35; 13.3, 33, 36;
14.4f., 12, 19, 28; 16.5, 16–19, 28. They are intentionally vague;
Jesus has foreknowledge of coming events, but to speak more
precisely would obscure the deeper meaning of them; Jesus will
soon have completed his task for which he came from God, and
so will soon return. But the time has not yet been reached when
it can be openly stated that the way of his return to God is the
Passion. The words fulfil the same function as the Passion predictions in the Synoptic Gospels; and the special use of the verb
go (*hupagein* here, but *poreuesthai* in 35) is found in Lk. 13.32f.
(*poreuesthai*).

34. seek me: this is a very common word in John, and there
may be a deliberate irony in the two ways of using it in this
chapter. In verse 11 the Jews were 'looking for' Jesus in the hope
of being able to arrest him; in 18 it meant 'desire, or strive for',
and this again was applied to evil intentions in 19f., 25 and 30.
Here it could mean seek in order to arrest, as in 11, but the

general tenor of the verse is that they will seek him because, too late, they want to have what he came to give. John may even be playing on the well-known promise of Jesus: 'Seek, and you will find' (Mt. 7.7). The saying has a parallel in the *Gospel of Thomas*, 38: 'Jesus said: "Many times you have desired to hear these words which I speak to you, and you have no other from whom to hear them. The days come when you will seek me and you will not find me"' (the Greek text is also preserved in Pap. Oxyrynch. 655).

where I am: i.e. in the glory of the Father; cf. 12.26; 14.3; 17.24.

35f.: The Jews (it is not clear whether this means the people or the Pharisees) repeat Jesus' words as if completely baffled by them. It is a device (used again in the related passage, 16.16–19) to compel the reader to look for the deeper meaning. In this case the Jews take what Jesus has said literally, as so often, and suggest that he may intend to travel to the Greek cities of the Mediterranean seaboard, where there were numerous colonies of Jews, and they even consider the possibility of a mission to the Gentiles themselves (notice particularly the word **teach**). For **the Dispersion among the Greeks,** cf. 1 Pet. 1.1. Though they have misunderstood Jesus' words, we cannot miss the forecast of the Church's Gentile mission, which John has in mind in placing this comment on their lips. Ironically their expression of incredulity is a prophecy of the truth; cf. 11.51f. John regards the Gentile mission as the fruit of the Passion (12.20–4). This fruitfulness is actually expressed in the verses which now follow.

JESUS IS THE GIVER OF THE WATER OF LIFE: WHO THEN IS JESUS? **7.37–52**

The pattern of the last section is now repeated—an item of teaching (37–9), a popular discussion (40–4), and the return of the officers and consultation of the Sanhedrin (45–52). It has already been shown that John has taken these units from previous work and reassembled them for his purpose. Now we must note the ways in which he has adapted them for their present position. In spite of the major break at verse 37, indicated by the change of date (10.22 is similarly awkward), there is no break of thematic continuity. The fruitfulness of the Passion, ironically indicated in 35f., is now stated in verse 39, which is a comment on the Wisdom invitation of 37f. The citation of Scripture in 38 may be taken to indicate that the theme of teaching is still in mind, so that, in passing on the Spirit, Jesus transmits the capacity to give the true teaching (so Odeberg); but this is not specifically said. The second paragraph, on the people's discussion, is almost a doublet of 25–31 (Brown takes it as such), but the point at issue is different. It is welded into its present context by: 'When they heard these words' (40), so that it forms a response to the revelation-discourse of 37–9. In the third paragraph the discussion about Jesus is brought into the circle of the Sanhedrin itself, and so makes the threat to Jesus' life more serious. It thus balances the obscure teaching on the Passion in 32–6, and prepares the way for the intense drama of the dispute in 8.31–59. At the close of it we shall again find that John leaves a hint which will link up with the next section (8.12).

It is very widely held that the invitation of verse 37 is related to the ceremonies of the feast of Tabernacles, which Jesus uses as a basis for his teaching. According to the Mishnah *Sukkah* iv.9 a golden flagon was filled with water from the pool of Siloam, and taken in solemn procession to the Temple to the sound of the trumpet. It was poured into a special bowl, which was used (with another bowl of wine) for a libation over the altar. Meanwhile the people circled the altar, carrying the *lūlāḇ* (a bundle of palm, myrtle and willow, with a citron). The origin of this ceremony, which is not mentioned in the OT, is unknown, but it was probably a rain-making custom, as the rainy season begins shortly after the feast in the Holy Land.

The Water of Life 37–9

37. the last day: scholars are undecided whether this means the seventh day or the eighth. Lev. 23.33–43 makes it clear that the feast really lasted seven days, as in the older legislation (Dt. 16.13–15), but adds a solemn rest day at the end, to be observed by a holy convocation, i.e. like a Sabbath, with its act of worship. On this day the *Hallel* was to be sung, as on other days of the feast, but the water-pouring, which had been done for seven days, was omitted, and also the music and dancing in the illuminated Court of the Women (see below on 8.12). Thus the particular feature which gives point to Jesus' words was missing on the eighth day, and the comparative quietness of it hardly merits the description **great** (i.e. the greatest). Hence many commentators, including

Bultmann, Brown and Sanders, assume that the seventh day is meant. Hoskyns, however, cautiously followed by Barrett, argues that **great** is appropriate to the eighth day, precisely because it attracted a large congregation, as a Sabbath, and of course this makes a suitable occasion for a sermon. We have the evidence of Josephus (*Ant.* III.247) that the feast was actually kept for eight days. Hoskyns goes too far when he suggests that the ceremony need not be taken as having anything to do with Jesus' words; after all, it would still be in everybody's mind. From the approach taken in this commentary, it might be better to say that John has used the feast as the setting for the teaching on the Water of Life because of the water-pouring ceremony, which he knew to be one of its features. But it still remains most probable that he means the eighth day.

proclaimed: cf. verse 28.

thirst: the invitation is strongly reminiscent of Isa. 55.1, considered in connection with 6.35; cf. also 4.14. Although the water drawn at Siloam was not drunk, Isa. 12.3 was chanted while it was being drawn: 'With joy you will draw water from the wells of salvation.' This suggests an eschatological interpretation, the ceremony being symbolic of a greater blessing to come. When Wisdom's invitation (Isa. 55.1) is applied to this, it implies that that promise is already fulfilled. This exactly suits the presentation of the teaching of Jesus in the Fourth Gospel. It is this present fulfilment in the person of Christ which differentiates it from straight apocalyptic (e.g. the use of Isa. 55.1 in Rev. 21.6; 22.17).

38. He who believes in me: so far all has been well. But now we come to one of the most intractable problems of the whole Gospel. Three interrelated factors have to be taken into account, the grammar, the source of the quotation, and the application of it.

Retaining the punctuation of *RSV* (so *NEB, mg*), **he who believes in me** has to be regarded as a suspended subject (nominative), picked up, after the parenthesis **as the scripture has said,** by the genitive **his** in the quotation itself. This is extremely awkward, but no more so in the Greek than it is in English, and cannot be declared to be impossible. But there is evidence in some Old Latin MSS. (d e) and Latin Fathers that the phrase was taken with the preceding verse. This has several advantages: (a) It gives a balanced couplet: 'If any one thirst, let him come to me: and let him drink who believes in me.' (So *NEB*.) (b) It means that

as the scripture has said is no longer encapsulated between
the suspended subject and its sentence, but comes between two
complete sentences. Hence it could refer back to verse 37, instead
of to the words of unknown source in verse 38. (c) It changes the
application of **his heart** (*NEB*: 'within him') in 38 from the
believer to Jesus himself. Barrett argues against (a) that it is not
at all well balanced as far as the meaning goes, for **thirst** and
believe are not synonymous. Also **he who believes in me** is
extremely common in John at the beginning of a sentence, and
never found elsewhere at the end (though here it is still exceptional
because of the *nominativus pendens* construction; Sanders, however,
adduces 6.39 as a fairly close parallel). Blenkinsopp escapes the
difficulty by taking this phrase as a gloss, derived from 'those who
believed in him' in verse 39, and inserted to specify the subject of
thirst. This takes as the quotation the words in verse 38, and
suggests that the application of it is to Jesus, and not to the
believer.

Before any attempt can be made to identify the source of the
quotation, it has to be decided which sentence is being referred
to: **scripture** (singular) must mean a particular passage, as
always in John. If the first phrase is taken with verse 37, it could,
as indicated above, be taken with the couplet as a general
reference to such a passage as Isa. 55.1 or Prov. 9.4f., without
needing exact quotation. Chrysostom took it to mean simply **he
who believes in me,** presumably thinking of Isa. 28.16, but this
is hardly probable. It is, in fact, difficult to resist the impression
that it refers forwards to **Out of his heart . . .,** and all modern
commentators take this view, even when they adopt the couplet
of (a). Unfortunately there is no single OT passage which corresponds with this.

The various possibilities can be arranged under two headings.
First there are those which assume that the quotation is to be
applied to the believer, as in the *RSV* punctuation. Prov. 18.4;
Isa. 58.11; Sir. 24.30–4 all contain the idea of Wisdom as a
fountain or river within Man; 1QH viii.16f. also gives a slight
parallel in the course of a poem which is built up on this theme.
Secondly there are those which assume that the quotation refers
to Jesus. Isa. 43.19f. and 44.3 promise water like rivers, the latter
passage actually equating it with the Spirit. The context of both
these passages carries a reminiscence of the water from the rock

in the Wilderness. As Paul already has a tradition of this as a type
of Christ (1 C. 10.4), it must be regarded as a serious possibility
that the same is meant here. If so, a variety of OT allusions to this
miracle can be brought into the range of possibilities, notably Ps.
78.15f. (Boismard thinks that John is actually citing an Aramaic
Targumic rendering of this passage). But the trouble with all
these proposals under both headings is that none of them has
anything corresponding with **out of his heart** (lit. 'out of his
belly', *koilias*). So another approach is to start from this, and take
it to mean the Temple rock at Jerusalem as the 'navel' of the
earth (cf. Ezek. 38.12; *B. Sanhedrin*, 37a). This would apply it to
various prophecies of the future fruitfulness of Jerusalem, notably
Ezek. 47.1–12; Jl 3.18; Zech. 14.8 ('living waters'; the passage is
a *haphtarah* reading at Tabernacles); cf. Rev. 22.1. It may be
observed in passing that Sir. 24.30–4, on Wisdom in the individual,
is based on the ideas of Ezek. 47.1–12. Some of these passages were
read in the Tabernacles season. But the equation Jerusalem (i.e.
Jesus, or the believer) remains unexplained. Torrey brilliantly
surmounted this difficulty by supposing a misreading of Aramaic
migawwah = out of the midst of her (i.e. Jerusalem), as *migaw-
weh* = out of his belly, involving no change in the consonantal text;
but then the equation is lost, and the text becomes irrelevant.
But this suggestion also points to another facet of the matter, that
'out of his belly' could be a too literal rendering of a phrase that
can also mean 'out of the midst of'. Along the same lines Jeremias
(*Golgotha*, p. 82) and Bultmann think of the Aramaic *gûph*, meaning literally 'out of his body', but also 'from himself' (but this
does not explain the choice of the Greek *koilias*). Finally, Bultmann
among others is favourable to the suggestion that the words are
to be connected with the flow of water and blood from Jesus' side
(*pleura*) in 19.34, to which a scripture citation is appended. But
this means that the attempt to find a particular passage for the
words in the present verse is being abandoned.

Most of the above suggestions presuppose that the application
is to Jesus, in common with the Latin and Syriac Fathers. Such
a Christological interpretation is natural, and almost inevitable
in the light of the discourse of chapter 4 (cf. *Gospel of Thomas* 13,
cited in the notes to 4.14). Many of the Greek Fathers, however,
follow Origen in applying it to the believer, and this becomes
inevitable if the traditional punctuation, as in *RSV*, is accepted.

This Eastern interpretation cannot be set aside as an attempt to deny the procession of the Spirit from the Son (Lagrange). In order to make a decision, John's own comment in verse 39 must be given due weight; it is not good enough to dismiss it as a 'parenthetical comment from a later viewpoint' (Brown). It stands or falls with the authenticity of the similar comments in 2.22 and 12.16, both of which Brown appears to accept. It implies that the believers' response to Jesus' invitation will not only satisfy their thirst (verse 37, cf. 4.14a), but will be a source within them, so that they too will be fruitful (cf. 4.14b). This agrees with John's teaching on the Spirit in 3.5–8 and in the Supper discourses (14.16f., 26; 16.7–14). We may add to this the point, which has not been generally noticed, that it is also implied by the hint of the Gentile mission of the Church (not of Jesus in person) given in verse 35. This leads to the conclusion that the traditional punctuation of verse 38 is to be retained and the quotation is to be applied to the believer along the lines of the Wisdom allusions. The vast range of possible Christological allusions points in the opposite direction, but John has not taken sufficient pains to signal this so clearly as to make it the decisive factor. The actual source of the quotation itself remains an insoluble problem.

39. the Spirit: for water as a symbol of the Spirit, cf. 3.6. There is no indication of an allusion to baptism this time, but the possibility is not ruled out. The eschatological idea of Isa. 12.3 (see above on verse 37) suggests that the water-pouring at Tabernacles might prefigure the outpouring of the Spirit, which is actually stated in *Gen. Rabba* lxx.8: 'Why do they call it the House of Drawing [a name derived from Isa. 12.3]? Because thence they draw the Holy Spirit.' The theme of teaching, which has been so important in this chapter, may be maintained if we can regard the gift of the Spirit here in the same light as the Supper discourses. In this connection, *Sifre* Dt. xi.22 may be quoted: 'When the disciple is like a well, then just as from the well flows out living water on all sides, so from that disciple will come forth disciples and their disciples.'

not been given: given is an addition in B 053 Old Latin, Syriac and Sahidic, for the majority reading 'was not yet'. It was added no doubt to exclude the idea that the Spirit did not yet exist. What John means is that the Spirit was not yet available to be 'a spring of water welling up to eternal life' (4.14), because Jesus was not yet glorified, i.e. had not passed through the events of his Passion Resurrection and Exaltation (cf. 12.16, 23; 13.31f.; 17.1, 5). There is nothing mechanical about this. It has already been shown in the discourse with Nicodemus that man can only be fully opened to the influence of God when he entrusts himself to Jesus, and makes response in him. But this belief in Jesus is defective unless the believer commits himself to him as crucified, risen and glorified. The same idea comes out very clearly in the Bread of Life discourse of chapter 6, though using a different range of imagery. The use of **glorified** to express the total redemption-event is derived from the picture of the Son of Man, who is given glory (Dan. 7.14); see above on 3.14.

Messianic Origins (ii) **40–4**

40. the prophet: i.e. of Dt. 18.15, as in 1.21. Here he is distinguished as an eschatological figure from the Messiah, as in the Qumran literature. Contrast the Samaritan ideas (4.19–25) and the apparent fusion of the Prophet and the Messiah in 6.14f. In spite of the fact that we are now concerned with a different literary stratum from 37–9, the dovetailing is excellent, for the eschatological implications of Jesus' invitation could well provoke this speculation.

41. from Galilee: the speculative question is introduced by *mē*; cf. verse 26. It has already been implied in verse 27 that the people know Jesus' place of origin. There may perhaps be a reminiscence of Nathanael's derisive question in 1.46. There seems to be no evidence of belief in a Galilean origin for the Messiah in Jewish sources. Thus the fact that Jesus came from Galilee could be held against the Church's claim that he was the Messiah. The present verse may well reflect actual controversy on this issue. The question was settled by the tradition that, though Jesus was brought up in Galilee, he was actually born in Bethlehem. John is evidently well aware of this, as the next verse shows. There he ironically makes the people say, as if it was not true of Jesus, the very thing which he knows to be true. Does the same kind of irony operate in the present verse? Is the question about Galilee to be simply answered in the negative on the grounds that John knows in any case that Jesus was not born there, or does he hold that it is true in spite of this, because the Messiah was to appear in Galilee? This is in fact probable, because there is other evidence that the early Church sought for scriptural warrant for the Galilean origin of the Messiah. This is indicated by the quotation of Isa. 9.1f. in Mt. 4.15f. In this messianic prophecy Galilee is mentioned as one of the northern districts in which 'a great light' shines at the birth of the royal child. We shall see, when we come to verse 52 and 8.12, that John had pondered on the implications of this text.

42. the scripture: the primary reference must be to Mic. 5.2, which alone asserts that the future king will be born in Bethlehem. This passage is quoted in Mt. 2.6, and thereby indicates (what has just been implied in the last note) that John is drawing on the pool of the Church's messianic scriptures. Though the Micah passage assumes that the king will be descended from David, it does not say so explicitly, so there may be allusion here to other messianic prophecies in current use (Isa. 7.13f.; 11.1; Ps. 18.50). Whether Jesus was actually descended from David cannot be certainly proved, but the Church quickly assumed that he was, perhaps as a result of the pressure of the kind of dispute which is illustrated here, and the Galilean and Davidic (Bethlehem) views were harmonized. Outside the Gospels the descent of Jesus from David is mentioned in Rom. 1.3 and Ignatius, Rom. vii.3; Eph. xviii.2. See on this issue J. Jeremias, *Jerusalem in the Time of Jesus*, 1969, pp. 284-97.

43f. Cf. 30f. It again means divided reactions of the people, and the officers of 32 and 45 are not within the purview.

Reactions of the Sanhedrin **45-52**

45. The officers: the narrative implies that they have come straight back after listening to Jesus for a while, but the change of date in verse 37 makes this impossibly awkward. We can only assume that, in reassembling his material, John has failed to remove the inconsistency. He *needs* to place this paragraph here, because he has finished with the popular discussion, which has been a prominent element of his material so far, and he is about to lead into the more intense situation of chapter 8.

47. led astray: cf. the note on verse 12. We notice that now the chief priests have quietly been dropped, though they were mentioned in 45.

48. authorities: cf. verse 26. They are here distinguished from **the Pharisees,** who are a larger group, but are probably equivalent to both the chief priests and the Pharisees of 45. The fact that they do not believe in Jesus is not merely an item from the Gospel tradition, but also a reflection of subsequent events. Though certain priestly families and Pharisees (e.g. Paul, and cf. Ac. 6.7) were converted, the failure of the first Christians to win over the ruling classes of Jews was undoubtedly a big factor in the eventual estrangement from the synagogue.

49. this crowd, who do not know the law: there is abundant evidence (cf. *SB* ii.494–521) that the rabbinic scholars felt superior to the common people, whom they regarded as the *ʿammē hāʾāreṣ*, the peoples of the land. This phrase originally referred to the inhabitants of Judea in the fifth century B.C. They were despised by the more zealous and sophisticated Jews who returned from the Babylonian Exile to rebuild Jerusalem; cf. Ezr. 4.4.; Neh. 10.28. Later the same phrase was contemptuously applied to the common people, who were not well trained in the niceties of the Law, and tended to be slack over its observance. Thus in *Aboth*, ii.6; v.10 the phrase *ʿam hāʾāreṣ* means 'an ignorant man', likely to be careless about the rules of ceremonial purity. So the fact that Jesus has won approval from some of the people is no recommendation from the Pharisees' point of view. **accursed:** cf. Dt. 27.26. Their ignorance is culpable.

50. Nicodemus: cf. 3.1. He has been an open-minded enquirer, and now represents a reasonable, unprejudiced attitude in contrast with the hardening opposition of the rest. His final appearance in 19.39 will show him as virtually a full believer. **who had gone to him before:** the phrase has many variations in the MSS., and is missing from ℵ* altogether. It is nothing unusual for a glossator to provide the obvious cross-reference, and so it should probably be omitted.

51. Does our law judge: the OT has many passages condemning partiality and other means of evading strict justice (e.g. Lev. 19.15; Dt. 1.16f; 17.4); etc. Unconsciously Nicodemus echoes Jesus' own admonition in verse 24.

52. from Galilee too: a sarcastic question with double meaning. By taking Jesus' part Nicodemus is behaving as if he belongs to this party which has come from Galilee. But, as the Galileans were of mixed racial stock, and only Judaized comparatively recently, it amounts to a term of abuse in this exclusive setting. Notice that the whole emphasis of the verse is laid on Galilee. The real question at issue, which is decisive for the attitude of the

Sanhedrin, is precisely the question which was raised by the people in verse 41, whether the Messiah can come from Galilee. **Search:** i.e. in the scriptures; cf. 5.39. Once again there is a deliberate irony, for John knows well that Jesus' Galilean origin is in accordance with the messianic prophecy of Isa. 9.1f.

no prophet: nevertheless the title Messiah is avoided. The Pharisees use the more general designation **prophet,** which in fact was applied to several possible claimants to messiahship in Galilee at about this time (cf. the notes to 6.14f.). It had long since been conjectured by Owen that the article should be inserted before **prophet,** so as to identify him with the Prophet of Dt. 18 (cf. verse 40). Now there have actually appeared two mss. which have the article, both of great antiquity, P[66] and P[75] (second and third centuries). Brown adopts this reading, but it is by no means certainly correct. It could easily be a copyist's insertion from verse 40 (where it is indisputably right), on the supposition that the Prophet and the Messiah are identical. It may be said in favour of it that it avoids the difficulty of the denial that Galilee was the home of a prophet, whereas the rabbis must have known that Jonah came from Gath-Hepher (2 Kg. 14.25), only three miles north of Nazareth; or that one would ever come from Galilee, which is contradicted by *B. Sukkah* 27b; *Seder Olam* R.21. On the other hand the place of origin of the Prophet appears not to have been a subject of speculation, whereas that of the Messiah certainly was. And the fact remains that there is no passage in the OT which says that a prophet **is to rise from Galilee.** The reading of this verb (*egeiretai*, present tense with future meaning) is to be accepted against E, G, H and L, which have perfect (*egēgertai*). For the use of this verb, cf. Mt. 11.11; Lk. 7.16.

[THE WOMAN CAUGHT IN ADULTERY **7.53–8.11**]

By a happy chance this fragment from an unknown work has been preserved in the ms. tradition of John. The fact that it is a piece of a more extensive collection is indicated by the first two verses, which appear to be the conclusion of another incident. The story itself tells how Jesus was able to deal compassionately with a woman, whose guilt rendered her liable to the death penalty. He neither condones her sin nor denies the validity of the law; nevertheless, he gives her an incentive to make a new start in life. There is no reason to doubt that an authentic tradition lies behind this story. It is free from the tendency to incorporate miraculous elements; it simply gives an example of the wisdom of a revered teacher, and as such is rather like some of the stories in the Talmud and other Eastern literature. The general tone of the story has more in common with the Synoptic Gospels than with John. The motif of special concern for the outcast is reminiscent of Luke (7.36–50; 8.2; 15.1f.; 19.1–10).

The MS. evidence may be briefly summarized as follows: It is *not* found in P^{66} P^{75} ℵ B L T and other MSS. of the Egyptian type (A and C doubtful, because of gaps); also N W X Θ, various cursives, a f l q, Syriac, Sahidic, some Bohairic; all early Fathers. It is inserted in the canonical position after 7.52 by D (a text notable for its interpolations) and the main body of MSS. on which the *textus receptus* is based (many of these mark it with an obelus or asterisk to indicate uncertainty); also some Old Latin texts, the Vulgate and some Bohairic; Latin Fathers (Ambrose, Ambrosiaster, Augustine). It is placed elsewhere in John by 225 (after 7.36); and by fam. 1 and a few others (after 21.24). It is placed in Luke by the Ferrar group (after Lk. 21.38). There are numerous textual variations, some of which suggest homiletic application, and so point to the ecclesiastical lectionaries as the primary means of its preservation.

If it originally belonged to a non-canonical Gospel, as seems probable, there are two possibilities among known works, but neither is very convincing. According to Eusebius (*HE* III.xxxix.17) Papias 'also told another story about a woman who was accused of many offences in the presence of the Lord, a story which is contained in the Gospel according to the Hebrews'. It is by no means certain that this refers to the present story at all, as the woman is not here accused of 'many offences'. But it may be a reference to the same story in a rather different form. But there is a much clearer reference to it in the *Didascalia*, a work on Church discipline written probably fairly early in the third century. Though the original Greek is lost, the revelant passage was incorporated in the late fourth-century *Apostolic Constitutions*, ii.24, only slightly adapted, as we can see from the Syriac *Didascalia*, vii: 'Wherefore, O bishop, . . . if thou receive not him who repents, because thou art without mercy, thou shalt sin against the Lord God; for thou obeyest not our Saviour and our God, to do as he also did with her who had sinned, whom the elders set before him, and leaving the judgement in his hands, departed. But he, the Searcher of hearts, asked her and said to her: *"Have the elders condemned thee, my daughter?"* She saith to him: *"Nay, Lord."* And he said unto her: *"Go thy way; neither do I condemn thee"* ' (Connolly's translation, p. 76). Seeing that the author of this work evidently knew the *Gospel of Peter*, Barrett suggests that this too may be a quotation from that work, rather than from the canonical Gospels. Connolly himself regarded it as from the *Gospel of the Hebrews*, on the strength of the evidence of Eusebius given above, but held that other signs that the author knew this work could not be proved. But as this reference to the story antedates all the MS. evidence of its inclusion in John, it is highly probable that it was included in *some* non-canonical work, which was circulating at this time in the region (probably Syria) where the *Didascalia* was written.

If the *Didascalia* fails to solve the problem of the source of the story, it none the less is most valuable evidence for the way in which it was saved and brought into the scope of the canonical tradition. For it is adduced as an example of mercy to be followed by the bishop in his administration of discipline in the Church. The Church in the second century, under pressure of persecution, tended to be rigorous in its attitude to moral offences; as the position eased, a gentler pastoral approach became both possible and necessary, and to promote this is one of the major concerns of the author of this work. It would thus seem probable that at about this time the story began to be read in the course of the liturgical lections,which sometimes include non-canonical extracts. By this means it came into the text of John, presumably coinciding with a course of readings from the Gospel. This is certainly the most probable explanation of the insertion of the story into the text of Luke in the Ferrar group, as the Byzantine lectionary has Lk. 21.12–19 and the *Pericope de Adultera* on successive days (Colwell and Riddle, *Prolegomena to the Study of the Lectionary Text of the Gospels* (1933), p. 19). The noncanonical story of the man working on the Sabbath (see the notes to 5.17), which is found only in D, may also have been preserved because of its relevance to questions of discipline.

This, however, is not likely to have been the original motive for recording the story in the first place. For the element of compassion to the sinner is not the real interest from the story-teller's point of view. Jesus' compassion towards sinners is a presupposition of the story, without which verses 4–6 would be senseless. The point is the skill with which Jesus maintains his own position without falling into the trap of publicly repudiating the Law. It thus belongs to the class of controversy stories represented in the Synoptic Gospels by the Tribute Money (Mt. 22.15–22 paras.).

It is not difficult to see why it was used in conjunction with John and found its way into the text of the Gospel at this point. The story ends: 'Neither do I condemn you', and in 8.15 Jesus says: 'I judge no one'. It makes an excellent illustration of the teaching of Jesus in this passage.

53f. Although it is clear that verse 53 is the conclusion of another story, it is part of the same sentence as verse 1, as is correctly indicated in *RSV, mg.* The scribe evidently felt it necessary to include the information that Jesus came to the temple from **the Mount of Olives,** and so transcribed the whole sentence. Otherwise we should not have known that this is an excerpt from a longer work, rather than a piece of floating tradition. The situation is comparable to the Synoptic account of the days immediately following the triumphal entry into Jerusalem. The closest parallel is Lk. 21.37f., i.e. immediately before the insertion in the Ferrar group. Verse 53, but not verse 1, is omitted by one Old Latin MS (ff[2]). John never mentions the Mount of Olives. Other non-Johannine expressions in the story are: 'early' (*orthrou*); 'scribes'; 'adultery'; 'placing her' (*stēsantes* used transitively); 'in the midst'; 'in the act'; 'bent down'; 'continued'; 'stood up'; 'him who is without sin'; 'one by one'; 'was left'; 'looked up'.

8.2. *all the people came . . .:* this part of the introduction is similar to Mk 2.13.

3. *The scribes:* frequently mentioned along with the Pharisees in the Synoptic Gospels, but never in John. It appears that they deliberately bring the woman to the large gathering around Jesus, instead of dealing with the case elsewhere (cf. verse 6). It is to this extent a 'put-up job', though the sequel shows that it was a real case requiring a decision which could not be lightly taken.

4. *Teacher:* Gr. *didaskale,* frequently used in addressing Jesus in the Synoptic Gospels, but never in John, though he uses the word in other ways.

in the act: the Greek is a technical legal term (*ep' autophōrō*). There would have to have been at least two witnesses for the case to be brought (cf. verse 17 below). We may reasonably conjecture that successful convictions, involving the death penalty, were not numerous. In this case the evidence is irrefutable, so that Jesus cannot evade the dilemma by suggesting that the case is unproven.

5. *to stone such*: the case being proved, it only remains to decide the penalty. This is laid down in Lev. 20.10 and Dt. 22.22 as death for both the man and the woman; in Dt. 22.24 stoning is prescribed for the particular case of a betrothed virgin who is within call for help and makes no attempt to resist the assault, and the penalty applies to both. It is possible that strangling was used for the cases for which stoning was not specified; this certainly was the case in later times (cf. *Sanhedrin* vii.4, 9; xi.1). Hence we might have to assume in the present case that the woman was a betrothed virgin. If the final words 'and do not sin again' are not original (see the notes on verse 11), there is nothing in the story to suggest that she was a hardened sinner or prostitute. It might then be the specially poignant case of a girl who had unwillingly submitted to assault, and now has to face the extreme penalty. But against this supposition it must be observed that **woman** (*gunē*) is an improbable word to use of a betrothed virgin; and the fact that there were witnesses who could have testified if she had submitted unwillingly suggests that she did not even pretend to be resisting the man when she was caught. In any case we have to assume that the man succeeded in making his escape. But there is good evidence that right up to NT times stoning was applied more widely than Dt. 22.24 implies. Apart from the earlier evidence of Ezek. 16.38-40; 23.45-8, there is the probable implication of death by stoning, or its regular substitute of throwing down a precipice, in the LXX text of Sus. 60-2 (not the text used in *RSV*), which takes it well into the first century B.C. (See J. D. M. Derrett, *NTS* x (1963-4), p. 11.)

6. *to test him*: for the phrase, cf. Mt. 19.3; Mk 8.11, and, for the idea of laying a trap, Mt. 22.15. But in what does the test consist? It has been suggested that the Jews could not impose the death penalty in Judea without the permission of the Roman procurator at this time. As under Roman law adultery was not a capital offence, there would be no possibility of enforcing the Mosaic law, unless the Jews acted in defiance of the Romans. Thus Jesus must either repudiate the Law of Moses or encourage the Jews to act illegally. This would make the issue somewhat

similar to that of the tribute money. But the case of Stephen
(Ac. 7.54–60) shows that stoning was still done on occasions even
after the time of Jesus, even if this was a matter of lynch law, and
strictly speaking illegal (see the notes on 8.59). But, whatever may
have been the case in the time of Jesus, this cannot be the point
at issue in this story, because there is not the slightest hint of it
either in verses 3f., where the facts of the case are laid before
Jesus, or in the subsequent development of the story. This is quite
different from the tribute money, where it is assumed from the
outset that Jesus preaches the sovereignty of God and does 'not
regard the position of men', i.e. even the position of Caesar
(Mk 12.14). Accordingly we must look for the terms of reference
in the facts that are given. These are simply that the woman is
guilty, and that the penalty is stoning, with the implication that
these is nothing to prevent the accusers from carrying it out. If this
is a test case, it must surely be that it brings into the open an
existing conflict between the known teaching of Jesus and the
requirements of the law, which he was bound to observe as a
faithful Jew. This is then most likely to be the well-known fact
that Jesus showed a particular regard for 'tax-collectors and sinners' (Mk 2.15–17). The behaviour of Jesus presented a direct
challenge to the strict Jews, and it was theologically based on his
preaching of the Kingdom. And it was extremely difficult to catch
him out in such a way as to undermine his whole position. This is
the view of Hoskyns, which seems to hold good, in spite of the
arguments of more recent studies.

bent down and wrote: this vivid detail has no parallel in any
other traditions about Jesus. Naturally there has been endless
speculation about what he was writing as he doodled on the dusty
pavement—the sins of the accusers, the decision he is going to
announce, a symbolic word of doom like the writing on the wall
(Dan. 5.24), a particular text appropriate to the situation
(Derrett suggests Exod. 23.1b)—but most commentators think
that he was doing this to play for time or to hide his feelings. The
one thing that is quite clear is that it indicates that he does not
wish to be involved in the matter, as the next verse shows.

7. *continued:* it seems not to be generally noticed that the
action of Jesus serves a direct function in the story. By taking
no notice and refusing to be drawn, Jesus has shown that he is
well aware that the whole thing is a trap. Brown is quite wrong to

suggest that the accusers seriously wish to know Jesus' verdict and would be likely to allow it to override the decision which has already been reached. So it is only after they have **continued to ask him,** compelling him to say something by their sheer persistence, that he speaks. And then his words are well weighed.

stood up: rather than resumed his sitting posture (verse 2). But *NEB* 'sat up straight' is to be preferred.

him who is without sin: for the implicit indictment, cf. Rom. 2.1, 22. The word used (*anamartētos*) conveys no suggestion that they might be guilty of the *same* offence.

first: Dt. 17.7 specifies, with regard to another offence, that: 'the hand of the witnesses shall be first against him to put him to death, and afterward the hand of all the people' (cf. also Dt. 13.9f.). Jesus, however, gives a new ruling. It is beside the point, however (*pace* Derrett), to suggest that he means it to be taken seriously as *halakhah*, to be accepted on the same terms as other rabbinic rulings. He is really telling the accusers to get on with the job. He does not deny that the correct decision has been made. But he turns it into a test of their own integrity: if they now proceed with the decision, they will appear self-righteous and ruthless, but Jesus will retain his reputation for mercy combined with truth to oneself before God.

8. *once more he bent down:* Jesus returns to his occupation to dissociate himself once more from the case and to allow his words to take effect. This is an essential feature of the story, and again it is unnecessary to speculate what he might have been writing (Derrett suggests Exod. 23.7a, which is cited in Sus. 53).

9. *they went away:* it is psychologically sound that the more experienced senior men would be likely to be the first to acknowledge the falsity of their position. Jesus helps them by tactfully not looking at them in their embarrassment. This verse has been subjected to embellishments in various MSS., adding 'being convicted by their conscience', 'each one', 'each one of the Jews', 'until all had gone out', 'until the last'. Some of these additions might be original.

10. *looked up:* the reading of Λ and the Ferrar group, whereas most MSS. have 'stood up' (or, rather, 'sat up straight') as in verse 7. Some insert 'when he saw no one except the woman'—a prosaic addition to account for Jesus' question. But of course Jesus knows perfectly well that they have all gone away! The

question is a delicate way of preparing the woman for his own
verdict.

condemned: the verb (*katakrinein*) means 'give a judicial sentence', and in this case indicates the decision to carry out the
penalty required by the law. The withdrawal of the accusers
shows that they have decided to drop the case. This means that, instead of trapping Jesus into an open denial of the Mosaic law, they
have capitulated to his own teaching on the nature of God's kingdom.

11. Jesus has won his point, and it only remains for him to dismiss the woman. When he says: **'Neither do I condemn you'** it
does not mean that he condones her sin, nor is it a declaration of
the divine forgiveness, but it merely shows that he, too, dismisses
the case, so that she is free to depart. The influence of ecclesiastical
usage has again caused some embellishments to the verse. Some
MSS. read 'go, and from now on', so as to avoid the impression that
Jesus condoned her conduct. A late Armenian MS. (quoted by
Bernard) attempts to reverse the whole implication of the story
by reading: 'Go in peace, and present the offering for sin, as in
their law is written.' But it must also be asked whether **do not
sin again** is not also an ecclesiastical addition, although it is
found in all MSS. But it is missing from the Syriac *Didascalia* (and
likewise the *Apostolic Constitutions*), although the author is clearly
quoting from the text of the story as it was known to him (hence
Connolly's italics, cf. p. 307 above). But it would have been very
relevant to his purpose of promoting a compassionate discipline
to include it, if he had known it. As the precise Greek phrase
(*mēketi hamartane*) occurs in 5.14, it is reasonable to suppose that
it was added at the same time as the story came into the MS. tradition of John. If the conclusion is read as in the *Didascalia* ('Go;
neither do I condemn you'), the story ends convincingly, keeping
entirely within its own terms of reference, and there is no feeling
that what Jesus is giving with one hand he is taking away with
another. It is in his *exercise* of the divine compassion rather than
in an admonition that he gives the real incentive for a better life
in future. She has already had a real fright, narrowly escaping the
death penalty.

JESUS IS THE LIGHT OF THE WORLD: WHO THEN IS JESUS? **8.12–30**
In this chapter, the question of Jesus' identity passes from theoretical considerations of the qualifications for messiahship to the

meaning of his special relation to God. This is set out in the discourse of verses 31–58, but the material which we now have to
consider is orientated towards this theme. Once more the triadic
structure which we have noticed in 7.15–36 and 37–52 is repeated
here to bring together distinct blocks of material. (a) Verse 12 is
a fragment of a revelation-discourse, comparable to 7.37. It is
related to the feast of Tabernacles by the illumination ceremony
(see below), and it appears to belong with the theme of chapter 9.
But its position here is far from accidental, as will be shown below.
(b) Next there is a discussion on Jesus' credentials as a teacher,
using the analogy of evidence admissible in a court of law (verses
13–20). This section at least arises from, if it did not actually
originally belong to, the discussion on the witness to Jesus in
5.30–47. But structurally it corresponds with 7.25–31 and 40–4,
and, like those two paragraphs, it concludes with a note about the
possibility of arresting Jesus. This again shows that John has edited
the piece for its present position. (c) In the third paragraph the
theme of Jesus' departure is reintroduced (verses 21–30). As in
7.32–6, the Jews take it literally, but this time they have a more
sinister suggestion to make about Jesus' possible motive, involving
an even heavier irony. This opens up a short discourse, in which
Jesus' movement is shown to be vertical rather than horizontal.
It is return to the Father by way of the Cross, and so reveals the
perfect accord between them, which was the starting-point of the
discourse of chapter 5 (cf. 5.19f.; 30). Thus the relation of chapter 8 to chapter 5 extends beyond the obviously similar material
of verses 13–19. It is truer to say that John has composed the
whole chapter on the basis of that discourse, in order to take its
themes further. It is thus most likely to be *new* work, unlike the
reassembly of bits and pieces in chapter 7, except for the one
verse of (a), the nucleus of (b) and the first two verses of (c).

The Light of the World 12

12. **Again:** cf. verse 21. This seems to be simply an editorial
link (as very frequently occurs in Mark), in order to suggest a
fresh occasion, which the context absolutely requires, with the
minimum of disjunction from the preceding paragraphs. There is
no indication who are meant by **them,** but the next verse mentions the Pharisees. We are left to assume that it is the same day as
the proclamation of 7.37, which is the last recorded saying of Jesus.

I am the light of the world: coming as it does at the beginning
of a new section, this famous saying could be taken as an introduction formula: Jesus arrives on the scene and announces who
he is. But it is much more likely to be intended from the start
as a qualification formula (cf. 6.35, and the reference there to
Bultmann); in this case it means: 'from me the world receives
illumination'. The idea is a central one in the Prologue, cf. 1.4f., 9,
and evidently belongs to the Wisdom Christology. Wisdom herself,
as the source of interior illumination, is regarded as superior to
the created light, and therefore to the whole of creation, in Wis.
7.26. In applying this title to himself, Jesus declares that, as a
teacher from God, he can illuminate men's minds with the knowledge of God. This is probably to be taken in an eschatological,
rather than in a timeless, way (cf. 6.35). The transition to the age
to come will be a theophany when the whole truth of God is
revealed, and when all the secrets of men's hearts are exposed
(cf. 1 C. 3.13). The light thus includes ideas of both revelation
and judgment. The point of Jesus' self-identification with the
light is that in his person both these functions of the end time are
anticipated. He is both the Revealer of God (1.18) and the
Revealer of men's hearts (the latter function being inseparable
from men's response to him (3.19–21)). We shall see that it is the
second aspect of the matter which is the real interest of John in
the use of this title. The idea of revelation of God, or of the truth,
is less prominent; both in verses 13–19 and in chapter 9, where
the idea of light is taken up again, the issue is right judgment
against spiritual blindness. Light is an idea which has vast ramifications in religious thought and literature. Barrett (pp. 277f.) has
given a most useful summary of Hellenistic, pagan, Jewish and
biblical ideas, all of which may have contributed something to
John's use of it as a very inclusive term. It is also necessary to add
the special use of light in the Dead Sea Scrolls, where it is intimately bound up with the issue of truth and falsehood (cf. the
notes on 1.5). This comes close to John's moral emphasis, and
explains how the thought in this verse also underlies the ensuing
discourse in 8.39–47, which is concerned with truth and falsehood.
The actual phrase **the light of the world** occurs in the Synoptic
tradition in Mt. 5.14, where it is applied to the disciples, whose
good works will make them like beacons in the darkness. This is
also a moral application of the idea, and it is possible that (as

with so many of such sayings) John derived this teaching ultimately from traditions of Jesus' words. The saying has two
parallels in the *Gospel of Thomas*: 24, where the idea of the beacon
is applied to the good Gnostic, and 77, where it is parallel to 'I
am the All', applied to Jesus. Two matters remain to be discussed.

The saying is included in the complex of material in the setting
of the feast of Tabernacles, and so it is only natural to see in it a
reference to the illumination of the Court of the Women in the
Temple (*Sukkah* v.2–4). At the end of the first day four huge
golden lampstands, which had been specially prepared, were filled
with oil and the large wicks (improvised from the priests' worn-out
clothing) were lit, to give brilliant illumination while singing and
dancing continued through the night until dawn; cf. Zech 14.7
(*Haphtarah* reading at this season; cf. the notes on 7.38). The
Mishnah is careful to point out that backs were turned to the
East, to show that there could be no suspicion of sun-worship,
though there may have been some such connection in the origin
of the custom. It is not clear whether this was repeated each night,
but certainly not on the night of the eighth day (cf. 7.37). In any
case the intricacy of the composition in these chapters does not
allow us to suppose that Jesus spoke these words actually in the
course of the feast, while this ceremony was in progress. But John
may well have had it in mind when he composed this material,
for the theme of light and darkness is present throughout (cf. 7.4).

This leads to the second point. For the aspect of this theme
which has been uppermost in chapter 7 has been the appearance
of the Messiah from obscurity (7.27f.). It was suggested in the
notes on 7.41 that John may well be darkly alluding to the messianic text Isa. 9.1f. Now the juxtaposition of a depreciatory comment on Galilee in 7.52, and of Jesus' announcement of himself
as the light in the verse immediately following, even more strongly
suggests that this text is in mind. This becomes still more probable
when we turn our attention to the rest of the verse, and compare it
with Isa. 9.2: 'The people who walked in darkness have seen a
great light; those who dwelt in a land of deep darkness, on them
has light shined.' Nevertheless the idea receives an entirely new
emphasis in John's hands, which marks the change from the theme
of the appearance of the Messiah to the new theme of exposure of
sin and falsehood by the light. **He who follows me** is a phrase
from the vocabulary of discipleship, and so the whole of the second

half of the verse forms a promise to the faithful disciple. It is
entirely probable that it has a basis in the tradition, cf. the more
naïve idea of the reward of discipleship in Mk 10.28f. paras. But
John has reworked the tradition, possibly with conscious reference
to Isa. 9.2. The promise of **the light of life** is defined by the
contrast with the alternative of continuing to **walk in darkness.**
Thus the acceptance of Jesus as the light has decisive moral consequences. Bernard draws attention to Barnabas, xviii, on the Two
Ways of light and darkness in the moral life, which are associated
respectively with the light-giving angels of God and the angels of
Satan. This is now known to be a derivative of the Two Spirits
doctrine of the Dead Sea Scrolls, and John here also belongs to the
same school of thought. 1QS iii.1–9 is especially close to John's
thought, and even includes the actual phrase 'the light of life' in a
comparable context. It means the illumination of men's minds by
perfect knowledge of God (cf. Leaney on 1QS iii.7), which is
precisely what is offered by Jesus.

The Witness to Jesus **13–20**

13. The Pharisees: not mentioned again in this chapter. John
has probably substituted this word for the more usual 'Jews' so as
to bind the dialogue to the preceding paragraph, in spite of the
fact that it relates to a different occasion.
bearing witness to yourself: in the context this can only mean
'making claims about yourself'. But before such momentous
claims can be accepted, they need some kind of confirmation. In
fact we are back in the situation of 5.31, which also follows far-
reaching claims. Jesus' words in that verse are now repeated almost
verbatim by his opponents. In 5.32ff. Jesus presupposed that his
witness to himself was invalid, and showed that he has the witness
of the Father; now we have the same point from a different point
of view. Jesus corrects the premiss that his witness to himself is
invalid by pointing out that the union between himself and the
Father is so close that the Father's witness and his own witness to
himself are really indistinguishable. Consequently this further
refinement of the issue of 5.30–47 deepens the sense of the unity
of the Father and the Son, and so helps to prepare for the discourse in the second half of the chapter.
14. for I know: the reason is not satisfying at first sight, but
it is necessary to bear in mind John's quasi-technical use of key-

phrases. At one level it would be absurd for Jesus to be the witness in his own case (5.31), but as he has come from the Father (verses 18, 23, 26–9), and is going to him by way of the Passion (verse 21, cf. 7.33), he alone has possession of the full facts on which his claim (to be the light (verse 12); to give life and to judge (5.21f.)) can be substantiated. If the Pharisees could understand the plan of redemption, in which Jesus is the protagonist, they would accept his teaching without insisting on external confirmation; it is God's plan, and God does not require witness from men (cf. 5.34). The vocabulary of this verse has the same deliberate vagueness as 7.33, and the relation between these verses shows that we cannot simply transport this section to chapter 5 without reckoning with careful reworking for the present context. Brown, recognizing this, suggests that this verse (from **for I know** to the end) and the next two verses belong to a different strand of material from the rest, which has affinities with chapter 5. But this fails to do justice to the care which has gone to the construction of the piece as a whole.

15. So far the topic of witness has been discussed without reference to judicial procedure. In 5.30–47 various forms of *evidence* were examined. Now Jesus is going to deal with the *witnesses* required for that evidence to have legal force. So here the idea of judging is introduced. The Jews **judge according to the flesh,** i.e. by the human methods of judicial procedure. For this use of **flesh,** cf. 1 C. 1.26; 2 C. 11.18; Eph. 6.5; Col. 3.22. When Jesus says **I judge no one,** it does not mean that he does not judge at all, in flat contradiction of 5.30, but that his judgment is performed on a different plane, and is not subject to the same standards. It is, of course, these words, taken very literally, which account for the insertion of the story of the woman caught in adultery (7.53–8.11) into the Gospel in the third or fourth century.

16. The verse follows the same pattern as verse 14. First Jesus corrects the impression given by the last words, then he asserts the validity of his judgment, and finally he gives the reason for it. The phrases are not quite identical, however. This time **true** is *alēthinē* ('real'), according to P75 A B D and the great majority of Egyptian and Caesarean MSS., whereas verse 14 has *alēthēs*. It is doubtful if there is any distinction (Barrett sees none), unless it be that John wants to say that Jesus' action of judging is authentic, quite apart from the truthfulness of the sentence he gives. It is a true act of judgment, even if it is given without witnesses; though

in fact there *are* witnesses, and, as already said in 14, their witness
is true. The reason which is given for this confidence in Jesus'
judgment, is the complete harmony between him and the Father.
This is exactly the same as the reason for the validity of his witness, already indicated enigmatically in 14b, and just about to be
stated explicitly in verse 18.

he who sent me: almost all MSS. read 'the Father', as in the
margin; but this is another case of a notable omission by ℵ* D
and Old Syriac (cf. 6.23). The motive for the insertion is obvious.
The omission is right, because it maintains to some extent the
obscurity of 14b, and yet the whole phrase prepares for the full
clarity of 18.

17. in your law: i.e. Dt. 19.15. Jesus says **your,** to dissociate
himself from it, because his judgment is not strictly comparable.
Nevertheless, arguing *ad hominem* as in 5.31, he can claim that this
requirement is satisfied in his case too.

18. This verse is the climax of the argument. It is more than a
debating point. It almost amounts to a revelation. The order of
words in the Greek is suitably impressive. Literally translated, it
reads: 'I am (*egō eimi*) one bearing witness to myself, and there
bears witness to me one who sent me the Father.' Notice the
chiastic structure, the *egō eimi* of self-revelation at the beginning,
and that **the Father** is held back to the very end. Assuming that
the omission in verse 16 is right, this is the first time that **the
Father** has been mentioned as such in the whole composite discourse of the feast of Tabernacles. This title at once arouses
interest, and dominates the rest of the chapter. Many scholars
have noted that the ideas and vocabulary of this verse also have a
remarkable similarity to Isa. 43.10 (more so in the LXX than in
the Hebrew). Further parallels to this passage will be observed in
verses 24 and 28. This may well be the case. It means that John
thinks of Jesus as performing the work of God—the salvation of
his people—which is the theme of the great prophecy of Isa.
40–55. This suits the eschatological emphasis of all John's thinking. The question of witness in this section is precisely a matter of
assurance that the eschatological claims which Jesus makes about
himself are really true. It is not a matter of timeless truths.

19. As usual, the Jews do not comprehend Jesus' allusive language, and assume that he means a human father. In his reply,
Jesus shows that the misunderstanding was bound to arise, because

of their lack of response to him. If they believed in him, they would know who his Father is, because of the essential unity between them, and then the question where he is would never arise.

20. the treasury: it is hardly likely that Jesus taught in the Temple strong-rooms, where the muniments were kept (1 Mac. 14.46–9: Josephus *BJ*, v.200). Barrett thinks that it means the place where the *shofar* chests stood for free-will offerings, probably outside the treasury in the Court of the Women, where the illumination ceremony took place (cf. Mk 12.41f., 'opposite the treasury'). Sanders points out that John can hardly be accused of inaccuracy when our own knowledge of the lay-out of the Temple is so slight. Bultmann takes this verse closely with 13–19, and regards it as the conclusion of the discourse of chapter 5. But the note that **no one arrested him** recalls 7.30 and 44, which suggests that the whole verse is an editorial link, to give a slight break between two blocks of material.

The Divine Witness to Jesus will be proved in the Passion **21–30**

21. Again: another sign of editing, as in verse 12. The rest of the verse is almost identical with 7.34, except that **and die in your sin** replaces 'and you will not find me'. As before, **seek** expresses the need which they feel when it is too late. The new feature in this verse makes it even more poignant. They will not only fail to find him, but they will lose their own hope of salvation. In terms of verse 12, they will remain in darkness without attaining the light of life. The phrase **die in your sin** is a legal one (cf. Dt. 24.16), and occurs in a context of personal and national salvation in Ezek. 3.19; 18.24, 26. All the issues in this chapter are set out in stark black-and-white tones; John allows no place for the shades of grey in which they mostly work out in practice.

22. Will he kill himself: once more the Jews misunderstand Jesus' obscure expressions, which we now know really refer to the Passion and subsequent exaltation. But this time, as in the last verse, the issue is intensified. They think he might mean suicide. Of course this is completely mistaken. But the irony of it is that he does mean his death. The OT is silent on the subject of suicide, and it is not clear what the Jews thought about it in NT times. It was certainly held to be right when honour was at stake; we can think of the last stand of the Jews at Masada in A.D. 73. Josephus, *BJ* III.375, declared it to be reprehensible at the end of

a long speech on the subject; but we may suspect a certain ten-
dentiousness, as he had himself gone over to the side of the
Romans.

23. From this starting-point in earlier material, John proceeds
to take forward the argument which has been begun in 13–19.
First he puts the contrast between Jesus and the Jews (already
indicated with regard to the ideas of witness and judgment in 13f.
and 15f.) in the most uncompromising terms. They are from the
parts **below,** i.e. **of this world,** whereas he is from the parts
above, i.e. **not of this world.** To a Hellenistic reader this would
sound like a radical dualism, the complete incompatibility between the eternal and the created orders, which can only be overcome by the saving knowledge which raises man to the eternal
realm. But we must interpret it in line with John's thought elsewhere. It is the modified dualism represented by the flesh/spirit
contrast of 3.6, and expressed in similarly spatial terms in 3.31.
The phrase, **this world,** here for the first time used in a bad
sense, means the world of men considered apart from God. It is
only evil in so far as it denotes men who refuse the response of
saving belief. The idea that the world is inherently evil or incapable of redemption is foreign to John's outlook. Barrett says that
the verse has been 'shaped in a popular Platonic mould', but
cites rabbinic parallels to the thought (p. 282).

24. Consequently the stark phrase of 21 can be modified. It
will not apply if the Jews will **believe that I am he** (*egō eimi*).
This is an 'I am' saying of a different kind from 6.35 and 8.12,
where there is a predicate. In this case the predicate has to be
supplied, as in Deutero-Isaiah, where the LXX translates *'anî hû'*
('I am he') by *egō eimi* ('I am'). We may thus suspect influence
here from Isa. 43.10 (cf. verse 18). Possibly the prophet was
making a play on words, for 'I am he' (*'anî hû'*) is reminiscent of
the traditional etymology of 'Yahweh' given in Exod. 3.14. But
he uses the phrase with a pregnant meaning, which is clear in the
context of the various passages where it occurs (Isa. 41.4; 43.10,
13, 25; 46.4; 48.12; cf. Dt. 32.39). Yahweh is the one who created
all things, who has raised up Cyrus to conquer Babylon, and who
will restore Israel. All his power is concentrated on this one fact,
that he is the one who saves his people. Now we have the same
phrase on the lips of Jesus in a parallel situation—that God, who
created all things through the Word, is the one who saves mankind

through him in the events of the incarnate life; cf. 3.16. We may, then, fill out the saying thus: 'I am the one through whom salvation is accomplished.' But the fact that the predicate is not expressed means that we must think of this in the most inclusive possible way. It includes everything Jesus has said about himself (Bultmann). On the other hand it is improbable that the words are intended to echo the I AM of Exod. 3.14 in a timeless and philosophical sense ('I am self-subsistent being'); but we shall have to consider this when we come to verse 58.

25. Who are you?: the Jews still fail to grasp the meaning. They think that the *egō eimi* requires a predicate, as if they could believe in Jesus if he was something other than he is. Hence Jesus' answer is not evasive, but necessary to the situation. They must either accept him for what he has already said about himself, or not accept him at all. Unfortunately the translation of Jesus' reply is highly problematical. The two possible ways of understanding it, given in the text and in the margin, correspond with this decisive either/or. Literally translated, the reply is: 'At the beginning [*tēn archēn*: adverbial accusative, *BDF* § 160] what also I say to you.' This expresses the unchanging nature of Jesus from the beginning, which accords with what he says. P⁶⁶ᶜ tries to ease matters by reading: 'I told you at the beginning what also I say to you [i.e. now]', which refers to the unchanging tenor of Jesus' words (this reading is cautiously favoured by Brown). The *RSV* text (and, roughly, *NEB mg*) is a fair paraphrase, but leans a little too far in the direction indicated by this reading. Read, therefore, 'Ever since the beginning I have been what I say to you' (cf. Barrett *ad loc.*). It is possible that there is a further echo of Deutero-Isaiah; cf. Isa. 41.4; 43.13. Since at least the time of Chrysostom it has been supposed that *tēn archēn* is a classical idiom for 'at all', and that the sentence is a question, as in *RSV*, *mg* (so *NEB* text). Though accepted by a number of modern scholars (e.g. Bultmann, Sanders), it is unlikely that John was familiar with classical Greek to the extent which this implies (cf. Davey, in Hoskyns, p. 335). Black's suggestion (p. 174 of 1946 edition) of misunderstanding in translation from an Aramaic original requires also rearrangement of the text, and so fails to convince.

26. I have much: i.e. the indictment implied by verses 21 and 24. Barrett suggests that **have** should be understood to mean 'can' (cf. the Greek of verse 6). The meaning of the verse is then similar

to verse 16: though Jesus could condemn the Jews for their lack
of response, he does not do so because he only speaks as the Father
instructs him, and this is nothing less than the message of salvation for the world.

27. this misunderstanding of the Jews indicates that the statement of 26b is to be further elaborated.

28. lifted up the Son of man: John's technical expression
for the Passion of Jesus as the manifestation of the divine glory,
now used for the first time since 3.14. In this verse the various
threads of the argument are drawn together. Here is the explanation of the mysterious 'going away' of verse 21. The Passion will
confirm what Jesus has already said about his identity, that **I am
he.** It will not only be apparent that Jesus is the Son of Man
(Bernard), or rather the agent of salvation in its fullest sense, as
indicated when the phrase was used in verse 24. It will also prove
the point just made in 26b. It will then be clear that Jesus does
not act in this capacity 'from himself' (**on my own authority;**
cf. 5.19, 30), but as he has been **taught** (cf. 7.14–17, 28, 35; 8.20).

29. The Passion will thus reveal the true relationship between
Jesus and God. The phrases recall 5.19–23. For **alone,** cf. verse 16,
where the same point was made in a context restricted to the
function of judging. As explained in 26a, Jesus does not wish to
confine his ideas to that, but to extend them to the widest possible
range. Sanders observes that it now becomes clear that the sending
of the Son by the Father does not entail separation from him.
The fact that Jesus is not alone, even in the darkness of the Cross,
will be emphasized in 16.32.

30. In the last two verses Jesus' self-revelation has reached a
climax, and this is suitably marked by the note that **many
believed,** cf. 7.31. Like verse 20, it makes a break before John
introduces a fresh block of material.

JESUS IS THE TRUE SON OF ABRAHAM: OPEN OPPOSITION **8.31–59**

We now come to the main teaching of this chapter, that, *because*
Jesus is the Son of God as just explained in 28f., he is the true son
of Abraham, whereas the Jews have forfeited the privileges of
descent from him because they are sons of the Devil. On the positive side, the discourse is concerned both with the disciples, who
by response of faith share in Jesus' sonship, and with the unique
sense in which Jesus is the Son of God. The latter aspect pre-

dominates in the final section of the discourse, so that the whole
builds up to a Christological climax, as so frequently happens in
this Gospel. For the paramount importance of descent and the
maintenance of racial purity in Jewish thought, cf. Jeremias,
Jerusalem in the Time of Jesus, pp. 271–302.

The issue is very similar to Paul's argument against the Judaizing Christians in Rom. 4 and Gal. 3–4. It is probable that Paul
based many of his arguments on disputes with the Jews, transferring them to the internal crisis of Judaizers within the Church.
John is not directly derivative from Paul, but rather reflects the
continuing debate between the Church and the synagogue. It is
unlikely that the main lines of the argument go back to Jesus
himself, though it may be claimed that John makes a legitimate
extension of the principles of Jesus' teaching. In a few places we
shall note items of teaching which appear to be based on traditional sayings of Jesus; they are the pegs on which the argument
is hung.

John's debt to Jewish moral dualism, especially as it is found
in the Two Spirits doctrine at Qumran, is very marked. We have
already been prepared for this by the theme of light and darkness
in 7.4 and 8.12. For John, as also for the men of Qumran, whether
a man is controlled by the Spirit of Truth (light) or the Spirit of
Error (darkness) depends upon his own personal response. But
John differs from Qumran, just as the whole of the NT does, in
the fact that the Spirit of Truth is the direct influence of God himself, demonstrated in the person of Jesus. That is why Christology
is central to John's position, and why response to Jesus is the
cardinal factor. It is Jesus, the one sent by the Father, who is the
Light of the World. So this discourse forces the reader to the most
fundamental moral decision as it poses the question 'What think
ye of Jesus?'

The Disciple is a Son, not a Slave **31–8**

31. who have believed in him: though these words are found
in all MSS., it is best to follow Dodd and Brown and to excise them
as a gloss. They have been inserted because Jesus' words in this
verse appear to be addressed to the 'many' of verse 30, encourag-
ing them to stand firm. But it quickly becomes clear that these
words are a general statement, laying out the foundations of the
new discourse, addressed to Jews who are decidedly hostile. The

construction of the verb with the dative (instead of *eis* and accusative) suggests the hands of a glossator. If the words are taken to be authentic, they have to be regarded as meaning that the Jews have given credence to Jesus' teaching without entrusting themselves to him, as in 6.30, where the dative is used. But this is not what John meant in the preceding verse.

If you continue: the same word as 'abide' in 15.7. Here, however, it is an anticipation of **continue** in the parable of verse 35, on the slave and the son. The 'truly, truly' opening in 34 is a sign of traditional material, and suggests that 35 is an adaptation of a genuine parable of Jesus (so Dodd, Jeremias). The parable expresses the privilege of sonship, which confers a permanent position in the household—i.e. in the house of our heavenly Father (cf. Rom. 8.15). John's application of it begins in verse 34, where the slave is identified with 'every one who commits sin'. One would expect the son to be 'every one who does righteousness', but John expresses this idea by the phrase: 'if any one keeps my word' (verses 51f.), or **if you continue in my word,** so as to bring it into close relation with Jesus himself. So also in this present verse **disciples** replaces 'sons', which the parable strictly requires. If this verse is read after verse 35, it will be seen at once how it forms an exposition of the idea of sonship. The reason why John has anticipated this part of the application is that he also applies the son to Jesus himself (verse 36). The main issue, however, is that of slavery, as we shall see in the next two verses.

32. know the truth: cf. verses 40, 44–6, where it becomes evident that John has in mind the contrast between truth and falsehood which is characteristic of the Two Spirits doctrine. Thus the disciples are under the control of the truth, which is conveyed by Jesus' words. This means that they are free from the opposite controlling factor, the spirit of error. John has thus aligned the contrast between slave and son in the parable with the Christian form of the Two Spirits doctrine. The word for **free** (both verb and adjective) occurs only here and in verses 33, 36 in the Fourth Gospel.

33. descendants of Abraham: the Jews claim to be the elect people of God on the grounds of descent. This is the presupposition of the Judaizers, whom Paul refutes in the argument of Romans and Galatians, cf. especially Rom. 9.7. Shallow reliance on descent from Abraham is condemned by John the Baptist

(Mt. 3.9 (= Lk. 3.8)) and by Jesus himself (Mt. 8.11f. (= Lk.
13.28f.)). The claim is here put forward to refute the suggestion
in the last verse that freedom can only be obtained by becoming
disciples of Jesus.

never been in bondage: this is certainly not true of the political
history of the Jews, and is ironical when spoken at a time when
Judea is under the direct control of a Roman procurator. But they
had always maintained their religious freedom, and in Roman
times they were allowed to practise their faith as a *religio licita*.
But even this does not go deep enough. It is yet another example
of a literal understanding which serves by contrast to draw attention to the real issue of spiritual freedom.

34. The Jews' question is the cue for Jesus to begin the exposition of the slave in the parable of the next verse. As we have seen,
he has already given one application of the son in verse 31. Here
he shows that it is a spiritual bondage that is meant by the slave.
to sin: these words are missing from D b, Sinaitic Syriac, and
Clement of Alexandria, and should undoubtedly be omitted as a
very early gloss (so Hoskyns, Sanders, *NEB*). The sentence answers
the question: 'Who is the slave [sc. of the parable of 35]?' The
further question: 'To whom is he enslaved?' will be raised in verse
38 and will not be answered until verse 44. There it will appear
that the answer is not sin personified, as the gloss implies, but the
Devil himself. Thus it cannot even be asserted, as for instance by
Barrett, that the gloss gives the correct sense of the passage.

35. The relation of this verse to the context has often perplexed
commentators, as it seems to interrupt the idea of slavery (verse
34) from which Jesus can give release (36). Bernard even suggests
that the whole verse might be a gloss. But the difficulties are
resolved by the recognition that it is a genuine parable of Jesus,
which John has used as the nucleus of the whole argument. In its
present position it sums up the discussion so far: just as a slave
has no permanent position, so those who commit sin suffer from
the disabilities of slavery, whereas a son has a permanent inheritance in his father's house, and so enjoys freedom like the disciples
of Jesus (verses 31f.). The article before **the slave** and **the son**
is the Semitic generic use, where English requires 'a' (cf. 5.19f.).
the son continues for ever: Omitted by ℵ W X Γ and some
other MSS., probably as a result of homoioteleuton.
36. the Son: the use of the capital letter is interpretative,

applying the son of the parable to Jesus himself. This would not be apparent in the Greek, which means that, because the son has a special position in the household, he can release slaves and give a share in the inheritance to whom he will. But the interpretation implied by *RSV* is correct, for this is not part of the parable itself, but direct address to the Jews. Jesus offers freedom, as already mentioned in verse 32. It will be true freedom (**free indeed**), because 'what the Son does will be ratified by the Father' (Bernard).

37. The idea that the son can give freedom in his father's house has shifted the thought from the identity of the slave and the son in the parable to that of their respective masters. When this is put in terms of spiritual sonship, as the argument requires, it is necesssary to abandon the strict logic of the parable itself. The Father of the Son (Jesus) is of course God, and this will be expressly stated in verse 42. The father or master (i.e. the controlling influence) of the slave (i.e. the Jews) must now be identified. First of all, Jesus accepts the Jews' claim of verse 33 that they are **descendants of Abraham,** but dismisses it as irrelevant to the real point at issue: descent is no criterion to decide spiritual paternity. Next he adduces the Jews' behaviour, to see what kind of controlling influence that implies; this is put in sharpest focus by the bald statement **you seek to kill me,** which not only refers to their attempts to arrest him, but also sums up their refusal to believe in him (for the important equation: 'to seek to kill' = 'to refuse to believe in', cf. the notes on 7.19). It is the logical consequence of the fact that **my words find no place in you.** This phrase is reminiscent of 5.38. The verb (**find . . . place,** *chōrei*) is unusual. In 2.6; 21.25 it is transitive, meaning 'hold, contain'. The intransitive use generally implies motion, either to withdraw or to make progress, hence Moffatt has 'makes no headway among you' (cf. *NEB*). But there is not much idea of motion here, and so *RSV* is to be preferred (so Bultmann, Sanders).

38. It follows that Jesus can now assert that he and they have entirely different fathers (controlling influences), corresponding with their entirely different conduct. Again we must remember that the Greek text had no capital letter for **Father.** The verse has numerous textual variants, indicating the difficulty which it caused to ancient commentators. There can be little doubt that the original text (represented only by P[66] B L 070) was: 'What I have seen from the father I speak: you also, then, what you have heard (P66: 'seen') from the father, do.' The final 'do' can be either indicative or imperative; Brown thinks that it is imperative, and this enables him to take 'the father' in both cases to be God; this makes the verse an appeal to the Jews to abandon their intention just exposed in the last verse. But this interpretation makes nonsense of the argument: the point is that (as Sanders puts it) 'conduct is the clue to paternity'. It is precisely to avoid the mistake of supposing that 'the father' is the same in both cases that many MSS. have inserted **my** or **your,** or both. This is the correct interpretation, though John does not yet wish to say who the father is in each case. This will be done in the next paragraph.

The Father of the Jews 39-47

39. The position is that the Jews' desire to kill Jesus indicates that they are slaves from the point of view of the parable, and also raises the question of their controlling influence, or 'father'. The Jews do not know what Jesus means, and doggedly reassert that **'Abraham is our father',** cf. verse 33. Jesus' reply recapitulates the criterion given in verse 37. This is not physical descent, but moral affiliation. What Abrahamic behaviour is, is not specified, but we already know that it is the response of faith which the Jews withhold, just as it is in Paul. Unfortunately the tenses of the verbs in Jesus' reply give rise to some difficulty. The *textus receptus* has: 'If you had been . . . you would have done . . .' (*ēte . . . epoieite*, or *epoieite an*). P66 and B have: 'If you are . . . do . . .' (*este . . . poieite*, presumably to be taken as imperative). But the best-attested text is a mixture (*este . . . epoieite*): 'If you are Abraham's children, you were (presumably) doing what Abraham did (when you sought my life, though that is not true to Abraham, and so spoils your case).' This is not sarcastic, but a statement of the grounds for a logical proof that the Jews' claim is inadmissible.

40. Jesus repeats the summary of the Jews' conduct from verse 37, so as to show that it excludes not only physical descent from Abraham, but also spiritual affiliation. At the same time he gives a fuller description of his own conduct than he gave in verse 38, reminiscent of 26b, and including the important word **truth** from 32. It is to be observed that the vague 'father' (= *RSV* 'my Father') of 38 has now become **God,** so that the question of Jesus' own affiliation is now implicitly settled.

41. your father: Jesus has excluded Abraham from consideration, but has not yet put forward an alternative. If his words are taken literally (which is what we should expect), they imply that the Jews are bastard sons. Hence they indignantly reply: **We were not born of fornication.** This is sufficient explanation of the saying, and it is not necessary to see in it a sneer at Jesus himself, as if the tradition of the Virgin Birth of Jesus was known to the Jews and explained away by them in this way (contrast 6.42). But the possibility of an ironical allusion cannot be excluded, because **We** in the Greek is emphatic; the next two verses immediately revert to Jesus' sonship; and a Jewish sneer of this kind is recorded in Origen, *contra Cels*. i.28. See also the notes on 1.13.

one Father, even God: the fatherhood of God is a commonplace of the OT, cf. Mal. 2.10. It appears that the Jews have taken the point that the argument is concerned with spiritual paternity, and so they naturally make this claim. Obviously it cannot be upheld, for the same reason as the claim to Abrahamic sonship fails. Ironically it is true of Jesus himself, and that in a deeper sense than the Jews will be ready to admit.

42. love me: the verb is here used for the first time since 3.35. It is a way of representing the opposite of 'seek to kill me' in 37, 40, and so describes the conduct which would be appropriate to the claim to affiliation to God. As in 40, the contrast between the Jews and Jesus is emphasized by another fuller description of his own position. This time, however, it is not a description of his behaviour, but of his affiliation to God, which that implied. The actual phrases are closely parallel to 7.28f., where Jesus' origin was under discussion in connection with messiahship.

43. Why: not a rhetorical question, but a challenge to the Jews to think out the implications of their failure to respond to Jesus. They **do not understand** Jesus' speech (**what I say,** *lalian*), because they are unable to submit themselves obediently to (*akouein* = **hear** in the Semitic sense of grasp and obey) his message (*logon* = **word**). The reason can only be that they are under the control of a quite different 'father', as the next verse will show. *RSV* **cannot bear to hear** misses the point, because it makes it more like 'do not like to hear', as in 6.60, which is the wrong nuance here. In fact the Greek only says: 'cannot hear'.

44. your father the devil: at last the answer to the question

of the spiritual affiliation of the Jews can be given. Their failure
to believe in Jesus leads to the conclusion that they are sons of,
or slaves to, **the devil.** But the Greek is very awkward. Literally
it means 'You are from the father of the devil', if the strict rules
of Greek grammar are observed, as 'the' must be omitted before
'father' if the two nouns are to be taken as in apposition (*BDF*
§ 268.2). According to Bauer (p. 127) some Gnostics actually took
it in this literal meaning. But the words must be in apposition,
and we must either assume that John is here following Semitic
usage requiring the article, or side with Bultmann in taking **the
devil** to be a gloss (better than omitting **father** with K and Old
Syriac).

your will: Greek has the verb: 'you will to do'; but we can
scarcely escape an allusion here to the 'inclination' (*yēṣer*) in the
rabbinic form of the Two Spirits doctrine (the inclination to good
and the inclination to evil). What Jesus has said about his own
relation to God applies *mutatis mutandis* to the Jews' relation to
their 'father'. Their behaviour corresponds with the essential
character of the Devil.

a murderer: the Devil is described in terms which explain the
Jews' attitude to Jesus. Two fundamental characteristics are
selected. The first is that **he was a murderer from the beginning,** which explains Jesus' insistence that the Jews seek to kill
him. The reference is presumably to Wis. 2.24: 'Through the
devil's envy death entered the world', referred to by Paul in
Rom. 5.12. Many commentators see here a reference to Cain's
murder of his brother Abel (Gen. 4.8), which was the first act of
sin after the fall of Adam. Brown is even favourable to the theory
of J. R. Diaz (*NT* vi (1963), p. 69f.) that John had in mind a
tradition that Cain was the son of Eve by the Devil, though there
is nothing in the text here to suggest this. In fact Cain would
hardly come into the picture, if it were not for the very clear
relation between this verse and 1 Jn 3.10–12, where Cain is mentioned as the primary example of the children of the Devil.
Moreover the rare word for murderer (*anthrōpoktonos*) is found in
the NT only here and in 1 Jn 3.15, where it obviously refers
back to Cain. But as far as the present verse is concerned, we can
only say that the reference might be to Wis. 2.24 or to Cain or
to both, but the text does not permit a definite decision.

no truth: the second characteristic of the Devil is his absolute opposition to the truth. This explains the Jews' inability to respond to Jesus (verse 43), who declares the truth from God (verse 40). The Devil's antagonism derives from the fact that **he is a liar and the father of lies** (lit. 'of it', i.e. of falsehood, *pseudos*, used in the phrase **When he lies;** the rendering 'of him' (i.e. 'and so is his father'), is possible, but would require the impossible 'father of the Devil' at the beginning of the verse).

The issue of truth and falsehood naturally reminds us of the Spirit of Truth and the Spirit of Error in the Qumran texts. But falsehood also accords with the central meaning of **'devil'** (*diabolos*), which means 'slanderer'. The corresponding verb (*diaballein*) means to bring charges against someone to procure a conviction, often in the context of a malicious act of false accusation. It thus makes a good translation of the Hebrew *sāṭān*, which means 'accuser', often with hostile intent. In the OT the Satan is one of the ministers of the heavenly court, whose function is to test men's integrity before God (Job 1–2), and so may entice them to sin (compare 1 Chr. 21.1 with the older version of the same passage in 2 Sam. 24.1); by NT times he is regularly regarded as the tempter (Mt. 4.1). He is described here as **the father of lies,** because of the father/son concept which is central to the whole argument.

45. At this point, having given the exposition of 38b, Jesus reverts to the subject of his own position, which is exactly the opposite (38a). **I tell the truth** (cf. 39) replaces 'speak of what I have seen' in 38a, so as to continue the thought of the preceding verse.

46. This verse is omitted by D and a few other MSS., probably simply by homoioteleuton, but perhaps because it seems to contradict the last verse. In fact it only makes the point more strongly, because Jesus' known moral integrity should be proof enough of his truthfulness, and if they still refuse to believe it can only be due to their submission to the Devil, or (as it is put in the next verse) to the fact that they 'are not of God'.

convicts is a forensic word (cf. 16.8), and recalls the setting of this discourse in an informal investigation by the Pharisees (cf. the editorial links of verses 12 and 20).

47. He who is of God: the phrase is general, referring to anyone who submits to God, by contrast with the Jews. But the singular suggests that it refers primarily to Jesus himself.

hears: again there is the Semitic nuance of 'obey, give heed to'. This verse rounds off the argument concerning the real spiritual affiliation of the Jews who oppose Jesus.

'Before Abraham was, I am' 48–59

This final section of the discourse has considerable dramatic power, but the argument is not easy to follow. As often happens, John now goes back to the beginning again in order to follow up another aspect of the matter in hand. He is now concerned with the positive aspect of the parable, 'the son continues for ever' (verse 35b), applied to the disciples, as in verses 31f. Another way of expressing their permanent continuance is to say that they 'will never see death' (51f.). The 'truly, truly' opening again indicates that this way of expressing it is taken from another saying of Jesus in the tradition. The argument then moves on to the unique capacity of Jesus to confer eternal life, which makes him superior even to Abraham, the father of the race. At verse 56 the course of the argument becomes extremely rapid and condensed, and the true interpretation is by no means certain. The solution adopted below is that Jesus maintains that Abraham had no such jealousy of his unique position; rather, as one who was faithful to God's word, he looked forward to the fulfilment of God's promise in Jesus' 'day'; and because he was open to God, he had his share in the eternal life which Jesus has now come to confer on believers; consequently he was alive to rejoice at Jesus' 'day'. In the next verse the positions are reversed, and it is suggested that Jesus was alive in the lifetime of Abraham—a misunderstanding which ironically hits on the truth. So in verse 58 the grand climax is reached, and Jesus reveals his essential existence from eternity.

48. a Samaritan: here used as a term of abuse, cf. the note on 4.9. It is generally taken to mean heretical, though the usage is unparalleled. The suggestion that it means illegitimate (cf. verse 41) is not convincing, because descent from mixed stock and illegitimacy are not the same thing. There is, however, some slight patristic support for this interpretation. But the meaning required by the context is 'mad', i.e. 'one of those mad Samaritans'. If this is right, one naturally thinks of Simon Magus (Ac. 8.10) and Dositheus, who operated in Samaria, claiming to be Son of God, and were considered mad by the Jews (Origen, *contra Cels.* vi.11). But this is too obscure and anachronistic to be altogether certain, and we must be content to admit that the precise reference is unknown to us. (Cf. Bowman (*BJRL* xl (1958), pp. 298–308. His own view is that the description is meant quite seriously, because the teaching of Jesus (as presented by John) is indebted to Samaritan traditions, cf. Introduction, p. 37).

have a demon: not the same word as 'devil' in verse 44, but the usual expression for insanity, cf. 7.20. It implies spirit-possession, however, so that the terms of reference of the whole discourse are maintained. Jesus' accusation that the Jews are under the control of the Devil is thus countered by the charge that he himself is under a controlling spirit, and so is out of his mind.

49. honour . . . dishonour: Jesus' sanity is proved by his reverence for the Father in contrast with the abusiveness of the Jews. Each side acts according to the principle laid down in verse 38.

50. glory: i.e. good opinion; cf. 5.41; 7.18. Jesus does not wish for glory for himself, for glory is due to God alone, who will condemn those who withhold it. Thus the thought is turned from the controlling influences to the results of allegiance to them in the reward of life or death. In the next verse Jesus will show by contrast the reward that awaits his disciples.

51. will never see death: in the context this implies: 'will not be condemned', by contrast with 50b (cf. 5.24). But it is put in the form of the reward of eternal life, so as to bring in the category of life and death in the ensuing discussion. The phrase is a variation of 'taste death' (*NEB*: 'know what it is to die' in both verses conceals the variation) which is actually employed in the next verse, when the Jews repeat the saying. This indicates that the whole verse is built on the saying of Jesus which is preserved in the Synoptic Gospels in Mt. 16.28 paras.: 'Truly, I say to you, there are some standing here who will not taste death before they see the Son of man coming in his kingdom' ('. . . see the kingdom of God come with power', Mk 9.1). This saying, which cannot be interpreted with certainty, seems to imply that the kingdom will come in the lifetime of Jesus' hearers. John has introduced two changes. **If any one keeps my word** replaces 'there are some standing here', which specifies who they are (i.e. his disciples; cf. verse 31). The second change can only be appreciated by a very literal rendering of the form in verse 52, i.e. 'If any one keeps my word, he will not at all taste death for ever.'

Here 'for ever' replaces 'before they see . . .' in the Synoptic saying. This is John's regular practice of making eternal life the equivalent of the kingdom of God in the tradition; cf. 3.3, 5,15. 'Taste death' occurs nowhere else in the four Gospels outside these related passages, but it is also found in Heb. 2.9 and in some rabbinic texts (*SB* 1.751f.). It is interpreted in a way rather reminiscent of John in the opening words of the *Gospel of Thomas*: 'These are the secret words which the living Jesus spoke, and [which] Didymus Judas Thomas wrote. And he said: He who finds the explanation of these words will not taste death' (cf. Pap. Oxyrhynchus 654 for the original Greek).

52. Now we know: exultantly the Jews renew their charge. The interplay of extreme contrasts is particularly effective, as John builds up the discourse to its climax. They call Jesus mad, but they are completely mistaken. Their scornful rejection of Jesus' words shows once more that by taking them literally they have quite misunderstood them. They speak of Jesus' promise of life as if it could be disproved by the fact of death. **Abraham** is mentioned, partly because his sanctity was such that, if anyone might escape death, he should certainly have done so; but chiefly to reintroduce him into the argument as the point of comparison in the contrast between Jesus and the Jews; **the prophets** are included, to bring in other OT saints, and to suggest the long lapse of time between Abraham and Jesus. It is unlikely that the objection is directed against the doctrine of the Resurrection as such, for this belief was held by the Pharisees in common with Jesus (against the Sadducees, who are not mentioned in the Fourth Gospel; cf. Mt. 22.23–33 paras.). It is rather an objection to the idea of continuing life without the intervention of death.

53. greater: for the argument, cf. 4.12.
our father: perhaps an addition. The words are omitted by D W, Old Latin and Old Syriac.
who died: the syntax is slightly awkward. The relative is the indefinite *hostis*, which must be regarded as replacing the usual *hos* (this is not infrequent, however; cf. *BDF* § 293), and it ought to be repeated after **the prophets.** Black (p. 74) accounts for this by an Aramaic construction, but the Greek is not impossible as it stands. D improves it by reading *hoti* ('for he died and the prophets died').
Who do you claim to be: not quite the same as 'Who are you?'

(verse 25). The Jews complain that Jesus is setting up himself as one greater even than Abraham.

54. Jesus refutes the suggestion by repeating the substance of verse 50. The Father **glorifies** him by effecting what Jesus does in his name (28f.).

your God: This is the reading of א B* D F, but many MSS. (P66 P75 B2 A I W Θ, Lake and Ferrar groups and *textus receptus*) have 'our God', thus using *oratio recta*, which adds to the vividness of the words (so *NEB*). It is a sarcastic reference back to verse 41, and leads into a brief recapitulation of the distinction argued in 39–47 in the next verse.

55. For **you have not known him,** cf. 43; for **I know him,** cf. 42; for **liar,** cf. 44; for **keep his word,** cf. 51. It follows from the argument of 39–47 that the Jews neither understand Jesus' teaching, nor know the Father from whom it is derived; and that Jesus both knows the Father and declares his words. Jesus is himself the model of discipleship, as will be shown more fully in the Supper discourses, and therefore he keeps the Father's words in the same way as the disciple must keep his.

56. Your father: Jesus is here speaking *ad hominem* (Barrett), acknowledging the Jews' descent from Abraham, as in 37, in spite of having refuted their claim to spiritual affiliation to him. There is thus a touch of irony about it.

rejoiced that he was to see . . . saw it and was glad: there are two distinct actions here, and much confusion has been caused by the failure of many commentators to keep them separate. The first happens in Abraham's lifetime. He **rejoiced** at the birth of his son Isaac (whose name means 'laughter'), Gen. 17.17. This is the fulfilment of God's promise, and is the beginning of the whole process of promise and fulfilment which is consummated in the Incarnation of Jesus. But perhaps we should see here a hint of the tradition that Abraham was vouchsafed a conspectus of the age to come (*Gen. Rabba* xliv.25; 2 Esd. 3.14). From this point of view Abraham was privileged **to see** Jesus' **day** (for **rejoiced that he was to see,** cf. *BDF* § 392.1(a)), just as Isaiah had prophetic vision of the future ('saw his, i.e. Jesus', glory', 12.41). Cf. also Lk. 10.23f.; Heb. 11.13. But why does Jesus go on to say **he saw it and was glad**? If this is not a redundant repetition of what has just been said, it must surely refer to the fulfilment of that vision in the coming of Jesus, and this must mean that Abraham is alive

in Paradise at the time (so Bauer, Sanders; denied by Hoskyns,
Brown). That this was a popular belief in NT times is attested by
Lk. 16.19–31. Thus Abraham did not 'taste death' in the sense
intended by Jesus in verse 51, for he has his share in eternal life.
And at the same time he acknowledges by his gladness that Jesus
is indeed greater than he.

my day: the phrase has two possible meanings: if we put the
stress on Abraham's rejoicing and connect that with the birth of
Isaac, then we may suppose that it means the Incarnation—the
birth of Isaac is prophetic of the birth of Christ (cf. Paul's argument along this line in Gal. 3.16); if, however, we think of the
preview of the age to come, we should expect it to have its apocalyptic meaning, and so it would mean the day of the Son of Man.
This in John's terminology could only mean the exaltation of
Jesus after his Passion (cf. 14.20, and the frequent use of 'the last
day'), which is still future at the time of speaking. But this interpretation (in spite of its wide support among modern critics) is
excluded, if Abraham has already had the joy of seeing the vision
fulfilled, as argued above. Hence we must take it to mean 'my
time (era)' (so *AG*, p. 348a).

57. However we understand the last verse, it is clear that it has
in some sense made Jesus and Abraham appear to be contem-
poraries. Whether Abraham saw the day of Jesus only from afar
(Heb. 11.13), or was alive in Paradise to witness it in actuality, he
has seen Jesus, and this suggests that Jesus has seen him. Taking
this last idea literally, it follows that Jesus was alive in the lifetime
of Abraham. This is the Jews' literal-minded reaction, which makes
them ask their incredulous question, so ironically close to the
truth. The reference to Jesus' age would be pointless if it were
not intended to mean that he was alive then.

fifty years old: this implies that Jesus is in his forties, which
hardly agrees with Lk. 3.23; hence Chrysostom and a few MSS.
read 'forty'. Irenaeus, however, takes it as evidence that the
ministry of Jesus was longer than is commonly supposed (*Adv.
Haer.* ii.22.6). But the implications of this round number should
not be pressed. It certainly has no connection with the forty-six
years of 2.20.

have you seen Abraham: a few important MSS. (P⁷⁵ ℵ* 0124
Old Syriac and Sahidic) have the reading in the margin, 'Has
Abraham seen you?' Bernard argues in favour of it, but nearly all

modern critics take it to be a correction based on the preceding
verse. In fact it ruins the transition from the idea of Abraham in
the time of Jesus in 56, to the idea of Jesus in the time of Abraham
in 58, which is the whole point of this verse.

58. Truly: the solemn formula brings the discourse to its
climax. It does not appear to indicate the presence of traditional
material on this occasion (cf. 6.47).

Abraham was: i.e. was born (lit. 'came into being'; cf. 1.3, where
the same verb (*genesthai*) was used).

I am: the striking change of tense and the use of the simple verb
einai (cf. 1.1, 2) put all the emphasis on the timeless condition of
eternal existence (cf. Ps. 90.2); so Jesus is pre-existent to Abraham.
The phrase (*egō eimi*) thus has a rather different nuance from
verses 24 and 28, where it required a predicate ('I am he'). It
does not, then, correspond with *'ani hū'* in Isa. 43.10, etc.; but
Hebrew idiom would have used simply the personal pronoun
(*'ani* or *'ānōki*); cf. Prov. 8.27.

The question then arises whether John intends the phrase to
convey a hint of the divine name I AM of Exod. 3.14. Odeberg
affirms this, on the grounds that this was current in Jewish mystical
language, but Bultmann shows that this would deprive the phrase
of its verbal force, making it simply a name, so that the phrase
would have to be an elliptical way of saying 'I am the I AM'.
Moreover John never simply identifies Jesus with God. The whole
point of the saying, as the grand climax of the discourse, is that
Jesus 'continues for ever' (verse 34), and therefore is the eternal
Son of God. It is in this sense that Jesus 'makes himself equal with
God' (5.18), and so incurs the charge of blasphemy (10.36). Thus
Jesus' sonship implies the Wisdom Christology expressed in the
opening words of the Prologue. In this chapter the successive *egō
eimi* sayings convey a deepening meaning, corresponding with the
unfolding of the argument: 'I am the light of the world' (verse 12)
becomes 'I am (he)', i.e. the light and all other possible predicates
which denote salvation (verses 24 and 28); and this in its turn
becomes the simple 'I am' of the present verse, denoting timeless
pre-existence.

59. took up stones: the spontaneous attempt to lynch Jesus
expresses with dramatic force the Jews' reaction to the electrifying
effect of his brief words. It implies that they feel that he has
'blasphemed the name of the Lord' (Lev. 24.16, where death by

stoning is prescribed as the penalty). Exactly how his words constitute blasphemy is not yet made clear. John will hold over the
issue for fuller treatment later on (10.31–9); indeed, he has not
even mentioned yet the charge of blasphemy. At this point the
repeated attempts to arrest Jesus (7.30, 44; 8.20) come to a head,
but still the time has not come; consequently Jesus is represented
as making his escape. Many readers of this verse are puzzled by
this attempt on Jesus' life, because it appears from 18.31 that the
Jews did not have the right to impose the death penalty; but it is
doubtful how far this was actually enforced, and it certainly did
not prevent occasional acts of lynching, as the case of Stephen
shows (Ac. 7.54–60). In the case of Jesus at the time of the final
Passover, there were special considerations: Pilate was present at
Jerusalem with the express purpose of keeping order and prevent-
ing a riot, so that it was essential to act in full agreement with the
ruling authorities. Whether John is right in suggesting that the
Jews attempted to lynch Jesus in Jerusalem on some earlier occasion is another matter. The construction of chapters 7 and 8 is so
artificial that we can hardly take this verse as reliable history.
But it may be dependent on an item of tradition such as Lk. 4.29f.,
which tells of an attempt on Jesus' life at Nazareth. This was a
matter of trying to hurl him from a promontory, and so is not
identical with John's source here (if he had one); but in fact in
NT times this was a recognized alternative to stoning, and more
commonly practised (cf. D. Daube, *The New Testament and Rabbinic
Judaism* (1956), pp. 303–8). The Lucan parallel has actually
affected the textual tradition, so that the *textus receptus* and
numerous MSS. add: 'and passing through the midst of them he
went away [= Lk. 4.30], and so passed by [= 9.1]'.

JESUS ENLIGHTENS MEN TO KNOW THAT HE AND THE FATHER ARE ONE 9.1–10.42

The healing of the blind man provides an element of relief after
the emotional tension of chapter 8. But at the same time it follows
naturally from the last chapter, and prepares the reader for the
vital teaching of chapter 10.

First the theme of the Light of the World (8.12) is taken up and
developed in the story of the blind man, which occupies the whole

of chapter 9. This is one of John's most brilliant compositions. It begins with the blind man, as it were, dazed by the new light which has just been given, hardly understanding what has happened to him, and yet subjected to cross-examination by the Pharisees, who show themselves hostile to Jesus. Gradually his own understanding is bathed in light, while their opposition hardens. Finally we discover that the roles have been reversed, so that the man sees with complete clarity to make his confession of faith, and the Pharisees show by their obduracy that it is they who are blind. The result is that the ground is prepared for the final revelation of the identity of Jesus, which will be given in chapter 10. This is the fact that he and the Father are one (10.30). This can only be understood and accepted by those whose minds have been enlightened, because it is known only through experience of the analogous relationship of believers themselves to Jesus. This point is asserted in the allegory of the shepherd and sheep in 10.1–18. But the allegory also takes into account the blindness of the Pharisees. They are 'blind guides' (Mt. 23.16), who 'shut the kingdom of heaven against men', and 'neither enter' themselves 'nor allow those who would enter to go in' (Mt. 23.13). They are not, therefore, in the right condition to accept the revelation of the unity of Jesus with the Father. It was bad enough when Jesus mysteriously asserted his pre-existence with the Father (8.58); now they make open charge of blasphemy. Although Jesus defends himself by an argument from Scripture, and also restates the unity between him and the Father in terms of mutual indwelling, they remain set in their determination to be rid of him (10.31–9). The debate of the whole central section of the Gospel (chapters 5–10) has now reached its conclusion with the issue which is proper to the trial before the Sanhedrin (see the notes on 10.22). The stage is set for the Passion narrative to begin.

So there is a logical consistency about these two chapters which confirms the care with which John has arranged his material for the purposes of his narrative. This does not, however, mean that we are free from the problems of minor inconsistencies and of possible displacements. No such problems arise with chapter 9. But there are real difficulties in chapter 10. The allegory of 10.1–18 gives the appearance of being a separate composition, and is fitted abruptly to the end of chapter 9. On the other hand, 10.19–21 clearly belong to the controversy of that chapter. Then there is a

time indication at 10.22, three months later than the last date
given, i.e. the feast of Tabernacles. In spite of this important
break, the allegory of shepherd and sheep is resumed in 10.26–9.
The simplest method of dealing with this is to remove 10.1–18
from its present position, and to insert it between 10.29 and 30,
as is done by Bernard and (with more complex minor adjustments)
by Bultmann. Reasons for rejecting this rearrangement have been
given in the Introduction (p. 49), and need not be repeated here.
Suffice it to say that the existing order of the material is thoroughly
characteristic of John's methods of composition. The allegory of
10.1–18 has the twofold object of discriminating between the true
and false guides and of supplying the grounds for the statement that
Jesus and the Father are one. The first of these two motifs attaches
it firmly to chapter 9. The second prepares for the dialogue in
10.22–39, and part of the exposition of the allegory is held over
for this section. But this section has such importance in its own
right, that it is necessary to mark it off from the preceding section,
and John does this by specifying a fresh occasion in 10.22. The
procedure is exactly what we should expect in the light of the even
greater complexity of the composition of chapters 5, 7 and 8.

If there are good grounds for believing that the Gospel never
existed without the arrangement of material as it now stands in
chapter 10, it does not necessarily follow that John has composed
it all at a single sitting. Chapter 9 is in any case complete in itself,
presumably based on one of John's homilies. The allegory of
10.1–18, 26–9 is likely to be another homily, which has required
rather more adapting to fit it to its present context. The rest of the
material belongs to the work of making the Gospel itself, and so is
to some extent editorial. It consists of two short pieces (10.19–21
and 40–2), and a fresh composition embodying part of the allegory
(10.22–39). It will be observed that the two short paragraphs have
much similarity to John's editing work elsewhere, and that 10.22–
39 has a clear relation to 8.31–59.

THE MAN BORN BLIND   **9.1–41**

At last John is able to make use again of a traditional story as the
basis of his teaching, as he did in chapter 5. The method in each
case is very similar: John uses a tradition which has clear links
with Synoptic passages, though he probably takes it from an independent source. As before, John adds to the tradition, almost as an

afterthought, the information that the miracle was done on the Sabbath. For this reason the man is brought before the Pharisees to explain the case in the absence of Jesus. In chapter 5, however, that was soon disposed of; Jesus renewed contact with the healed man, and the bulk of the chapter was devoted to a discourse which was only loosely attached to the opening episode. But this time the examination of the man replaces the discourse altogether, and the teaching is conveyed by means of an almost wearisome repetition of the facts of the cure. Jesus renews contact with the man only at the end of the chapter, in a short paragraph which brings to a head the two sides of the argument. Thus the teaching of the chapter, on spiritual sight leading to confession of faith in Jesus, and on spiritual blindness which refuses to believe, is kept within the terms of the narrative.

Nevertheless the chapter is not merely a narrative told with a theological purpose. Other related interests may be discerned. Firstly, the healing of the blind man can be regarded as a model of the experience of conversion, and therefore of the Christian practice of baptism. The idea of illumination occurs in the NT in connection with Christian initiation; cf. Ac. 9.17f.; Heb. 10.32; 1 Pet. 2.9. Hoskyns (pp. 363ff.) gives evidence of the use of this chapter in connection with baptism in the early lectionaries. John is not, of course, giving teaching on baptism as such; but his picture of the conversion experience may be influenced by his knowledge of Christian initiation, in which the notions of spiritual illumination and active confession of faith in Jesus are combined.

Secondly, it is difficult to resist the impression that the attitude of the Pharisees, especially the threat of excommunication in verse 22, reflects the actual situation obtaining at the time when John was writing. By A.D. 90 confession of faith in Christ meant perpetual exclusion from the synagogue (cf. Introduction, p. 37). It is extremely hard to imagine anything comparable to this in the lifetime of Jesus. From this point of view we may well suppose that John has the actual needs of the Church of his own day in mind as he writes.

Thirdly, the wider issue of spiritual blindness goes back into the Synoptic tradition, so that we need have no doubt of John's continuity with earlier teaching. At the end of the chapter (verse 39) John refers to the widely used proof text on blindness (Isa. 6.9), which he will himself quote at 12.40. It is referred to by Mark with

reference to his own special issue of the blindness of the disciples
(Mk 8.17), and then immediately after this he records a story of
the restoration of sight to a blind man (Mk 8.22-6) as a curtain-
raiser to Peter's confession of faith (Mk 8.29). This story has some
slight points of contact with John's account; the nearest parallel is,
however, the healing of Bartimaeus (Mt. 20.29-34 = Mk 10.46-
52 = Lk. 18.35-43), and the doublet of it in Mt. 9.27-31. John
is not likely to be much influenced by pagan parallels, though
these do show that such a miracle was generally felt to be within
the limits of the possible in the Hellenistic world as much as in
popular Judaism. Most commentators quote the following parallel
from a votive tablet found in the temple of Aesculapius at Rome
(W. Dittenberger, *Sylloge Inscriptionum Graecarum* (Leipzig, 1915-
24), 1173.15-18; and Adolf Deissman, *Light from the Ancient East*
(1911), p. 132): 'To Valerius Aper, a blind soldier, the god revealed that he should go and take the blood of a white cock,
together with honey, and rub them into an eyesalve and anoint
his eyes three days. And he received his sight, and gave thanks
publicly to the god.'

Jesus gives Sight to the Blind Man **1-7**

1. passed by: Gr. *paragōn*, a word never used elsewhere by
John (but cf. the spurious addition to 8.59). But it occurs in the
Synoptic parallel at Mt. 9.27 (cf. 20.30), and in other connections
in Mk 1.16; 2.14. Hence it probably belongs to John's source,
describing the journey of Jesus. Here it is a vague indication of a
new occasion, probably not intended to mean the same time as
Jesus escaped from the Temple in 8.59.
blind from his birth: D adds 'sitting', clearly as a result of the
influence of Mk 10.46 paras. None of the Synoptic parallels mentions blindness from birth. The detail is important for John's purpose, because he wishes to present the healing, not as an act of
restoration, but as a creative act by him who is the Light of the
World. That the words **from his birth** were not in his source is
indicated by the choice of phrase, instead of the Semitic 'from his
mother's womb' (Ac. 3.2; 14.8; *AV*, *RV*; obscured by *RSV*, *NEB*).
John's *ek genetēs* occurs in Justin, *Dial.* lxix, probably alluding to
this verse.
2. who sinned: the dialogue in 2-5 is best taken as John's own
composition, replacing the blind man's request for healing (Mk

10.47f. paras.). John reserves complete freedom of initiative to Jesus, as in 5.6. The question is a device to elicit the answer in verse 3b, and patently lacks the seriousness which it deserves. It is an academic question, perhaps taken from rabbinic disputations (cf. *SB* II.529). Assuming that suffering is due to sin, how is suffering from birth to be accounted for? It might be due to the sin of the parents (in spite of Ezek. 18.20), or it might be due to ante-natal sin (as, for instance, when a pregnant woman commits idolatry, involving the child in her womb in the act of bending in worship, *Ca. Rabba* i.41).

3. Jesus does not deny the principle, but asserts that in this case the man's condition serves another purpose. Although it is foreign to John's purpose to suggest here a general answer to the problem of suffering, the existential approach of Jesus is worth pondering, for it has a striking Synoptic parallel in Lk. 13.2, where again Jesus deflects the thought from the cause of suffering to its possibilities for God's purpose. In this case, then, it is **that the works of God** [his creative power] **might be made manifest** [come to light in Jesus' act] **in him**. Seen in this way, the healing will lead to faith in Jesus as the one who is sent (cf. verse 7) by God. The sickness of Lazarus is treated in exactly the same way in 11.4.

4. **We:** although 'I' would be expected in view of the following **me,** and has the support of the majority of mss., **We** is unquestionably right (so P⁶⁶ P⁷⁵ B ℵ D L W), even though all of these, except B and D, wrongly read 'us' in place of **me.** Most commentators are content to assert that the plural pronoun associates the disciples in Jesus' work (cf. 3.11), not realizing that this destroys the whole point of the saying. It is, as Dodd has recognized (*Historical Tradition*, p. 186), a piece of 'proverbial wisdom', and this becomes immediately apparent if we follow Bultmann in taking the typically Johannine **the works of him who sent me** as an addition which John has made for his use of it here. Without these words, **work** has no object in the first half, and so chimes in properly with the second half. The point, then, is exactly the same as the saying of R. Simeon ben Eleazar (*c.* A.D. 190): 'Work so long as you can and it is possible for you and it is still within your power' (*B. Shabbath,* 151b). But for John this is not a general piece of advice to the disciples, but a fact of crucial importance for Jesus himself, as the next verse will show. Hence the addition of **the works of him who sent me.** The saying has a close parallel in the Lazarus story (11.9f.) which Dodd rightly takes to be another example of John's use of a parable from his stock of tradition. It goes without saying that he has used the proverb in the present verse because the contrast of **night** and **day** admirably suits the theme of light and darkness.

5. the light: the article is omitted in the Greek: 'I am [*eimi* simply; not *egō eimi*] light for the world'. The reference is, of course, to 8.12; this is not a revelation-formula, but a plain statement of fact. Jesus does his work as the Light of the World while he is, as it were, shining. It is implied that the work must be done now, before it is too late, and it is impossible to avoid (*pace* Odeberg) the implication that it is the Passion which will bring on the darkness all too soon. The work that he has to do is something that he must do himself, and no one can do for him. It is not the kind of continuation of his ministry which the disciples, and the Church after them, will perform after his exaltation; it is a work which forms part of the revelation about himself, without which his full identity as the Son of God cannot be known. Hence he must seize the God-given opportunity to 'manifest the works of God' which the chance meeting with the blind man has provided.

6. As he said this: after giving such expressions of urgency, Jesus loses no time in performing the cure. At this point John resumes the narrative from his source, which must have contained the feature of the use of **spittle,** as in Mk 8.23. This was commonly thought to have curative properties in the ancient world (see Barrett, p. 296, for references); but in Mk 8.23 Jesus spat on the man's eyes, whereas here he makes an ointment by moistening the dust. This at first sight seems more like the eyesalve in the votive tablet quoted above, but it could hardly have the same effect; for, instead of acting as an emollient, it would obviously dry into a hard shell over the eyes (hence for **anointed** we must read 'put' (*epethēken*) with B; see below on verse 11). Such a procedure is so improbable that it compels us to assume that John has elaborated his source, which may have been much closer to Mk 8.23. His reason is clear. Jesus does exactly what was done in the creation of man in Gen. 2.6f. Hence we are to understand, as 'from birth' in verse 1 has already suggested, that the healing is a creative act. The gift of sight corresponds with the light of revelation coming into the world. John's account shows no sign of influence from Tob. 11.5–12, where Tobit's eyes are healed by anointing with the gall of a fish.

7. Siloam: this is the regular LXX form of the Hebrew *Šilôaḥ*, the pool where Hezekiah's conduit emerges in the southern end of the Tyropean valley (outside the present walls of Jerusalem); on the conduit, cf. 2 Kg. 20.20. Arab women still wash clothes at the pool. It is probably only coincidence that Lk. 13.4 mentions the collapse of a tower there, in a context which reflects the question in verse 2. The translation **Sent** (*apestalmenos*) follows a popular etymology. John here probably intends a symbolical allusion, i.e. Jesus himself. For in verse 4 it was said that the Father 'sent' (*pempsantos*) Jesus to do his work (John generally uses *pempein* for the active and *apostellein* for the passive without any distinction of meaning; cf. 13.16). This suggests that the command to wash at Siloam might be a veiled reference to baptism into the name of Jesus, the one who was sent (see Hoskyns, p. 355, for patristic exegesis along these lines). The fact that the water used in the feast of Tabernacles (cf. 7.37) was drawn from Siloam does not seem to be relevant here.

seeing: after this creative act and the quasi-baptismal washing, the man acquires sight for the first time in his life, and the story is complete. It remains to be shown in the sequel how it is also an act of interior illumination.

Questioning by the Neighbours **8–12**

8. as a beggar: many late MSS. read: 'that he was blind', an obvious correction for greater consistency. But although John has omitted from his narrative the detail that the man **used to sit and beg,** it must have stood in his source in the introduction to the story; cf. Mk 10.46 paras.

9. The variety of views expressed is reminiscent of the popular discussion in 7.12. The purpose of the whole of this vivid little paragraph is to draw attention to Jesus as the one who has done the cure. But when the man says **'I am [the man]',** using the simple phrase *egō eimi*, there are none of the grand overtones which it has on the lips of Jesus in 8.58, and it is a mistake to read them into it (against Marsh). We have seen that, even when it is spoken by Jesus, it has different emphases according to the grammatical structure of the sentence and the meaning of the context. The only near parallel to the present case is 6.20, which, like this, is purely factual.

10. opened: another word which may have been in the source;

cf. Mt. 20.33. 'To open the eyes' is the regular Semitic expression
for restoration of sight, and is frequent in the OT (e.g. Isa. 35.5).
It does not necessarily imply that the man's eyes were closed before
the cure—only that they were sightless.

11. The man called Jesus: this colourless description is not
accidental. The ensuing dialogue will show successive stages in the
enlightenment of the man's understanding about Jesus. But he
begins without any distinctive title for him. The fact that Jesus
has done the cure is the only clue to his identity.

anointed: there is no dispute about the reading here, and it is
probably the reason why nearly all MSS. have this word in verse 6,
instead of the original 'put', which is preserved only in B and a
very few others. **Anointed** (*epechrisen*; *NEB*: 'smeared') takes the
accusative, whereas 'put' (or 'apply to', *epethēken*; *NEB*: 'spread')
requires repetition of the preposition, which occurs both in verse 6
and in verse 15, where it is the undisputed reading. 'Put' occurs
in Mk 8.23, and so one might well think that it was found in John's
source. But it is possible that *epechrisen* (which occurs nowhere else
in the NT) was in the source, as it is not suitable to the application
of clay, but could well be used for rubbing in the spittle. It is this
word which is used for 'anoint' in the votive tablet mentioned
above, and in this case it is exceptionally construed with repetition
of the preposition.

received my sight: Gr. *aneblepsa* ('I saw again'), thus properly
indicating the restoration of sight which has been lost. Here again
the word is probably from the source, cf. Mk 8.24; 10.51f. paras.

12. For the question and answer, cf. 5.12f.

Examination by the Pharisees **13–17**

13. They brought: it is left to the reader to guess why this was
done; it is not *because of* the breach of the Sabbath, in spite of the
next verse. We have to assume that the people want a more careful
enquiry simply to establish the truth of what the man claims.

14. Now it was a sabbath day: the identical expression was
used in 5.9. The detail is no part of the original story, but is
inserted for the sake of the following dialogue.

15. again: referring back to verse 10, though the speakers are
different.

16. not from God: thus denying 8.40, 42. But what the Pharisees deny about Jesus is to be affirmed, and so this paradoxically

draws attention to the fundamental fact which compels the man to assert at least that Jesus is a prophet (verse 17).

the sabbath: it is not clear whether it is the labour of making the clay (verse 15) or the act of healing (cf. **do such signs** in the following sentence) which constitutes the offence. Making clay would fall under the prohibition of kneading (*Shabbath*, vii.2), and the *carrying* of 'water enough to rub off an eye-plaster' was forbidden (*ibid.* 8.1); but so was anointing an eye (*B. Abodah Zarah*, 28b), and the use of spittle for the purpose by a man who was fasting (*Y.Shabbath*, 14, 14d, 17f); healing a chronic, as opposed to a case of urgent need, was also forbidden (see above on 7.21). We are thus in the same dilemma as we were over this issue in chapter 5. But here we do not have to make a decision, as the matter is immediately dropped. It is only introduced to throw doubt on Jesus' integrity.

How can a man who is a sinner do such signs: the argument is reminiscent of Jesus' argument against the charge that he is in league with Beelzebul in the Synoptic tradition; cf. Lk. 11.15–20. **such signs** refers principally to the healing just described, but in a general way to other acts, as in 7.31. For **division,** cf. 7.43; 10.19.

17. a prophet: the man is thus compelled to make a confession of faith, and makes the most natural suggestion in explanation of the miracle; cf. 4.19; Lk. 7.16. There is no suggestion here that the Prophet of Dt. 18 is meant. On the other hand even to say that Jesus might be a prophet comes near to acknowledgement of him as the Messiah; cf. 7.52. This fact comes to the surface in verse 22, so that the next short paragraph, which appears to hold back the argument, in fact takes it a stage further.

The Parents give Evidence **18–23**

18. Before any decision can be reached about Jesus, it is necessary to establish that he actually had performed the miracle. The parents act as the two witnesses required by the law, to attest that such a miracle has occurred.

who had received his sight: probably a scribal addition (not in P⁶⁶* Lake group, 565, Old Latin, Old Syriac and Bohairic).

19. Only the first question can really be answered by the parents, and they duly give their witness in the next verse. The second question can only be a matter of opinion (i.e. a confession of faith, verse 22), because they were not witnesses of what had occurred.

21. he is of age: the minimum age for legal response was thirteen.

22. feared the Jews: cf. 7.13.

confess him to be the Christ: it is thus implied that the parents would have been ready not only to endorse the man's own estimate of Jesus as a prophet, but even to regard him as the Messiah cf. above on verse 17. They would thereby express the baptismal confession of faith (Ac. 2.36; 1 C.12.3), which must be upheld even in the face of persecution (Mt. 10.32f.). There is sacrifice involved in the decision of faith.

put out of the synagogue: the word (*aposunagōgos*) is not used in the NT except by John (cf. 12.42; 16.2). Excommunication from the synagogue was usually for thirty days (*niddûy*), but for very serious offences there might be a total ban (*ḥērem*). This would obviously apply to apostasy, and so commentators generally see here, not a reference to punishments for normal offences, but the actual situation which obtained after the expulsion of the Minim in the late eighties of the first century (cf. Introduction, pp. 36f.).

As the dialogue, which forms the bulk of this chapter, is to be regarded as a Johannine construction, only the miracle of giving sight to the blind man being based on earlier tradition, no historical problem arises. John speaks of the cost of discipleship in terms of the conditions with which his readers were familiar. It is unnecessary to take this and the next verse as the evangelist's addition to his source (Bultmann); they are, in fact, the point of the paragraph. For the practice of excommunication from the synagogue, cf. Barrett *ad loc.*

23. For the repetition, drawing attention to the gravity of the matter, cf. 13.11.

Second Examination of the Man 24–34

24. Give God the praise: not an admonition to ascribe the healing to God instead of Jesus, but an unusual way of adjuring the man to speak the truth; cf. Jos. 7.19; 1 Esd. 9.8; *Sanhedrin* vi.2. It implies that the Pharisees think he has been lying.

we know: we is emphatic. This is the Pharisees' confession of disbelief, now more definite than at the beginning (verse 16), just as the blind man's belief grows stronger.

25. The man's guarded reply, sticking to the bare facts, shows that he is still not ready for full confession of faith.

27. Do you too want to become his disciples: the question is introduced by *mē*, making it a tentative suggestion rather than an open taunt, though it is certainly meant to be ironical. The man is nettled by the repeated questioning, and we can feel the emotional temperature rising. This forces the issue to extremes. The word **disciples** is not only sarcastic, but also an indication of the contemporary reference of the dialogue. John's great concern with the meaning of discipleship will appear in the Supper Discourses.

28. reviled: the word is used of the abuse suffered by Christians in 1 C. 4.12; 1 Pet. 2.23.

disciples of Moses: not a usual designation of the Pharisees; but cf. Mt. 23.2, the beginning of a long indictment of the scribes and Pharisees for their blindness. For rabbinic references for the designation, see *SB* II.535. The confession of faith entails a decision between the old teacher and the new.

29. spoken: primarily in giving the Law. The Pentateuch frequently mentions direct address to Moses on the part of God. The implication is that, by sticking to their rabbinic tradition, the Pharisees feel secure. Jesus, on the other hand, is an unknown quantity; they are unwilling to accept that the healing of the blind man provides part of Jesus' credentials to be one who is greater than Moses. The argument has obvious affinity with that of 5.45–7, and the two passages have been conflated in the fragment of an unknown Gospel, quoted above in the notes on 5.39.

where he comes from: cf. Pilate's question in 19.9. Here, however, it is not just an expression of ignorance, but a negative way of asserting that Jesus is not from God (verse 16). The question whether he is a sinner (verse 24) is thus tacitly dropped, and attention is fastened on the more fundamental issue.

30. a marvel: the ironical surprise is similar to that of Jesus in 3.10. At this point the man himself becomes the teacher, echoing the kind of argument used by Jesus himself in other discourses.

31. First of all, the issue is put in general terms, using conventional ideas which can be taken as agreed on both sides. It was normally held that a sinner's prayers would not be heard, but the more righteous a man was the more certain he would be of a hearing (cf. Ps. 66.16–19; Jas. 5.16–18). It thus follows that Jesus is not a sinner, and indeed, in view of the magnitude of the miracle, that he is a specially righteous person. It is taken for granted that the work has been done by divine power in answer to prayer, though nothing was said about this earlier. There will be an example of Jesus praying before doing a sign in 11.41f.

a worshipper of God: Gr. *theosebēs*, only here in the NT, but cf. 1 Tim. 2.10 (*theosebeia*). It is a Hellenistic word. The usual Semitic expression is 'one who fears God', regularly applied to devout Gentiles who did not feel they could become proselytes, cf. Ac. 10.35. The present context permits this wider range of reference, but does not necessitate it.

32. Never since the world began: the OT has prophecies of restoration of sight, and Tob. 11.10–15 describes the healing of Tobit's blindness, but there seems to be no precedent for a case of **a man born blind.** There is perhaps here again a hint of the creation of light, the first act in the creation of the world (Gen. 1.3). Thus Jesus' act 'manifests the works of God' (verse 3).

33. The conclusion, that Jesus is **from God,** is put in negative form; cf. 5.30. It is the affirmation to which all the dialogue has been leading.

34. born in utter sin: the words are merely an expression of abuse, putting the point as strongly as possible; cf. Ps. 51.3–5. But again there may be a hint of the opening of the story in verse 2. **cast him out:** thus bringing the examination to an abrupt end, and indicating the final refusal of the Pharisees to believe. It suggests the excommunication mentioned in verse 22, and this in its turn implies that the man's affirmation in verse 33 is equivalent to a confession of faith in Jesus as the Messiah. Bernard objects that it cannot mean a formal act of exclusion from the synagogue, which would require a decision of the Sanhedrin. This may be so, but the story operates at two levels, that of the conditions in the time of Christ, and that of the later experience of the Church. Thus the informal expulsion of the man is symbolic, at least, of the later excommunication.

Spiritual Sight and Spiritual Blindness **35–41**

In this final paragraph Jesus is brought back on to the scene, and makes the paradoxical pronouncement which has been implicit throughout the preceding dialogue. The reader is enabled to identify himself with the blind man in his confession of faith as a true disciple, and so is prepared for the final revelation about Jesus in 10.30. At the same time the Pharisees' refusal of belief is shown to be culpable blindness, and their subsequent unyielding opposition to Jesus is accounted for.

35. found: evidently after a search, precisely because he has heard that they had cast him out (cf. 5.14). It is 'a meeting which issues in discipleship' (Hoskyns).

Do you believe: you is emphatic. The question is reminiscent of the 'scrutiny' which precedes the confession of faith in baptism (cf. Ac. 8.37, a liturgical interpolation into the story of Philip and the Ethiopian eunuch).

Son of man: we should expect 'Son of God', which is indeed the reading of the majority of mss. But this is explained as a change influenced by the baptismal confession of faith, whereas **Son of man** (P⁶⁶ P⁷⁵ B ℵ D W Sinaitic Syriac and Sahidic) is certainly to be accepted as the harder reading. In fact, John is probably saving up 'Son of God' for the climax in 10.36. We must not forget that, with characteristic *inclusio*, John has in the last two verses brought the thought back to the beginning of the chapter, and Son of Man is the appropriate title to use with the idea of doing the Father's works in anticipation of future glory. For the brief statement in verse 3, 'that the works of God might be made manifest in him', picks up the teaching of the discourse in 5.19–29, where there is explicit reference to the Son of Man (5.27). This thought has now been deepened by the introduction of the theme of the glory of the Son of Man in the Passion in 8.28.

We have had an example of a Sign which must be accomplished before the Passion overtakes him (verse 5). This theme will be renewed, with an even more emphatic warning about the darkness overtaking the light, in 12.34–6. This will be immediately followed by further reference to spiritual blindness, obviously closely related to our present paragraph (12.37–43). Finally we shall have the splendid announcement on the eve of the Passion: 'Now is the Son of Man glorified, and in him God is glorified' (13.31). Thus the reading **Son of man** here places the confession of faith in the larger frame of the special Johannine theology of the manifestation of the divine glory in the incarnate life of Jesus.

36. who is he: the question is put in, as so often, to heighten the effect. The respectful **sir** (cf. 4.19) is the attitude of the disciple, ready to receive the master's teaching; in spite of his splendid affirmation of verse 33, the man has still to learn the truth about Jesus contained in the title Son of Man.

37. Jesus' reply has exactly the same awe-inspiring effect as
4.26. His use of the third person to speak of himself increases the
sense of distance, and so of overpowering majesty. Like 4.26, this
is a self-revelation which puts the coping-stone on the whole
brilliantly constructed edifice. What follows is only comment,
though none the less important for that. It may be remarked that
4.26 has nothing corresponding with **you have seen him,** a
detail specially apt in the context of new sight.

**38, 39a. He said, 'Lord, I believe'; and he worshipped
him. Jesus said:** these words are missing from P75 ℵ* W b; also
from one Coptic MS. (Q). Bernard, writing before the discovery
of P75, thought the omission 'remarkable', but said it 'cannot be
original'; but it must now be considered most likely that the words
are a liturgical interpolation from the use of this chapter in connection with baptism at a very early date (cf. C. L. Porter in *NTS*
XIII (1967), pp. 387–94; and Brown). The Greek for **he said** (*ephē*)
is rare in John (only in 1.23 elsewhere); nor does the present **I
believe** occur again (contrast 11.27, where the Greek is perfect
with present meaning); and nowhere else does he have the word
worship (*proskunein*) with Jesus as object (contrast 4.20–4; 12.20).
Moreover **Lord** (*kurie*) here is the same word as 'sir' in verse 36,
but clearly has a different nuance. It is probable that the interpolation came in as a result of the similarity of verse 35 to the
baptismal scrutiny, and this also explains the reading 'Son of God'
there.

39. This verse should be the continuation of verse 37, and it
maintains the sense of solemnity of that verse. The order of words
places the emphasis on **judgment,** which is a function of the Son
of Man (5.27). The form of the word used here (*krima*) is exceptional in John, though it is common enough elsewhere, usually
applied to a judicial verdict. John normally uses *krisis*, which is
more suitable for the idea of discrimination, which seems to be
demanded here. But it may well be that he is thinking of the future
judgment, which is anticipated in the confrontation with Jesus in
his incarnate life; the response to Jesus *now* determines his verdict
as Son of Man in the future. In any case, we have here the basic
moral challenge which has already been clarified in 3.18–21.
Though the immediate reference of the words is to the blind man,
now able to **see,** and the Pharisees, who have now **become blind,**
the statement is universal in its scope.

those who do not see . . .: the words are based on Isa. 6.9, the standing proof text in the early church to explain the unbelief of the Jews; cf. 12.39f.; Ac. 28.25–7. It is the background of Paul's argument in Rom. 11.7f., where further related texts are adduced (Isa. 29.10; Dt. 29.4). It is widened to apply to unbelief in general in 2 C. 4.4; and to the dullness of the disciples in Mk 4.12 paras.

40. Some of the Pharisees: this is surprising, as verse 35 gives the impression that the conversation was in private. But, as happens elsewhere, John has lost sight of the needs of the story, and is more concerned with the theological issue. It is now necessary to turn attention to the unbelief of the Pharisees, to prepare for the discourse of the next chapter.

Are we also blind: the question with *mē* expects the answer no: 'Surely *we* are not blind?'

41. The answer is a play on two levels of the metaphor of blindness, i.e. incapacity to understand and wilful refusal to understand. If the Pharisees were really incapable of understanding, their 'blindness' would not be morally culpable; but in the foregoing dialogue they have claimed to be well-informed spiritual guides, and so (from John's point of view) they have no excuse. In the Synoptic tradition the blindness of the Pharisees is found only in Matthew (Mt. 15.14; 23.16–26); but the saying in Mt. 15.14, on the blind leading the blind, was originally more general in its application, and not directed to the Pharisees in particular (cf. Lk. 6.39). Matthew's teaching is probably influenced by the later rift between the Church and the synagogue, as in John. But, even so, the application is different, for in Matthew it is applied to the inadequacy of the Pharisees' teaching, whereas in John it is referred to their refusal to believe in Jesus.

guilt: lit. 'sin' (*hamartia*). Several MSS. (אcorr D L W 33 Sinaitic Syriac) have plural, 'your sins remain', implying that their behaviour is unforgivable. But this is not what John means. The point is developed further in 15.22–4.

ALLEGORY OF THE SHEPHERD: TRUE AND FALSE LEADERS   10.1–21

The allegory of the sheep and the shepherd makes an immediate appeal to the imagination. It provides the most endearing aspects of the Johannine portrait of Jesus, which otherwise tends to be remote and forbidding. In spite of being a highly wrought composition, it has sufficient links with the Synoptic tradition to ensure

that it has its basis in authentic memories of Jesus' teaching. In the
Synoptic Gospels there is the famous parable of the Lost Sheep
(Mt. 18.12–14 = Lk. 15.3–7), and Jesus' own address to the
disciples as his 'little flock' (Lk. 12.32); also the theme of the
scattering of the sheep in Mk 14.27 paras. The idea of the shepherd
is taken up once more in the Johannine appendix (21.15–17), and
in Paul's farewell speech to the elders of the Church at Miletus
(Ac. 20.28–30; cf. also 1 Pet. 2.25).

Behind these NT references there lies the wide use of this theme
in the ancient world. The shepherd as a metaphor for a ruler is
natural in a pastoral society, and is frequently found among the
peoples of the ancient Near East. In the OT there is a play on the
idea of David, the shepherd of his father's sheep, becoming the
shepherd of Israel (2 Sam. 7.7f.). But God himself is referred to as
a shepherd in the prophecy of the Exilic Age; cf. Isa. 40.11; Jer.
31.10; Ezek. 34.11–16; so Jesus is not only the descendant of
David, but acts as God's own representative. Moreover, Ezek. 34
begins with an indictment of the rulers of Israel as unfaithful
shepherds (verses 1–10), and even includes the idea of the new
David who is to come (verse 23f.) 1 Enoch 85–90 has a long and
tedious allegory of the history of the Jews in terms of sheep and
other animals.

These precedents show that John is building on a long-standing
tradition. It is not to be expected, however, that his work contains
no original features. Bultmann (p. 367) singles out the *lack* of
specifically messianic ideas; the relation of shepherd and sheep is
one of mutual knowledge, rather than that of ruler and people;
so also the door of the fold and the thieves and robbers have no
parallel in the OT. Bultmann thinks that John has derived these
elements from non-biblical sources, and quotes many telling parallels from the Mandean literature. The most important point is that
the shepherd is not messianic, but the Redeemer sent from heaven.
But in fact it is more likely that the influence is the other way
round, and that John has coloured the Mandean texts. The special
features in John's allegory are not derived from extraneous sources,
but arise from two factors which normally characterize his creative
work. The door and the thieves belong to the underlying parable,
and there is no reason to deny that this goes back to Jesus himself.
The 'truly' opening (verses 1 and 7) nearly always indicates the
use of authentic tradition, and there is no need to doubt that here.

Secondly, John naturally composes the allegory in the terms which
he always uses to express his Christology. The chief model is
Ezek. 34, in which God himself is the true shepherd. According to
John's theology, Jesus represents God; he is the focal point of God's
saving activity, and he brings men into relation with God through
their response of faith in himself. The moral unity of the Father
and the Son is the necessary presupposition of this teaching. The
idea of the messianic ruler would only confuse the issue by bringing
in different categories of thought. This is, then, not so much
omitted as suppressed in John's handling of the material, so that
the main lines of thought correspond with the teaching in the
Gospel as a whole.

All agree that John has one entirely new idea in his allegory, and
that is the shepherd's sacrifice of his life on behalf of the sheep.
This has a precedent in the *danger* to the shepherd in David's vivid
description in 1 Sam. 17.34f., but is more likely to be derived from
Christian meditation on the *sheep* in the prophecy of the Suffering
Servant (Isa. 53.6–8; cf. 1 Pet. 2.24f.). From this point of view
John stands in the main stream of the theology of the early Church.

In studying this section, it is important not to search for a uniform overall interpretation, for that would not do justice to the
nature of the composition. It is not so much an allegory as a discourse in monologue form. The closest parallel is 5.19–47, where a
parable from John's stock of dominical sayings is used as the basis
of a series of further reflections. Here the structure is indicated by
the break at verse 6. Verses 1–5 contain the parable, comparable
to 5.19–20a. It is to some extent allegorized, because it is not
simply drawn from life, but contains some features which presuppose the interpretation in terms of Jesus and those who believe
in him. The rest of the piece takes up features from the parable
successively, expanding and developing them—the door (verses 7–
9), the thief (10), the shepherd (11–13), the sheep (14–16)—and
these have further developments on the sacrifice of the shepherd
(17f.) and the safety of the sheep (27–9, a piece held over for the
next section). The one unifying feature in the rich growth of interpretation is the consistency of the Johannine theology. All other
considerations are subservient to that.

Further scrutiny of the parable (verses 1–5) suggests that it is a
fusion of two originally distinct parables. This has been persuasively argued by J. A. T. Robinson (*Twelve NT Studies*, pp. 67–75),

and subsequent writers have brought greater precision to the theory. The first parable (1–3a) is on access to the sheepfold; but there is room for some difference of opinion on the meaning this would have had as an independent parable in the eschatological perspective of the teaching of Jesus. The second parable (3b–5) is more straightforward. It is on the mutual confidence between shepherd and sheep, suggesting the *rapport* between Jesus and the outcasts, which angered the Pharisees (cf. Mk 2.15–17). It is not exceptional for parables to be preserved in pairs; cf. Mk 2.21f. (the New Patch and the New Wineskins). The Lost Sheep stands alone in Mt. 18.12–14, but is paired with the Lost Coin in Lk. 15.3–10, and the pairing is responsible for some degree of assimilation between them. This shows the kind of process which could lead to fusion, by telescoping the two stories into one.

The Parables 10.1–6

10.1. Truly, truly I say to you: these words are John's introduction, indicating authentic material, but not part of the parable itself.

he who does not enter: the first parable consists of a straight contrast between the man who **climbs in by another way,** and the man who goes through **the door.** The fact that the setting is a **sheepfold** is fortuitous, for an ordinary house would have made an equally suitable setting (cf. Lk. 12.39). The point is that there is a gatekeeper (verse 3), and so only a *bona fide* person will be allowed entry. It is obvious that a person who knows that he cannot be admitted by the gatekeeper, and yet attempts to break in, is likely to be **a thief and a robber.** But the one who gains entry has right to be there. In the setting of the sheepfold, he must be **the shepherd of the sheep.**

What was the original meaning of this parable? If the emphasis is laid on the setting, on the sheepfold and the shepherd, we must follow Robinson in taking it to be an urgent address to the Jewish rulers to attend to their spiritual responsibility before it is too late, for they must answer for their charge at the coming judgment. But the parable lays more stress on the integrity of the man who gains entry. This is reminiscent of Jesus' saying about the narrow gate (Mt. 7.13f. = Lk. 13.24). Both these Synoptic parallels have related material in the same context: Matthew goes on to speak of the false prophets, who are like wolves in sheep's clothing; Luke continues with the householder, who refuses entry to those who knock on the door too late.

Seen in the light of these passages, the parable is a warning to Jesus' *hearers*. They must be men of integrity and take heed of his teaching, if they are to win a place in the coming kingdom. The parable is drawn from life, using the familiar image of a farmstead with an enclosed courtyard in front of it. In an upland pastoral setting, this would be the sheepfold, where the sheep are brought in for safety at night. It would be a great mistake to allegorize these details, taking the fold as the Church and the sheep as the true believers, and so on. But in using this parable for his present purpose, it is clear enough that John has allegorized the shepherd and the intruder in terms of Jesus and the Pharisees; cf. verses 8f.; this is why he has made use of this material as the direct continuation from 9.41.

a thief and a robber: John uses **thief** (*kleptēs*) of Judas in 12.6, and **robber** (*lēstēs*) of Barabbas in 18.40; but the words probably stood in his source with no particular reference. For Synoptic parallels, cf. Mt. 24.43 = Lk. 12.39. The idea of the thief recurs in 1 Th. 5.2; Rev. 16.15.

3. gatekeeper: properly 'doorkeeper' (*thurōros*). The same word is used for 'the maid who kept the door' in 18.16. The doorkeeper is prominent in yet another of Jesus' parables on watchfulness (Mk. 13.33–7).

the sheep hear his voice: with these words the second parable is begun. We have to assume something like 'When a shepherd comes to the sheepfold' as the original opening, which has been suppressed in the fusion of the two parables. The whole of this second parable answers the question: 'Why do the poor and outcast, who refuse to follow the religious leadership of the Pharisees, listen to Jesus?' He replies by telling a parable about the intimate understanding between a shepherd and his own sheep (the Aramaic original would have said *the* shepherd; cf. 8.35). The use of this imagery serves a double purpose, for if the shepherd is taken as a symbol for God himself, as in Ezek. 34.11–16, it implies that Jesus is mediating to these people the pastoral care of God. Thus the parable is not merely a fanciful way of explaining his own behaviour, but carries with it a deeper meaning which could hardly be expressed openly (cf. the notes on 3.29f.). If this is a correct estimate of the original significance of the parable, it will be seen that John's handling of it is a legitimate drawing out of its implications, even to the climactic point of the unity of the Father and the Son (verse 30).

calls his own sheep by name: the intimate relationship is at once brought to our notice by the two observations that the sheep are **his own,** and that he **calls** them **by name.** If verses 1–5 are taken as a unity, it is natural to think of several flocks in the same fold, so that **his own** has an exclusive sense, the others being left behind. But Hoskyns is right to deny that there is any such implication here, even if the division into two parables is not accepted. The naming of individual sheep is reported to be common to this day among Arab shepherds.

leads them out: the verb (*exagei*) is colourless, and means rather 'brings them out'—probably simply holding the gate open while the sheep run out past him.

4. brought out: Gr. *ekbalē*, the same word as 'drove out' in 2.15 and 'cast out' in 6.37. It is used in the Koiné Greek with a much weakened sense (cf. *AG*, p. 237a). In colloquial English we would say: 'when he has got them all out'. Presumably he closes the gate behind them, before he goes before them. As he strides out, the sheep, who have been slightly dispersed on first emerging from the fold, flock together and follow him—as may be seen still in the Holy Land.

5. A stranger would never be able to do this, and would have the utmost difficulty in keeping them together, precisely because of the lack of the intimate relationship which has been described. The contrast between the shepherd and the stranger is entirely different from the contrast in the former parable, and is used differently in the following allegory (verses 12–13).

6. This figure: the Greek *paroimia* properly means a proverb or maxim, whereas *parabolē* (the Synoptic word, never used by John) means a comparison or illustration. But both represent the Hebrew *māšāl*, and may be regarded as synonyms in NT usage.

did not understand: cf. Mk 4.10–12 paras., including reference to Isa. 6.9, to which John has alluded in 9.39. The Pharisees' lack of understanding is the natural consequence of their wilful blindness.

The Allegory **7–18**

7. again: perhaps an addition (not in P⁴⁵ P⁶⁶ ℵ* W). If original, it would suggest a fresh occasion; cf. 8.12, 21.

Truly: the repetition of the opening of the parable is a sign that it is now to be expounded in detail. It seems less likely to be a pointer to fresh traditional material.

I am the door of the sheep: this is an *egō eimi* saying, and it occasions surprise by fastening on to an unexpected feature of the parable. We have to remember that, whether John was responsible for the fusion of the two original parables or not, he has presented them as one, and can be expected to maintain a uniform interpretation in his exposition. It is, then, surely to be expected that Jesus would identify himself with the shepherd from the start. Torrey (*Our Translated Gospels*, pp. 111–13) suggested an Aramaic basis which would make 'I came as the shepherd of the sheep' into 'I am the door of the sheep', merely by the alteration of one letter in the division of words ('*TY TRʿHWN* for '*TYT RʿHWN*); but this kind of mistake is hardly likely to cause the *harder* reading, which is in any case confirmed by verse 9, where the same mistake could not occur (accordingly Torrey deletes it). The Sahidic version reads 'shepherd', and this now has early Greek support from P75. But it still remains most likely that this is a copyist's correction.

We must, then, accept the text, and verse 9 must be taken in conjunction with it. There the title is reduced to: 'I am the door'. If we follow Bultmann in regarding the latter as the original form of the words, we should naturally regard it as a revelation-formula, e.g. 'I am the light of the world'. This would mean: 'You know what "the door" means as a religious symbol (the way of escape from the prison, the gate into heaven, etc.). Well, that is what I am!' In this case there is only the slightest connection with the parable, which has supplied the vocabulary, but not the meaning. But if we take the title in verse 9 as an abbreviated form of what we have in verse 7, the primary reference of **the door,** and for that matter **of the sheep,** is to specific words in the parable, i.e. verses 1 and 2. In this case the **I am** is merely an explanatory statement, the first of a series of identifications which are made as the parable is taken point by point. It does not have the rich overtones of a revelation-formula, but is a pointer to the interpretation of the parable.

8. All who came before me: Jesus begins by commenting on the idea of gaining entry, the point of verses 1–3a. He thus gives the contrast between false and genuine methods of admission. We must thus take verses 8 and 9 together, and verse 10 will be a second exposition of the same contrast (Brown makes the break after verse 8, taking 9 and 10 together; but this gives a less satisfactory analysis). These verses are an exposition of the door as the way into the sheepfold, and if this is identified with Jesus it means the response of faith which opens the way to eternal life (cf. 9.35). Those who attempt to show some other way of gaining eternal life are false (**thieves and robbers**), and the true disciples refuse to **heed them** (cf. 6.44, 65). But why are these false guides, who must at least include the Pharisees in view of the last chapter, described as **all who came before me?** There is some evidence for the omission of **before me** (P45 P75 ℵ* Old Latin, Vulgate, Sinaitic and Peshitta Syriac, Sahidic), but what we want is some expression corresponding to 'by another way' in verse 1. The early Gnostics applied the phrase to the OT prophets; Bernard thinks of messianic pretenders; Bultmann takes it to mean all possible predecessors—which is probably right, if we may qualify it to mean those whose teaching cannot be regarded as a preparation for Jesus himself.

9. Jesus repeats the identification of himself with **the door,** and naturally it is unnecessary to include 'of the sheep' this time, in the light of the last verse. He is the one through whom they gain eternal life, or, in the words of the allegory of Ezek. 34.14, they **find pasture.** For **saved,** which fixes the interpretation in terms of eternal life, cf. 3.17. It is unnecessary to go into the ramifications of the idea of the door in ancient mythology (well summarized by Barrett, pp. 308f.), because it is not allegorized as such. It is simply an item of the parable which John has used as a symbol of Jesus in terms of his own theology, and no other conceptions are either implied or required for the elucidation of the text as it stands.

10. The thief: at this point a new line of exposition is begun. Jesus has finished with the door, and now turns to consideration of **the thief** (verse 1b). Obviously he cannot identify himself with this figure of the parable; in fact, he has to dissociate himself from it. So the first half of the verse gives a sketch of the thief, and the second half describes Jesus himself in contrast. It is not yet stated that Jesus is to be identified with the shepherd; that would be to anticipate matters. He will come on to that in a third line of exposition in the next verse. The thief in this verse is only indirectly connected with the thieves and robbers of verse 8. In his usual way, already familiar to us from preceding discourses, John goes back to the beginning at each new stage in the exposition, though there is at the same time a continuity of thought which takes into account the part of it which has just been finished. So here the idea of the thief is thought through afresh entirely in the terms of the imagery of the parable, and the resulting description virtually makes a new subsidiary parable (hence the article should be understood generically, i.e. *a* thief); for it is literally true that a sheep-stealer **comes only to steal and kill** [lit. slaughter] **and destroy.** But the application of this imagery needs no explanation, for it has been made clear in verse 8, and in this respect there is continuity of thought. Thus Jesus teaches the deadly purpose of the false guides (cf. 8.44).

I came: the pronoun is emphatic, pointing the contrast. In this half of the verse allegory and application are completely merged, so that the words operate at both levels simultaneously. It may be said in passing that the capacity to do this with complete ease and assurance, as John does here, is one of the most effective of all homiletic devices. So here there is straight theological language, and not one word is drawn from the allegory. But the context demands that the unexpressed subject, **they,** is 'the sheep' of verse 8. What Jesus gives them has already been expressed in terms of the allegory in verse 9, and to this extent this half verse forms an exposition of that verse. Thus the reader at once thinks of the words in terms of the allegory, and is scarcely aware that they are so completely non-allegorical! And this makes the transition to the next verse, where Jesus is identified with the shepherd, natural and inevitable, though in fact the shepherd has not yet once been referred to in the exposition of the parable.

and have it abundantly: perhaps an allusion to the plentiful pasture described in Ezek. 34.25–31; or alternatively a reminiscence of the saying of Jesus in Mt. 13.12: 'To him who has will more be given, and he will have abundance . . .' These words are omitted by P[66]* D ff[2], probably by homoioteleuton.

11. I am the good shepherd: in the light of verse 10, we expect the introduction of the third item of exposition to go back to the parable afresh, to develop the new theme virtually into a new parable, but yet to maintain continuity with the main lines of the exposition. All these things duly happen in this verse. Taking yet another cue from verse 10, we may confidently treat the article as generic, i.e. I am *a* good shepherd. This makes sense of the adjective (*kalos*, properly 'beautiful'; we might say 'an ideal shepherd'). Thus the verse is not merely an exposition of the shepherd as he appears in the parable (verses 3f.), but takes up this theme to begin a new description, just as in verse 10 a typical thief was described. Again we must not read into the words an 'I am' saying of the revelation-formula variety. There is a great temptation to do so, for the **shepherd** is another word of evocative power in ancient religious language, just like the door. We can think of David, who 'was ruddy, and had beautiful eyes, and was handsome' (1 Sam. 16.12); and the very phrase 'beautiful shepherd' is applied to Moses or to God himself in some rabbinic texts (*SB* ii.536; cf. Isa. 63.11–14). But the content of the phrase is not derived from a character, or characterization of God, presupposed to be in the hearers' minds, and not provided by the parable itself. What constitutes a good shepherd is just about to be described in the verses which follow. The *egō eimi* opening is explanatory, as in verse 7, and does little more than pick up the emphatic 'I' (*egō*) of verse 10b.

lays down his life: this is the first especial characteristic of a good shepherd. A second one will be given in verse 14. Both are essential to John's theological exposition. This one is a clear reference to the Passion, and has had immense influence on Christian teaching on the Cross. None of the OT passages on the shepherd theme contains this striking feature. It is most reasonable to suppose that it is a result of applying the theme to Jesus, and would never have been thought of if he had not actually been crucified. It is thus an aspect of the allegory which is derived in the first instance from the application, adding a new element to the picture which the parable evokes. That the life of a shepherd really involved risk to his life is vividly expressed in the story of David (1 Sam. 17.34–7). But it is far more likely that the chief influence has been the Church's use of Isa. 53 to expound the crucifixion, a passage which at least includes mention of the sheep (Isa. 53.6) as those who benefit from the Servant's sacrificial death. Sanders points out that the unusual expression **lays down** (lit. puts) **his life** could mean *risks* his life (cf. Jud. 12.3; 1 Sam. 19.5), if it were not for the preposition **for** (*huper*), which has sacrificial overtones (cf. Mk 14.24; Lk. 22.19f.; Rom. 5.6–8). The construction is exactly the same in 13.37f. and 15.13.

   12. He who is a hireling: the Greek simply says 'the hireling' with the generic article once more. He is introduced to show by contrast the quality of an ideal shepherd. As in 10a, the description is entirely realistic, and contains no hint of a particular application. He is not the same as the thief of verse 10, nor is there any emphasis on the fact that he is paid for his services. The one important point is that he is a man **whose own the sheep are not.** He has the same responsibility as the shepherd, but he has not the same incentive to remain by his charge in the face of danger. The wicked rulers of the allegory in Ezek. 34.2–10 could be described in similar terms, but John is not indebted to this passage and has no intention of making a formal identification of the hireling with them. Nor is **the wolf** (*a* wolf, of course) to be identified with the devil (Sanders). The picture which John describes is obviously to some extent conventional, and capable of numerous permutations. The motif of 'fierce wolves' comes in quite independently in Paul's use of this imagery (Ac. 20.29).

whose own the sheep are not: the slightly awkward grammar of the relative clause (lit. 'whose are not his own sheep') is to be explained from the desire to use the exact phrase of verse 3.

13. He flees: inserted by *RSV* to complete the sense after the parenthesis of the last clause ('and the wolf, etc.'), which involved a change of subject. The later mss. similarly insert: 'The hireling flees'; cp. *AV*.

cares nothing: this not only explains the hireling's conduct, but also constitutes the essential point of difference between him and the ideal shepherd. This important fact has been reserved until after the description of the last verse, because it leads into the theme of the fourth stage of exposition in verses 14–16.

14. The identification of the ideal shepherd with Jesus is repeated, so as to give the second special characteristic. This is that he *knows* his sheep, and they know him, cf. verses 3b, 4. The parable has already given us some idea of what this means. It is a matter of mutual confidence, and of willing obedience on the part of the sheep. But there is an important difference between this part of the exposition and verses 11–13. Here it is put entirely in the first person. Just as in verse 10b, allegory and application coalesce completely.

15. as the Father knows me: it would be possible to make this a new sentence (continuing 'even so I know the Father'), and this is implied by the insertion of 'and' at the beginning of the

verse in P⁴⁵ (so *AV*). But it is better to take it as the continuation
of verse 14, as in *RSV*. The verse then gives two reasons why Jesus
is to be regarded as the ideal shepherd. The first is that the mutual
knowledge which expresses the relationship of sheep and shepherd
corresponds with his own relationship to the Father. Bultmann
(p. 382) stresses that this is fundamentally a moral relationship,
quite different from the mystical knowing in which the identities
of worshipper and deity are merged. This issue will be developed
in 14.7-11. The second reason is that Jesus passes the ultimate
test of an ideal shepherd: **I lay down my life for the sheep**
(cf. 15.13). This is the supreme act of obedience to the Father.

16. other sheep: now that the exposition has ceased to be a
fuller statement of the parable, the way is open for further detail
to be introduced, using the language of the allegory. So now the
sheep can be identified as those who respond to Jesus in his incarnate life, and it is inevitable that **this fold** should be taken to
mean the Jewish people who believed in him and formed the
primitive Church. The **other sheep,** then, are the Gentiles who
will believe as a result of the mission of the Church (**they will
heed my voice**). It is the divine purpose that **there shall be one
flock, one shepherd.** The idea is not quite the same as Ezek.
34.11-13, in which God gathers up the scattered sheep of the
Dispersion, though there is a certain parallel between them; cf.
7.35f. The same idea occurs in 11.52, where the gathering of the
scattered people refers to the breaking down of the barrier between
Jew and Gentile. But it is also possible that John is thinking of the
spread of heresy in the church, and the need to maintain Christian
unity; cf. 17.20ff.

there shall be: if the plural verb is read with the majority of
earlier mss. the meaning is 'they shall become'. But no hint is given
of the way in which they will become a unity, apart from the fact
that Jesus himself will **bring them.** Hence the text (supported
by P⁶⁶ and ℵ*) is to be preferred.

one flock: the 'one fold' of *AV* is derived from the Vulgate, a
tradition which is perhaps due to thinking of the allegory in terms
of the institutional conception of the Church, though the difference
is hardly significant.

17. the Father loves me: the allegory is now almost abandoned, as Jesus expands the point made in verse 15, that the
mutual knowledge of sheep and shepherd corresponds with that

of Jesus himself and the Father. It is impossible to maintain the
allegory in dealing with this essential theological issue. This verse
recapitulates verse 15 with two significant changes. The first is that
the relationship is now expressed with the verb to **love** (*agapān*).
The obedience of Jesus in laying down his life is an act of love,
and for this reason it is perfectly satisfying to the Father. The words
should not be misunderstood to mean that the Father's love is
dependent on Jesus' willingness to do this. The point is that it is this
act above all which expresses the perfect accord between them.
The second change is that Jesus now shows that the Passion, completely pleasing as it is, is not an end in itself. It has the further
object **that I may take** (i.e. receive) **it again.** It is, then, to be
followed by the Resurrection, whereby abundant life will be made
available (verse 10b). This thought will be taken up in verses
26–9.

18. takes: the harder reading 'took' (P[45] ℵ* B) is to be preferred (cp. *NEB*: 'has robbed me of it'). It can scarcely be a
reference to unsuccessful attempts on Jesus' life up to this point,
but is rather the perspective after the Resurrection, looking back
on the events. One can hardly miss the apologetic motive in this
insistence that the Passion was entirely voluntary. There is plenty
of evidence that the Church was embarrassed by the question in
debate with the Jews. We have seen that John frequently emphasizes that Jesus is always in control of his destiny. But here the
theological motive is uppermost; the central act of redemption is
done in obedience to the Father's **charge** (*entolē*, cf. 12.49f.; 14.31;
15.10). Jesus, the good shepherd, is the model for the sheep.

Reactions of the Jews **19–21**

19. again a division: cf. 9.16. This little paragraph is typical
of John's editorial writing, lightly touching on previous material
in order to maintain the plot. Instead of speaking of the Pharisees
(cf. 9.40), he slips into his usual designation **the Jews** for the
opponents of Jesus. This is one reason why it is improbable that
this verse should follow immediately after 9.41 (on displacement
theories, cf. p. 339). Another reason is that there would then be
no reference for **these words**, which must be a block of teaching,
rather than the single point made in 9.41, for which John would
have used the singular ('this saying'; compare 7.36 and 40 in
the Greek).

20. He has a demon, and he is mad: the phrases are synony-mous. This charge was made in 8.48. The repetition of it here is a hint that the tense situation of the context of that verse is to be renewed in the following discourse.

21. the blind: the adjective is plural in the Greek, and so only refers to the healing of chapter 9 in a general way, like the vague use of 'signs' in 7.31; 9.16. But the use of the plural reminds us of 9.40f., by contrast with the healing, and this may perhaps be John's intention. For the discourse of the next section will be a decisive test whether they can see or not.

JESUS AND THE FATHER ARE ONE   10.22–42

The central section of the Gospel closes with a tense meeting between Jesus and the Jews. The scene is similar to that of 8.48–59, and the subject under discussion is inevitable after that magnifi-cent assertion of Jesus' pre-existence. Now the question of his identity must be given a direct answer. The structure of the dialogue is similar to the Synoptic account of the trial of Jesus before the High Priest (cf. Mk 14.61–3 paras.). The Jews ask him whether he is the Messiah. He gives what amounts to an affirm-ative answer, but adds a further claim (in Mark it is his future glory as the Son of Man; here it is his union with the Father); this is regarded as blasphemy, and he is duly condemned. It is possible that John has constructed this section out of the trial traditions, because his own account of the trial before the High Priest lacks this vital piece, and Jesus is sent to Pilate without any adequate formulation of the charge against him; on the other hand, it transpires in 19.7 that it was precisely the issue discussed here which was the charge for which the death sentence was demanded (compare 19.7 with 10.33 and 36). The fact that part of the trial tradition is anticipated here should warn us not to press too hard the differences between John and the Synoptics in the trial narrative.

One of the features of John's trial narrative is the ironical way in which the Jews, in seeking to condemn Jesus, actually condemn themselves. This feature also belongs to the present section, be-cause of the way in which John has prepared the ground. The debate logically follows on 8.48–59, as we have seen. But the chap-ter on the blind man has shown up the wilful blindness of the Jews; it is for this reason that they do not accept his teaching.

The allegory of the shepherd has shown by contrast why the true believers can accept it, and has also provided the essential facts for a proper understanding of what he means. It is for this reason that a portion of the allegory has been held over to form part of the discourse.

The present scene has also been made to stand out by the time indication given in verse 22. It is possible that the theme of the Dedication bears a relation to the contents of the debate (see the notes on verse 36), just as Tabernacles may have provided the themes of water and light in 7.37 and 8.12, but this is by no means certain. But it is much more likely that the reason for giving this date is simply the fact that it falls halfway between Tabernacles and the final Passover, when the trial will actually take place. It thus suggests the approach of the Passion and contributes to the sense of mounting climax.

The Relation of Jesus to the Father 22–30

22. It was the feast: some of the earliest MSS. (P66c P75 B L W Sahidic and Bohairic) insert 'then' (*tote*). This word properly refers back to a time already mentioned, and on these grounds some have argued that the whole sequence from 9.1 is to be dated at this time. This would ease the difficulty of the reference in verses 26–9 to what has been said ostensibly some two months earlier—not that we need regard this as a difficulty in view of the similar phenomenon in 7.15–24. But Sanders has argued convincingly that the sentence originally had no connecting particle (the enclitic *de* of the majority of MSS. is missing from the Lake group, 565 and a few other MSS.). Thus *egeneto tote ta* has arisen by dittography from *egeneto ta*.

the Dedication: the feast of Ḥanukkah commemorated the rehallowing of the altar in 164 B.C., after its desecration by Antiochus Epiphanes three years earlier (1 Mac. 4.52–9; 2 Mac. 10.1–8; Jos. *Ant.* XII.316–25). It was held on 25th Kislev (December), and lasted eight days. The most popular feature was a ceremony with lights, following virtually the same form as the ceremony at Tabernacles; lights were also put in the windows of all the houses. This may perhaps have had a pagan origin in connection with the winter solstice. John's composition shows no sign of being influenced by this. Guilding (*op. cit.*, pp. 129–32) has attempted to find connections with the synagogue lections at this season, and

asserts that Ezek. 34 was a *haphtarah* in the second year of the
triennial cycle, about a month after the feast itself. John certainly
had Ezek. 34 in mind in making the allegory of the shepherd, but
nothing much can be built on this coincidence.

23. winter: the circumstantial detail (which at least shows that
John knew the date of the feast) is given to explain why Jesus took
shelter **in the portico of Solomon.** This was the colonnade
facing into the Temple area on the eastern side of the Temple of
Herod, and was one of the few portions of the pre-Herodian
structure to be retained in the new building (Jos. *Ant.* xx.221). It
is referred to in Ac. 3.11; 5.12, and these references imply that it
was known to be a meeting-place of the first Christians, where
they came into open conflict with the authorities.

24. gathered round: Dodd thinks there may be a literary
allusion to Ps. 118.10–12, where the same Greek word is used in
the LXX four times for 'surrounded' with hostile intent. This
psalm is quoted a number of times in the NT (e.g. Mt. 21.9; Ac.
4.11) in connection with the death and resurrection of Jesus.
But we cannot be sure of this allusion, as there is no hint of the
psalm in the context, and the word, though uncommon, is quite
natural.

keep us in suspense: lit. 'raise (*aireis*) our spirit (*psuchēn*)'. This
is generally taken to mean lift us up in expectancy, i.e. keep
us in suspense, but, as Barrett points out, this conveys a friendly
impression rather than hostility, which the context requires.
Hoskyns noted that the same words have just been used with a
very different meaning in 17f., and on this basis translates 'continue to take away our life'. The implication is that the Jews
realize that Jesus' teaching is a threat to their very existence, but
in their blindness they cannot see that it is necessary to die in
order to live. Hoskyns has not won support for this suggestion,
though Brown says it is 'not impossible'. Most, however, would
agree with Bultmann that it is 'scarcely credible'. Barrett quotes
evidence for the meaning 'provoke us to anger'. This gives a
much more satisfactory sense, though precise parallels are lacking.
The similarity of vocabulary to 17f. means nothing, as John uses
this verb with a variety of meanings.

If you are the Christ: the question has been discussed in 7.25–
31, 40–2, but has not been put to Jesus directly. The Jews have
asked him about his identity in 8.25, 53, but his answers have

been evasive. On the other hand, his teaching implies again and again that he has a unique relationship with God. That this can be expressed in terms of messiahship has been suggested by the allegory of the shepherd (cf. Ezek. 34.23). So now there is the straight challenge, and the question, and Jesus' answer in the next verse, are remarkably similar to the Lukan trial narrative (Lk. 22.67). The similarity of the answer should not be pressed (see the notes on the next verse), but the question is found in all three of the Synoptic Gospels at this point in the trial before the High Priest and it is probable that John is indebted to this tradition.
plainly: Gr. *parrēsia*, a favourite word with John (cf. 7.4).

25. I told you: although this sounds like Lk. 22.67: 'If I tell you, you will not believe,' the words have too Johannine a ring to be regarded as derived from a source; nor can we squeeze out the past sense of the aorist 'told'. In fact the nearest parallel to these words is the complaint of the blind man in 9.27. There may also be allusion to 8.25.
works: Jesus reminds the Jews of the argument of 5.36 on the witness of the works, now made even more compelling by the sign of giving sight to the blind man (cf. 9.3; 10.21).

26. At this point John has two things which he needs to do. He must make it clear that Jesus knows that the Jews *cannot* believe, in view of the preceding discussion on spiritual blindness, so that there is really no point in answering their question. But he must also give the answer, in spite of this, for the benefit of the reader and for the sake of giving the grounds for the final rejection. As the allegory of the shepherd has moved the concept of Jesus' identity to a deeper level than ever before, he can best give the answer on the basis of further aspects of it. The answer itself (which is not part of the allegory) comes in verse 30. The present verse is, then, an artificial link to reintroduce the theme of the shepherd. We have seen in verse 8 that the sheep are the true believers, so much so that they did not heed (lit. hear) thieves and robbers, whereas they do heed the shepherd's voice (verse 16). So the unbelief of the Jews, which is a refusal to hear and to obey (cf. 9.27) can be expressed extremely simply by saying **you do not belong to my sheep.** The thought of other animals, definitely excluded from the flock, had not occurred anywhere in the parable and its allegory, but the point is quite natural when allegory and application merge. At the end of the verse a great number of MSS. add: 'as I said to you' (P⁶⁶* joins the words to the next verse). They are presumably a gloss (not in P⁶⁶ᶜ P⁷⁵ B ℵ L W Θ), but they show the awkwardness felt by the reintroduction of the theme here.

27. Like the other items of the exposition of the parable in 7–18, this piece goes back to the beginning again, but builds on the thought of the allegory as a whole. So we now have a piece on the safety of the sheep, which is introduced by means of phrases entirely drawn from verses 3f. This piece maintains the use of the first person, which has been consistent since verse 14.

28. eternal life: the application draws in the first instance on verse 10, but the theme has gained a fresh dimension from the exposition in 14–18 on the sacrifice of the shepherd. It is because Jesus not only lays down his life but also takes it again (verses 17f.) that he is in a position to **give them eternal life.** The exposition passes beyond the terms of the allegory, referring to some of the great theological statements of the Gospel. For **they shall never perish,** cf. 3.16; 5.24; 8.51f., in all of which the Greek is very close. Yet immediately we return to the pictorial imagery with **no one shall snatch them out of my hand,** which is derived from verse 12. Thus the eternal safety of the sheep is ensured, because Jesus displays the two special characteristics of the ideal shepherd, his sacrifice for them and his intimate knowledge of them.

29. My Father: it remains to trace back this idea of the safety of the sheep to the plan of the Father, just as in verse 15 Jesus' knowledge of the sheep was traced back to his own relation with the Father. Their security is impregnable because the Father is the ultimate reality; so is fulfilled the prophecy of Ezek. 34.25–31. The allegory ends with the certainty of the security of the sheep with God.

Unfortunately, although this is obviously the meaning required by the context, the interpretation is complicated by textual confusion, as the margin shows. The question turns on the gender of **who** (*hos*), which is neuter (*ho*, i.e. which, or—as there is no antecedent—what) in B ℵ L W, and of **greater** (*meizōn*), which is neuter (*meizon*) in B A Θ X. *RSV, mg.* (so *NEB, mg.* (2nd version)), taking both words to be neuter, is thus only found in B, though it is supported by Old Latin, Vulgate and Bohairic. It is grammatically awkward, because **my Father** stands outside the relative clause of which it must be regarded as subject, but this is not unknown in John (cf. 7.38), although it gives an impossible sense. Sanders, accepting it as the harder reading, translates: '[They are] the greatest gift of all which my Father has given me', thus transferring the sense from the Father's power to the preciousness of the sheep. It is obvious, however, that the *textus receptus*, with *hos* and *meizōn* (so *RSV, NEB* text), cannot be original, because otherwise the other readings would never have arisen (for the same reason the theory of mistranslation of a presumed Aramaic original, advocated by Burney, is unacceptable). The truth of the matter can only be established if the transcriptional development can be explained satisfactorily. This is the merit of the note on this text by J. N. Birdsall (*JTS*, n.s., xi (1960), pp. 342–4). He shows that the neuter *ho* must be original, because it is likely to be attracted to the masculine to agree with **my Father**, but the change is not likely to work the other way round; but, in the process of copying the text by the method of dictation, the masculine *meizōn* would easily be heard as *meizon* (this is a well-known form of itacism), especially when there was the *ho* just before it. Hence the mixed text with *ho* and *meizōn*, as in ℵ L W (supported by the manifestly improved variant text of D), is to be accepted. This means that the true translation of this troublesome sentence is: 'My Father in regard to what he has given me is greater than all.' Out of numerous parallels to this idea, 6.39 and 17.24 are specially notable; in both cases the neuter singular is used in the Greek. Accepting this translation, we have the required sense in which **greater than all** refers to the incomparable power of God, and the rest of the verse follows logically, and suitably brings the allegory to its conclusion.

30. one: neuter; not 'one thing', but 'belonging to the same category', cf. 1 C. 3.8, where *RSV* renders the same word 'equal'. Although this statement is not an integral part of the allegory, it forms a splendid climax after it, and its meaning is defined by it as a most tender moral relationship. It has been prepared for by the whole series of Christological discourses in the preceding chapters; we may mention particularly the father/son parable of 5.19f. (cf. 5.30); the fact that Jesus' teaching is not his own but that of him who sent him (7.17); his obedience to death, which is pleasing to the Father (8.28); the parable of the son who has a permanent place in his father's house in 8.35; Jesus' knowledge of God, which is derived from his eternal and pre-existing relationship with him (8.55–8); and the fact that God has entrusted to him his own creative works (9.3). It is a unity which is conceived first and foremost in ethical terms. A further explanation waits to be given in verse 38 (though we have, in fact, already come across it in the later chapter 6), and that is the idea of mutual indwelling. This suggests that the unity of the Father and the Son is no passing and temporary concurrence of a common mind and purpose, but is essential and permanent. Beyond this we cannot go. John's attempt to express what he means in metaphysical terms comes in the Prologue, 1.1–3 (also a later strand). But inevitably this verse had momentous consequences for the Christological controversies of the third and fourth centuries (see Wiles, *Spiritual Gospel*, chapter 7).

The Charge of Blasphemy 31–9

31. The parallel with the situation at the end of chapter 8, where a major Christological statement provokes the reaction of stoning, underlines the importance of what has just been said. At the same time, it already implies the charge of blasphemy which is just about to be made, and this in its turn indicates that the Jews have misunderstood Jesus' words, taking them too literally. This will open the way to a closer definition of his meaning.

32. many good works: Jesus refers back to his explanation in verse 25. This seems perverse, because obviously the objection is to the statement of verse 30. But it is logical, because that statement depends upon the evidence provided by the divine acts which he has performed, and which should have evoked the response of faith. The word for **good** is exceptional (*kala* = beautiful, as in 'the good shepherd', verses 11 and 14), and may well be an intentional allusion to the allegory. For Jesus' acts are those of an ideal shepherd.

do you stone me: the present tense in this and the next verse must be taken as conative (i.e. 'do you mean to stone me'). There is no indication that stones were actually thrown.

33. blasphemy: this word and its cognate verb (verse 36) occur nowhere else in John. In the Synoptic Gospels Jesus is accused of blasphemy in the story of the paralysed man, as he appears to arrogate to himself the divine prerogative of forgiving sins (Mt. 9.3 paras.). Otherwise this charge is only made in the trial narrative (Mt. 26.65 = Mk 14.64; Luke does not specify blasphemy, perhaps designedly). It is thus probable that John is once more dependent on the trial traditions, as in verse 24. The law of blasphemy is given in Lev. 24.16. It is not easy to see what was felt to be blasphemous in Jesus' teaching. *Sanhedrin* vii.5, which rules that the law applies only if the *name* of God has been used, only considers the case of a man who has cursed God. But as that is an offence against God's honour, any statement which reduces his unique status as the Supreme Being might be held to be blasphemy, and probably was so under the stricter laws which obtained in NT times. Thus, in the case of Mt. 9.3 just mentioned, Jesus robs God's honour by claiming for himself a divine prerogative. Jewish anti-Christian polemic accused the Church of blasphemy on the grounds that the worship due to God alone was given to Jesus (Justin, *Dial.* xxxviii), and that God's sovereign power of redemption was ascribed to him. This latter point appears by implication in the Passover *Haggadah*, in a comment on Dt. 26.8: '*And the Lord brought us forth from Egypt*, not by means of an angel, nor by means of a seraph, nor by means of a messenger [cf. verse 36 below], but the Most Holy, blessed be he, himself in his glory; as it is said [Exod. 12.12]: *And I will pass through the land of Egypt in this night, and I will smite every first-born in the land of Egypt, both man and beast, and on all the gods of Egypt I will execute judgments; I am the Lord. And I will pass through the land of Egypt:* I myself, and not an angel; *and I will smite every first-born:* I myself, and not a seraph; *and on all the gods of Egypt I will execute judgments:* I myself, and not a messenger; *I am the Lord:* I am he ['* anî hû*'], and no other.' It has been suggested by Daube (*op. cit.*, pp. 325–9) that this final phrase is a direct polemic against the Christian ascription of the *egō eimi* to Jesus; cf. the notes on 8.24. Along these lines the reply of Jesus to the High Priest in the trial can be regarded as constituting blasphemy if the High Priest assumes that: 'you will see the Son of man sitting at the right hand of Power' (Mk. 14.62) is a way of saying: 'you will see *me* sitting . . .', so that Jesus occupies a position equivalent to that of God himself. That this is likely to be the solution to this vexed problem has recently been convincingly reasserted by M. D. Hooker (*The Son of Man in Mark*, 1967, pp. 172f.; cf. also T. Horvath, *NT* xi (1969), pp. 174–84). If this is right, then John's use of this feature of the trial narrative is closely related to it. For here the nature of the offence is specified in the charge that **'you, being a man, make yourself God'. God** here is without the article (though it was written by mistake in P⁶⁶*), and so is virtually adjectival, as in 1.1. The charge is the same as in 5.18, which in fact may be an allusion to

the charge of blasphemy in Mt. 9.3 paras. (see the notes *ad loc.*).
Here, as there, a literal interpretation of Jesus' words produces
the ironical situation that the Jews are formally justified in their
objection, yet what they say (when properly understood) is precisely the truth which John wishes to assert.

34. In his reply Jesus is not merely concerned to refute the
charge of blasphemy, but also to expand the teaching which has
been opened with the provocative statement of verse 30. First
he uses a scriptural argument to show that, even when it is taken
at its face value, it is an admissible statement, and should not incur
the charge of blasphemy. It is an *a fortiori* argument: if the
appellation 'gods' could be given by God himself to the persons
mentioned in the scriptural quotation, then 'God', or rather 'Son
of God', is a permissible title for Jesus, who has a special relationship with God. But this argument itself shows that he has a
deeper relationship with God than they. What this relationship
is can be seen by turning attention once more to Jesus' works.
This is the second point, and it leads to the conclusion that the
unity of Jesus with the Father is a mutual indwelling (verse 38).
in your law: your is omitted by P⁴⁵ א* D Θ Old Latin and
Sinaitic Syriac, and may be an addition from 8.17. The appeal to
the Law (properly the Pentateuch, but here applied to the OT
as a whole) suggests that John is here making use of an argument
from the current debate between church and synagogue. The
a fortiori argument is very common in the rabbinic use of Scripture.
The argument appears fallacious (unlike the example of this type
of argument in 7.23), because to prove that some people have
been *addressed* even by God himself as gods is irrelevant to the
point at issue, which is the actual *relationship* to God. It therefore
seems wrong to place it on Jesus' lips. But we do not know the
precise logical range of the mind of the incarnate Jesus; he
may have had no greater equipment to see the fallacy than his
opponents. Alternatively, it may be that he speaks *ad hominem*,
because those who make captious criticisms must be beaten on
their own ground. Or, more likely than either of these, the argument comes, as suggested above, from contemporary debate, and
John may have simply not realized that it was inappropriate on
the lips of Jesus.

But is the argument really so false? It is, after all, a matter
of words. It proves that words which are apparently equally

blasphemous pass unchallenged in Scripture itself. That at least is true. If Jesus is to be accused of blasphemy, the Jews must not just stop at the immediate impression given by his words, but must take care to make sure that they have first understood his meaning.

I said, you are gods: the quotation is from Ps. 82.6a. The transition from **gods** to Son of God at the end of the next verse becomes more acceptable when it is recalled that the parallel clause (Ps. 82.6b) reads 'Sons of the Most High, all of you'. Thus 'gods' and 'sons of God' are equivalents. If *they* are sons of God, then Jesus is all the more the Son of God.

35. to whom the word of God came: i.e. those whom God was addressing in the psalm. But who were they? In the psalm itself they appear to be the gods of the nations, who have not come up to Yahweh's standard of ethical justice, and so are demoted and 'die like men'. This is held by many modern scholars to mark an important stage in the Hebrew apprehension of monotheism. But in NT times, as we know from rabbinic evidence (*SB* II.543), they were held to be the divinely appointed judges of Israel, and so were in fact human beings. The argument on this basis is that some men, at any rate, have been called 'gods', and so the title Son of God is not blasphemous when applied to Jesus in a rather special way. Other evidence, especially the recently discovered scroll 11Q *Melchizedek*, suggests that they are the angels, and the downfall is that of the evil angels (Emerton, *JTS*, n.s., XI (1960), pp. 330ff.). On this interpretation the argument would be that, as the angelic messengers of God are called gods (even including the bad ones), then Jesus, as the special messenger of God (verse 36a), has a better right to the title. Although this explanation is attractive, especially as John shows other contact with Qumran ideas, the contrast between man and God in verse 33 makes the second the most likely interpretation. In fact angels are not mentioned in the argument at all, and play no part in John's Christology (1.51 is a special case), unlike the author of Hebrews, for whom the place of angels is an important consideration (so de Jonge and van der Woude, *NTS* XII (1965–6), p. 314).

(and scripture cannot be broken): i.e. it always remains in force, cf. 7.23. The same verb (*luein*) is used of overriding the Sabbath in 5.18. **scripture** means any particular passage of Scripture. The parenthesis is an admission that the text is excep-

tional; no one would have the audacity to say this without such
indisputable authority.

36. consecrated: Jesus speaks of himself in the third person,
using a careful choice of descriptive phrases. The verb for **consecrated** (*hagiazein*) means to set apart for sacred use, and does
not in itself imply a sacrificial act. John only uses it here and in
17.17, 19. In 17.19 the consecration of Jesus is for (*huper*, cf. the
note on verse 11 above) the disciples. This suggests that, in the
Incarnation, God has set apart, or sanctified, Jesus with a view
to the sacrificial act which he will finally accomplish. It is possible
that this word, which is admittedly rather unexpected, is an
allusion to the idea of the feast of the Dedication. It is used in
Num. 7.1, a lection read at the feast.

sent into the world: this is one of John's most frequent ideas.
For its force here we may compare particularly 3.16f., where
'gave' and 'sent' are synonymous, and 9.4, 7, where the emphasis
falls on the nature of Jesus' mission and the importance of completing it before the Passion. The word for 'messenger' (*šālîaḥ*) in
the passage from the Passover *Haggadah* quoted in the notes on
verse 33 exactly corresponds with the meaning of this expression
(cf. also 13.16). Both this and the preceding *consecrated* draw attention
to the Father's initiative, so as to imply Jesus' origin from him.

the Son of God: this is not exactly what Jesus had said, but the
use of 'Father' in verse 30 obviously implied it. Three reasons seem
to lie behind the choice of this title here. For obvious reasons
Jesus could not simply say 'I am God', as might be expected from
verse 33, but the fuller title maintains continuity with the quotation, especially if Ps. 82.6b was also in mind (it is not uncommon in rabbinic exegesis to quote only part of a text which is
under discussion). The title also belongs to the question of the
High Priest, referred to in verse 24: in Mk 14.61 he asks: 'Are
you the Christ, the son of the Blessed?' which Mt. 26.63 correctly
interprets as 'the Son of God'. Again, John uses this title extremely
sparingly, and it is all the more significant for this reason. It has
occurred hitherto at most five times: 1.34 (but read 'the Chosen
of God'); 1.49; 3.18; 5.25 (perhaps 'of God' is a gloss here);
9.35 (but here 'Son of man' must be read). In 1.49 it formed part
of Nathanael's confession of faith, which was the climax of the
series of confessions in the opening sequence of the Gospel. In
a moment we shall see another reference to this opening sequence

in the reference to John the Baptist. So it seems that here is a case of John's favourite *inclusio*. The grand finale of the central scenes, which have unfolded the truth about the person of Jesus, rounds off the series by recalling the point from which it started.

37. Jesus now reverts to the evidence of **the works** (verse 25), and thereby brings his assertion that he is the Son of God into line with the unanswered question to which it is related in verse 24. His assertion does not depend merely upon a spoken claim but upon acts which demonstrate that God is working through him. Once more we are reminded of the urgency to complete these works before it is too late, which was expressed in 9.3–5.

38. believe the works: if the Jews will but be willing to see God's loving plan and redeeming power in what Jesus has been doing, the wrangling over the meaning of words would be unnecessary. They would 'come to know and continue to know' (**know and understand,** cf. below) the truth which they refuse. There is a different kind of urgency here, the urgency of a final appeal, which perhaps reveals John's own despair at the fruitless verbal battles of the acrimonious debates between Christians and Jews in his own day. There is an echo of Ezekiel's 'Why will you die, O house of Israel?' (Ezek. 18.31).

know and understand: the note of appeal is maintained by the pathetic repetition of the same verb in aorist and present tenses (*gnōte kai ginōskēte*), which must be translated as above. This is the reading of P45 P66 P75 B L W Θ and the Lake group. Other MSS. either change the second verb to the more obvious 'believe', or, in the case of D Old Latin and Sinaitic Syriac, omit it altogether—both on prosaic stylistic grounds.

the Father is in me: in these simple words the unity of Jesus and God (verse 30), and the idea of his sonship (verse 36), are expressed in terms of mutual indwelling. The depth and intimacy of this relationship can be realized, because John has carefully prepared the ground by prefacing this discourse with the allegory of the shepherd. It is the most satisfactory way of describing the relationship, because it excludes any literal notion of the father/ son idea, like the family relationships of the pagan gods; nevertheless it preserves the logical priority of God, because the title **Father** is retained; it denotes a personal intimacy which forestalls any suggestion of ditheism; and as such it is as much an ethical statement as it is metaphysical.

39. Just as in 8.59, the climax is marked by the withdrawal of
Jesus when his opponents are on the point of arresting him. His
appeal has fallen on deaf ears, because of their spiritual blindness
(9.39–41).
Again is omitted by P45 א* D Old Latin, and may be a har-
monizing interpolation.

Jesus withdraws across the Jordan **40–2**

The chapter ends with a brief note of Jesus' movements, in order
to make a break between the series of disputes in chapters 5–10
and the beginning of the Passion narrative in chapter 12. As has
just been pointed out in the notes on verse 36, there is a deliberate
recalling of the early chapters of the Gospel, which makes this the
major division in the structure of the book. This has been to some
extent obscured by the insertion of chapter 11 in the second edition
of the work.

Jesus' withdrawal to Peraea brings him to roughly the same
position as he is at the corresponding point in Mark; cf. Mk 10.1,
which may be the tradition on which John has based these verses.
The situation is not really the same; in Mark Jesus is travelling
from Galilee by way of Peraea on his way to Jerusalem. After
healing the blind man at Jericho (Mk 10.46–52) Jesus comes to
Bethany (Mk 11.1). The insertion of chapter 11 means that John
brings Jesus twice to Bethany (11.1, 17; 12.1). But Jesus does not
enter Jerusalem until 12.12ff. (= Mk 11.1–10). This short paragraph also serves the purpose of drawing attention to the increasing number of Jesus' disciples, without whom the triumphal entry
into the city would hardly be explicable.

40. across the Jordan: this would reduce the risk of arrest,
as Peraea was part of the tetrarchy of Herod Antipas, along with
Galilee (cf. Lk. 3.1). The place referred to is Bethany beyond Jordan
(or whatever is the true reading at 1.28), roughly opposite Jericho.

41. John did no sign: the reference to the Baptist (who has
not been mentioned since 5.33–6) is not accidental. We are reminded of the whole course of Jesus' ministry, beginning with the
witness of the Baptist. The Gospel, as originally planned, began
with a deputation from the same Jewish authorities who have now
been questioning Jesus, and they had asked him: 'Who are you?'
He confessed, he did not deny, but confessed: 'I am not the Christ'
(1.20).

But now Jesus' life is in danger, because he has shown beyond any doubt that he is the Christ. It is thus possible that the people's words are intended to point to this contrast. Some thought that the Baptist might be the Messiah, but he **did no sign;** whereas Jesus' claim has been confirmed by numerous signs. But this interpretation does not make sense of the actual contrast in this verse, that, in spite of doing no sign, his testimony to Jesus **was true.** E. Bammel ('John did no Miracle', in *Miracles*, ed. C. F. D. Moule (1965), pp. 181–202) has suggested that the point is that, when the Baptist gave his testimony, he could provide no divine warrant of the truth of his words. Nevertheless, even though this important aspect of his credentials as a prophet was lacking, **everything that John said about this man was true.** John's words had to be taken on trust, and this makes them all the more convincing in the light of their subsequent confirmation. The situation is reminiscent of the reaction of the Samaritans in 4.42. Bammel sees in this verse a different approach from the references to the Baptist in the earlier chapters, where his subordination to Jesus is very strongly stated, and on this basis he suggests that (like the last verse) it is based on old tradition. But it is difficult to be sure about this. The great merit of Bammel's interpretation is that it gives a satisfactory explanation to the fact that **sign** is suddenly used here, whereas in the preceding discourse the word has been 'works'. The works *are* Signs, but, as we have seen in verse 38, they are much more than that: they are the acts of the good shepherd, who lays down his life for the sheep. One further point must be noted. What John the Baptist said about Jesus— that he takes away the sin of the world (1.29) and that he baptizes with the Holy Spirit (1.33)—has not yet come to pass. His sacrificial death and the gift of the Spirit still lie in the future. But the Baptist's statements were true, and the people now know this, not because of their actual fulfilment, but because of the revelation which Jesus has given about himself in the whole progress of these central chapters.

JESUS IS THE RESURRECTION AND THE LIFE   11.1–54

As the Gospel now stands, the story of the raising of Lazarus has a pivotal position in its structure. The series of discourses with the Jewish leaders is finished. Jesus has revealed the deepest meaning of his union with the Father. The Jews have accused him of blasphemy, and are seeking to arrest him. Jesus cannot now return to Jerusalem without exposing himself to serious danger. It is to be expected that he will lie low, until he chooses to appear once more at the feast of the Passover (12.1). From that moment the whole series of events of the Passion will be set in motion. We therefore expect that the Passion narrative will now begin, and will proceed without a break through to the Crucifixion and Resurrection of Jesus. But John does not fulfil our expectations; instead, he first gives us the Lazarus story in chapter 11, and then reshapes the introductory sequence of the Passion narrative in such a way that it belongs more obviously with the foregoing chapters than with what follows (chapter 12). In chapter 11 the continuity with 9 and 10 is maintained by light touches in the course of the narrative—the fact that the healing is 'for the glory of God' (verse 4), the theme of darkness and light (9f.), and actual mention of healing the blind man (37). It is linked theologically by the fact that the story is a revelation-event, incorporating and illustrating one of the great 'I am' sayings (25). It carries forward the plot of the Gospel as a whole by the fact that the raising of Lazarus is made the occasion for the decision of the Sanhedrin to put Jesus to death (verse 53). Chapter 12, after recounting two traditional items of the Passion narrative (1–19), picks up once more the theme of darkness and light (35f.). Then two final paragraphs repeat in fuller form the complaint of spiritual blindness (36b–43; cf. 9.39) and the final appeal of Jesus (44–50; cf. 10.37f.). The result is that the reader is left, as it were, hovering on the brink of the Passion. Then, with the utmost solemnity, the Passion narrative is begun with the measured steps of 13.1–3.

It will be argued below that the story of the raising of Lazarus (11.1–44) has been introduced by John only in the course of preparing the second edition of the Gospel (cf. Introduction, p. 50). But first it will be helpful to compare the Synoptic scheme. After the healing of the blind man outside Jericho (Mk 10.46–52), Jesus enters Jerusalem on Palm Sunday, cleanses the Temple, and as a result the chief priests and scribes determine to destroy him (Mk 11.1–18). This is followed by a block of teaching, before the main structure of the narrative is resumed with a repetition of the plot of the chief priests and scribes (Mk 14.1f.). Then comes the anointing at Bethany (Mk 14.3–9). The Last Supper follows immediately, and from there onwards John's narrative runs parallel with the Synoptic sequence. All these items, with the exception of the long block of teaching, are represented in John, but in a different order. The priests' plot comes first (11.47–53), then the anointing (12.1–8), and then the entry into Jerusalem (12.12–19). The cleansing of the Temple is omitted, because it has already been used in 2.13–22. But we observed that this passage contains various features which suggest a close literary connection with the account of the entry into Jerusalem. It thus seems likely that it belonged, at least in John's source, with the material which he has used in chapter 12, presumably immediately after 12.19. If this were so, we may take a further step, and consider the possibility that the priests' plot (11.47–53) originally followed the cleansing. This brings all the events into the same sequence as in Mark, except the anointing at Bethany, which in any case is more independent as far as the plot is concerned.

There is good reason to suppose that 11.47–53 should follow the cleansing of the Temple. According to John's presentation of the ministry of Jesus, the Jews have been actively hostile to him for some time. Now, however, something has happened to fill them with alarm. There is likely to be a breakdown in the uneasy relationship between the Jewish people and the Roman power, so serious that the Temple and other marks of national identity may be completely destroyed (verse 48). But the only reason given for this grave anxiety is a report that Jesus has brought to life a dead man. It is implied that, as a result of this, he is likely to win a very large following; this might lead to a political attempt to set up the messianic kingdom, and so would give rise to the danger which the priests now feel. But this danger has been present all along. It is difficult to see why the raising of Lazarus should suddenly make it more acute: the action itself contains not the slightest political overtones. On the other hand, the triumphal entry into the city and the cleansing of the Temple give only too obvious cause for alarm. Moreover, John's account of the cleansing includes a prophecy of the destruction of the Temple (2.19). According to the Synoptic tradition precisely this threat was held against Jesus at his trial (Mk 14.58 paras.).

The conclusion must be that John's source contained at least the triumphal entry, the cleansing of the Temple, and the priests'

plot in the same order as Mk 11.1–18, though it was probably
independent of Mark. John has disturbed this sequence so as to
introduce the Lazarus story. Before we ask why he has done this,
we must first decide when he did it; on the face of it, there is no
reason why he should not have done this in composing the original
edition of the Gospel, which is the time when he had the greatest
freedom in handling his sources. But although the story of Lazarus
has been written with some attention to its place in the total
scheme, it comes in very awkwardly after the finality of 10.22–42.
11.54 is similar to 7.1, just as 11.55–7 corresponds with 7.2–13,
implying that the comparatively independent story of 11.1–44 has
been inserted subsequently, just like the story of chapter 6; in
fact, 11.54 makes a suitable continuation from 10.42. Brown has
observed that 'the Jews' in the Lazarus story and in 12.9, 11 are
not the hostile authorities but the people of Jerusalem who are
favourably disposed to Jesus. No attempt has been made to weld
the account of the priests' plot into the great theological design
of 11.1–44. On the other hand, the continuity has been preserved
by editorial comments which can easily be removed without
damage to the rest of the material, i.e. 11.45f.; 12.1b, 2b, 9–11,
17f. The cleansing of the Temple has also been artificially inserted
into chapter 2 (see above, pp. 135ff.).

If we may assume that John has made these changes for the
second edition of his work, we must now try to see why he has felt
it necessary to do so. The fundamental point is that he has now
produced a homily on the raising of Lazarus, which is aimed at
making a profound emotional impact on the reader as he addresses
himself to the story of Jesus' Passion and Resurrection; this could
not be introduced into the sequence of the Gospel without disturbing the carefully ordered account of the mounting opposition to
Jesus. At 10.39 this has reached such a pitch that only the formal
decision to put Jesus to death remains to be described. This
followed naturally enough when the triumphal entry and the
cleansing of the Temple came immediately after chapter 10. These
two symbolic acts suitably followed the gigantic claims of 10.22–
38, and precipitated the priests' plot. Although it is a very different
kind of story, the raising of Lazarus illustrates these same claims
in a highly dramatic way. The artistic balance requires that it
should be followed by the counterpoint of the decisive action of the
priests. But if this is transferred to follow the raising of Lazarus,

the triumphal entry and cleansing of the Temple lose their point; they do not lead to anything. Consequently John has played down the importance of the triumphal entry, even making it a kind of appendix to the Lazarus story (cf. the notes on 12.17f.). He has removed the cleansing of the Temple to an entirely different point in the Gospel, where it can serve the theme of the opening chapters —i.e. the ending of the old order and the arrival of the new.

One consequence of these changes is that they have disrupted a theme which is very dear to John. This is the theme of the infinite fruitfulness of the Passion of Jesus. This has been enunciated in the shepherd allegory (10.14–16). In the original sequence it was represented in the crowds surrounding Jesus at his entry into Jerusalem and the idea of the new Temple replacing the old in the cleansing story. Then it was continued in John's handling of the tradition of the priests' plot (11.52). It can easily be seen how well the teaching of 12.20–6 followed on from this.

THE RAISING OF LAZARUS 11.1–44

The first two Signs which John recorded (2.1–11; 4.46–54) were simply told in a straightforward way, so as to form an implicit comment on the teaching which preceded them. The others (5.1–9; 6.1–21; 9.1–7)were told in the same kind of way, as the basis of a full-scale discourse, or equivalent teaching. The raising of Lazarus is unique in that everything is subordinate to the overriding aim of making the maximum emotional impact. It does not form a comment on the teaching of the preceding chapters, except in the most general way. The teaching is only a matter of a few verses (21–7), and comes at an early stage in the course of the narrative. The reader is kept in suspense as John uses one delaying tactic after another (the separate interviews of the sisters; the emotion of Jesus; his prayer at the tomb). The effect of the final scene, when Lazarus emerges from the tomb, is startling. Immediately the story is at an end; its point has been made. The reader cannot fail to see how this is a sort of dress rehearsal for the Resurrection of Jesus himself. Not that they are really the same thing. For this is a resuscitation to the life of the flesh, whereas the Resurrection of Jesus is a transition to the state of glory. But the details of the mourning women, the rock-hewn tomb closed with a stone, and the grave-clothes, with separate mention of the face-cloth, all have their counterparts in chapter 20, not to men-

tion the doubts of Thomas (verse 16; cf. 20.24f.). From this point
of view the story is the first element of a fresh example of *inclusio*,
the two resurrections of chapters 11 and 20 balancing each other
and encapsulating the entire story of the Passion. It will be
observed that this cuts across the presentation of the material in
chapter 12, which, as shown above, is aimed at tying it in with the
first half of the book.

   The emotional effect of the story, and its value as a preliminary
orientation of the reader's mind before the Passion narrative, are
clear enough; but how far does it contribute to the didactic purpose of the Gospel? One might say that it is the coping-stone on the
series of Signs. Jesus has dealt with a man's limbs (5.1–9) and
his eyes (9.1–7); now he deals with the whole man. But there is
no indication in the Gospel that John thought of the series in this
cumulative fashion. In fact he has already given a sign of new life
for the whole man in the healing of the official's son (see the notes
on 4.50). Alternatively, then, one might say that it is to give
teaching on the meaning of the Resurrection. But new life has
been the subject of chapters 3 and 4, and the discourse of chapter
5 was devoted to the function of Jesus as the giver of life. There
are, indeed, important points of contact between it and the
teaching of verses 21–7. The one thing that remains to be said is
that Jesus is himself the Resurrection and the Life (verse 25). The
point has already been made in the allegory of the shepherd
(10.17f., 27–9). But it is worth repeating in this highly dramatic
form. The story is thus expendable from the point of view of the
object of the Gospel; but it is a most valuable addition, nevertheless.

   Before going on to detailed commentary, we must face the
thorny problems of the sources and historicity of this fine composition. As the theologizing is minimal, it is not possible to
think of a Synoptic-type miracle story overlaid with Johannine
reflection (hence the failure of W. Wilkens, *TZ* xv (1959),
pp. 22–39, to reach convincing results). Bultmann's division, into
a story from the Signs-source and fragments of revelation-
discourses, does not allow for the radical recasting which has been
necessary for John's purpose. Nor will it do to suppose that John
has dreamed up the story from scattered hints in the Synoptic
Gospels; there is no Synoptic parallel to this story. On the other
hand, there are examples of resurrection miracles in the stories

of Jairus' daughter (Mk 5.21–43, paras.) and of the widow of Nain (Lk. 7.11–15).

But the points of contact with the Synoptic tradition are in the setting and the personal names. Lk. 16.19–31 records a parable, in the familiar style of the oriental moral tale, about a rich man and a beggar called Lazarus. Lazarus enjoys the blessings of eternal life. A supplement to the tale suggests that the rich man's brothers might repent if Lazarus were permitted to visit them, ending with the memorable pronouncement: 'If they do not hear Moses and the prophets, neither will they be convinced if someone should rise from the dead.' If there is a connection between this and Jn 11, it could be argued that John (or his source) has turned a parable into an event, as in the case of the Wedding at Cana (cf. the analysis, pp. 123-8). The setting here is the home of Martha and Mary at Bethany, and the latter is identified with the woman who anointed Jesus. These features of the story appear to be composed of various hints in the Synoptic Gospels, which were originally distinct, and have only come together at a later stage. Thus the two sisters are mentioned by name in the beautiful incident of Lk. 10.38–42, but the village is not named. It is clear, however, that Jesus is a long way from Jerusalem, so that the village is probably intended to be in Galilee. Luke's version of the anointing (Lk. 7.36–50) clearly distinguishes the woman from Mary Magdalene (Lk. 8.2), and again the location is in Galilee. On the other hand, Matthew and Mark have the anointing by an unnamed woman in the house of Simon the leper in Bethany in the beginning of the Passion narrative, as in John. It looks as if John (or the circle to which he belongs) has combined these various elements to produce the idealistic picture of the family at Bethany. Such a process is common enough in the history of traditions.

These facts must be evaluated in the light of John's use of sources elsewhere. All the previous healing miracles have had a basis in the tradition, and there is no reason to deny that this one has too, especially as other cases of raising the dead are recorded. But we cannot tell the form of the underlying tradition, because John has taken the details of the burial from his own account of the circumstances of the Resurrection of Jesus himself. A characteristic feature of the stories in chapter 20 is that John builds them around a particular person who has no special position in the traditions which he is using—the Beloved Disciple in the Petrine tradition (20.1–10); Mary Magdalene in the tradition of the women at the tomb (20.11–18); Thomas in the tradition of the assembly of the Apostles (20.24–9); cf. p. 595 below. In the same way, it seems likely that he knows of the story of Martha and Mary and has added Lazarus into this setting. His familiarity with the story of the two sisters is suggested by the characterization of them: Luke tells us that Mary 'sat at the Lord's feet', but 'Martha was distracted with much serving (*diakonian*)' (10.39f.); so in John Mary 'sat in the house' and later came to Jesus and 'fell at his feet' (11.20, 32), and 'Martha served (*diēkonei*)' at the supper in the anointing story (12.2). Brown suggests that their home actually was at Bethany, which has been obscured by Luke, because he incorporated this tradition into his travel narrative. The parable of the good Samaritan, which immediately precedes it (Lk. 10.30–7), takes as its setting the road from Jerusalem to Jericho, which passes through Bethany. But it is really more likely that John has located the home at Bethany because he identified Mary with the woman who performed the anointing there. He knows the Lucan anointing story, but not in the form in which we actually have it in Luke; and his identification of the Mary of the story of the two sisters with the woman of the anointing story owes nothing whatever to the mention of Mary Magdalene in Lk. 8.2. Mary Magdalene comes into chapter 20 from the Resurrection traditions, and there is not the least hint that John thinks of her as identical with Mary of Bethany. For the moment we may leave it an open question whether John had already fused the story of Mary and Martha with the anointing story in the first edition of the Gospel (which would explain why he subsequently brought this story into close proximity with the Lazarus story), or whether the family details of 12.1–3 have been added at the same time as he made the other alterations for the second edition (which in any case is the time when Lazarus first comes into 12.2). Finally, the connection with the parable of the rich man and Lazarus seems very remote; John's telling of the story is in no way indebted to this parable. But it is possible that the name Lazarus already existed in the traditional miracle on which his story is based; if so, there might ultimately be a connection between the Lazarus of a parable, who might return from the dead, and a man who was actually raised to life by Jesus.

If the above analysis is correct, we must suppose that John has created this magnificent scene in the following way. The setting has been provided by the story of Mary and Martha, and this has been located in Bethany on account of the anointing story, which already stood in John's first edition of his Gospel. The action has been taken from an otherwise unknown tradition of the raising of a man from death by Jesus, perhaps including the name Lazarus. John has not only fused these together, but has re-worked them with the narrative of the Passion and Resurrection of Jesus in mind. He has done this so thoroughly that the result is a fresh piece of creative writing. His special interests are apparent not only in the few theological statements, but also in the precise details of the story, and these are not confined to the obvious re-semblances to chapter 20, as the detailed notes will show. By this means the whole story has become an allegory of the Passion, Death and Resurrection of Jesus, relating them to the experience of every man, whom Lazarus represents. This is what gives to the story its lasting value. The only regrettable aspect of John's work is that it has deprived us of any hope of recovering the truth of what actually happened. All we know is that people in NT times felt that return to life was not impossible in certain circumstances, and that Jesus was credited with having raised the dead on one or two occasions. John himself had not the least doubt that this was so.

Lazarus is ill **11.1-4**

11.1. Now a certain man: for the Semitic style of opening a story, cf. 1.6.
Lazarus: this Greek form of *La͑zār*, the abbreviated form of the Hebrew name Eleazar (= God helps), is known from inscriptions and Josephus. The names **Martha** (*Mārᵉthā͗* = lady) and **Mary** (*Maryām* = Miriam) are also found in other sources.
Bethany (el-Azariyeh) is on the eastern side of the Mount of Olives, about two miles east of Jerusalem. According to the Synoptic Gospels, Jesus retired to this village when he came to Jerusalem on Palm Sunday (Mk 11.11 paras.).
2. The verse is an explanatory parenthesis, anticipating 12.1-8, from which all the vocabulary is drawn. It seems to imply that the anointing has already taken place, and that this is the reason why the sisters now turn to Jesus for help. But though the verse

is found in all MSS., it is probably an early gloss (so Bernard, Brown). Notice the non-Johannine use of **the Lord** (cf. 4.1; 6.23).

3. to him: if verse 2 is omitted, this must refer back to 'him' in 10.42.

whom you love: the phrase is unusual, but need mean no more than 'your friend' (so *NEB*). It is assumed without explanation that Jesus knew the family well. This verse is the basis of the theory that Lazarus is to be identified with the Beloved Disciple (cf. Introduction, p. 33); But the verb used is *philein*—cf. *philos* in verse 11; but *agapān* in verse 5. It is doubtful whether John discriminates between these synonyms, but the fact remains that *agapān* is nearly always used when the Beloved Disciple is referred to (the one exception is at 20.2). The fact that the story belongs to the second edition of the Gospel also weakens the case for this identification.

4. not unto death: i.e. Lazarus will not die, and so the sisters need feel no alarm, and Jesus need take no action (cf. verse 6). But the next words show that he knows that Lazarus will die, but that death will not be able to hold him: 'though he die, yet shall he live' (verse 25).

for the glory of God: Jesus can speak so confidently, because he interprets the circumstances in terms of his own vocation in the purpose of God. The sickness is **for the glory of God,** i.e. that God may get for himself praise. This will be achieved because death will be overcome. But there is a particular purpose beyond this: the divine act will be performed by the agency of Jesus himself. Thus God's power to give life will be displayed by the act of Jesus, in exactly the same way as in the case of the man born blind (9.3). The raising of Lazarus will not only redound to the glory of God, but will also display the glory of Jesus, who makes God known in his incarnate life. It will therefore form part of Jesus' revelation about himself, making known his true identity as **the Son of God** (see the notes on 9.5). The thought is similar to 9.3–5, but the word **glory** brings in a new emphasis. It is a special feature of John's presentation of the Passion as the supreme manifestation of the glory of God in Christ; cf. 12.23; 13.31. From this point of view the raising of Lazarus is a clue to the meaning of the Passion.

the Son of God: probably the original reading was simply **the**

Son, omitting **of God** (so P⁶⁶; 'his Son' is read by P⁴⁵ and some Old Latin texts, and by Sinaitic Syriac and Sahidic).

Lazarus is dead 5–16

5. loved: Gr. *ēgapa* (though D has substituted *ephilei*). See the note on verse 3. Many scholars think that this verse is a gloss (which would explain the change of verb), or is at least misplaced; Moffatt transposes it to precede verse 3. Barrett says that the intention of the verse in its present position is to soften the apparent carelessness of Jesus' behaviour.

6. So when he heard: resuming the narrative from verse 3 in such a way as to bring Jesus' action into line with his saying in verse 4. His spoken reaction was a denial of the sense of urgency. This is matched by his refusal to take action immediately; but, just as the real reason for his confidence was his knowledge of the deeper purpose of the event, so the real reason for his delay is to allow time for the situation to be reached in which this purpose can be fulfilled; cf. verse 15. Thus the whole of this paragraph forms a comment on the saying of verse 4. Jesus' delay is caused by the needs of the story, and is not merely intended to suggest that he remains in control of his own destiny, refusing to be swayed even by an urgent claim upon his friendship.

two days: cf. 4.40, where it simply seems to mean a short time without symbolical implications. Here it is the minimum time required for the story, as Lazarus was still alive when the sisters sent their message, but has been dead four days by the time Jesus comes to them (verse 17). It is improbable that John specifies this interval so as to make the resurrection of Lazarus take place on the third day. The whole point is that it happens on the fourth day, and the third day is never mentioned in the story.

7. The dialogue which now follows has been composed in full view of the larger context of the setting of the story in the Gospel, and owes nothing to either of the main sources (the story of Mary and Martha, and the raising of a dead man). John has modelled it on his previous work in 9.3–5, using another parable (verses 9f.) which may be a genuine saying of Jesus. The dialogue plays on the danger to Jesus' life incurred by his decision to restore the life of Lazarus, which in fact is to be a demonstration of his own conquest of death. So, to begin with, Jesus suggests returning into

Judea without giving any reason (but see below on verse 54), or referring to Lazarus.

8. seeking to stone you: cf. 10.31, 39. It has been deduced from this verse that Jesus' delay was precisely because of this danger, but this is not really likely, as Jesus appears to be unmoved by this consideration. The deeper object of this very natural response to Jesus' suggestion is to put him alongside Lazarus, as one who is in imminent danger of death.

9f. Jesus replies with a parable, comparable to 9.4. This allusive way of speaking is adopted in order to make the answer fit both levels of interpretation. The parable is about a traveller, who can find his way in the daylight hours, but is liable to have an accident in the dark. Structurally it begins with a rhetorical question, and then has two perfectly balanced sentences in antithetic parallelism. Each consists of three clauses. Bultmann regards the third in each case, which is a causal clause, as an expansion of the original. This is not unlikely, if we may judge from the very similar parable in Mt. 6.22f. (= Lk. 11.34–6). This has an opening statement ('The eye is the lamp of the body'), corresponding with the rhetorical question here. Then follow balanced clauses, as here, which are almost identical in the two gospels. But both have further expansions, which diverge considerably. The *Gospel of Thomas* 24 has a version of this parable without expansions: 'There is light within a man of light, and he (it) illumines the whole world (*kosmos*); when he (it) does not shine, there is darkness.' But, against Bultmann, it is altogether probable that the causal clauses in verses 9 and 10 had been added in the tradition before it reached John, because they introduce no theologizing. They may well be due to cross-fertilization from the similar parable in Mt. 6.22f., and they have been added to assist the interpretation. This means that we have no less than four levels of intepretation to deal with, two in the underlying tradition, and two in John's application of it in the present dialogue.

Taking the parable without the causal clauses, the parallel sentences of 9b and 10 are so obvious that all the emphasis is thrown on the question: **Are there not twelve hours in the day?** This follows the current way of reckoning time, in which the daytime is divided into twelve hours from sunrise to sunset, the night being divided into four watches (cf. the notes on 1.39). The point then is that action must be taken while the light lasts, just

as in 9.4. It is a parable of crisis, in which Jesus seeks to impress
on his hearers the necessity of taking prompt action before the
judgment falls. It is possible, but by no means certain, that
stumble is an allusion to the 'rock of stumbling' in Isa. 8.14,
alluded to several times in early Christian literature (cf. Rom.
9.32; 1 C. 1.23; 1 Pet. 2.6–8).

The addition of the causal clauses gives to this a more spiritual
and interior application. A man is safe in the daylight **because he
sees the light of this world,** i.e. the daylight enters into him
through his eyes (cf. Mt. 6.22). At night, however, **the light is
not in him** (the reading of D* 'in it', i.e. in the night, is due either
to erroneous copying or to misunderstanding of the meaning). So
he stumbles for lack of perception. The idea is reflected in the
Thomas logion. 'There is light within a man of light.'

John has used this parable in the first place as a response to the
disciples' fears expressed in verse 8. Jesus knows that he will be
safe (in spite of the danger of going about in Judea in broad daylight!), because he has the light in himself. Indeed he *is* the Light
of the World (8.12). The close similarity of vocabulary between
this parable and 8.12 suggests that John consciously intends the
reader to pick up this allusion. But we should not for that reason
conclude that **of this world** is a Johannine addition, as this
phrase is represented in the *Thomas logion,* which is certainly independent of John. This interpretation removes the sense of
urgency, which is present in both the first two levels, because
it means that the forces of darkness can have no power against
him who is the light.

But the urgency remains from another point of view, because
the light of the incarnate life of Jesus will all too soon be put out
(cf. 12.35f.). There may be twelve hours in the day, but Jesus'
hour will soon come (12.27), and then it will be too late to reveal his identity as the giver of life (cf. 9.5). Lazarus' illness was
not unto death in one sense, but he must die in another in order
that the Son may be glorified by means of it (verse 4). Thus the
parable has a specific reference to the situation of Lazarus, and
leads straight into the plain-speaking (or not quite plain-speaking!)
of the next verse.

Can we take one further step and find a fifth interpretation for
the benefit of the reader? This would be that John is teaching,
in the critical urgency of the situation, the need for the reader to

walk by the light of Jesus. This certainly seems to be true of 8.12, but it is doubtful if John has this aspect in mind here, as such an interpretation has little relation to the context. The parable is not inserted for general teaching, but to make an essential point in the dialogue.

11. Thus he spoke: John indicates a pause to allow the meaning of these cryptic words to sink in. For **friend,** cf. verse 3.

has fallen asleep: Greek *koimāsthai* (from which our word 'cemetery' is derived) is frequently used of death in classical Greek, and several times in the NT, e.g. 1 C. 15.6. John has deliberately chosen this word because of its ambiguity, cf. Mk 5.39: 'The child is not dead but sleeping' (where, however, a different Greek word is used).

to awake him: when he awakes, or rises from the dead, Lazarus will see the daylight once more. The night will be past, and the new day will dawn.

12. he will recover: lit. 'be saved', one of John's rare uses of the verb *sōzein* (cf. 3.17). It is regularly used in the NT for recovery from sickness. But the ambiguity remains, as the words could be translated: 'if he has died, he will be saved' (P[75] even reads *egerthēsetai*, 'he will be raised up', a definite allusion to resurrection). There is thus a delicate irony here, whereby the disciples say what will actually happen, without realizing it.

13. The explanation is required because, as just pointed out, the disciples' words are not free from ambiguity. John is using his favourite device of a literally-minded misunderstanding, and it is necessary to make this clear. It is also implied that, if this is the true state of affairs, and Lazarus has taken a turn for the better, Jesus' venture into the danger of Judea is unnecessary.

14. plainly: *parrēsia*; cf. 10.24.

is dead: the aorist *apethanen* is not an Aramaism, but does duty for the perfect, which is never used in NT Greek in the case of this verb. We have to assume that Jesus knows of Lazarus' death by his supernatural powers of insight.

15. for your sake: the death of Lazarus, which might be good cause for distress, is in fact cause for rejoicing, because it will enable Jesus to reveal the glory of God, as stated in verse 4. One might say that it is particularly fortunate that this has happened, because Jesus' time is short, and there will not be another opportunity for such a compelling act of revelation, as the parable has hinted. Although we shall see later that Jesus feels a real sympathy for the sisters in their sorrow, he can say to the disciples **'for your sake I am glad'**, because the whole future depends on establishing their faith before the decisive moment of his own death and Resurrection.

16. Thomas: outside the Fourth Gospel, he is mentioned only in the lists of the Twelve in the NT (Mt. 10.3 paras.). John makes him represent doubt concerning the Passion and Resurrection (14.5; 20.24–9). In 20.24 and 21.2 John adds **called the Twin** (*Didumos*), as here, translating the Aramaic name (*Tʾōmā*, 'twin'). The Greek form is known as a personal name, rather than a describer, from other sources, and (according to *AG*, p. 367b) Thomas existed as a Greek name, quite apart from its apparent equivalence with the Aramaic word for twin. This suggests that John gives the translation because the name Didumos was known in his circle, without intending to imply that he actually was a twin. The use of the Greek equivalent no doubt arose because the name was taken as a describer in order to identify Thomas with a person of another name, i.e. Judas the brother of Jesus. Thus the *Gospel of Thomas* begins in the Greek (Pap. Oxyrhynch. 654): 'These are the secret words which the living Jesus spoke and Judas who is also Thomas wrote . . .' In the Coptic the last phrase has become: 'and Didymus Judas Thomas wrote' (cf. the notes on 8.51). In the later apocryphal *Acts of Thomas*, 31, this has led to the grotesque suggestion that Judas was the twin brother of Jesus himself. But John shows no sign of this identification with Judas. **die with him:** Thomas's remark must be interpreted in the light of his doubt about the resurrection in 20.24–9, which belongs to the first edition of the Gospel, and so was written first. Thomas is not ready to 'believe' (verse 15). To go back into Judea is to court danger of death (verse 8), and so to share in the fate of Lazarus. He expresses the loyalty of a true disciple, but he does not know that the disciple must share the death and Resurrection of his Master. His words are thus yet another case of unwitting irony, and suitably close the dialogue.

Jesus and Martha: Doctrine of Resurrection **17–27**

17. four days: an important point, because it means that, according to Jewish belief, the physical death of Lazarus is irreversible; cf. verse 39. Today we know that irreversible changes take place in a matter of hours. But the pre-scientific Jewish view (shared also by other ancient peoples) was that the soul of the dead only finally left the body after three days. After this the effect of corruption made recognition of the person impossible, and this had legal consequences (for rabbinic references, cf. *SB* 11.544f.; see also Hoskyns, p. 200 and Barrett, p. 335). On this view it could be maintained that the Resurrection of Jesus on the third day allows the possibility that death was not finalized in his case. But if John is not free to alter that tradition, he can certainly make sure that Lazarus, the type of the Resurrection, was truly dead. Hence the insistence that the fourth day has been reached. There is no certain evidence that Jesus' Resurrection on the third day was asserted in order to make any suggestion of corruption impossible, though this may be implied by the use of Ps. 16.10 in Ac. 2.31; but the unexpected **four days** in the Lazarus story does suggest that, by the time John was writing, there were objections to the Church's doctrine, on the grounds that Jesus had never been properly dead. For evidence of John's need to combat Docetism, cf. Introduction, pp. 61ff.

18. two miles: lit. 'fifteen stadia'. The Greek *stadion* is about 200 yards, and the distance is thus a little less than two miles.

19. the Jews: not the hostile authorities, but citizens of Jerusalem (hence D reads 'many people from Jerusalem').

20. Jesus would be approaching the village from the opposite side, along the road from Jericho. The traditional house of the sisters and Lazarus is almost at the bottom of the steep track which was once the road from Jerusalem. Below it is the site of the Byzantine church, built to accommodate pilgrims when the house began to be a pilgrimage attraction, and a modern church has been built on its foundations. Originally there was a court between the house and the church, but this part of the site is now occupied by a small mosque, obscuring the Byzantine layout. **Martha . . . went:** it is natural that she should wish to speak with Jesus privately, away from the company of the mourners. The fact that John makes the sisters speak to Jesus separately is an artistic device, whereby the teaching (17–27) can be given separately from the action in which it is actualized (28–44). **Mary sat:** this was the correct posture when mourning; cf. Job 2.8, 13; Ezek. 8.14. But this may also be a hint of the underlying story of the two sisters; cf. Lk. 10.39.

21. would not have died: the teaching starts from the fact, already established in the previous signs, that Jesus can heal the sick. It now has to be shown that he is also the giver of life to the dead. Martha is a believer from the start, but she does not yet know the full range of Jesus' authority from God.

22. whatever you ask: the words are reminiscent of the Sermon on the Mount: 'Ask, and it will be given you' (Mt. 7.7). They will be echoed again in the Supper discourses (14.13, 14; 15.7, 16; 16.23f.). Martha presupposes that, because Jesus is a holy man, his prayer is sure to be granted (cf. the notes on 9.31). In the circumstances it is virtually a request that he should procure the restoration of Lazarus to life. It falls short of the faith required, because she does not see that Jesus is himself the divinely appointed agent of resurrection. This becomes clear in the following dialogue.

23. will rise again: the phrase is reminiscent of Isa. 26.19 (LXX), which perhaps is meant metaphorically, rather than literally of return to life. But Jesus is here stating the barest fact, to leave room for variety of interpretation. There are three ways in which these words could be understood: (a) he could mean a miracle of return to life, like the Synoptic raising stories, such as Martha has just asked for, and, indeed, such as actually happens in the event; (b) he could be referring to the general resurrection, as understood by the Pharisees and popular Jewish belief at this time. This is how Martha actually takes it (see the next verse); (c) he could be referring to a new quality of life beyond death, which is not tied to this eschatological and juridical concept, and is not merely resuscitation to the present form of existence. This is what Jesus does mean, as he will explain in verse 25. He will thereby open Martha's eyes to the truth, and evoke a more adequate confession of faith.

24. the resurrection at the last day: Martha states a view which is common in apocalyptic and rabbinic literature. One of the earliest passages where it is expressed is Dan. 12.2, which belongs to the time shortly after the Maccabean revolt (167 B.C.). At the end of the present age there will be a general resurrection, and the dead will be judged and suitably rewarded. This picture is grandly developed in 1 Enoch 41–57, and reappears in Rev. 20.11–15. But it also comes in a non-apocalyptic context in *Psalms of Solomon* 3.12: '. . . . This is the lot of sinners for ever; but those who fear the Lord will rise to eternal life, and their life shall be in the light of the Lord, and it shall never fail.' On internal grounds this composition is assigned to a date between 63 and 30 B.C.; it was written in Palestine, and has contacts of thought with both the Pharisees and the Dead Sea Scrolls. Martha's statement can thus be taken as representative of a considerable body of Jewish opinion. It was taken up into Christian thought, and has already formed the basis of John's treatment of judgment as a function of Jesus as the Son of Man in 5.28f.

25. I am the resurrection and the life: this magnificent assertion is to be understood in the same way as 'I am the light of the world' in 8.12. It is a qualification-formula, revealing a new characteristic of Jesus as the Wisdom of God. In this case it means 'through me men are raised up and receive eternal life'. This is true, according to John's theology, both from the point of view of the consistent eschatology, which is presupposed by Martha, and from the point of view of the special Johannine idea of the anticipation of the end in the life of Jesus, which will be expounded in the next sentence. In the resurrection at the last day (verse 24), the criterion for eternal life will be the response which each man has made to Jesus (cf. 5.22). But if a man responds to him now, he will be in an enduring relation to him, so that already he 'has eternal life; he does not come into judgment, but has passed from death to life' (5.24). The raising of Lazarus is to be a demonstration of this teaching, though it will be supremely demonstrated in Jesus' own death and Resurrection. It is thus urgently necessary to perform this miracle before he reaches the end of his incarnate life.

and the life: these words are missing from P[45] l and Sinaitic Syriac, and from quotations in Cyprian and Origen, and could perhaps be an addition from 14.6. But the phrase seems to be necessary for the following exposition, and so should not be deleted without stronger MS. support.

he who believes in me: from here to the end of the next verse we have the exposition of the *egō eimi* saying. It has two parts, corresponding with **resurrection** and **life** respectively. Belief in Jesus creates a relationship with God which can survive death (25b), and so removes death altogether from the spiritual life of mankind (26). Physical death there must be (25b), but from the point of view of life in God there is no death (26).

26. Do you believe this: it is vitally important that Martha should understand this, because the raising of Lazarus does not exactly fit the terms of reference. It could be taken to be merely the restoration of the *status quo ante*, whereby Lazarus returns to the old conditions of life with no solution to the problem of death. Only if Martha believes in Jesus as the Resurrection and the Life, in the way in which he has just expounded these terms, will she be able to understand the real meaning and intention of Jesus' act.

27. I believe: the perfect (*pepisteuka*) is used, as in 6.69 (contrast 9.38). We might expect her confession of faith to take the form of playing back to Jesus what he has just said, and so assenting to the propositions of verses 25f. In fact she makes an act of trust in Jesus personally, using a series of three messianic titles. Does this mean that she misunderstands him, or at least cannot rise to the height of faith which he demands? Bultmann rightly asserts that this is not John's intention here. It is the climax of this theological section of the chapter. To make confession of faith in the person of Jesus is to entrust oneself to the whole of his teaching, exactly as it is in the baptismal confession of faith, which Martha's words reflect. Her confession is thus confirmation of her acceptance of his teaching on the Resurrection. She uses the standard titles, which have all been introduced in the first chapter: **the Christ** (1.41), **the Son of God** (1.49; cf. 10. 36), and **he who is coming into the world** (1.27, 30). The last title is to be connected with the idea of the Coming One ('he who is to come') in Mt. 11.3 = Lk. 7.20. Bultmann regards it as the most important of the three, because it 'most plainly affirms the in-breaking of the beyond into this life' (p. 404). The actual phrase has closer parallels in 1.9 and 6.14. In 1.9 it has been transferred to the idea of the pre-existent Christ as the light of men, which is not directly relevant to the present context. In 6.14 it is applied to the Prophet, but in a context where this figure is not clearly distinguished from the Messiah (contrast 7.40f.). But we have no warrant to suppose that the Prophet is in mind here.

Jesus and Mary: Demonstration of Resurrection **28–44**

28. quietly: *RSV* here appears to follow the reading of D, Old Latin and Sinaitic Syriac (*siōpē* = silently), rather than the majority reading (*lathrā* = secretly). In either case it means 'privately' (cp. *NEB*: 'taking her aside'). This is necessary to the story, as the Jews who follow Mary (verse 31) are to be witnesses of the miracle without first receiving the teaching of Jesus on the Resurrection which would in some sense make it inevitable (cf. 4.51–3 for the motif of confirmation of a miracle).

calling for you: either we must presuppose that the dialogue with Martha included more than is recorded in verses 21–7, or we are to suppose that Martha regards the teaching as intended for Mary as much as for herself, though it is not for the other mourners. It would have been more natural if Jesus had come with Martha to the house, and then taken Mary aside for private conversation. But John's object is to bring the whole company to the graveside.

29. rose quickly: Mary's reaction is similar to the call of Levi (Mk 2.14 paras.). She comes to Jesus, wishing to receive instruction from the Teacher (verse 28). For her character as a model disciple, cf. Lk. 10.39, 42.

30. No reason is given why Jesus stayed where he was, but the fact that he does so fits in well with the progress of the story, for the burial-place would be outside the village, as Jewish custom required. So the Jews can assume that Mary is going to the grave, and that is why they accompany her. We have to assume that in any case Martha went with her, or at least joined in the general movement from the house to the grave.

31. to the tomb to weep: the verb (*klaiein*) implies unrestrained weeping and wailing. The whole phrase is similar to 20.11, where Mary Magdalene weeps at the tomb of Jesus. Although John appears not to identify the two Marys, he has, as we have seen, imagined the scene in the light of the Resurrection traditions. So Mary here is a blend of the Lucan tradition of the sister of Martha and of John's own account of Mary Magdalene.

32. fell at his feet: an act of supplication, rather than of worship; cf. Mk 5.22; 7.25. There may be a reminiscence of 'sat at the Lord's feet' in Lk. 10.39. A gesture similar to her action here may be implied in 20.16f., following Mary Magdalene's recognition of Jesus. This link between the two narratives would explain the unnecessary **and saw him** in the present verse.

Lord, if you had been here: Mary's speech is identical with Martha's, and thereby reminds the reader of the *whole* of the conversation leading up to Martha's confession of faith in verse 27. It thus amounts to a renewal of that confession of faith, on the basis of an intuitive understanding of the teaching which had evoked it. This again suits Mary's 'contemplative' character. From another point of view it suggests that the whole dialogue is to be repeated, which would be intolerable if actually carried out. But, as it is only a mere hint, it is capable of taking a different form, i.e. that the repetition should be found in the course of the narrative which follows. Jesus' response is not to give further teaching, but to act it out in performing the miracle.

33. deeply moved: Gr. *enebrimēsato*. This expression has caused much difficulty to commentators, because it is properly applied to indignation or anger, cf. Mk 14.5 ('reproached her', properly 'were indignant at her'). It is translated 'sternly charged' in Mt. 9.30; Mk 1.43; John uses the word again in verse 38. That the word caused trouble to early commentators is shown by P45 P66 D Θ, which have 'was troubled in spirit as if angry' (*hōs embrimoumenos*), evidently trying to soften it. But why should Jesus be angry? Hoskyns thinks that it is due to frustration at the unbelief of the Jews, who cannot rise to the teaching on life and death without making him resort to the exercise of miraculous powers. Barrett suggests that it is because he is forced to do an act which will make him liable to arrest before the proper time (his 'hour') is come. Sanders objects that all interpretations along these lines mean reading too much into the text. In fact there are three equivalent expressions, all of which refer to inner emotion: **deeply moved in spirit** and **troubled** (lit. troubled *in himself*) in this verse, and 'deeply moved in himself' in verse 38. Black, followed by Boismard, has suggested that both expressions in this verse are translation variants of one original Aramaic phrase. Certainly they have a Semitic colouring, and it is highly probable that John would never have used this difficult word, which he uses nowhere else, if he had not found it in his source for the story of the raising of the dead man. C. Bonner (*HTR* xx (1927), pp. 171–80) compared these two expressions, and also 'sighed' in Mk 7.34, with accounts of pagan thaumaturgists, expressing the energy required for doing a miracle. This may perhaps be right for the source, but is unlikely to be the way John imagined the situation. Indeed, it soon becomes clear that Jesus' emotion is that of grief (verses 35f.). Seeing that John has taken such pains to paint the whole scene in terms of Jesus' Resurrection, there is good reason to take this unexpected display of emotion in conjunction with 12.27, where Jesus' 'soul is troubled' at the thought of his own approaching death. We are thus driven back to the classic interpretation of this verse as a testimony to the human feeling of Jesus, who shares with all men in their pain and distress.

34. Jesus' question and the people's answer employ the same vocabulary as the angel's words to the women in Mk 16.6, another hint that the Resurrection traditions have been influential in the shaping of the narrative. John skilfully refrains from giving any reason why Jesus should ask where the tomb is. It thus allows the Jews to suppose that he wishes to join in Mary's wailing there (cf. verse 31). They have no idea what he will do when he arrives there.

35. Jesus wept: Gr. *edakrusen*, i.e. 'shed tears'. There is not the same connotation of extravagant wailing as with *klaiein* (verses 31 and 33 (twice)). It is probably only coincidence that both the time and place are so very close to those of another occasion when 'Jesus wept (*eklausen*)' as he drew near to Jerusalem (Lk. 19.41). For the tears of Jesus, cf. Heb. 5.7.

36f. Two reactions of the bystanders are given. First the compassion of Jesus is noted; **loved** (*ephilei*) is the verb used in verse 3. Brown notes the repeated emphasis on the theme of love in this chapter, and thinks that it is meant to suggest the love of Jesus for the Christian (cf. 13.1); it is closely allied to the thought of his compassion. The second reaction (verse 37) is the idea that Jesus' tears indicate that he has been powerless to save Lazarus from death, by contrast with the miracle in chapter 9. This misunderstanding of Jesus' emotion heightens the climax to which the story is leading.

38. deeply moved: Greek adds 'in himself'; cf. verse 33. It is obviously important to John that Jesus' emotion should be kept at the centre of interest. In fact it hides his real intentions to the last possible moment, as the next verse will show.

the tomb: this is described in terms similar to the sepulchre in which Jesus was laid. To say that the **stone lay upon it** implies that it was an underground cave with a flat stone over the opening but the Greek can mean 'fixed to it' (as in Barnabas xii.7), in which case the similarity would be all the greater. Both kinds of tomb, some with square stones and some with rolling stones, are found in the burial areas around Jerusalem.

39. Martha's response to Jesus' command seems to imply that she has not learnt the lesson which she has been taught about the

Resurrection, in spite of her confession of faith in verse 27. But this is not necessarily what John intends: Jesus has said nothing to indicate what he will actually do. All the signs are that his request is in some way connected with his grief. It would be quite natural to suppose that he wished to take a last look at his dead friend, regardless of the risk of ceremonial impurity from contact with the dead (this issue seems to have no part in the present narrative). Martha's reply is an equally natural response, if that is how his request is understood. She reminds him that decomposition of the body is advanced, so that it would be better not to look at it now. Anybody else might have given this information, and in a sense it is mere chance that Martha is the speaker. But John knows what he is doing: he has brought Martha back into the centre of interest to prepare for the sudden revelation of what Jesus is really about to do, which has been entirely hidden up to this point by the consistent preoccupation with Jesus' grief from verse 33 onwards.

an odour: Jewish burial customs included the use of spices to counteract odours at the time of death and burial; but this did not amount to the kind of embalming for preservation of the body practised by the Egyptians, and would do nothing to prevent decomposition.

four days: see the notes on verse 17. The repetition of this information at this point throws into relief the magnitude of the miracle which will now be performed.

40. you would see the glory of God: the reference is to verse 23, interpreted in the light of the revelation-saying of 25f. But the phrase is taken from verse 4. The miracle will prove that Lazarus' fatal illness was 'for the glory of God', because it will be a practical demonstration that Jesus is God's agent to give the Resurrection and the Life, the eternal salvation of mankind. It will also be a symbolic anticipation of Jesus' own Resurrection, in which God's glory is supremely made manifest. From this point there is no further mention of Jesus' emotion.

41. This is the only occasion when a prayer of Jesus is recorded in preparation for a miraculous act. But it has been assumed that such acts were done through God's power in answer to prayer in 9.31, and the blessing of the loaves before the feeding miracle had much the same character, even if it was just the 'grace before meals' (6.11 and Synoptic parallels). In this case the prayer con-

stitutes yet another element of the narrative which corresponds
with the established pattern of the Passion and Resurrection of
Jesus himself. We have seen that Jesus' grief reflects his own distress
before the Passion (12.27), which appears in the Synoptic tradition in the agony in the garden of Gethsemane. So the prayer begins
with the simple address **Father,** as in Mk 14.36, where the original
Aramaic *Abbā* is preserved. But there is a much closer link with
John's own magnificent composition of the prayer of Jesus in
chapter 17, where the opening words are almost identical with
Jesus lifted up his eyes and said, 'Father'. It is notable, in
view of the last verse, that the prayer of 17.1 continues: 'The hour
has come; glorify thy Son that the Son may glorify thee.' In the
prayer of chapter 17 the motif of inner struggle of the Gethsemane
prayer has been replaced by the certainty that follows the resolu-
tion of conflict, so that it is a calm and majestic direction of intention just before the actual test begins. This short prayer is also
a direction of intention before the conquest of death is acted out
in the raising of Lazarus. It is not a prayer for help; nor is it
primarily to show that Jesus 'does nothing on his own authority'
(5.30), so as to distinguish him from popular wonder-workers;
neither is it a kind of object-lesson for the bystanders (for, of
course, Jesus prays aloud), as if they would be converted by
being prayed for in their hearing. It is a prayer *for* the bystanders,
that they may have the perception to see in the miracle the glory
of God as enunciated in the last verse. If it is urgent that Jesus
should do this sign before his Passion, it is equally vital that its
true meaning should be recognized.

lifted up his eyes: the attitude implies a certain confidence
towards God; contrast the tax-collector in the parable of Lk. 18.13.
I thank thee: a common way of beginning a prayer; cf. the
prayer of the Pharisee in Lk. 18.11; the opening of Paul's letters
(Rom. 1.8; 1 C. 1.4; Phil. 1.3, etc.); the Qumran *Thanksgiving
Hymns* (1QH), which regularly begin 'I thank thee, O Lord . . .'
The word is *eucharistein*; cf. 6.11.

thou hast heard me: the certainty of a hearing is a frequent
motif in the Psalms (e.g. Ps. 6.8f.). Jesus' communion with the
Father is such that he need not actually formulate his request
(cf. Isa. 65.24: 'Before they call I will answer').

42. Though the prayer is unnecessary, and indeed for that
very reason has been put in the form of a thanksgiving, it gives

expression to the purpose of the miracle in relation to the witnesses of it. The prayer is spoken (**I have said this**) not for power to perform the miracle, but for **the people standing by,** that it may not fail in its effect, but **that they may believe that thou didst send me.** The way in which this is said so strongly implies that Jesus is only praying with an eye to the effect on the crowd, that Bernard adopts the weakly attested reading of Θ 'I do this' instead of **I have said this.** But it *is* for the sake of the crowd, because they must witness not only the miracle but also the communion between Jesus and the Father, which this prayer expresses, if they are to gain the truth from it. This is put in the form **that thou didst send me,** so as to draw attention to the Christological character of the act. It is yet another aspect of the revelation of the identity of Jesus, which needs to be known in its fulness for men to entrust themselves to him in faith (see on verse 4). The actual phrase, which is common in John (cf. 10.36), occurs repeatedly in the prayer of chapter 17. The motivation of Jesus in this verse is comparable to that of Elijah in the test on Carmel, cf. 1 Kg. 18.37.

43. cried with a loud voice: as if awakening Lazarus from sleep, cf. verse 11. Jesus acts out his future function as Son of Man at this dramatic moment, cf. 5.28f.

44. bound with bandages: Sanders gives a probable picture of what is meant, based on the admittedly not indisputable evidence of the Turin shroud. This was a length of cloth on which the body was laid, and long enough to come back over the head and down to the feet. Bandages were then wound round it to keep the limbs in position, the *sudarium* (face-cloth) having been tied under the chin to keep the jaw in place. It can be regarded as certain that John has mentioned these details in order to invite comparison with the grave-clothes of Jesus (20.7), where 'napkin' is the same word as **cloth** here. John seems to be quite unperturbed by the thought of Lazarus' movement under such conditions. If the difficulty occurred to him at all, he probably imagined that some degree of movement of the feet was possible, enough to make a gliding motion. This seems more likely than Hoskyns' idea of 'a miracle within a miracle', especially if the tomb was such as to allow horizontal movement, rather than coming up from below ground (see above on verse 38).

let him go: the practical command is comparable to Mk 5.43, where Jesus commands that Jairus' daughter should be given food. The ending of the story is abrupt. Nothing further needs to be said. The type of the Resurrection has been accomplished.

PLOT TO ARREST JESUS 11.45–54

After two editorial verses, creating a causal link between the raising of Lazarus and what follows, John recounts the plot of the Sanhedrin (verses 47–53). This corresponds with Mk 11.18; 14.1f. paras. John's version reflects his own vocabulary and interests, but contains two features which may be derived from independent tradition: one is the Roman threat (48), and the other is the unconscious prophecy of Caiaphas (50). The second of these is an application of what appears to be a proverbial axiom of statecraft to the situation described in the first. If Jesus' actions were interpreted in terms of political agitation, the threat would be real enough. We know from Josephus (*Ant.* XVII. 52–62; *BJ* II. 169–70) that Pilate showed less than the usual Roman respect for Jewish customs, so that the Jews were liable to be turbulent and restive under his procuratorship. Caiaphas not only had to exercise caution in controlling Jewish affairs, but also had to guard his own position, which was by no means secure, as other members of the High Priestly family were envious of his success in securing appointment. Thus his advice to the Sanhedrin on this occasion is convincing in the circumstances, and could well be based on correct historical reporting. Alternatively it could be the reason for the arrest of Jesus accepted subsequently by the Jews and advanced by them in debate with the Church. In this case John would have derived it from the discussions between Christians and Jews, to which he certainly seems to be indebted elsewhere in the Gospel. John reproduces the information with a touch of irony, for he knows that eventually the threat of verse 48 was only too tragically realized as a result of the political upheavals of the late sixties. He also sees an irony in the advice of verse 50, which he has taken pains to relate to the theology of the Passion.

Reactions to the Raising of Lazarus 45f.

45. Many . . . believed: a standard reaction (cf. 2.23, etc.), but specially important in view of verse 42. It is given as the reason for the Sanhedrin's fear of the growing influence of Jesus (verse 47). **who had come** is the participle (*hoi elthontes*) agreeing with **many,**

not, as we might expect, with **the Jews** (which would require genitive, *tōn elthontōn*; D characteristically makes this correction). Bernard therefore takes it to mean: 'many of the Jews [i.e. all those who had come, etc.] believed', so that those who tell the Pharisees about the miracle need not be those who have actually witnessed it. But this interpretation depends on too rigid an idea of the use of the participle in the *koinē* Greek, to which the exact standards of classical Greek cannot be applied.

46. some of them: if this means some of the Jews, it could be quite different people who have heard about the miracle from the believers (so Marsh). But it most naturally means some out of the 'many' of the last verse, and Bernard is reduced to supposing that they told the news without any wish to get Jesus into trouble. In fact, it is most likely that John means that not all the witnesses were convinced of the deeper meaning of Jesus' act, and that they reported it to the Pharisees so that they should take note of it in formulating an official attitude towards him, just as in 9.13. As so often in the Fourth Gospel, John imagines the position of the Pharisees in an anachronistic way (see below).

Meeting of the Sanhedrin **47–53**

47. chief priests and the Pharisees: replacing the chief priests and the scribes in the Synoptic parallels. In the time of Jesus **the Pharisees** were a party, which naturally included many of the lawyers (the scribes) and also some members of the principal priestly families. The fall of Jerusalem in A.D. 70 was the death-blow to the other Jewish parties, and the Pharisees emerged as the new leaders of the shattered people. John identifies them with the scribes, seeing the past in the light of the conditions of his own day.
The chief priests is a collective term for the High Priest and other members of his family, some of whom were deposed high priests, and others members of prominent priestly families, who according to J. Jeremias constituted a definite body in the temple organization (*Jerusalem in the Time of Jesus*, pp. 175–81). These men, with representatives of the scribes, and other elders in Jerusalem, formed the Sanhedrin, or **council** (Gr. *sunhedrion*), the Jewish governing body responsible for both religious and secular affairs under the Roman procurator.
What are we to do: for the deliberative use of the present indica-

tive, cf. *BDF* § 366.4. Perhaps the sentence should run on: '. . . seeing that this man, etc. ?'

Performs many signs is typical of John's vocabulary, and is not a direct reference to the raising of Lazarus (cf. 9.16). In the original edition of the Gospel it presumably carried a reference to the symbolic acts of the triumphal entry of Jesus and the cleansing of the Temple. In any case, the members of the Sanhedrin are in no doubt that his acts are intended to be the guarantee of divine appointment as the Messiah, and they think of this in terms of political realism. Hence their alarm at his increasing popularity.

48. every one will believe in him: at present it is clear enough that not everyone does; cf. verse 46. The words seem appropriate, if spoken in exasperation, though they are not necessary to the argument. On the other hand they could be taken as an ironical forecast of the future universal following of Christ. But they are missing from quotations of this verse in Augustine, Chrysostom and Cyril of Alexandria, and Boismard accordingly suggests that they are a gloss (cf. verse 50). The sentence certainly reads more convincingly without them.

the Romans will come: they will be forced to take final action if a messianic claimant gains such a large following that a large-scale rebellion is begun.

our holy place: the Greek omits **holy,** and without it **place** could mean the city of Jerusalem (so Sinaitic Syriac and Chrysostom). But its use in the specialized sense 'temple' (so *NEB*) is well attested (cf. 4.20), and is probably intended here (especially if this paragraph were originally preceded by 2.13–22). The fear is that destruction, or desecration, of the Temple would put an end to the Jewish religion, for which it was the centre, and that the national identity of Judea would be brought to an end, to prevent any further nationalist rising. Whether the following of Jesus was really so great as to suggest such an extreme danger is doubtful. If this verse is derived from Jewish apologetic for the death of Jesus, it may be coloured by the events of the Jewish War of A.D. 66–73, in which the Temple was destroyed.

49. Caiaphas: the High Priest in A.D. 18–36. He was the son-in-law of Annas (cf. 18.13), who had been deposed in A.D. 15 by the procurator Valerius Gratus, Pilate's predecessor. Apparently he did this to secure his own nominee as High Priest, but stability was not achieved until the year 18, when Caiaphas was appointed after three others had held office in quick succession. Meanwhile Annas retained an influential position in the Sanhedrin.

that year: this sounds as if the office was an annual one, but this was never true of the High Priests of Jerusalem. It has been suggested that John has mistakenly applied to Judaism the practice of Asia Minor, where the pagan high priests were appointed annually. The same practice also obtained in Syria. But John is usually well informed on Jewish affairs (in spite of his anachronism about the Pharisees), and is unlikely to make this kind of mistake. Hence most modern commentators follow the lead of Origen, and take it to mean: 'in that memorable year', i.e. of the Passion, in which Caiaphas' unconscious prophecy was fulfilled, cf. verse 51 (and 18.13f.).

50. understand: better, 'take into account'. To remember the general rule which follows would soon settle the quandary. It is possible, as Boismard has strongly argued, that the following words should be omitted: **for you, man,** and **for the people.** The short text then gives an excellent sense: **It is expedient that one should die, and that the whole nation should not perish.** The *textus receptus* has 'for us' (*hēmin*), but **for you** (*humin*) is read by P⁴⁵ P⁶⁶ B D L X Old Latin and Bohairic; the word is omitted by ℵ and 053, and also in 18.14, where these words are repeated; **man** (*anthrōpos*) is found in all texts, but is missing from 18.14; **for the people** (*huper tou laou*) is not found in some patristic quotations (Augustine, Chrysostom, Theodoret) and some Ethiopic texts, and may be an insertion, anticipating verse 51f. As it stands, *huper* must mean 'instead of' rather than 'on behalf of', which it does mean in 51f., and usually elsewhere in John; and *laos* for **people** is particularly awkward, being identical with **nation** (*ethnos*) used consistently in the rest of the paragraph. In fact John never uses *laos* except here and in 18.14, which may be a gloss (see the notes *ad loc.*). The grounds for the omission of at least this phrase are thus strong. It has probably been inserted to make the prophecy fit more closely its explanation in 51f.

51. that year: that is omitted by P⁶⁶ and D, the whole phrase by P⁴⁵ e Sinaitic Syriac. If original, it stresses once more the memorable occasion when these words were uttered. But the whole point of the verse is that it was because Caiaphas was **high priest** that his words were prophetic. They were not, then,

merely an ironical assertion of the truth, but a declaration by God,
even though Caiaphas did not realize this himself. There is some
evidence to suggest that there was a popular belief that the High
Priest might have prophetic powers by virtue of his office, in spite
of the fact that the official view was that prophecy had come to an
end with Malachi, the last of the OT prophets. It is in any case
clear enough that the possibility of prophecy was a live issue in
the popular assessment of Jesus. But Josephus tells us that John
Hyrcanus was held to have prophetic powers, at least in the sense
of foresight (*Ant.* XIII.299, cf. XI.327). If Caiaphas' words are taken
from a Jewish apologetic for the condemnation of Jesus, then the
idea that they were prophetic of Christian truth may well be the
Christian reply. Jesus did indeed **die for the nation.**

52. It is characteristic of John to extend the idea to the Gentile
mission as well. We have seen his interest in it in two passages
already: 7.35 and 10.16. This explanation of the advice of
Caiaphas gains greatly in its effectiveness if the whole paragraph
stood originally between the cleansing of the Temple, now placed
in chapter 2, and the reply of Jesus to the Greeks in 12.20–4, as
has been argued in the introduction to this chapter. In 2.19–22
Jesus speaks darkly of the destruction of the Temple (cf. verse 48
above), and this turns out to be a prophecy of his own death and
Resurrection. Then in 12.20–4 Jesus tells the representatives of the
Gentiles about the immeasurable fruitfulness of his sacrificial
death, for which this explanation of the prophecy of Caiaphas has
just prepared the reader.

the children of God: cf. 1.12. It is a way of expressing the privileges of the 'Chosen People' in a universal way, without suggesting the old limitation to the Jews (compare the 'other sheep' in
10.16). Paul uses this phrase in the Judaistic controversy (Rom.
8.16f., 21; 9.8).

scattered abroad: Gr. *dieskorpismena.* The idea is present in the
allegory of the sheep in Ezek. 34, but a different word is used.
But it is precisely this word which occurs in another related
passage, Zech. 13.7: 'Strike the shepherd, that the sheep may be
scattered.' This is quoted by Jesus to express his presentiment of
the flight of the disciples at the time of his arrest in Mt. 26.31
(= Mk 14.27). That John knew this application of this prophecy
is implied by 16.32. It is thus possible that the flight of the
disciples, which must have been a most embarrassing memory for

the primitive Church, was held to be not only a fulfilment of
prophecy, but also itself a prophetic act, presaging the dispersion
of the disciples on the Gentile mission, cf. Ac. 8.1-4. The death
of the Shepherd causes the scattering of the sheep; nevertheless it
is really the means whereby they are gathered together and made
one (cf. 10.16). The same theme of the gathering up of the
Gentiles has also appeared in a different form in 6.12, where it is
applied to the gathering up of the fragments of the loaves. The
link between that passage and this present verse appears very
clearly in the eucharistic prayer of the *Didache* (IX.4), which is
quoted in the notes to 6.12 (p. 243 above). In this prayer 'scattered'
(*dieskorpismenon*) is the same word as we have here. John will revert to this issue in 17.20ff.

53. from that day: all previous attempts on Jesus' life have
been spontaneous reactions. Now there is the definite decision of
the Sanhedrin. John's phrases are very close to Mt. 26.4.

Jesus withdraws to Ephraim **54**

54. The narrative requires that Jesus should return to his retreat before making his dramatic entry into Jerusalem on Palm
Sunday. This is not only the inevitable consequence of the decision
of the Sanhedrin which has just been described, but is also the
situation obtaining at the end of chapter 10. We might expect
Jesus to go back to Peraea (10.40), and so resume the Synoptic
position for his progress towards Jerusalem. But instead he goes
to another place, which cannot be located with certainty (see
below). On the other hand, in verse 7 Jesus had announced his
intention of going back into Judea, and although he did not give
a reason for doing so, it would be natural to suppose that it was
for the purpose of continuing his mission. This gives us the clue
for understanding the meaning of this verse in its original position,
before the rearrangements for the second edition. If it followed
immediately on 10.42, it means that Jesus was not merely in
hiding, but was continuing his work away from Jerusalem. First
he went to Peraea, and 'many believed in him *there*'. Then he
went **from there** back into Judea (**among the Jews**), but to a
place of relative obscurity (**no longer ... openly,** *parrēsia*), and
continued to work there. The situation is thus very similar to 3.22,
where Jesus works away from Jerusalem, but the reason is exactly
the same as in 7.1, where he went to Galilee to avoid the danger of

arrest. Notice that **went about** (*periepatei*) was used in 7.1, referring to Jesus' preaching ministry. Thus this verse makes an excellent continuation from 10.42, and it is unnecessary to take it (as, for instance, Brown does) as a doublet of 10.40–2.

Ephraim: the name means 'fruitful', and was applied to the central mountain range of Palestine, especially the fertile western slopes, including the ancient tribal district of Ephraim. But this provides no clue to the identification of the particular place mentioned here. There are three possibilities: (a) In Ru. 4.11; Mic. 5.2 Bethlehem (six miles south of Jerusalem) is called Bethlehem Ephrathah. It is very close to the southern part of the Judean desert, and it would not mean a wide detour for Jesus to pass through Bethany again on his way to Jerusalem (12.1). But it is too close to the city to be plausible, and there seems no reason why John should not write 'Bethlehem' (cf. 7.42), if this is what he means.

(b) Some MSS. avoid the difficulty by omitting **town** (P⁶⁶* Sinaitic Syriac), so that the name is applied to **country,** and the actual place is not specified. But D inserts *Samphourin* after **country,** which is obviously a misplaced gloss on **a town called Ephraim.** This might be intended to mean 'a town of Ephraim called Samphourin'. It has been conjectured that this is to be identified with Sepphoris in Galilee, five miles north of Nazareth. But it is impossible to suppose that this is right, as it is much too far off, and nowhere near the desert. Another conjecture is that *Samphourin* represents Syriac or Aramaic *šᵉmeh 'Ephraim* = **called Ephraim.** If so, it is probable that the scribe of D took it from a Syriac version in which it stood in the margin as a variant reading for *methqᵉrē' 'Aphrēm*, which is read by Sinaitic and Peshitta Syriac (not, then, dittography as Barrett suggests), evidently thinking that it was intended to be inserted into the text as the name of the country. He wrote it down as he heard it dictated, and had no idea what it meant.

(c) Much the best suggestion is that this is the Ephraim mentioned in 2 Sam. 13.23, five miles north-east of Bethel. It was on the border of what had been the province of Samaria, and was one of three towns ceded to Jonathan in 145 B.C. (1 Mac. 11.34, spelt 'Aphairema'). Of course in the time of Jesus Samaria was part of the province of Judea, only being treated separately in so far as the people of that region supported the schismatic worship on

Mount Gerizim. But the people as far south as Ephraim had always remained loyal to Jerusalem. It is the modern et-Taiyibeh, on the E. slope of the central mountain region, and so on the edge of the northern Judean desert. If this is right, we must suppose that the people of this place claimed that Jesus had worked there at some stage during his ministry.

stayed: Gr. *emeinen*, John's usual word, which may imply only a very short stay (cf. 1.39). It is read by P75 B ℵ L W—a strong combination—against the majority reading *dietriben* ('remained for a considerable time') only used elsewhere in 3.22; but its presence here may well be due to influence of that verse.

JESUS MUST BE SACRIFICED BEFORE HIS WORK IS ACCOMPLISHED   11.55–12.50

The section begins with the people wondering whether Jesus will come to Jerusalem for the Passover. The situation is very similar to 7.11–13. John is following his usual narrative technique of bringing Jesus to Jerusalem at the time of a feast; this time it is not merely a convenient device, but it is a fixed part of the tradition about Jesus. John's account of Jesus' arrival at Jerusalem thus links up with the Synoptic scheme and reproduces some of the important items of it. As the Gospel stands, these are only the anointing at Bethany and the triumphal entry, but we have already seen reason to believe that originally the latter was followed by the cleansing of the Temple and the priests' plot. John has retold all these traditional items in such a way as to point forward to the immense fruitfulness of the death and Resurrection of Jesus. This is the theme of the short discourse of 12.20–36a. Although this is a typically Johannine composition, it has an unusually high proportion of traditional sayings of Jesus with Synoptic parallels. This discourse does duty for the story of the Agony of Jesus at Gethsemane in the Synoptic tradition. It will be argued in dealing with this section that John was familiar with the Gethsemane tradition, but deliberately chose to present the material in a different way; it is a tradition which is concerned with the necessity of Jesus' sufferings. For John this is a point of theological importance, and it is no surprise that he therefore puts it into the form of a public discourse. Finally John adds two editorial com-

ments: a theological explanation of the unbelief of the Jews
(12.36b–43), and a summary of Jesus' teaching in the form of a
miniature discourse (12.44–50). These form the conclusion, not
so much to the chapter, as to the whole of the public ministry of
Jesus described in the preceding chapters.

Chapter 12 gives an untidy impression. This is partly due to
the varied kinds of material used, partly to the reshaping of it
when the story of Lazarus was inserted. It has suffered the removal
of the cleansing of the Temple and of the priests' plot. References
to Lazarus have been inserted into the narrative of verses 1–18.
It is also possible that the anointing at Bethany has been shifted
from a position later in the chapter, in order to bring it into closer
relation with the Lazarus story. If so, the date 'six days before
the Passover' (12.1) might originally have belonged to the entry
into Jerusalem. This would bring the time-scheme closer to that
of the Synoptics. In Mk 14 the anointing is immediately followed
by the treachery of Judas, revealing his avaricious nature in the
contract for money, and then the narrative goes straight on to
the Last Supper. John's account of the anointing incorporates the
theme of Judas' avarice, and contains several subtle anticipations
of the Last Supper, thus providing a kind of trailer for chapter 13,
as will be shown in the notes below. This aspect of the anointing,
which has not been generally noticed by scholars, would be much
clearer to the reader if the structural connection were closer. Once
recognized, it opens up the real possibility that John originally
composed his version of the anointing to come at the end of
chapter 12. This leads to the further possibility that the miniature
discourse of 12.44–50 is an afterthought, inserted only after all the
other changes had been made; this seems better than the suggestion that it has been accidentally transposed from elsewhere.
But it is impossible to arrive at certainty where so much guesswork
is required.

Before the Passover **11.55–57**

55. the Passover of the Jews was at hand: the same phrase
as at 2.13; 6.4. For the continuation from verse 54, cf. 7.2.
to purify themselves: preparatory rites of washing and atonement are referred to in Exod. 19.10, and were specially necessary
for those who had come from a distance; cf. Num. 9.6–12; Ac.
21.21–4 (a private vow). Pilgrims used to arrive in Jerusalem a

week before the feast for this purpose, Jos. *BJ* 1.229; VI.290. For
John's knowledge of such customs, cf. 2.6.

56. cf. 7.11. The question, **'That he will not come . . . ?',**
suggests that the people are very doubtful if Jesus will dare to show
himself publicly again, i.e. after the attempted arrest of 10.39
(or, in the present ordering of the material, after the decision of
the Sanhedrin in 11.53).

57. chief priests and the Pharisees: the phrase is taken
from 11.47, and may replace 'the Jews' in the original edition, cf.
7.13; 10.31. **Arrest** clearly refers back to 10.39. This is more
plausible, if the priests' plot has not yet taken place, as the
Synoptic account of it specially mentions that the decision to
put Jesus to death (cf. verse 53) was to be kept secret, to prevent
a popular demonstration during the feast.

THE ANOINTING AT BETHANY 12.1–8

After the questioning of the pilgrims in 11.56, we now expect
John to bring Jesus to Jerusalem. If Ephraim (11.54) is to be
identified with the place near Bethel, he would be coming from
the north, and would not need to pass through Bethany. However,
as things now stand, Jesus calls there first, and the vivid little
incident of the anointing is described. A woman, here identified
with Mary the sister of Martha, apparently moved by some
spontaneous impulse, pours an expensive perfumed oil over Jesus'
feet. When Judas objects to her extravagance, Jesus defends her
action as a symbolic anticipation of his burial.

Simple as the story is, it raises hosts of problems. John's version
is very close to that of Mt. 26.6–13 (= Mk 14.3–9), and it looks
at first sight as if he is actually dependent on both these accounts;
for 'pure nard' (*nardou pistikēs*) in verse 3 is a rare phrase found
only in Mk 14.3; whereas 'costly' (*polutimou*) in the same verse is
perhaps Matthew's word, and also verse 8 abbreviates Mark in
exactly the same way as Mt. 26.11. The only serious difference
from these accounts is that in John the woman pours the ointment
over Jesus' feet, and then wipes them with her hair, whereas in
Matthew and Mark she pours it over his head. But it is precisely
this feature which makes John appear to be dependent on the
very different, but obviously related, story of the woman who was
a sinner in Lk. 7.36–50. There the woman sheds tears over Jesus'
feet and wipes them with her hair (the phrase is precisely the

same as in John), and then, as a kind of bonus, anoints them as well. This is the one place in the Fourth Gospel where it really does seem as if John has all three Synoptics open before him as he writes, and picks a phrase from here and a word from there. But, just because it is unparalleled, such an idea can scarcely be entertained, and we must search for better and more convincing solutions of the problem.

The first prerequisite is to establish the relation between the Lucan story, which is set in Galilee, and the Bethany story of Matthew and Mark. Benoit and others have shown that they are really distinct, and should be traced to two entirely separate occasions. The Lucan story is about a penitent sinner, who allowed her tears to fall over Jesus' feet, thus rendering Jesus liable to ceremonial impurity through contact with a (possibly menstruous) woman. When the host raises this objection, Jesus delicately shows that his own acceptance of her act is tantamount to the forgiveness of God himself. This is quite different from the Bethany story, where there is no question of sin and forgiveness. The anointing of the head is a matter of pure luxury, as the disciples are not slow to point out, and the incident is only re-membered because of the macabre twist which Jesus gives to it. But it is clear that the Lucan story has been elaborated (presum-ably by Luke himself) by the introduction of details from the anointing story, i.e. 'brought an alabaster flask of ointment' in 7.37 and 'anointed them with the ointment' in 7.38 (cf. 46). There is also the name Simon for the anonymous Pharisee in 7.40, 43 (cf. Mk 14.3). Thus Luke gives the Galilee story with slight touches from the Bethany story. It is arguable that John gives the Bethany story with slight touches of the Galilee story quite independently of Luke. In this case we might suppose that John is not working from any of the Synoptic Gospels, but has an independent version of the Bethany story which has already been influenced by un-conscious assimilation to the other.

The exact verbal agreements with distinctive features in all three Synoptic Gospels cannot be entirely explained by the theory that John is using a source. This does not account for the precise agreement of Mt. 26.11 and Jn 12.8 against Mk 14.7, which Matthew was probably abbreviating (assuming the priority of Mark). We shall see, when we come to the relevant verses in the detailed commentary, that in all the cases of verbal agreement we must seriously reckon with the possibility of assimilation *after* the Gospels were written, in the process of transcription. This kind of contamination of the text is far more common than the average reader supposes, as a glance at the critical apparatus of a Greek NT text will show. There are positive grounds for explaining some, at least, of the verbal agreements in this way.

If the two Synoptic stories are originally distinct, we cannot use the Galilee story to explain the motivation of the anointing at Bethany, in which the theme of sin and forgiveness plays no part. But it does contain a useful little summary of polite behaviour on a convivial occasion in Lk. 7.44–6, which reflects customs known from numerous Jewish and classical sources. Luke mentions the washing of feet, usually done by a slave, the kiss of the guest by the host, and the anointing of the head to create a luxurious atmosphere. It is thus unnecessary to suppose that the anointing is in any way intended as an acknowledgement of Jesus' messianic status. Neither Matthew and Mark nor John show any sign of having this issue in mind, and it is a false track to interpret the story along these lines (against Barrett). The point of the story is that the woman's personal devotion to Jesus, expressed in an act of unnecessary luxury, is accepted by Jesus as an anticipation of his burial, so that the incident is prophetic of his death, and the joy of the moment is over-shadowed by the note of impending tragedy. In the event, according to the Synoptic tradition, Jesus' body was not anointed, as time was very short after the crucifixion before the Sabbath drew on. John, however, does mention anointing (19.39f.), but this does not alter the fact that he sees the woman's action as a symbolic anticipation of this.

Whether the woman was named in John's source we cannot tell for certain, but there is no strong reason for supposing that she was. John, however, has imagined the scene in the light of the story of Mary and Martha, which he has used for the setting of the Lazarus story. It is thus probable that this aspect of John's version was only added to it at the time when John made all the other drastic changes to chapter 12 for the purposes of the second edition of his Gospel.

John's most important adaptation of the tradition consists in a deliberate reshaping of it to make it an introduction to his own account of the Last Supper in chapter 13. Many commentators have noticed that Luke is careful not to confuse the washing of

Jesus' feet with the anointing of them, even though anointing of
feet instead of the head is unusual (Lk. 7.38). But John really
makes the anointing a sort of washing, so that the woman's action
anticipates the washing of the disciples' feet by Jesus himself in
13.3-11. Next John makes Judas voice the objection of the
disciples. Verbal links between 12.4-6 and 13.29 indicate that
John intends the reader to gain an insight into the character of
Judas, which will help to account for the theme of his treachery
which dominates the Last Supper (13.21-30). Finally, the closing
remark of verse 8 (if original) is reflected in the theme of Jesus'
departure (13.31-8).

1. Six days before the Passover: for the Greek construction,
cf. *BDF* § 213. If Good Friday is the actual day of Passover, this
could be either Saturday or (reckoning inclusively) Sunday. As
travelling on the Sabbath is unlikely, Sunday is to be preferred.
It is probable that this date originally introduced the account of
the Triumphal Entry (see above, p. 411).
Bethany: this is from the source; cf. Mk 14.3. The rest of the
verse and also verse 2 belong to John's secondary adaptation of
the material to fit in with the Lazarus story. For the style, cf.
2.1f. It is probable that **whom Jesus, etc.** (preceded by 'who
had been dead' in the *textus receptus*) is a gloss (so Bernard,
Barrett).

2. a supper: Gr. *deipnon*, used by John alone of the four
evangelists for this occasion *and for the Last Supper* (13.2). It means
the main meal of the day.
Martha served: cf. Lk. 10.40 and the introduction to the story
of Lazarus, p. 385 above.
those at table: Gr. *tōn anakeimenōn*, the technical term for reclining on couches for a formal meal, used again by John in
13.23, 28.

3. Mary: probably replacing 'a woman' in the source, as in
all the Synoptic parallels.
a pound of costly ointment of pure nard: the Greek and
Roman pound (*litra*) was equivalent to 12 oz., i.e. a little more than
half a pint. Only John has this detail, cf. 19.39. His word for
costly (*polutimou*) is found as a variant in Mt. 26.7 (for *barutimou*)
and in Mk 14.3 (for *polutelous*), slightly better supported in Matthew
than in Mark. But this seems to be a case of assimilation by copy-
ists, as suggested above. It is specially noteworthy as a case of

the influence of John on the Synoptic text. This opens up the possibility that **pure nard** (*nardou pistikēs*) is John's expression, and has come into the text of Mk 14.3 in the same way. It is missing from Matthew, and the whole phrase ('pure nard, very costly') is missing from Luke precisely at the point where both are clearly dependent on Mark, reproducing his 'alabaster jar of ointment' exactly. The whole phrase is also missing from one important MS., D. This MS. is notable for its additions and harmonizations, but its omissions are rare and important (cf. on 6.23 above). If, however, it is original in Mark, we must assume that John found it in his source. But it must also be noted that **nard** is missing *in John* from D, and also P66* and Old Latin. **nard** is the oil of an aromatic plant, and was imported from India, so that it was naturally very expensive. *Pistikēs* (here translated **pure**) is an adjective of uncertain meaning. It may be derived from the name of the nard plant (*AG* mentions East-Indian *piçita*) or of another substance mixed with it (perhaps ŏil of pistachio nuts); it could be from the root of *pisteuein* ('believe'), and so mean 'trustworthy', i.e. genuine and unadulterated (so 'pure'). This is not really supported by Aramaic *quštā'* (= 'truth'); when this word is used with 'nard', it is probably the transliteration of another aromatic plant (Gr. *kostos*); it may be the Greek equivalent of the Latin name of the plant, *spicatum* (hence our 'spikenard'), but the consonants do not correspond very well; the derivation from *pinein* = drink, i.e. 'potable' (*LSJ*) is scarcely credible. The choice must lie between the first two alternatives, and, until fresh evidence comes to light, no final decision is possible.

the feet of Jesus: although the anointing of the feet is not unheard of in ancient literature (cf. *SB* 1.427), it is clearly secondary in Lk. 7.38 and foreign to the Bethany story. What is extraordinary, however, is that Mary wiped his feet with her hair. And the unnecessary repetition of **feet** looks suspicious. It may be, as Bultmann suggests, that **and wiped, etc.,** is a later insertion from Luke, but there is no MS. evidence for this, and it still leaves the change from the head to the feet unexplained. But in 13.5 we read that Jesus 'began to wash the disciples' feet, and to wipe them with the towel'. The word for wipe (*ekmassein*) occurs in the NT only in these related passages (Lk. 7.38, 44; Jn 11.2; 12.3; 13.5). John seems to have imagined the anointing as washing of

the feet, for which drying with the hair would not be inappropriate. This suggests, as argued above, that John's source already contained the washing of the feet from the tradition which
lies behind Luke. But John wishes to retain the motive of the
Bethany story, that the woman's act is an anticipation of Jesus'
burial, and so he identifies the anointing with the washing. In
the Last Supper account Jesus' act of washing the disciples' feet
is the model of true discipleship. The connection may even extend
further to the fact that the woman in the story used by Luke
'loved much' (Lk. 7.47), for the commandment to 'love one
another' (13.34) is the rule for true disciples.

the house was filled: fragrance is a symbol of permeating influence, and so some commentators, both ancient and modern,
have discerned here a veiled allusion to the spread of the message
of Jesus throughout the world. It would thus correspond with the
saying of Mt. 26.13 (= Mk 14.9), which John has omitted, and carry
forward the theme of the Gentile mission, which we have seen
elsewhere in chapters 11 and 12. This idea would be more plausible if we could be sure that the anointing was supposed to have
the force of an acknowledgement of Jesus as the Messiah. But this
is too uncertain, and it is better to take this detail of the story as a
way of emphasizing the extravagance of the act (so Bernard,
Sanders).

4. Judas Iscariot: the description has variants (including the
addition of 'Simon' or 'son of Simon' in some MSS., and 'from
Kerioth' for **Iscariot** in D), as in 6.71. Before the insertion of
chapter 6 in the second edition of the gospel, the present verse
would have been the first mention of him. John has deliberately
substituted him for Mark's vague 'some' (Mk 14.4; Mt. 26.8 has
'the disciples'), with a view to the parallel of the Last Supper,
cf. 13.2.

5. Judas' objection is virtually identical with Mk 14.5, except
that Mark's 'more than three hundred denarii' has become the
precise sum (possibly 'more than' is Mark's own addition to the
source). The sum is equivalent to about £30 (*NEB*), but its
purchasing power would be far greater than it is today; cf. 6.7.

6. John here adds an explanatory note, which would probably
have no basis in the source. Barrett notes that **cared for** and
thief are reminiscent of the allegory of the shepherd (10.10, 13).
More significant is the fact that **had the money box** (*glōssokomos*,

properly a reed-box for the reeds of flutes) and **given to the poor** (verse 5) are repeated in 13.29. John is here showing the avarice of Judas, which was a fatal flaw in his character and led to his terrible act of treachery. The verse thus corresponds with Mk 14.10f., a necessary story detail, which John has unaccountably omitted from his Passion narrative (but see below on 13.27). **used to take what was put into it:** lit. 'used to lift what was thrown in', a colloquial expression for pilfering the contents.

7f. Jesus' reply is entirely derived from the source; cf. Mk 14.6–8. But by abbreviating it, John has obscured the line of thought. **Let her alone** is of course singular, being addressed to Judas rather than to a group. In Mark, Jesus first accepts the woman's act as a mark of particular regard for him. It is at this point that Mark has the contrast with the poor: **the poor you always have with you . . .** It leads to the first hint of the interpretation of the anointing which is still to come: **you do not always have me.** Only after this does Mark reach the real point, that, in doing 'what she could', she had unconsciously 'anointed Jesus' body beforehand for burying' (Mk 14.8). In John verse 8 comes lamely as an additional explanation. It is unnecessary, because the point of the story has already been reached. As the form of this verse is identical with Matthew's abbreviation of Mark, it may very well be a case of interpolation in the course of transmission of the text. For here we have the evidence of D once more (cf. the comment on 'pure nard', verse 3), supported by the Sinaitic Syriac, for the omission of the whole verse (the omission of part of the verse in P75 Λ*, however, is only due to haplography). Consequently Jesus' reply is even more abbreviated than appears at first sight, being confined to verse 7.

But what *does* Jesus mean? Literally the text reads: 'Let her alone, that (*hina*) she may keep (*tērēsē*) it . . .' This implies that she has some of the nard over, and instead of selling it for charity, she is to retain it for actual use at the burial. Though Bernard takes this view, it is rightly rejected by nearly all recent commentators, because it is obvious that she has used it all. This leaves two other possibilities: We may omit *hina* and read 'she has kept it' (*tetērēken*) with the later MS. tradition. This means that she has already done what would have been done at the burial of Jesus if there had been time, so that, although it might later be objected that he was not buried properly, her act has already made good that deficiency. But in John the anointing for burial is not omitted (19.39f.), and so this cannot be his meaning here. Or we may treat the *hina* as epexegetic, carrying on the sentence, not from the interjection: 'Let her alone', but from the question in verse 5, i.e. 'Let her alone! [The reason why she did not sell it and give the proceeds to the poor was] that she might keep it for the day of my burial' (hence read 'Let her alone; it was to keep it . . .'). This can hardly mean 'that she might have something to remember on the day of my burial', which would be against the usage of *tērein*. It means rather: 'she refused to give it away, so as to keep it for a special occasion, not [as Judas thinks—and for that matter probably also the woman herself] just for luxury, but for the day of my burial'. Without realizing it the woman has performed a prophetic act. The occasion is symbolically equivalent to the day of burial, and for this reason she was right to keep the ointment and use it in this extravagant way (cf. Brown, p.449). **burial:** the word (*entaphiasmos*), which is a rare one, is derived from the source. It has influenced John's account of the burial in 19.40 (*entaphiazein*).

A Plot against Lazarus **9–11**

9. the great crowd: presumably the pilgrims of 11.55. The paragraph, which has been inserted on account of the importance of the raising of Lazarus in John's reshaping of the material, is plausible but unconvincing. Having represented the raising of Lazarus as the reason for the decision to put Jesus to death in 11.45–53, John must tone down the importance of the entry into Jerusalem (verses 12–19), which would be quite enough to cause alarm, especially when the cleansing of the Temple was coupled with it. Thus the transference of the Bethany story to its present position draws attention to Lazarus. This public interest in him can then be given as 'the reason why the crowd went to meet' Jesus when he came to Jerusalem (verse 18), implying that otherwise it would not have been a sufficiently large demonstration to call forth the Pharisees' alarm. It must be accepted that John has got himself into difficulties by his rearrangements, and the idea that Lazarus should also be put to death is an unhappy consequence of his own work, deriving not from the tradition, but from the logic of the situation which he has produced.

10. The vocabulary is drawn from 11.53.

11. were going away: not literally, but metaphorically, i.e. forsaking Judaism for Christianity in a way that reflects the post-Resurrection situation. The verse as a whole is based on 11.45.

THE ENTRY INTO JERUSALEM   12.12–19

The splendid picture of Jesus' triumphal entry into Jerusalem is a fixed part of the Passion narrative, found in all four Gospels. John has recast it and abbreviated it drastically, so as to make it lead up to the quotation of Zech. 9.9 (verse 15), with a comment on the subsequent exegetical work of the Church (verse 16). This sounds rather lame. Barrett points out that the crowd has been in no doubt that Jesus came as the Messiah, and it is odd that the disciples should not be able to realize this until 'Jesus was glorified'. It sounds a little more sensible when the passage is read with the cleansing of the Temple (2.14–22) immediately following it, as was originally intended. For then the two events interpret one another, and it becomes clear that the death and Resurrection of Jesus are the key to understanding both of them. They could not be properly understood at the time, even though Jesus was openly hailed as the Messiah.

If verse 16 is the really important fact from John's point of view, we can work backwards from there to trace his theological aim in presenting this traditional episode in what seems to be an untraditional manner. In verse 15 the entry is seen to be a ful-filment of Zech. 9.9. This is actually a traditional item, but it will be argued below that it is not an original feature of the story, and that it is a mistake to suppose that Jesus was actually staging a fulfilment of this prophecy. It came into the tradition after the actual event, but before the tradition reached John. For John the point at issue is that it explains why Jesus chose to ride on an ass (verse 14). It seems a very topsy-turvy way of writing to mention this only *after* the crowd have hailed Jesus as the Messiah. Brown has observed that, by mentioning it at this point, John makes it a subtle correction of the people's nationalistic interpretation of messiahship. It indicates that Jesus comes in peace: 'My kingship is not of this world' (18.36). So we arrive at the beginning of the story. The crowd makes the demonstration, not Jesus. They go out to meet him, carrying palm branches and chanting a victory song (a quotation of Ps. 118, found also in the Synoptic accounts). It should now be clear what is in John's mind. The entry is a messianic act, but not in the sense which is implied by the popular acclaim. Jesus can only accept their Hosannas if it is recognized that he comes as the Prince of Peace. But what this means cannot be understood until he is 'glorified', i.e. until after the total redemptive sequence of death, Resurrection and exaltation as Son of Man (see the notes on 7.39, another of John's explanatory comments).

John's account is theologically motivated, and gives very little help in the task of reconstructing what actually happened. The fuller Synoptic versions of the story give a more plausible picture of the course of the events, but are not free from the tendency to elaboration. In Mark Jesus carefully arranges the procession to Jerusalem. He obtains an ass which has never been ridden before, because 'The Lord (i.e. God) has need of it.' As he enters the city the people cry: 'Blessed is the kingdom of our father David that is coming!' It is not necessary to suppose that Jesus is claiming to be the Messiah. It is rather a demonstration that the Kingdom of God is about to be inaugurated, and so forms the climax of the mission of the Apostles to proclaim the imminent arrival of the rule of God (Mk 6.7–13, paras. and related passages). The choice of the ass 'on which no one has ever sat' indicates that it is for a profoundly religious purpose (cf. 1 Sam. 6.7). It also implies that it is a coming in peace (SB 1.843), so that the modern tendency to think of it as a military coup is mistaken. A reference to the prophecy of Zech. 9.9 is not excluded, for that verse, taken with its continuation in the next verse ('he shall command peace to the nations') gives the warrant for the use of the ass as a sign of coming in peace. But the important point is that Jesus chose to ride on an ass, not in order to make the prophecy come true, but because it expressed the meaning of what he was actually doing. He was not staging a fulfilment of the prophecy in order to make people believe that he is the one to whom the prophecy refers. Consequently the prophecy plays no part in the Marcan account. The prayer of the people is addressed to God (Mk 11.10: 'Hosanna in the highest!'; or, Grant salvation, thou who art in the highest heaven). The beginnings of an interpretation of the event as a proof of the messianic status of Jesus only appear in Mk 11.9b, where the people's cry of verse 10, which is actually based on Ps. 118.26a, is anticipated by the insertion of the precise text of the passage. This draws attention to Jesus as the Coming One.

The application of Zech. 9.9 only comes in when we reach Matthew, and there it has influenced the details of the narrative. But in Luke also there are light touches which show that this prophecy is in mind (e.g. Lk. 19.38, where 'the King' is inserted into the quotation of Ps. 118.26a). John is aware of this interpretative tradition, but he has his own understanding of the idea of the Kingdom in terms of eternal life (cf. 3.3, 5, 16). Jesus is the Messiah, but this means to John that he is the giver of eternal life (cf. 4.14, 26). It is axiomatic that this cannot be properly understood before the Resurrection. In spite of the difference of terminology, John's understanding of the event is in striking agreement with what appears to have been its actual significance for Jesus. The arrival of Jesus is the signal that God has come to his own. And as in the preaching of Jesus God comes in mercy to the outcast and in judgment to the proud, so in John Jesus arrives as the one to whom are delegated the divine prerogatives of giving eternal life and executing judgment (5.21f.).

12. The next day: for the expression, cf. 1.29, 35, 43. See also the note on verse 1. The rest of the verse presupposes the situation at the end of chapter 11.

13. branches of palm trees: lit. 'palm fronds of palm trees', so that it is not strictly necessary to mention the trees. But the compound also occurs in *Test. Naphtali*, v.4. Palms do not grow commonly in the uplands, and they were usually brought up from the Jordan valley when required for ceremonial use. They were regularly used for the *lūlāb* at the feast of Tabernacles (cf. the notes on 7.2, 37), and 1 Mac. 13.51 tells how they were used in the victory procession after the capture of the citadel of Jerusalem in 141 B.C. Matthew and Mark do not mention palms, but suggest that the disciples spontaneously cut branches of the trees growing in the locality. This suggests that the event has been reinterpreted in the course of the transmission of the tradition as a victory procession, or more likely as an equivalent of the Tabernacles procession for the water-pouring. This is all the more probable, seeing that Ps. 118 was sung in connection with this ceremony. But if the palms only came into the tradition at a secondary stage, there is no warrant to assume that the entry of Jesus actually took place at the time of Tabernacles, six months before the Passover, as some scholars hold.

Hosanna!: the Greek transliteration of the Hebrew *hôšîaʿ-nnāʾ*

('Save us, we beseech thee!'), a liturgical cry in Ps. 118.25, thus immediately preceding the quotation which occupies most of the rest of this verse. The use of the Hebrew, instead of the LXX translation followed in the quotation, is more readily explained if the original tradition only contained Mk 11.10: 'Blessed is the kingdom of our father David that is coming! Hosanna in the highest!' This was based on Ps. 118.26, and included the liturgical cry from the preceding verse. The precise quotation, now given in Mk 11.9, came into the tradition later, as suggested above. Not unnaturally, 'Hosanna!' was inserted before it as time went on (so Matthew and John; in Mk 11.9 it is probably an interpolation, as it is omitted by D W and Old Latin, and it is not included in the corresponding point in Luke). The fact that Ps. 118 was used at the feast of Tabernacles does not mean that it was not used on other suitable occasions as well.

even the King of Israel: this addition to the quotation, explaining **he who comes** (cf. 11.27), is derived from Zech. 9.9, or from a related passage (see on verse 15). This has influenced John's text here in much the same way as in Lk. 19.38, though there is no interdependence between Luke and John at this point. The insertion of these words is important for John's purpose, because it is an explicit and unsolicited statement of the messiahship of Jesus on the part of the people, which will have a prominent place in the trial narrative.

14. found a young ass: i.e. appropriated one that happened to be handy. So far the demonstration has been entirely the spontaneous act of the crowd. We must assume that, according to John's picturing of the scene, the people have now met him as he approaches the city, and insist on bringing him in in triumph. The fact that Jesus rides an ass is important to John, for it is the key to the following quotation. It is thus reasonable to suppose, as suggested above, that John thinks of Jesus' action as in some sense correcting the crowd's nationalistic idea of messiahship. The word for **young ass** (*onarion*) is a diminutive form of the word for colt in the quotation, and not different from it in meaning; but John retains the tradition that the ass was new and unused (cf. Mk 11.2).

found probably comes from the source, cf. Mk 11.2, 4.

15. The quotation of Zech. 9.9 is composite and much abbreviated. Both these features are signs of careful exegetical work.

The text is based on the Hebrew, indicating that the work has been done in a Jewish-Christian environment. The opening words of the prophecy are: 'Rejoice greatly, O daughter of Zion! Shout aloud, O daughter of Jerusalem!' This has been not only reduced by half, but altered to read **Fear not,** probably under the influence of Zeph. 3.16. Other passages have been suggested, but this is the most likely on account of the contextual similarity. For the whole passage (Zeph. 3.14–20) makes an excellent commentary on Zech. 9.9, and Zeph. 3.15 may have supplied 'the King of Israel', which John has inserted in verse 13. The passage describes the blessings which will abound when God is present in the midst of the people as their King.

behold, your king is coming: here John's text follows Zechariah exactly; but after this it is abbreviated drastically. The prophecy continues: 'triumphant and victorious is he, humble and riding on an ass, on a colt the foal of an ass'. All the description of the King has been cut out, both his military glory and his humility. Attention is concentrated solely on the fact that he is **sitting on an ass's colt.** Here again the parallel phrases are reduced to one. But still the newness of the ass remains clear. It is this feature which has been the original reason why this passage has been correlated with the tradition of Jesus' entry into Jerusalem. Jesus arranged for an unused animal, because 'the Lord had need of it'; for only such would be suitable for a divine burden. The phrase in the prophecy, 'a colt the foal of an ass', appeared to reflect this, and so the connection between the event and the prophecy became established. John accepts, but appears not to stress, the *newness* of the ass, which is important for an earlier stage of the tradition. To him it is the fact that the King rides an *ass* which is the important thing.

16. His disciples . . . remembered: a vignette of the way in which the early Church's exegetical tradition was formed, which should be compared with 2.22. The application of the prophecy is an interpretation of the event. It defines the messiahship of Jesus in terms of what he eventually achieved. In the face of the disaster of the Cross, following so swiftly on the brief splendour of this event, the nationalist idea of messiahship could have no place in the disciples' thoughts. But they boldly proclaimed Jesus as the Messiah. One facet of their proclamation was the fact that Jesus had fulfilled the messianic prophecies in the events of his life. Jesus riding on a new ass is one event which can be linked with such a prophecy. At the same time, the nature of the messianic kingdom has to be redefined in line with Jesus' own teaching on the rule of God; it suits the idea of the king who comes in peace. Thus the interaction of memories of the life of Jesus, and scriptural passages which were seen to be prophetic of them, is the means by which the Church hammers out its doctrinal position. This is the process which lies behind the developed doctrinal position of John himself. It is also the process which is alluded to in this verse. John is careful to draw attention to the exact correspondence between what **had been written** in scripture about Jesus and what was actually **done to him.**

17. The crowd: this set of people is distinguished from the crowd which came to meet Jesus (verses 12 and 18). Apparently they have come with him from Bethany, and now they confirm the popular acclaim by bearing witness to the great event of the raising of Lazarus. This and the next verse must certainly be regarded as additions to the story, along with all the other references to Lazarus.

18. Not only does this group draw attention to the raising of Lazarus, but now it transpires that it was news of this miracle which had inspired the pilgrims in Jerusalem to take the initiative in making the demonstration in the first place. This is patently artificial, but it suits John's purpose for the second edition, in which the miracle is the reason for the priests' decision to put Jesus to death.

19. The Pharisees are alarmed at the popularity of Jesus. The verse is a comment on the event as a whole, and not just evoked by the last two (additional) verses. Originally it formed a punctuation mark between the entry into Jerusalem and the cleansing of the Temple. The thought is then picked up at the meeting of the Sanhedrin, now placed at 11.47f., where the growing popularity of Jesus is the reason for deciding to take action. But in the present order of the text it suggests that, in spite of the fact that the decision has been taken to get rid of Jesus, the Pharisees fear that it will be impossible to carry it out. This verse has its Synoptic counterpart in Mk 11.18.

the world: i.e. everybody. But perhaps the expression is also intended to convey a hint of the universal salvation, cf. 11.52.

DISCOURSE ON SACRIFICE 12.20–36a

The raising of Lazarus and the entry into Jerusalem (or—to put it in terms of the original plan—the entry into Jerusalem and the cleansing of the Temple) are grand events which point forward to the future glory of Jesus in the Resurrection. At the same time they precipitate his death. In the unconscious prophecy of Caiaphas (11.50–2) these two themes merge into one. The death of Jesus is the means of new life for all the scattered children of God. Jesus' resurrection 'in three days' (2.20f.) includes more than the raising of 'his body' (i.e. himself; see the notes on 2.21). It effects salvation for all. Having brought this point to expression (in the original ordering at 11.52, but even in the present arrangement it is hinted at in 12.19), the moment has arrived for John to explain *why* the death of Jesus is necessary to achieve salvation. John starts with the widest scope of salvation: he introduces for the first and only time 'some Greeks', representatives of the Gentile Church which is to be. They cannot, of course, 'see Jesus' (verse 21), for the time of the Gentile mission has not been reached. But their presence inspires Jesus to give a parable, the seed which dies in order to be abundantly fruitful. This is followed by a short collection of sayings on the cost of discipleship. All these verses (23–6) have contacts with the Synoptic tradition. At verse 27 the scene changes. Jesus is now in the presence of 'the crowd'. He gives expression to the inner struggle involved in facing death, using words which reflect the Gethsemane tradition of the Synoptic Gospels; this moves the thought to the level of spiritual conflict. His death is the conquest of the spiritual powers, and by its attractive power involves men in his spiritual victory (verses 31f.). Finally the audience is warned that it is their own spiritual conflict which is at stake, for it is the crucial moment in the age-old struggle between light and darkness (verse 35f.).

The reader is now in a position to understand the chapters which follow. He will know that they are more than the history of a brave man who was condemned to death and was crucified and rose again from the dead. He will know that it is a history in which his own destiny before God is involved.

Death Leads to Life 20–6

20. Now among those . . . were: the Semitic-style narrative opening, as at 11.1.

Greeks: the word denotes all those who came within the orbit of Greek culture, and so often means Gentiles in Acts and the Pauline Epistles. It does not mean Greek-speaking Jews, who are designated Hellenists (Ac. 6.1). But it can be applied to proselytes (Jos. *BJ* VII.45) and to 'devout' Gentiles like Cornelius (Ac. 10.1f.) who were deeply attracted to Judaism because of its high monotheism and strong ethical basis, but were unwilling to be circumcised, and so break with their family background to become proselytes. As representatives of the Gentile Church, it is probably the latter who are meant here.

21. Philip: as he has a Greek name, it is possible that he was Greek-speaking—or at least that John thinks so, and so has chosen him for his role here. He has a similar 'missionary' role in 1.43–5, and is mentioned with Andrew in 6.5, 7. **Beth-saida** was to all intents and purposes within the Galilean setting of Jesus' ministry, though actually just over the border of Gaulanitis, part of the tetrarchy of Philip the brother of Herod.

see Jesus: the choice of word, natural as it is in the context, may be intended to anticipate the motif of 20.29. For the Church of the Gentiles had to believe without seeing Jesus.

22. Andrew: he also appears as a 'missionary' in 1.40–2. Jesus' reply is apparently addressed to these two alone. Alternatively Jesus may already be in the presence of the crowd of verse 29.

23. The hour is come: this verse is the text on which the whole of the ensuing discourse is hung. Brown thinks that its proper continuation is verse 27, so that 24–6 are an insertion (by John himself) into his original composition. But it is quite usual for John to refer back to the beginning of a discourse when he wishes to introduce a fresh stage in the argument. In this case he repeats the idea of **is come** in the emphatic 'now' in verse 27, and again in verse 31 for the next stage.

hour: according to 2.4 this is the time when Jesus manifests his glory, but the exact moment is unspecified. In 7.30 and 8.20 it is identified with the time when he is to be arrested. Now the decision of the Sanhedrin has been taken, and so the moment has almost arrived. It is the moment that will set in motion the whole process of the Death and Resurrection by which the Son of Man will be glorified. This will be the vindication of Jesus, already anticipating his heavenly glory as the Son of Man of Dan. 7; cf. 3.13f.; 8.28; 12.34; 13.31.

for . . . to be glorified: a final clause with *hina* ('in order that he may be glorified'), weakened to mean 'when he will be glorified'. But, in Semitic style, John does not distinguish sharply between purpose and consequence. It is the predestined moment.

24. Truly: characteristically John begins the first consideration of his text with an item from the tradition of the sayings of Jesus, indicated by the **truly** opening. In fact the first consideration is a collection of such sayings. They are all concerned with the idea of 'glorified' in verse 23. Glory follows the 'hour' of Jesus: and so in the same way abundant fruit follows the 'death' of a seed, eternal life follows the abandonment of one's life, a share in Jesus' glory follows the total generosity of true discipleship. Thus the seed parable of the present verse sets out the principle in general terms. Verse 25 applies this to personal behaviour. The argument requires that this is in the first instance a reference to Jesus' understanding of his own vocation, although it is the rule for disciples as well. Then in verse 26 the idea of discipleship is made explicit.

a grain: lit. 'the grain', the Semitic generic use of the definite article. The parable is probably a genuine saying of Jesus, but if so it is likely that the application has changed. The vocabulary is reminiscent of the seed parables of Mk 4, particularly the Sower (Mk 4.3–8) and the Seed Growing Secretly (Mk 4.26–9). These are concerned with the harvest of the Kingdom, but not with the necessity of death. On the other hand the grouping together of this parable with traditional sayings on the cost of discipleship suggests that it was applied to the idea of 'losing one's life in order to save it' from the first. It is a short step from there to the application of it to Jesus' own premonition of death, and his faith that his death will nevertheless be immensely fruitful.

These ideas are well within what we know of the teaching of Jesus, and consequently it can be confidently asserted that John has scarcely distorted Jesus' meaning here. On the other hand, Paul takes up this same parable and puts it to a new use as a metaphysical argument for the resurrection of the body (1 C. 15.35–41, especially 36f.: 'What you sow does not come to life unless it dies. And what you sow is . . . a bare kernel, perhaps of wheat or of some other grain'). There is no hint of this in John. The idea of the 'death' of the seed which is buried in the ground is a natural one, and there is no need to drag in the vast ramifications of the mythology of dying and rising gods of the vegetation cults of the ancient world in order to explain this parable. This would only come into question if Bultmann is right in assuming a Gnostic basis for the Johannine discourses. But the terms of reference are ethical and not metaphysical here, so that such ideas are excluded.

much fruit: cf. 15.1–8. The context into which John has inserted the parable implies that he is thinking of the Gentile mission. To this extent he goes beyond the original meaning of the parable, but it is a legitimate extension of it. It is this issue which explains why he has chosen to make the idea of death leading to life the theme of the *first* consideration of the text in verse 23, rather than the theme of the awfulness of the 'hour', which comes in the second (verse 27).

25. The principle enunciated by means of the parable is now applied to the personal behaviour of the Kingdom, i.e. that one must abandon one's life (life as a personal possession, apart from God) in order to gain one's life (life in its full meaning, in fellowship with God). The saying has close parallels in no less than five Synoptic passages: Mt. 10.39; 16.25; Mk 8.35; Lk. 9.24; 17.33. Dodd (*Historical Tradition*, pp. 338–43) has analysed John's text in relation to these, and concludes that John is using an independent form of the saying which has all the marks of authenticity. This did not include **in this world** and **for eternal life,** which are explanatory additions in typical Johannine vocabulary, and relate the saying to the present context of death and resurrection. Jesus' death will produce 'much fruit', and in facing death he is putting into practice this rule of behaviour.

loves . . . hates: these seem strong words, but according to Semitic usage they do not have the emotional intensity which we should give to them, when they are used as opposites. They merely express contrasting attitudes, and therefore preference; cf. Mt. 6.24.

26. If what Jesus does is the rule for all disciples, it follows that they will also share his glory. This is how it comes about that his death produces 'much fruit'. This saying does not have such close parallels with the Synoptic tradition, and indeed appears to be secondary, because of the amalgamation of distinct themes. We can begin by removing the last sentence. The second **if any one serves me** simply resumes the first, so as to make

the Father will honour him an exposition of **where I am, etc.**
This leaves two imperfectly balanced sentences. (a) **If any one
serves me, he must** (lit. let him) **follow me.** This mixes the
ideas of serving and following. They are both ways of speaking of
discipleship, and both occur in Synoptic sayings which have
thematic connection with verse 25. For **serves** (*diakonē*), cf. Mt.
20.26–8 (= Mk 10.43–5): 'Whoever would be great among you
must be your servant (*diakonos*) . . . even as the Son of man came
not to be served but to serve (*diakonēsai*), and to give his life a
ransom for many.' For **follow,** cf. Mt. 16.24 (= Mk 8.34): 'If
any man would come after me, let him deny himself and take up
his cross and follow me.' It is obvious that the saying here is an
adaptation of this second parallel, rather than the first. In fact it
is doubtful if the first is really relevant at all. **Serves** replaces
'would come after'. It is likely that it has come into the saying as a
result of the fusion of it with the second sentence, which we must
now examine. (b) **And where I am, there shall my servant**
(*diakonos*) **be also.** This has no close parallel. But a servant
(usually *doulos*) is a common enough character in the Synoptic
parables to justify the supposition that this sentence is a relic of
a saying or parable on the theme of reward for service. The
thought is most closely represented in Mt. 25.21, 23: 'Well done,
good and faithful servant . . . enter into the joy of your master.'
But compare also Mt. 24.45–7; Mk 13.34f.; Lk. 17.7. As the
vocabulary has no specially Johannine traits, it is likely that the
fusion took place in the pre-Johannine tradition. The result of the
fusion is that Jesus is represented as both the example and the
reward of discipleship. This suits John's purpose admirably.

Jesus Faces Death **27–30**

27. Now. resuming 'the hour is come' (verse 23).
is my soul troubled: the second consideration takes up what
would logically be the first point to deal with, the fact that the
appointed moment has arrived (or almost arrived). And it is a
moment of horror. So John makes use of the Gethsemane tradition. He expresses the emotion of Jesus in a phrase which recalls
11.33. It is certainly derived from the Psalms, possibly Ps. 42.6
(cf. the Synoptic parallel, 'my soul is very sorrowful' = Ps. 42.5a,
LXX) or Ps. 6.3 (cf. the next words, **save me,** = Ps. 6.4, LXX).
It is thus clear that John is not directly dependent on the Synoptic

version of this tradition, but rather on a variant form. In both cases the Psalms have been quarried to provide the words which express Jesus' emotion. This is just what we should expect. So also the writer of the Qumran *Thanksgiving Hymns* often uses psalm-tags in this way (e.g. Ps. 42.5a occurs in 1QH viii.32). The fact that John knew the Gethsemane tradition, in a form comparable to that of the Synoptists, is indicated not only by Jesus' withdrawal to the garden in 18.1, but also by the reference to his 'cup' (cf. Mk 14.36) in 18.11. See also the notes on 11.41.

And what shall I say: the quandary of Jesus is an index to the inner tension which he suffers. What follows can either be taken with a question mark at the end (as in *RSV*, *NEB*, *mg*), meaning Shall I make this kind of prayer? Or it can be taken with a full stop, so that it actually is the prayer which Jesus first prays (so *NEB*, text). In either case it is dismissed as soon as it has been brought to expression.

Father: cf. Mk 14.36 ('Abba, Father') and 11.41 above.

save me: another psalm-phrase; cf. Ps. 6.4.

from this hour: this not only refers back to verse 23, but also belongs to the Gethsemane tradition, from which, indeed, John may have derived his special use of the word. For in Mk 14.35 (alone of the Synoptists, but Mt. 26.39 definitely shows knowledge of it) we read: 'He . . . prayed that, if it were possible, the hour might pass from him.' But in the next verse the actual prayer is: 'Remove this cup from me.' The hour appears to be the moment of trial, the cup the sufferings which it brings.

No: lit. 'but', exactly as in Mk 14.36 ('*yet* not what I will'). The whole point of the story of the agony of Jesus is his triumph over the natural shrinking from the suffering that lies ahead.

for this purpose: i.e. to bring salvation. The irony is that Jesus cannot be saved from suffering, for it is the appointed means of achieving salvation.

28. glorify thy name: just as 'not what I will . . .' in Mk 14.36 reminds us of the clause: 'Thy will be done' in the Lord's Prayer, so these words recall 'Hallowed be thy name' (rendered 'Glorify your name' in a recent translation of the Lord's Prayer). It means 'act for your own glory', and so is roughly equivalent to the Synoptic words. In 13.31 we shall find that God wins for himself glory in the glorifying of the Son of Man. So in this petition Jesus acknowledges that he must go forward into the test of his 'hour'

so that he may be glorified as Son of Man (verse 23). Some MSS.
read: 'glorify your Son', but this is probably a correction on the
basis of verse 23 by those who found the expression difficult to
understand.

a voice came from heaven: cf. the Synoptic account of the
baptism of Jesus (Mt. 3.17 paras.), and also the transfiguration
(Mt. 17.5 paras.). But it is unlikely that John has either of these
in mind, as the following words bear no relation to the divine
utterance on these occasions. Nor is this a contradiction of the
impossibility of direct sight or hearing of God, which was asserted
in 5.37. It is a sound which can be variously understood as
thunder or an angel speaking, and which is interpreted in the
typically Johannine words which now follow. Possibly John's
source already contained some kind of assurance that Jesus'
prayer was heard, comparable to the strengthening angel in the
spurious verses which have come into the text of the Lucan account (Lk. 22.43). As Barrett points out, it is absurd to say that
the 'voice has come for' the crowd (verse 30) if it can be confused
with a thunder-clap—unless, that is, the noise of thunder is itself
sufficient to indicate divine assurance. But this may well be what
John means. The Greek word for **voice** (*phōnē*) means any kind
of noise, and does not necessarily denote speech. The Hebrew
qôl is similar, and when applied to God often refers to thunder
(cf. 1 Sam. 7.9f.: '. . . . And the Lord answered him . . . The
Lord thundered with a mighty voice . . .'). If this is the case here,
the actual words are an interpretation of the reassuring sound,
which re-echoes from the vault of heaven the words Jesus has
himself just spoken. God has **glorified** his name in that Jesus
has 'accomplished the work which thou gavest me to do' (17.4). He
will glorify it again in the final act which is just about to take
place (cf. 17.5).

29. If the above interpretation is right, the people's idea **that
it had thundered** must be taken to mean that John does not
wish the reader to suppose that this was a case of direct speech
from God, contrary to 5.37. That denial still holds good. But the
vivid belief of first-century Judaism in heavenly messengers suggests another possibility, that **an angel has spoken to him.**
This provides a middle way between regarding the sound simply
as thunder and interpreting it as direct speech of God, as the form
of the words in verse 28 implies. The mention of an angel raises

the question whether something like Lk. 22.43 stood in John's source; but the connection is not close enough to admit of a certain answer.

30. for your sake: as in 11.42, which has a close connection with this passage, Jesus does not himself require an external answer, because of his intimate relation with the Father. But he welcomes it, because it ratifies openly the spiritual victory which he has won in the agonizing moment of the prayer in verse 27.

The Conflict of Light and Darkness **31–6a**

31. Now: the third and final consideration of verse 23 starts from the fact that, morally, the victory is already won. It is the moment of **judgment of this world,** i.e. of this present age (*hā-ʿôlām haz-zeh*). The turning-point from the present world-order to the next, which is inaugurated with the eschatological judgment, has already been reached—or at least is anticipated in this decisive moment. It is therefore the moment when **the ruler of this world is cast out.** Obviously this is a reference to the Devil, called by the same title in 14.30 and 16.11, though there is no precise parallel for it in Jewish literature. But that it belongs to the Jewish background (ultimately derived from Iranian influence, Bultmann, p. 431, n. 2) need not be doubted, for the idea it represents agrees with that of the Angel of Darkness (Spirit of Error) in the Qumran Two Spirits doctrine (see above on 8.44). Cf. also Rev. 12.9, and especially 1 Jn 5.19. The title itself may be compared with 'the god of this world' in 2 C. 4.4 and 'the prince of the power of the air' in Eph. 2.2; cf. 6.12. It occurs in the form 'the ruler of this age (*aiōn*)' frequently in Ignatius (Eph. xvii.1; xix.1; Mag. i.3; Trall. iv.2; Rom. vii.1; Philad. vi.2). This is clearly an exact equivalent of John's phrase, but independent of John.

cast out: i.e. from his position of usurped authority. We are to assume that his fate is imagined in line with current apocalyptic speculations. But John is interested only in the fact of the devil's defeat, not in the pictorial details. Some MSS. (Θ Old Latin, Sinaitic Syriac, Sahidic) have 'cast down', bringing the thought into line with the Lucifer myth (Isa. 14.12–15; Rev. 12.7–9; cf. Lk. 10.18).

32. lifted up: the reverse aspect of the conquest of 'the ruler of this world' is that Jesus himself gains the mastery over all mankind,

and so God's plan of salvation is achieved. The words thus
refer primarily to the exaltation of Jesus as Son of Man (for this
is the hour 'for the Son of man to be glorified', verse 23). But the
phrase is carefully chosen, because it can also refer to the Cross
(3.14; 8:28). The victory, however, does not override man's will.
Jesus will gain the mastery, but it will not be by force. For the
Cross **will draw** (6.44) men by spiritual attraction. **All men**
(*pantas; panta* = all things, read by P^{66} ℵ* D Old Latin and
Vulgate, can hardly be right) denotes the universal scope of salvation, thus bringing in the thought of the Gentiles once more.

33. John does not wish to leave the matter merely as an assertion of victory. The point of the whole discourse is that the death
of Jesus is the necessary means of gaining it (cf. verse 27). The
double significance of 'lifted up' allows the meaning 'die on the
cross', and it is essential to make this clear. The paradox of the
situation is that both meanings are applicable. It should be
observed that the idea of the death of Jesus is only possible if
death on the cross is meant. 'Lifted up' could hardly be applied
to stoning.

34. The objection of the people, which is reminiscent of 7.27,
40-2, presupposes that they are fully aware that Jesus is alluding
to his death. It thus seems likely that we have here another item
of Jewish and Christian debate, in which the fact of Jesus' death
is held to be inconsistent with the Church's claim that he is the
Messiah. The people know that Jesus speaks of himself as the
Son of Man (this is clear in the opening text, verse 23), and their
manner of speaking tacitly identifies the Christ with the Son of
Man (rightly, according to both Jewish apocalyptic and Christian
teaching). **The law** (i.e. the OT) has many passages in which it
is asserted that **the Christ remains for ever,** if these words are
taken to mean eternal dominion; cf. Ps. 89.36; 110.4; Isa. 9.6f.;
Ezek. 37.25. The same idea is applied to **the Son of man** in
Dan. 7.14, which Hoskyns takes to be the actual passage intended
here. The argument is very clearly put by Trypho the Jew in
Justin *Dial.* xxxii: 'These and such like scriptures, sir, compel us
to wait for him who, as Son of Man, receives from the Ancient of
Days the everlasting Kingdom. But this so-called Christ of yours
was dishonourable and inglorious, so much so that the last curse
contained in the law of God fell on him, for he was crucified.'
The question is, then, whether one who is to be crucified can be

identified with the Messiah/Son of Man who **lives for ever.** It is
not, as Bernard and Barrett argue, that Jesus' idea of the Son of
Man does not fit with the established idea of the Messiah, so that
by claiming to be the one he cannot be the other. The contrast is
between what **the law** says and what **you** (emphatic) **say.** The
final question is, then, 'Who is this Messiah/Son of Man you are
talking about? (Certainly not the one we have heard about!)'

35. Jesus does not answer the question. Such misunderstanding
would never arise if the people responded to his teaching, and
now the judgment is imminent (verse 31) and it is too late to
begin all over again. So Jesus tells a parable, which forms a final
appeal to them to believe in him before it is too late. This parable,
which may be based on authentic tradition, is clearly a variant of
9.4 and 11.9f., and also has close links with 8.12. (a) The parable
is a word-picture of a traveller at sunset. He must make an effort
to finish the journey before the darkness overtakes him, or he will
lose his way. This is obviously a parable of crisis, comparable to
the parables of watchfulness in Mt. 24.42–51. (b) The opening
words, **The light is with you** (or, according to the best MSS., 'in
you', cf. 11.10) **for a little longer,** indicate the interpretation
which John places on the parable. The light is Jesus as the revelation of God (cf. 8.12), and **a little longer** refers to the approaching Passion (cf. 7.33; 16.16–19). The special mode of revelation
embodied in Jesus' life and ministry will soon be withdrawn. If
not accepted now, the chance of salvation will be lost. (c) It
seems probable, especially in the light of verse 31, that John also
has in mind the cosmic implications of the situation. The light
and the darkness are the cosmic forces which contend for the
possession of mankind. The people must either open themselves
to the light (identified with Jesus), or else be overwhelmed by the
darkness. This interpretation is implied by the use of the same
imagery in the Prologue (1.5), and also by the next verse.

36a. light . . . believe in . . . sons: the close connection with
the Prologue is maintained; cf. 1.9–12.
sons of light is a Semitic phrase ('people who are full of light';
cf. 'son of Belial' = worthless fellow). But it naturally carries with
it the implied contrast with those who are sons of darkness (cf.
1 Th. 5.5 and Eph. 5.8). In Lk. 16.8 the sons of light are contrasted with 'the sons of this world (lit. age)', where 'this age'
evidently has the same significance as John's expression in verse 31.

The sons of light and the sons of darkness are constantly contrasted in the Qumran literature (see especially 1QS iii.13–iv.26). For John God is light (1 Jn 1.5), and Jesus is the revealer of light. So the verse means: 'While Jesus is still available, entrust yourselves to him as the revelation of God, so that you may become God's children' (cf. 1.12).

THE BLINDNESS OF THE PEOPLE AND SUMMARY OF THE TEACHING OF JESUS 12.36b–50

The parable of verse 35 has turned the thought away from the particular disputed point to the wider issue of response to the Gospel as a whole. The references in it to the Prologue make an *inclusio*, bringing all the first twelve chapters under the heading of response to the light. John's final comments before beginning the Passion narrative drive the same point home. First, after symbolically putting out the light by making Jesus hide (36b), he explains the unbelief of the Jews in terms of blindness (verses 37–43). John is here following an established tradition of scriptural exegesis to cope with this problem, which we have already come across in 9.39. Secondly he appends a summary of the teaching of Jesus in the form of a monologue (verses 44–50). It is still concerned mainly with the theme of response. It starts with the metaphor of the light. Then the moral authority of Jesus' message of salvation is traced back to his unique relation to the Father. This paragraph presents two problems. (a) Jesus has no audience for his words. This has suggested to some commentators that the paragraph is not in its proper context. Bernard therefore transfers it to follow verse 36a. Bultmann attempts to reconstruct a discourse on the Light of the World, taking chapter 9 as the introduction, then 8.12, and finally 12.44–50 as the discourse based on this verse. (b) But these theories of transposition, apart from their intrinsic improbability, only make the second problem more acute. This is the fact that this paragraph falls below the standard of creative writing usual in the discourses. Almost every phrase has been used elsewhere, so that the whole paragraph appears to be a cento of Johannine sayings. Brown thinks that it is an unattached fragment of a discourse, perhaps a variant of 3.16–19, with which it has much in common. Its insertion here then has to be attributed to a later editor. If, however, John has felt the need to explain the unbelief of the Jews in verses 37–43, it is at least appropriate to put the opposite point, the value and the validity of belief, by contrast. The lower level of composition can be explained by the fact that it *is* a summary, drawn from the preceding chapters, and is not a piece of creative writing. John has used the verb 'cried out' (*ekraxen*) in a similar way of the Baptist in 1.15. There also it referred to the burden of the message in general, and was not attached to a particular occasion. For the possibility that this paragraph was composed specifically for the second edition; cf. p. 411 above.

Israel's Blindness 36b–43

36b. hid himself: this note, typical of John's editorial writing, is not so much a repetition of 11.54, denoting withdrawal from danger, as a symbolic statement that the period of public teaching is ended. Jesus will no more speak openly (cf. 7.3–10). It thus makes a suitable point to tackle the problem of unbelief.

37. signs: John usually uses this word in his editorial summaries. They are the revelatory acts which back up the teaching of Jesus and prove that he is the Messiah (see the notes on 10.41).

38. that the word . . . might be fulfilled: John's explanation takes the form of citing a prophecy (Isa. 53.1), introduced by this fulfilment-formula, which will recur with his quotations from now on. It is almost identical with the formula used by Matthew (e.g. Mt. 4.14). Its Semitic character is shown by the final clause, in which consequence and purpose are not clearly distinguished (cf. verse 23). The unbelief of the Jews is felt to be tragically inevitable. It is just what the prophet said would happen. Therefore even this is, in a sense, part of God's predetermined plan. John uses two quotations to make this point, both widely employed in primitive Christianity. First Isa. 53.1 foretells the *fact* of unbelief. Then, in verse 40, Isa. 6.10 provides the *reason* for unbelief. The second quotation must be considered primary from the point of view of the history of early Christian exegesis. The first differs from it in two important respects: (a) The text of Isa. 53.1 agrees exactly with the LXX, whereas that of Isa. 6.10 is abbreviated and based on the Hebrew. This implies that the work of exegesis, which began in Aramaic-speaking circles, has been carried over into the Greek-speaking community where of course the LXX is in use (so Paul's quotations are normally close to the LXX). It is at this stage that Isa. 53.1 has been brought into relation with Isa. 6.10 as a commentary on it. (b) The application of Isa. 53.1 to unbelief is secondary, for primarily this is part of the Passion prophecy, explaining why, contrary to expectation, the Messiah should suffer (cf. Lk. 24.26). The verse (which expects the answer 'no one') should be referred to this specific issue, whereas here it has been given a general application to the whole of Jesus' ministry. So also Paul independently applies the first half of the very same verse to the apostolic preaching in Rom. 10.16.

39. Therefore: the *RSV* punctuation wrongly makes it seem as if this sentence refers back to the preceding quotation. In fact it refers forward: 'This is the reason why it was not even possible for them to believe, viz. that Isaiah also said . . .'

40. Cf. 9.39, where other NT citations of the passage are listed in the notes. There the allusion was to Isa. 6.9, here to 6.10. It has been tailored to fit the application to spiritual blindness by the removal of all unnecessary phrases. First we notice the alteration of tense and subject of the opening words (past indicative with God as subject, instead of imperative, addressed to the prophet; so also LXX has past with the people themselves as subject). This is a permissible rendering of the Hebrew (infinitive absolute). More important, the sequence—heart, ears, eyes—has been changed to **eyes . . . heart** (the ears are omitted). So also sight comes before hearing in the non-LXX version of Isa. 6.9 of 9.39 and of Mk 4.12. This is because sight is the point of interest. Perception precedes understanding. John retains this sequence in the clause starting **lest,** whereas the original reverses the triad— eyes, ears, heart—for the sake of chiasmus. Only in the last phrase (**for me to heal them**) is John's text conformed to LXX, possibly replacing the interpretative non-LXX text of Mk 4.12 ('and be forgiven'), which was not so suitable for the present application. It will thus be seen that John's rendering is no mere loose quotation from memory, but is a Palestinian non-LXX form with strong Semitic colouring, though beginning to undergo modification in the direction of conformity with the LXX.

hardened: Gr. *epōrōsen* (= 'petrified'). The use of this word for the hardening of the heart (i.e. of the understanding), hence for obtuse insensibility, in Mk 6.52; 8.17; Rom. 11.7; 2 C. 3.14, and of the noun in Mk 3.5; Rom. 11.25; Eph. 4.18, may in every case go back to the occurrence of it in this important non-LXX form of Isa. 6.10. But P⁶⁶ P⁷⁵ ℵ W read here *epērōsen* (= 'maimed'). Sanders says this is original, the other being due to conformity with the NT texts cited. But it is also a variant at Mk 8.17; Rom. 11.7; Job 17.7 (LXX), which suggests a tendency to alteration in this direction. *Epōrōsen* is far more likely as a rendering of the Hebrew.

41. because he saw his glory: this is the reading of P⁶⁶ P⁷⁵ ℵ A B against the majority, which have 'when', and Θ Ferrar group and Coptic, which have 'because (or when) he saw the glory of God'. But these are corrections, to turn the verse into a kind of footnote, to tell the reader where to find the quotation. But John means that the theophany of Isa. 6.1ff. was a sight of the glory of the Logos (cf. 1.14, 18 and the notes on 5.37). He can also say that Isaiah **spoke of him,** because he 'saw the last things . . . and revealed what was to occur in the end of time' (Sir. 48.24f.). John is in line with the established Christian conviction that the OT prophecies all find their fulfilment in the Christ-event. So we have here a hint of how it came about that the Isaiah quotation could be applied to the present situation.

42. Nevertheless: the complaint of verse 37 has been too sweeping, for indeed John has repeatedly mentioned that there were those who responded to Jesus, including **many even of the authorities** (*archontōn*). This probably merely refers to Nicodemus (3.1; 7.50), but may also look forward to 19.38f., where Joseph of Arimathea is mentioned with him. The rest of the verse is virtually identical with 9.22, referring in fact to conditions which belong to a later time.

43. praise: the same word as 'glory' in verse 41 (*doxa*). See the notes on 5.44 and 7.48. It is a bitter comment on the quite natural hesitation of men in influential positions, who cannot lightly go against the opinion of the majority of their colleagues. John tends to see issues in black-and-white contrast, and does not easily make allowances for anything in between. His attitude is no doubt affected by the hardening opposition between Church and synagogue in his own day.

Summary of the Teaching of Jesus **44–50**

44. cried out: the verb used in 1.15 (see the introduction to this section) and 7.28, 37 ('proclaimed').

He who believes: the monologue begins with the authority of
Jesus, summarizing the argument of 5.19–47 (note especially
5.23). But the closest parallel to this and the next verse is yet to
be given in 13.20, a 'truly' saying, which (we have learnt to
expect) is derived from the tradition. In this case there is the
important evidence of Mk 9.37 paras. and Mt. 10.40; Lk. 10.16.
It is not too much to say that these sayings lie at the root of John's
Christology. See further on 5.23; 13.20.

45. sees: belief and sight are closely correlated in the Fourth
Gospel; cf. 6.40. Just as blindness leads to unbelief, so sight leads
to faith. John repeats the substance of 44 in this form, so as to
resume the light and darkness theme in the next verse.

46. light into the world: cf. 1.5; 8.12; 12.35f. Notice that
remain replaces 'walk' in the earlier passages, suggesting the
abiding effect of the decision for or against Jesus.

47. The purpose of Jesus' mission is not negative. So the unbelievers are not judged by him, but rather find themselves self-
condemned. This does not mean that Jesus does not perform the
function of judging (contrast 5.30), nor that his judgment differs
fundamentally from men's judgments (cf. 8.15), but that he does
not really *condemn* people (*krinein* means both judge and condemn),
for they condemn themselves. Thus **does not keep** (*phulassein* here
exceptionally for *tērein*) **them** (*NEB*: 'pays no regard to them')
refers to those who do not respond to the message of Jesus, not to
failure to keep specific commandments. Marsh aptly compares
the man who built his house on sand (Mt. 7.24–7). But the sentence has not unnaturally been misconstrued to mean keeping
commandments, and so the **not** (*NEB*: 'no') has been omitted by
P⁶⁶ᶜ D Θ and others, implying that Jesus *does* judge those who disobey. Many other MSS. ease the sense by reading 'believe' instead
of **keep.** The last part of the verse is almost a straight repetition
of 3.17.

48. It is now explained how the unbelievers are self-condemned.
Their response to **the word that I have spoken** during the
public ministry (or during its proclamation by the church) has
decided the final issue already. It is the correlative of the great
affirmation of 5.24. The thought sounds harsh. But John is not
concerned with the rights and wrongs of a doctrine of final
separation from God. His one object is that the reader should
make his decision now.

49. not . . . on my own authority: cf. 5.30; 7.16f. The soliloquy ends with a reassertion of Jesus' authority. In verses 44f. it was asserted that belief in Jesus is equivalent to response to the Father. Here the ultimate significance which has been attributed to Jesus' message is traced back to his obedience to the Father. It is the principle enunciated in 8.28f., which covers not only his teaching but also his acts, especially his acceptance of the Cross. **Commandment** (*entolē*) was applied to the Cross in this way in 10.18.

50. eternal life: the sentence is extremely condensed, summing up the process that has been set in motion by the coming of Christ: the Father's **commandment** is set out in Jesus' word, and, where there is response to it, it leads to **eternal life.** This takes the summary of the preceding chapters through to the fruitfulness of the Passion, cf. 12.23-6. But even so, this grand statement is not the last word. The final thought is of Jesus' humble obedience to the Father: **What I say, therefore, I say as the Father has bidden me.** This recalls the spiritual struggle of 12.27ff. At the same time it prepares the way for the theme of humble service in the Last Supper narrative of the next chapter. Jesus' obedience to the Father is not only the guarantee of the authenticity of his message. It is also the model for those who hear the message, the proper condition for a true response. This will be expounded in 13.12-20.

THE LAST SUPPER: JESUS AND THE DISCIPLES (i)
13.1-38

John's account of the Last Supper shows, perhaps more than any other part of the Fourth Gospel, his highly individual approach to his task as an evangelist. It is vividly imagined, like his best narrative-writing elsewhere, so that the reader can easily picture the scene. His dramatic skill, wringing every ounce of irony out of the situation, is superb, as he handles the theme of the traitor in the midst. It is evident that he writes on the basis of sources which were comparable to the Synoptic Gospels, so that what he says has a foundation in the tradition. But it is equally clear that he writes with a specific purpose, which is not identical with that of the Synoptic writers. His approach to the tradition is wholly dominated by his preoccupation with the theme of discipleship. The story begins with Jesus washing the disciples' feet (verses 1–11), and this is made the basis of a discourse on the relation of master and disciple (12–20). Then comes the questioning about the traitor, in which all the emphasis goes on the enormity of betrayal of trust involved in the breach of table fellowship (21–30). Finally the new commandment to love one another (31–5) and the forecast of Peter's denials (36–8) bring up further aspects of discipleship. But this is not all that John has to say on the subject. He has for good measure appended the Supper discourses, occupying the next three chapters, and the prayer of Jesus in chapter 17, which is another version of the Gethsemane prayer specially composed with this issue in mind. Obviously the subject of discipleship is one of immense importance to him. It can scarcely be doubted that it is because the state of the Christian community in his own day gives him deep concern.

Consequently, although the Supper has been expanded to a disproportionate length, the approach is selective. John does not use it as a basis for revelation of the person of Christ. The themes of the first half of the Gospel, including those of the necessity of the death of Jesus and the meaning of the Resurrection, are presupposed. John is looking forward to the actual life of the Church, when Christians know themselves to be united with Christ through their possession of the Holy Spirit. John pictures the scene at the Last Supper from the point of view of the problems of living together in the Christian community. It is as much a scene of the eucharistic assembly of the Church as of Jesus and the Twelve in the upper room.

The surprising thing about the narrative is that the institution of the Eucharist, which is the central feature of all the parallels (Mt. 26.17–30; Mk 14.12–26; Lk. 22.7–39; 1 C. 11.23–6), is omitted altogether. A glance at the Synoptic accounts, especially Luke's, will show, however, that the issues which John *does* take up are prominent in them too. But the complete silence of John on the Eucharist demands an explanation. It is scarcely likely that John's account of it fell out accidentally at the time when, according to the transposition theories, the material of chapters 13–17 was disarranged (Bernard). Nor can we seriously entertain the suggestion that the Eucharist was unknown in John's circle, for religious meals are too well attested both in Judaism and in the early Church for this to be probable. The Eucharist is certainly implied in 6.52–8. If these verses are to be ascribed to an ecclesiastical interpolator, why did he not make the much more obvious and necessary interpolation in chapter 13? It has been argued that John's reticence is due to the *disciplina arcani*, the rule that the most sacred truths are not to be divulged to outsiders, like pearls before swine. John's omission of the story of the baptism of Jesus might be explained in the same way. But John holds back nothing in this way (cf. 18.20), and in any case the rule of the *disciplina arcani* cannot be proved to go back before the third century (Justin seems quite unaware of it). Barrett, Sanders, Lohse (*NTS* VII (1961), pp. 110–25) and others explain it along the lines of the need to correct a false emphasis on the sacrament of the Eucharist. It is necessary to stress the word of Jesus which gives meaning, rather than the symbolic act which can become mere magic or ritualism. Bultmann asserts that the prayer of chapter 17 originally came after 13.30, and was intended to be a substitute for the words of institution. But this is contrary to John's literary method. John corrects false emphases by his special dialogue-feature, the deliberate misunderstanding which leads to revelation of the truth. In fact he has done precisely this in connection with the Eucharist in chapter 6. Even if that only belongs to the second edition, it is still hard to see how his silence in chapter 13 actually does anything to correct false ideas. It leaves his readers to go on holding them in blissful ignorance. Hoskyns consistently takes the line that John's readers are familiar with the Synoptic Gospels, and so assumes that John leaves it out, in common with much else, as he wishes only to concentrate on particular points. So John presupposes the Eucharist. This explanation cannot now be accepted in the face of the considerable evidence that John did not know the Synoptics in the form in which we have them. We can only be sure that he knew such items of the tradition as he actually mentions. However, if 6.52–8 is not an interpolation, there is good reason to believe that he was familiar with this item. It is probably better to assume that he can presuppose it because of the setting which belongs to all John's discourses, the Eucharist itself. If the Gospel is based on homilies preached at the eucharistic assembly, it is likely (if not absolutely certain) that the words of institution would be recited in the course of the liturgy itself, as they are in all except one of the known liturgies of the ancient Church. On this basis Hoskyns' point of view is right. In his homilies John selects a particular theme for treatment. When he works them up into a Gospel he does not necessarily use all the narrative material at his disposal. For his Last Supper account he has used a homily on the subject of table fellowship which is based on the tradition known to us from the Synoptic Gospels. The fact that it is a sacred meal is clear enough. The words of institution are not included, because they are not relevant to the theme of the homily. On the other hand the idea of communion comes into other homilies (chapter 14, mutual indwelling; chapter 15, the allegory of the vine; cf. Mk 14.25; chapter 6, the bread of life). But it is structurally impossible to include the words of institution at any of these other points. There is an equally glaring omission at 18.1, where Jesus goes to Gethsemane according to the Synoptic scheme, and not a word is said about the agony for which alone it is memorable. But of course John uses the Gethsemane material elsewhere, as we have seen. And by transferring it to other positions (chapters 12 and 17) John has had to put it into quite a different form. This is exactly what he has done with the tradition of the words of institution. He had no idea what a disproportionate part these words would play in the theological controversies of the Western Church; otherwise no doubt he would have made sure of fitting them into chapter 13 somehow. His teaching would have still been the same.

One other point of introduction must be faced. John makes it quite clear that he does not regard the Last Supper as the Passover meal. The Synoptists are equally definite that it was. Is John altering the Synoptic tradition, and if so what is his reason? Alternatively, does the Synoptic tradition alter the original tradition, and if so why? No solution is satisfactory which does not answer *all* these questions. The motive in both cases is to bring the death of Jesus into close relation with the celebration of the Passover; cf. 1 C. 5.7f. The early Eucharist was not tied to the Passover, an annual celebration, but was held weekly, if not daily (Ac. 2.42, 46), but it gained its significance from the death and Resurrection of Jesus at Passover time. The Eucharist was a continuation of the fellowship meals of Jesus and the disciples, which certainly did not begin (and end) with the Last Supper. The Passover significance, so to speak, which must now attach to that meal can be secured either by making the meal itself the

Passover (Synoptics), or by timing Jesus' death which it com-
memorates with the slaying of the Passover lambs (John). If
John's timing is right, the Last Supper has subsequently acquired
the status of the Passover meal, in spite of destroying the exact
correlation of Jesus' death and the slaughter of the lambs, and in
spite of the fact that the Eucharist did not need to be invested
with this status. This is scarcely convincing. If the Synoptics are
right, John has abandoned the identification of the meal with the
Passover in order to gain the correlation with Jesus' death. This
change coincides with the reduction of the account of the Last
Supper to the eucharistic words, which may be used at any sacred
meal where bread and wine are blessed (e.g. 1 C. 11.23–6).

The *prima facie* case goes against John. We must now turn to
hints in the narratives themselves. First, the haste to conclude the
trial before the Sabbath (Synoptics) or before the feast-day (John).
According to the laws in the Mishnah (*Sanhedrin*, iv.1), neither of
these is possible. In capital cases the trial must be held during the
day-time, and the verdict of guilty cannot be given until the next
day, and it must also be in the day-time. Hence a trial may not
even be held on the day before the Sabbath, for this would still
mean convening the court for the verdict on the Sabbath itself.
The same rule applies to feast-days, which for this purpose are
treated like Sabbaths. But these rules do not necessarily apply so
early as the time of Jesus. Trial during the night and verdict on
the same day may still have been permitted in exceptional circumstances. Moreover the tractate *Yom Tob* (or *Betzah*) shows
that the application of Sabbath rules to feast-days was still in
dispute over a number of issues. Although it records no dispute
over trials (5.2), the rules may have been more flexible in the
time of Jesus. If so, the Synoptists may be right to represent the
trial on the feast-day; John may reflect the influence of later
legislation. Secondly, the narrative even of John himself appears
to reflect the customs of the Passover meal. Reclining at table,
the giving of the morsel, and the fact that it was night, all suggest
this (for details see the notes). It looks as if John's homily pictured
it as Passover, even though his narrative framework denies it. If
so, he has made the change himself in the course of constructing
his Gospel, but has not followed it through consistently. Thirdly,
the same inconsistency appears in 19.31, where John agrees with
the Synoptics that the next day was to be the Sabbath. But by

his reckoning the Sabbath is in fact the feast-day, and he notes this fact in parenthesis. Comparison with Mk 15.42 suggests that there was no indication that it was the feast-day in his source.

An ingenious attempt to cut through these problems has been made by A. Jaubert (*La Date de la Cène* (1957)). She holds that more than one system of reckoning the date of the Passover existed in NT times. This could be deduced from patristic references, but their reliability as evidence was until recently open to doubt. But now the Dead Sea Scrolls have revealed a sect which apparently followed the fixed calendar of the *Book of Jubilees*, whereby Passover is *always* on Wednesday (the meal, then, on Tuesday night). If Jesus and the disciples used the same calendar, the Last Supper would have been a real Passover, but on Tuesday. The death of Jesus was on the eve of the official Passover, Friday, as John asserts. This leaves Wednesday and Thursday for the trial and verdict before the eve, as the Mishnaic law requires. Everything fits—except for one vital factor: John himself is completely ignorant of this scheme. He still has the trials during the night and early morning, and the death of Jesus on the same day. It is difficult to eradicate the impression that the death of Jesus on the eve of the Passover is a purely Johannine invention, dictated by his theological interests, regardless of the traditions which he was actually handling (cf. 1.29; 19.36).

Finally, Lk. 22.15f. has been taken as evidence that the meal was not the Passover, but some kind of preparation for it (not, of course, the Kiddush, as that was not a preliminary meal, but the blessing of the meal itself; cf. J. Jeremias, *The Eucharistic Words of Jesus* (1966²), pp. 26–9). But this is by no means the most likely interpretation of this perplexing passage; cf. Mk 14.25 paras.

JESUS WASHES THE DISCIPLES' FEET 13.1–20

John's story of the Last Supper begins with an action which is not a special part of the Passover ceremonies as such, but is a normal feature of eastern hospitality (cf. Lk. 7.44). But of course it should have been done on arrival, not after all have taken their places for the meal (verse 4). This at once singles it out as something out of the ordinary. What is more surprising is that Jesus performs the task himself. It was the task of a slave, though sometimes a disciple might wash the feet of a rabbi (*SB* II.557). The lesson is obvious: in the Kingdom of God the roles are reversed. The point is made explicitly in verses 13–15. It exactly corresponds with the words of Jesus in Lk. 22.27: 'For which is greater, one who sits at table, or one who serves? Is it not the one who sits at table? But I am among you as one who serves.'

The Lucan parallel is striking, and at once raises the question whether the episode is based on authentic tradition, or has been created by John out of the Lucan saying, or one similar to it. We can be confident that he did not take it simply from the Lucan narrative. John's narratives of the Passion and Resurrection have certain features in common with the special material of Luke, it is true. But these are better explained on the assumption that John's available source material included items which have also been used by Luke. In this case there was a tradition similar to Lk. 22.27 in the Last Supper material. It cannot be excluded that this may have been accompanied by an anecdote in which Jesus put this into practice in a symbolic action, as here described. The saying in Luke is attached to the dispute between the disciples on their future positions in the kingdom (Lk. 22.24–6). This has a parallel in Mt. 20.25–8 (= Mk 10.42–5), which does not include the saying of Lk. 22.27. The theme of the master serving the servants also appears in Lk. 12.37, again an addition to its context; cf. also Lk. 17.7–10. It is thus arguable that there were various sayings on this topic including an anecdote in which Jesus demonstrates the point. Of course this may have been evolved from one of the sayings, but if so this might well have happened before it reached John. There is no reason to suppose that he simply invents it. The incident is unknown from other sources, except for a reference to the lost *Gospel of the Hebrews* in a medieval *History of the Passion of the Lord*, presumably based on John (see on verse 5).

The original tradition probably included only the information in verses 4, 5, 12–15. Brown takes the whole of verses 2–11 as a unit, regarding 12–15 as a second interpretation of the washing. But this disregards John's methods of building on traditional material, expanding it with dialogue, and often singling out a particular person (cf. his handling of the resurrection traditions in chapter 20). Here the dialogue in verses 6–11 relates the washing to the doctrine of the unique sacrifice of Jesus on the Cross. Then further teaching in 16–20 draws out the implications of Jesus' example of humility for the theology of the Church.

The Foot-Washing **1.1–11**

1.1 before the feast: the expression is similar to 12.1, but without specifying which day. The sequel, however, shows that John means the night before the Passover.

when Jesus knew: lit. 'knowing', as in verse 3. The circumstances which give meaning to the foot-washing are first put in general terms, applying to the whole history of the Passion. The piling up of participial clauses is unusual in John, and gives a most solemn effect. The circumstances are **that his hour had come;** cf. 12.23. Here, as there, the phrase is construed with *hina*. This means that he must now **depart out of this world,** i.e. from the present age (*hā-ʿōlām haz-zeh,* cf. 12.25). It is thus an eschatological event, anticipating the transition to the Age to Come (*hā-ʿōlām hab-bāʾ*). Jesus goes **to the Father;** cf. 7.33. He has completed his earthly ministry, apart from the one remaining act of the Passion itself. This is expressed in the words **having loved** (cf. 3.16) **his own** (cf. 1.11) **who were in the world.** The reference is to all believers, 'his own sheep' (10.3f.), not just to the disciples, though in the present context they represent them. The word **loved** has been chosen to describe Jesus' ministry to prepare for the new commandment of verse 34.

What applies to the ministry applies *par excellence* to the Passion itself. Jesus **loved them to the end.** Bernard points out that the aorist **loved** must refer to a specific act, and takes it to mean the foot-washing as a special manifestation of Jesus' love. But it is only one supporting item (cf. verse 34). There is a double meaning in **to the end,** for it can be meant literally (cf. Mt. 10.22, and 19.30 below), or it may mean 'completely' 'to the uttermost' (cf. 1 Th. 2.16), and both ideas seem to be present here.

2. during supper: having set out the circumstances of the Passion, John now sets out the circumstances of the supper, to some extent going over the same ground. This phrase corresponds with 'before the feast of the Passover' in verse 1. The timeless **during supper,** for AV 'supper being ended', is certainly right (reading *ginomenou* with ℵ* B W against the majority *genomenou,* which is a natural change in transcription). For **supper,** cf. 12.2.

when the devil: the attendant circumstances are mentioned in the reverse order, so that we now have the counterpart to the last point made in verse 1, although it is the complete antithesis to it. The juxtaposition of Jesus' love, which is the rule of true discipleship, and the Devil's mastery over Judas, is extremely effective. This is the first hint of the irony which runs through the entire chapter. This note about Judas is one of the special links with the Lucan material. All three Synoptics mention Judas' act of betrayal immediately before recounting the Last Supper. Lk. 22.3, however, begins with the words: 'Then Satan entered into Judas called Iscariot . . .' That John knew these precise words is shown in verse 27, where he actually says 'Satan entered' when he takes up this idea again. Here he uses his own vocabulary. For **devil,** cf. 8.44 (also 6.70). **Put** is *ballein* ('throw') in the weakened sense, which is very common in John (cf. 5.7; 12.6; 13.5; 18.11; 20.25, 27). For another example of John's use of a traditional saying twice, first with his own vocabulary and secondly with traditional vocabulary; cf. 8.51f. It follows that verse 27 decides the meaning, that **the devil had . . . put it into the heart of Judas . . . to betray him,** which is the text read by nearly all mss. But the reading of B ℵ* is to be preferred, in spite of apparently giving a different meaning: 'the devil had already put into the heart that Judas . . . should betray him'. This seems to mean the Devil's own heart, i.e. he had made up his mind (so Barrett). But this makes nonsense of the word **put,** and Bernard is surely right in asserting that John intends what the *received text*, smoothing out the grammar, actually says. **Iscariot, Simon's son** shows the same textual variations as in 6.71; 12.4.

3. **knowing:** cf. verse 1. We now have the counterpart to the first part of that verse. So **that the Father had given all things into his hands** corresponds with 'his hour had come'. But whereas that referred to the predestined moment, this refers to the predestined function. To Jesus is given the responsibility of taking the action by which the world's redemption is achieved. In the context of the foot-washing this heightens the paradox of his example of humility. The phrase is almost identical with 3.35, which also refers to Jesus' unique responsibility. Finally the paradox is pressed home by showing how this moment, which is the start of the Passion, is the turning-point in the grand movement of redemption, that Jesus **had come from God** (7.28; 8.42), and now **was going to God** (7.33; 8.21f.).

4. **rose from supper:** at last the anecdote begins. Jesus **rose**

from the meal, because he had been reclining, as was customary
for the Passover (see below on verse 23).

laid aside his garments: it is fanciful to see here a symbol of
'laying down' his life (10.11, 15, 17f.), though the same verb is
used. Jesus strips for action, like a slave.

    5. a basin: Gr. *niptēr.* By chance this word is never used else-
where in classical or *koiné* Greek (*AG* mentions one Cyprian
inscription from Roman times where it occurs). Brown insists
that the word means a pitcher, as washing was always done by
pouring. For **wipe,** cf. 12.3. Apparently the *Gospel of the Hebrews*
said that Jesus kissed the disciples' feet as well as washing them,
perhaps on the analogy of Lk. 7.38.

    6. Simon Peter: only mentioned so far in 1.40-2, 44, and
6.8, 68, but he will have a prominent part in chapters 18–21. To
John Peter is one who does not understand the necessity of the
Passion. He represents faith without understanding. It is possible
that John has constructed the dialogue here with the parallel of
Peter's failure at Caesarea Philippi in mind (Mk 8.31–3 paras.).
That John knew this tradition is indicated by 6.66–9. The dia-
logue also balances that of verses 36–8.

do you wash my feet: the words **you** and **my** are juxtaposed
in the Greek, emphasizing the paradoxical reversal of roles.

    7. afterward: this is said too emphatically to mean 'in a
minute or two', i.e. at verses 12–14. In any case that is an explanation of the fact that Jesus does the menial task, which is not the
point at issue, though Peter thinks it is. For Jesus here is referring
to the meaning of the washing as such. That is significant itself,
and demands explanation. But this can only be given in the light
of subsequent events, and obviously that means the Passion and
Resurrection. Thus the **now/afterward** contrast alerts the
reader to see in the act of washing the feet something to do with
the meaning of the Passion.

    8. never: this is very emphatic. Peter persists in thinking only
of the impropriety of being washed by his Master.

you have no part in me: Jesus puts the opposite point just as
strongly. Being washed by Jesus is necessary to being counted one
of his company (for the phrase, cf. Mt. 24.51, which means literally
'he will set his lot with the hypocrites'). Evidently this is symbolic
of a cleansing action which confers membership in Christ. We
begin to think that John must be referring to the sacrament of

baptism, which is described by Paul as participation in Christ's Death and Resurrection (cf. Rom. 6.1–11). This is denied by Bernard and Bultmann, but accepted by Barrett and Sanders. The question turns on the interpretation of verse 10.

9. also my hands and my head: Peter's response is evoked by the thought that he might be excluded from his part in Jesus, and so amounts to a strong expression of loyalty. Apparently he thinks of the washing quantitatively, as if more washing would secure a better place. But of course John is constructing the dialogue with his usual skill. Peter's misunderstanding is designed to show that the washing means something different from ordinary washing, cf. 4.10–15.

10. The reply of Jesus is difficult to interpret because of textual confusion. The words **except for his feet** are omitted by ‭א‬ c Vulgate and Origen. The variants in other MSS. betray uncertainty. The textual evidence thus suggests that they are not original, but have been added in an attempt to clarify the sense. The short text is accepted by Barrett, Bultmann and Hoskyns, and is certainly to be preferred if it will yield a suitable meaning. In fact it produces an excellent sense, when two observations are borne in mind. The first is that it is not a direct reply to Peter's exclamation, but a proverbial saying or parable (Bultmann). The second is that the verbs for **bathed** (*louesthai*) and **wash** (*niptein*) are not contrasted, but are synonyms, as so often when John uses pairs of words (Barrett). The saying can thus be translated: 'He who has washed does not need to wash, but is clean all over.' In other words, there is no need to wash twice (cp. *NEB*). In the present context this means that the foot-washing represents an act which is done once for all, and Jesus can comment **'you are clean'.** In the light of the Passion and Resurrection the disciples will know that this means atonement. They are cleansed from sin once and for all (cf. 1.29). The reference to baptism is made no clearer. But what John is saying is certainly close to the theology of baptism. The additional words in the *textus receptus* have given rise to grotesque contortions of exegesis. The plain meaning (probably intended by the interpolator) is that a person who has had a ritual bath at home before coming to the dinner (a well-attested Jewish custom) only needs to have his feet washed on arrival, and is ceremonially completely pure. But Holtzmann took it to mean that standing in water up to the ankles for baptismal infusion is

sufficient in place of total immersion! Even Sanders argues that the
bath means the cleansing effect of Christ's death, but this still
leaves the need for a further token washing of the feet, i.e. the
sacramental act of baptism whereby the benefits of his death are
appropriated by the individual. Bernard thinks that the washing
of the feet alone is quite sufficient for the real purpose that Jesus
has in mind, i.e. the lesson in humble service which he will give in
verses 12–15. This renders the whole dialogue with Peter futile.
but not all of you: from John's point of view Judas is self-
excluded from the atoning efficacy of Jesus' death. In spite of
being washed like the rest, his heart is not true (verse 2), and he
can have no part in Jesus. John is preparing the reader for the
fact that even his participation in the Eucharist will be of no
avail (verse 27).

  11. he knew who was to betray him: cf. 6.70f. The rest of
the verse is missing from D and the Palestinian Syriac version,
and may be a gloss. But the repetition is certainly effective.

The Example of the Master 12–20

  12. The anecdote is resumed after the intrusion of the dialogue
of verses 6–11. The act of washing finished, Jesus reclines once
more (**resumed his place**) and addresses the assembled company. It is a monologue, beginning with a rhetorical question.

  13. Teacher and Lord: the words are, ungrammatically,
nominative with the article, perhaps representing the Semitic
vocative (*BDF* §§ 143, 147.3). They correspond with *rabbi* and
mari, both titles of respect. It is noteworthy that Jesus does not
repudiate these titles. He is not arguing for the abolition of rank
and authority in the Church.

  14. There is independent evidence that the details of the Passion
narrative were used for moral example in the instruction of cate-
chumens in 1 Peter, where slaves are specially singled out for
mention (1 Pet. 2.18–25). In 1 Tim. 5.10 to have 'washed the
feet of the saints' is one of the qualifications for the order of
widows in the Church.

  16. Truly: the exposition of the foot-washing as moral example
is ended, but John now gives further teaching on the basis of it.
He uses for this purpose a traditional saying (indicated by the
truly opening), which has a close parallel in Mt. 10.24 (cf. also
Lk. 6.40). The Matthean context is persecution, so that the saying

makes the point that the disciples cannot expect to escape the obloquy which is accorded to their Master. John knows that this is its context, as he uses the saying again to teach precisely this lesson in 15.20. Mt. 10.24 pairs disciple and teacher, servant and master. John (or his source) has varied this to **servant** and **master, one who is sent** (*apostolos*) and **he who sent him** (*pempsantos*). The word *apostolos* (Hebrew *šālîaḥ*) has a quasi-technical meaning for an accredited representative (cf. K. H. Rengstorf, *TDNT* I, pp. 413–20). It is also the word 'apostle' regularly applied to the Twelve in the Synoptic Gospels and Acts, but never in John. But no doubt there is an intentional allusion to the status of the Twelve here. For the synonymous use of *apostellein* (passive forms) and *pempein* (active) in John, cf. 9.4, 7.

17. The point is driven home with a beatitude, which has a faint parallel in Lk. 11.28, and may have a traditional basis. The words **if you do them** are missing from e and Sinaitic Syriac, and may be a gloss (Barrett notes that **them** has no particular reference; it does not quite mean: 'if you act upon them, i.e. these things I have spoken'). The emphasis which John places upon this teaching may well be due to his concern at the growing tendency to abuse authority in the Church of his own day.

18. The beatitude of verse 17 appears to apply to all the disciples, just like 'you are clean' in verse 10. So here again Jesus must correct himself, because it does not apply to all. Judas has put himself outside the scope of the blessings that result from true discipleship. This context of thought raises the thorny question why Jesus should have made the mistake of including Judas in the first place. John will not allow that it was a mistake: **'I know whom I have chosen.'** (For **chosen,** cf. 6.70; 15.16.) But this does not prevent him from recording that Jesus' foreknowledge of Judas' failure caused him the greatest distress (verse 21). The situation was not so simple that Jesus could expose his intentions and take action to avoid the consequences. According to John's narrative, Judas has still done nothing treacherous as yet (see the notes on 12.6). This does not happen until verse 27, and we shall see that John probably intends the giving of the morsel to be a last appeal by Jesus to him to reconsider his intentions. That means that Jesus always knew Judas would betray him, but always hoped that he would not. Nevertheless, on reflection it could be seen by the early Church that it was inevitable. And John here reproduces a scriptural explanation of Judas' conduct which is derived from this reflection. Judas' treachery was extremely embarrassing to the early Church, and gave rise not only to a special work of scriptural exegesis, but also to a Judas-legend associated with it (Mt. 27.3–10; Ac. 1.16–20). John here gives one of the texts used in this work. The argument is: Certain texts show that there will be a traitor; Judas actually was a traitor; therefore, when Judas betrays Jesus, **it is that the scripture may be fulfilled.** As before (12.38) consequence and purpose are confused. What is seen to have been inevitable by hindsight is represented as known by foresight.

He who ate my bread: the quotation is from Ps. 41.9. Again the non-LXX form of the text suggests that it has been selected in a Palestinian milieu. This psalm—one of many which could be applied to Jesus as the righteous sufferer (cf. 12.27)—was specially valuable for the problem of Judas, because it stresses the enormity of the breach of table fellowship on the part of the psalmist's enemy. It is precisely this motif which accounts for the prominence of the theme of the traitor in all the Last Supper narratives. There is probably allusion to the same verse of Ps. 41 in 'one who is eating with me' and 'one who is dipping bread in the same dish with me' in Mk 14.18, 20. Mark's repeated 'with me' is likely to be the true text in John's quotation (i.e. 'He who ate bread with me . . .'), as in P⁶⁶ℵ A D W Θ and the *textus receptus* (so *NEB*), against **my** of B C L, which brings the quotation into closer conformity with both the Hebrew and the LXX. On the other hand the majority reading could be due to assimilation to the Synoptic parallels.

has lifted his heel against me: the Hebrew and LXX have 'has made great the heel against me', and the exact meaning of this is disputed (caused me a great fall by tripping me up?), and some editors suspect textual corruption. John's quotation is interpretative, and perhaps means 'has kicked me from behind', i.e. treacherously (cf. G. B. Caird, *JTS*, n.s. xx (1969), p. 32). *NEB* 'has turned against me' is too weak. Barrett's 'has shaken off the dust from his feet against me in scorn' is hardly right, though E. F. F. Bishop (*ET* LXX (1958–9), pp. 331f.) claims that to lift up the heel—i.e. show the sole of one's foot—is regarded by Arabs as an insult.

19. The failure of Judas might well cast doubt on Jesus' dis-

cernment, and so on his status as God's own representative. To
forestall such an objection John emphasizes Jesus' foreknowledge
once more, and shows that it leads to the opposite conclusion,
that Jesus *is* the one sent by the Father. This is expressed in a way
that is familiar enough, but rather unexpected in the present context, that **you may believe that I am he** (*egō eimi*). It is precisely
the same argument as 8.28 (see the notes on 8.24 for the special
use of *egō eimi*). That passage almost certainly contained allusion
to the theology of Deutero-Isaiah, especially Isa. 43.10. One aspect
of this theology is that Yahweh is known to be the real God, by
contrast with the idols of Babylon, because his word uttered in
prophecy comes true, and he has foreknowledge of the saving
events (cf. Isa. 43.9–13). It thus looks as if John has thought
through the argument from prophecy, which he has taken over
from the Church's exegetical tradition, in the light of Deutero-
Isaiah. He is thus able to see the almost petty concentration on
scriptural fulfilments, such as he has just reproduced, in the larger
and deeper perspective of the total plan of redemption. This verse
will be substantially repeated in 14.29.

   20. he who receives any one whom I send: the final words
of exposition of the foot-washing disregard the digression introduced by the Judas theme, and revert to the subject of discipleship. It is a comment on *apostolos* in verse 16, drawn (as the **truly**
opening implies) from the tradition. The connection is so close
that one cannot escape the conclusion that these two sayings had
already been linked together in the underlying tradition, before
John welded them into his Last Supper narrative. John has already
used this saying in rather different forms in 5.23; 12.44f. It is
found in a number of different forms in the Synoptic Gospels.
Dodd argues persuasively that John is not dependent on them, but
on an independent tradition, which he has not altered significantly
in introducing it into its present context (*Historical Tradition*, pp.
343–7). The saying comes in the Synoptic tradition in two different, but related, connections: in Mt. 10.40 = Lk. 10.16 it is
included in the mission charge of the Twelve, and so addressed to
them directly. This seems to be a particularized form of what is
still a general saying in John, although he means it to have the
same reference to the Twelve personally. But the general form
survives in Mk 9.37 paras., where it is used to inculcate humility.
In fact the situation is very similar to that which has produced

the whole story of the foot-washing. It is a dispute among the
disciples about future greatness (cf. Lk. 22.24–7). But in this version Jesus points to a child, and says that even a child should
receive the respect due to himself if it has his authority as his
accredited representative, and similarly his own authority is derived from God. Hence he cannot claim any greatness for himself,
apart from his position as the Father's deputy. The child is a
secondary feature of the saying, so that the original form may have
been: 'Whoever receives anyone in my name receives me; and
whoever receives me receives him who sent me.' The meaning of
'in my name' (*epi to onomati mou*) is uncertain, but John's **whom I
send** may well be the correct interpretation of it. As a proverbial
saying it is most naturally taken to be an explanation of Jesus'
own authority, i.e. just as anyone I might send would be received
as if it was I myself, so I only claim respect inasmuch as it is due
to God, whose representative I am. Naturally it has also been
applied to the position of the Apostles.

QUESTIONING ABOUT THE TRAITOR 13.21–30

The account of the Last Supper in Matthew and Mark consists
only of two items. First there is the questioning about the traitor,
then the institution of the Eucharist. Mark's version (Mk 14.18–21)
already shows the profound feeling of horror caused by Judas'
breach of the intimate trust of table fellowship. Jesus does not
say who the traitor is, but speaks of him with the greatest emotion:
'It would have been better for that man if he had not been born.'
Mt. 26.21–5 follows Mark almost word for word. But he is un-
satisfied that the identity of the traitor has not been indicated.
So he adds a verse in which Judas himself asks: 'Is it I?', and
receives the answer 'You have said so.' Lk. 22.21–3, however,
tones the whole issue down, and places it after the institution of
the Eucharist. Whether John would have sided with Mark or
Luke over the latter point we cannot tell (but see on verse 26).
But it is clear enough that he is working on a tradition which has
its closest parallel in Mark. There is the same desire to designate
the traitor, as in Matthew, but it is handled in a different way.
It is done by means of a little episode, in which the Marcan saying
of Jesus, 'one who is dipping bread in the same dish with me'
(Mk 14.20; cf. verse 18 above) is put into practice as a secret
sign to the Beloved Disciple and Peter. We are again faced with

the question whether the episode has a factual basis, or has been worked up from the saying. In this case the latter seems more probable, because (a) where John runs parallel to Mark he makes repetitive use of the vocabulary of the source; (b) the verses peculiar to John tend to employ quotations of what he has written elsewhere; (c) the whole has been written in such a way as to produce the greatest emotional effect from the irony of the situation (compare John's very free handling of sources for emotional effect in chapter 11).

This section introduces the Beloved Disciple, whose identity has never been satisfactorily solved. The question is discussed at length in the Introduction (pp. 31–4). Here it need only be pointed out that he is evidently intended to be regarded as one of the Twelve, but that he is deliberately not named (contrary to John's usual practice). This is because he represents a truer ideal of discipleship than Peter himself, the traditional leader among the Apostles. Thus he is historical in the sense that he is one of the Twelve who were actually with Jesus at the Last Supper, and he is not to be regarded as a mythical extra person. But he is fictitious in that the nameless portrait of him has been created by John precisely because he needed an ideal disciple as a foil to Peter and as an example to the reader. He comes into the Gospel here for the first time, because John is preoccupied with the problem of true and false discipleship in his presentation of the Last Supper traditions. In the present context he performs an essential function for the mechanics of the story, and at the same time provides a sharp antithesis to Judas Iscariot. He represents the perfect communicant, whereas Judas 'eats and drinks judgment upon himself' (1 C. 11.29).

21. troubled: a phrase from John's Gethsemane tradition; cf. 11.33; 12.27. Mk 14.19 mentions only that the disciples were 'sorrowful', but a similar expression is applied to Jesus at Gethsemane (Mk 14.34).

testified: as a witness in a court of law. The following words are almost a formal accusation, though the accused is not named. They are identical with Mk 14.18. This time the **truly** opening is not merely an indicator of the use of source material, but actually belongs to the source (so also in verse 38).

22. In Matthew and Mark the disciples each ask 'Is it I?', but John has varied this part of the tradition for the sake of the story.

In so doing he has brought it closer to Lk. 22.23, but there is no literary connection.

23. lying: the Hellenistic custom of reclining for a formal meal had been to some extent adopted by the Jews, and became obligatory for the Passover. So the Passover Haggadah states: 'On all other nights we eat and drink either sitting or reclining, but on this night we all recline.' The same verb (*anakeisthai*) is used for 'sits at table' in Lk. 22.27. It is a probable, but not certain, indication that the Supper is the Passover meal. Each lay on the left elbow. The most distinguished guest, or most favoured person (**whom Jesus loved**), would be at the host's right, and in order to speak to him would need to bend his head back close to the host's breast, thus making an entirely secret conversation possible. The positions of Peter and Judas are not specified, though it has been assumed by some that Judas was next to Jesus on the left side. **breast:** lit. 'bosom'; cf. 1.18. The use of this word and **loved** are intended to suggest a very special intimacy. Not only is the Disciple in a position to have a private word with Jesus, but he is also all that Judas is not, a loyal companion who understands the mind of the Master. For **loved,** cf. 11.3; 13.1, 34.

24. Peter: he acts as spokesman for the whole group; cf. 6.68. For **and said, etc.,** the *textus receptus*, supported by P⁶⁶ A D W Syriac Peshitta and Sahidic, has: 'to ask who it would be of whom he spoke'. ℵ combines both forms. This seems to be an attempt to improve the sense, bringing out the suggestion of **beckoned** (lit. 'nods') that Peter made signs without actually speaking.

25. breast: here the usual word (*stēthos*) is used. The question **who is it** corresponds with Mk 14.19.

26. The verse is based on the tradition as found in Mk 14.20, 'It is one of the twelve, one who is dipping [bread] in the same dish with me,' combined with the quotation in verse 18, 'he who ate my bread . . .' Mark has brought out the enormity of Judas' evil intention by drawing attention to the fact that he dips in the common dish. But John has taken the idea further by suggesting that Jesus, as host of the meal, himself dipped a tasty morsel in the dish and gave it to Judas as a special mark of favour. It is probable, in view of verse 18, that **morsel** here means bread. The Passover Haggadah, however, mentions only the dipping of the bitter herbs in the sauce, and so Barrett assumes that this is what is meant here. If it is bread, it must be assumed that the bread has already been blessed and broken, and so it may be argued that John's narrative implies that the institution of the Eucharist has already taken place. But it is also possible that the special significance was only attached to the bread at the second breaking of it, after the conclusion of the meal proper, before the grace and the Hallel psalms, though this seems much less likely. Mk 14.20 (where the word 'bread' is not actually in the text), could refer to the preliminary dish of vegetables dipped in vinegar, which (in the Passover only) precedes the breaking of of bread; alternatively Mark's participial construction represents a future ('one who is about to dip'). It is doubtful if John concerned himself with the niceties of detail in evolving this scene.

to whom I shall give: this is a clear case of the repetition of a pronoun in a relative clause in Semitic style (cf. Black, p. 101).
he gave it: B ℵ^corr C L have 'took it and gave it', perhaps through influence of the institution narrative (Barrett).

27. It should now be clear to the Beloved Disciple who the traitor is, but he does nothing about it. He has done his part, and the interest has shifted to Judas himself. If the morsel could be interpreted as a mark of favour, it could be a final appeal to Judas to reconsider his intentions. It is the moment of decision. Up to this point no irrevocable step has been taken (for John has not recorded the transaction of Mk 14.10f.). But the intention of betrayal has been forming in his mind. The giving of the morsel is a plea for loyalty. By refusing it he makes the decision to go through with the betrayal. John puts the point briefly and effectively by using once more the Lucan saying (Lk. 22.3) which he has already used in verse 2, this time keeping closer to the underlying text (**Satan entered**). It is as if the two Spirits, the good represented by Jesus and the evil by Satan, have been struggling within him for possession of his heart, and at this point he gives himself to Satan.

do quickly: now that Judas has reached the point of no return, there is nothing to be gained from further appeals; and in veiled language Jesus tells him to go through with his intention. He can have no further place in the fellowship of the meal. His departure, and the fact that Jesus is evidently in control of the situation, is enough to excuse the Beloved Disciple for his inaction (which Barrett finds reprehensible). The situation in Mt. 26.25 is far more unsatisfactory from this point of view.

28f. The ignorance of the disciples, presumably shared even
by the Beloved Disciple, who does not know the meaning of Jesus'
cryptic words, is intended to convey to the reader a hint of the
reason for Judas' failure in discipleship. John has already referred
to the motif of avarice in the growth of the Judas legend, when
he introduced this idea into the story of the anointing at Bethany.
He here reproduces the same material. For **money box,** cf. 12.6;
and for **give something to the poor,** cf. 12.5. The latter could
be taken to be an allusion to the custom of generosity at the
feast of the Passover (Jeremias, *Eucharistic Words*, p. 54). But **'Buy
what we need for the feast'** implies that the feast is yet to take
place, according to John's theory of the timing of the death of Jesus.

30. it was night: by referring back to **the morsel,** John
reminds the reader that Satan has entered into Judas. Satan represents the cosmic power of darkness. Judas' departure into the
night dramatically illustrates his final turning away from the light.
The fact that it is night-time again implies that the meal is the
Passover, which was eaten later than the usual time, on account
of Exod. 12.8 (so *Zebahim* v.8). John retains this detail from the
tradition (cf. 1 C. 11.23), in spite of the fact that it does not agree
with his own timing of the meal.

The New Commandment and the Coming Failure of Peter
13.31-8

John's narrative of the Last Supper concludes (if we discount for
the moment the Supper discourses) with two short paragraphs,
which correspond with the two preceding sections on Jesus as the
model of discipleship (1-20) and on failure in discipleship (21-30).
Structurally they recall the Lucan scheme, in which Jesus promises
the Twelve prominent positions in the coming Kingdom, and
then goes on to foretell Peter's denials (Lk. 22.28-34). But there
are no obvious literary links. The paragraph on the new commandment of love (31-5) has the typical Johannine vocabulary.
Its closest links are with his own presentation of the Gethsemane
material in 12.23-36. The paragraph on Peter (36-8) is also in
thoroughly Johannine style, except for the last verse, which shows
links with both the Marcan and the Lucan forms of the saying.

The relation of these two paragraphs to the following chapters
raises certain problems. It is fairly clear that they introduce some
of the themes which will be discussed in the Supper discourses at

greater length. In particular, the commandment to love one another is worked out in the allegory of the vine in chapter 15. Then in 16.5 Jesus says: 'None of you asks me, "Where are you going?"', although this is precisely the question which Peter has asked in 13.36. There is also the inexplicable 'Rise, let us go hence' in 14.31. Bernard gains a more logical arrangement by taking chapters 15 and 16 after 'Jesus said' in 13.31. This finishes with the thought of the scattering of the disciples (16.32), which is precisely the issue which introduces the forecast of Peter's denials in Matthew and Mark, while Jesus and the disciples are on the way to Gethsemane. Accordingly Bernard places 13.31b–8 at this point, and then goes on to chapters 14 and 17. Bultmann has a similar scheme, but takes chapter 17 first, regarding it as a substitute for the institution of the Eucharist. Then comes 13.31–5 as the introduction to chapters 15 and 16. This allows an even closer juxtaposition of the themes of the scattering and the denials, as only 13.36–8 has to follow chapter 16. Chapter 14 concludes the whole complex. As with all the other proposed transpositions, these rearrangements only gain consistency at the cost of creating fresh problems, as will be noted when we study these chapters. But the chief difficulty is that the material is treated as if John had planned the whole complex as a unity, whereas in fact the contents are loosely strung together with very little progression of thought, however the chapters are arranged. If it can be accepted that John picks up one theme after another for further development, without giving much attention to the overall unity, there is no reason to abandon the order which has come down to us.

The New Commandment 31–5

31. gone out: Judas' exit has removed an alien element from the company. It is dark outside, but inside there is the light of Christ. The verb **glorify** (*doxazein*), used five times in this and the following verse, strongly points the contrast, for it is a word which suggests light.

Now is the Son of man glorified: the words have a triumphant ring, again sharply contrasting with the preceding moments, when Jesus was 'troubled in spirit' (verse 21). It is the same contrast as in 12.27f., to which this verse is closely related. The departure of Judas on his vile errand recaptures the sense that 'the hour has come' (12.23). Jesus suddenly sees the whole process of his Death and Resurrection as accomplished. The transition to the state of glory, which he has spoken of as due to happen in 'a little while, (verse 33; cf. 12.35) is now imminent, and consequently the disciples must already learn how to live in the light of it (verses 34f). There is an artistic balance between the repetitiveness of 31f. and 34f. which suggests that the two are causally related. The mutual love of the disciples will be the earthly counterpart to the mutual glorification of the Father and the Son. This is the perspective from which we may understand the emphasis on **glorified;** this verb is in the aorist in both its occurrences in this verse. The Son of Man *has been* glorified, and in him God *has* revealed his glory. These do not refer to past events (i.e. the foot-washing as a symbolic anticipation of the Passion (Sanders)), but are more like the prophetic perfect of certainty (Bernard). It is as if the act has been already done.

32. if God is glorified in him: these words appear to be otiose, and are in fact missing from important early MSS. (P⁶⁶ B ℵ* C* D L W Old Latin, Sahidic and Bohairic). Barrett and Hoskyns regard them as a dittograph, which has become a fixed part of the textual tradition through the influence of Origen. But omission by haplography is so natural, that it is wiser to retain them as the harder reading. Moreover they are not really redundant. For the clause is conditional, turning the proposition of the last verse into the grounds on which a further logical inference may be drawn. G. B. Caird (*NTS* xv (1969), pp. 265–77) has argued that when God is the subject of **glorified** it is frequently not a true passive but more like an intransitive verb, and best translated 'has revealed his glory'. He also maintains that **in him** must be local. It is *in Jesus crucified* that God reveals his glory. Now comes the further point. *If* that has been done (for verse 31 views it as already past), then it follows that Jesus in his turn will gain glory *in God*, as he is exalted as Son of Man to the glory of the Father. Here the verb is future, for the exaltation follows the crucifixion. But logically the two events are simultaneous, for they are the reverse sides of the same coin. Therefore John adds that God will **glorify him at once.** The whole point of the seeming tautology of these verses is to express the mutuality of the glory of God in the Passion of Jesus and the glory of Jesus in God. The ideas put so concisely here will be expanded in the Prayer of chapter 17.

33. Little children: the diminutive (*teknia*) is used seven times in 1 John, always when the writer is addressing his readers. But this is its only occurrence in the Fourth Gospel. John has his readers in mind here, as well as the disciples in the upper room. This impression of contemporary pastoral concern continues throughout the Supper discourses.

a little while: cf. 7.33; 12.35. Just as at 12.35, Jesus has to correct the impression that the moment of glorification has in fact arrived. For the 'now' of verse 31 refers to the beginning of a process, which consists of **going** in two senses, first to the Cross and then to glory. There is a deliberate cross-reference here to the teaching of 7.33-6; 8.21-9. The process effects the transition of Jesus from the earthly to the glorified state. It involves detachment from normal human contact with the disciples. The result is that they themselves will live in a new relationship with him. This will be the subject of the discourse of chapter 16. For the moment John simply uses this theme briefly in a bridge-verse, so as to be able to pass straight on to the mutual love of the disciples, which he wishes to bring into close relationship with the mutual glory of the Father and the Son.

34. A new commandment: it is difficult to see what is new about it, seeing that it is embedded in the Jewish Law (Lev. 19.18), referred to in the Summary of the Law (Mt. 22.39 paras.). Indeed the fact that, in one sense, it is not new is taken into consideration in the exposition of this commandment given in 1 Jn 2.7-11. The word for **commandment** (*entolē*) is common in 1 John and in the homiletic writing of the Supper discourses. But **new** (*kainē*) occurs in the Gospel only here and in 19.41, where the context is quite different. In the context of the Last Supper it may well carry an allusion to the eucharistic words ('the new covenant in my blood', 1 C. 11.25). Even though the word 'new' seems not to be an original part of the Synoptic version of the eucharistic words, the idea of the New Covenant, prophesied in Jer. 31.31-4, was probably present from the first. The idea of the renewal of the Sinai covenant, in a new and deeper sense, is not confined to this passage, but is presupposed in Deuteronomy and in many passages in Ezekiel. It formed the basis of the spirituality of the men of Qumran, as is expressly stated in the introductory parts of both the *Manual of Discipline* and the *Damascus Document*. There is a Christian exposition of it in Heb. 8-10; cf. also 2 C. 3.7-18. In

any case, **new** here refers to the new situation which is created
by the sacrifice of Christ, in which the conditions of the Age to
Come are already anticipated.

that you love one another: this is the moral consequence of
table fellowship. The point has added force, if it is correct to see
here an allusion to the eucharistic words. But John has made the
connection sufficiently clear by his use of the verb *agapān* earlier
in this chapter. Jesus' own love of the brethren was asserted in the
solemn opening of the narrative (verse 1), and so the idea, coming
again at the end of it, makes a characteristic Johannine *inclusio*.
But it also occurred at the centre of the chapter, where the disciple
'whom Jesus loved' (verse 23) is contrasted with Judas, the disciple who denies love.

as I have loved you: the past tense is to be interpreted in the
same way as the aorists in verse 31. It is a reference to the Passion
as the conclusion of Jesus' ministry, regarded as already completed
(cf. verse 1), not simply to the foot-washing as an example
(Bernard). The mutual love of the disciples is the rule for the new
era, when the Father and the Son are glorified in each other, and
so constitutes the earthly counterpart to their relationship.

35. As such it will be a Sign to the world. The argument based
on the foot-washing (verses 13–20) is presupposed. Henceforth
Jesus will only be known through his representatives. Their
mutual love is their only credential. These thoughts will be worked
out in greater detail in the discourse of chapter 15.

Peter's Denials are Foretold 36–8

36. where are you going: the idea of **going** belongs not
only to John's own special vocabulary (cf. verse 33), but is also
found in the Synoptic tradition of the Last Supper, using John's
verb *hupagein*: 'For the Son of man goes as it is written of him'
(Mk 14.21 paras.). To John the important point is that this is a
way which Jesus must tread alone. This has been touched on
briefly in verse 33. Now, in completely characteristic style, John
makes Peter pick up this point, and by misunderstanding it opens
the way to further elucidation of it. Peter **cannot follow** Jesus
now, as he goes to his death. But, as a result of what Jesus will
achieve, he can **follow afterward,** in the post-Resurrection life
of the Church. The thought (but not the vocabulary) is similar to
Jesus' reply to Peter in verse 7; **follow** is a special word in the

language of discipleship; cf. 12.26; it does not necessarily indicate martyrdom, but the next verse shows that this is within the range of thought. In fact there may be here an ironical allusion to Peter's martyrdom, which was known to John (cf. the Appendix, 21.18f.).

37. I will lay down my life: at this point the reference to martyrdom becomes explicit. Peter uses precisely the same words as Jesus has used of himself as the Good Shepherd (10.11–18). The same expression will be used in a more general application in 15.13 (this is one reason why it seems unlikely that this paragraph originally followed chapters 15 and 16). Peter's protestation is closer to Lk. 22.33 than to Mt. 26.33 (= Mk 14.29), though there are no verbal links. Cf. also verse 9.

38. Peter may even follow to the point of martyrdom 'afterward' (verse 36), but the point is that he cannot do so now. He is still prone to temptation, and needs the cleansing of the Passion, which has been done symbolically, but which is yet to be actualized (cf. verse 10). John shows his present weakness, and by implication that of all the disciples, by introducing the Synoptic tradition of the forecast of Peter's denials. The text, including the **'truly'** introduction, is derived from the tradition. It has points in common both with Mk 14.30 and with Lk. 22.34 (which is based on the same tradition, in spite of the fact that the preceding verses are independent of Mark). John does not include Mark's 'twice' for the cock-crowing, which is only found elsewhere in a Fayyum papyrus fragment closely related to Mark. As this is unlikely to be an additional feature, but rather one which would naturally be omitted in transmission, it excludes interpretation of the cock-crowing in terms of the third watch of the night (cf. Mk 13.35). John records the fulfilment of this prediction in 18.17, 25–7. It may be remarked that the appearance of Peter at the beginning and end of the chapter is another example of *inclusio*.

THE SUPPER DISCOURSES: JESUS AND THE DISCIPLES (ii) **14.1-16.33**

The narrative of the Last Supper has had a contemporary relevance, because it has been concerned with the meaning of discipleship. The final section (13.31–8) has briefly introduced themes of crucial importance for the well-being of the Christian community. These cry out for further expansion and explanation. We know that the departure of Jesus (13.33) means his return to the Father, but we need to know what that means for those whom he must leave behind. Jesus has given the commandment to love one another (13.34), but has not gone into this in detail. Nor has he shown how the disciples' behaviour is to be a witness to the world (13.35). Peter has been told that he will follow the Master 'afterward', even perhaps by the way of martyrdom (13.36), but as the Passion of Jesus is a unique event, we need to know what this means in the practical life of the Church. It is obvious that the essential point which must be established is the precise relationship of the disciples to Jesus in his state of glory. It must also be shown how they are to carry on the work of his mission, which has been accomplished in one sense, but still remains to be begun as far as the Gentiles are concerned (11.52; 12.20–4). These are matters of contemporary concern. They could only be dealt with by the device, not uncommon in ancient literature, of inserting table-talk into the narrative. But as the element of dialogue in these chapters is slight, they are perhaps best regarded as a farewell speech (cf. below on chapter 17).

A quick glance through the contents of the discourses shows that they correspond with 13.31–8 in the reverse order. Chapter 14 answers the question of Peter, 'Where are you going?' (13.36). Jesus goes to the Father (14.1–11). His departure entails a new relationship between him and the disciples. His earthly mission will be accomplished through them (14.12–14) with the aid of 'another Counsellor' (14.15–17). They will not be separated from him, but will share in his own relationship with the Father, expressed in terms of mutual indwelling (14.18–24). These facts about the future are made known in advance, so as to sustain the disciples at the time of the shattering experience of the death of Jesus, which is imminent at the time of speaking (14.25–31). With chapter 15 we come to the exposition of the commandment to the disciples to love one another, which has been given in 13.34f. This consists of the allegory of the vine (15.1–17). Moreover, just as the love of the brethren is to be a witness to the world (13.35), so the work of the disciples under the Counsellor's guidance will make an impact on the world, including the real possibility of the witness of martyrdom (15.18–16.15). At 16.16

we come to an exposition of the intentionally obscure 'little while' of 13.33. This again, like the conclusion of chapter 14, leads to an assurance that all shall be well, an assurance which can carry the disciples through the time of testing. Finally chapter 17, the Prayer of Jesus, which is closely related to the Supper Discourses, takes up the thought of the glorifying of the Son of Man in 13.31f.

From the above very brief analysis it might be supposed that John has deliberately arranged his material to correspond with 13.31–8 on a chiastic plan. But this cannot be the case, because the relation between them is more complex. Chapter 14 has all the themes of 13.31–8 ('glorified', verse 13; 'a little while', verse 19; 'love', verses 21–4). It comes to a suitable conclusion. 'Rise, let us go hence' (verse 31) presupposes that the Passion narrative (18.1) is to follow. Similarly the special concern of chapter 14 ('Where are you going?') is repeated in 16.5, leading to the same teaching on the new relationship with Jesus and the work of the Counsellor. We have already noticed that the conclusion of chapter 16 is similar to that of 14. If we reject the transposition theories advocated by Bernard and Bultmann (see above, pp. 442ff.), it is reasonable to suppose that there are two alternative versions of one discourse, the first being chapter 14 and the second chapters 15 and 16. This is the view of Barrett, Sanders and Brown. In this case the second discourse might well belong to the second edition of the Gospel. This is suggested by the fact that there are places where John appears to be correcting possible misunderstandings arising from the teaching of chapter 13 (see the notes on 15.15, 16, 20). It also reduces the force of the objection that 16.5 presupposes that the question of Peter in 13.36 (and Thomas in 14.5) has not yet been asked, for it removes the structural relation between these passages. But in any case the objection has no weight, because Jesus answers the question so fully in the teaching of chapter 16 that it is scarcely possible for Peter to ask it after this—or, for that matter, for Jesus to speak in the way that he does in 13.33. Here it may also be mentioned that the conclusion of the second discourse (16.29–33) has a double relation to the preceding material. It obviously corresponds closely with the ending of the first discourse, 14.25–31. But it also employs the same kind of irony as the forecast of Peter's denials in 13.36–8, and is dependent on the same range of underlying tradition (see the

notes on 16.32). If 13.36–8 is transposed to follow it, a new difficulty arises inasmuch as Peter's protestation in 13.37 is totally
unaware of the flight of all the disciples, which Jesus has forecast in
16.32. On the other hand, if the two pieces are left in their present
positions, they make another example of *inclusio*, as the same irony
begins and ends the discourses.

The most perplexing problem of the Supper discourses is presented by the introduction of the Counsellor (Paraclete). He is
identified with the Spirit, whose coming has already been referred
to in 7.39 as a direct consequence of Jesus' entry into glory. But
the title Paraclete is not used of him outside the Supper discourses.
Its meaning in connection with the Spirit is disputed, and it is
difficult to see why John has chosen it at all. Evidently he felt it
necessary to use this unusual designation in the particular context
of these discourses. But this raises another problem, whether the
Paraclete passages (14.15–17, 26; 15.26f.; 16.5–15) really belong
to the discourses. Windisch regarded them as secondary insertions,
which must be taken together as a separate continuous piece. But
although the relevant passages in chapter 14 can be removed
without difficulty, in chapters 15 and 16 they are very closely
bound up with the context. It is more likely that they are a distinct range of source material, which John has used in composing
the discourses (so Schnackenburg, Sanders). This theory is helpful
to Bultmann, because, if 14.16 comes from the source, it does not
spoil his contention that chapter 14 originally followed chapters 15
and 16, even though 14.16 is clearly the *first* mention of the
Paraclete. But, accepting the existing order, we can still assert
that the discourses are based on several homilies, which John has
pieced together for inclusion in the Gospel. The sources are in fact
John's own homilies: the longer discourse of chapters 15 and 16
thus incorporates much of his Paraclete homily. On the other
hand, it is very probable that the passages in chapter 14 were
only added in at the time of the second edition, when he composed
the second discourse. For the choice and meaning of the title see
the notes on 14.16.

The theory that the Supper discourses are based on homilies at
the Eucharist disposes of the problem of historicity. We need not
suppose that they were actually spoken by Jesus in the course of
the Last Supper. This would only be possible if they were based on
eye-witness reports which were not available to the Synoptic

writers. It is in any case most unlikely that Westcott is right in supposing that chapters 15 and 16 were spoken after leaving the Upper Room, and before reaching Gethsemane (he suggested actually in or near the Temple precincts, connecting the allegory of the vine with the golden vine carved on the Temple gates). The theory that these discourses embody teaching given to the disciples after the Resurrection (recently argued afresh by Stather Hunt) has been encouraged by their liturgical usage in the Church between Easter and Pentecost, for which they are certainly appropriate. But it not only runs up against the difficulty of eye-witness reporting, but also involves the supposition that John has recast them to suit the perspective of the eve of the Passion, which cannot be eliminated from them in their present form. But it is better to treat them in the same way as the other discourses of the Fourth Gospel, as John's own composition on the basis of his eucharistic homilies, which have a core of traditional words and teachings of Jesus not necessarily tied to this occasion. As usual, the 'truly' sayings (14.12; 16.20, 23) indicate the use of such material. Also the discourses contain parables in 14.2; 15.1ff.; 16.21. One of these, the allegory of the vine, may well be connected with the eucharistic words of Jesus known from the Synoptic Gospels. Then the teaching on persecution and the function of the Holy Spirit has a close parallel in the Synoptic tradition. There are quotations of sayings already used by John (15.20), of the Christian use of the OT (15.25), and of the Synoptic narrative (16.32). The integral connection of the discourses with what John has already written in 13.31–8 has already been noted above.

THE FIRST DISCOURSE   **14.1–31**

A brief analysis of the contents has been given above, p. 466. The discourse starts abruptly (D inserts: 'And he said to his disciples', perhaps from lectionary usage). But there is really no break after 13.31–8, which has already been in discourse-style. Peter's interruption at 13.36 has parallels in the discourse itself (verses 5 and 8). The reassuring words with which the discourse begins are needed after the disturbing language of 13.33 and 36 and the sharp rebuke to Peter. The reassurance is picked up again at the end (verse 27). It sets the tone of the whole discourse.

The Way to the Father **14.1–7**

14.1. hearts be troubled: a variation of the phrase used in 12.27; 13.21; it has a close verbal parallel in Ps. 55.4. The distress of the disciples is occasioned by the premonition of Jesus' death, but this is scarcely distinguished from their bewilderment at his speaking of it in terms of withdrawal, and this in its turn reflects the problem of the church serving an apparently absent Master. **hearts:** singular in the Greek, according to Semitic idiom (so also verse 27).
believe in God, believe also in me: both verbs are rightly treated as imperatives, in continuity with the preceding clause, though both could be translated indicative (as in the margin). The call to put away fear is a call to put faith in God; and therefore to put faith in Jesus himself, because of the relation between them which is just about to be expounded. The emphasis falls on **also in me** in the Greek on account of the chiastic structure.

2. many rooms: it has to be assumed that the distress of the disciples concerns Jesus' departure. The first point which Jesus makes is connected with the *destination*. For this purpose he uses the metaphor of a guest-house. Just as the Temple was regularly called the house of God (cf. 2.16), so heaven was pictured as a palace by many ancient peoples. 1 Enoch 39.4f. tells of 'the dwelling-places of the holy, and the resting-places of the righteous'. It is, then, easy to apply to heaven a word-picture of an earthly domestic situation: someone goes on ahead to the hotel, books rooms for all the party, and returns to fetch them when all is ready. We have had another domestic parable in 8.34f. Whether this parable goes back to Jesus himself is hard to say; Hoskyns suggests that it has been formed out of Jesus' instructions to the two disciples to go ahead and prepare the Passover in Mk 14.12–16 though the only verbal link is the obvious word 'prepare' (*hetoimazein*). The primary emphasis here is on the **many rooms,** i.e. there is accommodation for everyone. It is quite conceivable that Jesus should have spoken of the universality of God's love in this way, against the exclusivism of the Pharisees. But the language is Johannine, and the parable has been adapted and turned into a metaphor for its specific application here. **Rooms** (*monai*) is the noun corresponding with the verb 'abide' (*menein*, cf. 15.5ff.), and is picked up again in verse 23 (where it is translated 'home').

It thus means 'abiding' (cf. 1 Mac. 7.38, where 'let them live no longer' is literally 'do not give them abiding'), and so here 'abiding places'. It does not refer to lodging-places along the way or to different departments in heaven on arrival.

would I have told you that I go: the punctuation in *RSV* (adopted by Bernard, Bultmann, Sanders) makes the words refer back to something said previously. This must be 12.26, a saying about the reward for faithful discipleship. The usual punctuation is: 'If it were not so, I would have told you; for I go to prepare a place for you.' This gives a weaker sense, but accords better with John's idiom, and is to be adopted (so Barrett). The first sentence is not entirely pointless, for it reinforces the assurance of verse 1. Then the clause with 'for' (*hoti*) announces the next point for consideration. The particle *hoti* is omitted in the *textus receptus*, supported by P⁶⁶* Θ and Old Latin, probably because of uncertainty about the interpretation.

3. I will come again: the metaphor is continued. Jesus will first go and prepare the rooms, and then go back to welcome the guests. It is natural to think of this as the Parousia, or Second Coming. But if Jesus' departure is his death, then the return is his Resurrection, and the reception of the guests is the mutual indwelling which will obtain in the post-Resurrection situation of the Church (verse 23). The use of the sustained metaphor is a device whereby both these interpretations can be left open at this stage. **Where I am** in the last clause gives just a hint that the apocalyptic idea is being adapted to the timeless situation (as we know, the End Time in John's view is anticipated in the personal history of Jesus).

4. the way: the **where** clause starts the verse in the Greek, taking up the thought from the last verse in much the same way as verse 3 was linked to verse 2. But it is changed to **where I am going** in order to turn attention from the destination to the *route*. The resulting sentence is not good grammar, either in Greek or in English, according to the short text of *RSV* (= ℵ B W). The long text of the margin is very well attested, but is to be rejected as an attempt to ease the grammar, inspired by the following verse. Apart from an allusion to Isa. 40.3 in 1.23, **way** (*hodos*) occurs only in this and the next two verses in the Fourth Gospel, and never in the Johannine Epistles. This is surprising, considering the wide range of meaning of this word in general and the importance

of the idea of 'going' in John's presentation of the Passion. Moreover there is some evidence that in the early days Christianity
was called 'the Way' (Ac. 9.2—a title that may well be taken
from Isa. 40.3. It was used also at Qumran to designate the
sect (cf. 1QS ix.17f., 21; CD i.13)), before it became clearly distinguished from the main body of Judaism. But the fact that the
word here comes as a non-Johannine intruder suggests that we
should look for a specific saying in the underlying tradition to
account for it (see below on verse 6).

5. Thomas: introduced here without further description (D
characteristically adds: 'called Didymus'), and no more distinctive than the other disciples mentioned in the Supper discourses. His function as an 'honest doubter' only becomes clear
in 20.24–9, the passage on which the second edition reference to
Thomas in 11.16 is based. He takes Jesus' words and treats the
two elements of them separately, first the destination and then the
means of access. As the first is unknown, it follows that the second
remains uncertain.

6. I am the way, and the truth, and the life: this magnificent statement goes far beyond the scope of the question, and even
appears to deflect the argument. It is elucidated in the following
words, which specify the destination as the Father, and the
means of access as Jesus himself. Thus the centre of interest has
been shifted from Jesus' personal 'going', i.e. the Passion, to the
'going' of the disciples, which is the Christian way of life. They
follow Jesus by adhering to his example of obedience even to
death (**the way**). The next words (**and the truth and the life**)
are explanatory of this (cf. the paraphrase of *NEB*). It is a matter
of believing in him as the one sent by the Father (**the truth**),
and existing in the relationship which he creates between them
and the Father, a relationship which is not ended by death (**the
life**). On the last point, cf. 11.25. The three terms of the statement
should not be taken progressively, as by many of the Fathers (the
way and the truth leading to life, or the way leading to truth and
life); nor should they be taken as virtual equivalents in Christian
experience as by Bultmann (the paradox that the way and the
goal are the same). As an *ego eimi* saying, it is not a revelation-
formula (i.e. 'You know the religious meaning of the way . . .;
this is what I am'), but an explanatory statement, identifying a
feature of the parabolic metaphor of the opening verses. It is thus

very similar to the 'I am' sayings of the allegory of the Door and
the Shepherd (10.7, 11). It was observed in the commentary on the
Door (10.1) that the idea it expresses has a Synoptic parallel in the
saying of Jesus about the narrow gate (Mt. 7.13f.). But this also
includes the way and the life: 'For the gate is narrow and the way
(*hodos*) is hard, that leads to life . . . .' In the OT the way (Heb.
dérek) is frequently used in a moral sense (the way of the just, the
way of the righteous, etc.), and naturally Wisdom exhorts men to
'keep my ways' so that they may 'find life' (Prov 8.32, 35). Seeing
that John does not use *hodos* elsewhere, it is probable that he is
dependent on a particular saying which embodies these Semitic
ideas, a saying very like Mt. 7.13f., if not that actual one. It is
true that way, truth and life are all words which have an essential
place in the language of personal religion, but it is entirely unnecessary to say that John has derived the present saying from Hellenistic or Gnostic religion. It is a false track to interpret it in terms of
the mystical ascent of the soul to God. It is a moral union, which
makes the End Time present (see above on verse 3).

no one: the apparently exclusive notion rests on the unique position of Jesus as the one sent by the Father. The idea has already
been stated in 10.1, 8f., so that we have here another connection
with the Shepherd allegory. John's Logos doctrine in the Prologue
ensures that there is no narrow exclusivism here.

7. Having explained the way of access in verse 6, Jesus now
takes the first part of Thomas' question, which is concerned with
the destination. The metaphor of the house is dropped, and with
it the notion of heaven as a separate realm unrelated to present
existence. The destination is simply the **Father** (cf. verse 6b). If
Jesus is the way to the Father, then to know Jesus is to know the
Father too. But this is not simply a timeless truth, because the
situation is that Jesus' bodily presence is about to be withdrawn.
But this will not break the relationship which he has established.
Jesus is addressing the disciples (the verbs are plural). The text of
B C*, adopted by *RSV*, gives a false understanding, and really
amounts to a reproach, as Barrett points out, as if they have failed
to know Jesus properly, and therefore fail to know the Father. But
we should certainly follow P[66] ℵ D* (reading *egnōkate* and
gnōsesthe for *egnōkeite* and *an ēdeite*), and translate: 'If you have
known me, you will know my Father also.' (= *NEB, mg.*). The
rest of the verse then follows naturally: **Henceforth** (i.e. after

Jesus' departure) **you know him and have seen him.** This reading is adopted by Hoskyns, Bultmann, Barrett, Sanders, Marsh, Schnackenburg: Brown is undecided, but suspects that the reading in the text is due to the influence of 8.19.

Jesus and the Father 8–11

8. Philip: cf. 1.43; 12.21f. In the last verse Jesus has introduced a new expression of the relationship with the Father. Knowledge is replaced by *sight*. In religious language sight is the fullest and most direct form of knowledge. It is the summit of religious aspiration (cf. Exod. 33.12–23; Ps. 27.7–14). This new point demands elucidation, and so John, in his usual way, gives an uncomprehending comment on the part of Philip as the lead-in. Many commentators see in his words an allusion to Exod. 33.18.

9. There is a sense of urgency about Jesus' reply which suggests that Philip's confusion is shared by John's fellow-Christians, whom John is most anxious to instruct properly. Here we have the reproach which was not merited in verse 7. The whole life of Jesus (considered as a single whole, if the strict meaning of the reading of א* D W: *tosoutō chronō* = **so long,** is pressed) has been the revelation of the Father, who may not be seen by any other means (cf. 1.18). Thus what was said in verse 7a in terms of knowledge can equally be put in terms of vision (cf. 12.45).

10. I am in the Father: the claim that God may be seen in Jesus can only be substantiated by the relationship between them. This is a relationship of mutual indwelling. Jesus on his side never speaks on his **own authority,** as he has said repeatedly, but only and wholly in obedience to the Father. The Father on his side **does his works,** i.e. is active in the world, in and through Jesus. So, by the submission of himself to the Father, and by the Father's initiative in working through him, Jesus can claim to be the revelation of the Father. For **dwells** (or abides, *menein*), cf. verse 2. But the exact nature of this relationship is not defined. There are three possibilities. (a) The mutual indwelling might be mystical union, comparable to the experience of the mystics, implying absorption in the divine. This is excluded by the fact that the context is not at all concerned with the inner life of Jesus. (b) It might be a moral union, the supreme example of the relationship which the disciples themselves may expect to have with God. In this case Jesus is not different in kind from other men. (c) It might be a metaphysical union, in which Jesus is differentiated from all other men by the fact that he is the self-expression of God. This is certainly implied in the Prologue. It is probably a mistake to choose between (b) and (c). Jesus, in John's view, is different from other men, but the relationship between him and God is comparable to the moral union which is possible between them and God. This will become clear in the climax of the argument in verse 23. The whole issue is central to John's theology, and has already been dealt with in discussion with the Jews in 10.31–9.

11. or else believe me: *pisteuein* with the dative, i.e. give credence to me, just as at the beginning of the verse. But this time **me** should probably be omitted with P⁶⁶ P⁷⁵ א D L W Old Latin, cp. *NEB*. Jesus requires belief in the relationship between him and the Father, because it is the basis on which the disciples may follow the Christian way (verse 6). There is, however, a concession to those who find it difficult to accept, because (like Philip) they misunderstand it. If they consider the works just mentioned, they will be led to the same conclusion. This is not a lower level of belief, but an easier route to the same belief; cf. 5.36, and especially 10.38.

The Mission of the Disciples **12–14**

12. As before in verse 8, the next item of the discourse picks up the word which concluded the last one, in this case the **works.** Jesus now expounds the place of the disciples (verse 3, but the metaphor is not resumed) to show how they are associated with him after his departure. As their works are the works of Jesus, they will be just as much the activity of God in the world as his own acts were. Moreover they will be **greater.** This does not, of course, mean better than those of Jesus, but more extensive, for it is through the mission of the disciples that the work of Jesus is to be extended through the world and down the ages; the phrase is an unmistakable allusion to 5.20. The thought in that passage was more complex, because it referred to the full scope of the divine activity in Jesus which will only be reached in his final glory as the Son of Man, though it is revealed in miniature in the works of his earthly life. The mission of the disciples fills in the gap. It is, of course, still Jesus who is at work when they do these things, but they act on his behalf from the time that he has **to go to the Father.** The allusion to 5.20 provides, too, the clue to the use of the **truly** formula in this verse. For **he . . . will also do the works that I do** echoes the parable of the apprenticed son in 5.19 (the similarity is closer in the Greek than in the English), and is probably an adaptation of it.

13. ask: Jesus' works are always the result of prayer, which expresses the unity of his will with the Father's (cf. 11.41f.). In the same way the disciples' continuation of his mission depends on prayer, and naturally this is done with the invocation of **my name.** This does not mean the invocation of a powerful name in order to effect a magical spell (though such practices were frequent in the ancient world), but the use of Jesus' name as the grounds for the certainty of an answer. The disciples have a right to do so, because they are his representatives. Their prayer is presumably addressed to the Father (inserted as object of **ask** in a few MSS.), and we expect the Father to give the answer. So it comes as a surprise that Jesus says **I will do it** ('he will do it' is read by one minuscule). But the unity of the Father and the Son, described in verses 9-11, means that Jesus is still the agent of the Father's will, even after his departure from the world. The works of God are revelatory acts (probably miracles are meant) which have already been demonstrated in Jesus' life as his functions as the Son of Man, and will continue to be *his* acts in the new situation. So the Father will still **be glorified** (reveal his glory) **in the Son** (of Man). The argument is still closely related to the discourse of chapter 5; but there is also a definite allusion here to 13.31f. This explains why Jesus speaks of himself in the third person as **the Son.**

14. if you ask: the marginal addition 'me' is very well supported textually (P[66] B ℵ W Θ Vulgate and Syriac Peshitta), and should be retained. It has been omitted in the *textus receptus* for consistency with the preceding verse, and to avoid the contradiction with 16.23. But it marks a further stage in bringing round the argument to the mediatorial capacity of the glorified Jesus. The disciples pray as his representatives (**in my name**), and Jesus provides the answer as the agent of God. Obviously to address such prayer to Jesus himself is no different from praying to the Father, because of their mutual indwelling. So the way is open for verses 16 and 18, in which the emphasis is placed on the initiative of Jesus. The whole verse is missing from the Sinaitic Syriac, and some late Greek and Latin MSS., either by haplography, or because it was felt to be redundant (Barrett).

The Promise of the Counsellor 15–17

15. If you love me: having described the place which the disciples will occupy after the Resurrection—as Jesus' representatives on earth—in verses 12–14, Jesus goes on to expound what he means by saying that he will come again and take them to himself (verse 3). It will depend on the existence of a loving relationship between him and them, which will create a mutual indwelling comparable to his own relationship with the Father. There is probably an intentional allusion here to 13.34f. The plural **commandments** thus refers to the manifold applications of the one commandment to love one another (compare 15.10 and 12). For **you will keep** (B L Sahidic, Bohairic) most texts, including A D W Θ, read imperative, but this scarcely affects the sense. P66 and ℵ have subjunctive, making the whole verse the protasis, which is awkward unless 'and' is inserted between the clauses (so Brown). These are transcriptional variants, and future indicative probably represents John's intentions best. The thought of the whole verse is repeated in verse 21, after Jesus has explicitly mentioned his return in verse 18. It is thus a serious possibility that verses 16f., on the Counsellor, have been added at a later stage (see above, p. 468). They fit into the context very well, because they show how Jesus uses his initiative to provide the disciples with the essential equipment for their task as his representatives; but they spoil the consistency of the exposition, which is leading up to the mutual indwelling of the Father and Jesus and the disciples, by anticipating the idea of indwelling with regard to the disciples and the Spirit.

16. another Counsellor: the essential point to grasp is that the picture of the future which this discourse paints leaves an important gap, which John can fill with his doctrine of the Counsellor. Jesus is the way to the Father and also the revelation of the Father. But he is withdrawn from the disciples' sight. They will perform his mission with security, because of the mutual indwelling which unites them with him. But he will no longer be their visible teacher and guide. But primitive Christianity had a vivid sense of possession of the Holy Spirit, maintaining the life of the Church in the interval before the Parousia (cf. C. K. Barrett, *JTS*, n.s., 1 (1950), pp. 1–15). This is an experience which overcomes the difficulty of the absentee Lord. There is still an identifiable divine

presence when the presence of Jesus is withdrawn. John has referred to this experience in 7.39. The modern reader may well
feel let down at this point, for he is not vividly conscious of having
the Spirit, and so the problem for him remains unsolved. For him
it has to be a matter of faith that, if he loves Jesus and keeps his
commandments (verse 15), he is open to the influence of the
Spirit, and may bring forth his fruits (cf. 1 C. 13; Gal. 5.16–24).
This is not a modern problem, but goes back to John's own time.
It is notable that John lays very little stress on the extraordinary
manifestations of the Spirit which were valued in the early days
(miracles, prophecy, tongues, etc., cf. 1 C. 12).

Against this background it is at once clear that **another Counsellor** should not be translated 'another one, a Counsellor', as if
the title were not just as much applicable to Jesus himself as it is
to the Spirit (to do so goes against Johannine usage, cf. J. Behm,
TDNT v, p. 813). The whole point is that the Spirit performs
the functions which Jesus has done in the flesh, so enabling the
disciples to continue his mission. **Counsellor** (Gr. *Paraklētos*) has
been chosen precisely because it can be applied to both (cf. 1 Jn
2.1, where it is translated 'advocate'). It was obviously necessary
to find a word which, while being capable of being applied to
both, was not exclusively associated with either. What, then, does
it mean? (a) *Advocate* (*NEB*) i.e. the defending counsel in a legal
case, is suitable for the function of Jesus in 1 Jn 2.1, and accords
with Jewish usage (it occurs as a loan-word, *Pᵉraqlît*, in Hebrew
and Aramaic, e.g. *Aboth* 4.11). But this is too limited for John's
idea of the Spirit. In 16.8–11 he has a forensic function, but as
accuser rather than advocate. (b) *Intercessor* is really more suitable
in 1 Jn 2.1 than advocate (cf. R. E. Brown, *NTS* XIII (1967),
pp. 113–32), as Jesus stands before the Father. But the Spirit is
present with the disciples to help them. (The loan-word *pᵉraqlît*
occurs also in this sense in the Targum to Job, where it represents
the Hebrew *mēlîs* (= intermediary). The latter word is found in
the Dead Sea Scrolls for an interpreter. It can also be applied,
at least by implication, to the angelic spirits. John is surely indebted to this wide use of the term, though his own presuppositions
preclude identification of the Paraclete with an angelic figure (see
on verse 17). For details see G. Johnston, *The Spirit-Paraclete in the
Gospel of John*, pp. 80–118). (c) *Helper* might then be right. It corresponds with the verbal meaning from *parakalein*, to call to one's

side, and accords with Greek usage. The Mandean texts, on which Bultmann relies, speak of a helper in this way. But this is too weak, if the title is intended to represent the specific function of the Spirit as a substitute for Jesus' earthly presence. (d) *Comforter* (*AV*) or *Consoler* is suggested by Job 16.2, where LXX has *paraklētores* and Vulgate *consolatores*. From this point of view the Paraclete brings consolation when Jesus goes away (cf. 16.6, 7). But it is not a word that can be applied equally to Jesus and to the Spirit, as the present verse demands, and comfort is a very minor role in the Paraclete's activities. Barrett, however, argues that comfort and consolation are especially associated with the preaching of the gospel of salvation (cf. Isa. 40.1f.; 52.7–10. The LXX uses *parakalein* in the first passage). As the Paraclete is to be the disciples' guide in their mission, this is a suitable meaning. It fails to convince, because John himself never uses the corresponding verb. (e) *Counsellor* (*RSV*) is presumably an attempt to combine several of these meanings, using a word which retains the rhythm of the *AV* 'Comforter'. But if this is the aim, it is probably best to follow the example of Jerome and to be content with transliteration: 'Paraclete'. The decision about the real meaning of the word depends on the prior question whether it is a describer or an intentionally vague term to represent a substitute for Jesus. If it is a describer, it must convey some idea of the actual functions which the Spirit does. Otherwise it need only mean '[another] one at your side to call on'. From this point of view *Helper* is surely an adequate translation. The word is drawn from the Jewish background, but here (as there) it does not denote one particular figure. It can be applied to Jesus just as much as to the Spirit. For the background of thought in the Synoptic tradition, see the notes on 15.26 below.

17. the Spirit of truth: cf. 15.26; 16.13; 1 Jn 4.6. In the last-mentioned passage there is a direct contrast of 'the spirit of truth and the spirit of error'. This recalls the Two Spirits doctrine of the Dead Sea Scrolls: 'He has created man to govern the world, and has appointed for him two spirits in which to walk until the time of visitation: the spirits of truth and falsehood' (1QS iii.17–19; the words quoted in the notes on 3.6 immediately follow). The title 'spirit of truth' occurs also in *Test. Judah* xx.1 (see below on 15.26). John has inserted this title (though we should have expected the Holy Spirit, as in verse 26) in apposition to 'Counsellor' in the last verse, precisely because the latter is not self-explanatory. John's idea of the Spirit is certainly related to that of the Qumran texts, but is not identical with it. Whereas he speaks of the Devil in 8.44 in a way which exactly corresponds with the spirit of error (or angel of darkness) of the Qumran texts, he does not speak of the Holy Spirit as an angel (hence he does not make the equation spirit of truth = angel of light). But he does think of the Holy Spirit as personal, and for his present purposes it is necessary to emphasize that the Spirit is a reliable guide (14.26; 15.26; 16.13). This point does not come out here, as at this stage John is only concerned with the *presence* of the Spirit in the disciples.

whom the world cannot receive: men can only be open to the Spirit if they are in the right relationship with God (cf. verse 15). Hence **the world** (i.e. the world of men apart from God and in opposition to him; cf. 8.23) **cannot receive** him; **it neither sees him** by observation of his effects in the works which the disciples will do in the name of Jesus, **nor knows him** by inward apprehension, as they do. On the other hand, the disciples **know him** already, and only need to be told the true meaning of their experience, because **he dwells** (abides, *menei*) **with you** in the corporate life of the Church, and is (*estin*, B D* W) **in you** as individuals (**will be,** *estai*, is clearly a correction of the more difficult 'is').

Mutual Indwelling **18–24**

18. desolate: lit. 'orphans'. Jesus' departure might leave the disciples feeling as if they have lost their father, like pupils after the death of their rabbi (*Mekilta* Exod. 13.2) or like the followers of Socrates (Plato, *Phaedo* 116a). But not if they understand his return, which has been promised in verse 3.

19. a little while: instead of using the allegory of the house, Jesus takes up his usual veiled way of speaking of his death, last employed in 13.33. The verse describes the conditions which will follow this event. **The world will see me no more,** because he has died. But the disciples **will see me because I live** on account of the Resurrection. Note that it is best to take the causal clause closely with the preceding words (not, then, as in *RSV* and *NEB*, as the grounds for the next statement). Sanders even suggests taking it as 'you will perceive me, that I am living' (the same construction as in 9.8), depriving it of all causal force. But then the next words have to be taken improbably as a separate sentence, whereas the Greek says quite simply 'and you will live' (for **you will live also**) as a continuation of the causal clause. The disciples will see Jesus because of the Resurrection, but this is something in which they also share. John is introducing the reciprocal idea in preparation for the next verse. Evidently he wishes to guard against a false notion of the Resurrection, as if it were an event only affecting Jesus. He is anxious to show how it has a continuing effect upon the church and upon the life of the Christian.

20. In that day: cf. 16.23, 26. The phrase belongs to the vocabulary of eschatology (cf. Mt. 7.22; Lk. 17.31), but the End Time is anticipated in the day of Jesus' Resurrection. Nothing is said about the actual experience of the disciples at the Resurrection. The interest is entirely concentrated on their inward apprehension of the new state of affairs which will then obtain, a triple mutuality of Jesus and the Father and the disciples. Thus Jesus, on his return, takes them to himself (verse 3), into the relationship which he himself has with his Father (verse 10). Obviously verse 17, on the indwelling Spirit, is an awkward intrusion into the progress of thought, but it does not involve any contradiction. For the mutual indwelling of Jesus and the Father and the disciples is a way of expressing the *relationship*, whereas the indwelling of the Spirit is a way of expressing the *effect* of this relationship.

21. The rest of the paragraph is an exposition of this statement of mutual indwelling. It is important to remember that John has not actually said that the return of Jesus is his Resurrection, though it is obvious to us. It is still possible to assume that he is speaking of the Parousia, especially in view of the eschatological associations of 'in that day'. So he now goes back over the argument, and brings the issue to the surface by making it lead up to the idea of Jesus 'manifesting himself' to the disciples. He begins by repeating verse 15, but as a general statement and in the reverse order. This lays down the essential condition (**loves me**) for the mutual indwelling. It can now be restated in terms of a loving relationship. To be in the Father (verse 20) is the same thing as to **be loved by my Father,** and to be in Jesus is to be the object of his love, so that he says **I will love him.** But then there comes a tail-piece, which is really the theme for the next verses (just as

in verses 7, 11, 19): **and manifest myself to him.** It is not clear
whether this is a consequence, following on **will love him,** or is
yet another way of saying the same thing, so that Jesus' love and
self-manifestation are identical. The word for **manifest** (*emphani-
zein*) is not a technical term of apocalyptic, and is no doubt intentionally ambiguous. It is used of God's appearance to Moses in
Exod. 33.13.

22. Judas: the use of this name is one of the points where it
seems that John had traditions which were also available to Luke,
as it does not occur in the apostolic lists of Mt. 10.3; Mk 3.18,
but only in Lk. 6.16; Ac. 1.13, replacing Thaddaeus. The parenthesis (**not Iscariot**) may be a very early gloss. The Curetonian
Syriac reads 'Judas Thomas', Sinaitic simply 'Thomas', which
gives an alternative method of avoiding confusion with the traitor
(for the identification of Thomas with Judas, the brother of Jesus;
cf. the notes on 11.16). It is difficult to see any reason why John
should mention this name, except from a liking for variation, as
Peter, Thomas and Philip have all played their parts.
to us, and not to the world: Judas refers back to verse 19 for
the distinction between the world and the disciples. If Jesus meant
by **manifest** the Parousia, it would naturally be taken to be an
event visible to all (cf. Mt. 24.27). If, then, Jesus is speaking of
something that only the disciples can experience, he must mean
a different form of manifestation. In fact it is an anticipation of
the Parousia, and thus another way of coping with the problem
of its long postponement (cf. the notes on verse 16).

23. Jesus' answer does not deny the universal manifestation at
the Parousia (on the Johannine eschatology, cf. Introduction, pp.
57f.). Instead he retraces the argument of verse 21, speaking in
a timeless way, without the eschatological 'in that day' of verse 20.
We still have to assume that he means the time from the Resurrection onwards, as suggested by the 'little while' of verse 19.
The new feature is that **we will come to him and make our
home with him** replaces 'I will manifest myself to him', and so
must be taken to be an exposition of it, as required by Judas. It
is a form of manifestation which is not accessible to the world
(hence not the Parousia), nor confined to a privileged few among
Christians (hence not the Resurrection appearances), but is open
to all who have the right dispositions for union with God. It must,
then, be an interior apprehension of Jesus and the Father in the

hearts of those who love Jesus. This can hardly be a mystical experience of an esoteric kind, which would not be accessible to all. It is more likely to be something akin to the Pauline concept of being 'in Christ', a faith-union maintained by the imagination and the will (excellently described by J. Lindblom, *Gesichte und Offenbarungen* (1968), chapter 7).

we will come to him and make: D e Curetonian Syriac read singular: 'I will come . . .', presumably to bring it into line with verse 21.

home: Gr. *monē*, the same word as 'rooms' in verse 2. Thus the place which Jesus prepares in the Father's house turns out to be in the soul of the Christian, because of the mutual indwelling. Thus John, using once more the device of *inclusio*, brings the exposition to an end by alluding to the opening metaphor.

24. As an afterthought, Jesus adds the opposite, that the relationship fails when the disposition of love is not present. This is only mentioned so that he can assert that the message (**word**), i.e. the entire teaching of this discourse, is derived not from himself but from the Father. This is an echo of verse 1: 'Believe in God, believe also in me.'

Conclusion 25–31

25f These things I have spoken to you: a resumptive phrase, which is used four times, in slightly varying forms, in the second discourse (15.11; 16.1, 25, 33). Here it marks the break between the sustained exposition of verses 1–24 and the concluding comments, which are more directly concerned with the situation of the disciples on the eve of the Passion. The fact that Jesus has given this teaching **while I am with you** is most important, for it provides the clue to the divine purpose in the terrifying event which is just about to take place. This verse belongs closely with verse 26 the whole of which is a parenthesis, referring once more to the post-Resurrection conditions, and so breaks harshly into the natural progression of thought. Like the previous verses on the Paraclete (16f.), they are probably a second edition insertion. It anticipates what will be said in 16.13 about the teaching function of the Paraclete (it is this function which justifies the title used in verse 17, the Spirit of truth). Here the emphasis is on a particular aspect of this function, that of recalling to the disciples' minds the teaching which Jesus has already given (D ruins the sense by

changing **all that I have said** into 'all that I may say'). The
insertion is no doubt prompted by the emphatic way in which
Jesus asserts that the necessary teaching has already been given.
As before, the non-technical title **Counsellor** has to be explained
by appositional phrases, **the Holy Spirit** (only here in this form
in John. But possibly 'Holy' is an early scribal addition; it is
missing from Sinaitic Syriac), and **whom the Father will send
in my name,** i.e. as my representative (cf. verses 13f.). The
teaching function of the Spirit appears in the Synoptic tradition
in connection with persecution (cf. Lk. 12.12: 'For the Holy Spirit
will teach you in that very hour what you ought to say'). See the
notes on 15.26.

27. Peace: the Hebrew *šālôm* is used both as a greeting and as
a farewell. It has a much richer content than our word peace,
denoting also health and prosperity. As a valediction it is a
bestowal of blessing, and so conveys a certain power which can
remain with the disciples (cf. Mt. 10.13 = Lk. 10.6). So **leave**
virtually means bequeath (Barrett; cf. *NEB*: 'My parting gift'). In
the light of the foregoing discourse, Jesus' blessing carries with it
the whole positive content of the abiding effects of the Resurrection
which he has described. Hence it is **not as the world gives,** a
perfunctory farewell devoid of real power. Therefore Jesus can
repeat the reassurance of verse 1, but even more emphatically.

28. I go away: having recalled verse 1, Jesus reminds the disciples of the metaphor of departure and return used in verse 3.
This was expounded in verses 18–20 in terms of the situation
which will follow the Resurrection. But nothing was said there
about the actual event of the Resurrection, nor of the disciples'
reaction to it. Now, on the basis of what he has said, they should
be in a position to rejoice at his departure. The word translated
rejoiced (*echarēte*) has perhaps been chosen to suggest the usual
Greek form of greeting (*chaire*). The idea will be treated more fully
in 16.16–23. When rightly understood, Jesus' departure is cause
for joy, because it completes his earthly assignment from the
Father.

for the Father is greater than I: Jesus is aware that his mission
is entirely derivative from the Father and done in obedience to
him. In spite of the horror of the Passion, he has nothing to fear,
because he has surrendered himself to the Father (12.28), and the
Father is in control of events. The sentence is thus intended to

confirm the assurance which Jesus has already given to the disciples. It is a metaphysical statement only in so far as the concept
of sonship necessarily implies subordination to some extent. It does
not mean that Jesus is a lesser kind of being, not truly divine. But
inevitably this verse played an immense part in the Christological
controversies of the third and fourth centuries (cf. Hoskyns, pp.
462–4; Wiles, *The Spiritual Gospel*, pp. 122f.).

29. Jesus has been describing the conditions of the future. But
first he must undergo the Passion. It is not quite clear whether he
means that the forewarning will help the disciples to maintain
faith at the time of his death, when all seems to be lost, or whether
he is referring to the time after the Resurrection, when the fulfilment of the whole pattern of events will confirm his teaching.
Either way, we have here the argument from prophecy in words
very similar to 13.19.

30. the ruler of this world: i.e. the Devil. For this title see
the notes on 12.31. He **is coming** in the march of events leading
up to the Passion, of which the traitor's behaviour is one item
(13.27).
He has no power over me: lit. 'he has nothing in me'. This
corresponds with a Hebrew idiom, to have no claim or charge
against a person in a legal sense (*SB* II. 563). Bultmann (p. 630, n. 6)
argues that it is also good Greek. Jewish thought about the Devil
frequently uses forensic metaphors (see the notes on 8.44). From
this point of view the Passion is not thought of as a struggle in
which Jesus emerges as the victor, but as a court of law in which
his innocence is proved. The readings 'he will find nothing' (K
Origen) and 'he has nothing to find' (D) bring out the legal sense
(cf. 19.4).

31. I do governs both **so that the world may know that I
love the Father** (which comes first in the Greek) and **as the
Father has commanded me.** But they are really equivalents,
for the Father's bidding is precisely the act which proves Jesus'
love for him. *RSV* rightly takes this closely with the preceding
verse. The case against Jesus is conducted openly, so that it may
reveal the loving relationship between him and the Father, which
is the ground for the salvation of all men. For salvation also consists in a similar loving relationship, as the whole of this discourse
has shown. So the final reassurance to the disciples is the fact
that the Passion is the divine act of redemption.

Rise, let us go hence: these words are found in all MSS., and indicate that originally the Passion narrative continued after this point (cf. 18.1). Apart from **hence,** the identical words are found in Mt. 26.46 (= Mk 14.42), at the end of Jesus' prayer in Gethsemane, immediately before the arrival of the traitor. John has thus most probably taken them from the tradition which he has used for 18.2–11. Obviously they are quite inconsistent with the continuation of the discourses in chapters 15–17. Attempts to avoid this conclusion have been made both by ancient and modern commentators. Hoskyns (p. 465) quotes the spiritualizing interpretation of Cyril of Alexandria, which would take the phrase closely with the earlier part of the verse: 'Arise, let us remove from death unto life, and from corruption to incorruption.' Westcott (see above, p. 469) thought that the following discourses were delivered after Jesus had left the upper room. Torrey assumed that there was a continuous Aramaic original, so that **rise** is an error for 'I will arise' through the loss of a single letter by haplography from the preceding sentence. But then **let us go** has to be changed to 'and I will go'. It still does not give a convincing sense.

THE SECOND DISCOURSE 15.1–16.33

Apart from the insertion of the verses about the Paraclete, the first discourse has been a consistent and orderly treatment of the theme of the departure of Jesus. The second discourse gives a less unified impression. It seems to have been composed from a variety of homiletic pieces, which John has preached on different occasions, and now brings together and welds into a supplementary discourse, to take further the exposition of 13.31–8. The Paraclete passages are obviously one of these pieces. But the allegory of the vine (15.1–17) and the teaching on persecution (15.18–25; 16.1–3) may have had a separate existence. So also the exposition of 'a little while' (16.16–22).

As before, the discourse starts without any introductory words. But this again creates no problem, because Jesus is still the speaker. What is more disconcerting is the fact that the first verse looks like the exposition of a parable, which has not been given (cf. 10.7). If the *Sitz im Leben* of the allegory of the vine is the eucharistic assembly, it may be that there was no parable comparable to 10.1–5. Instead it may be a sustained metaphor based on the eucharistic words of Jesus: 'Truly, I say to you, I shall not drink of the fruit of the vine until that day when I drink it new in the kingdom of God' (Mk 14.25; cf. Lk. 22.18). It is communion in the one cup which lays upon the disciples the obligation of mutual love (13.34f.). This is precisely the point which Jesus is expounding in the allegory of the vine.

Although most editors are prepared to admit that the allegory has some connection with the Eucharist, there are plenty of other sources for the imagery, which must be taken into account, and their effect on the interpretation assessed.

Bultmann points out that there is no mention of the wine; it is all about the tree. He therefore assumes that it is derived from the mythological Tree of Life, which in some mythologies (e.g. the Mandean) is a vine. He also mentions the Christian idea of the cross as the Tree of Life, often identified with a vine, though this can certainly be explained entirely from biblical categories. But strangely enough the word life does not occur once in 15.1–17 (except of course verse 13). The allegory is entirely concerned with personal relationships, so that the categories of thought are moral, not Gnostic.

The same observation throws doubt on the much more widely accepted view that John has in mind the biblical and rabbinic usage of the vine as a symbol of Israel, cf. Isa. 5.1–7; Jer. 2.21; Ezek. 19.10–14; Ps. 80.8–16; *Lev. Rabba* xxxvi.2 (*SB* II. 563). John is speaking of the relationships which will exist in the Church, but he is not saying that the Church is to be the New Israel, and there is not the slightest indication that his thought is running along this line. The allegory comes close, it is true, to Paul's metaphor of the wild olive (Rom. 11.17–24), but John is not here concerned with the problem confronting Paul. Only by a forced exegesis of 15.6 can the notion of the rejection of the apostate Israel be brought into the interpretation. John is not contrasting the old with the new.

The teaching of Jesus in the Synoptic Gospels gives us no help. The parables of the labourers (Mt. 20.1–16) and of the wicked husbandmen (Mk 12.1–9 paras.) are set in a vineyard, but the vine as such gets no mention. The only time that Jesus uses the word is in the oath at the Last Supper quoted above. It should be noted that the phrase 'the fruit of the vine' occurs also in the Jewish blessing of wine at meals: 'Blessed art thou, O Lord our God, King of the universe, Creator of the fruit of the vine.'

It seems best to take the allegory on its own terms, as a meta-phorical use of the details of viticulture to expound the command-ment of 13.34f. We may legitimately ask whether there are any factors in the situation of the Last Supper which might suggest the use of such a metaphor. As already mentioned on p. 469, Westcott thought of the carved vine on the Temple gates. But the eucharistic benediction over the wine is sufficient to account for it.

The True Vine 15.1–11

15.1. I am: an explanatory statement, like 14.6—what Bult-mann calls a recognition-formula (cf. the notes on 6.35). Just as in 10.7, 11, Jesus identifies himself with a major item of the par-able. In this case, the parable can be imagined from the mention of the vine in the eucharistic words, which may be assumed as the immediate setting of the allegory. For **true** (*alēthinē*), cf. 1.9. If a vine is used as a symbol of spiritual realities, then it stands for Jesus himself, and any other identification would be misleading. For the purposes of the allegory the Father represents **the vine-dresser.** But this detail should not be pressed further than the context requires, for it does not correspond with the real relation-ship between Jesus and his Father, expounded in chapter 14.

2. First there is a description of the work of the vinedresser. He cuts out the dead wood, so that the fruit-bearing branches may be more productive. We can guess that the branches are the disciples, but this is not actually stated until verse 5. There is no warrant to identify the dead wood with unbelieving Jews or apostate Christ-ians, who are not mentioned at all in the exposition which follows. There is perhaps a play on words in **takes away** and **prunes** (*airei* and *kathairei*). If so, it is an indication that the piece is not based on an Aramaic original. The verb *kathairein* is commonly used for ceremonial cleansing, but it is quite correct in an agri-cultural context (Barrett refers to Xenophon, *Oeconomicus* xviii.6; xx.11).

3. clean: precisely because the allegory starts from some refer-ence to a vine, the parable has only come in after the initial identification in verse 1. Now Jesus identifies the branches, not formally, but by implication, because he addresses the disciples as if they are the branches. The word **clean** (*katharoi*) gives the application of prunes (*kathairei*) in the parable, taking advantage of its double meaning. The pruning process has already been done in the case of the disciples by the teaching of Jesus (cf. 17.14, and cp. 5.38; 8.37). There may be a cross-reference here to 13.10, where the same word is used.

4. Abide in me, and I in you: this is the classic expression of mutual indwelling, using the language of chapter 14 (the verb *menein* and the ideas of 14.11, 20, 23). The imperative denotes a moral union. The imperative force can hardly be extended to **and I in you,** which must then be equivalent to saying 'as I am in you' (Marsh). This goes beyond the allegory, because a branch has no moral power to abide in the vine. But Jesus is making the point that only the branches which are not 'taken away' (verse 2) can bear fruit. We are not yet told what he means by fruit.

5. I am the vine: the new start, repeating verse 1a, indicates the introduction of a fresh theme, like the new start in 10.11. This is to be the exposition of the fruit. The pruning of the branches which are not cut out of the vine has already been explained, and now we are ready to discover how they can bear more fruit (thus **much** corresponds with 'more' in verse 2). As a preliminary condition, Jesus repeats with greater emphasis the essential prerequisite of mutual indwelling, because he himself, as the stock of the vine, alone can channel the sap to the branches. As Jesus is speaking metaphorically rather than allegorically in the strict sense, there is no concentration on the details.

6. If a man does not abide in me: the preliminary point is pressed home even more strongly by a reminder of what happens to the unfruitful branches; **as a branch** explains the metaphorical **cast forth,** which is not intended to be taken literally. Jesus is not talking about excommunication. The rest of the verse tells what happens to branches which are thrown away. They wither for lack of sap, and their only usefulness is for firewood. Again, Jesus is not talking about eternal punishment; all he is saying is that a disciple who breaks fellowship with him is useless.

7. ask: the imperative is the reading of B. Most texts, including ℵ and Θ, read future, 'you will ask'. Others misunderstand the construction and read infinitive ('whatever you wish to ask will be done'). The meaning of the verse is similar to 14.13. It is concerned with prayer in connection with the disciples' mission. As a result of their close association with Jesus they are in a position to continue his mission in obedience to the Father, exactly as he has done it himself. This is what Jesus means by bearing much fruit.

8. It follows that the Father reveals his glory (**is glorified**) when the disciples fulfil Jesus' mission. **That** (*hina*) is explanatory, not purposive (cf. 12.23).

and so prove to be: lit. 'you will become', reading future (*genēsesthe*) with ℵ A and the majority of MSS., against subjunctive (*genēsthe*) of B D L Θ and perhaps P⁶⁶. As future, it means 'when the Father's glory is revealed in that you bear much fruit, it will be seen at the same time that you are disciples *of mine*'. As subjunctive, it is 'the Father's glory is revealed in this way, namely that you bear much fruit and thereby prove to be disciples of mine'. There is not much difference, but the first is to be preferred, as the second is probably assimilation to the subjunctive **bear** (*pherēte*).

9. At this point the metaphor is abandoned, and the mutual indwelling of verse 4 is expounded as a loving relationship, so bringing the exposition round to the commandment of 13.34. The aorist verbs (**loved** twice) are to be explained by that verse and by 13.31. Jesus is speaking from the perspective of the completed act of salvation, in which the Father's love for him, and his own love for the world, are expressed. The idea of abiding in the vine must not be misunderstood in a quasi-physical sense, for it is a personal relationship, for which the Father and Jesus himself provide the model.

10. my commandments: cf. 14.15, 21. The loving relationship of mutual indwelling is pre-eminently a moral union. Hence love is shown by the voluntary keeping of the Master's commandments.

11. These things I have spoken to you: cf. 14.25. As before, the phrase brings the thought from the future to the present situation of the disciples. The **joy** which Jesus has in looking forward to the completion of his task is to be shared by the disciples, and can be shared by them now, in view of the glimpse into the future which he has given to them, though it will not be fulfilled (**full**) until the time of the Resurrection. For the theme of joy in relation to the expectation of the Resurrection, cf. 14.28; 16.20–2, 33. *RSV* rightly places this verse at the conclusion of the first paragraph. It is not an introduction to what will come next.

Love One Another **12–17**

12. my commandment: the plural was used in verse 10, but now the thought is narrowed down to the single, all-embracing commandment of 13.34, here repeated almost verbatim. The relation between this verse and verse 10 is such that it is clear that the new paragraph is to be a further explanation of the idea of bearing fruit in the allegory. But John never quite manages to show how the continuation of Jesus' mission by the disciples and their love for one another are integral parts of the same thing. He leaves them in awkward juxtaposition, cf. verses 16 and 17 below. But he has certainly grasped the point that the internal life of the Church and its mission to the world are inseparable.

13. greater love (*agapē*): this incomparable description of true friendship is given as a general truth, almost as a proverb. The idea is not entirely without pagan parallels (cf. Bultmann, p. 542, n. 4). Paul in Rom. 5.7f. argues that the love of Jesus goes beyond even this. But whatever its background, John has thought it through for himself, so that it is completely in Johannine language and closely bound up with his teaching.

lay down his life: cf. the Shepherd (10.11, 15-18) and Peter (13.37).

friends (*philōn*) means those whom he loves (*agapān*; for the virtual identity of these synonyms, cf. 11.3). Although it is expressed in general terms, it is of course a self-portrait of Jesus himself, as the model for the mutual love of the disciples.

14. friends: the word opens up a fresh thought, which gives greater precision to the exposition of the loving relationship of mutual indwelling. To say **you are my friends** means no more than 'I have loved you' in verse 9. But the use of the word **friends** makes possible a further distinction within the concept of mutual love, as the next verse will show.

what I command you: read **what** singular (*ho*) with B, i.e. 'the thing which I command you' (viz. 'to love one another').

15. servants: probably the margin 'slaves' is the better translation, for the verse is concerned with status. In the ancient world slaves often reached high positions at court and enjoyed the close affection and confidence of their masters. But this could not alter the fact that they had no rights against their owners. John has referred to the condition of slavery in 8.35; see also Philemon. Here John takes as the normal situation of a slave the fact that he **does not know what his master is doing,** which may not apply to all slaves, but certainly would be regarded as the usual state of affairs. Friends on the other hand have a mutual intimacy

and confidence on equal terms. Jesus has given the disciples this
kind of confidence in imparting to them the full message of salvation from the Father. It may well be that John is here correcting
a false inference from his use of the analogy of master and slave to
teach the example of Jesus in 13.16, which he has taken over from
the earlier tradition.

16. You did not choose me: but the analogy must not be
pressed too far. The initiative always rests with Jesus himself. The
disciples' part is that of response to a love already given, and as
such entails submitting themselves voluntarily to his will in loving
obedience. There can never be any suggestion of a disciple laying
claim to Jesus' friendship in order to use it for his own ends. The
verb for **choose** has been used in 6.70 and 13.18 in connection
with the embarrassing fact that Judas was one of the Twelve. After
the allusion to 13.16 in the last verse, we can scarcely miss an
allusion to 13.18 here. Jesus chose Judas, but he failed to abide in
the vine. The rest, however, have been **appointed** (a Semitizing
use of *tithenai* not uncommon in the NT, cf. *AG*, s.v. '*tithēmi*', 1.2b)
that they **should go and bear fruit.** Here **go** is not the Aramaic
idiomatic auxiliary usage (i.e. go on bearing fruit), but is meant
literally, to go on mission. It is also a false interpretation to read
into **go** the special meaning of Jesus' departure (i.e. his Passion),
for the phrase is too weak to bear the sense of 'go the way of the
Cross', even though that will indeed happen, as we shall see in the
next section.

whatever you ask: as before in verse 7, and also in 14.13, the
disciples' prayer is for grace to continue Jesus' mission. They pray
in my name, i.e. as his representatives, and therefore the answer
is assured. The reference is not to prayer in general, but is strictly
parallel to **go and bear fruit** (the clauses beginning **so that** and
that are co-ordinate *hina* clauses, both dependent on **appointed**;
cf. Barrett).

17. This: the Greek is plural: 'these things', presumably meaning the contents of verse 16; so that the verse is not an exact
equivalent of verse 12. It is more like the effect of verse 11, picking
up the whole of the paragraph, and relating it to the actual situation of the disciples at the Last Supper. So **to love one another**
is the substance of all that Jesus has been saying, and it is the
command that is given at the Supper (13.34). In fact it is only
by referring back to 13.35, and seeing this section as an exposition

of it, that we can see the connection between the command to love
one another and the mission to the world.

The Hatred of the World 18–25

18. If the world hates you: the mission of the disciples is continuous with that of Jesus himself. The thought of love suggests its
antithesis, hate. It is thus a suitable point to insert teaching on the
world's hatred, which has its basis in warnings of persecution preserved in the Synoptic tradition. The most important Synoptic
parallel is Mt. 10.17–42, immediately following the mission charge.
For this sequence contains not only the hatred of the world (Mt.
10.22), but also versions of the sayings in 13.16 (just about to be
quoted in verse 20) and in 13.20, as well as teaching on the Holy
Spirit which clearly lies behind the idea of the witness of the
Counsellor in verses 26f. It is thus evident that the present section
of the second discourse is at once an exposition of further facets of
the Last Supper account of chapter 13 and a Johannine version of
the traditions which have also come together in Mt. 10 (partially
found also in Mk 13.9–13; Lk. 12.2–9 and other passages). John
relates these warnings directly to the sufferings of Jesus, using a
scriptural quotation from the Church's exegetical work, with
which he concludes the paragraph (verse 25).
know: the verb can be either imperative or indicative, but the
imperative is better, because this is new teaching, not referring
back to what the disciples already know. On the Semitic use of the
love/hate antithesis, see the notes on 12.25. That the world **hates**
Jesus, in so far as it does not respond to him, is inevitable by the
reasoning of 3.18–21. Jesus has ascribed the mounting opposition
in the time before the Passion to the hatred of the world (7.7).

19. I chose you out of the world: the choice of the disciples
(verse 16) has put them into the same category as Jesus himself,
and so they are removed from the category of men who separate
themselves from God (John's meaning of **the world,** cf. 14.17).
There is no warrant here for an 'other-worldly' outlook, as if the
disciples are to contract out of involvement in the ordinary affairs
of men. But by their incorporation into Christ they form a distinct
category in society.

20. Remember: Jesus reminds the disciples of his own words
in 13.16, which are quoted exactly. This is yet further proof that
the second discourse has been composed as a commentary on

chapter 13. There the saying was used to teach the proper exercise of authority among the disciples, after the model of Jesus himself. Here it is applied to persecution: the servant cannot hope to escape what even his master cannot avoid. This is the meaning which the saying has in its Matthean context (see Mt. 10.24f.).

persecute . . . keep: note the correlation between **persecute** and **hate** on the one hand, and **keep** and **love** on the other. On the positive side, to love Jesus and to keep his commandments are constantly brought together (cf. verse 10). The master/servant saying applies both ways, to the success of the disciples' mission and to the persecution which it evokes.

21. At this point the centre of interest changes. Jesus has finished speaking of the persecution of the disciples (at least for the moment), and now turns to consider the *reason* for the world's hatred. The world does not hate the disciples for themselves, but because they are *his* disciples.

on my account: lit. 'on account of my name'. John frequently has 'in my name', but the phrase with the preposition *dia* (on account of) occurs nowhere else in the Fourth Gospel. It is thus reasonable to suppose that he has taken over the whole phrase from his source; in fact, it occurs in Mt. 10.22 ('you will be hated by all for my name's sake'), just before the saying quoted in the last verse.

because they do not know: in typical Johannine language Jesus traces the world's rejection of himself to its failure to recognize the Father himself. This has been argued at length in chapter 8 (cf. especially 8.19, 54f.).

22. The world's opposition is thus a wilful refusal of the light. The argument here recapitulates the discourse on blindness of chapter 9, especially 9.41. The word for **excuse** (*prophasis*), only here in John, usually means a (false) pretext in the NT, but here it means a valid reason, as often in classical usage.

23. Barrett points out that this epigrammatic verse is the negative counterpart to 13.20b, which is based on a traditional saying. In view of the connection between the present section and 13.16ff., it may well be that John has actually modelled this verse on that saying. The point is that the world's hatred of Jesus is actually equivalent to hatred of God, however much it may profess to be devoted to him, because Jesus' teaching (verse 22) is entirely derived from him. The world was not only ignorant of God (verse 21), but actively hostile to him.

24. the works: in the argument of the central chapters, the works of Jesus have been specially important, because they are the acts of God, and so back up his claim to divine authority in his teaching, cf. 10.37f. (also alluded to in 14.11). His unique position as the Son of the Father has been proved by the fact that these divine acts are **works which no one else did.** They were not just the miracles of a wonder-worker, but acts which were done in obedience to the Father in order to reveal the glory of God (9.3). It was bad enough to refuse the teaching of Jesus (verse 21). It is even worse to refuse the revelation of God which has been given through his acts. As it is (**but now,** as in verse 21), the world cannot plead ignorance, for they have seen God act in Jesus, and in rejecting Jesus they have rejected God.

25. It is to fulfil: lit. 'but that the word . . . may be fulfilled . . .' The sentence is elliptical. For the final clause with *hina*, cf. 12.38. Here, as there, the introductory formula suggests that John is making use of an established scriptural explanation of the opposition to Jesus, which he now applies both to the hatred of the Father which it necessarily entails, and to the hatred of the disciples which follows from it. The quotation **is written in their law** (cf. 8.17; 10.34). There is a touch of irony here, that the Jews' rejection of the one sent from God is foretold in their own sacred scriptures. The quotation uses the language of the LXX, but does not quite tally with any single passage; the nearest approximations are Ps. 35.19; 69.4; Ps. Sol. 7.1. Of these Ps. 69.4 is to be preferred, because this psalm is widely used in the NT, and quotations from it occur elsewhere in John (see the notes on 2.17; also 19.28–30 below). Obviously the words quoted here would have been used in the first instance to account for the rejection and suffering of an innocent man, and so to combat the notion that Jesus in any way deserved to die. But John has generalized the application, to make it account for the rejection of the total message and work of Jesus.

The Witness of the Counsellor 26–7

26. It is against this background of the world's hatred that the disciples have to carry out their mission, but they will have the Counsellor to help them. Again the parallel with the warnings of Mt. 10 is striking. It seems that John has the material in reverse order, or elects to change the order in making use of it. For the world's hatred (verses 18–25) comes last in Matthew (Mt. 10.22). The inner speaking of the 'Spirit of your Father' has already been mentioned in Mt. 10.20, and the violent persecution of the disciples (= Jn 16.2) earlier still in Mt. 10.17f. The progression of thought is more logical if the order in Matthew is followed, for it explains the connection between persecution and the witness of the Spirit, who comes to the aid of the disciples when they have to make their defence. It should be observed how the background of the Paraclete passages in Mt. 10.20 (= Mk 13.11), in which the Spirit is to act as advocate or helper, goes some way to explaining why John has chosen this unusual title (see the notes on 14.16; cf. Brown, pp. 699f.). The rather illogical order in John is probably due to the fact that he has taken and developed this item for a separate homily, before bringing it and the rest of the material together for the second discourse.

As before in 14.16 and 26, it is necessary to provide an explanation of the title. **The Spirit of Truth** is clearly suitable in view of his function of bearing witness. **Who proceeds from the Father** is not really different from 'whom the Father will send' in 14.26. Jesus, too, was both sent by the Father and came from the Father (8.42; 13.3). But this phrase was incorporated in the Nicene Creed, to express the special metaphysical relationship of the Spirit to God; and the controversy between the Eastern Orthodox Churches and Western Christendom over the *filioque* clause stems from the fact that the text of this verse does not include the words 'and from the Son'. Needless to say, John could have no idea that his words would become the subject of such a long-standing theological dispute. (For a modern treatment of the problem, cf. V. Lossky, *The Mystical Theology of the Eastern Church* (1957), pp. 44–66.) **he will bear witness:** there is a notable parallel in *Test. Judah* xx.5: 'The spirit of truth testifies all things, and accuses all.' The context of the passage is the struggle of the Two Spirits in the soul of man (see above on 14.17). Hence it refers to the exposure of the heart of man and the accusation of him before God. Something akin to this will appear below in 16.8–11. Here, however, although it is clear that there is a fundamental community of thought, the application is quite different. Jesus is promising the assistance of the Spirit, to inspire the disciples to defend the faith in time of persecution. It probably means legal testimony in a court of law, as in Mt. 10.20.

27. you are also witnesses: the disciples can bear witness, not only because they will receive special inspiration of the Spirit, but also because of their unique experience as men who have been personally associated with Jesus **from the beginning.** This means from the start of Jesus' ministry, as in 16.4, not from the creation (as in 1.1; 8.44). There is probably a reference here to the special function of the apostles as witnesses of Jesus (cf. Ac. 1.21f.; 5.32), and therefore as guarantors of the gospel message.

Persecution **16. 1–4a**

1. I have said all this to you: the words in the Greek are identical with 'These things I have spoken to you' in 14.25. They are characteristic of John's editorial style in piecing together these discourses. Each time they relate the theme under discussion to the need to give advance warning before the Passion. Here the theme of persecution is resumed from 15.20. In 15.21–5 the reason for the world's hatred has been explained. Then there has been the slight digression on the witness of the Paraclete. Now Jesus gives some idea of the nature of the persecution which may be expected. It is necessary to do so, for unless the disciples are forewarned they will be in danger of **falling away.** This verb (*skandalizein*) is the same as 'take offence' in 6.61, but not used elsewhere in the Fourth Gospel. As a non-Johannine word in an editorial verse, it may well be derived from John's source. As we have seen (pp. 46of.) John knows the form of the prediction of Peter's denials as it is found in the Synoptics, though he has only used it for the final saying in 13.38. But in Mk 14.27–31 paras. Peter's protestation of loyalty, which provokes the prediction, is a response to Jesus' warning that 'You will all fall away (*skandalisthēsesthe*).' There will be another allusion by John to this very same verse in 16.32. As John sees it, the danger which it denotes will be due to loss of nerve in the face of violent persecution. Thus he uses this item of the Last Supper traditions to introduce his development of traditional sayings about persecution.

2. out of the synagogues: cf. 9.22; 12.42. The warnings in Mt. 10.17f. (= Mk 13.9) visualize trial and punishment by the synagogue, but do not actually mention excommunication. They also refer to putting the disciples to death, but without giving the motive specified by John, that it is thought to be **offering service** to God. The idea that 'one who sheds the blood of the godless is like one who brings an offering' (*Num. Rabba* xxi.4) illustrates the lengths to which fanaticism can go. Christians themselves have only too often been guilty of this in the course of history. John writes from the point of view of the time after the exclusion of the Minim, when Jewish Christians could no longer join in the worship of the synagogue (cf. Introduction, p. 37).

the hour: usually this refers to the moment of Jesus' Passion (cf. 13.1). Here, as also in verse 4, it means the moment of trial, when the disciples themselves undergo their corresponding share in the Passion.

3. The irony of the situation is that the opponents of the church actually think that such behaviour is acceptable to God. The reason for this tragic misunderstanding has already been given in 15.21–5, and so the ideas of 15.21 and 24 are briefly repeated. This verse is missing from the Sinaitic Syriac, perhaps because it began with the same Syriac particle as verse 4 (Barrett).

4a. I have said these things to you: the same words again as in verse 1. The whole sentence has the same meaning, but in positive form. Instead of 'falling away' the disciples will **remember that I told you of them** and so be prepared to hold fast.

their hour: i.e. the time of these things. **Their** (*autōn*) is only read by B A L Θ Ferrar group and a few minuscules and Old Latin and Vulgate, probably because of confusion with **of them** (also *autōn*), which is also omitted in some MSS. Both are likely to be original. Cp. Lk. 22.53: 'This is your hour, and the power of darkness.'

The Function of the Counsellor 4b–11

4b. So far the second discourse has been concerned with the way the disciples are to behave in the future, abiding in Jesus' love (15.1–17) and ready to face persecution (15.18–16.4a). Now John turns to the theme of the necessity of Jesus' departure, which was the major concern of the first discourse in chapter 14. For this purpose he uses two distinct kinds of material, on the work of the Paraclete (verses 7–15) and on the joy of the new relationship which is to be established (16–24). Thus the Paraclete material is an extension of the idea found in 15.26, that the Spirit inspires the disciples at the moment of trial. It becomes a full-scale exposure of the world, presumably through the disciples' preaching (7–11), and a comprehensive instruction of their minds (12–15). In order

to introduce this wider application and to get away from the particular theme of persecution, John has constructed a quasi-
dialogue, in which Jesus alone is the speaker, using three elements
from other parts of the larger context. (a) The editorial **these
things** picks up the idea of the present warning from verses 1
and 4a. (b) The theme of 'going' in verse 5 is taken from 13.33,
36, which has provided the text for chapter 14. (c) The disciples'
sorrow in verse 6 is taken from the material which is yet to be used
in verses 16-22.

from the beginning: cf. 15.27. So far Jesus himself has been the
disciples' teacher, but he must now prepare them for the conditions which will follow his departure to death and to glory.

5. now I am going: there is an intentional ambiguity, as the
words can apply equally to Jesus' death and to his future glory.

none of you asks me: there is a formal contradiction with 13.36
and 14.5, but (as shown above, pp. 461 and 467) this is not such
as to warrant theories of transposition. Barrett insists on the present
tense **asks.** The unspoken question forms the transition from the
apprehensiveness of verses 1 and 4 to the explanation of the reason
for Jesus' departure in verse 7. It thus performs the function of a
literalistic question to introduce a deeper explanation, which is
such a frequent device in the Johannine discourses. But it is put in
this unusual form of a suggestion by Jesus himself, so as not to
anticipate the dialogue of verses 16-19, which John is using as his
model for the quasi-dialogue at this point.

6. sorrow: the mistake of taking the idea of departure too
literally is shown up by the emotion of the disciples, which would
be quite unnecessary if they really understood the teaching which
is just about to be given. The word **sorrow** is taken from the
material to be used in verses 20-2.

7. truth: John's editorial work shades off into the Paraclete
material, which really begins in verse 8. First there is an echo of
the Paraclete's other title, the Spirit of truth, corresponding with
his special function of guiding the disciples 'into all the truth'
(verse 13). Thus when Jesus says **I tell you the truth,** it is more
than an asseveration (i.e. 'It is true, and not false, what I am
going to say to you'). It is an imparting of the truth, an exposition
of the plan of God, an instruction of the same order as the Spirit's
future guidance.

to your advantage: the same word as 'expedient' (*sumpherei*) in the unconscious prophecy of Caiaphas (11.50; 18.14). The argument which follows is extraordinary, suggesting as it does that Jesus and the Spirit cannot be present to the disciples at one and the same time. (Brown, p. 710, too readily assumes that this is what John actually means.) It is inevitable that we should detect an apologetic motive here. John is dealing with the problem of the absentee Lord (cf. Ac. 3.21). The presence of the Spirit in the Church is the guarantee (cf. 2 C. 1.22; 5.5) of the union of the disciples with Christ, who is in heaven. On the other hand, if we do not press the negative aspect, that **the Counsellor will not come to you** unless **I go away,** but concentrate on the positive aspect, that **if I go, I will send him to you,** the argument is consistent with John's theology. For (a) John conceives the chief function of the Spirit to be producing in the disciples the works which Jesus has done in his incarnate life; and (b) the departure of Jesus (i.e. his death) must be accepted by the disciples as an essential element of their response of faith, if they are to be capable of receiving the Spirit (cf. 3.1–15).

the Counsellor: further explanation of the title is unnecessary in view of the close proximity to 15.26. Here, as there, Jesus himself **will send** the Paraclete, although he actually proceeds from the Father, because Jesus in his glory remains the agent of the Father's will (cf. the notes on 14.13).

8. when he comes: i.e. to the disciples. What follows is the work of the disciples, which they will do in continuation from the ministry of Jesus. In fact it is the deeper meaning of the witness which the Paraclete will give to the world through them, already referred to in 15.26. For this witness will have a decisive effect upon the world. Unfortunately the way in which John describes this work in the following verses is so obscure that there is wide disagreement among scholars about its precise interpretation. John has sacrificed clarity to gain an artificial balance of clauses.

he will convince . . . of sin: John uses the same phrase (*elenchein peri hamartias*) as in 8.46: 'Which of you convicts me of sin?' This would seem to mean: 'he will find the world guilty in a matter of sin'. If we ask what the wrongdoing consists in, the answer appears to be provided in verse 9, that 'they do not believe in me'. The difficulty is that the other verses cannot be simply co-ordinated with this. The world cannot be found guilty **of righteousness and of judgment,** nor does the world's righteousness consist in

the fact that 'I (Jesus) go to the Father, etc.', or its judgment in
the fact that 'the ruler of this world is judged'. Bultmann avoids
the difficulty by ascribing these other elements (i.e. verses 8b, 10,
11) to the redactor. But this only shifts the problem from the author
to the redactor, who still must have thought that what he had
written made reasonable sense. We must therefore seriously question the meaning of the particles in this and the following verses.
'To convict of (*peri*) sin, that (*hoti*) they do not believe' (Büchsel),
makes good sense for verse 9, but is impossible for verses 10 and
11. But *elenchein*, which originally meant 'to scorn' and so 'to expose
as evil', was weakened by NT times to 'expose' in general, and is
so used by John himself in 3.20. The phrase could thus mean,
'He will expose the world concerning sin, etc.', i.e. bring to light
the true meaning of these concepts in the world. In this case *peri*
means 'concerning' or 'in regard to'; and the *hoti* clauses in verses
9–11 must be translated 'in that'. Thus the Paraclete reveals the
real nature of sin, in that it is rejection of Jesus; of righteousness,
in that it has been demonstrated in Jesus' obedience to death; and
of judgment, in that the archetypal act of judgment has taken
place in the moment of his Passion. These verses are explained
along these lines by Westcott, Bernard and Lightfoot. But a more
satisfactory sense is gained, if *hoti* is translated 'because'. This has
the advantage of retaining the meaning 'convict' for *elenchein*, as in
8.46. On this view all three elements are different aspects of the
same thing, viz. the condemnation of the world. It is convicted of
its own sin because of its unbelief; of *God*'s righteousness, which is
vindicated in the just condemnation of the world, because of God's
saving act in the passion of Jesus; and of judgment, because that
was the decisive act for all time, so that the issue has already been
decided. This view is taken by Hoskyns, Bultmann, Barrett,
Strathmann, Blank, Marsh and Brown (so also the paraphrase of
NEB).

  The last view is attractive, but labours under the difficulty that
righteousness is out of line with **sin** and **judgment,** because it
is the righteousness of God and not of the world. But if **sin** and
righteousness are interpreted along the lines of the special use
of their Semitic equivalents in judicial contexts (see the notes on
verses 9 and 10), they can be translated 'guilt' and 'innocence',
and so both be applied to the world. **Judgment** is then the judicial
verdict. The verses on this view include the possibility of the

salvation of the world. For the world is shown up as guilty because of its unbelief, but as innocent (if it does believe) because of what Jesus has done; and as under judgment, because the decisive factor for a judgment has already taken place. A view very similar to this is argued by Mastin (who here takes over from Sanders; see Bibliography).

9. sin: according to John's usage **sin** (*hamartia*) is a quality. This is clear in 9.41, where *RSV* has 'guilt'. But it also applies in 8.46, which does not mean 'Which of you convicts me of actual sin?', but rather 'Which of you finds me guilty (of the implicit charge of speaking falsehood)?' John does not use the usual biblical (LXX and NT) words for guilty (*adikos, anomos, asebēs*), though he once has the noun *adikia* in a legal context (7.18, translated 'falsehood'). In biblical Hebrew the adjective *rāšāʿ* (wicked) has a verbal form *hiršîaʿ* (to make wicked), which is regularly used in judicial contexts for 'to find guilty', 'to condemn'. Its opposite is *hiṣdîq* (to make righteous), used for 'to find innocent', 'to acquit'. It is the use of 'righteousness' in verses 8 and 10 which suggests that John is here using *hamartia* in the sense of 'guilt' as a synonym for *adikia* (cf. 1 Jn 5.17: 'All wrongdoing [*adikia*] is sin [*hamartia*]'). John's use has a precedent in Gen. 42.21, where 'we are guilty' (*ʾašēmîm ʾanaḥnû*) is rendered *en hamartia esmen* by the LXX.

because they do not believe in me: John is referring to the moral response to God, who is made known in Jesus. From this point of view failure to believe is a wilful refusal, and so is culpable (cf. 3.18). The intellectual difficulties of the honest unbeliever do not come within John's purview at all.

10. righteousness: John never uses this word (*dikaiosunē*), which is central for Paul, outside the present context, though it occurs in the phrase 'to do right' in 1 Jn 2.29; 3.7, 10. Instead he generally has 'truth' where 'righteousness' might have been expected (3.21; cf. 4.23f.; 8.32, 44; 14.6; 17.17, 19; 18.37f.). It is thus unlikely that the word refers to moral perfection in an abstract way. Rather, the forensic context places it firmly in the realm of judicial vocabulary. In late Judaism the status of man before God was regularly thought of in judicial terms. The eschatological picture of the final judgment is clear evidence of this. But it is now known that Paul's special concept of justification by faith must be seen against this background, and that it has its root in Jewish thought, especially in the Dead Sea Scrolls (cf. 1QH iv.30–7; vii.16–19, 28–31; 1QS xi.10–15). If John normally avoids this word, but found it necessary to use it here, it is reasonable to suppose that it was the best word he could think of to express the opposite of *hamartia* (guilt). In doing so he was not dependent on Paul (as was supposed by Hatch, *HTR* xiv (1921), pp. 103–5), but on the Jewish background of thought which both share.

because I go: obviously the verdict of acquittal would be given if the world believed, just as it is pronounced guilty when it withholds belief. But it is not belief as such which procures the acquittal but what it is that is believed. It is the fact that God has taken action for the salvation of men (3.16), and that belief is not merely intellectual assent but a matter of entrusting oneself to God on the grounds that he has done so. This divine action is the total Christ-event, which comes to its climax in Jesus' return to the Father by way of death and resurrection. In the setting of the Last Supper this can be put in the form that we have here: **I go to the Father,** i.e. the work of salvation is accomplished; **and you will see me no more,** i.e. you will remain in the world to make known this fact, and so to bring it to bear upon the lives of men. For it is in the mission of the disciples that the Paraclete convicts the world, exposing men's hearts for the verdict one way or the other, according to their response.

11. judgment: this word (*krisis*) has a wide range of meaning in the Fourth Gospel. In 3.19, to which the present passage is clearly related, it means the criterion. In 5.24 (a verse which may be regarded as the Johannine counterpart to the Pauline doctrine of justification by faith), it means the act of judging, which the believer by-passes. In 5.27 'to execute judgment' means to give the verdict. In 5.29 it means condemnation, which John has here expressed by *hamartia*. But the present verse is evidently modelled on 12.31, and there the meaning is the judicial act. Here, however, the context requires the meaning 'judicial verdict', which would normally be represented by *krima* (but John does not distinguish these words, cf. 9.39). The work of the Paraclete in the Church will have a decisive effect. Men cannot be confronted with the fact of salvation without making a choice one way or another. The moment of choice is the occasion when the divine judgment becomes an inescapable reality to them. John has presented this idea in universal and timeless terms in 3.18–21. In 5.22–9 he put it in

terms of consistent eschatology, with the important modification
that the End Time is anticipated in the life of Jesus. Here it is the
particular application, at any time in the future, of what has been
done in Christ and remains to be fulfilled in the End Time.

because the ruler of this world is judged: it is clear from
12.31f. that the departure of Jesus, just mentioned, and the expulsion of the Devil are the reverse sides of the same coin. The mythological language puts the event of Christ into the cosmic setting of
the total sweep of history. **is judged** (lit. 'has been judged',
kekritai) is said from the point of view of the post-Resurrection
situation. The issues need not be debated afresh, when the Paraclete does his work of judging, because they have been settled by
the decisive act which has already been done. Comparison with
12.31 ('cast out') shows that **judged** here means condemned.

The Spirit of Truth 12–15

12. yet many things: the second function of the Paraclete is
to give further instruction to the disciples. There may be an apologetic motive at work here, for John is aware that his presentation
of the Gospel is the fruit of reflection on the original tradition, and
could be criticized on these grounds. But it is also true that heretical teachers are at work, and it is necessary to indicate the limits of
legitimate doctrinal development (cf. 1 Jn 4.1–3).
bear: a metaphorical use of *bastazein*, to carry a burden; cf. Ac.
15.10 (contrast Mt. 11.30); Gal. 5.10; Rev. 2.2f.

13. When the Spirit of truth comes: lit. 'when he, the Spirit
of truth, comes'. The pronoun is masculine, agreeing with the
implicit *ho Paraklētos*, whereas **Spirit** is neuter, placed in apposition
to it. Thus the personal character of the Spirit is maintained. The
title now comes into its own, because it is essential to John's purpose that the Spirit **will guide you into all the truth.** The mss.
show some confusion about the meaning of these words; the reading of ℵ D L W: 'in [i.e. by] all the truth' suggests trustworthy
guidance, whereby the disciples will be kept safe from deviation.
It is accepted by Barrett because of its good attestation, but it may
be due to the influence of LXX usage. The Vulgate's 'will teach
you all truth' suggests passive reception of revealed truths on the
part of the disciples. But the text (supported by B A) implies a
process of bringing them to full apprehension of the truth, which
is what the context demands. There are good OT precedents for

guide (*hodēgein*). The verb is used with God as subject (Ps. 25.5: 'Lead me in thy truth'); with the Spirit (Ps. 143.10: 'Let thy good spirit lead me'); with Wisdom (Wisd. 9.11: 'she will guide me wisely': cf. 10.10, 17). So in the same vein Philo speaks of the Spirit's guidance (*Mos.* ii.265) and in *Test. Benjamin* vi.1 'an angel of peace [i.e. the good spirit in the Two Spirits doctrine] guides' man's 'soul'. Naturally in the Fourth Gospel itself it has been Jesus himself who has declared the truth hitherto; cf. 8.40, 45f. In fact, as we shall see in the rest of the verse, John thinks of the Spirit's guidance exactly in the same way as he thinks of the teaching of Jesus.

he will not speak on his own authority: this is the claim which Jesus has constantly made about himself; cf. 8.26–8, 38, 40, 42; 12.49; 14.10. The Paraclete is similarly no independent force, but the transmitter of the Father's will. The future tense is read even in the dependent clause by B D W and others (i.e. 'whatever he will hear' for **whatever he hears**), and this is right, for Jesus is speaking of the future conditions when his own presence is withdrawn. This teaching includes not only what is already known, but also **the things that are to come.** This rather unexpected phrase may well be an allusion to Isa. 44.7, where the truth of God is proved by contrast with the falsity of the idols from the capacity to predict the future. It refers, then, to the prophetic gift, which was recognized as one of the spiritual gifts in the primitive Church, cf. Ac. 21.10f.; 1 C. 12.10 (so Bernard). But this is thought of not just from the point of view of the unknown future, but of the whole range of eschatological events, which have been anticipated in Jesus, and remain to be worked out through time in the life of the Church.

14. That this is what is meant by 'the things that are to come' is evident from the clarification which is now given. The Paraclete **will glorify** Jesus by maintaining and impressing upon the disciples what has been accomplished by Jesus, and by actually performing Jesus' own mission through them. The Paraclete **will take** what is proper to Jesus, and **declare it to** the disciples, so that they may make it known to the world. Hence (as Bultmann points out) the Paraclete does not so much bring new knowledge as the power of Jesus' word, which is ever new in the process of confronting fresh ranges of hearers.

15. All that the Father has is mine: this verse (missing, presumably by homoioteleuton, from P⁶⁶ א*) is not simply aimed at expressing the complete unity between the Father and the Son, which remains unbroken in the new situation when the Spirit is the effective agent in the furtherance of Jesus' mission. It is rather concerned with the complete identity between the mission of Jesus and the mission of the disciples under the Spirit's guidance. The whole of God's will for mankind has been expressed in Jesus. The disciples cannot expect to have such an all-inclusive endowment as was seen in him. They **will take** of **what is mine** (the Greek has partitive *ek*), according to the measure that each may be able to receive. Whatever they achieve, it is only a part of what is given to Jesus by right. But none the less it is *his* mission which they will be empowered by the Spirit to perform. The future belongs to Jesus as well as the past. So 'the things that are to come' are already known in principle from the revelation of God in his incarnate life; and the 'many things' that the disciples 'cannot bear now' are only authentic if they maintain continuity with what has already been given.

Sorrow Turned into Joy 16–24

16. A little while: the change of theme, probably involving the employment of material from another homily, is abrupt. But the theme has been prepared for in the introductory part of the preceding paragraph, verse 6. John is dealing with the necessity of Jesus' departure. It is 'expedient' because of the coming of the Paraclete (verse 7). But it is also cause for joy, because of the new and lasting relationship which it will establish between Jesus and the disciples. This has already been treated in the first discourse at some length. But in the course of it John used the mysterious **little while** (14.19; cf. 7.33; 12.35; 13.33) in a way which was open to misunderstanding. He there implied that the moment of Jesus' death, which is about to happen in **a little while,** would be the removal of him from the sight of the world, but not from the sight of the disciples. But in fact they too **will see me no more.** It is only after a further period, **again a little while,** that they **will see** him in a new sense. It is clear that John means the Resurrection (cf. 14.19). He thus correlates his teaching with the conventional Christian teaching of the Resurrection on the third day. The death of Jesus is to John the fundamental thing, for it reunites Jesus with the Father. Thus the condition for the new relationship with the disciples is fulfilled. But he can make a concession to the conventional view, in as much as the disciples only become aware of the new relationship in the Resurrection experience. And this happened on the third day. Thus the vague **little while** here corresponds with the traditional time-lag between death and Resurrection. We may observe how John is once more correcting misunderstanding in this second discourse (cf. 15.15, 20). At the end of the verse most MSS. and versions add: 'because I go to the Father', which seems to be required by the next verse. But the textual grounds for omission are strong (P⁵ P⁶⁶ B ℵ D L W Old Latin). But if these words do not belong to the present verse, how can the disciples quote them in verse 17? This question forces us to look further back, and we duly find *both* 'you will see me no more' *and* 'because I go to the Father' in verse 10. This at once solves the problem of the abrupt introduction of the new theme. John has adopted his customary technique of picking up a phrase from a previous paragraph and subjecting it to more detailed exposition. The whole of the new paragraph expresses the triumph which was just hinted at in verse 10.

17. The conversation-piece is designed to narrow down the issue to the obscure phrase **a little while.** The disciples repeat what Jesus has said in verse 16, and then they add the phrase out of verse 10, in order to show that they *do* understand the idea of Jesus' departure and return. At least they realize that to say **you will not see me . . . you will see me** is the same thing as **I go to my Father.** It is the act which puts the finishing touch on the work which Jesus came to do, and forms the subject of their message to the world (verses 7–11). What remains to be explained is the time indication used in connection with it, and this is repeated in verse 18 as the one real question at issue. In fact the idea contained in **because I go to the Father** is not taken up in what follows, so that it is scarcely necessary to include it in the present verse. Mastin suggests that it is inserted in order that the equivalence of the two themes should not be lost to view.

18. What does he mean by: lit. 'What is this that he says', as in verse 17. But 'that he says' should probably be omitted with P⁵ P⁶⁶ ℵ* D* W Ferrar group, Old Latin and Sahidic. The verse shows other signs of confusion in the MSS. no doubt because of its repetitiveness, and **what he means** at the end of the verse should perhaps be omitted with B.

19. When this chapter is read aloud the repetitions become almost ludicrous. John is holding up the climax so as to give the greatest solemnity to the solution to the disciples' quandary.

20. The answer is given simply by a change of metaphor, which certainly helps to clarify the issue, though it still does not amount to plain-speaking. The **truly** opening suggests, as usual, that John is building on a traditional saying. This is no doubt the parable in verse 21. The present verse is part of the application of it, which is given by anticipation so as to form an exposition of the statement in verse 19 (= 16). The parable depicts the sudden change from severe distress to triumphant joy in the common experience of childbirth. There is no mention of the disputed 'little while', but the parable implies that it is comparable to the period of labour. But before the parable is given, Jesus speaks of the experience of the disciples in terms which suggest mourning for one dead, and thereby fixes the interpretation as his own death and Resurrection. The disciples will not see him, because he must die. What is grief to them makes the world (here regarded as hostile to God) temporarily jubilant. But then they will see him: **sorrow** for one dead **will turn into joy** at the discovery that he is alive; cf. 14.19, 27f. Thus the Resurrection on the third day corresponds with the renewed sight of Jesus after a little while. It may then be the case that John's 'little while' is actually what lies behind the conventional description of the Resurrection as 'on the third day' (e.g. Lk. 18.33) or 'after three days' (e.g. Mk 8.31). For this may be derived from the literal application of some such phrase as 'after two or three days', meaning 'a little while' (cf. Hos. 6.2, which may lie behind these expressions).

21. The last verse has changed the thought from the theme of being lost to view and then restored to sight to the theme of death and new life. It still has not explained the little while. This is done by means of the parable of childbirth, which is admirably suited to the new theme. The metaphorical use of the ideas of childbirth is frequent to the OT. It generally occurs in a bad sense, with reference to the pains of the mother. A good example is Isa. 26.16–19, where the people complain that they were 'like a woman with child, who writhes and cries out in her pangs, when she is near her time'. This is followed by the promise 'thy dead shall live, their bodies shall rise', which is a metaphorical use of the idea of resurrection to suggest national revival; but the childbirth metaphor

has been dropped. But in Isa. 66.7–14 the future prosperity of
Zion is foretold with a striking use of the idea of childbirth, in
which delivery of the child is so fast that the pains of labour are not
even experienced. Turning to the Dead Sea Scrolls, we find an
even more impressive parallel (1QH iii.9f): '. . . She labours
in her pains who bears the Man. For amid the throes of Death she
shall bring forth a man-child, and amid the pains of Hell there
shall spring from her child-bearing crucible a Marvellous Mighty
Counsellor; and the Man shall be delivered from out of her throes'
(Vermes' translation). This appears to be the birth of the Messiah,
with its obvious allusion to Isa. 9.6, but it forms part of a much
more complex poem on the coming eschatological cataclysm, from
which the messianic *people* will emerge (for the interpretation of
the passage, cf. M. Black, *The Scrolls and Christian Origins* (1961),
p. 150). This eschatological use of this imagery was later taken up
in the Jewish doctrine of 'the pangs of the Messiah'. There is no
parallel to this in the Synoptic record of the teaching of Jesus, but
there is no reason to doubt that he could have used this imagery in
a similar way to express the arrival of the New Age. The verse may,
then, be a genuine parable about the coming Age, which John has
taken over as the central item of teaching in this paragraph. That
it is based on an Aramaic original is implied by the generic article
with **a woman** (lit. the woman), the idiomatic use of **her hour**
(cf. 12.23), and the use of 'man' (*anthrōpos*) for **child.** Bernard is
mistaken when he seeks to allegorize the details, making the
woman's pains equivalent to the sorrow of the disciples. The point
of the parable is simply the sudden transition from grief to joy.

22. I will see you again: as it stands, the phrase refers to the
Resurrection appearances of Jesus. But we know from the larger
context that he means the establishing of a permanent relationship
(cf. 15.1–11, and note the reminiscences of 10.29 and 15.11 in the
final words, **no one will take your joy from you**). There is
probably a literary allusion to Isa. 66.14: 'You shall see, and your
heart shall rejoice.' The change from 'you shall see' to **I will see
you** may be intentionally directed to turning the thought away
from the Resurrection appearances to the abiding relationship
which is achieved by Jesus' death and resurrection.

23. In that day: this eschatological phrase has been used in
14.20 to denote the Resurrection as the time when the new conditions of the End Time are established. John here moves the

thought still further away from the idea of seeing Jesus. He is
preparing for the point that the disciples' relationship with the
risen Jesus gives direct access to God. So the next few verses are a
repetition of the ideas of 14.12–14. The transition of thought is
effected by a subtle use of the verb to **ask.** Two different Greek
verbs are used. First we have *erōtān* in the phrase **you will ask
nothing of me.** It could mean to pray, but it could also mean to
ask questions. The meaning 'you will not need to ask me any more
questions' is accepted here by Barrett, Brown and Mastin, though
in fact *erōtān* is used for 'pray' in verse 26 below. Otherwise the
verb *aitein* is used throughout, and it certainly means here to ask
in prayer. The meaning 'ask me no more questions' for the first
phrase is probably right. It avoids contradiction with 14.14, and
suitably expresses one aspect at least of the disciples' future joy;
for all has been revealed to them, or at least will be through the
Paraclete (verse 13). It is also implied by verse 30, referring back to
this verse. But the thought of asking carries with it the idea of
prayer, and it is natural to go on to explain the nature of prayer in
this new situation. It is precisely because the disciples now have
the right to pray to the Father **in my name** that it can be said
that free access to the Father is one aspect of the post-Resurrection
situation.

Truly: what John has to say on this subject is once more based
on a traditional saying, though as before it is not actually reproduced until the next verse. This is the famous 'Ask, and it will be
given you . . . for everyone who asks receives . . .' of the Sermon
on the Mount (Mt. 7.7f. = Lk. 11.9f.). Mt. 18.19f., on the efficacy
of prayer 'where two or three are gathered in my name', should
also be compared. The saying needs to be modified by the addition
of **in my name** (see the notes on 14.13). The disciples' requests
cannot be answered indiscriminately. The position of **in my name**
differs in the various MSS. The majority take this phrase with **ask
anything of the Father,** as in the next verse. But *RSV* follows
P5vid B ℵ C* and Origen in taking it with **he will give** (*NEB*,
mg.). This may well be right, as its unexpectedness tells in favour
of it. It means that the Father will grant the disciples' requests on
account of Jesus' own relationship with him, in which the disciples share. This is another consequence of the post-Resurrection
situation.

   24. Hitherto: Of course the disciples, like all religious people, have been accustomed to pray to the Father, but only after the Resurrection will they do so **in my name,** i.e. as Jesus' representatives. Both the asking and the receiving are to be done in Jesus' name, because the Resurrection unites him to the Father without breaking the relationship with the disciples. On this basis of complete reciprocity it is possible to quote the traditional saying in its unadorned simplicity: **'ask, and you will receive'.** The result is that the joy of the disciples, experienced in the moment of his Resurrection, is continually maintained, as they benefit by the lasting consequences of it.

Access to the Father 25–8

25. I have said this to you: the same resumptive phrase as in 14.25; 15.11; 16.1. As before, it draws attention to the contrast between the moment of speaking on the eve of the Passion and the new conditions which will apply after the Resurrection. This is the moment to which **the hour is coming** refers (contrast the use of the same phrase in verse 2). The meaning of the relationship between the disciples and the Father, which has been handled from the point of view of prayer in verses 23f., is now developed by contrast with the present situation. During his earthly life Jesus has taught the disciples **in figures** (*en paroimiais,* cf. 10.6), i.e. obscurely, because his bodily presence has overshadowed the spiritual relationship which will exist after the Resurrection. So the promise to **tell you plainly** (*parrēsia*) **of the Father** does not refer to further teaching to be given in similar fashion in the course of the post-Resurrection appearances, but to the direct knowledge which will result from the mutual indwelling which will then be established. This could be expressed in terms of the doctrine of the Paraclete, as in 14.26; 16.12–15. But John is here using the range of material about prayer in Jesus' name, which is concerned with the same conditions, but must be regarded as drawn from a different homily.

26. In that day you will ask in my name: these words briefly summarize verses 23f., which are now to be clarified. It is important that the disciples should realize that praying in the name of Jesus is not intended to imply that he is an intermediary in order to gain entry into the forbidden territory of the presence of God. When Jesus says **I do not say . . . that I shall pray the Father,** he may be correcting a misunderstanding of 14.16, where he says 'And I will pray the Father', though this is a Paraclete passage. Alternatively it may be a correction of a false impression about his position as *himself* the Paraclete with the Father (1 Jn 2.1), or similar teaching. But the truth of the matter is that, precisely because the disciples pray as his representatives, they have direct access to the Father, because of his own union with him.

27. the Father himself loves you: this direct access is most simply expressed by the idea of the loving relationship of mutual indwelling, cf. 14.21. **Loves** here is *philein* (both times), but it is not distinguished from *agapān* used elsewhere in these discourses. Obviously it is a two-sided relationship. The fact that the disciples have the right disposition for it is proved by their attitude to Jesus: **you have loved me and have believed that I came from the Father.** Indeed this belief shows that they are already the recipients of the Father's love, in as much as it has been expressed in the incarnation, which they acknowledge. It is probable that we should read 'that I came from God' (*theou*, P5 P66vid *ℵ A Θ 33; *tou theou*, Γ Δ W Lake and Ferrar groups and most later MSS.) instead of **from the Father** (B ℵcorr C* D L), which seems to be due to assimilation to the next verse (so *NEB*). But D W omit the phrase in the next verse altogether, running on the sentence. Barrett takes this shorter text to be original. But the repetition with slight variations (a different word for **from**) is quite in John's style.

28. The future relationship of the disciples to the Father results from the historic act of God in Christ. To John the Incarnation and the Passion are the two foci of this act. He has mentioned the Incarnation in the last verse. Now he expands his words to take in the Passion, using his favourite idea of Jesus' departure. He thereby brings the thought back to the actual circumstances of the setting of the discourse, which will conclude with the reader prepared for the continuation of the Passion narrative. **The world** here has a neutral sense, as in 10.36.

Conclusion **29–33**

29. now you are speaking plainly: the conversation makes a bridge between the high level of thinking in the preceding discourse and the Passion narrative, from which the prediction of the scattering of the disciples is taken (verse 32; cf. p. 497 above).

When it comes to the point of the arrest, John fails to mention
the flight of the disciples (but cf. 18.8). But he is clearly aware of
the tradition of it preserved in the Synoptic Gospels, and it is in
one sense an embarrassment to him. For obviously the disciples
would have stood firm if the above teaching had actually been
given at the Last Supper, and if they had understood it and
accepted it. The gulf is so wide that it can only be bridged by a
subtle use of irony. First the disciples claim that they have understood Jesus' teaching, although in fact they have not done so. They
suppose that Jesus is **speaking plainly,** but the whole point of
verse 25 was that this could only apply *after* the Passion.

30. Next they confess that Jesus knows **all things** (cf. verse 15),
so that they do not even need to ask him for anything. The word
for **question** is *erōtān*, and it clearly refers back to 'you will ask
nothing of me' in verse 23. But the idea of asking in prayer is not
excluded. Again the disciples have missed the fact that this is one
of the new conditions which will operate 'in that day'.

by this we believe: finally they take up and affirm for themselves
the confession of faith which Jesus has applied to them in verse 27.
But this too is defective, because it does not include mention of
Jesus' return to the Father (verse 28). In fact this is the cardinal
factor for the establishing of the new relationship between the
disciples and the Father. The disciples have confessed faith in the
deepest teaching of the discourse about the future situation, but
they have failed to recognize that the crucifixion must come first.
It is not surprising that Jesus now queries their confession of faith
by challenging them with their own share in the coming suffering,
which is the real test of faith. The irony is just the same as it was
with Peter in 13.36f.

31. Do you now believe: the ironical question is expressed
without an interrogative particle, just as in 13.38. Bernard rightly
points out that the emphasis falls on **now** (*arti*), but he is wrong
to deny that this is a question. The point is that the disciples have
not really reached true belief. John has a practical purpose in
these verses, for he wishes his readers to be prepared for the test
of persecution.

32. The hour is coming: Jesus means the Passion, as in verse
25, but from the point of view of the readers it carries with it the
time of persecution, as in verse 2. It is put emphatically and
urgently (**indeed it has come**; some MSS. add 'now'), because it

is the point which the disciples have so lamentably missed in their
confession of faith.

scattered: Gr. *skorpisthēte*. Although the simple verb is used, it can
hardly be doubted that this is an allusion to the quotation of
Zech. 13.7 in its non-LXX form (*diaskorpismena*), on which the
Synoptic prediction of the flight of the disciples is based (Mt.
26.31 = Mk 14.27). The compound verb was used by John in
11.52 (see the notes *ad loc.*). The use of this quotation in the earlier
tradition is to be ascribed to the apologetic need to account for the
disciples' desertion of their Master, which must have been a source
of grief and embarrassment to them. Cf. also verse 1.

not alone: the flight of the disciples is a dark note on which to end
the discourses. It is required by the narrative. But this must not
be allowed to spoil the effect of the discourses, which have been
designed to give reassurance to the Church under threat of persecution. It is true that the disciples will leave Jesus alone. But his
isolation at this moment is offset by his close union with the Father,
which has been the foundation of the teaching of these chapters,
and is the ground for the final note of triumph. The vocabulary in
which this is expressed is thoroughly Johannine, and has a close
parallel in 8.29. It is possible that John here is intentionally correcting a false understanding of the cry of dereliction in Mt. 27.46
(= Mk 15.34). But this can be no more than surmise.

   33. I have said this to you: cf. verse 25.

peace carries with it the notion of lasting well-being and blessing,
as in 14.27.

have tribulation: D Old Latin and some Greek Fathers have the
future verb, but the present is probably intentional, as the conditions of the church in John's own time are in mind. The word for
tribulation (*thlipsis*) is the same as 'anguish' in verse 21. It carries
with it the idea of the eschatological birth pangs.

overcome: this verb (*nikān*, cf. *nikē* = victory) is a military term,
rarely used in the NT and only here in the Fourth Gospel. But
it occurs in 1 Jn 2.13f.; 4.4; 5.4f. The last reference is specially
close to the present passage. The use of this verb draws attention
to the cosmic significance of the Passion, cf. 12.31. The past tense
is appropriate, because Jesus has already won the spiritual victory
in principle (12.27–36). It also expresses certitude with regard to
the future, when the redemptive work of Christ will be the accomplished fact which continually gives assurance to the Church.

So the discourses end with the reassuring note with which they began, but it has now become the sound of triumph.

THE PRAYER OF JESUS 17.1–26

Although the Supper discourses have been skilfully brought back to the point in the narrative where they began, and all is set for the account of the arrest of Jesus, the story is again held up by another long insertion. According to the Synoptic Gospels Jesus went with the disciples to Gethsemane ('as was his custom', Lk. 22.39) in order to pray (Mt. 26.36 = Mk 14.32). The introduction of a prayer of Jesus thus agrees with the Synoptic tradition, though it is placed before he goes to Gethsemane (18.1), where apparently nothing happens until the arrest. John had removed the prayer from the Gethsemane account, as he wished to use it as the basis of a theological explanation of the meaning of the Passion at an earlier point (12.27–36). But it is evident that the Gethsemane tradition made a profound impression on him, and that his understanding of Jesus in his relation to the Father owes much to it. The prayer of chapter 17 has slight links with it, but it is at this deeper level of John's Christology, and of his attempt to enter into the mind of Jesus, that his work is chiefly indebted to it.

The purpose of the composition, and the reason for inserting it into the narrative at this point, may be deduced from the contents. First Jesus prays for himself, that the crowning act of his earthly ministry may indeed lead to the glorious conclusion which God has intended (verses 1–5). Next he prays for the disciples, that they may be protected and upheld in their mission, which is the continuation of his own (verses 6–19). It is in connection with the mission that Jesus uses the language of sacrifice, which has earned for the whole piece the title of The Consecration Prayer (Westcott, Hoskyns). After this it is entirely natural that Jesus should go on to pray for the Church of the future, which will be the fruit of the disciples' mission (verses 20–3). Here the whole emphasis falls on the overriding need to maintain the unity of the Christian community, echoing the New Commandment of 13.34f. Finally Jesus prays for the union of all, both the disciples and the Church of the future, in his ultimate glory in the presence of the Father, thus drawing together the threads of all three of the preceding sections (verses 24–6).

The prayer is thus primarily an act of intercession, and it is only in this sense that it can be called the Highpriestly Prayer, a title which has been applied to it from Cyril of Alexandria onwards. It fittingly concludes the account of the Last Supper, summing up as it does the whole purpose of John's presentation of the narrative, in which the meaning of discipleship has been the dominant theme. It is shot through with a sense of urgency, which betrays John's concern for the state of the Church in his own day. The Church is faced with internal disruption. It is beset by danger from within, as well as by the threat of persecution from without, which has been the subject of much of the Second Discourse. This internal danger is the divisive effect of false teachers, if we may judge from 1 Jn 2.18ff. There is the risk that the whole work of Christ may fail in its effect. From this point of view the prayer is a final plea of the Master himself. It is not without reason that it has become the charter of the Ecumenical Movement in the twentieth century.

This last observation draws attention to the literary genre of the prayer. It is a final message, a sort of last will and testament. Bultmann points to the farewell messages of the Revealer in the Gnostic literature. Dodd (*Interpretation*, pp. 420-3) shows how, in the Hermetic literature, a prayer or hymn of the Revealer is itself the final revelation, whereby the initiant attains salvation. But although the prayer might well be taken in this way by a Hellenistic reader, it cannot be regarded as actually modelled on such pagan prototypes. As we have seen, it is really an afterthought, inserted at a late stage in the process of the composition of the Gospel, which was originally planned without it. But the literary device of a final message can be found within the Bible itself—Jacob (Gen. 49), Moses (Dt. 33; but in fact the whole of Deuteronomy is a farewell speech), Samuel (1 Sam. 12), and Paul (Ac. 20.17-38). It is a device whereby the author hopes to produce moral effect by the emotional impact of the situation. From this point of view it gives insight into the author's deepest aims, and accordingly this chapter has been studied by E. Käsemann as the clue to the purpose of the Fourth Gospel as a whole (*The Testament of Jesus* (1968)). Käsemann stresses the importance of knowledge (verses 3, 25f.), and thereby reaffirms Bultmann's interpretation of John as basically a gnosticized Christianity. But John has no wish to pull Christianity from its roots in the historic events of the Incarnation and of the Passion and Resurrection, however difficult

they may be for modern men to believe. The knowledge which
Jesus imparts is not separable from those events. They alone give
the basis of a right understanding of his unique position in relation
to men, so that they may live in union with him. And this is a
moral union, carrying with it mutual obligations. It is a unity
which is modelled on the relation of Jesus to the Father himself.

John has produced his desired effect by presenting this vital
teaching in the form of a prayer of the Master. Is it a free composition of his own, using his utmost imaginative power to enter into
the mind of Jesus at this solemn moment before the Passion? Or is
it based on authentic tradition? Most editors argue for some degree
of authenticity, but on slender grounds. Verbatim reporting of
what was said at the Last Supper is as improbable for this chapter
as it was for the Supper Discourses. The language is Johannine
throughout. Both phraseology and subject matter are closely related to the Supper Discourses and to John's writing earlier in the
Gospel. The prayer-style, with its characteristic address 'Father!',
is modelled on the Gethsemane prayer (possible allusion in verse
24) and on the Lord's Prayer (probable allusion in verse 15). The
prayer as a whole has its closest parallel in Mt. 11.25-7 (= Lk.
10.21f.). But this, as has been remarked above (p. 221), seems to
have entered so deeply into John's Christological thinking, that it
can only be regarded as a general background influence to his
composition here. Precise allusions to it are lacking.

The fact that the prayer cannot be securely traced back to Jesus
himself in no way detracts from its value. It is precisely because of
the convincing way in which John has penetrated the mind of
Christ that many Christians are reluctant to deny its authenticity.
John writes from within the Christian experience, perhaps two
generations after the events he describes. In the meantime that
experience has not lost its vitality. John has a vivid sense of the
union with Christ which his words describe. He feels that he has
the aid of the Paraclete (16.12–15). He can say with Paul 'we have
the mind of Christ' (1 C. 2.16). Jesus has left no records of what
was going on in his own mind, and many authors, both ancient
and modern, have speculated about his inner consciousness. To
some extent their reconstructions reflect the mind and temper of
their own times, and the same is true of John's. From this point
of view Christ is a changing personality, relating himself to each

generation in the way that is appropriate to its particular needs. There is always the risk of serious distortion. But it can confidently be asserted that John's picture is free from such distortion. It is consistent with the impression of Jesus' personality which can be gained from the more varied evidence contained in the Synoptic Gospels. But, in the last analysis, it stands or falls with the Christology of the Fourth Gospel as a whole.

Prayer for Jesus' own Glorification **1–5**

1. these words: the whole of the Supper discourses.
he lifted up his eyes: the attitude for prayer, cf. 11.41, a passage which is closely related to the present verse. Both are dependent on the Gethsemane tradition. For the simple vocative **Father,** cf. Mk 14.36. For **the hour,** cf. Mk 14.35. John has already made good use of this in 12.23, 27; 13.1; 16.32. In fact the last-named passage provides the link between the prayer and its actual context. The prayer starts from the fact that **the hour has come.** This is what gives it such urgency. It is the Gethsemane moment. But instead of being the moment of inner conflict, it is the time when Jesus demands the fulfilment of all that he has worked for in his life on earth. Without pleading or hesitating he boldly uses the imperative: **Glorify thy Son.** These words recall, and are intended to recall, 13.31f. As applied to himself, **glorify** suggests the Son of man imagery. The glorification of Jesus is at once the completion of his mission and the vindication of his obedience even to death. Jesus can make this demand, because it accords with the Father's will (12.28). He does not demand it for himself, but so **that the Son may glorify thee.** For the Father's glory is revealed most fully in the same act. The almost nervous anxiety with which Jesus repeats this demand in verse 5 expresses the crucial importance of what is now to be accomplished.
2. since thou hast given: it is not just Jesus' own position which is at stake. It is the salvation of all men, whose eternal destiny has been committed to his charge. The expressions used are Semitic, and suggest that John is adapting conventional apocalyptic phrases, appropriate in a Son of Man context. For **power** (*exousia*), cf. especially 5.27, which seems to be a direct reminiscence of Dan. 7.13f. **All flesh** is a common Hebrew phrase for humanity; cf. Isa. 40.5: 'The glory of the Lord shall be revealed, and all flesh shall see it together.' The Semitic character of the

writing (which, however, does not necessarily point to an Aramaic original) is continued in the neuter singular for **all whom** (i.e. 'the whole lot which' instead of 'all those whom'; cf. 6.39), and the *casus pendens* construction, picked up exceptionally by the masculine plural pronoun (*autois*) instead of neuter singular. For the whole sentence, cf. 1.12.

eternal life: this is John's regular substitute for 'the kingdom of God' in the earlier tradition; cf. 3.3, 15f. It is therefore true to say that the first two verses of the prayer correspond with the opening of the Lord's Prayer: 'Our Father who art in heaven, hallowed be thy name. Thy kingdom come.' But the absence of verbal allusions forbids us to say that John has actually used it as his model. Here the prayer is more urgent and insistent. The success of God's plan for all mankind hangs upon this moment. This consideration anticipates the prayer for the disciples and the Church which is to follow.

   3. And this is eternal life: the verse is clearly an explanation of **eternal life,** and accordingly must be taken as a parenthesis. Barrett calls it a footnote. What is more difficult to decide is whether it really comes from John's hand, or is a later gloss. The designation **Jesus Christ** is not characteristic of John, occurring only here and in 1.17 (where, too, the authenticity of the verse is disputed). On the other hand the personal address to the Father is maintained, which would be unexpected in a footnote, and there is no difficulty in Jesus' reference to himself in the third person, continuing from verses 1 and 2. So it may be that only **Jesus Christ,** which are the last words of the sentence in the Greek, are an interpolation, though there is no MS. authority for their omission. But it must still be remarked that **the only true** (*alēthinon*, cf. 1.9) **God** is an expression unparalleled in the Fourth Gospel. It splendidly voices Jewish monotheism. The whole verse, however, has a Johannine ring, and in fact has its closest parallel in 1 Jn 5.20. The crucial question, however, is whether this is a truly Johannine exposition of eternal life. To say that it consists in knowing suggests the Hellenistic and Gnostic concept of salvation. But John has the whole weight of the OT behind him, if he means that the knowledge of God is an essential prerequisite to salvation (the idea is specially characteristic of Hosea, cf. Hos. 4.6; 6.3, 6). Indeed, it was observed in connection with 1.10 that John thinks of knowledge Semitically in terms of relationship, rather than Hellenistically in terms of intellectual apprehension. At the end of the prayer we shall find great stress laid on knowledge as the grounds of relationship (verses 25f.). The verse may be a clumsy gloss, aimed at bringing this opening statement into line with the conclusion. But it remains possible that it is a true part of John's composition, intended to give a hint of the final statement of salvation —hence another example of the Johannine *inclusio*.

4. I glorified thee on earth: Jesus now gives the grounds for his urgent demand. There are two stages in his mission of revealing the glory of God. First there is the whole of his work on earth, **the work which thou gavest me to do.** This has been **accomplished.** Now it must be followed by the second stage, the glorification of the Son of man, without which it remains incomplete and unconvincing. For the two stages of the revelation of the divine glory, cf. 12.28.

having accomplished: the participle (read by B ℵ W) is to be preferred to the majority reading of the finite verb 'I have accomplished'; for the meaning is causal: 'I have glorified thee *in that* I have accomplished . . .'

5. and now: a technical expression to introduce the plea after the relevant facts have been stated, both in judicial (eg. Isa. 5.3, 5) and liturgical (e.g. Dan. 9.15, 17) compositions (cf. A. Laurentin, *Biblica* XLV (1964), pp. 168–97, 413–32). The request takes the form of a repetition of verse 1, but this time Jesus speaks of himself in the first person. But what is remarkable about it is the fact that the glorifying for which Jesus prays is conceived of as the restoration of a pre-existing glory. The phrases **in thy own presence** and **with thee** are almost identical, and are certainly identical in meaning. Jesus does not simply pray for vindication as the Son of Man, but for the completion of a process which can be very easily expressed in Gnostic terms, the descent and return of the Revealer from the heavenly realm. But although John's thought closely resembles this kind of mythology, it has its roots in Jewish tradition (cf. Introduction, pp. 40ff.). The resemblance is due to the fusion of two originally distinct concepts, the descent of wisdom and the ascent of the Son of Man. The pre-existent Wisdom did not have a glory like that of the Son of Man in his enthronement in Dan. 7, but she was 'beside' (*para*, the same preposition as John uses here) God, 'rejoicing before him always' (Prov. 8.30). But this is how John thinks of the glory of the Son of man. It is a matter of intimate personal relationship, rather than splendid robes and royal state. In the final reckoning, it can only be expressed in terms of love (verse 24).

before the world was made: possibly an allusion to Prov. 8.23f. The idea will be taken up once more in the conclusion, verse 24. John's thought here agrees with the Prologue (1.1–3), though he does not use the same expressions. The thought of the verse as a whole, especially in the light of the pivotal moment of the Passion, is comparable to Phil. 2.5–11.

Prayer for the Disciples **6–19**

6. I have manifested thy name: an unusual variant expression for 'I glorified thee' of verse 4. Jesus' earthly work has consisted in revealing the character of the Father, making known his glory, cf. 12.28 and also 11.40, both of which are related to John's handling of the Gethsemane tradition. Brown seems to be on the wrong track when he takes this to mean 'revealed what thy name is', and then proposes that the name so revealed is *ego eimi*, I AM. Here, as in 12.28, there may be a reminiscence of 'Hallowed be thy name' in the Lord's Prayer. But the point of the present verse is the restricted range of the work, not to all men, but **to the men whom thou gavest me out of the world.** This means those who have been receptive, as explained in the Prologue (1.12). **The world** (*kosmos*) is the world of men. Actually only the disciples are meant, for they are the people who have responded to Jesus during his ministry and will be his agents for the further extension of his work.

thine they were: there is a sense in which all men belong to God, because he has made all and desires the salvation of all. But there is a special sense in which those who respond to him through belief in Jesus belong to him. They have always been his and know it, whereas those who refuse to respond will deny that they ever belonged to him. The paradox is put very clearly in 3.16f. There is no rigid doctrine of predestination here, though the tendency of Semitic thought to see the whole contained in the beginning gives the impression of such a doctrine. See the notes on 6.37, 44f.

they have kept thy word: word (*logos*) in this chapter, as often elsewhere in the Gospel, means the divine message. Here the verb **kept** further defines it as the commandments (14.15, 21), and of course we must think primarily of the commandment to love one another (13.34). For this is the special mark of discipleship, the moral implication of the response to the revelation of God's name. Here and in the next two verses Jesus speaks from the perspective of the Resurrection, when the disciples' failure (16.32) is past, and the constitutive factors of discipleship are firmly planted in them, so that their loyalty no longer hangs in doubt. The prayer which follows can then be directed to the particular needs of the disciples, which they can recognize and see for themselves. The Christian reader is expected to see himself in their company, and to take to heart what is to be said.

7. Now they know: in 16.30 the disciples claimed this for themselves, and the words meant nothing, for they failed to reckon with the Passion. But once that is over their knowledge is real, and it means that their discipleship is self-conscious and deliberate. They are prepared to take seriously the implications of the divine message which has been entrusted to them.

8. the words: not *logos* but *rhēmata* ('sayings'), the various specific injunctions of the divine message (*logos*). The disciples have accepted the full implications of the revelation of God in Jesus. It is thus put most emphatically that they recognize the source of Jesus' sayings in God himself. **Know in truth** and **have believed** are not to be distinguished, as if knowledge was different from blind faith. Both verbs express the appropriation of divine truth with the heart and mind and will. So also **that I came from thee** and **that thou didst send me** are completely synonymous ways of expressing the Incarnation.

9. I am not praying for the world: before making his petition on behalf of the disciples, there is a further distinction to be made. It is not that Jesus has no concern for the world at large. On the contrary the safety of the disciples, for which he is just about to pray, is essential for the eventual salvation of the world (cf. verse 23). But just for this reason prayer for the disciples comes first. Jesus is just about to return to the Father, and he entrusts his entire mission to them. If they were to fail, it would render all his own work useless. Thus Jesus' anxiety for his glorification, which completes his own personal and unique work, extends to the disciples as they take over his mission. At the moment when Jesus prays for them everything is hanging in the balance, for the critical hour has come. This anxiety makes itself felt in the emphatic way in which Jesus repeatedly asserts that **they are thine.** It is the

Father's own purpose for mankind which is at stake, and his own chosen agents whose welfare Jesus prays for.

10. all mine are thine, and thine are mine: these words are really parenthetical, explaining why the disciples, who obviously belong to Jesus himself (verse 6), are the Father's. The pronominal adjectives are neuter plural ('all my things, etc.'). This is not the same as verse 2, where the neuter singular was used to express the totality of men, considered as a single entity. The point here is the complete community of possessions between the Father and Jesus, which entitles him to say of the disciples 'they are thine'.

I am glorified in them: it is probably best to take these words as the continuation from verse 9. They add further point to Jesus' anxiety on behalf of the disciples. It is not only because, as *his* disciples, they are *the Father's* disciples, but also because their mission in relation to him is analogous to his own in relation to the Father. Just as God has revealed his glory in Jesus ('in him God is glorified', 13.31f.), so the disciples will reveal the glory of Jesus. Their mission is the earthly counterpart to the glorification of Jesus as Son of Man in the presence of the Father, so that the prayer of verse 5 cannot be fulfilled without the granting of the prayer for the disciples too. **Glorified** (*dedoxasmai*) is the perfect tense, still thinking of the disciples from the point of view of their stability after the Resurrection.

11. And now: the Greek (which does not include **now,** cf. *NEB*) is not the same as in verse 5, and the meaning is different. The first half of the verse is still part of the preamble, explaining the conditions which make the prayer so urgent. For the situation, which follows the critical moment of Jesus' departure, is that he is separated from the disciples: **I am no more in the world, but they are in the world.** They may have all the qualities which have been ascribed to them in verses 6–8, so that they are far more capable of standing on their own than is actually the case on the eve of the Passion (16.32). But they will no longer have Jesus' bodily presence with them. Not all Jesus' reassurances to the disciples in the Supper discourses can alter the fact that the new situation is thereby completely different from the old. It may be 'expedient' for them that he should depart, and it may lead to a deeper and truer joy than they have ever experienced before, but it means that they will have to depend upon their inner resources without physical contact with Jesus. They are like children come of age and ready to leave home, unaware of the dangers that lie before them as they venture forth.

Holy Father: Jesus resumes the opening invocation as he makes his petition on behalf of the disciples. The adjective **holy** is suitable, though in fact rare in invocation of God. Here it is perhaps an intentional anticipation of the theme of consecration with which the prayer for the disciples will conclude (verses 17–19), just as 'righteous' in verse 25 is related to the content of the prayer. This form of address appears in the eucharistic prayer of the *Didache* (x.2): 'We give thee thanks, Holy Father, for thy holy name, which thou hast made to tabernacle in our hearts, and for the knowledge and faith and immortality, which thou hast made known unto us through thy Son (*paidos*) Jesus.' As has been pointed out in the notes on 6.12, it is probable that the prayer in the *Didache* has been influenced by the Fourth Gospel.

keep them in thy name: the prayer is for the protection of the disciples. This theme continues until verse 15, where the same verb is used (*tērein*). The name of God is his revealed character. It is not quite clear whether Jesus means 'keep them *by* thy name', i.e. protect them according to your own duty as Father (cf. *NEB*: 'protect by the power of thy name'), or 'keep them *in* thy name' as a place of security, i.e. keep them safe in their profession of faith in the revelation which they have received (cf. *NEB*, *mg.*: 'keep in loyalty to thee'). The latter seems preferable in view of the next verse, and from comparison with the corresponding phrase in verse 17, 'in thy truth'. Brown asserts that both meanings are intended.

which thou hast given me: here we encounter textual difficulties. These words until the end of the verse are missing from the Sinaitic Syriac and some Old Latin MSS. (a b c e ff² r¹). P⁶⁶* retains **which thou hast given me,** but omits **that they may be one, even as we are one.** But then in verse 12 P⁶⁶ omits 'which thou hast given me', supported by ℵ* and Sinaitic Syriac. The omission of **which thou hast given me** in both these verses can be explained by the difficulty of understanding what it means. That it was felt to be difficult is indicated by the change of **which** to 'whom' (i.e. the disciples) in this verse by D² N and some Latin texts, and in verse 12 by a great number of MSS., including C³ A D Θ Lake and Ferrar groups, Latin and Syriac Peshitta. But this may be accounted for by the influence of 18.9, which alludes to verse

12, though not quoting it exactly. It is clear, then, that the harder reading **which thou hast given me** is to be retained, even though we may suspect that the phrase was originally only found in one or other of the two verses rather than in both. If we are right in supposing that **name** here is virtually equivalent to 'revelation of the Father', the relative clause becomes quite natural, for it emphasizes the fact that this revelation has been entrusted to Jesus. His prayer for the protection of the disciples is a matter of personal interest to himself, for they are now the guardians of the revelation which he has received, and which it was his mission to make known. Thus these words betray the same concern as 'I am glorified in them' in the last verse.

that they may be one, even as we are one: Barrett argued for the omission of these words on the strength of the Sinaitic Syriac text alone, before it received support from the publication of P66. The Greek words are very brief (lit. 'that they be one thing as we'). The thought is not taken up in the remainder of the prayer for the disciples, which is wholly concerned with their protection as guardians of the revelation. It is not impossible that John should drop a hint of the theme of the later part of the prayer (verses 20–3) at this point, but it must be admitted that the words interfere with the general sense. Moreover John never elsewhere questions the unity of the disciples, whereas we have the precedent of 10.16 for the theme of the unity of the Church.

12. While I was with them: the future need of the disciples is emphasized by the contrast with the conditions which must now cease. Jesus himself was their protector. On the textual problems of **which thou hast given me,** see the notes on the last verse. **I have guarded them:** the verb (*phulassein*) is rare in John (only here and 12.25, 47), and properly applies to military guard. It may be simply due to the need for a synonym of **kept** (*tērein*). But the following words suggest that the Shepherd allegory may be in mind. The idea that **none of them is lost** occurs both in 6.12 and 10.28 ('perish'). It is presupposed that the failures of Peter (13.38) and the rest of the disciples (16.32) will have been made good. But the same cannot be said of Judas Iscariot. But this exception is covered by the fulfilment of **scripture** (a particular passage, presumably Ps. 41.9 quoted in 13.18), and so can be discounted. **the son of perdition:** there is a play on words in the Greek (lost, *apōleto*, and the son of loss, *apōleias*). The phrase **son of perdition**

is a Semitic idiom for 'the man destined for perdition'; cf. 2 Sam.
12.5, where 'deserves to die' is literally 'is a son of death'. But it
can also mean 'the man under the influence of the power of destruction', its agent from birth, cf. Isa. 57.4. In 2 Th. 2.3 we have
precisely the same title for the final enemy in an apocalyptic passage ('. . . and the man of lawlessness is revealed, the son of perdition'). His appearance is the signal for the last onslaught of evil
before the Parousia and the inauguration of the eternal Kingdom.
It is thus likely to have been a conventional title, even if limited
in currency, in Jewish-Christian apocalyptic speculation, denoting
the final enemy. The passage in 2 Thessalonians implies that he is
not the Devil himself, but a sort of incarnation of evil, one in whom
the Devil has absolute sway, and whose destruction represents the
collapse of the Devil's final attempt to thwart God's will. John
very likely had these apocalyptic overtones in mind in using this
title for Judas.

13. But now: resuming verse 11a, in order to put the other
side of the contrast. As before, this is not the technical 'and now'
which was used in verse 5. It is a matter of the changed circumstances brought about by Jesus' departure. On the brink of leaving
(this is the force of the Semitic-style present for future in **I am
coming,** and often in chapters 14–17) Jesus does all he can to
make sure that the disciples are prepared for the change. Prayer
on their behalf is one thing that he does. It is not clear whether
these things I speak in the world is a reference to the prayer,
which should have an educative effect on the disciples as they
hear the Master communing with the Father, or whether it is a
reference to the Supper discourses as a whole. Either way, the object
is to make the transition as smooth as possible, so that the disciples
may continue Jesus' mission and have the joy of reaping a rich
harvest. The words **my joy fulfilled** are a verbal allusion to
15.11; 16.24. This tips the scales in favour of the Supper discourses
for **these things I speak.**

14. I have given them thy word: cf. verses 6–8. Their
equipment is complete, and so Jesus does not have to pray for the
supply of any deficiencies in their preparation. He has no anxiety
on this score. But the danger lies in the fact that their vocation and
ministry to continue his mission sets them apart from the rest of
the world of men (as already noted in verse 9), and incurs its
hatred. Here again there is allusion to the Supper discourses, this

time taking the forecast of 15.18-25 as accomplished fact. The past tense **has hated** is strictly illogical at this point but may be intended to recall the quotation in 15.25. (*NEB* 'hates' is inaccurate.) For the purpose of the prayer it is necessary to assume that the hatred of the world is already operative.

even as I am not of the world: these words anticipate verse 16, and are better omitted as a further embellishment (cf. verse 11). They are not found in P66* D 69 Old Latin and Sinaitic Syriac, thus adding the important support of D to the same witnesses for omission in verse 11. Further omissions at this point are not likely to be original, and can be accounted for on transcriptional grounds. Both verses 15 and 16 are missing from a few minuscules, but this is simply because of the general acceptance of the insertion of the words here from verse 16, which led to homoioteleuton. Verse 16 alone is missing from P66c, but this is surely due to the corrector's confusion in attempting to make good the deficiency of P66* in verse 14. He crossed out verse 16 when he should not have done.

15. I do not pray: one way of preserving the disciples from harm would have been for Jesus to take them with him on his return to the Father, but that would be to miss the point of the creation of the apostolic band. They are to 'go and bear fruit' (15.16). Therefore they cannot be taken **out of the world,** though their special relationship with God sets them apart from it. But the essential thing is that they should not be overcome by the world. They need to be kept **from the evil one.** This is the one indisputable allusion to the Lord's Prayer. Just as in Mt. 6.13, the genitive *ponērou* can be either masculine ('deliver us from the evil one') or neuter ('deliver us from evil'). Here the word, whether personal or impersonal, denotes the active power for evil in the world which is expressed in the world's hostility to the disciples. The personal interpretation is supported by John's use of the same word to mean the Devil in 1 Jn 2.13f.; 3.12; 5.18f. But it is taken impersonally in what appears to be a further allusion to this chapter in the eucharistic prayer of the *Didache* x.5: 'Remember, Lord, thy Church to deliver it from all evil (*rhusasthai autēn apo pantos ponērou*) and to perfect it in thy love; and to gather it together from the four winds . . .'

16. In a way quite similar to the discourses, Jesus now takes up the point in verse 14, which was the reason for the petition which he has just made, and repeats it in order to draw out a further consequence of it. So he first explains that the disciples' separation from the world puts them in a position analogous to his own during his earthly ministry, i.e. **even as I am not of the world.** This point is much more effective as the lead-in to verses 17–19 if these words are not included in verse 14.

17. Sanctify: the verb *hagiazein*, instead of the classical form *hagizein*, is largely confined to the LXX and literature dependent on it. The same verb is translated 'consecrate' in verse 19. It means to bring a thing or person into the sphere of the sacred, and so to dedicate to holy use, not necessarily in the form of offering sacrifice. So it is used metaphorically of Jeremiah's vocation to be a prophet from birth, Jer. 1.5. John has used this verb of the dedication of Jesus inherent in the incarnation in 10.36. So the disciples need to be men apart, consecrated men. This can be done if they are preserved **in** (or by) **the truth,** i.e. by the continuing effect of God's **word** (message) in their minds, for **thy word is truth. Truth** here (the presence or absence of the article with it appears not to be significant, cf. Mastin *ad loc.*) is another way of speaking of the revelation of God in Christ with which the disciples have been entrusted, like 'name' in verse 11. It draws attention to the capacity of the revelation to counteract the evil influence of the world, which tends to falsehood; cf. 8.44ff. The petition is thus the reverse side of the prayer for safety from the evil one (verse 15). It is a prayer for their preservation in the truth which they have received. Brown regards **thy word is truth** as a parenthesis (perhaps a quotation of Ps. 119.142). The verse runs on much better without this phrase.

18. send: in this verse the verb *apostellein* is used, as in 10.36. In the context it is virtually a synonym of 'sanctify'. Both words refer to the sacred mission which was first laid upon Jesus, and now has been passed on by him to the disciples. To fulfil so high a calling will require the utmost loyalty and devotion. So now Jesus prays that they may not fail to profit by his own example of self-sacrifice.

19. for their sake: very rarely the verb *hagiazein* (Heb. *qaddēš*) is used of a sacrifice, when that is the appropriate means of consecrating the animal concerned (so in the case of the consecration of the first-born (Exod. 13.2; Dt. 15.19)). So in this verse the verb takes on the notion of sacrifice because of the phrase **for their sake** (*huper autōn*). The preposition *huper* unmistakably introduces a sacrificial connotation. John has used it in the context of laying down one's life in the Shepherd allegory (10.11, 15–18), in the unwitting prophecy of Caiaphas (11.51f.), and in the Vine allegory (15.13). He has also used it in an allusion to the eucharistic words of Jesus in 6.51. It is quite possible that its presence here is a reminiscence of the eucharistic words (cf. Mk 14.24; 1 C. 11.24). Bultmann even regards this verse as the Johannine interpretation of these words (which he assumes that John wishes to detach from their sacramental associations). But what is unprecedented in Jesus' words is the fact that he says **I consecrate myself.** In any other context it would mean making oneself holy by carrying out the prescribed ceremonial ablutions, as in Exod. 19.22. But here the sense demands that we take it to mean 'offer myself as a sacrifice on their behalf'. This again suggests that John is building on the tradition of the eucharistic words, which he paraphrases for the present context.

that they also may be consecrated: it is not suggested that the disciples will be sacrificed in the same sense as Jesus, but his sacrifice will be their constant inspiration to maintain their separation from the world and their devotion to their mission. The unique sacrificial act of Jesus is undertaken so as to have the lasting effect desired in the petition of verse 17.

Prayer for the Future Church **20–3**

20. The structure of the prayer is similar to that of the allegory of the Shepherd. It is only after describing the shepherd's care of the sheep, culminating in the idea of self-sacrifice on their behalf, that John mentions the 'other sheep', briefly introducing the theme of unity (10.16). So he now turns to **those who believe** (the present tense with future meaning, as often in these chapters) **in me through their word,** as the disciples pass on the message.

21. that they may all be one: this is the only petition on behalf of the Church. The fact that it is stressed so strongly here, whereas the idea did not even need to be mentioned in the prayer for the disciples (if we omit the final words of verse 11), shows that this is a burning issue for John. To him disunity is a denial of the faith. The grounds on which Jesus has made all the petitions in this chapter have been the analogy between his own relation to the Father and the Church's relation to himself. So his unity with the Father must be reflected in the life of the Church. It is the

doctrine of mutual indwelling, in which Jesus himself is the middle
term of two overlapping unities, his union with the Father and
his union with his brothers in the world, which was described in
individual terms in 14.18–24.

that they also may be in us: this is the reading of P⁶⁶ᵛⁱᵈ B C* D
W Old Latin and Sahidic. The rest have 'may be one in us', presumably by influence of the beginning of the verse.

that the world may believe: cf. 13.35. A disunited Christian
community denies by its behaviour the message which it proclaims. We may note here that John thinks of the salvation of the
world as a real possibility (cf. the notes on 16.10). Brown draws
attention to the structural parallelism of this verse and verses 22f.
Each consists of a petition (**that they may ... be one**), the
grounds of the petition in the unity of the Father and the Son
(**even as ...**), repetition of the petition on this basis (**that they
also may be...**), and a further consequence of this (**so that the
world ...**). Thus verses 22f. draw out the implications of what
has been said in verse 21.

22. glory: Jesus' glory consists in his function as the revealer of
God (1.14), displayed through every facet of his life and teaching.
He has passed this on to the disciples not only by entrusting to
them the message of salvation, but also by creating in them a form
of life which bears witness to it. As was pointed out in the notes
on verse 5, John thinks of the glory of Jesus as primarily a matter
of relationship. As the revealer of God he reflects God's glory, and
this is only possible because of the special relationship between
them. And John thinks of this relationship in terms of moral union.
So the necessity for the unity of Christians can be deduced from
their commission to bear witness to Jesus in his relation to the
Father.

23. I in them: the verse puts more briefly what was said to the
disciples in 14.20f. The analogy between Jesus indwelling the
disciples and the Father indwelling Jesus (one side only of the
mutuality in each case is expressed) requires taking the disciples
as a single entity. The analogy would not hold if the disciples were
so divided that they could not be taken as one whole. So it is vital
that they should **become perfectly one.** The Greek is literally
'that they may be completed into one', using the same verb as
'accomplished' in verse 4 (*teleioun*, elsewhere only used in 4.34;
5.36; 19.28). Bultmann and others think that this is an eschato-

logical statement. The unity of the Church is a given fact which
has an ultimate quality. It has to be realized and progressively
attained. The unity which marks the life of the Church now is a
sign of its final unity at the consummation. But John's other uses
of the word suggest that to him it means 'to do fully'. The language is not specifically eschatological, but relevant to all times.
The prayer is that the disciples 'may form a perfect unity'.

and hast loved them: the witness of the Church's united life is
not merely a confirmation of the revelation of God in Jesus, but
also a sign that the object of that revelation is being achieved.
It displays and effects God's love for mankind. There is nothing
difficult about this thought, which has already been expressed in
14.21, 23. But the interpretation is not certain, because of the
reading of D and some Old Latin texts (a b r¹), 'I have loved
them', which in Greek involves merely the omission of one letter
(*ēgapēsa* for *ēgapēsas*). This aligns the final thought with the beginning of the verse, where D has reversed the phrases to read 'thou
in me and I in them', so that the progression is that the Father
loves Jesus in sending him into the world and Jesus loves the
Church which is the product of his sending of the disciples. This
is surely an attempt at improvement on the part of D, which in
fact fails to recognize that the verse is really leading to a climax.
The point is that the Father's unity with Jesus, and his unity with
the Church, leads to the conclusion that **thou . . . hast loved
them even as thou hast loved me.** And so the purpose of
Jesus' mission is complete. The reading of D is supported by Syriac
Peshitta in its pointing of the text, which is identical with the
Sinaitic Syriac. But it is not certain that this was the intention of
the Sinaitic Syriac, as the difference of reading is not visible in an
unpointed text.

Final Appeal 24–6

24. I desire: Gr. *thelō*, translated 'I will' in Mk 14.36. The
repetition of **Father** in close proximity with this word suggests that
there is here a further case of ultimate dependence on the Gethsemane tradition. If so, John deliberately changes 'not what I will'
into **I desire,** because here there is no tension between Jesus' will
and the Father's. Jesus' prayer coincides exactly with the Father's
will.

whom thou hast given me: Another case of neuter singular for the relative and of *casus pendens* construction, as in verse 2. Most editors take this to be the continuation of the prayer for the Church, but the reference is now universal, applying both to the disciples (verse 6) and to the future believers (verse 20). It is a general conclusion to the whole prayer.

with me where I am: i.e. in the presence of the Father. Jesus is referring to the ultimate goal, when the temporary conditions indicated in verses 11 and 15 have finished. This goal is that all men may **behold my glory** as the exalted Son of Man, which nevertheless is the end term of the Father's **love** for Jesus in the beginning of time as the pre-existent Wisdom (cf. verse 5).

foundation: though the word was not used in verse 5, it is a conventional expression, found ten times elsewhere in the NT.

25. O righteous Father: as in verse 11, a descriptive adjective is used, which reflects the character of the appeal that is about to be made. **Righteous** (*dikaios*) is extremely rare in John (only elsewhere at 5.30, 'just', and 7.24, 'right'), cf. the use of 'righteousness' in 16.8, 10. As a juridical word it suggests that the notion of vindication is present, which is suitable to the use of the Son of Man imagery in the preceding verse. The point is that Jesus' own cause is just, and therefore he makes his final appeal on the grounds of the Father's justice. The following words can then be expected to expose the justice of Jesus' cause. It rests on two facts. First, **the world has not known thee,** which shows that Jesus' mission has been and is indispensable for the Father's own purpose. In the Greek this phrase is introduced by *kai* (and), which implies a 'both . . . and' construction (in this construction the first clause is sometimes concessive, 'though . . .'). But the construction is not maintained. For the second fact, Jesus continues: **but I have known thee,** and then continues with co-ordinate clauses with 'and'. We should thus continue: 'and these have known that thou didst send me, and I have made known to them . . .' The second fact is, then, that in the situation of the world's ignorance Jesus has taken these precise steps to make the Father known. That is why it is so essential that his prayer should be granted. Barrett and Brown take **but I have known thee** as an important parenthesis in the midst of the 'both . . . and' construction, making **and these know** co-ordinate with **the world has not known thee.** But Mastin preserves the sense better by translating 'although the world . . . *yet* I . . . *and* these'.

26. The great emphasis on the verb 'to know' in these last two verses is to be explained along the lines indicated in the notes on verse 3. To John it not only refers to the giving and receiving of a revelation, but also to the establishing of a personal relationship. Jesus has known the Father (verse 25), because there has always been a loving relationship between them (verse 24). The disciples have known, i.e. recognized, that he alone can reveal God, and on this basis he has **made known to them thy name**—God's revealed character, which will be shown later in the verse to be love. Such is Jesus' urgency that he is not content to leave it at that, but promises that he **will make it known** in the future by the means that are appropriate after his return to the Father, and have been outlined in the Supper discourses. This is in order to establish and to maintain the relationship between them and God comparable to his own: **that the love with which thou hast loved me may be in them** (cf. verse 23). Love is thus to be a quality of each of them, which is evinced in the mutual relationship between them. But if there is divine love in them, then it is the same thing as saying **I in them,** for Jesus is himself the area of overlap between the unity of the divine love and the unity of all those who believe. The prayer ends with the substance of the new commandment of 13.34f., now raised to the status of the theological justification for the entire work of redemption (cf. above on verse 1). By this final allusion to the Last Supper account, John once more brings his material to a suitable point for the continuation of the narrative.

THE TRIAL AND DEATH OF JESUS 18.1–19.42

At last John resumes the flow of the Passion narrative. It has the same essential outline as that of the Synoptic Gospels—the arrest in the garden, the trial before the High Priest, into which is woven the story of Peter's denials, the trial before Pilate, the crucifixion and death of Jesus, and the rapid burial in the rock-hewn tomb by the good offices of Joseph of Arimathea. When we come to details there are some serious differences. John omits the agony in the garden—but we already know his reason for that (cf. p. 410). He appears to have two examinations of Jesus by the Sanhedrin, once before Annas (18.13–23), and once before Caiaphas (18.24),

though the latter is not described and there may be some dislocation of the text. The scourging and mocking of Jesus come improbably in the middle of the trial before Pilate (19.1–3), instead
of being after he has given sentence. There are two notable dialogues between Jesus and Pilate, which have no parallel in the
Synoptic accounts and bear all the marks of John's genius as a
creative writer (18.33–8; 19.8–11). His account of the crucifixion
omits much of the Synoptic detail, but introduces the consignment
of Jesus' mother to the care of the Beloved Disciple (19.25–7)
and the piercing of Jesus' side after his death (19.31–7). Finally
he brings in Nicodemus to help Joseph of Arimathea, and they
anoint the body of Jesus, contrary to the Synoptic tradition.

The general similarity between John and the Synoptics can be
accounted for by the fact that the Passion narrative acquired a
comparatively fixed form at a very early date. But it was subject to
revision and expansion in the light of further reflection and new
accessions of information (whether historically reliable or not).
Matthew works on the basis of Mark, but feels free to introduce the
Judas legend (Mt. 27.3–10) and the dream of Pilate's wife (Mt.
27.19). Luke appears to have access to a non-Marcan account, which
includes the examination of Jesus by Herod not found in the rest
(Lk. 23.6–12). The second century apocryphal *Gospel of Peter* not
only has legendary accretions but also indulges in crude and improbable alterations of fact, while nevertheless preserving the
same general outline.

The differences between John and the Synoptics can be explained from two main causes. First, it is not a foregone conclusion
that he was actually using one of them as we know it. There are
many important contacts with Mark, but also he seems to know
some details which are otherwise only recorded in Luke. Bultmann
is probably right in asserting that he has a written source, which
is not identical with Mark. Vincent Taylor attempted to demonstrate that two written sources (which he designated A and B) lie
behind Mark's Passion narrative. It has been suggested that John
used *one* of these sources. But in fact John has details from both
A and B, and omits items from both. The theory is thus not helpful
in the task of uncovering John's underlying source. See the discussion in Brown, pp. 787ff. Presumably this also contained the features which were later taken over by Luke. But he may also have
had further items of tradition, and not have been confined to a

single continuous source. We must also reckon with the fact that some of his assertions may be deductions from general knowledge of procedure. It seems certain that he introduces topographical details from familiarity with the sites.

The second cause is that John is a creative writer. His approach to the tradition here is exactly the same as to the Last Supper. He uses all his dramatic skill to distil every drop of irony out of the situation. In his hands the narrative becomes a series of unforgettable moments. John sees the Passion as the decisive moment of the Gospel. It is the hour for Jesus to be glorified, and so Jesus remains in control of events until they are triumphantly completed (19.28–30). It is the time of 'the judgment of this world' (12.31), and even the worldly power of Pilate is shown up to be derivative from God and subject to his will (19.11). It is the moment when unbelief is exposed as resistance to God himself, and those who condemn Jesus in fact condemn themselves (19.15). Just as in chapter 13 the material was organized to bring out the fundamental issues of discipleship, so here the charge that is laid against Jesus is made the basis of a consideration of the true meaning of kingship.

It is therefore not to be expected that John's narrative is altogether factually reliable. In any case his theological interests have led him to treat his sources with some degree of freedom. But it is not to be taken for granted that even his sources were entirely accurate records. In his book *On the Trial of Jesus* (1961) Paul Winter develops the view of Hans Lietzmann that only Mark contains factual information, and even much of his narrative is legendary. On the other side A. N. Sherwin-White (in his *Roman Society and Roman Law in the New Testament* (1963), pp. 24–47) argues that John's presentation of the trial is not impossible and cannot be lightly dismissed. In any case it cannot be assumed that all non-Marcan tradition is valueless. The possibility that John contains some better information than Mark is not to be dismissed out of hand. But what is more to the point is to decide the criteria for assessing the various components of the Passion narrative, whether John's or Mark's.

The very bare outline given at the beginning of this section (p. 533) is reflected in the Passion predictions; cf. Mk 8.31; 9.31; 10.32–4. With these may be compared 1 Tim. 6.13, which anticipates 'suffered under Pontius Pilate' in the creeds. These passages not only give a clue to the solution of the problem *why* these things happened. They also indicate the quick answer to the question *what* happened. They suggest that the Passion narrative follows a basic pattern, and there is no compelling reason to doubt its historical reliability.

This basic pattern is filled out in two ways. First there are fairly detailed descriptions of each separate event, what happened before the Sanhedrin, what happened before Pilate, etc. Secondly there are isolated traditions which have to be fitted into it at some suitable point. The denials by Peter are an obvious instance.

Both these kinds of material may depend in the first instance on eye-witness reporting, though it is liable to have suffered some degree of distortion in course of transmission. But both also may in some respects derive from a general knowledge of procedure, whereby it can be asserted, for example, that the soldiers took Jesus' clothes because this was a recognized perquisite. Modern attempts to evaluate the Passion narrative largely depend on the comparison of the records with what can be known about procedure from reliable sources.

Apologetic needs very quickly turned the attention of the early Church to the fulfilment of Scripture, and Pss. 22 and 69 were specially exploited in order to account for the details of the Passion. It is sometimes assumed that details have been fabricated on the basis of OT prophecies alone (e.g. the two robbers crucified with Jesus have been supposed to be dreamed up on the basis of Isa. 53.12). But in no case is this the best explanation. There is always a basis either in earlier tradition or in known procedure. Then the tendency is for the application of an OT text to take control over the further development of the detail. We shall see this in the case of the dividing of the clothes in 19.23f.

Even before Mark's narrative was written the tendency had begun of shifting the blame for the crucifixion away from Pilate and on to the Jews. John's highly dramatic handling of the trial before Pilate shows a definite advance in this direction by comparison with Mark. The reason for this is not anti-Semitism, but the practical need for the Christians to be on good terms with the Romans, in order to be allowed to practise their religion unhindered. It must be shown that Jesus was not really held to be guilty of sedition by Pilate, even though he condemned him to death.

Evidently the formation of the Passion narrative is highly complex. John's handling of it shows a remarkable balance of fidelity to underlying traditions and adaptation to the great theological design of his Gospel. His account has greater depths than appear on the surface. For we must not forget that he has timed the death of Jesus to coincide with the slaying of the Passover. By this means he not only has the overt motif of kingship, but the hidden motif of the death of Jesus as the paschal sacrifice.

Modern discussion of the trial of Jesus is concerned for the most part with two questions of procedure, with which the credibility of the Gospel narratives stands or falls. The first is the trial before the Sanhedrin at night, which is contrary to the rules laid down in the Mishnah. Some consideration has been given to this question in the introduction to chapter 13 (p. 445). The second is the assertion, very prominent in John (18.31), that the Jews did not have the right to impose the death penalty (cf. the notes on 8.59). Winter, following Lietzmann, contends that the Sanhedrin did have this right, so that it would not have been necessary to send Jesus to Pilate. On this basis, he argues that the account of the trial before the Sanhedrin is wholly fictitious, that Jesus was taken direct to Pilate after his arrest without any intervention of the Sanhedrin, and that the introduction of the tradition of the trial before the Sanhedrin is the first stage in the exoneration of Pilate and the transferring of blame to the Jews. Sherwin-White presents the opposite case, claiming that municipal authorities were refused capital jurisdiction throughout the Roman Empire, and that although the Sanhedrin had exceptional powers, it could only put men to death in the limited sphere of maintaining law and order within the Temple precincts. Stoning might sometimes happen as a matter of lynching (8.59) and would be approved in the case of sexual offences (8.5). Failing further decisive evidence, it seems best to accept the arguments of Sherwin-White that it was necessary for the Sanhedrin to hand Jesus over to the Roman procurator to ratify and execute the sentence of death, as is implied by the synoptics and explicitly stated by John (see further p. 556 below).

THE ARREST 18.1–12

The tradition used by John is not likely to have been very different from that of the Synoptics (Mt. 26.30–56 paras.), though it may have contained some unique features. John omits the prophecy of the flight of the disciples and of Peter's denials, which Matthew and Mark place during the walk to Gethsemane, because he has used them in his account of the Last Supper (13.36–8; 16.32). He is here in line with Luke, though not dependent on him. He also omits the agony of Jesus on arrival, having used this tradition in 12.27ff. This leaves his Gethsemane narrative defective, for he gives no reason why Jesus went there. But in fact he includes an allusion to the agony in verse 11. In his account of the arrest John has no mention of the kiss of Judas. Instead he has a dialogue between Jesus and the soldiers which has all the marks of Johannine style. It is designed to show that Jesus is in complete command of his destiny. The little detail in Mk 14.47, to the effect that someone attempted armed resistance and cut off the ear of one of the soldiers, has been expanded with circumstantial details. Comparison with Matthew and Mark suggests that these are due to legendary accretion, which took a variety of forms. What we have in John was probably already in his source.

18.1. the Kidron valley: this valley (lit. 'winter torrent' or '*wadi*', only carrying water in the rainy seasons) runs down from the east side of Jerusalem under the Temple area and continues under the spurs of the original Jebusite city of Jerusalem (now outside the medieval walls on the south side). The Tyropaean valley, which originally was the western boundary of the Jebusite city, runs into it just below the Pool of Siloam (cf. 9.7), and then only a little further south it meets the deep valley of Hinnom (Gehenna), which comes down from the W. side. The traditional site of the upper room, where the Last Supper was held, is at the highest point between these two valleys, a little to the west of the head of the Tyropaean. If the identification is correct, it would be necessary for Jesus and the disciples to cross the Kidron valley some way to the south of the Temple area, and proceed along the other side northwards until they reached the old road to Bethany leading up the Mount of Olives on the east side.

Kidron: the correct reading is *tou Kedrōn* (A S Δ Sinaitic and Peshitta Syriac). The name is from a Hebrew root meaning 'black'. It is mentioned in the OT at 1 Kg. 2.37; 2 Kg. 23.6, 12. As the Greek transliteration is almost identical with *kedros* = 'cedar', it gives the impression of a false agreement. Hence most MSS. erroneously read either *tou Kedrou* (ℵ* D W) or *tōn Kedrōn* (B C Θ and most others), both with support from the versions.

a garden: John does not mention Gethsemane (Mt. 26.36 = Mk 14.32) by name. But it means 'oil-press' and so denotes an olive orchard on the slopes of the Mount of Olives. Very few olive trees grow there today, but some ancient specimens are still to be seen in the traditional site. The name was probably not included in John's source. It is also omitted by Luke.

2. often met there: there is a narrative defect in Matthew and Mark, in that Jesus goes to Gethsemane apparently without any prearrangement, so that it is not explained why Judas was able to choose this spot for the arrest. Luke therefore inserts: 'as was his custom' (Lk. 22.39). John independently gives a similar explanation. As the vocabulary is Johannine, it is probably his own addition, not found in the source.

3. a band of soldiers: John here has an important difference of detail from the Synoptics. All are agreed that Judas brought with him a body of armed men sent by the Temple authorities. Only John mentions in addition **a band** (*speira*) **of soldiers.** These are Roman soldiers. The *speira* corresponds with the Latin *cohors*, usually consisting of 600 men (so Mt. 27.27 = Mk 15.16, 'battalion'; Ac. 10.1; 21.31; 27.1, 'cohort'). But in other literature it is often used for the Latin *manipulus*, a body of 200 men. But verse 12 implies that the cohort is meant here. John gives the impression that the Temple authorities obtained the help of the Roman garrison from the outset. These troops were stationed in Jerusalem to prevent a civil disturbance during the festival, when nationalist feeling was liable to run high. If Pilate granted their help, it can only be that the High Priest had already consulted with him, and represented to him the danger of a political coup on the part of Jesus. But then it would be expected that Jesus would be taken in charge by Pilate from the first. Mastin concludes that Pilate must have permitted the High Priest to have charge of him, so as to be able to prepare the case before sending him to Pilate for trial in the morning. But this is pure speculation. But it is possible that John has introduced the soldiers into the traditional account for a symbolic reason. Bultmann points out that the arrest is the moment of the arrival of 'the ruler of this world', who nevertheless 'has no power' over Jesus (14.30). In the trial narrative the world's power against Jesus is incarnated not in the Jewish leaders, but in the Romans (cf. 19.10f.). So in the arrest Jesus gives himself up to the representatives of both ecclesiastical

and secular power, and his real supremacy in regard to both is
established from the first.

some officers from the chief priests and the Pharisees: that
John is adapting his source in this verse is clear from the expressions he uses to describe the Temple guards, which have been
conformed to his own practice elsewhere; cf. 7.32.

lanterns and torches: only John has this detail. He has already
told us that it was night (13.30). The detail may already have been
included in his source; it is obviously correct.

4. knowing all: the awe-inspiring effect of Jesus in what follows is prepared for by the note that he already knew what would
result, so that he meets the situation with dignified calm. So also
in 13.1, 3 Jesus' foreknowledge is mentioned to give solemnity and
deliberation to the scene. However, D Ferrar group and Sinaitic
Syriac read 'seeing all' (*idōn* for *eidōs*), and Barrett is inclined to
accept it as more likely to be corrupted into the characteristic
feature of supernatural knowledge. But the reading is probably
due to the influence of the similar, but entirely independent,
phrase in Lk. 22.49.

came forward: John has now abandoned his source, and con-
structs the dialogue with typical dramatic effect. First Jesus takes
the centre of the stage under the full glare of the lights. He asks
'Whom do you seek?' (the same words as Mary Magdalene in
20.15), thus taking the initiative.

5. of Nazareth: here and in verse 7, and also in 19.19, John
uses the adjective *Nazōraios*, which is more common in the NT
than the adjectival form *Nazarēnos* (the more obvious formation
from Nazareth). In fact it probably has a quite separate origin.
Both are derived from the Hebrew *nāṣar* = watch (for Nazareth,
'lookout place'; cf. the notes on 1.45). *Nazōraios* could thus mean
'an observant' and be applied to a religious sect or party. In fact, it
seems to have been applied to a pre-Christian Jewish sect, to the
Christians themselves (Ac. 24.5), to Jewish-Christians, and to the
Mandeans, at various dates and in various forms. Black (p. 199)
has suggested that it was used in connection with the Baptist's
followers, and so came to be applied to Jesus and his followers too.
But apart from Ac. 24.5 its use in the NT is confined to Jesus himself, and as such it is most naturally taken to be synonymous with
Nazarēnos. It thus seems likely that the *form* of the adjective has
been influenced by the existing use of *Nazōraios* in another connec-

tion, but that in Christian currency it always denoted connection
with Jesus the Nazarene. For further details, cf. O. Cullmann in
IDB III.523.

I am he: the Greek *egō eimi* could be a simple acknowledgement
of identity, as in 6.20. On the other hand there may well be the
richer, awe-inspiring overtones of 8.24, 28; 13.19. The matter is
complicated by the fact that there is slight MS. support (B a) for
reading: 'I am Jesus'. It is argued that the common abbreviation
for Jesus *IS* might have dropped out before the next word
ISTĒKEI (**was standing**). But as so often, this argument works
both ways; and it is at least as probable that the name has come
into the text of B by dittography of *IS*. That this is the case seems
certain from the repetition of *egō eimi* in verse 6, where there is no
MS. authority for the insertion of the predicate. It is precisely this
repetition which makes the *egō eimi* stand out so effectively, and
justifies Bultmann in calling it a 'recognition-formula'—as he says,
'the Revealer speaks!' That John is building up to a climax is
indicated by the odd position of the next words: **Judas, who
betrayed him, was standing with them.** This is put in here
specially to hold up the narrative, and make the repetition in verse
6 necessary. At the same time it is dramatically effective. For this
is the moment when Jesus and Judas meet again after the tense
and agonizing final appeal in 13.21–30. Judas is confronted with
the one whom he has betrayed, who foreknew that this would happen and told the disciples of it actually in his presence: 'that when
it does come to pass you may believe that I am he (*egō eimi*)'
(13.19). Thus the *egō eimi* here can be taken as a cross-reference to
this verse in the Last Supper account, intended to call to mind the
tragic irony of the situation.

6. The reaction of the soldiers is the normal effect of a theophany; cf. Dan. 10.9; Ac. 9.4; 22.7; 26.14; Rev. 1.17. It can
scarcely be regarded as an historically reliable detail, however
awe-inspiring and majestic Jesus was on this occasion. It is John's
way of expressing the theological fact that Jesus is above all earthly
power. Hence he yields himself voluntarily into the hands of his
captors.

8. The unbearable tension has been broken by Jesus' renewal
of his original question, which leads to yet another *egō eimi*, as he
recalls what he said before. But this time it has been deflated of
its mysterious quality, and comes out as a matter-of-fact acknow-

ledgement of identity. Then, in the most businesslike manner, he
proceeds to arrange for the safety of the disciples. It is too much
to say, as many commentators do, that Jesus pays for the safety
of the disciples with his life. For he is going to his death in any case.
Actually John is correcting the earlier tradition here. According
to Mt. 26.56 (= Mk 14.50) the disciples ran away out of fright.
We know from 16.32 that John was familiar with this tradition.
John wishes to show that even this feature of the narrative falls
within Jesus' complete control of events.

9. to fulfil the word which he had spoken: cf. verse 32. The
comments of this kind (cf. verse 14 and 12.33) are taken to be
redactional glosses by Bultmann. But they are perfectly consistent
with John's presentation of the Passion. Like the Synoptic writers
(Mt. 26.56; Mk. 14.49; Lk. 22.37) he lays great stress on the fulfilment of Jesus' destiny in the events of the Passion, but he extends
the idea not only to the scriptures (see below on 19.28–30) but also
to Jesus' own words. In this case, however, it is objected that the
verse betrays a prosaic misunderstanding of Jesus' teaching. In
6.39 (which stands closest to the present text) and 10.28f. the same
words are applied to the eternal salvation of the disciples, and
even in 17.12 they refer to their spiritual safety up to the point of
Jesus' departure. But now they are applied to their physical safety.
But this is not necessarily a matter of misunderstanding. If chapters 6 and 17 both belong to the second edition of the Gospel (cf.
Introduction, p. 50), the reference must be to 10.28f. (the similarity is clearer in the Greek than in the English). This is part of
the allegory of the Shepherd, but also included in a context which
has definite contacts with the trial narrative (see the notes on
10.24). If John is correcting the earlier tradition of the flight of
the disciples, it would be natural for him to think of the Shepherd
allegory because of the proof text which belongs to that tradition:
'I will strike the shepherd, and the sheep will be scattered' (Mk
14.27 = Zech. 13.7). John cannot allow that the Good Shepherd
should be so careless; indeed it is for the sake of the sheep that he
gives his life. Consequently the scattering of the disciples, which is
a fixed item of tradition, has to be represented as Jesus' own way
of ensuring their safety. His act is not a substitute for the securing
of their eternal salvation, but a symbolic anticipation of it.

10. Simon Peter: only John makes this identification. This incident is a classic example of the expansion of a tradition with

circumstantial detail. Mk 14.47 simply says: 'One of those who stood by drew his sword, and struck the slave of the high priest and cut off his ear.' There is no reason to doubt this rests on authentic reminiscence; but the story has grown in the telling, and it is scarcely possible to determine whether the additional material has any factual basis. The naming of Peter is dramatically skilful, as it enables John to link up this tradition with the denials of Peter (verse 26). Precisely for this reason, it is difficult to resist the conclusion that John has added this feature himself. The fact that it was the **right ear** which was damaged agrees with Lk. 22.50. But John is not dependent on Luke, because he knows nothing of the special Lucan development that Jesus healed the wound. This feature, then, belongs to John's source, to which Luke also had access. The name **Malchus** is peculiar to John. It means 'king', and was a fairly common Semitic name, particularly among the Nabataean Arabs. It is tempting to see a symbolic meaning in it, and so an intentional irony, in view of the fact that kingship will be the dominant theme in the trial before Pilate. But this temptation is to be resisted, because John would certainly have provided the translation if this were his intention, as he has done in the case of Siloam (9.7). So it is more likely that John found it in his source.

11. The response of Jesus to this attempt at resistance has a parallel in Mt. 26.52–4; but there is so little verbal similarity that it is unlikely that John is dependent on Matthew. It is better again to suppose that John's source has a development comparable to Matthew's, which circulated in various forms. The similarity is not confined to **Put your sword into its sheath** (= Mt. 26.52a), for John also refers to the statement of Jesus that it would be inappropriate for his followers to fight on his behalf in verse 36 below (cf. Mt. 26.53f.).

sword: the word *machaira* is used in all four Gospels. Properly it means a dagger. The historicity of the entire incident has been thrown in doubt on the grounds that it was forbidden to carry weapons on Passover night, which for many purposes was subject to the same restrictions as the Sabbath. But R. Eliezer ben Hyrcanus (c. A.D. 80–120) explicitly permits this on the grounds that a man's weapons are 'his adornments' (*Shabbath* vi.4).

the cup: whatever comment of Jesus John found in his source at this point (and it may be that it contained something like verse 36), he has substituted words which belong to the tradition of the agony of Jesus, before the arrival of Judas and the soldiers. The phrase-ology is distinctively Johannine, but the vocabulary is entirely from the source (cf. Mt. 26.39, 42; Mk 14.36). John has not used the metaphor of the Cup previously, though he presupposes that his readers will understand it. Apart from the connection with the eucharistic cup (cf. 1 C. 11.25), which suggests sacrificial usage as part of the background of thought, there is also the idea of the cup of God's wrath as a metaphor of suffering as punishment in the OT (e.g. Isa. 51.17–22; cf. Rev. 16.1). It is used simply as a metaphor for suffering in Jesus' reply to the sons of Zebedee (Mt. 20.22 = Mk 10.38). With this saying John maintains the character of Jesus as one who submits voluntarily to his captors in complete obedience to the Father. There is a similar, but inde-pendent, use of the prayer of the agony at this point in Lk. 22.53.

12. captain: Gr. *chiliarchos*, properly the leader of 1,000 men, but regularly used for the commander of a cohort, cf. verse 3.

JESUS BEFORE THE SANHEDRIN AND PETER'S DENIALS **18.13–27**

In common with the other three gospels, John next describes the examination of Jesus before the Sanhedrin, and includes the story of Peter's denials in the course of it. But his account raises a num-ber of problems, and no solution has been put forward which is completely satisfactory.

(a) The account is not self-consistent. Jesus is first sent to Annas, who, as a deposed High Priest, could be called 'the high priest' (verses 15, 16, 19, 22), though it is natural to suppose that John means Caiaphas, whom he explicitly calls the High Priest in verses 13 and 24. For the position of Annas, see the notes on 11.49. But Jesus is not sent to Caiaphas until verse 24. As the text stands, we have to assume that Annas presided at a preliminary hearing, and that the references to the High Priest are to him. Nothing is said about the examination by Caiaphas (verses 24 and 28). Meanwhile the story of Peter's denials is divided into two parts. The first denial takes place during the hearing by Annas (verses 15–18), the second and third after Jesus has been sent to Caiaphas (verses 25–27). We are forced to assume that John imagines that both hear-ings took place in the same house. Otherwise the second part of the story of Peter's denials loses its connection with the proceedings.

(b) The account is not compatible with the Synoptic tradition. Mark records a definite trial before the High Priest (only Matthew

gives the name Caiaphas (Mt. 26.3, 57)). First Jesus is charged
(Mk 14.55), then the evidence of witnesses is taken (Mk 14.56–9),
next Jesus is cross-examined (Mk 14.60–2), and finally he is
sentenced to death (Mk 14.63f.). At this point the denials of Peter
are described, evidently intended to be contemporaneous with the
trial (Mk 14.66–72). At daybreak the Sanhedrin is convened once
more, in order to take the case to Pilate (Mk 15.1). It seems, then,
that there were two meetings of the Sanhedrin, both presided over
by Caiaphas. The first was a formal trial, the second the preparation of the case to take before Pilate. Luke, however, gives a different scheme. Jesus is brought to the house of Caiaphas during the
night, and Peter's denials are recorded at that point (Lk. 22.54–
65), but there is only one meeting of the Sanhedrin, which is at
daybreak. This is the formal trial (Lk. 22.66–71). John can only be
harmonized with Mark if we assume, first, that he is wrong in
supposing that Annas presided at the first hearing, and, secondly,
that this hearing was in fact a formal trial. But John can more
easily be harmonized with Luke, if we assume that Luke has
simply not recorded the hearing by Annas (which happened while
Peter was in the court), and that John has simply not recorded
the formal trial before Caiaphas. But this is impossible, because
John agrees with Mark in sending Jesus to Pilate at daybreak
(verse 28). We therefore have to resort to a compromise. John has
a preliminary examination by Annas, not included in the Synoptic
accounts. The trial before Caiaphas took place during the night,
as Mark asserts, but John thinks of it as lasting until morning, so
that he does not have the Sanhedrin reconvened before the case
is referred to Pilate. This omission is understandable, seeing that
in any case John gives no details of the trial, wishing to pass on
quickly to the trial before Pilate.

(c) The account is defective. Jesus is sent to Pilate without having been condemned by the Sanhedrin and without a formal
charge (cf. verse 29). But it becomes clear from 18.33 and 19.7
that the Synoptic trial tradition is presupposed in the presentation
of the case to Pilate. We thus have to assume that John has
deliberately omitted the formal trial by the Sanhedrin. But we
have already seen that John has made use of this tradition earlier
in the Gospel, at Jesus' confrontation with the Jews at the feast of
Dedication (10.22–39; cf. p. 365 above). It can therefore be argued
that John thinks of the trial as having already taken place; that the

condemnation has been decided in Jesus' absence at a further
sitting of the Sanhedrin in 11.47–53; and that it only remains to
prepare the brief for the hearing by Pilate. But before we jump to
the conclusion that this is what John intends, and then take an
even bigger leap and decide that this is historically true, against
the Marcan tradition, we must pay attention to John's literary
procedure. For his use of the trial tradition at a climactic stage in
the series of central discourses is comparable to his use of the
Gethsemane tradition in 12.27ff. In this case it was clear all along
that John's source agreed with the Synoptics, but that he altered
it out of theological considerations. So in this case it seems that
John has placed the trial tradition in chapter 10 to make it the
climax of Jesus' self-revelation, but omitted it (or rather substituted
the examination by Annas for it) in the present chapter so as to
direct the interest entirely towards the dialogue with Pilate. This
leads to the conclusion that John's source contained the trial
tradition, as in the Synoptics, and that he has deliberately altered
his material for his theological purposes.

(d) The account is not historically probable. (i) Although Annas
might well be present at the meeting of the Sanhedrin, along with
other members of the High Priestly family (cf. Ac. 4.6), one would
expect Caiaphas to preside personally in a matter of such importance. It is not as if Caiaphas was not available. Bultmann, following Wellhausen, argues that in one of John's sources Annas was
incorrectly represented as the High Priest, instead of Caiaphas.
John's account is thus the result of the combination of two incompatible versions. It is possible, however, that both Annas and
Caiaphas were mentioned by name in John's source (cf. Lk. 3.2),
and the subsequent examination was intended to be understood
as presided over by Caiaphas. If so, John has mistakenly taken the
term 'High Priest' to mean Annas, and so inserted verse 24 in order
to get the position right for verse 28. (ii) There is another historical
improbability in the defence of Jesus before the High Priest in
verses 20f. He makes a dignified reply to the implicit suggestion
that he has been plotting in secret, but he speaks as if no witnesses
are to be brought. But the law required at least two witnesses
(cf. 8.17), and the Synoptic tradition is clear that two witnesses
were brought, even though it claims that they were false. In fact,
verses 19–23 have a strongly Johannine ring, and seem to replace
rather than to reproduce what was contained in the source.

(e) John's account cannot be mended by transposition. The simplest solution is to transpose verse 24 to the middle of verse 13, so that Annas transfers Jesus to Caiaphas immediately on his arrival. Then all the rest of the action takes place under the presidency of Caiaphas, and there is no change of scene until verse 28. This solution is found in one minuscule (225). But this still leaves unexplained why the soldiers went to Annas in the first place. The Sinaitic Syriac has a more complex arrangement: 13, 24, 14–15, 19–23, 16–18, 25–7. This not only brings Jesus to Caiaphas at the outset, but also brings the two paragraphs about Peter together. Both texts are probably motivated by the desire to bring John more into line with the Synoptics. For a modern suggestion along the same lines, cf. Introduction, p. 49.

(f) John is certainly recasting his source. His account of Peter's denials seems not to have been much altered. But it is certain that it was one piece in his source, because the division of it into two involves the repetition of the end of verse 18 at the beginning of verse 25 (accordingly the Sinaitic Syriac omits the repeated words). Verses 19–23 replace the source material, and it is natural to suppose that they are a substitute for the trial tradition, cf. (c) above. This passage has connection of thought with 7.14–26. This suggests that John's aim is to represent the trial by the Sanhedrin as a miscarriage of justice. This is consistent with the final exposure of hypocrisy (19.15).

Annas and Caiaphas **13f.**

13. First: Gr. *prōton*, a mark of John's style (1.41; 2.10; 7.51; 10.40; 12.16; 15.18; 19.39), and so perhaps not in his source, which may have had the examination before Annas and Caiaphas together; cf. (d) above.
father-in-law: John is our only source for this piece of information; there is no reason to doubt it. For the rest of this verse and verse 14, cf. the notes on 11.49–51. For **die** many texts read 'perish' (apolesthai) which may be original; if so, **for the people** may be a gloss. The point is repeated here to suggest the outcome of the trial and its saving purpose.

Peter Denies Jesus (i) **15–18**

15. followed: the word is found in Mk 14.54 paras., and no doubt stood in John's source. The tradition that Peter hung about the court-room, but was too afraid to profess his allegiance to Jesus, is generally recognized as authentic. It has been told by Peter himself in the first instance, presumably, to encourage others to show a firmer loyalty when similarly pressed. But this does not mean that it has been free from the tendency to embellishment. The *three* denials correspond with the style of folk-lore (M. Dibelius, *From Tradition to Gospel*, 1934, p. 216).

another disciple: So P60vid P66 B ℵ* A Dsuppl W Ψ. Nearly all other MSS. have the article, as if 'the other disciple' is already known to the reader. Schnackenburg calls this a notable variant, attesting the identification of this disciple with the Beloved Disciple (who is referred to as 'the other disciple' in 20.2–4, 8) from an early date in the interpretation of the Fourth Gospel. It is perhaps on the basis of this verse that Polycrates asserted that John 'was a priest wearing the *petalon* (the gold plate attached to the high priest's mitre, Ex. 28.36)' (Eus. *HE* III.xxxi.3). But, in any case, the identification is unlikely, because elsewhere John gives adequate description to avoid confusion (cf. 19.26), and also has a definite purpose in mentioning the Beloved Disciple. Here the absence of the article in the best textual authorities, and the fact that the disciple has no part to play once he has gained entry for Peter into the court, tell strongly against it. What we can deduce from the use of the same phrase in 20.2ff. is that **[an]other disciple** is Johannine diction. This suggests that he was not mentioned in John's source. John assumes (or perhaps knows, if the assumption is correct) that the public were not admitted to the High Priest's court, and feels the need to explain how Peter was able to gain admittance. So he imagines a disciple who was **known to** (i.e. an acquaintance of) **the high priest,** and so could gain access. According to the *Gospel of the Hebrews*, John used to supply fish to the High Priest's court, when he worked for his father Zebedee.

court: Gr. *aulē*, used only here in the trial narrative. But it comes at the corresponding point in the Synoptics (cf. Mk 14.54), and so belongs to the source.

16. A further sign of John's writing is the unnecessary repetition of **who was known to the high priest.**

the maid who kept the door: lit. 'the portress'; cf. 10.3. In the next verse we have a fuller phrase (lit. 'the maid the portress', *hē paidiskē hē thurōros*), using the same word *paidiskē* as Mk 14.66, 69. Again it looks as if John is elaborating the tradition, or perhaps

this detail was already found in his source. Variant readings of
these phrases in the Sinaitic Syriac have been taken by Black and
Boismard to point to an Aramaic original behind John. For it
reads 'the porter' and 'the maid of the porter' respectively. This
gives a good sense, as one would expect a male porter at such
a place and time (but cf. Ac. 12.13). The Greek text could have
been derived from the Aramaic by dittography of one letter (both
times, of course). But the Syriac and its derivatives (Tatian,
Ethiopic) may have arisen from confusion of the Greek, as *thurōros*
has the masculine ending, and is only shown to be feminine here
by the article.

17. Are not you also: the question with *mē* implies cautious
assertion (cf. 4.29), and so constitutes a challenge. **You also**
appears in the Synoptic version (Mk 14.67 paras.), but there it is
a definite statement. As the doorkeeper, the maid scrutinizes
Peter as he enters. This is a variant development from the Marcan
version, where Peter moves out into the gateway after the first
challenge.

I am not: Gr. *ouk eimi*—a flat denial, as in verse 25 and Lk. 22.58.
Cf. John the Baptist, 1.21. There is no warrant in the text for
drawing a sharp contrast with the *egō eimi* of Jesus in the account
of the arrest. In Mark, Peter prevaricates. D. Daube (*Theology*
LXXII (1969), pp. 291–304) asserts that prevarication would be
considered less reprehensible than outright denial by Jewish
moralists, and notes the way Peter's three replies in Mark build up
to a climax. But for John the flat denial is necessary, as Peter would
otherwise hardly gain entry.

18. a charcoal fire: this is a feature of the Synoptic story,
which uses the same word for **warming himself** (cf. Mk 14.54).
John mentions this *after* the first denial, so as to break off the story
where the characters are stationary, before inserting his account
of the High Priest's examination of Jesus. But the detail may well
have been mentioned in this order in his source.

Jesus before the High Priest **19–24**

19. The high priest: evidently John means Annas, though in
verse 15 the reference was certainly to Caiaphas in John's source
(cf. Mk 14.54). There is no difficulty about Annas, as an ex-High
Priest, being referred to in this way. But the suggestion, commonly
expressed, that the case would have been referred to him by Jews,

because they still felt he was the *real* High Priest and distrusted
Caiaphas as a tool of the Romans, is not convincing. The arrest
has been the result of a plot by the chief priests themselves, and
there is not the slightest hint that Caiaphas was left out of it—
rather the reverse (11.47–53).

about his disciples and his teaching: the vocabulary is typical
of John, here and throughout the paragraph. But the noun **teaching** (*didachē*) only occurs elsewhere at 7.16f., to which this dialogue
is clearly related.

20. openly: a favourite word of John's (*parrēsia*; cf. 7.4).

taught in synagogues and in the temple: the similarity to
Mk 14.49 paras., Jesus' protest at the time of his arrest, can
scarcely be accidental. As John has deliberately departed from his
source in the account of the arrest, it is reasonable to suppose that
it contained this feature, which he now uses as a basis for his
substitute for the trial tradition. The addition of **in synagogues**
(the word is singular in the Greek) may be a reference to chapter
6. But the whole of Jesus' public teaching thereafter has been given
in the Temple in chapters 7–10 (cf. especially 7.26). For **in secret**
(*en kruptō*), cf. 7.4. According to John's presentation of the Gospel,
Jesus can justly claim that the teaching on which the indictment
is based in the trial tradition was given in public (10.22–39).

21. Ask those who have heard me: the words are comparable to a Lucan insertion into the trial tradition, Lk. 22.67f.: 'If
I tell you, you will not believe; and if I ask you, you will not
answer.' But there is no verbal dependence on either side. Jesus
appears to be demanding that testimony should first be taken from
witnesses, as legal procedure requires, and as is actually recorded
in the trial tradition.

22. struck Jesus with his hand: lit. 'gave a *rhapisma* [a blow
with the hand] to Jesus'. The trial tradition in the Synoptics ends
with abusive treatment of Jesus. Mk 14.65 concludes: 'And the
guards (*hupēretai*, the same word as John's **officers**) received him
with blows (*rhapismasin*).' The similarity may be accidental, but
John may be building on something similar in his source. For this
incident has been subject to development. In Mt. 26.67f. the
rhapismata of Mark have been included in the game of blindfold
which immediately precedes Mark's remarks about the guards (so
Matthew adds 'slapped', *errhapisan*, before 'Prophesy!'). But John,
or his source, takes it to be a rebuke for abusing the High Priest,

which was forbidden under the law of Exod. 22.28. The situation
has a close parallel in the case of Paul (Ac. 23.2–5). The action is
evoked by Jesus' refusal to give a direct answer to the question of
verse 19, which is taken to be evasion.

23. Jesus' response to this attack amounts to a reassertion of his
claim in verse 21. It was no evasion, for he is willing to have witnesses called. On the other hand he has been abused without witness to the wrong. There must be proof that he meant to be con-
tumacious, if the guards' action is to be allowed. The protest of
Jesus is reminiscent of 7.24 and 8.46, though not related to either
verbally; and invites comparison with Paul once more, cf. Ac.
25.11. It has been suggested that the shaping of this paragraph
owes something to Christian experience of persecution. However
that may be, John's purpose is to give the impression of unreasoning
hostility on the part of the Jewish authorities, in preparation for
their part in the trial before Pilate.

24. to Caiaphas: this verse is the cause of all the difficulties in
our attempts to make sense of John's narrative. But it cannot
lightly be set aside on that account. For the view that it arises from
a mistake on John's part in handling his source; cf. (d) in the
introduction to this section. Mastin supposes that Jesus is sent to
Caiaphas simply to keep him under guard until the morning.
Barrett thinks that this verse corresponds with Mk 15.1.

Peter Denies Jesus (ii) **25–7**

25. warming himself: cf. verse 18, and compare Mk 14.54
with Mk 14.67. The questioners are presumably the group of
servants and officers who had lit the fire (verse 18). John creates
the sense of climax by varying the questioners. All four evangelists
agree that a maid asked the first question. For the second, Mark
has the same maid, Matthew another maid, Luke 'someone else'
(the Greek pronoun is masculine). The question here is almost
identical with the question in verse 17; the answer **'I am not'**
precisely the same.
denied: the key word of this tradition; cf. 13.38; Mk 14.30f., 68,
70, 72, paras.

26. For the third denial Matthew and Mark have the whole
company as questioners, Luke simply another man. The reader's
interest is heightened by the fact that Peter is almost exposed, because he is recognized as a Galilean. Mark and Luke fail to indicate

what was distinctive about him, but Matthew takes it to be his
Galilean accent, revealed in his previous replies (Mt. 26.73). John,
but probably not his source, achieves the same end in a more
dramatic way, making a most effective climax. One of the company, who is **a kinsman of** Malchus, **whose ear Peter had cut
off,** claims to have seen him at the time of the arrest. There Peter's
face had been visible in the glare of the torches, here it is seen by
the light of the fire. Thus very skilfully John uses the one tradition
to enhance the other, although originally they circulated separately, without any cross-reference (cf. the notes on verse 10). For
garden, cf. verse 1.

   27. again denied: cf. Mk 14.70 (the second denial). John here
is characteristically brief. There is no reference to Peter's self-
imprecation and curse, nor to his tears of remorse when the cock
crows and brings him to his senses. There is nothing further to
record, because Peter apparently got away with it. The climax
has been reached in the sense of personal danger given by the last
verse. It is only necessary to say that Peter denied once more, and
that **the cock crowed.** These words are identical in all four
Gospels. Bernard argues that it is not meant literally, but refers to
the third watch of the night, called 'cockcrow' (Mk 13.35), when a
blast was given on the *buccina*; but against this see the notes on
13.38. There is no article with **cock** in Greek. There is a sequel to
this tale in the Johannine Appendix, 21.15–17.

JESUS BEFORE PILATE   **18.28–19.16**

In spite of all difficulties, what follows is recognizably a trial, comparable with the trial described in the Synoptic Gospels. In all
four Gospels Pilate begins by stating the charge in the form of a
question addressed to Jesus: 'Are you the King of the Jews?' John,
however, precedes this with a paragraph (18.28–32) in which
Pilate first asks the representatives of the Sanhedrin the nature of
the charge. This is also supplied in the special material of Luke
(Lk. 23.2), where the 'many things' of Mk 15.3 are specified.
Although this must be regarded as an authentic item, omitted by
Matthew and Mark, John's version of it is entirely independent
of Luke, and handled in such a typically Johannine fashion that
we cannot even be sure whether he had anything corresponding
with it in his source. In any case he uses it in order to draw attention to the necessity of crucifixion (verse 32). Then, when the

charge has been read in verse 33, John replaces the short non-committal 'You have said so' of the Synoptic tradition with an important discussion on the meaning of kingship, arising from the form of the charge. Whatever lay in John's source at this point, this is undoubtedly his own composition. It really holds up the proceedings, for the charge should be followed by the evidence of the Sanhedrin. This is briefly indicated in Matthew and Mark (cf. Mk 15.3–5), but omitted by Luke and John, both of whom represent Pilate as saying: 'I find no crime in him' (18.38, cf. Lk. 23.4). This may indicate a common source, though John knows nothing of the transfer of the case to Herod, which now follows in Luke.

It is at this point that the real difficulties begin. All four Gospels agree that Pilate was convinced of Jesus' innocence (for Matthew and Mark, cf. Mt. 27.18, 23 = Mk 15.10, 14). But then the extraordinary transaction is proposed, whereby Pilate offers to release Jesus as a kind of amnesty to maintain popular favour, and it is revealed that the people already desire this clemency to be exercised in favour of a criminal called Barabbas. According to the Synoptists, Pilate gives way to the people, and condemns Jesus to be crucified. The trial is over. The soldiers take Jesus, mock him as a king, and lead him off to crucifixion. It appears that Pilate has allowed fear of a popular disturbance to override justice. This suits the apologetic character of the trial narrative, which seeks to give the impression that Jesus was not found guilty by the Romans (cf. p. 537 above). But a further look at Mark shows that Pilate is satisfied that Jesus has admitted the charge of claiming to be the King of the Jews (Mk 15.9, 12). He is not convinced that Jesus has actually committed insurrection, but that does not prevent him from believing that Jesus is a politically dangerous person. The accusations of the Sanhedrin, which are based on the charge of blasphemy (Mk 14.64), cannot be lightly brushed aside. If Pilate has to release Barabbas, he dare not let this man live as an even more potentially dangerous threat to the Roman peace.

Returning to John, we find that as soon as Pilate has declared Jesus guiltless he suggests the release of the prisoner, and the crowd asks for Barabbas (18.39f.). Then comes the scourging and mocking, which in the Synoptics is rightly recorded after the trial is over (19.1–3). But not in the case of John. It is only at this point that the chief priests speak, and this is not so much to give evidence of the charge as to renew it more insistently. What follows is a battle of nerves, in which Pilate gradually yields to them because of the implied threat to his own position (19.4–12). Only then does he give the sentence (19.13–16). It can scarcely be claimed that this is an historical picture. For one thing, the mocking as an interlude during the trial is extremely improbable. Secondly, the conversation of 19.4–12 should follow 18.38, Pilate's first declaration of Jesus' innocence. Most important of all, the whole of 19.1–16 is dominated not so much by narrative interest as by the emotional effect of a devastating dramatic irony, in which the Jews finally acknowledge Caesar to be their king, in order to be rid of Jesus, their true King. But this very fact explains the alteration of the historical sequence, which has been made subservient to building up to a momentous climax. And whether John is using tradition from a non-Synoptic source or not, his explanation agrees with what has been said above to account for Pilate's action, that he believed that Jesus claimed to be King of the Jews and saw in this a serious political threat. Sherwin-White is prepared to admit that John is right in representing the chief priests as using Pilate's personal insecurity as a lever to secure condemnation (cf. below on 19.12).

Jesus Brought to Pilate on a Capital Charge **28–32**

28. from the house of Caiaphas: *RSV* is interpretative here. The Greek simply says 'from Caiaphas' (so *NEB*). He is not mentioned by name again, but the following account always speaks of the chief priests in general.

the praetorium: the technical term for the procurator's official residence, mentioned also in Mk 15.16 para. Pilate normally used the Palace of Herod at Caesarea. It is disputed whether his residence at Jerusalem was the Palace of Herod near the Jaffa Gate or the Antonia Fortress at the NW. corner of the Temple area. The evidence of Philo and Josephus suggests that it would usually be the Palace of Herod. But it is possible that he stayed at the Antonia at the time of Passover, because the huge crowds of pilgrims and the nationalist feeling of the occasion made this the most likely trouble spot, where his personal control was most needed. The modern discovery of the Lithostrotos under the convent of the Sisters of Sion (see on 19.13 below), and the long-standing tradition of the *Via Dolorosa* beginning at this point (though the so-called *Ecce Homo* arch at the same site was actually built later

than the time of the crucifixion) make the Antonia the most
natural interpretation of John's account (so Lagrange). But there
is no conclusive evidence. The arguments for and against the
Antonia are very fully presented by Vincent and Benoit respectively in *RB* LIX (1952), pp. 513–50.

It was early: Sherwin-White holds that it is altogether probable
that Pilate would attend to judicial business early in the day. It
would thus have been necessary to prepare the case before dawn,
if the whole affair was not to be held over until another day. Luke's
timing of the trial by the Sanhedrin in the morning (Lk. 22.66)
necessitates cramming in so much activity, including the examination by Herod, before the sixth hour (12 noon; Lk. 23.44) that his
scheme cannot be regarded as reliable.

might not be defiled: the dwelling-places of Gentiles were
regarded as unclean (*Oholoth* xviii.7). Normally ceremonial purity
could be restored the same evening by taking a bath. As the
Passover was not eaten until evening, the insistence on remaining
outside would appear to be unnecessary. But the chief priests may
have feared the possibility of contracting seven-day uncleanness,
which could arise from a variety of causes (*Kelim* i.4). Alternatively
eat the passover might refer to the sacrifices on the day following
the Passover itself, which were eaten during the day-time, if this
detail belongs to John's source and accorded with the Synoptic
timing of the Last Supper and the crucifixion (full discussion in
SB II.837ff.). In any case this allusion to Jewish customs is not
found in the Synoptic accounts, and so is derived either from
John's source or from his personal knowledge of Judaism. From
the point of view of the 'staging' of the trial, it allows him a most
effective alternation between public dealing with the chief priests
and private conversation with Jesus on the part of Pilate. It also
increases the irony of the whole situation, in which the Jews are
more concerned with ceremonial purity than with moral integrity.

29. Pilate: first mentioned here, as if well known to the reader
(cf. Mk 15.1). Pontius Pilate was procurator of the tetrarchy of
Judea from A.D. 26 to 36, when he was recalled, largely because of
the trouble caused by his unsympathetic handling of Jewish
affairs. The trial narratives tend to give a better picture of him
than was really the case, by contrast with the Jewish leaders. Very
properly he asks first for the accusation, as Roman law required.

30. Instead of the answer which must surely have been given (cf. Lk. 23.2), and which is implied in Pilate's question in verse 33, John represents the chief priests as prevaricating in a scarcely credible fashion. **This man** (*houtos*) is not the same phrase as in verse 29, and carries a pejorative nuance. From previous experience of Johannine dialogue, we may assume that the answer of the chief priests has been carefully worded with a view to the point which John wishes to make clear. The next two verses are in Johannine vocabulary throughout. By stating only that Jesus is an evildoer, the seriousness of the charge is intentionally left open.

31. your own law: as matters stand, no reason has been given why the case should not fall within the competence of the Sanhedrin. Only when the Jews reply that **'It is not lawful for us to put any man to death',** does it become clear that this is a capital charge. The question whether the Sanhedrin possessed the *ius gladii* at this period has been briefly mentioned above, p. 537.

The Jewish evidence (summarized by Barrett, pp. 445f., on the basis of J. Juster, *Les Juifs en l'Empire romain* (1914), II, pp. 127–49) tells both ways: (i) the *Mishnah* includes regulations for the death penalty, as if the Sanhedrin had the right to enforce them, and includes an actual example (*Sanhedrin* vii.2); but this is a case of adultery, for which the decision of the local authority would be likely to be confirmed by the procurator (cf. Jn 8.5). (ii) Josephus (*Ant.* xx.200–2) tells of the stoning of James the brother of Jesus by order of the Sanhedrin, while the procuratorship was vacant; but the new procurator, Albinus, did not approve, and the High Priest was deposed. (iii) Gentiles who entered the sacred inner courts of the Temple were executed; but this must be regarded as a concession to Jewish religious feeling and consideration for the need to prevent the possibility of a highly inflammable situation.

The Roman evidence is the common practice of the Roman Empire, which shows that only in exceptional cases was the local municipal power allowed full jurisdiction, including the death penalty, and that was as a reward for conspicuous loyalty to the Romans (Sherwin-White, p. 36).

The New Testament evidence is (apart from the present passage) the woman taken in adultery (Jn 8.5), the stoning of Stephen (Ac. 7.58), and the refusal of Paul to be tried at Jerusalem (Ac. 25.10). Stephen is certainly tried by the Sanhedrin, but his death is equally certainly a matter of lynching while the procurator is away from Jerusalem. Jn 8.5 is best taken as a case of lynch law,

which nevertheless would be upheld if the case was referred to the
procurator, on the grounds that the *lex Iulia de adulteriis* now took
cognizance of the offence, and the local customs should be maintained. Paul's refusal to go to Jerusalem does not imply that he
would there be tried in the absence of the procurator (in spite of
Winter's long argument to the contrary), for Festus never suggests
that he would not be conducting the case himself ('before me', Ac.
25.9). It is, then, a refusal to go where his opponents have most
opportunity to exert pressure behind the scenes. The upshot of
these various lines of evidence is that, even if the Sanhedrin occasionally got away with execution by Jewish methods, it could
not have done so while Pilate was actually in the city to prevent
disturbances, nor could it ever have claimed the right to do so.

32. For John this fact has theological significance. The case is
referred to Pilate, because it is a capital charge. If he condemns
Jesus, death will be by the Roman method of crucifixion. The
transference of the case to Pilate is thus necessary for the meaning
of the death of Jesus to be displayed. For only if he is crucified
will he be 'lifted up'; cf. 3.14; 8.28; 12.32. There is no reason to
ascribe this verse to the redactor (Bultmann). It is the point of the
whole paragraph.

The Kingship of Jesus 33–8a

33. 'Are you the king of the Jews?': the words are identical
in all four Gospels. There can be no doubt that this was the charge
which was brought to Pilate, and that he condemned Jesus on the
strength of it. It is not excluded that there were subsidiary charges
(cf. Lk. 23.2). Obviously it would carry serious political implications from Pilate's point of view. The accusation rests on the fact
that Jesus had claimed, or was thought to have claimed, to be the
Messiah ('anointed'), a title which was reserved to the Davidic
King and, to a limited extent, to the High Priest. From a Jewish
point of view such a claim would not of itself involve a criminal
offence, though its truth might be contested. But in the Synoptic
trial before the Sanhedrin, reproduced by John in 10.24, 33,
Jesus interpreted it in terms of the Son of Man imagery, claiming
a right to sit on the throne of God himself (Mk 14.62 paras.) He
was thus condemned on the grounds that the form of his messianic
claim involved blasphemy. This Jewish objection to Jesus' claims
will be referred to in 19.7. But we should not jump to the conclusion

that the Jews condemned Jesus for one thing, but referred the case to Pilate for another. The charge remains the same, that Jesus claimed to be the Messiah. But if the Sanhedrin had not been convinced that in Jesus' case it involved blasphemy, they might have been prepared to dismiss the case. In deciding to refer it to Pilate they were not bound to give the religious grounds for their decision, in which Pilate would not be interested. It was sufficient that Jesus had admitted the charge, which would secure condemnation without bringing in the religious issues. Nor is it to be supposed that the Sanhedrin opposed Jesus purely on religious grounds. The conviction of blasphemy ensured condemnation, but the Sadducees (including Caiaphas, and most of the leading members of the Sanhedrin) were genuinely concerned to maintain good relations with the Romans, and so shared Pilate's fear of the political consequences of a claim to messiahship. Their motives may have been mixed, but they were not guilty of duplicity.

34. of your own accord: the phrase is characteristic of John, just as the structure of the dialogue follows his established patterns. It can scarcely be considered probable that Jesus replied to the charge by asking Pilate where he got it from. But the purpose of the question is to introduce the idea of distinctions in the meaning of kingship. So first Jesus asks if the charge is the result of Pilate's own observation and thought or comes from hearsay. The whole conversation can be regarded as a commentary on the noncommittal 'You have said so', which is Jesus' reply to the charge in all three Synoptics. If it is asked whether Jesus is a king, the answer can only be that he is and he is not; it depends what is meant by kingship.

35. Pilate brushes aside responsibility for thinking of this issue, and asks for facts. The verse performs the function of the overliteral misunderstanding, by which John so frequently prepares the way for a deeper understanding of the issue under discussion.

36. not of this world: cf. 8.23; 17.16. The preposition **of** (*ek*) means not only 'from', 'originating from', but also 'on the side of', 'belonging to'. Speaking strictly in Jewish terms, the contrast would be one of temporal succession. Jesus' kingdom is not to be understood in terms of the Present Age (*hā-ʿôlām haz-zeh*) but belongs to the Coming Age (*hā-ʿôlām hab-bāʾ*). But John thinks of it in terms of simultaneous orders of being (Gr. *kosmos* = **world**). But this is not to be taken in a metaphysical sense, but as spheres of relationship. Jesus' kingdom is not a kingdom of the world of men apart from God, but a kingdom of men in relation to God; not secular, but spiritual. For the Kingdom understood in this way military action is not appropriate—a fact which the Church has not always remembered.

my servants would fight: this explains why Jesus would not allow the use of the sword at the time of his arrest (verse 11). The words are comparable to Mt. 26.53, but there is no verbal link.

but: the Greek has 'but now' (omitted by *NEB*), i.e. 'but as it is', as in 17.13.

from the world: lit. 'from there'. Jesus still has not said where it *does* belong.

37. 'So you are a king?': the question is introduced by a particle (*oukoun*) which occurs nowhere else in the NT. When accented on the first syllable, it has negative force, but expects the answer yes: 'Are you not a king?—Yes, of course I am.' But when accented on the second syllable, it loses its negative force and becomes inferential. It may then be a statement: 'So you *are* a king!'; or a question: 'So you *are* a king, are you?' (For the three possibilities, see Moule, p. 165.) All three have found favour with various scholars, but the last seems best. It suits the situation that Jesus has denied the charge, and yet left the way open for affirmation of it in another sense.

You say that I am a king: it is impossible to escape the impression that **you say** (*NEB*: 'is your word') is an allusion to the answer as given in the Synoptics, 'You have said so' (*NEB*: 'The words are yours'), for the Greek (*su legeis*) is precisely the same. It is widely held among scholars today that this expression can only be a refusal to admit the charge (*BDF* §§ 277.2, 441.3). But what is expected is a frank avowal. To get round the difficulty, scholars have suggested taking **that I am a king** as a separate sentence ('*You* say so. For I am a king; for this I was born . . .'), or turning the whole thing into a question ('Do you say that . . .?'). Neither of these expedients is convincing. But John probably means (and the emphatic position of the pronouns in the Greek supports this) a denial of the charge in one sense and an avowal in another, i.e. '*You* say that I am king in a political sense; but *I* say so in the sense that for this I was born, etc.' So, in familiar Johannine phrases, Jesus explains that the reason why he **was born** and has **come into the world** is to gather around him the company of those who are **of the truth,** i.e. on the side of the truth, as opposed to being on the side of the world. It comes as a surprise to the ordinary reader that Jesus should express the spiritual meaning of the kingdom in this way. But it accords with the basic idea of spheres of relationship, using the Two Spirits doctrine which is fundamental to John's thinking. The kingdom consists of those who are open to the Spirit of Truth, as opposed to those who are under the influence of the Devil ('the father of lies', 8.44; see the whole passage, 8.39–47, and note how this verse echoes 8.47). But the phrase **hears my voice** reminds us of the Good Shepherd; cf. 10.16, 27. This saves the exposition from losing touch with the essential character of kingship, that it implies personal allegiance to one man. The allegory of the Shepherd beautifully illustrates the meaning of the kingship of Jesus.

38a. 'What is truth?': it is not to be supposed that the meaning of Jesus' kingship is confined to the one item of proclaiming the truth. But by concentrating on this one element, John can round off the dialogue with this rhetorical question. Just as in verse 35, Pilate dissociates himself from the challenge implicit in Jesus' words. He has, then, already lost his integrity, and his subsequent behaviour in sentencing an innocent man to death is explained.

Jesus or Barabbas? **38b–40**

38b. 'I find no crime in him': these words are almost identical with phrases in Lk. 23.4, 14, 22; the repetition in Luke is probably due to the insertion of the Herod episode. This phrase is strong evidence that John's source differed to some extent from Mark, but was known to Luke. It is Pilate's summary of the case, and in Luke rightly precedes the giving of the sentence, which in all three Synoptics is bound up with the affair of Barabbas. John maintains these connections, though he makes the whole sequence less plausible by inserting a fresh examination of Jesus in 19.4–11. Moreover the declaration of Jesus' innocence at the present stage in the trial is premature, as no witnesses have been called. But John's account appears convincing at first sight, because Jesus' own statement has provided evidence that he has not committed a political offence. This is the fact that he had offered no resistance at his arrest (verse 36).

39. you have a custom: so also Matthew and Mark. But there is no evidence for this as a regular practice. This may be the reason why Luke makes no mention of the custom in his version of this tradition (Lk. 23.17 is an addition to the original text). On the other hand there is nothing improbable in the idea that Pilate should make a gesture of good will to the people by releasing one political prisoner whom they regarded as a hero on occasions. His relations with them were far from cordial, and an occasional act of generosity could do much to reduce tension. Barrett cites what little classical evidence there is for an act of mercy of this kind, but points out that the release of a prisoner on a capital charge would require imperial dispensation. It is possible that this had happened at least once before, and that the people regarded this as a precedent for a further demand. According to Mk 15.8, the people happened to come up ('came up' is the text, against the *textus receptus* 'shouted out') at this crucial moment, and made the demand. It is implied that Pilate proposed to release Jesus in response to them, hoping to gain the support of the people against the pressure of the chief priests to condemn Jesus. But the chief priests organized the popular feeling to ask for Barabbas, and so the artifice failed. This seems more likely than Matthew, who makes Pilate take the initiative in proposing the alternatives, Barabbas or Jesus. In Luke the people have been summoned along with the chief priests (Lk. 23.13). Pilate then announces his intention of releasing Jesus, but the people cry out: 'Away with this man, and release to us Barabbas' (Lk. 23.18). Presumably the people have interpreted Pilate to mean that he intends to pardon Jesus, and feel that if he is prepared to do that he should rather release their favourite. John's version stands midway between Mark and Luke. This suggests once more that his source is not Mark, but contains a developed form of the tradition which is moving in the direction of Luke. That John is here reproducing his source with very little change is indicated by the fact that he makes no attempt to build on this item of tradition. He only seems to include it because of its firm place in the tradition, and then after verse 40 he drops it like a hot cake. His source accords with Mark in the mention of the custom and in Pilate's question: **'Will you have me release for you the King of the Jews?'** These words are almost identical with Mk 15.9. The agreement with Luke comes in the next verse, where the people cry out for Barabbas, thus mentioning him for the first time, and the description of Barabbas only comes after that. The final element in the source at this point, the demand that Pilate should crucify Jesus, which agrees with both Mark and Luke, is held over by John until 19.6 and the grand climax at 19.15.

40. cried out: John uses *kraugazein* (as also at 11.43; 12.13; 19.6, 12, 15) instead of the more common *krazein*, which probably stood in his source (cf. Mk 15.13f.); **again** also comes from the source (cf. Mk 15.12f.; Lk. 23.20), and is not really appropriate in the text as it stands, for no previous cry of the people has been mentioned. **'Not this man, but Barabbas!'** has its closest parallel in Lk. 23.18.

Barabbas: a common Aramaic name ('son of Abba'). If the name is a true patronymic we should expect another personal name to precede it, and there is an ancient tradition, found in some MSS. and versions of Mt. 27. 16f. (Θ Lake group, Sinaitic and Palestinian Syriac), and commented on by Origen (Klostermann XI, pp. 255–7), that his name was Jesus! This tradition cannot be lightly dismissed. It is clear that the name is likely to have been removed out of reverence, rather than inserted. Moreover it is probable that it stood in the original text of Mark. For Mk 15.7 reads literally 'there was the one called Barabbas', which sounds very strange in Greek without mention of the personal name first. Hence it is widely assumed that the original text was 'there was Jesus called Barabbas' (so Rawlinson, Cranfield, Nineham). There is nothing improbable about it, for Jesus (*Yēšûaʿ*, an abbreviated form of Joshua, *Yehôšūaʿ*, in the OT) occurs frequently as the name of Jews in the first century (cf. Col. 4.11, where 'Jesus who is called Justus' is exactly parallel to Mark's phrase). But what is much more questionable is the attempt, often made in reconstructions of the trial narratives, to explain this perplexing episode, and the condemnation of Jesus, as due in part to Pilate's confusion, when dealing with two men of the same name (cf. Winter, p. 99). Mt. 27.17, reading: 'Jesus the son of Abba or Jesus who is called Messiah', gives the impression of absolute clarity, as the surname or describer is carefully retained. But of all this both John and Luke appear to know nothing. We must assume that their common source did not include the personal name. Probably the distaste of Christian readers for the application of it to such an unsuitable person in such shocking juxtaposition with Jesus Christ had already brought about its suppression. But if only John had known of it, we can guess the irony he would have got out of the situation! Finally, the equation Barabbas = son of Abba (i.e. 'son of the father') is uncertain. 'Son of the father' invites further speculation about underlying ironies, but the evangelists are unaware of such. But some MSS. read: 'Barrabas', i.e. *Bar-Rabbā(n)* = son of the teacher (so the *Gospel of the Hebrews*, in a fragment in Jerome, *Comm. in Mt.* 27.16). This must be regarded as much less likely as a patronymic, and is not supported by the Syriac, which uses the Aramaic form (*Bar-'Abbā'*). But there is other evidence that Barabbas may not have been the man's actual name, but a title for a character in a ritual drama of the mocking of a king. This will be considered in the notes on 19.2f.

a robber: both Mark and Luke assert that Barabbas had taken part in an insurrection and committed murder. Hence this probably stood in John's source too. For the sake of brevity he uses the word **robber** (*lēstēs*), which is used in Josephus both for a bandit and for a revolutionary. This may well be the meaning of the word in Jesus' protest at his arrest in Mk 14.48. The word may also have been in John's source for the arrest (which he has drastically altered), and so chosen for use here by influence of it. It is also possible that he intends to allude to the allegory of the Shepherd (10.1, 8), as the allegory has already been echoed in the trial narrative, and the application would be apt. John now drops the subject, wishing to reserve the sequel for the build-up to the climax at 19.15. It is left to the reader to assume that Pilate acceded to the people's wishes, and released Barabbas.

Ecce Homo **19.1–11**

19.1. scourged him: Roman law knew of various grades of flogging (Sherwin-White, pp. 27f.). There was a lighter form to accompany a warning when a man was released (cf. Lk. 23.22), and a more severe form after sentence had been given, as the first stage of the punishment (cf. Mk 15.15). John's source is thus nearer to Mark than to Luke at this point. But by holding over the end of the Barabbas episode, which was in fact the giving of sentence against Jesus, John has produced an impossible sequence. Mastin, who rates the historical value of John's trial narrative very highly, is compelled to suppose that there has been some dislocation, whereby the scourging and mocking have been removed from their original position at the end of the trial. But it is quite clear that John has done this deliberately, regardless of the correct procedure (perhaps not knowing it). He wants to use the mocking as the jumping-off point for the dialogue which follows it, and of course the scourging goes with it.

2. John's account of the mocking has many verbal agreements with Mk 15.17–20. If, as seems probable, it was in the source which he has used in common with Luke, we must assume that Luke has deliberately omitted this item. Just as, at the end of the trial by the Sanhedrin, the Jewish guards taunted Jesus as a prophet (Mk 14.65), so now the Roman soldiers, knowing the charge against him, mock him as a king. There is nothing odd about this, but speculations are aroused by the fact that Philo recounts something similar during political disturbances at Alexandria in A.D. 39 (*In Flaccum*, 36–9). Public feeling was aroused by the fact that the city was expected to accord royal honours to Agrippa, when he was on a visit to Alexandria. One of many insults was the idea of dressing up a poor half-wit Jew called Karabas as a king, and paying him mock homage. This was followed by unrestrained mob violence against the Jews, the whole affair being a particularly nasty example of anti-Semitism. The mocking is described with details almost identical with the mocking of Jesus, and the name of the victim is strikingly similar to Barabbas. It has thus been suggested that Barabbas and Karabas are garbled forms of a cult name for a king-substitute, and that the mocking is derived from an ancient ceremonial involving the ritual slaughter of the king, actually slaying the substitute instead (for further details and criticism, cf. Nineham on Mk 15.16ff.). But the evidence is far too slender. The similarity of names may be pure coincidence. Philo tells us that the people got the idea of the mocking from theatrical performances. There really seems to be no connection between the two events at all.

a crown of thorns: the great tradition of Christian art represents this as a twist of thorny twigs, which gives the impression of physical cruelty. But it is simply part of the dressing-up, and the Gospels give no indication that it was painful. There is therefore much to be said for the suggestion of H. St J. Hart (*JTS* n.s., III (1952), pp. 66–75) that it means here the spiky leaves of a frond of a palm tree, used to represent the radial crown of a king in the likeness of the sun and its rays, the *sol invictus* of pagan mythology. The **purple robe** is an obvious symbol of royalty (perhaps a military cloak?). Mt. 27.29 adds a reed-stalk as a sceptre, though

Mk 15.19 refers to this only as a sort of stick used by the soldiers
to bait Jesus. The unfortunate Karabas was given a paper crown,
a mat for a robe, and a papyrus-stalk for a sceptre.

3. The salute of the soldiers is the same as Mk 15.18, except that
John uses the nominative with article for **king,** instead of the
vocative. This retains the idea of 'so-called King' without admit-
ting that Jesus has a right to the description (cf. J. H. Moulton,
A Grammar of New Testament Greek, 1 (1908), pp. 70f.).
struck him with their hands: the mock homage appears to
consist of coming up as if to swear allegiance and suddenly hitting
Jesus instead. John uses his own phrase (lit. 'gave him blows',
rhapismata, as in 18.22), probably abbreviating the source. The
mockery is not so much cruel as crude.

4. Theatrically this is a most impressive moment. Pilate emerges
from the praetorium and announces that he is about to bring out
the prisoner. All eyes are fastened on the portico, and Jesus appears, dressed up as the king he claims to be. If this took place at
the Antonia, it would have been somewhere near the position of
the famous Ecce Homo arch, though in fact this arch was not in
existence then, as the Antonia was rebuilt about a century later
by Hadrian. But it is extremely difficult to take this incident as
historical: as we have seen, the mocking must certainly have been
done after the trial was over; Mark asserts that the robe was removed, and presumably the radial crown too, before Jesus was
escorted from the praetorium to go to the place of crucifixion. It
is also hard to see why Pilate should wish to bring Jesus out if the
trial was not yet finished. Nothing is said about taking him back
in again, though he is in the praetorium at verse 9. Pilate has
already tested popular feeling, and discovered that the people
want Barabbas, not Jesus. To bring him out now, already arrayed
as a laughing-stock, could only invite a ribald and hostile response,
the very opposite of the conditions required for a considered judgment of the case. The motive given, 'that you may know that I
find no crime in him', which is virtually a repetition of verse 38,
is extremely lame and scarcely plausible. But if John was allowing
his imagination to run beyond the probabilities of the situation, it
is easy to see why he has done it, why indeed this *coup de théâtre* was
irresistible. The mocking is too magnificent as a piece of dramatic
irony to be left to the comparative privacy of the guardroom.
Just as the dialogue on kingship between Jesus and Pilate was a

commentary on the charge in 18.33, so the dialogue between Pilate
and the Jews on who has the royal power is introduced by the
presentation of Jesus before them in the trappings of kingly state.

5. Pilate said to them, 'Here is the man!': lit. 'Behold the
man!' (Lat. *ecce homo*). The declaration makes the whole scene
even more impressive (the fact that this whole sentence is missing
from P⁶⁶* a e ff¹ r² is perhaps accidental). But it adds nothing to
the real course of the trial. So we must ask what effect John desires
to produce. All turns on the interpretation of **the man** (*ho anthrōpos*). To Pilate himself it would be far from complimentary—'the
poor fellow!' is Bernard's paraphrase. Barrett and Mastin argue
that it is meant to suggest 'Son of Man' to the reader, so that
Pilate, like Caiaphas, is an unconscious prophet. This is possible,
for the Aramaic *bar nāšā'* (lit. 'son of man') simply means 'man',
and the literal translation in NT usage is adopted to preserve the
reference to the heavenly figure of Dan. 7.14 (cf. the notes on 5.27).
The veiled allusion then prepares the way for the objection in verse
7, for the blasphemy of Jesus' messianic claim consisted precisely in
his expectation of sharing God's throne as the glorified Son of Man.
On this interpretation it has to be maintained that John could not
use the full expression here, as it would be inappropriate on
Pilate's lips. Another possibility is that there is an allusion to an
OT prophecy, Zech. 6.12: 'Behold, the man whose name is the
Branch.' In verse 2 John's text agrees with Mt. 27.29 against Mark
in adding 'put it on his head' with reference to the crown, though
there are very slight differences of grammar and word order which
suggest independence. This apparently independent development
can be explained if the crowning was being interpreted as a fulfilment of Zech. 6.11, where the prophet is instructed to 'make a
crown, and set it upon the head of Joshua (Gr. Jesus) the son of
Jehozadak, the high priest'. As soon as this is done the prophet
is to make the declaration 'Behold, the man . . .', as above. For
'man' the LXX has *anēr*, but this does not destroy the allusion. On
this interpretation Pilate is unconsciously showing that the prophecy has been fulfilled, in fact he acts the part of the prophet. But
this can remain no more than a suggestion, because John has provided no indication that there are deeper issues here. The prophecy of Zech. 6.12 is applied to the incarnation of Jesus by the
early Fathers, e.g. Justin, *Dial.* cvi; cxxi.

6. crucify him: here John picks up the sequel of the Barabbas episode, which he had abandoned after 18.40, only it is the chief priests and the officers who cry out instead of the crowd. For the repetition; cf. Lk. 23.21. This verse makes an *inclusio* with verse 15, bringing the whole of the intervening dialogue together as an enlargement of Mk 15.12–15, or whatever corresponded with it in John's source.

'Take him yourselves and crucify him': this is obviously impossible, and is presumably intended to be sarcasm on the part of Pilate, exasperated at the opposition to his decision, which he quotes once more in the words of 18.38. Once more, the deeper reason is likely to be that it moves the dialogue in the direction which John requires for the climax to which he is leading.

7. a law: the law against blasphemy, Lev. 24.16, cf. the notes on 10.33 (hardly the law against false prophets (Dt. 13.1–5), as suggested by Wead, *NT* xi (1969), pp. 185–9).

ought to die: if Pilate had meant the last remark seriously, the Jews could have put Jesus to death, in spite of the official position. But there is no real suggestion on either side that the conditions of 18.31 do not apply. The point here is that, even if Pilate can find no case against Jesus, the Sanhedrin have condemned him under their own laws, and they are really applying to Pilate for leave to impose the death penalty. This does not, however, mean that the Jews now suddenly alter the charge. It is rather an explanation of the deeper meaning of the same charge. Pilate has acquitted Jesus of plotting against the state in order to fulfil his role as King of the Jews. But Jesus has admitted to being King in another sense. What this sense is, is now revealed: it is the kingly status of **the Son of God.** In the Synoptic trial before the Sanhedrin the charge of blasphemy was levelled against Jesus' use of the Son of Man imagery to defend his messianic position (cf. the notes on 18.33 above). But in John's own version of this tradition it was put in the form of a claim to be the Son of God (see 10.33–6). But this also has its place in the Synoptic trial tradition (Mk 14.61 paras.). The fact that blasphemy has to be inferred in the present verse strongly suggests that John expects the reader to have the argument of 10.33–6 in mind. Just sufficient of it is recalled to bring the title **Son of God** into the dialogue at this point.

8. the more afraid: the comparative here should be treated as a superlative ('exceedingly afraid', Mastin). From the point of view of Pilate the idea was not so much blasphemy as a real and awesome possibility. Pagan mythology has plenty of examples of gods appearing as men (cf. Ac. 14.11f.).

9. So Pilate re-examines Jesus. The question now is no longer 'What have you done?' (18.35), but **'Where are you from?,'** i.e. 'What is your real origin?'

gave no answer: John's dramatic skill continues to serve him well. Taking a cue from the silence of Jesus before his accusers (cf. Mk 15.4f.), he uses this facet of the tradition to force Pilate to reframe the question in such a way as to produce the most devastating answer. For the question of Jesus' origin cannot be dissociated from the question of the source of authority. It was universally held in the ancient world that a ruler's authority was ultimately derived from the sovereign authority of God (cf. Rom. 13.1–5). In order to extort an answer to his question, Pilate attempts to exert his authority, only to discover that he is confronted with one who is himself at the source of all authority. The tables are turned, and Pilate is judged by the one whom he judges.

10. I have power: Gr. *exousia* ('authority', i.e. power in the political sense rather than power as physical strength). Pilate's unqualified claim to be above reason and justice, like an absolute monarch, makes him ascribe to himself almost the divine prerogative which is actually true of Jesus. For the nature of Jesus' authority, cf. 5.19–29.

11. Jesus pricks the bubble of Pilate's conceit by reminding him of the derivative character of all earthly power. **You would have** should probably be 'you would have had' **no power over me,** implying that Pilate would then not have been in a position to speak as he does now. This depends on the text of B W Θ and most MSS., reading *eiches* (omitting the particle *an*, as at 8.39), against *echeis* of ℵ A and a few others.

from above: i.e. from God, cf. 3.31. The **no** in the words **no power** is very emphatic. It is implied that, without divine support, Pilate would crumble before Jesus. And this can only be because of what he is in himself. He *is* from above. So there is an implicit answer to the unanswered question in verse 9.

therefore he who delivered me: Jesus is willing to acknowledge that, if Pilate is true to his derived authority, and remembers its true source, he is not to be blamed for carrying out his duty, even though it will be the sentence of death. For even that is the fruit of the divine will. What is so serious and so poignant is the fact that Jesus stands before Pilate as a result of men's unbelief, of their refusal to accept him as the one who came forth from God and was sent into the world by him, i.e. as the Son of God. It is not clear whether **he who delivered me** refers to Judas or to the people of the Jews, or just to Caiaphas. It has been almost a technical term for Judas whenever the verb (*paradidonai*) occurred earlier in the Gospel (6.64, 71; 12.4; 13.2, 11, 21; 18.2, 5), but it has been used of the Jews handing Jesus over to Pilate at 18.30, 35f. As this verse is to some extent exonerating Pilate, it is best to take it in line with the whole tendency of the dialogue to cast the blame on the Jews, and so to mean the people as a whole (so Bultmann). **Sin** here certainly means 'guilt', cf. 9.41; 16.9.

No King but Caesar 12–16

12. Upon this: probably 'because of this' (*ek toutou*, only here and 6.66). Thoroughly alarmed by Jesus' words, Pilate now really wants to release him. But he is in a difficult position, because, although he has cleared Jesus of the political aspects of the charge, the Jews' explanation of it in verse 7 has not been refuted. Pilate is not willing to face the challenge of Jesus' claims (cf. 18.35, 38), but he can only resist the argument of the Jews if he actually takes Jesus' part. So now we see him reluctantly going through the formality of giving sentence, putting off the fatal decision until the last possible moment, when he is forced to condemn Jesus out of consideration for the implications of the decision for his own personal position.

cried out: cf. 18.40; 19.6.

Caesar's friend: the phrase is virtually a technical term for an imperial representative (Sherwin-White, p. 47), perhaps implying an honour conferred on Pilate (E. Bammel, *TLZ* LXXVII (1952), cols. 205–10). The people's response to Pilate shows a new turn in the argument. It has now moved away from the question of Jesus' guilt to the issue of Pilate's position. This has been prepared for by verse 11. Jesus has fastened the blame for the crime of the crucifixion on the one (or the people) 'who delivered me to you'. The people now proceed to show their true colours by a persuasive piece of hypocrisy—for they themselves hate the Roman rule. But their argument depends on the other part of verse 11. Pilate's authority is derived from Caesar, and depends on his good pleasure. But Jesus has claimed a kingship not of this world, which can be regarded as a rival to the power of Caesar. Thus, it is suggested, to release Jesus is tantamount to taking sides against Caesar.

13. sat down: the verb could be transitive, i.e. Pilate made Jesus sit on the judgment seat. Loisy was the chief exponent of this view, arguing that this scene is a further mockery of Jesus, as in verse 3. This could be supported by the similarity between 'Here is your King!' in the next verse and the *Ecce homo* of verse 5. This supposition cannot be dismissed out of hand, because two independent references to the mocking include this motif, the *Gospel of Peter* 7: 'And they clothed him with purple, and set him on the seat of judgment, saying, "Judge righteously, King of Israel" '; and Justin, 1 *Ap.* xxxv: 'They tormented him, and set him on the judgment-seat, and said, "Judge us." ' It is clear that these go back to an embellishment of the tradition of the mocking. It is also possible that this began as a result of interpreting our present verse in John precisely in this way. But it cannot be proved that it is in fact derived from John, in spite of the similarity of wording. And even if it does stem from this verse, it does not prove that John intended to use the verb transitively. He only uses this verb (*kathizein*) elsewhere at 12.14, and there it is intransitive (cf. also 8.2), as it is also throughout the NT. But it is in any case unlikely that John means a further act of mockery at this point. The moment is far too serious. Pilate is just about to give judgment. The act is so momentous that the date and time are carefully recorded (verse 14). In the event the judgment is not stated in so many words, but it is unmistakably implied in verse 16. It is thus altogether probable that John means that the official positions were taken up, Pilate sitting on the judgment seat, and Jesus standing before him. **The pavement:** Gr. *lithostrōtos*, a street or square paved with stones or mosaic. One of the most exciting discoveries on the site of the Antonia fortress is the vast paved area under the convent of the Sisters of Sion, which answers to the description of the *lithostrōtos*, and was supposedly in existence in the lifetime of Jesus. C. Kopp, *The Holy Places of the Gospels* (1963), pp. 372f., gives evidence to suggest that this pavement may not have been laid until the rebuilding by Hadrian in A.D. 135; cf. Brown, p. 882. Visitors are shown the scratch marks on the stones where the soldiers played the Game of the King, a kind of board game like ludo, which suggests some connection with the mocking of Jesus. But whether this is the place John is referring to depends on the vexed question of the identification of the praetorium with the Antonia. But the details given here certainly give the impression that John knows the place he is describing.

Gabbatha: this is not a translation of *lithostrōtos*, but the **Hebrew** (really Aramaic) name for the place. Varius suggestions about the meaning of the name have been made, the best being the Aramaic *gabbᵉṭā'* = ridge (L.-H. Vincent, *RB* XL (1933), pp. 83–113; LIX (1952), pp. 513–30; W. F. Albright in *The Background of the NT and its Eschatology*, ed. W. D. Davies and D. Daube (1956), pp. 158f.; *id.*, *The Archaeology of Palestine* (1960), p. 245). This suits the position of the Antonia, on high ground north of the Temple.

14. Preparation of the Passover: Preparation (*paraskeuē*) translates the Hebrew for 'evening' in the technical sense of the time before the Sabbath begins, when preparations have to be made, on account of the cessation from work (so Jos. *Ant.* XVI.163). It can also be applied to the eve of a feast-day, when Sabbath rules apply. Here it means the eve of Passover, according to John's scheme, but he uses it in 19.42 of the eve of the Sabbath, which is in fact the same day (in the Synoptic scheme the Sabbath is the day after Passover).

the sixth hour: i.e. noon. Mk 15.25 says that Jesus was actually crucified at the third hour (9 a.m.). But the period of darkness began at the sixth hour (Mk 15.33). It is useless to try to harmonize these discrepancies (confusion between numerical signs has been suggested; cf. Barrett *ad loc.*). It is more likely that the third hour was not in John's source. There is nothing corresponding with Mk 15.25 in either Matthew or Luke. Thus either John has found **the sixth hour** in his source in some connection, and so has incorporated it into his composition here, or he has estimated the time, so that the death of Jesus may coincide with the slaying of the Passover lambs, which took place between 3 and 6 p.m.

Here is your King!: the situation repeats verse 5. The people have not seen Jesus since that dramatic moment, because he has been in the praetorium (verse 9). Now he emerges once more, but presumably no longer wearing the purple robe and the crown, and Pilate once more points him out to the people. But significantly the words are changed: instead of the scornful 'man', Pilate says **your King.** There is no mockery of Jesus here: it is rather a taunt to the people, bringing the irony of the whole affair to a point. As far as Pilate himself is concerned, it is almost a confession of faith, for he cannot bring himself to deny that Jesus is King in a sense which impresses and frightens him. But to the people Jesus represents a possible fulfilment of their messianic hopes, a possible rallying-point for their anti-Roman feeling, one whom they should acknowledge as sent by God, if only they would believe. Pilate knows that they do not accept any of this, but he is equally well aware that what Jesus stands for comes close to their own most cherished hopes. The whole course of John's brilliant handling of the dialogue has led up to this intensely meaningful moment, where so few words can comprise so much. The pronoun **your** dissociates Pilate himself from the issue, and throws it back to the people.

15. So at last, by his own much more impressive route, John lands up at the point in the Synoptic tradition, and no doubt in the source which he is following, at the conclusion of the Barabbas episode; cf. Mk 15.12–14, and verse 6 above. For **Away with him,** cf. Lk. 23.18 (where, however, the tense is different). In John's presentation of the tradition, the cry of the people has been convincingly evoked by their rage at the taunt implied in Pilate's words. What he has to say next is calculated to enrage them still further. **Your King** receives all the emphasis, by its position before **shall I crucify** in the Greek, and by the straight repetition of the words of the taunt just made. The reply, then, of the chief priests (speaking, of course, on behalf of the people, as throughout this dialogue) is not a considered answer, but a cry of anger and exasperation: **We have no king but Caesar.** No Jew could say this with a clear conscience. Only God is Israel's King (Jg. 8.23; 1 Sam. 8.7), and his anointed one (Ps. 2.2) is vicegerent of God who is the true King. So with splendid irony John makes the Jews utter the ultimate blasphemy in the same breath as their final rejection of Jesus. And if Pilate does not agree with them, he will find himself in the wrong (verse 12).

16. to them: this is impossible, as John understands perfectly well that the Roman soldiers took Jesus to be crucified (verses 23 and 25). But the subject of the verbs in 17f. is not expressed, and yet it must be the soldiers and not the Jews. **To them** (*autois*), applied to the Jews, appears in Mk 15.15, but in connection with the release of Barabbas ('for them', dative of advantage). The next words in Mark, 'and . . . he delivered him to be crucified', are identical with John, apart from his insertion of this phrase. But Lk. 23.25 has 'but Jesus he delivered up to their will'. It looks, then, as if *autois* stood in John's source, as dative of advantage (hence *NEB* rightly paraphrases: 'to satisfy them'), and Luke, working from the same source, has clarified it by changing it to 'to their will'. The omission of the soldiers as subject in verse 17 can be explained by the fact that John now omits the scourging and mocking from his narrative, having used it in verses 1–3.

THE CRUCIFIXION 17–30

John's account of the crucifixion has a unique character. All the details which add horror to the scene in the Synoptics are omitted. There are no taunts by the bystanders, no mention of the darkness at noon, no cry of dereliction. There is a pervading calm, like an Italian primitive painting. John retains the tradition, already well established, of building up the picture on the basis of customary procedure, interpreted in the light of the Passion psalms (Pss. 22 and 69). In fact he enhances this for the sake of his theological purpose. For through the Passion Jesus remains a majestic figure, and the control of his destiny which has been emphasized hitherto is now taken up into the thought of accomplishment. The Scriptures which foretell God's will are fulfilled, and the work of redemption is brought to its completion.

Though he drops so much from the tradition as it has come to us in the Synoptics, John adds to his narrative two items of special material. The first is the dispute about the title on the Cross (verses 19–22). This carries forward the dialogue on kingship from the trial narrative, and so is likely to be John's own embellishment of the tradition (Mk 15.26 paras.). The second item is the unique episode in which Jesus consigns his mother to the care of the Beloved Disciple. Again there is a starting-point in the tradition, in the mention of the women near the cross (Mk 15.40 paras.). But, as always, the Beloved Disciple is unknown from the parallels, and his presence coincides with theological issues of great importance to John. In this case the story, told with the utmost simplicity, suggests a new beginning at the moment when all is over. John's creative hand is more evident than any signs of historical tradition, though the possibility that it is based on fact cannot be excluded.

Jesus Crucified at Golgotha 17f.

17. bearing his own cross: the word translated **cross** (*stauros*) means a stake stuck into the ground. The use of it by the

Romans as a method of execution developed from the practice of
placing a beam (Lat. *patibulum*) across a criminal's shoulders, and
attaching his hands to the ends, so as to make him a laughing-
stock, unable to help himself. (It has long been surmised that in
practice the nailing must have been done between the bones of the
forearm, just above the wrists. The recently discovered remains of
a man crucified near Jerusalem in the first century show clear
traces of nailing in this position. See the articles by V. Tzaferis,
J. Naveh and N. Haas in *The Israel Exploration Journal* xx, i–ii
(1970), pp. 18–59, and plates 9–24, especially plate 22.) This was
then fixed to the top of a stake, where he might hang until he died.
Cross here thus properly means the *patibulum*, as the stakes were
left permanently at the place of crucifixion. It appears that Jesus
simply carried it, and was not nailed to it until the place was
reached. This has parallels in Greek literature, e.g. Charito (2nd
cent. A.D.) says 'each one used to carry the cross (*stauros*)' (cf.
AG, p. 772a). Various suggestions have been made for the emphasis on **his own** (better 'for himself', reading *heautō* with
P⁶⁰ P⁶⁶ᶜ ℵ L W, or *hautō* with B, instead of *heautou*). It is generally
taken to be a deliberate alteration of the tradition that Simon of
Cyrene was made to carry the Cross, but as John was not using
Mark, he may not have known this tradition. In any case it is
likely that Jesus carried it himself to begin with, even if he needed
help later. Another idea is that it is intended to guard against the
heretical notion of Basilides (Irenaeus, *Adv. Haer.* I.xxiv.4) that
Jesus, as being divine, could not have died on the cross, and it was
actually Simon who suffered in his place. But this again presupposes that John knows the Simon tradition. A third view is that
John intends a parallel with Isaac in Gen. 22.6, carrying the wood
to be used when he himself is sacrificed, which is noted as a type
of the crucifixion in Barnabas vii. But John gives no hint that this
is in his mind. The best suggestion is that of Dodd (*Historical
Tradition*, p. 124f.) that the phrase is to be connected with Lk.
14.27: 'Whoever does not *bear his own cross* and come after me,
cannot be my disciple.' The vocabulary is precisely the same as
John's here. This implies that the Passion narrative is being used
for moral example, and this passage has, in John's text (perhaps
his source), begun to be influenced by this usage.
Golgotha: Aram. *gulgoltā'* means a skull. It is more likely that the
place got this name from its shape than because it was a burial

area. It was an absolute rule among the Jews that a burial-ground
should be outside a city, as its use rendered it an 'unclean' place.
The traditional site of Golgotha (or Calvary, as it is often called,
from the Latin for skull, *calvaria*) is included within the Church of
the Holy Sepulchre. Subsequent history since the spot was identified in the early fourth century has made it so unrecognizable
that many modern pilgrims are perplexed and disappointed by it.
But in NT times this site was certainly outside the walls, which did
not extend northwards to anything like their present extent. The
Church of the Holy Sepulchre covers what was once steeply slop-
ing ground containing cave-tombs at the west end (the Rotunda;
cf. notes on verse 41 below), and the skull-shaped hill at the south-
east corner (the chapel of Golgotha). But most of the rock was cut
away around these two sites in the time of Constantine, so as to
make a large level area for gatherings of pilgrims. They were still
further reduced in the course of the centuries. However, glass
panels show the bedrock rising to a considerable height *within* the
east wall of the building, with a crack running down it, which
is said to be due to the earthquake mentioned in Mt. 27.51.
The identification of the site is thus possible, but by no means
certain.

18. two others: all four Gospels have this detail. It is necessary
for John to include it, because of his special material in verses
31–7. Mk 15.27 says that the men were 'robbers' (*lēstai*) like
Barabbas, cf. 18.40. They could have been political prisoners. The
fact that they are only mentioned at this point, without any hint
of their existence having been given in the previous narrative, has
suggested to some that this detail is fictitious, aimed at providing
a fulfilment of Isa. 53.12: 'He was reckoned with the transgressors.'
This reference is actually inserted into the text of Mk 15.28 in
many MSS. The words are quoted in Lk. 22.37, but significantly in
a different context. This fact, and the lack of verbal allusion to the
text of Isaiah in the account itself, make it improbable that it was
simply invented on the basis of the OT passage, though it would
explain the note that the two men were **one on either side**
(John's phrase is Semitic, used in the LXX at Num. 22.24). It is
possible, of course, that they were already hanging on crosses when
the party with Jesus arrived, though this is contrary to the impression given by Mark. John himself makes no attempt to draw attention to the fulfilment of Scripture at this point, and appears to

know nothing of the Lucan tradition of the one who repented (Lk. 23.39–43).

The Title 19–22

19. a title: it was customary to display the nature of the crime as a deterrent to others. John says that it was preceded by the name, **Jesus of Nazareth** (for the phrase, cf. 18.5). So also Mt. 27.37: 'This is Jesus the King of the Jews.' This was done by Pilate's orders. It is hardly likely that John means that Pilate carried it out himself, though his words give this impression. Barrett says that **wrote** here means 'caused to be written' (cf. 21.24).

20. John reports that the title was in three languages. This may well have been the case. The same information is given in Lk. 23.38, relegated to *RSV, mg.*, because the words are missing from P75 B אcorr C* L Old Syriac and Sahidic. But the support is strong, so that this is not necessarily a case of the influence of John on the text of Luke. It is possible that it comes from the source common to Luke and John. For John it may have had symbolic significance, foreshadowing the Church's mission to Jews and Romans and Greeks. But the information that **many of the Jews read** it is mentioned to explain the objection in the next verse.

21. The fact that the charge is true gives John the chance for a further irony. The title is intended to warn men that anyone who makes claim to be **King of the Jews** must expect the same ghastly punishment. But it can be taken to be a proclamation of the messiahship of Jesus. Naturally the chief priests object, and ask for it to be modified (cf. verse 15). There is no indication that John found this detail in his source.

22. With magnificent finality, Pilate refuses to make any alteration. Though it can be interpreted as mere stubbornness on his part, or perhaps as a calculated insult to the chief priests, it is certainly intended to imply that the title was true and unalterable, and can be regarded as a concealed confession of faith by Pilate, cf. verse 14. The title is retained, not only as the grounds for crucifixion, but also as the proclamation of the Gospel.

The Parting of the Garments 23–5a

23. his garments: the word is taken from the quotation in the next verse. In Mark this is the first of a series of details which are expressed in terms of the Passion psalms, in this case Ps. 22.18.

Thus the motif of fulfilment of Scripture in this instance is not in doubt (contrast verse 18). But the incident must equally certainly be accepted as historical, as it is known that it was customary for the soldiers on duty to share out the personal belongings of an executed man (Sherwin-White, p. 46). So the present passage is particularly instructive for the growth of the Passion story. The parting of the clothes is a fact, known either from an eye-witness or from general knowledge of procedure. No one would bother to mention it, if someone had not observed that it made a fulfilment of the prophecy of Ps. 22; or rather Ps. 22 was applied to Jesus, and then it was raked through to see if any details corresponded with what actually happened. So in the Synoptic accounts Ps. 22.18 has determined the words in which this detail is told. John's use of this tradition takes the development further in two ways. (a) He spells out the allusion by providing the quotation with fulfilment formula, in addition to using it as the basis of his text. This tendency appears in the textual history of Mt. 27.35, where the Western text has inserted the quotation from Jn. 19.24. (b) He uses the quotation as a basis for further detail of the incident. Thus at this stage the quotation has begun to have a creative effect upon the tradition itself. Once this position has been reached, it is very easy to suppose that the detail is pure invention on the basis of the quotation. But in fact this is a false inference. The tradition of the two robbers in verse 18 is an example of a detail where the OT allusion has not yet begun to influence the text.

four parts: it is implied that a squad of four soldiers carried out the sentence; cf. Ac. 12.4, where 'squads' properly means groups of four (*tetradion*). The word for **part** (*meros*) is taken from 'parted' in the quotation (*diemerisanto*).

tunic: it is at this point that John, or possibly his source, creates a new detail on the basis of the quotation. Naturally, by the convention of Hebrew poetic parallelism, the two halves of the quotation are intended to be synonymous. To part the garments and to cast lots on the clothing are one and the same act. In taking the two halves separately, and applying them to different actions, John is not guilty of failure to understand Hebrew parallelism (Barrett), but is taking advantage of it to fill out the tradition. What he builds on the basis of it is plausible. He cannot be accused of being fanciful. The **tunic** (*chitōn*) was the garment worn next to the skin. It could be a kind of shift cut out of a single piece of cloth, with a hole for the head and arm-holes. But as it is regarded as equivalent to 'clothing' (*himatismos*) in the quotation, which can refer to outer garments of fine quality, it is not impossible that John wishes the discerning reader to see a parallel with the long outer robe of blue of the High Priest. Josephus (*Ant.* III.161) tells us that it was woven without seams, and had a vertical slit for the head and slits at the sides for the arms. Philo (*Fug.* 110–12) regards this robe as a symbol of the Logos, who unites all things into a seamless unity. A reference to Jesus as High Priest seems unlikely, as this theme receives no attention by John; but Barrett thinks there could be symbolism along the lines of Philo with regard to Jesus' universal mission (cf. 11.52). Even this has not the slightest hint in the text. It is wiser to follow Bernard, who denies that there is any intention of alluding to the High Priest's robe. The tunic is said to be **without seam** simply to explain why the soldiers cast lots for it.

24. Let us not tear it, but cast lots for it: John does not use the same words as the quotation, because he wishes to make the distinction between the two halves of it clear. Parting in the first half could imply tearing. But the quotation says that on one item of clothing (the word is singular in the quotation, though really intended as collective) a different method was used. The words of the quotation itself exactly follow the LXX, which has in any case supplied the form of the text in Mk 15.24. It is fulfilled in every detail, and so suits John's purpose of suggesting that in the Passion all that God has appointed is accomplished. **So (25a) the soldiers did this.** It was their contribution to the plan of God.

Mother and Son **25b–7**

25b. But standing by the cross: now we have the contribution of others (note the *men* and *de* construction in the Greek). We expect it to be another scriptural fulfilment. This is possible, for the tradition that the women, who had cared for Jesus and the disciples, were looking on at a discreet distance is another item which becomes influenced by the Passion psalms. Thus Lk. 23.49 shows signs of conformation to Ps. 38.11. John's **standing** (*heistēkeisan*) agrees with Luke against Matthew and Mark, so that the process may have begun in John's source. But he has made no attempt to draw attention to it.

his mother: she is never named in John; cf. 2.1; nor is she mentioned here in the Synoptic parallels. Only **Mary Magdalene** is common to John and Mark; she will figure in the Resurrection narrative (20.1–18). Though she is not identified with Mary of Bethany, she fulfils a similar symbolic function (cf. the notes on 11.32). **His mother's sister** and **Mary the wife of Clopas** (two persons are probably meant) are only found in John, though they could perhaps be identified with Salome and Mary the mother of James the less and of Joses (Mk 15.40). John's source differs, and Luke omits the names at this point. But the connection between John and Luke lends support to the identification of Clopas with Cleopas in Lk. 24.18. Hence this Mary, and also Mary Magdalene, are named because they also attest the resurrection. Even the presence of the mother of Jesus at the Cross contains this motif, if the ensuing verses may be taken to imply that she is to be included in the list of the primitive Church, as in Ac.1.14.

26. the disciple whom he loved: last mentioned in 13.23, unless he is to be identified with the disciple in 18.15. As the character who represents 'faith with understanding', he is well suited to the role that is now assigned to him. A great depth of meaning is indicated by means of a very few words, composed with the utmost restraint. There is no hint of emotional aspects. Apparently Jesus is making sure that his death will not leave his mother desolate, and so he arranges that his filial duty should be done by this disciple (cf. the fifth Commandment, and Jesus' comment on it, Mk 7.9–13). But this is only implied. What is actually said is that they should be in a new relationship. His mother loses her Son, but she gains a new son, one who most fully knows the mind of the Son whom she has lost. Considering what has been said in the Supper discourses about the new relationship which is to follow Jesus' death, it is natural to interpret this in the light of 16.7: 'It is to your advantage that I go away.' From this point of view the mother/son relationship of Mary and the Beloved Disciple has a quality which could not have existed if Jesus had not been crucified (see further on 20.8, 17). Loisy opened a false path of exegesis when he tried to interpret this incident allegorically, taking Mary as the synagogue and the Disciple as the Church. Bultmann is equally astray when he takes Mary to be the Jewish-Christian Church and the Disciple the Church of the Gentiles.

The incident is concerned with the Church because it is concerned with the future, but the point is the new life which results from the death of Jesus, a quality of life which transcends physical barriers.

27. to his own home: this is the basis of the theory that the Beloved Disciple is to be identified with John Mark. For the primitive Church met at the house of John Mark's mother, whose name was Mary (Ac. 12.12; there is no suggestion that she was not his natural mother). On the whole question see the Introduction, pp. 31–4. The argument is precarious, because it rests on correlating the incident with hints in the Lucan writings, and it is clear that Luke has no knowledge of it at all. The vocabulary of verses 26 and 27 is typical of John, and shows no signs of dependence on a source. The piece takes the obviously appropriate theme of filial piety, and uses it creatively to suggest that the death of Jesus is not so much the end of his work as a new beginning. This is what (by contrast with the soldiers) those who stood by the Cross did.

'It is Finished' **28–30**

28. finished: the formal introduction is reminiscent of the more elaborate opening at 13.1. It gives an impression of solemnity, suitable to the necessarily brief description of the actual death of Jesus. The word **finished** (*tetelestai*, from *telein*, only here and in verse 30, but not to be distinguished from John's usual *teleioun*) is the key-note. So much has been said about Jesus' works and deeds in previous chapters, that the word can only mean 'achieved', 'accomplished', in a positive, even a triumphant, sense. One thing only remains to be done. Jesus must take a sip of vinegar **to fulfil the scripture.** We should rather say, to *complete* the Scripture, for here in this one place alone John replaces the usual word for fulfil (*plēroun*) by *teleioun*, to finish (though ℵ D^suppl Θ Lake and Ferrar groups read the usual *eplērōthē*; P66* omits the whole phrase). This can hardly mean to bring the OT to an end, but rather to bring to completion what is appointed in Scripture for Jesus as the agent of God's will. Thus John takes the detail of the vinegar, found also in the Synoptic tradition, and uses it as a symbol of the fulfilment of all relevant scriptures, and so of the completion of Jesus' work.

'I thirst': this is not an exact quotation, but in view of the next verse it is certainly to be taken as an allusion to 'for my thirst', Ps. 69.21. That Jesus felt unbearable thirst as he hung on the Cross is altogether probable. But by emphasizing the aspect of fulfilment, John suggests that this detail has theological significance. The motive could be anti-Docetic, to show the reality of Jesus' sufferings (cf. Introduction, pp. 61ff.). But as John reduces this aspect of the Passion narrative, it is more likely that he has a different motive. The most probable explanation is that this item of the tradition appealed to his sense of irony. Jesus had said: 'Whoever drinks of the water that I shall give him will never thirst' (4.14). This water is the Spirit, to be given after he is glorified (7.39). But before he can give it, he must himself suffer thirst.

29. vinegar: as the parallels in Mt. 27.48 = Mk 15.36 show, this is another item which is told in scriptural language, i.e. Ps. 69.21: 'They gave me poison (gall) for food, and for my thirst they gave me vinegar to drink.' This suggests that the act of providing vinegar is regarded as something cruel; but in fact there is nothing cruel about it, for the vinegar (sour wine) of the ancient world was wholesome and refreshing. It is the application of the quotation which gives the impression of cruelty (cf. Mt. 27.34, where Mark's 'myrrh', which was definitely intended to reduce the pain of the act of crucifying, has been changed to 'gall' by influence of this quotation). The motif of cruelty also seems to be present in allusions to this detail in Barnabas vii.5 and *Gospel of Peter* 16. But this is not so with John: he is interested in it as fulfilment, and so as divine necessity.

hyssop: a famous difficulty, because the plant is quite unsuitable to the purpose. A reed-stalk (Mark) would be much more likely. One MS. (Θ) neatly avoids the difficulty by conflating John with Mt. 27.48: 'They put a sponge full of the vinegar with gall and hyssop on a reed.' Hyssop (*NEB, mg.* 'marjoram') was in fact used for flavouring wine. The most commonly accepted solution (Dalman, Lagrange, Bernard, Field, Moulton and Milligan, Goodspeed, Bultmann, Dodd, *NEB* text) is that the reading *hussōpō* is a primitive error for *hussō* = javelin, arising from reduplication of two letters where it runs on to the next word (i.e. *HUSSŌPŌ-PERITHENTES* for *HUSSŌPERITHENTES*). This reading actually occurs, probably by accident, in one late minuscule. It is easy to see why this error arose, for hyssop is a common biblical word, whereas the other is rare, and does not occur in the Greek Bible. It may be said in favour of **hyssop** that it could be an allusion to the ceremonial of the Passover, in which it was used for the sprinkling of the blood on the doorways of the Hebrews' houses (Exod. 12.13). It could, then, be a reminder of the timing of Jesus' death, intended to suggest its sacrificial meaning (cf. verse 36 below). If John had wanted to say 'javelin' he would presumably have used *lonchē* (spear) as in verse 34. But the reading of Θ shows that the difficulty is not a modern one. 'Javelin' was suggested by Camerarius in the sixteenth century, and may well be right.

30. 'It is finished': Gr. *tetelestai*, the same as in verse 28. Mk 15.37 says that Jesus 'uttered a loud cry'. Though this could mean the cry of dereliction, recorded in Mk 15.34, it is taken as something different by Matthew ('cried *again* with a loud voice', Mt. 27.50). Both Luke and John omit the cry of dereliction. For John at any rate it would have spoilt the calm triumph of his presentation of the Passion. Luke mentions the loud cry and then supplies a suitable psalm-verse (Ps. 31.5), which occurs again in the martyrdom of Stephen (Ac. 7.59), and is alluded to in connection with persecution in 1 Pet. 4.19. It is probable that he has supplied it from Christian usage. John does not mention the loud cry, but *tetelestai* is presumably his idea of what the cry was. It makes a most appropriate ending to his account of the crucifixion, combining the awful finality of that moment and the triumphant note of completion. Presumably he imagines that Jesus said it with an upward, heavenward, look, for he (alone of the evangelists) has the detail that Jesus then **bowed his head.**

gave up his spirit: not the usual phrase for 'expire' ('breathed his last' (Mk 15.37; Lk. 23.46)), and not quite the same as Mt. 27.50 ('yielded up his spirit'). The verb **gave up** (*paredōken*) at least implies a voluntary act. This is probably the reason for John's choice of word. Jesus maintains control right up to the last breath. But it could mean 'handed over the spirit' (**his** is not expressed in the Greek), and so refer to the gift of the Spirit, which is the consequence of his death. This is an attractive idea, but John actually describes the donation of the Spirit in 20.22, and on these grounds it is rejected by Bernard and Mastin. In order to have this meaning it requires that there should be an indirect object (i.e. the disciples). But here, if one must be supplied, it must surely be God himself to whom Jesus entrusts his spirit. If this is right, there may be, as Barrett suggests, a hint of Luke's 'Father, into thy hands I commend my spirit!'

THE DEPOSITION AND BURIAL   **19.31-42**

The meaning of the death of Christ now receives a commentary in the form of a declaration of faith in all four Gospels. Matthew and Mark very briefly give the testimony of the centurion: 'Truly this man was the Son of God!' Luke alters it to: 'Certainly this man was innocent!' John, however, has a unique incident which serves a similar purpose. It arises from the fact recorded in Mk 15.44 that Pilate had to send the centurion to certify that Jesus was dead, before he could hand over the body to Joseph of Arimathea. On this basis John tells how a soldier pierces the side of Jesus, and there is an emission of blood and water. The importance of this surprising phenomenon is conveyed in two ways. First there is an emphatic personal testimony from the author, addressed directly to the reader (verse 35). Secondly two passages are quoted from the OT (verses 36f.). It will be argued in the notes below that verse 35 is probably not an original part of John's composition at this point, but is to be connected with the addition of 21.24f. which makes the Beloved Disciple the author of the Gospel. But the two Scripture texts (which may be compared with 12.38-40) are certainly original, and are intended to indicate the theological meaning of what happened. The first explains why Jesus' legs were not broken, the second why his side was pierced. The latter does little to elucidate the significance of the flow of water and blood in verse 34, though it may suggest an interpretation in terms of spiritual cleansing. It is doubtful whether the passage in 1 Jn 5.6-8, about the witness of the water and the blood and the Spirit, can provide a solution to the problems of this verse, being itself extremely obscure and hard to interpret. But there may well be some connection between them. More will be said about this in the notes. It is evident that John regards this incident as highly significant, but—in spite of verse 35—it by no means follows that it is derived from eye-witness reporting. Like the parting of the garments, it seems rather to be based on knowledge of procedure, in this case the giving of a *coup de grâce* to certify death; and in the same way the application of an OT quotation to it has to some extent controlled the formation of the tradition. It may be noted here that Mt. 27.49b, describing the spear-thrust *before* the death of Jesus, is a spurious insertion from John.

The account of the burial, which follows in verses 38–42, keeps fairly close to the Synoptic tradition. The main difference is that Nicodemus is brought in as Joseph's assistant. It will be remembered that he figured in chapter 3 in the discourse on the new birth of baptism. But he remained an uncommitted disciple (cf. 7.50). His presence at the burial can be taken as a gentle hint that he now commits himself to faith in Christ crucified. If the water and the blood in the preceding paragraph denote spiritual cleansing, then his assistance at the burial may be intended to provide the reader with a cross-reference to chapter 3, where the theme was first handled. This is all the more likely, if John has no basis in the underlying tradition for bringing Nicodemus into the story.

Both incidents thus begin to take the Gospel story beyond the death of Jesus to the experience of the Resurrection. This will be continued in the next chapter, where the traditions are treated in such a way as to give a wider and deeper understanding of this experience.

The Piercing of Jesus' Side 31–7

31. the day of Preparation: for the technical term, cf. verse 14 above. The phrase is taken directly from John's source, cf. Mk 15.42, where it is explained as 'the day before the sabbath'. John says it was **a high day** (lit. 'great day', as in 7.37). By this he presumably means the feast of the Passover, which was observed to some extent as a Sabbath, and in this case, according to his reckoning, actually fell on the Sabbath. But even by the Synoptic reckoning the description would be suitable, as the Sabbath in the week of Unleavened Bread had the special observance of the offering of a sheaf of barley (Lev. 23.11). Originally the feast of Unleavened Bread always began on a Sabbath, but when it was timed to begin with the Passover, which was dated by the full moon, this opening ceremony was held over until the Sabbath within the week (cf. R. de Vaux, *Ancient Israel*, p. 492). In the Synoptic time-scheme this Sabbath fell on the day following the Passover.

to prevent the bodies from remaining on the cross: according to Dt. 21.23 the body of a hanged man must be removed by nightfall on the day of his death, because of the risk of rendering the land 'unclean' (cf. the notes on verse 17). If a criminal were still alive on the sixth day of the week, there was the possibility that he might die on the Sabbath, and then the body could not be removed because of the Sabbath laws. The only solution to guard against this contingency was to hasten death artificially, and so remove the body before the Sabbath began. This would apply to any Sabbath, but was even more necessary at the festival time. Hence the request of **the Jews**—presumably the chief priests are meant.

that their legs might be broken: the *crurifragium* seems to have been a cruel way of hastening death by a shock which jerked the unfortunate victim violently. It has been argued (e.g. by Barbet) that the death would actually be caused by asphyxiation, as the whole weight of the body would now have to be taken by the outstretched arms, making respiration almost impossible. But it is doubtful if it would necessarily have this effect. It seems more likely that death would be caused by bleeding from the rupture of the main arteries. There is no hint of the *crurifragium* in the Synoptic Gospels. In Mk 15.44 (on this verse see below) Pilate simply ascertains from the centurion that Jesus is dead, but nothing is said about the death of the two robbers. Thus, on grounds of procedure, it is probable that formal request was made for the hastening of death for all three in this way. On the other hand, it is precisely because John's information accords with the needs of Jewish custom and known Roman procedure, that we cannot be certain that he is relying on actual reporting, rather than on what 'must have been' the case. The skeletal remains of a crucified man, referred to in the notes on verse 17, show that the *crucifragium* was carried out in his case, both legs being broken (plate 23).

32. As the two robbers are still alive, their legs are broken. *Gospel of Peter* 14, disregarding the technical reason why this was done, says that the soldiers refused to break the legs of the penitent robber 'that he might die in torments' as a reprisal for taking Jesus' part. It is quite correct that the *crurifragium* would be a welcome release from a lingering death in extreme misery and torture.

33. already dead: but it was unnecessary in the case of Jesus, because the tradition is unanimous that he died before the time

of Sabbath drew on. It has always been difficult to explain why
Jesus died in such a short space of time; in spite of the strain and
torture, a man in normal health would linger on for days. Mk 15.44
tells of Pilate's surprise at the speedy death of Jesus. As the language of Mk 15.44f. has some unusual features, and as neither
Matthew nor Luke has anything corresponding with these two
verses, it is probable that they are a primitive insertion into the
text of Mark, ante-dating all MSS. (so Nineham). If so, this does
not lessen the importance of the observation, which is clearly
independent of John. It means that the problem had already been
raised, at any rate by the time that John was writing, in more than
one quarter. But it would not be wise to attempt an answer. We
cannot break through the schematized time-scheme of the Passion
narratives to find out exactly how long Jesus actually hung on the
Cross. We know nothing of his physical and emotional condition
at the time. Asphyxiation, for the reason given above, is one
medical explanation, but is perhaps less likely when the legs were
not broken. Sudden heart failure seems more plausible. If so, the
truth may still rest with R. W. Dale's contention (*The Atonement*,
Appendix, Note D) that Jesus died quite literally of a broken
heart.

34. The spear-thrust cannot be intended to cause death, but to
certify it, unless it is 'mere spite or casual cruelty' (Barrett) on the
part of the soldier concerned. If the soldiers arrived only minutes
after Jesus expired (verse 30), emission of blood would still be
possible. The water might be a collection of fluid in the lung. It is
doubtful if a single blow would cause these to flow in such a way
that an observer would notice the two different kinds of liquid.
But if John is writing on the basis of a knowledge of procedure
rather than of first-hand information, it is only necessary to suppose that he thought this result to be possible and imagined it in
this way. His motive in recording it cannot be simply to combat
the Docetists (cf. Introduction, p. 61), though that may well be
a subsidiary motive; for it would not be necessary to mention
the water in addition to the blood for this purpose. But the water
is important if his desire is to suggest the theological meaning of
the death of Jesus as the opening of a fountain of grace (see below
on verse 37). No sooner is Jesus' sacrifice complete than the flow
of life for the world begins.

blood: apart from 1.13, which is irrelevant here, blood is only

mentioned in the Fourth Gospel in 6.53–6, where it certainly refers
to the wine of the Eucharist as a sacrament of the sacrificial death
of Jesus. Hence many commentators take the present verse to be
symbolic of the Eucharist, by which the benefits of the death of
Christ are appropriated in the life of the Church. But it is doubtful
if John would refer to the Eucharist by mentioning the blood of
Jesus alone (cf. G. R. Beasley-Murray, *Baptism in the New Testament*
(1962), p. 241). It is more likely that he means it in the same
sense as 1 Jn 1.7: 'The blood of Jesus his Son cleanses us from all
sin.' This agrees with the Baptist's description of Jesus as 'the
Lamb of God, who takes away the sin of the world (1.29). John
thinks of Jesus as the true paschal lamb, and (as a result of inner-
Christian development) ascribes to him the efficacy of an atoning
sacrifice (see the notes on 1.29).

water: this is generally regarded as a symbol of baptism. But
although 3.1–15 has baptismal overtones, water is generally a
symbol of the Spirit, so again a sacramental interpretation is not
absolutely required. Mastin, taking the blood to mean the Eucharist, complains that it is the wrong order to place baptism *after* the
Eucharist. We might get round this difficulty if we could follow
Boismard in actually reading 'water and blood' here (*RB* LX
(1953), pp. 348–50), but Schnackenburg points out that in the
few texts and patristic citations where this occurs it is almost
certainly due to the influence of 1 Jn 5.6. But the difficulty does
not arise, if blood does not refer to the Eucharist. On the other
hand the thematic connection with 1.29 is an argument in favour
of the baptismal interpretation. The flow from Jesus' side is symbolic both of his atoning death and of the act whereby men are
put in relation with it. Several further points remain to be
considered:

(a) It is tempting to see this verse as a fulfilment of 7.38f.,
especially if 'out of his heart' refers to Jesus rather than to the
believer. But not only is the latter point doubtful, but also it is
wrong to see the fulfilment of 7.39 at this moment. That comes in
20.22, as was argued in connection with verse 30. 'Out of his
heart' (lit. 'belly', *koilia*) is not the same as **his side** (*pleura*).
There is no clear connection between the two passages.

(b) Rabbinic tradition (*Targum Pseudo-Jonathan* on Num. 20.11;
Exod. Rabba iii) connects the striking of the rock by Moses in Num.
20.11 with his capacity to turn water into blood (Exod. 4.9). The

rock is applied to Christ in a baptismal context in 1 C. 10.4. It also features in the wonders commemorated in the Passover Haggadah. Along these lines it can be argued that the connection between blood and water is ready-made in rabbinic exegesis, so that we only have to do with one application here, i.e. baptism. This line of interpretation fails to convince, however, because it presupposes too much exegetical erudition as common ground between author and reader.

(c) The verse obviously has some kind of connection with 1 Jn 5.6–8, which may therefore be expected to elucidate it. It is indeed quite possible that the first Epistle is by the same author as the Gospel, and that this passage is to some extent indebted to our present verse. It comes in a context of witness to faith that Jesus is the Son of God, which is precisely the testimony of the centurion after the crucifixion, but also of course the baptismal confession. Water and blood are mentioned in connection with Jesus, and then the Spirit is brought in as witness, making a triad. The most important difference from our verse here is that the water and the blood are not said to flow from Jesus. He 'came *by* water (*di' hudatos*) and blood'. This was 'not *with* the water (*en tō hudati*) only, but with the water and the blood'. It may be that the author means Jesus' baptism and his death, considered as two key events, which are nevertheless related. If he is writing against Docetists, who accepted the baptism but not the reality of the death, the emphasis on 'not with the water only' is readily explained. In verse 8 we find that 'there are three witnesses, the Spirit, the water and the blood'. The reference here is generally taken to be the continuing witness to these realities in the life of the Church: 'The apostolic teaching is authenticated against all false teaching by a threefold testimony: the living voice of prophecy, and the two evangelical sacraments' (C. H. Dodd, *The Johannine Epistles* (1946), p. 131). So also Schnackenburg (*Die Johannesbriefe* (1962[2]), *ad loc.*), who lays great stress on the report of Ignatius (*Smyrn.* vi) that the Docetists 'believe not in the blood of Christ' and as a consequence 'abstain from Eucharist and prayer, because they allow not that the Eucharist is the flesh of our Saviour Jesus Christ, which flesh suffered for our sins'. In spite of Beasley-Murray's arguments to the contrary (see above), it is difficult to resist the sacramental interpretation of 'blood' in this verse (1 Jn 5.8). But this does *not* mean that it already has this connotation in 1 Jn 5.6, and still less that it has it in Jn 19.34. It may well be that 1 Jn 5.6–8 is inspired by our present verse, but that does not warrant reading back into it all that the later passage contains. It only shows that the eucharistic interpretation is consistent with what is said here (i.e. the atoning efficacy of Christ's death), and can natur-ally arise from it when it is thought through afresh in another context.

35. This verse is missing from one Old Latin (e) and one Vulgate (Codex Fuldensis) MS.; but this is certainly insufficient warrant to strike it out of the text. But this does not mean that it is an original part of John's composition. Comparison with 21.24 suggests that it is an interpolation by the later redactor, who added the Appendix. Both these verses are based on the vocabulary of 3.11. Alternatively the verse may be an expansion by the redactor of an originally shorter sentence, consisting of the first two clauses. These would then be translated: 'He who saw it has borne witness, and his testimony is true' (*alēthinē*, cf. 7.28). The subject would then obviously be the soldier who pierced Jesus' side, giving his testimony. So it would be the Johannine counterpart to Mk 15.39 paras. The expansion then begins **he knows, etc.,** and at this point **he** is emphatic, represented by the pronoun *ekeinos*. As it then goes on to second person address, **that you also may believe,** it is inevitable that we should take **he** to be the author of the Gospel, using the third person for a veiled self-reference. Thus the author commends the soldier's testimony to the careful attention of the reader. If, however, the whole verse is an inter-polation, it is only natural to take **he** to mean the eye-witness, who then is not the soldier. On the basis of 21.24 it is generally supposed that this must be the Beloved Disciple, and this leads to the conclusion that the piercing of Jesus' side was seen and attested personally by the author. But this is most improbable, for the Beloved Disciple has gone home in verse 27, and there is nothing in the text to indicate that he has come back again. Other suggestions, that **he** means God or Christ himself, are scarcely plausible. The connection between this incident and 1 Jn 5.6–8 makes it likely that the reason for the interpolation, whether of the whole verse or only of the second half of it, is the need to combat Docetism. The purpose **that you may believe** is similar to 20.31. But whereas that, which is the authentic ending of the Gospel, is concerned with the total message of the Gospel, this is confined to the particular importance of belief in the significance of the flow of blood and water.

36. these things took place: here we have the real reasons why John has recorded the event of this paragraph, and it becomes clear that in any case verse 35 is a parenthesis, interrupting his composition. First he shows that the fact that Jesus was spared the *crurifragium* was necessary for the completion of the scriptural pattern of prediction.

Not a bone of him shall be broken: the words use the vocabulary of the LXX, but cannot be traced with certainty to one particular passage. It is possible that they were drawn originally from Ps. 34.20, which describes the providential protection of the righteous man. This, then, could have been selected, because it forecast the perfect state in which Jesus rose from the dead; his body, though dead, remained intact for the Resurrection. There is evidence that this thought was a real concern of Jews in the first century, when belief in the bodily resurrection was vivid and widespread (cf. Daube, *op. cit.*, pp. 307f.). But the text has been conformed to some extent to Exod. 12.46 or Num. 9.12, where almost exactly similar words are used for the regulations of the Passover—the lamb must be roast whole with no bones broken. Jesus is the true Lamb of God (1.29), and so this quotation applies not only to verses 32f., but also to the flow of blood in verse 34, as the blood is drained off by the Jewish method of ritual slaughter, and so made available for sacrificial sprinkling. The omission of the *crurifragium* and the piercing of Jesus' side belong together. Both are equally necessary to establish the sacrificial meaning of his death.

37. They shall look on him whom they have pierced: this is a quotation of Zech. 12.10, but the text differs from the LXX. It is, however, the same as Rev. 1.7, where the passage is quoted, and agrees with the later Greek versions (Aquila, Symmachus, Lucian and Theodotion) and with quotations of Justin (*Dial.* xiv.8; xxxii.2; lxiv.7; cxviii.1; *1 Ap*. lii.11) in the use of *exekentēsan* for **pierced** (the standard LXX reading 'danced in triumph' depends on a misreading of the Hebrew). There is also clear allusion to the same passage of Zechariah in Mt. 24.30. The use of this text in Mt. 24.30 and Rev. 1.7 indicates that John is here drawing on an existing tradition of biblical exegesis. As John alone has the piercing of Jesus' side (for Mt. 27.49b, see p. 584

above), it must be assumed that originally the passage was chosen to explain the piercing of Jesus' hands (wrists) and feet with the nails. It thus accounted for the crucifixion of the Messiah, as opposed to any other method of execution. John's new application of this prophecy has the more positive purpose of suggesting the meaning of the emission of blood and water. But what he intends this to be can only be decided when the subject of **they shall look** has been identified. It is not a foregone conclusion that it is the same as the subject of **they have pierced.** It is true that both Mt. 24.30 and Rev. 1.7 take it this way, so that in the eschatological judgment it is those who have crucified Jesus who look on him in his glory and mourn for their wicked deed, according to the continuation of the passage, which describes a mourning ceremony (Zech. 12.10–14). But in the rabbinic tradition, in which the prophecy is applied to the slaying of the Messiah ben Joseph (*B. Sukkah*, 52a), it is not taken this way, and there seems no reason to do so here. As the subject is unspecified (it can hardly be simply the soldiers), it can be people in general, including those who did the act of crucifixion, but not confined to them, just as in Zech. 12.11f. it is the whole people of Israel who see and who mourn (in fact Rev. 1.7 makes just this distinction). Then, immediately following this passage, Zech. 13.1 tells of the opening of a fountain 'to cleanse them from sin and uncleanness'. It is surely this fountain which is symbolized by the flow of water in verse 34. Thus John omits the theme of judgment, and leaves the reader gazing on the open side of Jesus, which is the source of universal cleansing. It is not essential to hold that John has Zech. 13.1 in mind in order to establish this interpretation, for water is already present in the context to define the object of the piercing in terms of cleansing. But it is certainly wrong to import the idea of judgment (Mastin, following C. F. D. Moule, *JTS*, n.s., x (1959), p. 258, n. 3; *NT* v (1962), p. 182, n. 4), for which there is no warrant in the context at all.

The Burial **38–42**

38. Joseph of Arimathea: nothing is known of him apart from this incident (= Mk 15.42–6 paras.). His home is generally identified with Ramathaim-zophim (Samuel's birth-place, 1 Sam. 1.1), the modern Rentis, 25 miles NW. of Jerusalem.
a disciple of Jesus: John coincides with Matthew in omitting

Mark's important information that Joseph was a member of the Sanhedrin and in saying that he **was a disciple of Jesus.** But the phrases are not identical, and there is probably no dependence on Matthew. John probably means that Joseph was a member of the Sanhedrin, like Nicodemus (cf. 7.50), but he is abbreviating his source, which may have contained much the same information as Mark. For **secretly, for fear of the Jews** is John's own diction, cf. 20.19. Joseph makes his request to Pilate, as in the Synoptic account. Some mss. (א* N W Old Latin, some Sahidic) have plural verbs for **he came and took,** but this is probably a case of anticipating verse 40.

39. Nicodemus: if, as is probable, he was not mentioned in the underlying tradition, John would seem to have brought him in partly because he makes an obvious pair with Joseph (both are public men and both are secret disciples), and partly because of the thematic connection of the last paragraph with chapter 3. These secret believers now come out into the open, carrying forward the idea of confession of faith latent in the piercing episode. **who had at first come to him by night:** these words have a number of variants in the mss., and may be a gloss (cf. 7.50).

mixture: Gr. *migma*. There are textual variants, but the only important one is *heligma* = roll or package, read by B א* W, a strong combination. This reading is recommended by Barrett as the harder reading. It means that the myrrh and aloes have to be regarded as herbs or crystals of the resinous gum from the two aromatic plants, i.e. in a dry, not a liquid, form. But it must be said against this that there seems to be a literary connection between John's handling of the burial tradition and his version of the anointing at Bethany (cf. 12.3, 7), where a liquid is used. The huge quantity (100 *litra* = nearly 8 gallons, or 75 lbs dry measure) is obviously an exaggeration. Brown tentatively suggests that it is to give the idea of a royal burial, citing the vast quantity of spices used in the burial of Herod the Great (Jos. *Ant.* xvii.199).

40. linen cloths with the spices: the Synoptics say that the body was only wrapped in a shroud, because there was very little time before the Sabbath. Mk 16.1 tells how the women bought spices (*arōmata*, the same word as John uses here) in order to anoint the body as soon as the Sabbath was over, or rather in the morning light of the next day, as the evening would be too dark.

This agrees with the Sabbath rules, which allow the preparation for anointing during the Sabbath, but not the lifting which would be needed for doing the task (*Shabbath* xxiii.5). Mark thus clearly implies the use of ointment or oil rather than dry materials, and this also accords with Jewish custom. But if John means dry materials, we must imagine that the **spices** are sprinkled between the linen cloths, rather than anointing. The word *arōmata* itself cannot decide the issue, as it refers to the scent given off by the plants concerned, and could be applied equally to either liquid or dry preparations made from them. The word for **burial custom** (*entaphiazein*) seems to be an allusion to 12.7, and so suggests anointing. Thus the prophetic act of the woman at Bethany has its fulfilment in the work of Joseph and Nicodemus. For the method of wrapping the body, cf. the notes on 11.44, where, however, **linen cloths** (*othonia*) was not used. This word will appear again in 20.6f. By saying that the embalming was done at the time of the burial, John deprives the story of the empy tomb of the narrative connection which it has in Mk 16.1 (it is also spoilt by Matthew, who omits the embalming altogether). We cannot tell whether this is due to his source or to his own way of imagining the situation, because he has recast the material considerably. Possibly he (or his source) assumes that a rich man like Joseph would not dream of burying Jesus without performing all the proper customs. John is aware, however, that haste was necessary (verse 42).

41. In this verse the source shows through John's writing more clearly, and it gives another object-lesson in the development of a tradition (cf. the notes on verse 23). Mark only says that a rock-hewn tomb was used, with a rolling stone in front of it, such as can be seen in several ancient burial-places around Jerusalem. He gives no indication of its location. Matthew adds that it was a new tomb, which Joseph had had carved out for himself. Luke, obviously independently, says that 'no one had ever yet been laid' in it. John appears to combine Matthew and Luke by saying that it was **a new tomb where no one had ever been laid.** This is best explained as due to the source common to Luke and John, containing **new** independently of Matthew, though it is omitted by Luke. The motive for these elaborations of the simpler tradition preserved in Mark is presumably the feeling that it would be unsuitable for the body of Jesus to be laid in a tomb alongside previous burials.

garden: this detail (using *kēpos*, as in 18.1) is only found in John, and there is no means of telling whether it stood in his source. It would be a mistake to attach symbolic significance to it (the Garden of Eden has been suggested, but that would probably be *paradeisos*; though it is translated *kēpos* in Aquila and Theodotion). In fact this detail is necessary for John's special Resurrection narrative (20.15). The garden would probably be an orchard, as in 18.1, and this would not be impossible in a tomb area close to Golgotha. The traditional site is in fact very close to the Golgotha site (see above on verse 17). Excavation has shown that there were burials in the area. It is now covered by the Rotunda at the west end of the Church of the Holy Sepulchre. Much of the rock was cut away to level the floor in the time of Constantine. A cube of the original rock was left in the centre of the Rotunda, containing the rock-hewn tomb believed to be the actual tomb where Jesus was laid. Most of the cube subsequently disappeared, so that the only piece of original rock now remaining is the shelf on which the body lay. This is now covered by marble slabs for protection, and so the actual rock is not visible. The cube has been replaced by a marble chapel containing the shelf in the inner chamber (the Holy Sepulchre). The outer chamber (the Chapel of the Angel) contains a marble pedestal in the centre, supporting an ancient piece of stone which is said to be all that remains of the rolling stone. Although so sadly cut about and altered beyond recognition, it remains possible that this is the genuine tomb of Jesus, though this can never be established with certainty.

42. Preparation: from the source; cf. Mk 15.42; Lk. 23.54, and see the notes on verse 31.

THE RESURRECTION 20.1–31

From the hints that appeared in the crucifixion narrative we are prepared to find that the chief interest of this chapter lies in the use of traditional material to convey the meaning of the experience of the Resurrection of Jesus. One way in which this can be expressed is that it is 'life in his name' (verse 31). But this has already been expounded in the substance of the Gospel itself, both in the Signs which have formed the basis of the account of Jesus' ministry and in the teaching to the disciples in the Supper discourses. All that remains to be done now is to explain more clearly the nature of the act of faith by which the life in Christ may be appropriated. So John uses once more the homiletic technique which was so effective in his account of the Last Supper. Various traditions are retold in such a way as to present one theme to the reader. In chapter 13 it was the theme of discipleship. In this chapter it is the act of faith.

For this purpose John had at his disposal three traditions concerning the Resurrection. The first is the discovery of the empty tomb by the women, in this case by Mary Magdalene alone (verses 1f.). The second is a visit of Peter to the empty tomb (verses 3–10). The third is the appearance of Jesus to the assembled Apostles (verses 19–23). In each case John has expanded the underlying tradition by bringing into it a particular person, who is the subject of John's own elaboration of it, and embodies his real interest in the nature of the act of faith. In the first case, John's source seems to have included an appearance of Jesus to the women, as in Matthew, a feature which is not found in Mark or Luke, or in the apocryphal *Gospel of Peter*. John has made this the foundation of the beautiful story of the appearance of Jesus to Mary Magdalene (verses 11–18). In the second case he has added the Beloved Disciple to the tradition about Peter, incorporating him into his version of this tradition in verses 3–10. In the third case he has taken up the motif of the incredulity of the disciples as the basis of the anecdote about Thomas (verses 24–9). In each case there is considerable repetition of phrases which belong to the underlying tradition, a feature which we have observed before in John's creative writing (e.g. 11.33–8). It is also characteristic of his method to save up a detail of the basic story as the nucleus of a further expansion (e.g. 19.6–15, taking up 'Crucify him!' from the Barabbas story). This applies to both the appearance to Mary Magdalene and the story of Thomas. We must now try to estimate John's sources in relation to the Synoptic Gospels.

(a) The story of the women at the tomb is found in all three Synoptic Gospels (Mk 16.1–8 paras.). John's version of it, in verses 1f., 11–18, has close connections of vocabulary and expression with all three accounts, as will be shown in the notes below. The most notable similarities are with Mt. 28.1–10, not only in the appearance of Jesus himself, more or less repeating the function of the angels earlier in the narrative, but also in the exceptional designation of the disciples as 'my brethren' (verse 17, cf. Mt. 28.10), and in the command: 'Do not hold me' in the same verse (contrast Mt. 28.9). F. Neirynck ('Les Femmes au Tombeau: Étude de la rédaction Matthéenne', *NTS* xv (1969), pp. 168–90) sees a line of development from Mark through Matthew to John. But it cannot be supposed that John is simply dependent on Matthew because he shares certain phrases with Mark against Matthew, and also agrees with Luke against both in speaking of two angels. If John is still using the source which he has in common with Luke, which certainly seems to be the case with the other two traditions, we must assume either that Luke has disregarded the appearance to the women or that John has derived this element from another source. The latter is much the more probable conclusion. Neirynck holds that Matthew has developed this item out of the vision of the angel in the Marcan account. But Matthew reproduces that too. The similarities between the vision of the angel and the appearance of Jesus risen are such that it is probable that they are alternative versions of the same experience. This suggests that Matthew has not developed this item out of Mark, but drawn it from his stock of special traditions. It is an independent item. This leads to the conclusion that the same item has come to John in a form slightly differing from Matthew, and that he is not dependent on Matthew in making comparable use of it. The idea that Mary Magdalene alone had this experience is peculiar to John ([Mk 16.9–11] is part of the spurious ending of Mark, and is certainly dependent on John). We therefore have no means of checking its historical worth. It remains possible that it has a factual basis, but certainty is impossible.

(b) The visit of the disciples to the tomb is mentioned in a general way in Lk. 24.24. But Lk. 24.12 describes how Peter alone went to the tomb and 'saw the linen cloths by themselves.' The vocabulary is very close to Jn 20.5ff. This verse (Lk. 24.12) is missing from D a b d e l r[1], Marcion and the Diatessaron, and so is regarded by many scholars as an interpolation based on John (hence it is relegated to the margins of *RSV* and *NEB*). But—by contrast with Mk 16.9–11—it is devoid of everything Johannine, and, whether it is an interpolation or not, it is much best explained as the source from which John has constructed verses 3–10. It is accepted as an authentic part of Luke's text by A. R. C. Leaney (*NTS* II (1955), pp. 110–14; *Commentary*, 1958, pp. 28–31), K. Aland (*NTS* XII (1966), p. 206), and E. Earle Ellis (*ad loc.*). But even if Westcott and Hort are right to call it a 'Western non-interpolation', it must be regarded as independent of John, and inserted into the rest of the MSS. of Luke to justify the statement of Lk. 24.24. It is notable that it does not include an appearance of Jesus to Peter. This, however, is good tradition (Lk. 24.34; 1 C. 15.5), although it is not described in the resurrection narratives of any of the four Gospels. The motive for the tradition of Peter's visit to the tomb is to establish the fact that, though it was empty, the body of Jesus could not have been stolen, because the grave-clothes were still there (against the suggestion, therefore, of Mt. 28.13). Whether the tradition is founded on historical fact again cannot be decided with certainty. It is evidence which cannot be scientifically confirmed, and it does not have the value of a personal statement of Peter himself or of eye-witness reporting. Whether it is accepted or not depends on the reader's presuppositions with regard to the nature of the resurrection of Jesus. John himself seeks to turn attention away from historical evidences to the experience of the Church (verse 29). For a modern discussion of the problem, see *The Significance of the Message of the Resurrection for Faith in Jesus Christ*, edited by C. F. D. Moule (*SBT*, 2nd ser., 8 (1968)).

(c) The appearance to the disciples has as its main purpose their commissioning for their apostolic task. Variant forms of this tradition are found in Mt. 28.16–20 and [Mk 16.14–20] (a primitive piece included in the spurious ending). But John is closest to Lk. 24.36–49. A common, and perhaps surprising, feature of these traditions is the incredulity of the disciples. The Lucan narrative has the motif of the display of Jesus' wounds in order to compel belief. John takes over this theme, but leads the reader beyond it. Much of Luke's writing at this point is characteristic of his own style and vocabulary, so that it is clear that he has done as much reworking of the source for his own ends as John has. The conclusion is inevitable that John is using the same source as Luke, but independently of him. We do not have this tradition in its original form, but it is vouched for again by Paul in 1 C. 15.5. The motif of incredulity may have begun as an expression of fear on the part of the disciples, for fear is the stock reaction to a theophany. The doubts arise from the unusual nature of the experience, which is disturbing and creates the need for reassurance.

This is clearly expressed in Lk. 24.37–9. The situation is comparable to the miracle of Jesus walking on the water (6.19f.). In the legendary expansion of this story in Mt. 14.28–31 Peter begins to sink because he doubts (*edistasas*). This clearly refers to lack of confidence in the divine power, rather than intellectual doubts. It is precisely the same word (used nowhere else in the NT) which occurs in the Matthean version of the appearance to the disciples for 'doubted' (Mt. 28.17). The application of this tradition to intellectual doubt belongs to a secondary stage in its employment, when objections are raised to the Christian proclamation of the bodily resurrection of Jesus.

The first Christians believed that the grave could not hold Jesus, but that he was raised to the glory of the Father. This was thought of in a simple and literal manner as a bodily resurrection. So the tomb was bound to be empty, and when Jesus was seen in his post-Resurrection glory, it was felt to be his bodily presence, almost as in the days of his earthly ministry. When the Church spread into the Greek world, it had to come to terms with quite different presuppositions. To the Hellenistic mind, as to the Gnostics later, salvation was identified with escape from the material body; consequently the idea of the bodily resurrection was offensive. Paul shows in 1 Corinthians that the flesh/spirit dualism of the Hellenistic view could lead to the most serious moral consequences, horrifying to a Jew with his flesh-and-spirit, integrated, notion of personality. Hence the later shaping of the Resurrection traditions tends to lay greater stress on the materiality of the risen Christ, in order to combat these views.

John shares the Jewish presuppositions, but he is aware of those of the Greeks. The fact of the empty tomb and the marks of the crucifixion in Jesus show the continuity with the past; the appearance behind locked doors shows the new capacity for universal presence. John writes at a time when the Resurrection traditions belong to the past, but he interprets the present experience of the Church in the light of them. The essential point for him is that the Christian is in a vital personal relationship with the risen Christ, the mutual indwelling expounded in the Supper discourses. The Resurrection narratives are handled in such a way as to lead to the response of faith by which this relationship is established. For John the proof of the Resurrection is to be found in the 'life in his name' (verse 31) which follows on belief. The traditional

narratives are not so much proofs as pointers towards the interpretation of the Christian experience of life in Christ, who is the
same Lord who revealed the Father and died and was glorified.

Peter and the Beloved Disciple **20.1-10**

20.1. the first day of the week: the Greek uses the cardinal
number instead of the ordinal. This is probably a Semitism (*BDF*
§ 247 (1)). Also the plural *sabbata* for week is likely to be due to
confusion with the emphatic state of the singular in Aramaic
(*šabbᵉṭā'*). The whole phrase is from the source, exactly as in Mk
16.2. It really means the first day after the Sabbath, i.e. Sunday.
The days of the week are not named in the Bible.

Mary Magdalene: she is mentioned along with others in all
four Gospels, cf. 19.25. Mark and Luke say that they came to
anoint the body of Jesus, Matthew simply that they came to see
the tomb. John gives no reason for the visit. But his silence suggests that his source stood nearer to Mark, but he has had to omit
the intention of anointing, because that has been done already.
early: *prōï*, as in Mk 16.2.

the stone had been taken away: John's colourless **taken away**
(*ērmenon*) perhaps replaces a phrase using 'rolled away' in the
source, as in Mark (cf. 11.39, 41). John has not mentioned **the
stone** in describing the burial. He probably thinks of it as square
rather than round. The tradition that it had been removed soon
gave rise to speculations how it had happened. In Mt. 28.2 it is
done by an angel in the presence of the women. The *Gospel of
Peter*, 35ff. describes it rolling back of its own accord during
the night, when two heavenly messengers arrive to lead Jesus
out triumphantly. But in the first instance it is simply a necessary
corollary of belief in the bodily resurrection. Obviously Jesus has
to open the door in order to come out. The fact that it might not
be possible to open it from the inside is not considered. The
raising of Lazarus, although it is resuscitation rather than resurrection in the theological sense, illustrates how the Jewish Christian
mind would imagine what happened. For another explanation see
the next verse.

2. ran: this comes at the *end* of the story of the women at the
tomb, cf. Mt. 28.8, where it replaces Mark's 'fled'. But as Mary
Magdalene is distressed, John is not dependent on Matthew for
this detail. His source may have had the motif of fear, as in Mark.

All the main part of the story is omitted by John, as he holds it over for the expansion in verses 11–18. But he presupposes the angel's instruction to the women (Mk 16.7) in that Mary goes to **Simon Peter.**

the other disciple, the one whom Jesus loved: thus John carefully refers the reader to 13.23; 19.26, in order to intimate the identity of **the other disciple** who figures in the ensuing story. The phrase means another besides Peter, and there is no good reason to identify him with 'another disciple' in 18.15 (see the notes *ad loc.*). Although Lk. 24.12 only mentions Peter for the visit to the empty tomb, the plural is used ('some of those who were with us') in the summary in Lk. 24.24, so that one or more others may have been mentioned in John's source. Alternatively John may be taking up the reference to 'his disciples' along with Peter in Mk 16.7. **Loved** here is, exceptionally, *ephilei*, cf. on 11.3 above.

They have taken the Lord: the Lord is respectful, cf. verses 13 ('my Lord') and 16 ('Rabboni'). **They** is impersonal, replacing a passive construction. Mary means that the body of Jesus has been stolen. Barrett draws attention to an edict of Claudius against the activities of those who break into tombs. The legend of the soldiers in Mt. 28.11–15 shows that this idea was put forward in Jewish circles to refute the Christian teaching of the Resurrection, with its emphasis on the empty tomb.

we do not know: the plural **we** suggests a group of women, as in the source.

where they have laid him: the phrase comes from the source (cf. Mk 16.6), where it refers to the shelf where Jesus had been laid.

3. Peter is mentioned first, as he is the subject of the underlying tradition.

4. John builds up the story by reduplicating what was said of Peter alone in the source. Lk. 24.12 says: 'Peter rose and ran to the tomb.' Here this has become a race between the two men. The Beloved Disciple's arrival **first** (often fancifully ascribed to his more youthful vigour) is probably intended as a hint of his being the first to believe in the Resurrection; cf. verse 8.

5. stooping . . . the linen cloths: the entire phrase is identical with the continuation of Lk. 24.12. As John applies it to the Beloved Disciple, he will have to repeat it when Peter arrives (verse 6). The fact that the grave-clothes are still there proves that Mary is wrong to suppose that the body has been stolen. The only possible explanation of the facts is that Jesus has risen from the dead. Bultmann points out that in this tradition there is no mention of the angels (one or more) who are a fixed element of the story of the women. The two traditions have grown up separately. John manages to unite them without glaring inconsistency.

but he did not go in: there is nothing about entry into the tomb in Lk. 24.12. This feature is part of John's delaying tactics, so as to build the narrative up to a climax.

6. following: cf. 1.37–43. Barrett suggests that the word here may be more than a narrative detail, and intended to emphasize the fact that the Beloved Disciple takes the lead in reaching faith. Then **went into the tomb** replaces 'stooping to look in' of the source. This is simply to advance the action beyond verse 5. John characteristically varies the word for **saw** (*theōrei* instead of *blepei*).

7. the napkin: cf. 11.44. John here introduces an item which is not found in his source, in much the same way as he expands the tradition in 19.23f. He thinks of the grave-clothes in detail, and singles out the **napkin** (*soudarion*) for mention. The fact that it was **rolled up in a** [lit. 'one'] **place by itself** shows that all the linen cloths were perfectly tidy. **rolled up** really means 'wrapped', as in Mt. 27.59 = Lk. 23.53 ('wrapped it [the body of Jesus] in a linen shroud'). The word (*entulissein*) is not used elsewhere in the NT. In 11.44 John used a different word (*periededeto*) for 'his face wrapped with a cloth (*soudarion*)'. On this basis it could be argued that John means here that the napkin was still wrapped round, as it had been when it was bound round Jesus' face. This would lead to the conclusion that John means that the grave-clothes were undisturbed by the Resurrection. Jesus had passed through them, and not even the face-cloth had been moved. This interpretation is denied by Bernard, Hoskyns and Mastin, probably rightly. Hoskyns quotes Chrysostom for the opinion that the fact that the grave-clothes were neatly folded up adds further evidence that there was no tomb-theft involved. The robbers might perhaps have stripped off the cloths, but they certainly would not have left them so tidy. John's use of *entulissein* is not quite correct (neither *MM* nor *LSJ* quote a precise parallel) but it is probable that he derives the word from the vocabulary of burial customs.

8. saw and believed: John does not say what the Beloved Disciple believed. He means that he drew the only possible conclusion from the facts, and the reader is expected to be able to do the same. The Disciple has reached Resurrection faith without an appearance of Jesus. According to the source (Lk. 24.12) Peter 'went home wondering at what had happened'. John perhaps means to imply this of Peter, by contrast with the Disciple, but omits to say so. Alternatively we are to assume that the Disciple communicated his faith to Peter, cf. verse 6. It is completely mistaken to allegorize the two men as symbols of the Church, Peter representing Jewish Christianity and the Disciple the Gentile Church (Loisy, Bultmann), in their apprehension of faith; or to see in them types of the ministry, Peter being the pastoral ministry and the Disciple the prophetic ministry, which specially characterizes the milieu of John (Kragerud). John is not interested in such polemical questions. He is concerned that *the reader* should believe, and sets the Beloved Disciple before him as the first example for him to follow. *His* kind of faith will be commended by the risen Jesus himself in verse 29. This holds good in spite of the formal contrast between this verse ('saw and believed') and verse 29 ('have not seen and yet believe'). Brown (pp. 1005f.) makes too much of this contrast, which needs to be understood in the light of John's recasting of the traditions in the chapter as a whole (cf. p. 595 above).

9. It is important at this point to see what John is doing. That Jesus should rise from the dead has not so far even been thought of. The tomb has been found empty. Mary Magdalene drew the wrong conclusion, that the body had been stolen. The Beloved Disciple has understood it correctly, and so come through to faith, but the substance of his faith has still not been formulated. Here at last John tells us what it is, but at the same time he explains why it took time for the truth to dawn on the disciples. It was only at a later stage still, when they began to reflect on the whole sequence of events after faith in the Resurrection had been reached, that they could see it in terms of a pattern of scriptural fulfilment. This is a thoroughly Johannine idea (cf. 2.22; 12.16). But the language of this verse sounds more like Luke than John. Leaney has plausibly suggested that it comes from the source. It would fit in perfectly after Lk. 24.12. This is possible, but Leaney is on less sure ground when he suggests that 'he did not know' (*ēdei* ℵ* Old

Latin) is the true reading here for **they did not know** (*ēdeisan*), for it is more likely to be due to assimilation to the singular verbs in verse 8. On Leaney's view the subject would, of course, be Peter.

the scripture: this must refer to a particular text, but John gives no indication of what he has in mind. Most commentators suggest Ps. 16.10, cf. Ac. 2.27.

10. to their homes: the verse is certainly adapted from 'he went home' in the source (Lk. 24.12). **To their homes** (*pros hautous*) is an unusual idiom, found in both passages. It is foreign to John's style, for he would certainly write *eis to idia* as in 1.11; 16.32; 19.27. Black (pp. 102f.) takes it to represent the Aramaic ethic dative, i.e. 'got themselves back', but Mastin points out that the same phrase occurs in the LXX of Num. 24.25, where it means 'went on his way' (Heb. *hālak lᵉdarkō*). But there may well be an Aramaic original behind the source used by John.

Mary Magdalene 11–18

11. stood: it seems to be forgotten that Mary has left the tomb, though it is possible to get round the difficulty by imagining that she followed the two disciples back to the tomb. But it is really due to imperfect interweaving of two separate traditions. John is now back at the situation of verse 1, and what follows is the material which was omitted from the story of the women. As no motive has been given for Mary's visit to the tomb, the **weeping** could be the purpose of it. She has come to the tomb to give vent to her grief (cf. 11.31). But in fact there is another reason (verse 13).

stooped to look: the same Greek word (*parakuptein*) as in verse 5, belonging to the other story. It is used of the women in *Gospel of Peter*, 55f., probably in dependence on the Fourth Gospel. The verb is from a root meaning to bend, and so implies at least an inclination of the head, if not of the body, in order to see (see the note in Mastin, p. 423, n. 2).

12. two angels: John's source agrees with Lk. 24.4 in specifying **two** (cf. also Ac. 1.10), but with Mk 16.5 in saying that they were **in white** and were **sitting** inside the tomb. **Where the body of Jesus had lain** is a variant of 'where they have laid him' in Mk 16.6, which John uses at the end of verse 13. **One at the head and one at the feet** is a phrase in Semitic style (Black,

p. 108; cf. 19.18), and probably also belongs to the source. For **angels** Luke has 'men', but he refers to them as angels in Lk. 24.23; Mark has 'a young man', Matthew 'an angel', and *Gospel of Peter*, 36f. 'two men' and 'both young men'. These differences are not significant, as angels were imagined as young men in NT times. What distinguishes them from human beings, and shows them to be heavenly messengers, is the exceptional brightness of their clothing. For the belief in angels, cf. 12.29 note. John only refers to angels when he is reproducing a source. **Two** is omitted by ℵ* e, probably by accident.

The fundamental fact of the original tradition is that one or more of the women had a vision, in which she saw an angelic figure and received assurance that Jesus had risen. The fact that the figure conforms to conventional ideas does not mean that it is merely a literary fabrication, for this is a constant feature of ecstatic visions (cf. Lindblom, *op. cit.*, chapter 5). It is the message which forms the core of the experience. It is possible that the reason why the later versions of this tradition (John; Lk. 24.4; Ac. 1.10) have *two* angels is that their function is thought of in terms of the legal requirement for valid witness (cf. 8.17). Meanwhile another development of this tradition is that the angel was none other than the risen Christ himself. Although at a theological level there could be no confusion between Christ and an angel (Heb. 1.1–14, however, faces the possibility and danger of it), the pictorial idea of Christ in glory would not be very different. For again exceptionally bright clothing predominates (cf. the accounts of the Transfiguration, and also Rev. 1.12–20, undoubtedly describing an authentic ecstatic vision). This is not to say that primitive Christian experiences of the risen Christ are *only* ecstatic visions. The Johannine emphasis on personal relationship with him, the Lucan on eucharistic fellowship with him, and the Pauline on being 'in Christ', show that there is far more to it than that. But in the actual narrative before us it is difficult to resist the conclusion that we have an alternative development of the tradition of the vision of the angel, because both in John and in Mt. 28.9f. the function of the risen Christ is precisely the same as that of the angel. It is to tell the women to bring the message of the Resurrection to the disciples. Mt. 28.10 simply repeats the gist of Mt. 28.5–7, though with just sufficient difference to suggest that this is not due to Matthew himself, but to a parallel and separate develop-

ment from the other tradition. John only begins the dialogue with
the angels in verses 13f., and then repeats it in verse 15. The
actual message of the angel(s) is omitted, so as not to spoil the
climax in verse 17.

13. Woman, why are you weeping: for **woman** (omitted
by *NEB*), cf. 2.4. The source probably continued 'whom do you
seek?' as in verse 15 (it is actually added here by D and Sinaitic
Syriac), cf. Mk 16.6; Lk. 24.5. But John holds it over until the
repetition in verse 15. John omits the stock reaction of fear on the
part of Mary. This suggests that **why are you weeping** replaces
something like 'fear not!', in order to take up the motive mentioned in verse 11. Mary's reply simply repeats what she had said
to Peter and the Beloved Disciple in verse 2, with 'we do not
know' corrected to **I do not know. For where they have laid
him,** cf. Mk 16.6 and the notes above. Mary's distress is caused
by her supposition that the body of Jesus has been stolen. It has
not occurred to her that he might have risen, as she lacks the
insight of the Beloved Disciple. At this point the angels disappear
from the story, and their intervention appears to have been
unnecessary; this is because John now continues with the other
tradition which he shares with Matthew.

14. The sudden appearance of Jesus conforms to the general
pattern of the Resurrection traditions. For **Jesus standing,** cf.
verses 19 and 26, and Lk. 24.36. For Mary's failure to recognize
Jesus, cf. 21.4, 7, 12; Lk. 24.16, 31, 37f.; Mt. 28.17. John uses this
feature very effectively to suggest a gradual unfolding of the truth,
comparable to the gradual realization of the Beloved Disciple in
verses 4–8.

15. Whom do you seek: see the notes on verse 13. The words
probably come from the source used at that point, rather than
from the tradition of the actual appearance of Jesus. Mary's idea
that he might be **the gardener** (*kēpouros*, only here in the NT) is
simply derived from the setting of the tomb in a garden (19.41);
this is John's favourite device of literal misunderstanding, given
a new kind of application. The gardener would be a neutral
person, not identified either with the disciples or with the hostile
Jews. It is most unlikely that he would remove the body, but
Mary is clutching at a straw. Her words form a third repetition
of verse 2, with change of 'taken' to **carried** (*ebastasas*), which
perhaps is meant to convey the notion of stealing (cf. 12.6).

16. Mary: the moment of recognition is the moment of personal address. In verse 15 Jesus had used the conventional 'Woman'. Now, like the Good Shepherd, he calls his own by name, and she turns to him, because she knows his voice (10.3f.). In the light of the Supper discourses, where personal relationship receives so much emphasis, we can see how important this is for John's understanding of the Resurrection. The sight of the risen Lord is a personal confrontation which involves relationship. In the story of Thomas we shall see how this applies even when there is no actual sight.

She turned: this seems illogical, for she has already turned to face Jesus (the verb is the same as in verse 14). But the Sinaitic Syriac reads instead 'she recognized him'. Black (p. 255) thinks that this corresponds with the original Aramaic at this point, and that **turned** in the Greek is due to a misreading on the part of the translator (cf. also M. É. Boismard in *L'Évangile de Jean*, Recherches Bibliques III (1958), p. 47). But it is much more likely to be an attempt to remove the difficulty (Barrett, Mastin). John probably imagines that she had half turned away as she spoke before, which would be very natural in the circumstances. Now the mention of her name startles her to face Jesus directly.

Rabboni: the pronunciation indicated by the Greek is *rabbūni*. The usual rabbinic pronunciation is *ribbōnī*, but the word occurs in the recently discovered Palestinian Pentateuch Targum with this precise pronunciation (Black, pp. 20–4); but, as J. A. Fitzmyer (*CBQ* xxx (1968), p. 421) has pointed out in a review of Black's work, this still does not prove that John gives the pronunciation as it was in the time of Jesus, as the vocalization belongs to a later time, and the Aramaic consonants (*rbwny*) can be pronounced either way. It is one of a variety of lengthened forms of *rabbi*, indicating greater respect and deference than the simple form (it is used for 'my lord' both times at Gen. 44.18 in the Palestinian Targum). Its only other occurrence in the NT is at Mk 10.51, where it is obscured by *RSV* 'master' (*RSV, mg* 'rabbi'). John is quite correct in supposing that a woman would use this form, whereas male disciples use the simple *rabbi* (1.38). It is impossible to tell whether he uses it here on the basis of his source, or from his personal knowledge of Jewish manners. It would be quite wrong to build anything on the fact that *rabbūni* is sometimes used in addressing God (*SB* II.25), for there is no suggestion of an ascription of divinity to Jesus, as the parenthesis **which means Teacher** (cf. 1.38) shows. Mary anticipates Thomas' 'my lord', but not his 'my God' (verse 28). At the end of the verse ℵ³ Θ Ψ Sinaitic Syriac add 'and she ran up to touch him', an insertion suggested by the next verse.

17. Do not hold me: the command is only intelligible if Mary has made some move to do so. It thus seems likely that John's source had something corresponding with 'took hold of his feet' in Mt. 28.9. But it still remains difficult, for in verse 27 Jesus actually invites Thomas to touch him. Hence Bernard conjectured that the original words were 'fear not!' (*mē ptoou*, corrupted to *mē haptou mou* as in B, ultimately changed to *mē mou haptou* as in all other MSS.). This verb for 'fear', though rare, is found at Lk. 24.37. But this makes the connection with **for I have not yet ascended** inexplicable. According to the Jewish idea of bodily resurrection presupposed by John, Jesus is touchable, and perfectly able to invite Thomas to handle him. His command to Mary has nothing to do with the ethereal nature of his body, but is concerned with establishing the proper relationship which must exist from now on. Jesus goes to the Father by way of his death, and in doing so makes possible the mutual indwelling which has been described in chapter 14. The Resurrection appearances attest the new situation, but they are not a substitute for it. The desire to hold Jesus must be restrained, because it is an attempt to recapture the conditions of the incarnate life in place of the universal and abiding relationship which is the object of his mission. Mary has experienced something of this in the moment of recognition. When Jesus says **'I have not yet ascended to the Father'**, this is in one sense untrue, for he has already gone to the Father through his death. It is only true inasmuch as the appearances are an accommodation to the needs of the disciples while they adjust themselves to the new situation. Meanwhile it is important to explain that the new relationship is not dependent on physical contact.

go to my brethren: it is this phrase above all which requires the supposition that John was using a source which also lies behind Mt. 28.10. Whether it was originally intended literally to refer to Jesus' brothers, or metaphorically to the disciples, is not clear; but for John at any rate it must mean the disciples (contrast 7.5). In fact it takes on a positive significance, as Jesus goes on to speak of **my Father and your Father.** It suggests the new family of

the Church (cf. 19.26f.), in which the disciples referred to each
other as brothers (Ac. 1.15; 9.17; etc.). The point is pressed home
by the synonymous phrase **to my God and your God:** it is the
family of the divine fellowship. The phrases are beautifully
balanced. They express both the separateness of Jesus as one in a
class by himself and his closeness as belonging to the same group.
John could hardly do more to express the prime importance of
personal relationship in his teaching on the Resurrection. Bultmann
notes how the repetition of phrases enhances the emotional impact.
I am ascending: the Greek word is often used literally of going
up to a feast (5.1; etc.), but the only places where it is comparable
to the present passage are 3.13 and 6.62. But in those contexts it
refers to the Passion of Jesus and his glorification as the Son of
Man considered as a single act, just like 'going to the Father' in
the Supper discourses. The Resurrection appearances are, as it
were, brief stops in this single movement, and in that sense Jesus
has not yet ascended. But John is not thinking of an occasion in
the near future when 'the Ascension' will take place according to
the Lucan scheme (Lk. 24.51; Ac. 1.9f.). Jesus is really ascending
now. The present verb has future meaning, as often in John, but
it is consequent on the present. This message replaces the Matthean instruction to the 'brothers' to assemble in Galilee (Mt.
28.10; cf. Mk 16.7). It is John's way of announcing that the era
of the Resurrection has begun.

   18. went and said: the word for **said** (*angellein*) means to
give a message, and occurs in compound forms in Mt. 28.8, 10;
Lk. 24.9; and the spurious verse [Mk 16.10], based on this passage.
John's narrative here links up with the ending of the other tradition of the visit of the women to the tomb. Characteristically John
omits all mention of the emotional effect of the message on the disciples. The lack of co-ordination between **'I have seen the Lord'**
(direct speech) and **that he had said these things to her**
(indirect speech) has led to some variation in the textual tradition. The phrase 'to see the Lord' is a feature of the following story,
and is probably taken from it (verses 20, 25, 28f.).

The Disciples 19–23

   19. of that day: John agrees with Luke in timing the appearance to the disciples on Easter night (repeating **the first day of
the week** from verse 1), and placing it in Jerusalem, contrary to

the instructions in Mk 16.7. But the tradition of an appearance in
Galilee is taken up in the Appendix (21.1). It is probable that
Luke's scheme is a result of concentrating the scattered items of
information into an ordered sequence, in accordance with his
idea that the Church worked outwards from Jerusalem (Ac. 1.8).
But it is intrinsically probable that the disciples should return to
Galilee after the feast of Passover and Unleavened Bread was
over, and it is really not difficult to imagine moments of awareness
of the Resurrection both in Jerusalem and in Galilee at various
times (cf. Moule, *op. cit.*, pp. 4f.). The connection between the
appearances of Jesus and the eating of a meal in Luke (Lk. 24.30,
35, 41–3) suggests that he has in mind the presence of Christ in
the eucharistic assembly of the Church. This applies to John too
(21.13), and the timing of the Thomas episode (verse 26) suggests
the pattern of regular Sunday worship (cf. Rev. 1.10). Thus the
traditions of actual appearances are related to the Church's wor-
shipping life, in which the meaning of the Resurrection is realized,
and this connection has to some extent shaped the form of the
traditions themselves. The spurious ending of Mark also has the
setting of a meal for this tradition ([Mk 16.14]). We are not told
where the disciples were. It is natural to suppose that it is the
upper room where the Last Supper was held, but this is only
surmise. We are also not told how many disciples were there. Lk.
24.33, 36 implies not only the apostles but also the whole number
of disciples in Jerusalem, which had risen by the time of the
Ascension to 120 people (Ac. 1.15). Whatever we make of this
figure, Luke certainly cannot be accused of exaggeration! But in
verses 24f. below John gives the impression that he means just the
Twelve, or rather the eleven, reduced to ten by the absence of
Thomas. But as Bultmann points out, we would never suspect
that one was missing in the present paragraph, as John fails to
prepare for this further anecdote. He evidently intends the group
to be considered as a whole. But, as the Supper discourses have
shown, John thinks of the Apostles as the nucleus of the Church
of the future, not as a ruling class within the Church. What follows
is important for the Church's doctrine of the ministry. But it does
not necessarily presuppose a distinction between priesthood and
laity.

for fear of the Jews: cf. 19.38. The motive is a natural one, but
it is introduced here to emphasize the miraculous character of

Jesus' arrival. This does not mean that his body is ethereal, able to pass through locked doors. It means rather that he can make himself present at any time and place 'where two or three are gathered in my name' (Mt. 18.20, where the larger context is the Christian assembly, cf. below on verse 23). When he does appear, his body is quite normal and solid.

stood among them: here John begins to reproduce his source, represented also in Lk. 24.36.

and said to them, 'Peace be with you': The normal greeting, but with immeasurably greater depth of meaning; cf. 14.27. The whole sentence is found at the end of Lk. 24.36 in all MSS. except D and Old Latin (a b d e ff² l r¹) and may well belong to the source. Aland (*art. cit.*, pp. 206–8) argues that it is an original part of Luke's text, in spite of the opinion of many modern critics (so it is relegated to the margin in *RSV* and *NEB*), because further expansions in other MSS. are inexplicable without it, though of course this is not decisive. If it is an early interpolation from John, it must be regarded as less likely to belong to the common source. For the diction is Johannine, as we have seen, and he has a motive for inserting it in that he wishes to hold over the theme of in-credulity (= Lk. 24.37f.) for the Thomas story. The fact that he has deliberately omitted this element here is proved by the next verse.

20. Throughout this verse John keeps fairly close to the source, as the Lucan parallel shows. In Lk. 24.39 Jesus says 'See my hands and my feet' in order to allay the uncertainty of the dis-ciples. The wounds of crucifixion prove the continuity between the dying Jesus and the risen Lord (for the nailing of Jesus to the cross, not mentioned in the actual crucifixion narratives, see J. Blinzler, *The Trial of Jesus* (1959), pp. 264f. 'Hands' includes the wrists and forearms in Hebrew and Greek usage, cf. the note on p. 574. The skeletal remains there referred to also include the feet, fastened to the *suppedaneum* (footrest) of the cross by means of one large nail through the two heels). In John this invitation to the disciples is again held over for the Thomas story (verse 27), but John retains the motif in the much weaker statement: **When he had said this, he showed them his hands and his side.** The change of 'feet' to **side** depends on John's own special item in 19.31–7, so that the present occasion makes a fulfilment of the text of Zech. 12.10 there quoted. John's statement has also found its way into the text of Luke, with side duly changed to feet, in most MSS. of Lk. 24.40. This time the evidence for omission is slightly stronger, for it includes besides the MSS. mentioned in the last verse both Old Syriac texts (Curetonian and Sinaitic) and Marcion.

were glad: Gr. *echarēsan*. Another feature from the source, cf. 'for joy' (*apo tēs charas*); Lk. 24.41.

the Lord: this title is never normally used of Jesus, except in personal address (cf. the notes on 4.1). John may have found it in his source. Alternatively, it may be used here and in verse 25 in order to prepare for Thomas' confession of faith (for the primitive confession 'Jesus is Lord', cf. 1. C. 12.3).

21. At this point John characteristically repeats himself before introducing his own version of the commissioning of the disciples. This is a fixed element of the variant traditions, cf. Mt. 28.18–20; [Mk 16.15]; Lk. 24.47–9; Ac. 1.8. But John uses his own words, cf. 17.18. As Luke also recasts this item to suit his own theology, we cannot recover what stood in the source here. The commissioning is of the disciples in the name of the whole Church for its mission to the world. It is not an ordination to a position of authority within the Church for an internal ministry, though this is not excluded. The disciples, and the whole Church following them, carry on the mission of Christ, which he received from the Father.

22. he breathed on them: with this symbolic action Jesus fulfils the expectation of 1.33 and the promise of the Paraclete (cf. also 7.39). **Breathed** (*enephusēsen*) occurs only here in the NT. Nearly all commentators see in it a verbal allusion to Gen. 2.7, where 'God formed man of dust from the ground, and breathed (LXX *enephusēsen*) into his nostrils the breath of life.' The same verb is also used in Ezekiel's vision of the dry bones (Ezek. 37.9). This suggests that John sees the constitution of the Church after the Resurrection as a kind of new creation. Thus both meanings of 'sent' in the last verse, i.e. the incarnation of Jesus and his work of redemption, apply to his sending of the disciples. They are created anew as well as being given a task to perform. Indeed they cannot perform it unless they have this inbreathing.

Receive the Holy Spirit: Receive (*labete*) is the same word as 'take' in the eucharistic words (cf. Mk. 14.22), but it is very doubtful if there is any intentional allusion, as it is an extremely common word. The full phrase **Holy Spirit** (**the** is not in the

Greek and should be omitted) is rare in John, and strongly suggests a reference to 1.33 (where also 'the' should be omitted). The
disciples are baptized with Holy Spirit, having experienced the
death and Resurrection of him who was endowed with Holy Spirit
when he symbolically anticipated his death and Resurrection at
his baptism in Jordan. For the connection between Jesus' baptism
and his death, cf. the notes on 1.29. There remains the question
whether the giving of the Holy Spirit belongs to the original story
at this point, or has been introduced by John himself. There is
nothing corresponding with it in Mt. 28.16–20 or [Mk 16.14–18].
But Lk. 24.49; Ac. 1.8 make special mention of the promise of
the Holy Spirit, shortly to be fulfilled at Pentecost. This may well
be a Lucan adaptation of something much closer to John in the
source. For John the gift of the Spirit is a direct consequence of
the death of Jesus, like the Ascension, not a separate event.

23. With the gift of the Spirit, Jesus directs how it is to be used.
The commission in the parallels is much broader. Mt. 28.19f.
speaks of evangelizing, baptizing and teaching. [Mk 16.15f.] is
also concerned with evangelizing, but then goes on to make a
contrast ('He who believes and is baptized will be saved; but
he who does not believe will be condemned'). This gives a vague
parallel to John, and, as will be shown below, is not far removed
from his meaning. Lk. 24.47, though heavily rewritten in Lucan
style, agrees in making 'repentance and the forgiveness of sins'
the substance of the Gospel which is to be preached (cf. Ac. 2.38;
3.19; 10.43; 13.38). As the language of the verse is Semitic in
style, there is good reason to believe that John here preserves an
item of the source untouched.

are forgiven .. are retained: these verbs are in the perfect tense,
implying a timeless state of affairs which will obtain in the future
(for the first verb, *apheōntai*, however, present with future meaning
is read by W Θ and the majority of mss., i.e. *aphientai*; this is
perhaps supported by the unusual form *apheiontai* of B*, though
Barrett thinks it is intended to be perfect). The most difficult
feature of the saying is the use of *kratein* for **retain.** The verb
means to hold or grasp. The metaphorical use of it for withholding
forgiveness is unparalleled. It is clear that the saying is a variant
of the giving of 'the power of the keys' to Peter in Mt. 16.19,
which is adapted to apply to all the apostles in Mt. 18.18. This
saying in its turn is unmistakably based on Isa. 22.22. J. A.

Emerton (*JTS*, n.s., XIII. (1962), pp. 325–31) has postulated a
reconstruction of the Aramaic original which plausibly accounts
for the variations between Matthew and John, and solves the
problem of *kratein*. He starts from Isa. 22.22, and shows that 'to
shut' (Aram. *'aḥad*, also 'hold, retain') and 'to open' (Aram. *peṭaḥ*,
also 'loose') could both lie behind 'bind' and 'loose' in Matthew
and **retain** and **forgive** in John. Matthew's version appears to
apply the saying to excommunication or to the issue of a binding
doctrinal decision (as in rabbinic usage), John's to the discipline
of penance. But although the saying in John has figured promi-
nently in connection with penance in Christian history, it is by no
means certain that this was its original application, or even that
this is what John intends in the present context. It is difficult to
believe that Jesus established among his followers a rigid internal
penitential discipline, comparable to that of the Qumran Sect,
when his preaching to the 'tax-collectors and sinners' was so open.
That was a later development, though it already appears in Mt. 18.
But the present context concerns the mission of the disciples (verse
21), a task for which the Paraclete was specifically promised
(verse 22; cf. 16.8–15). This supports the suggestion of Mastin
(p. 434) that the saying is to do with the mission preaching. The
disciples preach repentance and the forgiveness of sins in preparation for the rule of God. To those who respond forgiveness is
assured, and ratified by God himself ('in heaven', Mt. 16.19). But
to those who refuse, there is the divine warrant for asserting that
their sins remain unforgiven (cf. [Mk. 14.16] quoted above). This
interpretation not only suits what is likely to have been the original
meaning of the saying, but also John's actual intention in reproducing it here from his source. But we can hardly suppose that
John does not think *also* of preaching within the life of the Church,
so that the notion of an internal ecclesiastical discipline is not
altogether excluded (cf. 1 Jn 1.5–2.6).

Thomas 24–9

24. Thomas: for his function, cf. 11.16; 14.5. The verses which
follow are largely spun out of the preceding paragraph, using the
motif of incredulity, which has so far been omitted (cf. Dodd,
Historical Tradition, pp. 145f.). The information that Thomas was
not present on Easter night is as unexpected as it is unexplained.
25. We have seen the Lord: see above on verse 20.

the print . . . the mark: the MSS. vary between *tupos* (= impression, print, mark) and *topos* (= place). For the first word *tupos* is well supported, and should be retained. For the second it is better to read *topos*, the place of the nails, with A Θ Latin and Syriac texts (so *NEB*). The verse is clearly built on verse 20.

I will not believe: we must assume that the disciples showed some signs of unbelief when Jesus first appeared, but John purposely omitted this item (cf. verses 19f.). The wish to handle Jesus' wounds, in order to achieve certainty, was contained in the source at that point (cf. Lk. 24.39). The Lucan passage is alluded to by Ignatius, *Smyrn.* iii.2: 'And when he came to those with Peter, he said to them, "Take and handle me, and see that I am not a bodiless demon." And at once they touched him and believed, being joined to his flesh and spirit.' Ignatius is here writing against the Docetists. John, too, may have this heresy in mind, but this is not the purpose of his use of this tradition. It is, in fact, to show that the confession of faith (faith, of course, in the one who *really* died and rose to glory) is a more sure way of 'being joined' to the risen Lord than any amount of handling the resurrected body.

26. Eight days later: the next Sunday, cf. above on verse 19. The remainder of the verse reproduces verse 19 almost exactly.

27. The invitation of Jesus not only goes back over the phrases of verse 25 (suggesting that Jesus has been the unseen listener to the conversation), but also corresponds with the invitation in the source; cf. Lk. 24.39. This explains the unexpected **see my hands,** which does not quite tally with verse 25, but agrees precisely with Luke, except of course that the verb is singular. But whereas it is meant literally in Luke (though the disciples are not said to take advantage of the chance to handle Jesus), here it is clearly ironical. It is a challenge. The believing disciple does not need to touch him.

faithless: Gr. *apistos*, only here in John. It is probably due to the source, for the equally uncommon verbal form *apistoun* is a feature of this tradition, occurring in [Mk 16.11, 16]; Lk. 24.11, 41, and the noun *apistia* is found in [Mk 16.14].

28. Thomas' confession of faith is comparable to Mary Magdalene's to begin with, for **My Lord** (*mari*) is a title of honour which can interchange with 'Teacher' (*rabbūni*). But it goes beyond it inasmuch as **Lord** is regularly applied to God, as in English, and this is clinched by the completion **and my God.** It corresponds with the confession of faith of the pious Psalmist (e.g. Ps. 91.2). But there are precise parallels to the whole expression in pagan religious literature, the most notable being the requirement of the emperor Domitian (A.D. 81–96) that he should be addressed as 'our lord and god' (*dominus et deus noster*, Suetonius, *Domitian*, 13). As this is roughly contemporary with the Fourth Gospel, it is certainly possible that John has it in mind: Jesus is one to whom these titles may be properly applied. But it still occasions surprise, for although the confession 'Jesus is Lord' (1 C. 12.3) is well known to be primitive, the application of the word 'God' to Jesus is rare in the NT. Outside John the only sure cases are Tit. 2.13; Heb. 1.8f. (OT quotations applied to Jesus); possibly also 2 Pet. 1.1; 1 Jn 5.20; very doubtfully Rom. 9.5 (a doxology). It begins to be common in the epistles of Ignatius. The fact that it is first attested in the use of quotations and in liturgical pieces based on the OT suggests that it arises from the frequent combination 'the Lord God' in the OT, especially where the LXX is used, in which 'Lord', *Kurios*, regularly replaces the divine name. But this means that the restraining influence of rigid Jewish mono-theism is beginning to weaken, so that the word can be more generally applied to Jesus. It does not mean a fundamental change of doctrine. The confession 'Jesus is Lord' means more than the use of a title of honour. It means that Jesus is exalted to the throne of God, as his statement in the trial narrative implies (Mk 14.62), which was the basis of the High Priest's accusation of blasphemy. This was treated by John in 10.22–39 (see espe-cially the notes on 10.33). It is also the consequence of the Wisdom christology of the Prologue (cf. 1.1), whereby the Christ event is related to God in his dealings with the world, both as Creator and Redeemer. Jesus was both 'with God' and also 'was God'. As one who was 'with God', he could be thought of separately from him, and this is most easily understood by using the idea of the Father and the Son. But the union between them is such that Jesus can say 'I and the Father are one' (10.30), so that 'He who has seen me has seen the Father' (14.9). It is in this sense that 'my God!' is an appropriate expression of faith in Jesus as the exalted Lord. The act of belief not only puts Thomas into rela-tion with the risen Lord, but also with the Father himself.

Thomas' confession takes up the Christology of the whole of the Fourth Gospel. It starts from the personal relationship, which was so beautifully expressed in the experience of Mary Magdalene, and shows the full range of what that personal relationship implies. Thomas' confession is not so much a counterblast to the conceit of a Roman emperor as a summary of the Gospel as a whole. The synonymous repetition with **and** serves to express the emotional impact of confrontation with Jesus, cf. verse 17 above and the confession of Nathanael, 1.49.

29. It goes without saying that John has abandoned his source, though Mt. 28.17 says that the disciples worshipped Jesus when he appeared to him—another indication that this tradition has been shaped within the context of the Christian assembly. But now the final comment must be attributed to the pen of John himself. The question **'Have you believed?'** is taken by Barrett, against the authority of the minuscules, as a statement, so also *NEB*, but comparison with 1.50 and 16.31 suggests that this is wrong. It is slightly ironical, challenging Thomas to examine the nature of his belief, even though he has made confession of faith. Thomas did not, after all, find it necessary to touch Jesus. It would have been a better quality of faith still, if he had not found it necessary even to see him (cf. 1 Pet. 1.8). Brown (p. 1050) strenuously denies that John means that faith without sight is *better*. The point is that those who have not had the privilege of seeing the risen Jesus are no worse off than those who have. Though I agree with Brown (against Bultmann) that John has no wish to belittle the importance of the Resurrection appearances, or to deny the reality of them, perhaps he misses the real significance of Thomas in John's hands. Being absent when Jesus appeared to the disciples on Easter night, Thomas was virtually in the position of the Christian who has not seen the risen Jesus, and he should not have needed a further appearance in order to come to faith. Obviously John has the reader in mind in making this point. Consequently he gains the most universal reference by putting the final statement in the form of a beatitude in didactic style (cf. 13.17). This is the real purpose of the Thomas episode, and indeed of John's presentation of the Resurrection traditions as a whole.

Conclusion 30f.

30. John's purpose of presenting the story of Jesus Christ in such a way as to evoke the response of faith is now finished. It only remains to round off the narrative with this brief conclusion, in which his purpose is expressed with the greatest directness and economy of expression. Hoskyns perversely argues that this is not the end of the book, but merely a summary of the chapter; this is to save chapter 21 as an integral part of the Gospel, but its addition is better explained in other ways (see below). **Many other signs** cannot be confined to the Resurrection appearances, as this would require, but refers to the various narratives in the whole of what precedes (specifically the revelatory acts which lead the discerning to faith; cf. 10.41; 12.37), suggesting that John has used only a selection of the possible material. Bultmann draws attention to this as a literary device for the conclusion of a book, citing Sir 43.27–33 and 1 Mac. 9.22 (which, however, is modelled on the conventional summaries in the Books of Kings). It is important that the signs have been performed **in the presence of the disciples,** for they have now been commissioned to carry on Jesus' task (verse 21), and they will do so as witnesses to what they have seen and heard from him (15.27).

31. **that you may believe:** the verb is aorist subjunctive in nearly all MSS., but the true reading is probably present (B ℵ* Θ). This strictly means 'that you may continue to believe', as opposed to 'come to believe' implied by the aorist. Barrett relates this to the problem of the destination of the Gospel, whether it is addressed to believers or to the unconverted. But it is hazardous to build anything on such a fine point of detail, as John does not use tenses with absolute precision. Mastin points out that in 1 Jn 5.13, which is closely related to this verse, and definitely addressed to believers, the aorist is used.

that Jesus is the Christ: this is the key question for the Jews (cf. 1.41; 4.29; 7.26; 10.24), and to confess Jesus to be the Christ could lead to exclusion from the synagogue (9.22; 12.42). As far as the question of destination is concerned, the use of this title as a central item of belief means only that John presupposes a Jewish element in his Christian readership. It does not entitle us to draw the conclusion that he writes to convert the Jews.

the Son of God: this title, too, has Jewish origins as a messianic title (cf. the notes on 1.49), but it would be far more meaningful to a Hellenistic reader than 'Messiah', and in John's handling of it has taken on much more far-reaching implications. It sums up the whole meaning of John's Christology, for which the Father/Son

relationship is central, and, as we have just seen in connection
with Thomas, is the substance of the confession of faith whereby
salvation is appropriated (cf. 3.16).

life in his name: life has the broad connotation of eternal
salvation common in religious language (see the notes on 1.4).
This life consists in fellowship with God, and it is effected for the
believer through Christ, the overlapping point of the mutual indwelling of Father and Son on the one hand, and Son and disciples on the other (14.21). Hence **in his name,** which cannot
be taken with **believing** on account of its position and the use of
the preposition *en* instead of *eis*, must be taken closely with **you
may have life.** It has the same meaning as in 14.13. There it
properly denotes 'by the invocation of my name'. But it is thought
of much more in terms of vital contact, and is really a way of
saying 'through your relationship with me'. It is this saving relationship which John sets before the reader as he brings his Gospel
to an end.

THE APPENDIX   21.1–25

The addition of this chapter, so vividly written and appealing to
the imagination, poses a host of problems. One thing is clear at
the outset. As it comes after the conclusion to the Gospel, it cannot be regarded as part of the formal structure of the book. But
as it is included in all MSS., it is certainly not a late addition. It
has been added soon after the rest was written, possibly at the
time of publication to a wider audience than the immediate
circle for whom the Gospel was written.

A brief survey of the contents will show the problems which
have to be faced. First there is the story of the miraculous catch of
fish (verses 1–14). This is so similar to Lk. 5.1–11, that there must
be some connection between them. But for Luke it is a call story,
at the beginning of Jesus' Galilean ministry, for John it is a Resurrection appearance. So there is the problem of the underlying
tradition. But there is also a problem of handling. Some of the
details appear to be purely allegorical (e.g. the 153 fish, verse 11),
so that the line between fact and fiction is not clear, and the
author's intentions are obscure. Moreover the story itself does not
quite hang together. Jesus does not need the contribution of the

disciples, although he asks for it (verse 10), as he already has fish and bread, which he shares with them (verses 9 and 13). Accordingly some commentators think that the story is a fusion of two or more traditions. Finally, although it is said to be the third appearance of Jesus to the disciples, it gives the impression of being the first. If so, it could perhaps be the occasion which was foretold in Mk 16.7, where the disciples, and Peter in particular, are directed to go to Galilee. The *Gospel of Peter* actually has this arrangement, as it records no appearance to the disciples in Jerusalem, but then begins the story of the miraculous catch of fish, after describing the disciples' return to Galilee after the feast. Unfortunately the MS. breaks off just at the start of the story, and the rest is lost.

Next there is the commissioning of Peter (verses 15–17) and prophecy of his martyrdom (18f.). The link between this paragraph and the preceding story is tenuous, so that it is scarcely likely that they belonged together in the underlying tradition. Bultmann thinks that verses 15–17 form a special tradition of Peter's leadership of the church, comparable to Mt. 16.17–19. Jesus asks Peter the same question: 'Do you love me?', three times. This is normally taken to be a delicate allusion to Peter's three denials during the trial of Jesus, so that the story concerns Peter's reinstatement to apostleship. Bultmann again denies this, on the grounds that there is not the slightest verbal reference to it in the text. As was pointed out above (p. 548), folk-lore loves to have things in threes, so that this feature is not sufficient to ensure the connection. The veiled forecast of Peter's martyrdom raises the question whether the writer actually knows the tradition that he was crucified or not. The one thing that is certain about it is that death in a manner comparable to that of Jesus himself is presented as the fulfilment of true discipleship.

Thirdly there is a short continuation of the dialogue, in which Peter asks about the future of the Beloved Disciple (verses 20–3). This has been prepared for by the mention of this disciple in the early part of the narrative (verse 7), though he was not specified in the opening list in verse 2, and clearly did not figure in the underlying tradition. Jesus' answer presupposes the belief, known to be current in the early Church, but not at all characteristic of the Fourth Gospel, that some of the disciples would remain alive until the Second Coming of Jesus. The answer is obscure, and so is the comment which follows. It remains uncertain whether the writer means that the Beloved Disciple is dead at the time of writing, or wishes to combat the implications which some have drawn from his long life, which still continues. But of course this also raises the question whether the Beloved Disciple is to be thought of as an historical person or not, and so the problem of his identity is brought to the surface once more. Moreover the comparison between his future and the fate of Peter gives rise to another problem, whether these personal relationships reflect ecclesiastical disputes. It is possible that the Church of the Johannine circle needs to defend its position against those who claim to derive their authority from Peter. This could be a burning issue, if the Johannine theology were held to be heterodox.

Before the end of the Appendix is reached, there is a solemnly attested statement that it was the Beloved Disciple who was the writer. It is natural to take verse 24 to refer to the whole Gospel, but it could mean only the Appendix. Barrett regards this verse as an integral part of the preceding narrative, as he sees a parallel between Peter's witness by way of martyrdom and the Disciple's by way of the written word. This suggestion would be more convincing if verses 18f. had used the vocabulary of witness, but even so verse 24 would still need to be framed rather differently to make a formal parallel. As it is, it has obvious links with 19.35, which seems to be wholly or partly an interpolation. It is best to take it as an additional note, and so it is more likely to be by the editor who appended 21.1–23 to the rest of the Gospel than by the writer of verses 1–23 himself. The conclusion (verse 25) in any case presupposes that the Appendix has been added to the Gospel and refers to the whole.

It is one thing to raise the problems, but it is another to find the answers. The first thing that must be established is the integrity of the chapter. It has already been shown that verse 25 is a final addition, only added after the rest has been joined to the end of the Gospel. Verse 24 seems to have been the work of the editor who was responsible for appending it, if the above remarks are correct. It implies that it is his belief that the Beloved Disciple is the author of the Gospel. The plural attestation 'we know' suggests that his belief is shared by his fellow-members of the Johannine Church. As it is scarcely conceivable that they did not know who the author was (if the homiletic view of the genesis of the Gospel

is correct, they had listened to him preaching again and again),
it follows that they identify the Beloved Disciple with the one
whom they know so well as the author of the book. But it does
not follow that they were correct. For—passing back now to verse
23—there is certainly some misunderstanding about the fate of
the Disciple. It is significant that the question is not given a
straight answer, for this implies that it is a question which should
never have been asked. It has been argued in the Introduction
(pp. 33f.) that the same applies to the identity of the Beloved
Disciple. It is not the author's wish that this should be the subject
of speculation, and he would probably have been horrified to find
that his enthusiastic audience actually identified the Disciple
with himself. If so, it is unlikely that the identification would be
made before his death. Hence the Appendix was presumably only
added by the writer of verse 24 after his death. This explains
why it was not felt possible to insert it before 20.30.

But this still does not solve the problem of the author of verses
1–23. At this point purely technical matters have to be considered.
Do the style and vocabulary indicate whether he is the same
writer as the rest of the Gospel or not? (a) The form and structure are typical of John. A Synoptic-type episode is retold to make
a particular effect, which may be foreign to the original story—
in this case the theme of feeding in verse 13 (so the healing of
chapter 5 leads up to the Sabbath issue, which is foreign to the
basic tradition). This becomes the basis of further dialogue. The
final point ('Follow me!' verse 22) is intended to make a moral
impact on the reader. (b) Apart from a number of words demanded by the subject, and presumably mainly furnished by the
source, there are several words and usages which conflict with
John's practice in the Gospel (see the lists in Barrett, p. 479;
Bultmann, p. 701): verse 1, *epi* for 'by', and *phaneroun* ('revealed')
of a Resurrection appearance; verse 3, *hupagein* with infinitive
('going fishing'); verse 4, *prōïa* for *prōï* (= early, 18.28); verse 5,
paidia, 'children', for the disciples; verse 6, *ischuein* for 'to be able',
and *apo* causal ('for'); verse 8, 'not far' instead of 'near'; verse 10,
apo partitive ('some of'); verse 12, *tolmān* ('dared') and *exetazein*
('ask'); verse 15, *pleon* for 'more'; verse 20, *epistraphēnai* for
'turned'; verse 22, *heōs* without further particle for 'until', and *ti
pros se* for 'what is that to you?'; verse 23, 'the brethren' for the
Christian community (but cf. 20.17). These differences are not

all equally significant. Some simply belong to the source of the miracle-story. Really important differences are not sufficiently numerous to be decisive against Johannine authorship. Barrett judges that they do indicate a separate occasion of writing (presumably some time later), but not a different writer from the rest of the Gospel.

If the conclusion is sound that John himself wrote verses 1–23, and if it is accepted that he had no intention of revealing the identity of the Beloved Disciple, it follows that the idea of a conflict of ecclesiastical jurisdictions is ruled out. The contrast between the two disciples in verses 15–23 is not a mirror of Church polemics, but a way of teaching discipleship. The key word is 'following' (verse 20, cf. 20.6). Peter is generally regarded as the greatest of the Twelve, and he does indeed receive the prime responsibility for the Church (verses 15–17). Moreover, his loyal discipleship has gained him the most coveted prize, that of imitating his Master in death as well as in life (for it is difficult to resist the impression that verse 18 is a prophecy *ex eventu*). But still the Beloved Disciple is the better model, for he remains a loyal follower, he seeks no place of authority (for none is mentioned), and his end is in obscurity, without the glamour of a martyr's crown. John uses the language of consistent eschatology when he makes Jesus say 'until I come', but it does not necessarily entail a conflict with the teaching in the Gospel itself. The words could be simply an allusion to 14.3. Thus John answers the questions which have arisen among his fellow-Christians about the Beloved Disciple, or rather refuses to answer them. It was necessary to do so by contrast with Peter, because Peter is a known personality, whereas the Disciple remains a mystery. There is a teasing allusiveness about the whole piece, which indicates that John does not wish to be drawn on the subject. He does not want to say anything which would turn attention away from the real function and purpose of the introduction of this character into the Gospel story.

The same allusiveness attaches to the miracle-story with which he prepares the way for the dialogue on discipleship. It is possible that verse 1 and 14 are editorial additions or adaptations, to bring this essentially independent homily into line with chapter 20. The allegorical touches in verse 11 are not unnatural, seeing that the Church's mission is the task of disciples. It is probably a

mistake to suppose that the story is a fusion of traditions. The
theme of the meal, in which Jesus himself provides the food
(verses 9, 12a, 13), is not a separate story, but a new feature
introduced specially to lead into the theme of feeding in verses
15–17. It is universally recognized that this is intended to be
symbolic of the Eucharist; this would be specially appropriate if
the homily were delivered in the course of the eucharistic celebration. The special vocabulary in these verses comes from the
feeding of the multitude in chapter 6. If we discount these verses
and the obviously Johannine additions in 7a and 12b, what remains is a story of a miraculous catch of fish very similar to Lk.
5.1–11, though verbal contact is slight. In fact Luke has altered
the underlying tradition just as much as John has, though in
different ways. Most scholars hold that John is right to present it
as a Resurrection story. A. R. C. Leaney (*ET* LXV (1953–4), pp.
381f.; commentary *ad loc.*) has shown that Luke's story is a fusion
of the call of the disciples in Mk 1.16–20 and a tradition comparable to Jn 21.1–14. He argues that Luke intentionally inserted
the tradition at this early point, so as to take the commissioning
of Peter right back to the original call, just as Matthew takes it
back to Caesarea Philippi (Mt. 16.17–19). This makes Peter's
position stronger than Paul's, for Paul could only rely on a Resurrection appearance for his position (Ac. 9; 1 C. 9.1; cf. O. Cullmann, *Peter: Disciple, Apostle, Martyr* (1962²), p. 60). Bernard goes
too far when he claims that Lk. 5.8 ('Depart from me, for I am a
sinful man') presupposes Peter's denials, and so attests the post-
Resurrection position. On the other hand we cannot be sure that
Mk 16.7 refers to this story, as it seems rather to mean a special
assembly, as in Mt. 28.16, in spite of the *Gospel of Peter*. But it is
enough that the beginnings of a Petrine legend are already dis-
cernible in the Synoptic Gospels. The story of the catch of fish, in
which Peter is the chief actor, began to circulate early as one of
the post-Resurrection traditions. John and Luke share the same
underlying tradition, if not an identical source. The fact that the
Lucan version is less allegorical than John's may be due to Luke's
more 'naturalistic' handling. The same motive of the future mission of the Church is operative in both. Whether the tradition
has a foundation in history is impossible to say. Mastin suggests
that it began as a meditation—it might be better to say a genuine
visionary experience—in which Peter's new-found confidence after

the Resurrection opens up the prospect of abundant missionary success under the risen Master's help and guidance. And so it remains today, in its practical application in the life of the Christian.

The Miraculous Catch of Fish **21.1–14**

21.1 After this: the editor has used a simple conventional expression to link the Appendix to the preceding narrative. The position of **again** varies in ℵ and W, and the word is omitted by G Sinaitic Syriac and Sahidic. It is probably a later addition. The editor has taken **Jesus revealed himself . . . to the disciples** from verse 14, probably also his own addition to the homily. The word for **revealed** (*phaneroun*) has been used in 1.31; 2.11 (which may be the model for verse 14); 3.21; 7.4; 9.3; 17.6, but not in chapter 20. Reference to these passages will show that the use here is not characteristic of John. On the other hand **by the Sea of Tiberias** may be part of the original opening (cf. 6.1). The unusual use of *epi* for **by** even suggests that John took over the phrase from the source (cf. also the notes on 6.19).

2. The list comprises seven men, and does not include mention of the Beloved Disciple, so that his presence in verse 7 comes as a surprise. For this reason Bultmann thinks that the list is from the source, but there are indications that John has adapted the source. The compound name **Simon Peter** is typical of John's usage, **Thomas called the Twin** recalls 11.16; 20.24, and **Nathanael** is unknown outside the Fourth Gospel (1.45). That he is **of Cana in Galilee** is new information. It could be a false deduction from 2.1, following immediately on Nathanael's call. But it could equally well be what John meant in the first place, though he did not mention it in chapter 1. On the other hand **the sons of Zebedee** have never been mentioned in the Gospel. In view of their close association with Peter in the Synoptic Gospels (e.g. at the Transfiguration), they may well have been in the source at this point (cf. Lk. 5.10). It is tempting to identify the **two others** with Andrew and Philip (1.40, 43), but there seems no reason why John failed to give their names if this is what he meant. In fact it is much more likely that he has purposely not named these two, so as to leave the question of the Beloved Disciple unanswered. The traditional identification of him with John son of Zebedee is of course a possibility on the basis of this list,

but it is more likely that John means him to be regarded as one
of these two unnamed disciples. (Lagrange evades the difficulty
by treating **the sons of Zebedee** as a gloss to identify the **two
others.**) The opening of the story in *Gospel of Peter* 60 reads: 'But
I Simon Peter and my brother Andrew took our nets and went
back to the sea; and there was with us Levi the son of Alphaeus,
whom the Lord . . .' This is a reference to Mk 2.14. The fragment
gives no help in reconstructing John's source.

3. I am going fishing: Gr. *hupagō halieuein.* The infinitive with
hupagein is contrary to John's style. But again it is most reasonable
to suppose that he is here simply reproducing his source. For
halieuein = to fish, only here in the NT, cf. *haleeis* (= 'fishermen');
Mk 1.16f.; Lk. 5.2. The story presupposes that the disciples have
returned to their trade, after the shattering events in Jerusalem.
But as this is necessary *scenario* for the symbolic tale itself, it would
be hazardous to take this as historical evidence.
We will go with you: cf. 'there was with us', using the same
preposition *sun*, in the *Peter* fragment. John is still following his
source.
got into the boat: this phrase, using the same words, has been
adapted by Luke to apply to Jesus (Lk. 5.3), unless he has taken
it from the parallel in Mk 4.1, with which he has fused the opening
of the story.
that night they caught nothing: cf. Lk. 5.5: 'Master, we toiled
all night and took nothing!' Evidently the night was considered
the best time for fishing. In any case it ensures that the fish are
fresh for the market in the morning. The detail could be symbolical, representing the fruitlessness of working on mission without the light of the Master's presence, but such an interpretation
is not actually required by the text.

4. day was breaking: Gr. *prōïas . . . ginomenēs,* reading present
with B C* A L against the majority reading *genomenēs* (= when
morning was come). This phrase, with the form *prōïa,* occurs in
Mt. 27.1, where Mk 15.1 and Jn 18.28 have *prōï* (cf. 20.1), and
may well belong to the source.
stood on the beach: the same Greek words occur at Mt. 13.2,
improving the Marcan parallel; but no contact with John is likely,
as the setting is different. Jesus always stands for the Resurrection
appearances (20.14, 19, 26).
did not know: Luke's recasting of the tradition does not permit

this detail, which, with verses 7 and 12, suggests that there has been no previous appearance of Jesus. But as the words are identical with 20.14, and as verse 7 is plainly John's own work, comparable to the theme of the Beloved Disciple's belief in 20.8, it is more likely that John has introduced this item into the story himself. The theme of gradual recognition is typical of John. It belongs not only to the story of Mary Magdalene, but also to 20.19–28, though the division of this tradition into two occasions has to some extent obscured it. The failure of the disciples to recognize Jesus now, even though he has appeared to them twice in Jerusalem, can be explained in two ways, both of which are probably operative. Firstly, John's idea of the Resurrection appearances presupposes that Jesus is not immediately recognizable, except to the eye of faith, so that gradual apprehension is the rule. Secondly, as he gave this homily some time after the completion of the Gospel, it was not necessary for him to have strict regard for consistency. It is a feature which is primarily a matter of literary technique. At the present stage in the narrative it could be simply due to the lack of sufficient daylight, and so seems quite natural.

   5. Children: Gr. *paidia*; contrast 13.33 (*teknia*). But it occurs in 1 Jn 2.18; 3.7 (variant), and can scarcely be regarded as foreign to John's style. As a familiar, diminutive form it implies the master/disciple relationship, not quite suitable for a stranger. The word is used of a boy in 4.49 and of a newborn baby in 16.21. *NEB* changes it here to 'friends'.

   have you any fish: the question is introduced by *mē*, which regularly expects the answer 'no', 'of course not', as at 18.35. But here it is better to take it as a cautious assertion, as at 4.29; 7.26, and perhaps even *mēti prosphagion* (instead of *mē ti prosphagion*) should be read. This would mean, 'Surely you have a bit to eat?', i.e. have not been completely unsuccessful. The word *prosphagion* originally meant a relish to eat with bread, usually fish. It is thus exactly equivalent to *opsarion*, which John will use in verses 9f., 13 in dependence on 6.9 (*q.v.*). According to *MM*, p. 551f., both words were used quite generally for fish in NT times. But in the next verse the regular word for fish (*ichthus*) will be used, as in Luke and presumably the source. But it is possible that *prosphagion* in this verse stood in the source too.

   6. Cast the net: cf. Lk. 5.4, where the same word (*diktuon*) is used for 'nets'. Luke omits **on the right side of the boat,** as his version is differently structured, but in John it is necessary to convey the idea of a distinction from the fruitless efforts which have just been made, and this must also have applied in the source. In Greek usage the right side is the lucky side, but it is doubtful if this idea plays any part here. In both Luke and John the success of the fishermen is due entirely to their obedience to Jesus' word. They already display the first quality of discipleship. After **you will find some,** the following addition, based on Lk. 5.5, is ready by P⁶⁶vid ℵc1 g² Ethiopic and Cyril of Alexandria: 'But they said, "We toiled all night and took nothing; but at your name (word ℵc1) we will cast it." '

for the quantity of fish: quantity (*plēthos*) is translated 'shoal' at Lk. 5.6. *apo* = **for** is not necessarily a Semitism but corresponds with Semitic usage (the whole phrase *apo tou plēthous* is used by LXX at Gen. 16.10 for M.T. *mērōb*, and elsewhere). As *ischuein* for **were . . . able** is not found elsewhere in John, these phrases may well go back to the source.

7. At this point John's narrative diverges fundamentally from Luke's. Hitherto the differences could be explained for the most part by the fact that Luke has altered the opening in order to unite it with the tradition of Jesus' use of a boat as a pulpit, which occurs independently in Mk 4.1f. But now the sequence of events is differently imagined. In Luke the nets are breaking under the strain, and have to be hauled into the ship (the second boat, belonging to James and John, may be a Lucan addition deriving from the call story of Mk 1.16–20, with which the *end* of the story has been fused). The climax comes when Peter prostrates himself before Jesus in amazement (Lk. 5.8f.). In John Peter's reaction is recorded first, and the net is towed to shore, miraculously remaining intact in spite of the strain (verse 11). John's narrative is defective, because we are not told what happened when Peter reached Jesus. Something is missing between verses 7 and 11. But even allowing for some recasting on the part of both evangelists, it looks as if their sources differed, so that the two accounts attest variant forms of the tradition. In the present verse John's creative hand is evident in the fact that **that disciple whom Jesus loved** is suddenly brought into the story. Characteristically he knows from what has happened that **'It is the Lord!'** although Jesus remains unrecognizable on the shore (cf. 20.8). For **the Lord** as a designation of the risen Jesus, cf. 20.18, 20, 25, 28, and verse 12 below.

put on his clothes: lit. 'tied round himself the outer garment', presumably tucking it into his belt in order to wade through the water. The verb is the same as in 13.4f.; the noun is not used elsewhere in the NT. While working Peter **was stripped,** i.e. wearing only a small undergarment, but he must be properly dressed when he goes to pay homage to Jesus. Brown, following Lagrange, imagines that Peter was already wearing the outer garment, but nothing underneath, so that he simply tucked it up in order to swim ashore. Barrett cites *Y. Berakoth*, 2, 4c, 38 for the fact that a person not decently clothed could not give a greeting (which is intrinsically a religious act).

8. about a hundred yards off: lit. 'two hundred cubits'. The Sea of Galilee shelves steeply where the hills come down to its banks, but the plain of Gennesaret at the NW. corner gives a gentler approach, with shallow water for some distance. Jesus and the disciples are associated mostly with places at the northern end of the lake. The use of the non-Johannine **not far,** instead of the very common 'near', should perhaps be attributed to the source.

9. got out: *apobainein*, as a technical term for disembarkation, is used only here and in Lk. 5.2 in the NT.

a charcoal fire: cf. 18.18. **There** (*keimenēn*), lit. 'lying', is a very common verb in John. It has been read as *kaiomenēn* ('burning') by the Old Latin (*incensos*), a natural variant not likely to be original. **Fish** here and in verses 10 and 13 is *opsarion*, which was used by John in 6.9, 11. It occurs nowhere else in the NT. It is not quite clear whether Jesus was cooking the **bread** along with the fish, or had it close by. It is another indication that John is using the tradition of the feeding of the multitude at this point. Apart from the opening words, this verse cannot be regarded as part of the underlying story. It introduces a totally new theme, and spoils the continuity, because the fish have yet to be brought to land. As explained above, John has done this so as to bring in the theme of feeding in verses 15–17. The meal is a quasi-Eucharist. Jesus has taken the initiative, because he is the giver of the spiritual food—which is himself (6.35). The bread fixes this interpretation, but a fish also is a frequent symbol of the Eucharist in early Christian iconography, although of course never actually used as the matter of the sacrament.

10. Bring some of the fish: the request is addressed to all, but in the next verse Peter is the one who acts. So he is to con-

tribute to the meal, like the boy in 6.9. Bernard suggests that this
was necessary, because Jesus was only cooking enough for himself.
But we are not told that any of the fish which was brought was
actually used. In fact this verse seems to be merely a link, in
order to work in verse 11, which comes from the source. It is to
be noted, however, that the partitive use of *apo* for **some of** is
unparalleled in the rest of the Gospel.

11. The new theme in verse 9 really deprives this verse of its
real function in the story. This was to arouse wonder at the plentiful result of obedience to Jesus' word. The original motive was
the Church's mission. But by placing it between verses 9 and 12,
John reinterprets it in the light of the feeding miracle, so that it
now suggests Jesus' abundant pastoral care. The verse appears
legendary by comparison with Lk. 5.6f. The catch is not only
numerous in quantity (but is 153 really so phenomenal?), but consists of **large fish** (*ichthus*, as in verse 6). Moreover **the net was
not torn.** As John has altered the symbolism to apply to the
internal pastoral ministry of the Church, it is natural to see in
this a reference to John's vital interest in the maintenance of the
unity of the Church. Commentators are generally agreed about
this. But if it reflects John's concern, the question arises whether
he has altered the source, which may well have said that the nets
were breaking under the strain, as in Luke.

a hundred and fifty-three of them: the precise figure, as opposed to a round number, compels us to assume that it has a
symbolical meaning. As we do not know whether John found it
in his source, or introduced it himself, we cannot tell whether it is
in any way related to his particular interests. Before setting out
some of the solutions which have been proposed, it may be as
well to observe that the figure must represent totality in some way,
because the catch prefigures the ultimate universal salvation
through the church's mission (cf. 11.52). (a) We can first discount
ecclesiastical interpretations which are based on the fact that the
number is a multiple of three, e.g. $3 \times 50 + 3$, and relate it to
the doctrine of the Trinity. According to Hoskyns (p. 556) Origen
and Augustine interpreted it along these lines. But the doctrine
was not sufficiently formalized in John's time to be the basis of
symbolic numbers. (b) Jerome, in his Commentary on Ezek.
47.9–12, asserts that the ancient naturalists held that there were
153 species of fish, and so it symbolizes all the races of men.

R. M. Grant (*HTR* XLII (1949), p. 273) has shown that Jerome
is wrong about this, and so this explanation, attractive as it is at
first sight, fails. (c) The figure may be a case of *gematria*, i.e. the
sum of the numerical values of the letters of a name which it is
intended to disguise. But here the possibilities are endless. Bultmann (p. 709, n. 2) mentions the Hebrew *hā-'ôlām hab-bā'* (= Age
to Come) which gives 153, and the Greek *Simōn* = 76 plus
Ichthus = 77 (i.e. Peter and Jesus, who is represented by the fish-
symbol). Much more appealing is the suggestion of J. A. Emerton
(*JTS*, n.s. IX (1958), pp. 86–9; n.s., XI (1960), pp. 335f.). He takes
into account the connection with Ezek. 47.9–12 observed by
Jerome, and also the much more important mathematical property
of 153, that it is the triangular of 17, which was recognized at least
as early as Augustine (*Tract. 122 in Joh.*). The triangular number
means the sum of 1 + 2 + 3 . . . up to 17, which can be represented by an equilateral triangle of dots on a base line of 17 dots
(diagram in Hoskyns, p. 553). According to Ezek. 47.10 the waters
of the Dead Sea will become fresh as a result of the stream which
will flow from the Temple in the restored Jerusalem, and 'fishermen will stand beside the sea; from En-gedi to En-eglaim it will
be a place for the spreading of nets; its fish will be of very many
kinds . . .' Emerton found that the *gematria* for the Hebrew of
Gedi = 17 and of Eglaim = 153. Various forms of the Greek
transliterations of these names in the LXX will also yield the
total of 153, but if the *gematria* is on a Greek basis the 17 is left out
of account. (d) The point of the number is that it is the triangular
of 17. This is put at its simplest by Hoskyns, who holds that the
required notion of totality is provided by the sheer mathematical
perfection of the number, without any symbolical meaning attaching to it. Barrett, Grant (art. cit.), and Mastin prefer to include
symbolism in the basic number 17. It is the sum of 10 and 7,
both symbolical of perfection. They would not go so far as
Augustine, and say that there is a reference to the Ten Commandments and the Sevenfold Gift of the Spirit. But, if the solution
is to be found in the number 17, yet another possibility may be
offered, which seems not to have been suggested before. The context invites comparison with the feeding miracle, and the symbolical interest of this verse in the future totality of the Church
invites comparison with John's symbolical interpretation of the
leavings from the meal (6.12). The next verse (6.13) says that

12 baskets were filled with the fragments of the 5 loaves, omitting all mention of the 2 fish. The sum of 12 and 5 is 17. Just as the leavings typify the universal feeding of the future, so the catch of fish typifies the universal population which is to be fed.

None of these solutions is really convincing. They all require that the number should be regarded as code-language, for which John can expect his readers to have the key. Hoskyns thinks of them as 'educated Greeks' who could appreciate the mathematician's interest in a number for its own sake, but this is a gratuitous assumption. Nor can we take refuge in the naturalistic explanation favoured by Bernard, that the fish were duly counted so as to share out the takings, and the number happened to be remembered exactly (each man gets 22, except one, who has 21). For the story has too complex a history for such a naïve approach. It is best to agree with Bultmann, that the number is certainly symbolical, but that it remains inexplicable. To say that 'a correct interpretation [of the narrative] depends upon a correct interpretation of the significance of the number 153' (Hoskyns, p. 553) is a wild exaggeration. The number naturally arouses curiosity, but the story still makes its point clearly enough without any solution to the problem.

12. Come and have breakfast: Gr. *deute aristēsate*. *Deute* was used by John at 4.29, and is fairly common in the NT in connection with an invitation to dine. *Aristān* (only here and verse 15, and Lk. 11.37) is good Greek for 'to have breakfast'. These words belong to John's shaping of the narrative to recall the feeding miracle. It must be supposed that **come** is meant literally, and that there is still some distance between Jesus and the disciples, including Peter. The next words betray hesitancy on their part. They know, of course, that it is Jesus. But they are also beginning to realize who Jesus *is*—he is **the Lord.** The question '**Who are you?**' seems to have the same exploratory intention as in 8.25. It does not mean that they find Jesus unrecognizable. If it were spoken, it would have to be answered with the evocative *egō eimi*, 'it is I'. But **none** of them **dared ask. Dared** (*tolmān*) is not used elsewhere in John, but there is a similar idea in 4.27, suggesting the awe of the disciples. The word for **ask** (*exetazein*) is rare in the NT, and not used elsewhere by John. Their question does not need to be asked, because they already know the answer, that Jesus is the Lord. In other words, by the time that they reach

personal confrontation with Jesus they are ready to make the confession of faith, which the Beloved Disciple had anticipated in
verse 7.

13. Jesus came: so the breakfast is an act of communion with
the Lord who is known by faith (cf. Lk. 24.30). It is not clear
whether **came** denotes movement, because of the disciples' hesitation, or is pleonastic, derived from Semitic usage (as we say in
English 'I have gone and done it' = 'I have done it'). The rest
of the verse is an abbreviated version of 6.11, clearly modelled on
it directly. Consequently 'when he had given thanks' is inserted
before **gave** by D, with support from the Syriac and some Old
Latin texts, making the liturgical allusion more prominent.

14. the third time: the reference is to 20.19 and 26, the appearance to Mary Magdalene being discounted, because the writer
is concerned with appearances to the disciples. Several factors
indicate that this verse is an insertion by the editor responsible for
adding the Appendix to the rest. Firstly, it is only required when
this homily ceases to be an independent piece. Second, the story
is treated as an appearance to the assembly of the Apostles,
although only seven were concerned. Thirdly **revealed** (*phaneroun*) is used in a non-Johannine way (cf. verse 1), but may well be
derived from 2.11. The enumeration helps to counteract the impression, inherent in the story itself, that this is the first appearance of Jesus to the Apostles. As the verse is similar in form to 2.11
and 4.54, it is tempting to place this story in the same sequence.
It would then be the third in the series of Signs, and so would most
suitably fit the Lucan position in the early ministry, rather than
the Resurrection (so Spitta, Goguel, Fortna). But the above analysis of the story makes this impossible, and the word 'sign' (*sēmeion*)
could scarcely have been omitted, if this were so.

Peter the Pastor **15–17**

15. finished breakfast: the dialogue between Jesus and Peter
has been prepared for by the theme of feeding in verses 9–13, but
the only verbal link is the repetition of the verb *aristān* from verse
12. Otherwise the setting of the meal on the seashore is forgotten
altogether. In verse 20 the disciples seem to be walking along. It is
thus clear that this section has no inherent connection with the
preceding story.

Simon, son of John: cf. 1.42. Many MSS. have 'son of Jona' in

all three verses, but this is probably due to assimilation to Mt.
16.17. **John** is the reading of B ℵ W; the use of the patronymic
adds solemnity to the address. The case for connecting the threefold repetition of the dialogue with the three denials of Peter in
the Passion narrative does not rest on the content of the dialogue,
which provides no hint of a cross-reference. It rests rather on the
fact that it is closely related to the prophecy of Peter's martyrdom.
For this has already been introduced by implication into John's
handling of the tradition of the denials in 13.36–8. John not only
made Peter profess his willingness to die a martyr's death, but he
put it in words which were derived from the allegory of the Good
Shepherd. If John could link martyrdom, shepherd language and
denials in his recasting of the earlier tradition in 13.36–8, it is
difficult to believe that the present passage has no relation to that
paragraph, seeing that we have here further shepherd language
as well as the theme of martyrdom. Moreover the threefold repetition here is not simply the triadic structure of folk-lore, but receives
explicit emphasis and actual comment (verse 17). It is a fact which
demands explanation. And explanation is given darkly, in the
forecast of martyrdom which follows. But if we must admit that
the three-ness of the dialogue compels us to see here a rehabilita-
tion of Peter so that he may 'follow afterward' (13.36) to death,
we can agree with Bultmann that the real purpose of the dialogue
is the commissioning of Peter for his pastoral authority over the
Church. But then it will not be necessary that the threefold repetition was already found in the source of this tradition. The nucleus
need have been no more than a simple word of commissioning,
like the isolated verse used in 20.23. It should not be forgotten
that John's interest does not stop at the giving of authority to
Peter, but is much more taken up with the meaning of discipleship.
do you love me: this phrase has been the cause of endless controversy. For there are variations of vocabulary in both question
and answer in the three verses. The same applies to the words of
commission, **'Feed my lambs'** etc., but in this case the variations
are clear in the English. The variations in the question and answer
concern the words to **love** and to **know,** as follows:

15. 'Do you love (*agapās*) me?' 'You know (*oidas*) that I love
       (*philō*) you.'
16. 'Do you love (*agapās*) me?' 'You know (*oidas*) that I love
       (*philō*) you.'

17. 'Do you love (*phileis*) me?' Peter was grieved because he
said . . . 'Do you love (*phileis*) me?'—'You know (*oidas*)
everything; you know (*ginōskeis*) that I love (*philō*) you.'

The controversy concerns the question whether there is any distinction of meaning intended between *agapān* and *philein*, both
translated **love.** (a) That there is *no* distinction is the view most
commonly held today (Bernard, Barrett, Bultmann, Hoskyns,
Lightfoot, Mastin, Brown). This agrees with John's characteristic
liking for pairs of synonyms, which he tends to use without any
apparent discrimination (cf. Introduction, p. 45). Elegant variation seems to be the reason for the different forms of the commission, and is the obvious reason for the different word for 'know'
in verse 17. Moreover none of the early Fathers, not even Origen,
perceived any distinction of meaning in the present context. (b)
Westcott argued that *agapān* is a higher form of love than *philein*.
It is the love of the will, not simply the affection of the heart.
This gives an appealing interpretation to the dialogue. For Peter
cannot quite match up to the selflessness of Jesus' demand. At the
third question Jesus reduces the demand to Peter's level, out of
his own loving concern—but only to foretell that Peter will ultimately reach the height of it when he imitates the Master in his
death. This view has been enthusiastically presented in the recent
commentary of Marsh. But it suffers from the initial improbability
that it means a descending instead of a rising scale, which would
naturally be expected if there is a distinction in the words. (c)
Appreciating this point, E. Evans (*Studies in the Fourth Gospel*, edited
by F. L. Cross (1957), pp. 64–71) has argued that *philein* denotes
the higher kind of love, for it is more inclusive, going beyond the
notion of mere satisfaction which adheres to *agapān* in the earlier
classical usage. But this is exceedingly dubious as regards the
Fourth Gospel, and is hardly borne out by such passages as 13.34f.;
17.23–6, where *agapē* and *agapān* are used. (d) There may be no
distinction of meaning, but the variation may be intended to
allow a wider range of literary allusion than would be possible if
one word only were used. The relation of this section to 13.36–8
suggests that there is reminiscence also of 13.34f., and for this
allusion *agapān* had to be used. 15.12 and 17 show that it is a
stereotyped formula. But in 15.13 we read, 'Greater love (*agapē*)
has no man than this, that a man lay down his life (cf. 13.37) for

his friends (*philōn*).' This is the sort of love which Peter will display. The use of *philein* permits allusion to this important related text, where a word of the same root occurs.

more than these: this can mean either 'do you prefer me to these things (i.e. the fisherman's way of life)?', or 'do you love me more than these men do?' The use of *pleon* with genitive for **more than** (only here in John) seems decisive for the second. If it had been the first, John would probably have used *mallon ē* as at 3.19; 12.43. The phrase is disregarded in Peter's reply, and is dropped in the next two verses. It may have been put in here only to ease the connection with the preceding section (so Bultmann; Brown agrees). It does not of itself prove the primacy of Peter among the Apostles, though this is presupposed by the personal commission which will now be given.

Feed my lambs: the variation of verb—feed, tend, feed (*boske, poimaine, boske*)—and of noun—lambs, sheep, sheep (*arnia, probatia, probatia*)—is probably not significant. Many MSS. read *probata* for *probatia* (C* D also have it for *arnia*), but this is no doubt due to assimilation to chapter 10. Bernard argues on the basis of the Syriac, which uses three different words, that there is an ascending scale (the lambs, the young sheep, the whole flock), and so accepts *probata* in verse 17, but the textual evidence for it in this verse is no stronger than in verse 16. The imagery of shepherd and sheep for pastoral responsibility is conventional; cf. Ac. 20.28. In the context it follows naturally from Jesus' own act of feeding the disciples. But the commission probably has some basis in the tradition, a parallel to Mt. 16.18f. But if the connection between these verses and the denials of Peter is well founded, the threefold repetition must be attributed to John himself.

17. For the variants in this verse see above. Evans holds that the second **know** (*ginōskeis*) supports his theory of *philein* as the higher form of love, i.e. 'now that you use *philein* yourself, you are beginning to realize what I mean when I use this verb for my reply'. But if there is a distinction, it is between knowing as a fact (*oidas*) and knowing in a feeling and intimate way (*ginōskeis*). This indeed suits the increased emotional content of this verse. For Peter is **grieved** (= sorrowful, 16.20ff.) that Jesus puts the same question three times (not, of course, that a different word for love is being used). Jesus disregards this protest. It is enough that he has made Peter make the same profession of personal loyalty three times. So the stain of the three denials is wiped away. Peter can now assume the responsibility of being chief shepherd of the Church.

Peter the Martyr 18f.

18. The **truly** opening maintains the solemnity of the charge. It also marks the transition to the theme of martyrdom. Although this has a close link with verses 15–17 through the allusion of the whole section to 13.36–8, it played no part in the tradition of the commissioning of Peter on which these verses have been built. So now the formula indicates the use of a separate item of tradition. Previous experience has shown that this is often an authentic saying of Jesus. There will be a genuine saying at the end of the next verse ('follow me'), but it is impossible to achieve certainty about the present verse. Bultmann is probably right in supposing that it is based on a proverb ('in youth a man goes freely, wherever he likes; in old age a man must let himself be taken where he does not wish to go'). The point of the proverb is that the decision to go (i.e. to follow?) must be taken while there is still freedom of action; if left until later, it may be too late. It is thus conceivable that John found it in a collection of sayings on discipleship, similar to Mt. 8.18–22 = Lk. 9.57–62, where the key word is 'follow' (*akolouthein*), and each of the sayings embodies a proverb. Whether it goes back to Jesus himself or not, it has certainly been incorporated into the tradition in connection with discipleship. But it has been adapted by John, as the next verse explains, to apply to the death of Peter. He has put it into the second person and altered the tenses of the verbs from timeless present to past and future. He has also expanded it with symbolic detail. In the first half **you girded yourself** may be an allusion to verse 7 ('put on his clothes'), where a compound form of the same verb was used. It is inserted simply to make a foil to the expansion of the second half, **you will stretch out your hands, and another will gird you.** It is these words which are intended to give the clue to the manner of Peter's death ('by what death', verse 19). Most commentators (not Bultmann, however) see here a reference to crucifixion. The phrase 'to stretch out the hands' is used of Jesus' crucifixion in the early Christian literature (e.g. Barnabas xii.2, where Exod. 17.12 is alluded to as a type of the crucifixion; cf. xii.4, quoting Isa. 65.2), and the same verb is applied to crucifixion by the pagan writer Epictetus (early second century) and perhaps by Josephus (*Ant.* xix.94). The only difficulty is that it precedes the action of the helper. But this is not insuperable, for the sequence intended may be (a) stretching out the arms along the cross-beam, (b) having the arms tied to it with ropes, and (c) being hauled up on to the stake (for details of crucifixion, see above, p. 574; and for the use of ropes, cf. Blinzler, *op. cit.*, p. 250). But the language is carefully chosen to preserve the picture of the helplessness of an old man.

19. The parenthesis is an integral part of the text, and is essential to John's purpose, for the hint of Peter's crucifixion is too obscure to be perceived by the reader without it. We need not doubt that John really believed that Jesus had made this prophecy. For, if the proverb of verse 18 is a genuine saying on discipleship, it could be understood in this way even without the symbolic expansions. The words here are identical with 12.33, except that **he was to glorify God** replaces 'he was to die'. This simply picks up an idea which was already in the context of 12.23–33, and which is repeated with great emphasis just before the Petrine material in 13.31–8. But it is significant, because always hitherto the subject of 'glorify' has been either God or Jesus. In fact to glorify God with man as subject is not uncommon outside John, and simply means to give praise to God. But as Peter's death is to reproduce the act by which Jesus most fully revealed God's glory, it is impossible to doubt that John means here that it reflects the meaning of Jesus' death, on the principle that true discipleship continues Jesus' mission (17.10). Such is to be the privilege of Peter.

follow me: at last the real point of the narrative is reached, in the words which form the essence of the original call of the disciples (1.43). The theme has been under the surface all along. It is explicit in Luke's version of the miraculous catch of fish (Lk. 5.11), but whether it came into the source at John's disposal we cannot tell. But he has certainly recast it in order to lead up to this theme. Peter's pastoral responsibility has been given to him with no emphasis on the superiority of his position. Rather, he is to feed the flock in exactly the same way as Jesus has himself just done, which means that his office is thought of in terms of discipleship. Finally he has been promised the supreme expression of discipleship in following his Master to the Cross. All this starts with following Jesus now. The command is addressed to the reader as much as it is to the Apostle.

There remains the question whether these verses have historical value for the question of the martyrdom of Peter. Barrett, Cullmann (*op. cit.*, p. 88) and others think that they are an important early testimony to this tradition. Even Bultmann, who denies this, is aware that the present passage is not trying to impose belief in Peter's martyrdom on the reader, but rather presupposes it (p. 714, n. 1). Verse 19a views it not as a future possibility but as something that has already happened, just like 12.33. It is the natural inference that John has good grounds for writing in this way. And it is only if some such fate were already overtaking the Apostles that the final section of the homily has any real point.

The Beloved Disciple 20–3

20. following: just as verses 15–19 were linked to the preceding story by theme and catchword, so we have the catchword link here in **following,** and the continuation of the theme of the fate of the disciples. **Following** (omitted by ℵ* W ff²) implies that the party is now on the move, but John has no interest in the physical circumstances; he uses the word because it belongs to the language of discipleship. **Turned** (*epistrapheis*) is the compound verb. Elsewhere John uses the simple verb (1.38; 12.40; 20.14, 16). If the verse is modelled on 1.38, he may be consciously varying the vocabulary, as **saw** is a quite different word, though frequent elsewhere.

the disciple whom Jesus loved: his presence has been briefly prepared for in verse 7, where the same phrase was used. The fuller description of him which occupies the remainder of the verse is almost identical with 13.25, the vocabulary being entirely derived from it and its surrounding context. Though it is found in all mss., the use in it of **the supper** as a cross-reference looks suspicious, and Bultmann may well be right in supposing that it is an early gloss. Whether this is so or not, the object of the full description at this point (contrast verse 7) is to remind the reader of the special place of intimacy with Jesus which the Disciple enjoyed. This explains why his fate is a matter of particular interest. There is no suggestion in the text that it is because he holds a position of ecclesiastical responsibility comparable to Peter.

21. Peter's question is an ellipsis, and extremely vague (lit. 'as

for this man, what?'). It is only the answer in the next verse
which shows that it is concerned with his fate.

22. If it is my will that he remain: in strict grammar this
is not a hypothetical possibility, but what Jesus actually does
intend (*BDF* § 373 (1)). But it is probably meant to be ambiguous,
leaving the matter open. So in the next verse it is denied that
this is Jesus' intention. **Remain** (abide, *menein*) must mean 'remain alive' in the present context. There is a close parallel in
1 C. 15.6. But it is possible that the verb has been chosen because
of its richer associations in the Supper discourses.

until I come: the verb is present, where future, or better subjunctive, might be expected. The simple *heōs* for **until** is good
Greek, but not found elsewhere in John. Jesus apparently speaks
in terms of consistent eschatology, referring to his second coming.
There is plentiful evidence that in the early days of the Church
it was believed that Jesus would come again quickly, while many
of the first generation of Christians were still alive (cf. 1 Th.
4.13–17; perhaps also Mk 9.1). As the Apostles and other early
Christians (typified here by Peter) died off, an acute problem
was raised, calling for careful reappraisal of the accepted patterns
of belief. In the Fourth Gospel John uses the language of consistent eschatology, but he sees the End Time anticipated in the
events of Jesus' death and Resurrection. But this allows for the
idea that he who is to come has already come, so that the relationships which will characterize the End already exist, as John has
explained in 14.3. There may well be an allusion here to the
prayer in the eucharistic liturgy, *maran atha* ('Our Lord, come!')
(1 C. 11.26; 16.22; Rev. 22.20). Thus the Beloved Disciple abides
with Jesus always, whether in life or in death.

what is that to you: the expression is comparable to 2.4. It
implies that Jesus is not willing to give a direct answer to Peter's
question. It was an intrusion into Jesus' sphere of private knowledge, and should never have been asked. Peter must accept the
fact that the Beloved Disciple has a special intimacy with Jesus,
and should strive to emulate it. He will do this by his own loyal
discipleship. So the only possible answer is that he should look to
himself: '*You* [*RSV* fails to translate the emphatic *su*] **follow me!**'

23. The interpretation of this verse depends on one's estimate
of the identity of the Beloved Disciple. If it is assumed that
he was a member of the church where the Fourth Gospel was

produced, it speaks of him as one who is known to **the brethren** (for this designation of the Christian community, cf. 20.17). In this case the author is either warning them that they should not count on his remaining with them for ever, as if he would never die; or else he is explaining to them that, though he has in fact died, they should not have expected it to be otherwise. The latter view is more commonly held. If on the other hand the Beloved Disciple is an idealization of one of the Apostles, and for that very reason must always remain unnamed and unidentified, the speculation among the brethren obviously cannot be answered. It has been suggested in verse 22 that, unlike Peter, he might fail to win the martyr's crown, but his discipleship is none the worse for that. Nor does it mean that he **was not to die** (*apothnēskei*, present tense with future meaning). The rebuke of Peter in verse 22 applies to the brethren too. It is possible that **brethren** is used to suggest both the immediate circle of the disciples, as in 20.17, and the church where John preaches and writes. So this verse makes an epilogue to the story, which also points its application to the readers. They too must cease to indulge in wild speculations about the Beloved Disciple and attend to their own discipleship. For indeed that is John's object in creating this character in the first place. His reticence about him has a definite purpose. It is his hope that each reader will be so drawn by the Gospel to believe in Jesus and to follow him, that he will discover *himself* in the true discipleship of the Beloved Disciple.

Editorial Conclusion **24f.**

24. This is the disciple: in spite of trying to turn attention away from the Beloved Disciple, and of exhorting his listeners to attend to their own discipleship, John has left an aura of mystery around this figure, which is bound to provoke further speculation. Some are left wondering whether after all the Beloved Disciple is not John himself. Who else so obviously fulfils the part? Who else was so close to the mind of Christ? It can be well imagined how rapidly this belief would develop after John's death, when his restraining hand (so clear in the last two verses) was removed. Accordingly the decision was taken to publish the Gospel to a wider audience. The Appendix was added to the completed work both as a precious addition, worthy to be preserved with the rest, and also, and indeed primarily, to guarantee the authenticity of this highly individual work. So the editor adds this note, which is comparable to the opening of the *Gospel of Thomas* (cf. above p. 392). He asserts that John was not only **the disciple** of the Appendix, **who** therefore **is bearing witness to these things,** but also that he is the one **who has written these things; these things** can only refer to the Gospel as a whole, because the Beloved Disciple has not only participated in the action described in the Appendix, but has figured in some of the preceding chapters. If he bears witness to the conversation in verses 20–3, he bears witness to the other scenes in which he was present. Moreover there is no suggestion that he merely supplied the information, and got someone else to write the Gospel (like Pilate in 19.19). For, even if an amanuensis was employed, the point of this assertion is that the written form of the Gospel exactly corresponds with the Disciple's eye-witness testimony. Finally the community in which the Gospel was produced countersigns the editor's statement about his witness: **we know that his testimony is true.** The plural subject is important. If the reference had been merely to the true interpretation of Jesus' words just given in verse 23 (so Dodd, *JTS*, n.s., IV (1953), pp. 212f.), the third person would have been maintained ('he knows that he tells the truth', 19.35). The **we** takes the sentence outside the structure of the Gospel, so that it represents the *imprimatur* of the church in which it originated. The need to attest the Gospel in this way may well have been due to fear that it would not easily win wide acceptance. That this fear was justified is confirmed by the fact that it was first appreciated only in heretical circles (cf. Introduction, p. 28). It may be felt that this verse is a poor attestation, seeing that the eyewitness remains anonymous. But J. Roloff (*NTS* xv (1968–9), pp. 129–51) has shown that the anonymous figure of the Teacher of Righteousness in the Dead Sea Scrolls serves a similar function, as the authoritative teacher of the Qumran Community. We cannot, however, draw from this parallel the further conclusion that the Johannine Church had correctly understood the identity of the Beloved Disciple (against Brown). The story of the Woman taken in Adultery (7.53–8.11) is placed after this verse by the Lake group and a few other MSS.

25. The conclusion is presumably from the same hand as verse 24. It is missing from ℵ*, but then written in by the same copyist, so that its omission there must be considered accidental. It is obviously based on 20.30f. The editor was bound to try to make it a more grand conclusion, to avoid anticlimax. But he has only succeeded in producing an exaggerated literary conceit, which is not to be taken seriously. Barrett cites as parallels 1 Mac. 9.22; *Exod. Rabba*, xxx.22; Philo, *Post*, 144, and of course numerous others could be found. The **I suppose** does not conflict with 'we know' in the preceding verse, being merely a stylistic device.

The result is that the conclusion fails to impress. It was a mistake to tamper with John's own conclusion. The best advice that a commentator can give is to invite the reader to turn back once more to 20.30f., and to allow John himself to have the final word.

INDEX

INDEX